BOOKS BY Leslie A. Marchand

BYRON: A PORTRAIT (1970)

BYRON: A BIOGRAPHY (1957)
3 volumes

THESE ARE BORZOI BOOKS
PUBLISHED BY ALFRED A. KNOPF INC.

BYRON: ...

BYRON

A Portrait

LESLIE A. MARCHAND

NEW YORK
Alfred A. Knopf
1970

THIS IS A BORZOI BOOK
PUBLISHED BY ALFRED A. KNOPF, INC.

Library of Congress Catalog Card Number: 76-111252

Manufactured in the United States of America

First Edition

To Marion

Preface

IT MAY BE PRESUMPTUOUS to call this biography "A Portrait" of Byron, but the presumption is lessened by the fact that the lines of the portrait are drawn from his own revelations in verse and prose, while the natural colors are filled in from ample recollections by his contemporaries. What I have tried to do is to distill the essential Byron from the mass of biographical material now available, incorporating what is most interesting and significant from what I could find and what others have published since my three-volume *Byron: A Biography* appeared in 1957. Those who want further details can find them in the three volumes and in other recent biographical studies.

I have given what explanation and interpretation seemed necessary, but have tried not to obtrude my "philosophy of Byron" on the reader. I have seen little reason to paraphrase Byron when I could quote him. The trenchancy of his letters can seldom be bettered in modern prose. I have plagiarized myself freely from my longer biography when the statement there expressed my present views. I have modified it when I thought it could be made more accurate or more clear, or when new evidence has changed my judgment.

I have gained some fresh insights and have incorporated some new details from such recent biographical studies as Doris Langley Moore's *The Late Lord Byron* and Malcolm Elwin's *Lord Byron's Wife*. And I have added some hitherto unpublished details concerning Byron's residence in Rome and his name on a column at Delphi. My aim has been to give the essence of Byron's dramatic career and engaging personality in a single volume drawn from the most recent research and authentic sources. I am content to let the reader make his own judgments of Byron's character.

My indebtedness to Byron scholars and others in several countries, who have assisted my work either by their publications or by personal favors and information, is indeed considerable. I gave credit in the Preface to *Byron: A Biography* to those who aided me in my original research. I can do no more than add here the names of those who have assisted me personally in various ways in the preparation and writing of the present volume.

In England, Mrs. Doris Langley Moore has been helpful in calling many biographical details to my attention. And I am grateful for the encouragement and interest of Mr. Malcolm Elwin, now engaged in editing the Byron papers in the possession of the Earl of Lytton, Byron's great-great-grandson. Mr. William St. Clair first called my attention to Byron's name recently rediscovered on a column at Delphi. My English publisher, Mr. John Grey Murray, a direct descendant of Byron's publisher and an enthusiastic admirer of the poet's life and letters, has helped me in many ways.

In Italy, Sra. Vera Cacciatore's researches in the records of the Keats-Shelley Memorial led me to the authentication of Byron's residence in the Piazza di Spagna in Rome in 1817.

I am indebted for assistance in Greece to Mr. Francis R. Walton, Librarian of the Gennadius Library, and to his assistant, Miss E. Demetracopoulou; to Mr. P. Laurence O'Keeffe, Head of Chancery, the British Embassy, Athens; and to my friend of many years, Nassos Tzartzanos.

In America, I am particularly grateful to the John Simon Guggenheim Memorial Foundation and to its president, Gordon N. Ray, for a Guggenheim Fellowship in 1968–9, which enabled me to do research abroad. I am also grateful to Professor Allan Davis of Hofstra University for putting secretarial assistance at my disposal while I held the John Cranford Adams Chair of English, and to Miss Lynea Bowdish for typing the first draft of this book. Mr. Herbert Weinstock, my editor at Alfred A. Knopf, has helped with many pertinent suggestions. And the editorial assistance of my wife Marion has been of inestimable value.

Acknowledgments

FOR PERMISSION TO QUOTE from copyrighted books my thanks are due to the following:

Jonathan Cape, Ltd., and John Murray—for quotations from *The Last Attachment,* by Iris Origo, 1949.

Malcolm Elwin, Macdonald & Co., Ltd., and Harcourt Brace & World —for quotations from *Lord Byron's Wife,* by Malcolm Elwin, 1962.

Yale University Press—for quotations from *Lord Byron's First Pilgrimage, 1809–1811,* by William A. Borst, 1948.

John Murray—for quotations from books and manuscripts in which he holds copyright.

The Clarendon Press—for quotations from *The Letters of Percy Bysshe Shelley,* edited by Frederick L. Jones, 1964.

Princeton University Press—for quotations from *Medwin's Conversations of Lord Byron,* edited by Ernest J. Lovell, Jr., 1966; and *Lady Blessington's Conversations of Lord Byron,* edited by Ernest J. Lovell, Jr., 1969.

University of Oklahoma Press—for quotations from *Mary Shelley's Journal,* 1947; *The Letters of Mary W. Shelley,* 2 vols., 1944; and *Maria Gisborne & Edward E. Williams,* 1951. All edited by Frederick L. Jones.

Doris Langley Moore, John Murray, and J. B. Lippincott Co.—for quotations from *The Late Lord Byron,* by Doris Langley Moore, 1961.

Harvard University Press—for quotations from *Byron, Shelley and Their Pisan Circle,* by C. L. Cline, 1952.

Professor Willis W. Pratt—for quotations from his *Bryon at Southwell* (University of Texas Byron Monographs No. 1), 1948.

The Earl of Lytton—for quotations from *The Life and Letters of Anne Isabella Lady Noel Byron,* by Ethel Colburn Mayne (published by Constable & Co., Ltd., 1929); and *Astarte,* by the Earl of Lovelace (new edition by Mary Countess of Lovelace, published by Christophers, 1921).

Contents

Illustrations

following page 202

1. Byron at about the time he left Harrow for Cambridge.

   (Oil painting by an unknown artist, National Historical Museum, Athens. Photographed and reproduced with the permission of the Director of the Museum, Mr. Meletopoulos.)

2. Admiral Byron, grandfather; the Byron family coat of arms; and Captain John Byron, father.

   (From old prints.)

3. Mrs. Catherine Gordon Byron, mother.

   (From a portrait by Thomas Stewardson, in the Murray Collection. Courtesy of John Grey Murray.)

4. Newstead Priory, Nottinghamshire.

   (From an engraving of a painting by Paul Sandby, R.A. Courtesy of Newstead Abbey Collections, Nottingham Public Libraries.)

5. Harrow School.

   (Engraved by J. Stadler from a painting by William Westall. Courtesy of Pierpont Morgan Library, New York.)

6. Mary Chaworth.

   (From a miniature, artist unknown, in the Munster Collection, Newstead Abbey. Courtesy of the Nottingham Public Libraries.)

7. Byron, 1807–9.

   (Engraved by Edward Finden from a painting by George Sanders.)

8. John Cam Hobhouse.

   (Engraved by James Hopwood from a drawing by Abraham Wivell.)

9. Mrs. Spencer Smith.

   (Engraved from a portrait by John William Wright.)

10. Ali Pasha.

    (Engraved by William Finden from a drawing by Frank Stone.)

11. House of Nicolò Argyri, Ioannina, Byron's residence in 1809.

    (Engraved by F. C. Lewis; designed by C. R. Cockerell. From Thomas S. Hughes: Travels in Sicily, Greece and Albania, 1820.*)*

12. Monastery at Zitsa.

    (From a photograph by the author.)

MAPS

THE BYRONS

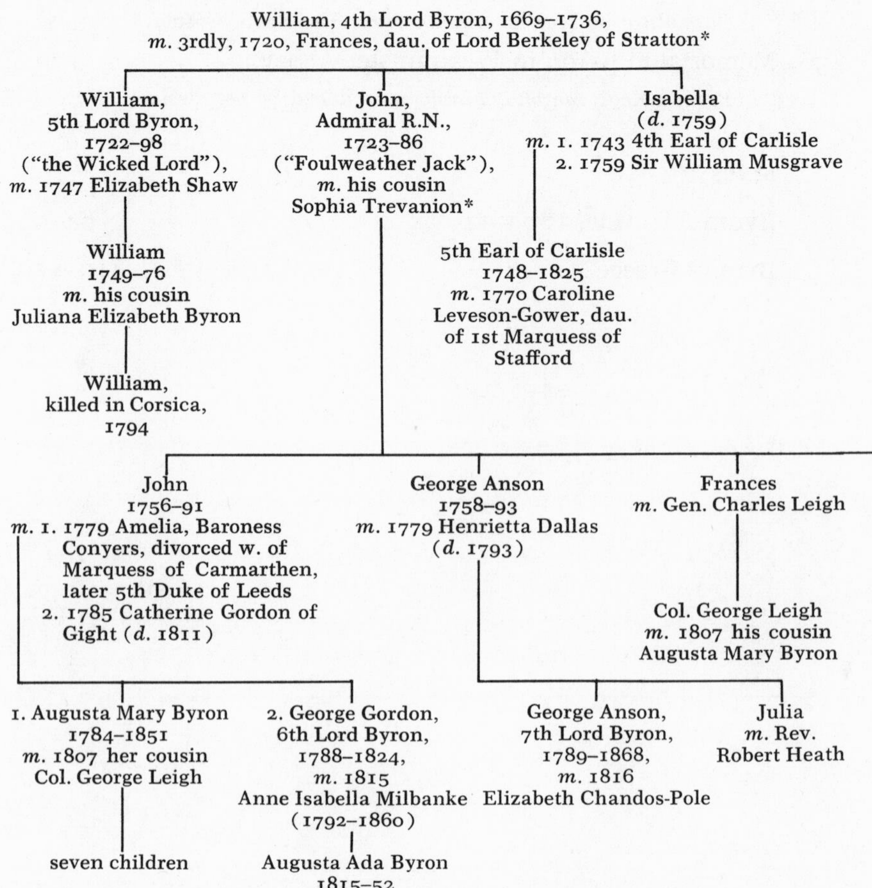

*Lord Berkeley of Stratton had two daughters; the elder married John Trevanion, of Carhays, Cornwall, the younger the 4th Lord Byron.

Juliana Elizabeth
m. 1. her cousin Hon. William Byron
2. Sir Robert Wilmot, Bt.

Robert John Wilmot
1784–1841
m. 1806 Anne Horton

Augusta Barbara Charlotte
m. Vice-Admiral Christopher Parker

Sir Peter Parker
1786–1814
killed in action

Margaret Parker
d. 1802

Sophia Maria
unm.

THE NOELS

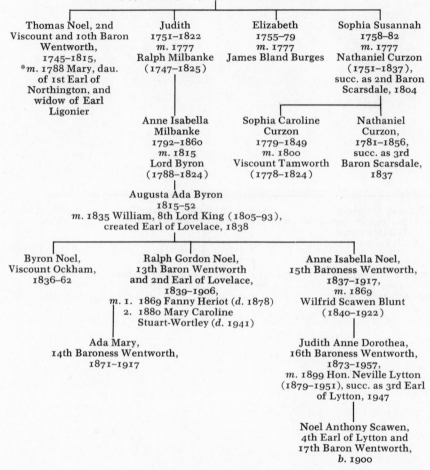

Sir Edward Noel, 6th Bart., 9th Baron and 1st Viscount Wentworth, 1715–74,
m. 1744 Judith (*d.* 1761), dau. of William Lamb

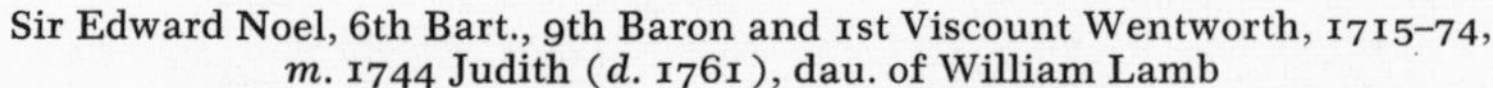

Thomas Noel, 2nd Viscount and 10th Baron Wentworth, 1745–1815, **m.* 1788 Mary, dau. of 1st Earl of Northington, and widow of Earl Ligonier

Judith 1751–1822 *m.* 1777 Ralph Milbanke (1747–1825)

Elizabeth 1755–79 *m.* 1777 James Bland Burges

Sophia Susannah 1758–82 *m.* 1777 Nathaniel Curzon (1751–1837), succ. as 2nd Baron Scarsdale, 1804

Anne Isabella Milbanke 1792–1860 *m.* 1815 Lord Byron (1788–1824)

Sophia Caroline Curzon 1779–1849 *m.* 1800 Viscount Tamworth (1778–1824)

Nathaniel Curzon, 1781–1856, succ. as 3rd Baron Scarsdale, 1837

Augusta Ada Byron
1815–52
m. 1835 William, 8th Lord King (1805–93),
created Earl of Lovelace, 1838

Byron Noel, Viscount Ockham, 1836–62

Ralph Gordon Noel, 13th Baron Wentworth and 2nd Earl of Lovelace, 1839–1906,
m. 1. 1869 Fanny Heriot (*d.* 1878)
2. 1880 Mary Caroline Stuart-Wortley (*d.* 1941)

Anne Isabella Noel, 15th Baroness Wentworth, 1837–1917, *m.* 1869 Wilfrid Scawen Blunt (1840–1922)

Ada Mary, 14th Baroness Wentworth, 1871–1917

Judith Anne Dorothea, 16th Baroness Wentworth, 1873–1957, *m.* 1899 Hon. Neville Lytton (1879–1951), succ. as 3rd Earl of Lytton, 1947

Noel Anthony Scawen, 4th Earl of Lytton and 17th Baron Wentworth, *b.* 1900

*Though the 2nd Viscount Wentworth left no legitimate issue, he had by Catherine Vanloo (*d.* 1781) a daughter, Anna Catherine, who married Vincent Hilton Biscoe in 1790, and a son, the Rev. Thomas Noel Noel (*b.* 1775), who married Catherine Smith in 1796.

THE MILBANKES AND THE MELBOURNES

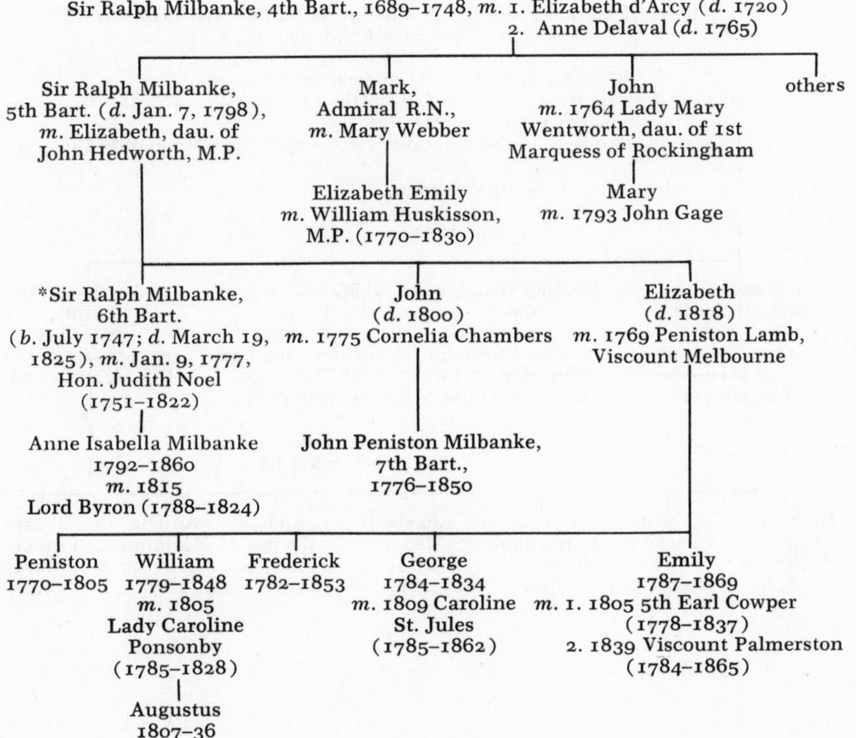

*Sir Ralph Milbanke took the name Noel instead of Milbanke by royal licence, May 20, 1815, in accordance with the terms of his wife's inheritance from her brother, the 2nd Viscount Wentworth, who died April 17, 1815.

AUGUSTA LEIGH'S FAMILY CONNECTIONS

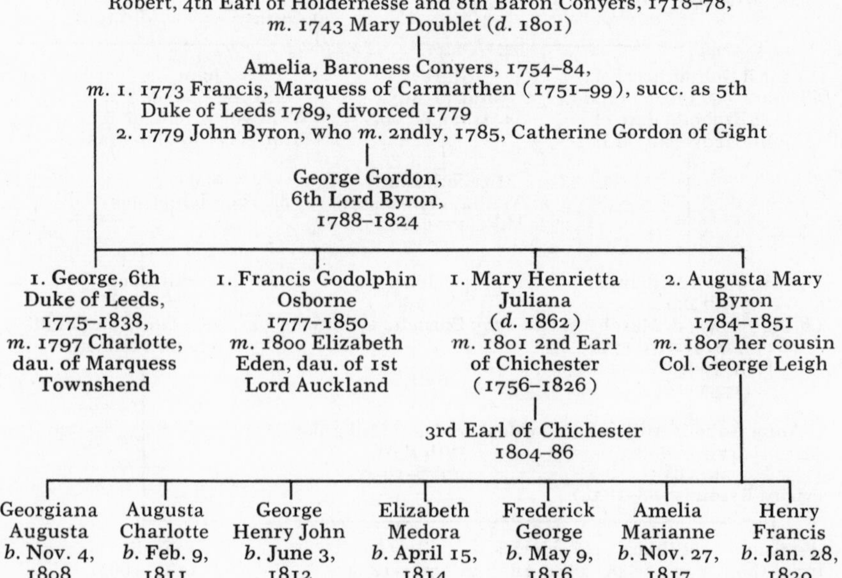
Robert, 4th Earl of Holdernesse and 8th Baron Conyers, 1718–78,
m. 1743 Mary Doublet (*d.* 1801)
Amelia, Baroness Conyers, 1754–84,
m. 1. 1773 Francis, Marquess of Carmarthen (1751–99), succ. as 5th Duke of Leeds 1789, divorced 1779
2. 1779 John Byron, who *m.* 2ndly, 1785, Catherine Gordon of Gight
George Gordon, 6th Lord Byron, 1788–1824
1. George, 6th Duke of Leeds, 1775–1838, *m.* 1797 Charlotte, dau. of Marquess Townshend
1. Francis Godolphin Osborne 1777–1850 *m.* 1800 Elizabeth Eden, dau. of 1st Lord Auckland
1. Mary Henrietta Juliana (*d.* 1862) *m.* 1801 2nd Earl of Chichester (1756–1826)
2. Augusta Mary Byron 1784–1851 *m.* 1807 her cousin Col. George Leigh
3rd Earl of Chichester 1804–86
Georgiana Augusta *b.* Nov. 4, 1808
Augusta Charlotte *b.* Feb. 9, 1811
George Henry John *b.* June 3, 1812
Elizabeth Medora *b.* April 15, 1814
Frederick George *b.* May 9, 1816
Amelia Marianne *b.* Nov. 27, 1817
Henry Francis *b.* Jan. 28, 1820

BYRON: *A Portrait*

NOTES

Asterisked notes at the foot of the page are explanatory or of general interest; the superior characters [n] in the text refer to notes of bibliographical or scholarly interest (chiefly source identifications), which are indicated by page and line at the back of the book.

CHAPTER I

To 1788

The Byrons and the Gordons

GEORGE GORDON, the sixth Lord Byron, was born with a lame foot on January 22, 1788, in poor lodgings in London. He was descended from two of the most erratic and colorful strains of the British aristocracy. Though he was later sometimes inclined to boast of his mother's descent from James I of Scotland, his imagination was stirred more by the long line of his paternal ancestry. The first members of the Byron family in England are supposed to have been Ernegis and Radulfus (Ralph) de Burun, large landholders in the north in the time of the Conqueror. Little is known of them until the time of Henry VIII, when the picturesque Newstead Abbey in Nottinghamshire came into the possession of Sir John Byron through the favor of the King. His natural son, "Little Sir John with the Great Beard," succeeded to the title by the grace of Queen Elizabeth, who knighted him in 1579, and he became something of a legendary character for his lavish entertainment (he maintained a troupe of players).

A later Sir John Byron, a faithful though not a very successful general of Charles I, was created Baron Byron of Rochdale in the County of Lancaster on October 24, 1643. This first Lord Byron lost most of his property in the Civil War and followed Charles II into exile. He was apparently rewarded with horns, for Pepys mentions his second wife, Eleanor, as having been the seventeenth mistress of Charles II.[n] His older brother Richard inherited the title and bought back the Abbey, which had been sequestered by Parliament.

William, the fifth Lord, entered the Navy but later retired to Newstead where his extravagances made him notorious. He had already earned the reputation of a rake in London. At Newstead he built a small castle on one of the lakes, which was darkly hinted to be the rendezvous of unspeakable orgies. He also built two turreted forts on the banks of the upper lake and waged mimic warfare upon them from small armed vessels. He was commonly referred to as "the Wicked Lord Byron" after he killed his kinsman and neighbor, William Chaworth, in a duel in a London club in 1765, following a drunken argument on the best way to preserve game. He was acquitted by his peers after a trial in the House of Lords and retired to the Abbey. In his misanthropy following the elopement of his son with an impecunious cousin, the old lord denuded the forests of his estate of their ancient oaks, and had twenty-seven hundred deer killed in the park and sold in the markets.

The "Wicked" Lord Byron's brother John, grandfather of the poet, was scarcely less spectacular, though considerably more genial. In 1740, at seventeen, he entered the Navy as a midshipman. The shipwreck, starvation, and hardships he encountered on a voyage to the South Seas he described in his *Narrative*, published in 1768. In 1748 he married his first cousin, Sophia Trevanion, long an intimate friend of Mrs. Thrale and a favorite of Dr. Samuel Johnson. By the time Byron was promoted to the rank of Vice-Admiral (1778), he had encountered so many storms that he came to be known as "Foulweather Jack." On shore his amorous adventures supplied lurid stories for the gossip columns of the time. But before the old Admiral died in 1786, his eldest son, John ("Mad Jack"), had so far exceeded him in gallantry, in scandal, and in extravagance as to cause the old seaman to disinherit him.

Born at Plymouth on February 7, 1756, John Byron, father of the poet, went to Westminster School and later to a French military academy, where he probably learned the language and acquired a taste for the "pastimes and prodigalities" that made him notorious while still a young man. With a commission in the Guards he served for a time with the British forces in America. But by 1778 he seems to have disposed of his captain-lieutenancy and retired to London to pursue the life of fashion. In that year the handsome Captain eloped with the accomplished and beautiful Lady Carmarthen, wife of Francis, then Marquis and afterwards fifth Duke of Leeds. She was the only child of the last Earl of Holderness, who had just left her an estate that yielded £4,000 a year, a very considerable added attraction, for the Captain had already outrun the purse and patience of his family. After the Marquis divorced her, they were married and went to France to escape the éclat of the scandal and the Captain's creditors.

That the madcap Byron was devoted to his heiress in his fashion seems probable, for they lived together in France until her death on January 26, 1784. She bore him three children, the last and only one to survive beyond infancy being Augusta, the poet's half-sister, born in 1783. The poet later replied to the accusation that his father's "brutal conduct" had caused his wife to die of a broken heart: "So far from being 'brutal,' he was, according to the testimony of all those who knew him, of an extremely amiable and (*enjoué*) joyous character, but careless (*insouciant*) and dissipated. . . . It is not by 'brutality' that a young Officer of the Guards seduces and carries off a Marchioness, and marries two heiresses. It is true that he was a very handsome man, which goes a great way." [n]

Captain Byron was soon sufficiently recovered in spirit and immersed in debt to leave the carefree life of Paris for the chilly shores of England, once more in search of an heiress. Knowing that the happy hunting ground for fortunes in the marriage market was to be found in the ballrooms of Bath, he appeared in that city in the spring of 1785 and no doubt cut a considerable figure, his natural grace heightened by French manners and speech. He met and soon turned the head of Catherine Gordon of Gight. Though her fortune of more than £23,000, "doubled by rumour," may not have been the largest in the Bath market, certainly it must have seemed the most accessible to the blasé, suave Captain. Catherine Gordon was an inexperienced Scottish girl of twenty. Though in the bloom of youth, she was rather plain and coarse, awkward and provincial, with a broad Scottish accent. With his elegant dancing Captain Byron swept the poor country girl off her feet, and on May 13, 1785, for the second time he was united with an heiress.

That branch of the Gordon family from which Catherine was most proud to be directly descended dated from 1490, when

Sir William Gordon traded the lands of Aboyne to his elder brother for the estate of Gight, which lay in the valley of the River Ythan about thirty miles north of Aberdeen. Sir William was the third son of George, second Earl of Huntly, by his second wife, Princess Annabella Stuart, daughter of James I of Scotland.

The Gight Gordons were among the most notorious of the Scottish lairds for their defiance of law and order. The wars of the Covenant gave the Gordons a happy chance to enter into some large-scale raids. Like the Byrons in England, they were Royalists, and they combined politics with plunder. By the beginning of the eighteenth century, the establishment of the more stable government and the cooling of the hot blood of the clans gradually developed more sober traits in the Gordons of Gight.

The eleventh laird fathered fourteen children before he was drowned in the River Ythan in 1760 under circumstances that suggested suicide. The twelfth laird, George Gordon, had three daughters, but only Catherine was living when her father died in 1779, leaving her heir to a moderate fortune, a decaying castle, and a curious combination of ancestral traits.

The bride of Captain Byron had few endowments to compensate for her plainness and the rolling gait that made her conspicuous. She had been brought up by her grandmother Margaret Duff Gordon, a pious and ignorant old woman. Catherine was fond of gossip and was given to fits of melancholy followed by capricious outbursts of passion that found vent in some choice epithets in the dialect of her native Buchan. Sir Walter Scott recollected seeing Catherine Gordon at the theater in Edinburgh before her marriage when she became hysterical at the acting of Mrs. Siddons in *The Fatal Marriage*, "harrowing the house by the desperate and wild way in which she shrieked out Mrs. Siddons's exclamation, in the character of Isabella, 'Oh my Biron!' . . . The remarkable circumstance was, that the lady had not then seen Captain Byron." [n]

Though Mrs. Byron's letters were often forceful and direct when the subject moved her, her spelling and grammar displayed an astounding illiteracy. And yet she read widely, had shrewd critical good sense (even in judging her son's poetry), and liberal Whiggish sympathies.

Where the Byrons spent their "treacle-moon," as their son

later called the days following his own "fatal marriage," is not known. No doubt it was financed by the heiress and was spent somewhere far from the Captain's creditors. But by July 1785 they were back in Scotland and established at Gight.

By the middle of the summer Catherine, it seems, was already frightened by the Captain's free spending, but she could never resist him and he proceeded to lay waste the Gordon inheritance. For almost a year they continued to live in the ancient and already dilapidated castle. The reputation Johnny Byron had earned among his neighbors is indicated in a popular ballad of the time:

This youth is a rake, frae England is come,
The Scots dinna ken his extraction ava;
He keeps up his misses, his landlords he duns,
That's fast drawn the lands o' Gight awa'.[n]

By the summer of 1786 Captain Byron had indeed squandered the lands of Gight away. The £3,000 in cash which Catherine Gordon had when she married had been spent, and her other disposable property sold at a sacrifice on forced sale. And within a year £8,000 had been borrowed on a mortgage on Gight. After a futile attempt to get something from the estate of his father, the Admiral, who died in April, the Byrons settled for a time in Hampshire, where duns were less likely than in London.

Mrs. Byron's plight was pitiable. Completely under the spell of her handsome husband, she appealed to her kinswoman Miss Urquhart, urging her to have the commissioners who sold Gight settle £10,000 on her "in such a manner that it would be out of Mr. Byron's power to spend, and out of my own power to give up to him. . . . I should not wish to appear in it myself, or Mr. Byron should know that I wrote or spoke to anybody upon the subject, because if he did he would never forgive me. . . ."[n] But when the estate was finally sold the following year, at least half of the purchase price of £17,850 disappeared to pay the Captain's most pressing debts.

By September 1787, Captain Byron had escaped to France, and his wife, then "big with bairn," soon followed. By that time Byron was without a sou and was glad to have her remittances from Scotland. The short sojourn of Mrs. Byron in France could not have been very happy. While her husband spoke French and was at home in French society, she knew not a word of the language. The Captain's daughter by the Marchioness, Augusta, then four years old, was taken from his sister and put under her care. The pregnant woman nursed the child through a serious illness and was still loyal to the Johnny Byron who had almost ruined her. When her time approached, Mrs. Byron returned to England accompanied by Augusta, whom she soon placed with the Marchioness's mother, Lady Holderness. She stopped briefly in Dover and then, alone in London, took lodgings for her accouchement.

CHAPTER II

1788–1798

Scottish Boyhood

CONSTANTLY HARASSED BY financial worries, Mrs. Byron rented a furnished back drawing room on the first floor at 16 Holles Street,[n] a respectable but inexpensive lodging in the short lane connecting Oxford Street and Cavendish Square. At her own request, the Scottish commissioners doled out her allowance in small bits. She wrote the Edinburgh agent on January 2: "I don't want much and if there was to be large sums it would be thrown away as it was before." [n]

The Captain arrived in England early in January, drawn no doubt not so much by the imminent birth of his child as by the fact that Mrs. Byron's small allowance was his only sure and easy source of supply. For the next few months he played hide-and-seek with his creditors, venturing into London to wheedle money from his poor wife on Sundays, when by English law the debtor had immunity. It is unlikely that he dared the duns to witness the birth of his son on Tuesday, January 22, 1788.

Mrs. Byron's first and only child came into the world with a physical handicap that caused him throughout his life much bodily suffering and mental agony, and that probably did more to shape his character than it will ever be possible to calculate. He was born with a deformed right foot. Despite all the controversy that has raged over Byron's foot, the evidence of his parents and of the doctors who attended him points to its being a true clubbed foot, the heel being drawn up and the sole of the foot turned inward.[n] John Hunter, a noted anatomist and surgeon who had specialized in the study of the rupture of the Achilles tendon, was called in for advice[n] and recommended a special shoe that he thought would enable the boy, when old enough, to walk without difficulty, though he offered no hope of an actual cure.

On February 29, Mrs. Byron took her son to be christened in the nearby Marylebone parish church. The child's father was nowhere about, and she gave the child the name of her own father, George Gordon. The poor woman was haunted constantly by money worries. Her husband owed £1,300 and "discharging the present debts would only be paving the way to the accumulation of fresh ones."[n]

A settlement was finally made in March, securing £4,222 of Mrs. Byron's remaining capital against further inroads of creditors. Of this, £3,000 was invested at 5 per cent under the care of trustees for Mrs. Byron, the principal being inalienable during her lifetime, and £1,222 was left as a burden on the estate, the annual interest (£55 11s. 1d.) going as a life annuity to her grandmother Duff. Sometime in the summer of 1789 Mrs. Byron left London for Aberdeen, where she and her baby could live comfortably enough on the £150 secured her under the settlement.

Soon after, with creditors close on his heels, Captain Byron fled again to Scotland, and by August he had moved into the small lodging his wife had taken in Queen Street. In these close quarters, with Agnes Gray, a pious Bible-reading Presbyterian maid, to look after the little lame boy, the Byrons lived an uneasy and cramped existence. The Captain was no longer master of Gight, where the evening punch and the pipes playing until midnight had made the raw Scottish winter less unbearable. He, the most amiable of men in good company, became irritable. He finally found relief by taking quarters at the opposite end of Queen Street, from which he visited his wife and drank tea amicably with her. Though she could fly into a tantrum when he asked her for money, Mrs. Byron often indulged in ridiculous displays of affection for her Johnny Byron. And the same extremes of uncontrollable anger and demonstrative affection marked her behavior both then and later toward her son, who had a temper equal to his mother's. Scolded one day for soiling a dress he had just put on, he stood for a while in silent rage and then tore the garment from top to bottom.

As soon as he could get a draft from his sister, Mrs. Leigh, the Captain sought more congenial society. When he was gone, Mrs. Byron was desolate. She assuaged her passionate grief by a mingled hatred and love of the son who reminded her of him. "My mother," the poet recalled, "when she was in a rage with me, (and I gave her cause enough,) used to say, 'Ah, you little dog, you are a Byron all over; you are as bad as your father!' "[n] But the next moment she was covering him with kisses.

Mrs. Byron's annuity had been reduced to £135 by the necessity of paying off a debt of £300 she had incurred while her husband was in Scotland. And he apparently returned once more in September 1790 to wheedle another hundred pounds, from the capital left to pay the annuity of her grandmother, to enable him to go to France. We next see him at Valenciennes, in the house owned by his sister, dallying with chambermaids and actresses. His wife and son never saw him again.

Captain Byron's letters to his sister read like some of those written by his famous son later from Venice during his dissipations in the Carnival: "As for me, here I am, and in love with whom? A new actress who is come from Paris. . . . I believe, I have had one third of Valenciennes, particularly a Girl at L'Aigle Rouge, an Inn here [.] I happened to [be] there one day when it rained so hard. . . . She is very handsome and very tall, and I am not yet tired."[n]

In desperation Mrs. Byron swallowed her pride to the extent of asking his sister, Mrs. Leigh, for a loan of £40, for her income had been arrested by creditors, "all owing to the debts I became bound to pay for him for the extravagant way he would live when he was here. . . ."[n] Mrs. Leigh must have been touched by this pathetic appeal, sealed in red wax with the motto of the proud Gordons: "*Je ne change qu'en mourant.*" But Jack Byron was only interested in money for his desperate needs. Writing to his sister on February 16, 1791, he spoke cavalierly of his wife and made the only reference to his son to be found in his correspondence: "With regard to Mrs. Byron, I am glad she writes to you. She is very amiable at a distance; but I defy you and all the Apostles to live with her two months, for, if any body could live with her, it was me. . . . For my son, I am happy to hear he is well; but for his walking, 'tis impossible, as he is club-footed."[n]

By the summer Jack Byron had sunk to the lowest depths of degradation and debt. His self-made tragedy came to an end on August 2, 1791, perhaps by suicide. He had made a will, ironically appointing his son, George Gordon, "heir of my real and personal estate, and charge him to pay my debts, legacies, and funeral expenses."[n]

When Mrs. Byron received the news of his death, her cries could be heard in the street. She wrote Mrs. Leigh: "I do not think I shall ever get the better of it;—necessity, not inclination, parted us, at least on my part, and I flatter myself it was the same with him; and notwithstanding all his foibles, for they deserve no worse name, I ever sincerely loved him. . . ."[n] The boy was three and one-half years old when his father died. He later told Thomas Medwin: "I perfectly remember him; and had very early a horror of matrimony, from the sight of domestic broils. . . ."[n]

Mrs. Byron drew her shattered life together with a great deal of courage, and lived within her narrowed income. She devoted herself unselfishly to the care of her lame son. She had written to Mrs. Leigh in London for aid in getting "a proper shoe for George's foot."[n] She later gave more details of her son's deformity: "George's foot turns inward, and it is the right foot; he walks quite on the side of his foot."[n]

The boy early developed a sensitivity to his lameness, perhaps because his mother upbraided him for it in her exasperated moods. A nurse, encountering Agnes Gray and her charge on one of her walks, remarked: "What a pretty boy Byron is! what a pity he has such a leg!" His eyes flashing with anger, the child struck at her with his little whip, shouting, "Dinna speak of it!"[n]

Mrs. Byron borrowed enough to furnish a flat of her own, taking the whole first floor at 64 Broad Street, a respectable thoroughfare in the heart of the new town, and she sacrificed her own comfort to give her son every advantage her poverty permitted. The chronological vagueness of early accounts of Byron's childhood has left the impression that his mother habitually threw the firetongs at his head or broke dishes over it. But most of these performances belong to his obstreperous youth in England. In his early years, George, though mischievous, high-strung, and sensitive, had a loyal and affectionate nature.

Byron's curious combination of aristocratic pride and liberal sympathy may have come from his mother. He wrote John Murray in later years: "My Mother (who was as haughty as Lucifer with her descent from the Stuarts . . .)" was "always reminding me how superior *her* Gordons were to the Southron Byrons."[n] And on the other side she sympathized with the people's cause in the French Revolution. She wrote Mrs. Leigh in 1792: "I fancy you and I are on different sides, for I am quite a Democrat and I do not think the King, after his treachery and perjury, deserves to be restored."[n]

And the whole environment of Byron's Aberdeen years conditioned him to the views of the lower-middle-class Scottish world with which he was daily associated in the streets and later at school. Though she was related to some of the best families in the northern counties, Mrs. Byron recognized that now she was only a poor relation.

Certainly there was nothing aristocratic about the first school to which she sent her son. In a narrow lane known as Long Acre, very near to the house in Broad Street, a Mr. John Bowers kept a mixed and noisy school in a grimy warehouse-like room, poorly lighted, with a low ceiling and dusty floor. Here the little boy with the red jacket and the nankeen trousers spent a fruitless year with the dapper "Bodsy Bowers." In his reminiscences of Aberdeen, Byron wrote: "I learned little there, except to repeat by rote the first lesson of Monosyllables—'God made man, let us love him'—by hearing it often repeated, without acquiring a letter."[n] During the next year, under more competent instructors, he learned to read. And he began the study of Latin in Ruddiman's Grammar.

In 1794, when Byron was six, news came of an event that was to change the whole course of his life. The "Wicked" Lord Byron's grandson had been killed by a cannon ball in Corsica and George Gordon had become heir presumptive to the title and estates of his Byron ancestors. Mrs. Byron began to hold her head a little higher and to visit with more confidence some of her aristocratic relations.

During the term of 1794–95 young George was sent to the Aberdeen Grammar School in the Schoolhill, a short walk from

Broad Street. The low one-storied gray stone structure then housing 150 boys was built in 1757. The only branch of study was Latin, taught in the traditional manner that made lessons a deadly chore. George Bayron Gordon, as his name was entered on the rolls (indicative perhaps of the pronunciation of the Aberdonians), did not exert himself and remained in the respectable middle of the class, though in the fourth form he had risen to fifth from the top of a group of twenty-seven boys. Writing was an "extra," which he studied at Mr. Duncan's writing school.

Byron had already begun to read widely before he left the Grammar School. He later recalled: "Knolles, Cantemir, De Tott, Lady M. W. Montague [sic], Hawkins's Translation from Mignot's History of the Turks, the Arabian Nights, all travels, or histories, or books upon the East I could meet with, I had read, as well as Rycaut, before I was *ten years old*." Knolles's *Turkish History,* he said, was "one of the first books that gave me pleasure when a child; and I believe it had much influence on my subsequent wishes to visit the Levant, and gave, perhaps, the oriental colouring which is observed in my poetry." After these books, he wrote, "I preferred the history of naval actions, Don Quixote and Smollett's novels, particularly Roderick Random, and I was passionate for the Roman History. When a boy, I could never bear to read any Poetry whatever without disgust and reluctance." [n]

Yet, under the tutelage of Agnes Gray, Byron had come to know and like the poetry of the Psalms. And with her, and later with her sister May, he had read with some thoroughness the books of the Bible. "I am a great reader and admirer of those books," he later wrote John Murray, "and had read them through and through before I was eight years old,—that is to say, the *Old* Testament, for the New struck me as a task, but the other as a pleasure." [n]

The story of Cain and Abel early captured his imagination. When he was eight years old, he read Gessner's *Death of Abel* with delight. The fascinating idea that he was predestined to evil was strengthened by his reading a semi-Gothic novel by John Moore called *Zeluco* after its misanthropic hero-villain, who was fated to perform dark deeds by forces beyond his control.

No doubt Byron thrashed more than one boy who dared to

make references to his lameness, though he had so far overcome his sensitivity as to take part in games which required running. And in a mood of bravado and kinship with another boy similarly handicapped he could say: "Come and see the twa laddies with the twa club feet going up the Broad-street."[n]

While Byron mingled freely with his classmates on a plane of equality, his mother had already begun to make him conscious of his superior destiny, not only as a descendant of the Gordons, but also now more particularly as heir to the Byron peerage. When a visitor flatteringly said that she hoped some day to read his speeches in the House of Commons, the boy replied proudly: "I hope not; if you read any speeches of mine, it will be in the House of Lords."[n]

There is record of at least one visit to the boy's great-grandmother, Margaret Duff Gordon, at Banff, perhaps in the summer holiday of 1795, the year in which Mrs. Byron had her son's portrait painted by John Kaye of Edinburgh. The demure, almost angelic profile of the seven-year-old boy with curly hair down to his shoulders, posed artificially as an archer, gives no indication of his mischievous nature.

It may have been in that year also that Byron first met his distant cousin Mary Duff. Years later he wrote in his diary: "I recollect all we said to each other, all our caresses, her features, my restlessness, sleeplessness, my tormenting my mother's maid to write for me to her. . . . I certainly had no sexual ideas for years afterwards; and yet my misery, my love for that girl were so violent, that I sometimes doubt if I have ever been really attached since. . . ."[n]

In 1795 or 1796, Byron was taken for a holiday to the valley of the Dee about forty miles above Aberdeen, near Braemar. The beautiful Deeside invited rambling and Loch-na-garr and Morven were visible in the distance. It was there that he came to love the Scottish highlands and countryside. He wore the Gordon tartan, dark blue crossed with lighter shades of green and blocked off with thin yellow lines. Except for an occasional flare-up, his mother treated him indulgently, and allowed him much freedom. The estuaries of the Dee and the Don gave him ample opportunity to practice the swimming that early became his favorite sport because in it his lameness was no handicap.

Exciting news came from England just after George's tenth

birthday: the fifth Lord Byron was dead. The day after he was told that he was now the sixth Baron Byron of Rochdale, he asked his mother "whether she perceived any difference in him since he had been made a lord, as he perceived none himself."[n] The greatest embarrassment came at school when the master sent for him, gave him some cake and wine, and told him that he was now a lord. Byron told his friend Hobhouse later that "the little treat and the respectful manner of the master gave him at once high notions of his new dignity."[n] When his new title, "Dominus de Byron," was pronounced without warning in the classroom and he was silently stared at by his fellows, he burst into tears.

Mrs. Byron's London agent, Mr. Farquhar, had recommended his friend John Hanson of Chancery Lane to handle her affairs. After conferring with the old lord's executor, Hanson discovered that her expectation of £2,000 a year from the estate was an illusion; there would not even be enough to bury the old lord after all debts were paid. He had died on May 21, but it was August before the Byrons could arrange their affairs in Scotland and start for a new life in England. Mrs. Byron's only resources for the journey came from the sale of her furniture for £74 17s. 7d.

Despite Byron's later romantic recollections of his Scottish childhood, it is difficult to know what the young lord's feelings were on leaving his homeland. He recorded in his journal in 1813: "I differed not at all from other children, being neither tall nor short, dull nor witty, of my age, but rather lively—except in my sullen moods, and then I was always a Devil."[n] But there was softness in him, and shyness, and an amiable desire to please and to be liked. He could be an agreeable companion, despite the fact that he was already a spoiled child. His childhood in Scotland was happy enough to make it the liveliest part of his later nostalgic dreams. At the phrase "Auld Lang Syne," he wrote, all Scotland flew up before him:

But I am half a Scot by birth, and bred
A whole one . . ."[n]

CHAPTER III

1798–1801

The Young Lord

FOUR MILES SOUTH OF Mansfield at the edge of Sherwood Forest, about 130 miles from London on the Great North Road, the coach from Aberdeen carrying three eager passengers stopped at the Newstead tollgate. Mrs. Byron, enjoying the drama of the occasion, asked what nobleman lived on the adjoining estate. "It was Lord Byron's, but he is dead," the woman at the gate replied. "And who is the heir now?" the proud mother asked. "They say it's a little boy that lives in Aberdeen." May Gray, now Mrs. Byron's maid, exclaimed: "This is him, God bless him!" and turned to kiss the embarrassed young lord.[1] They had gone two miles along a road that passed forlorn stumps of once great oaks, and farms sadly run down, when they saw the gray walls of the old Abbey facing a lake. The ruins of the Gothic church gave a romantic charm to the massive structure.*

Swinging around the fountain, which had been removed by the earlier Byrons from the court of the cloister and placed

* The Priory of Newstead had been founded by Henry II, probably between 1163 and 1173. The Canons Regular of the Order of St. Augustine built a handsome gray stone Gothic church and, adjoining it, the extensive halls of the Priory surrounding a square cloister enclosing an open court with a fountain in the middle. Sir John Byron, when he acquired the Priory from Henry VIII, had no difficulty in converting it into an extensive country estate, perhaps with the aid of stones from two sides of the church, for when the poet first saw Newstead in 1798 nothing remained of it but the front or west wall and the south side of the nave, which was also the wall of the main structure of the Priory.

before the entrance, the young lord and his mother were greeted by Mr. and Mrs. John Hanson, Mrs. Byron's London agent and his wife. As they looked over the park and the spacious but gloomy halls, their determination to dwell in this seat of the Byrons was strengthened. But their lawyer tried to dissuade them, for on the rear side of the court the building was roofless, and the monks' reception hall and the grand refectory were stuffed with hay for the cattle that had been stabled in the entrance hall and the Priory parlor.

The creditors of the old lord had seized everything, including much of the furniture. The 3,200 acres of the estate were so encumbered that the total income from rents, then not exceeding £850 a year, had been drained by debts. To make the necessary repairs to the Priory and the long-neglected farm buildings, to survey the property and set new rents, and to disentangle the legal knots tied in it under the fifth Baron's regime would take most of the income for at least the first year.

But it was the end of August and the park was lovely. The two lakes glistened and "Folly Castle" and the forts offered irresistible attractions to a ten-year-old boy. And after the cramped quarters in Aberdeen, the spaciousness of the monastic ruins appealed equally to his romantic mother. Reluctantly they drove on to Nottingham, where Byron relations were waiting to receive them.

But the boy's wishes were granted. It was decided that Mrs. Byron could live at Newstead, at least until affairs were settled, repairs made, and a suitable renter found for the manor. Hanson installed them in the dilapidated Abbey with what furniture there was, and he saw a good deal of his charge in the days that followed. He introduced the boy to the Clarkes at Annesley Hall. Mrs. Clarke had a little girl by her first husband, Mr. Chaworth, a descendant of the man who had been killed by "the Wicked Lord Byron" in the famous duel. But Mary Chaworth was two years his senior and Byron's thoughts were still in Scotland with Mary Duff. Hanson said jokingly: "Here is a pretty young lady —you had better marry her." "What, Mr. Hanson," Byron replied, *"the Capulets and Montagues intermarry?"* [n]

In a short while the young lord was happily settled as a nobleman on his country estate. He was proud of the Byron arms, with the mermaid and the chestnut horses surmounting the ancient motto: "Crede Byron." With a generous hand he dealt out largess to his relations in Nottingham. On November 8 he addressed his aunt, Mrs. Parker, daughter of the Admiral, to let her know that "the potatoes are now ready and you are welcome to them whenever you please."[n] And he sent a young rabbit to Mrs. Parkyns, a friend of his aunt.

The next year he was staying with the Parkyns family in Nottingham, where he was receiving treatments from Lavender, a practitioner who called himself a surgeon, and who apparently tried to straighten the boy's deformed foot by rubbing it with oil and screwing it up in a machine that gave the patient excruciating pain. He wrote his mother a letter that shows how seriously he was taking his responsibilities as a young nobleman. He suggested that Mr. Rogers, the tutor of the Miss Parkynses, could attend him every night. ". . . if some plan of this kind is not adopted, I shall be called, or rather branded with the name of a dunce, which you know I could never bear."[n] Dummer Rogers did take over the instruction of the young lord for several months, introducing him to parts of Virgil and Cicero.

On holidays and at other times Byron returned to Newstead to play the grand seigneur. The fifth Baron's pistols were fascinating playthings. The boy imitated his predecessor by practicing pistol shooting (a habit which he continued through life) and by always carrying small loaded pistols in his waistcoat pockets.

Hanson had induced Byron's kinsman, the Earl of Carlisle, to act as his guardian. And on the attorney's next visit to Newstead in the summer of 1799, he saw the necessity of separating the spoiled boy who had so much promise from his mother and putting him into an environment of both kindness and discipline where he could get a more systematic education. Moreover, it was evident that Lavender was merely torturing the child without doing him any good, and it was important to take him to London, where his foot could be examined by competent medical men. When the attorney left Newstead in the second week in July, he took Byron with him in his carriage, May Gray being sent along to look after the bandaging of his foot.

Byron saw London for the first time since infancy on July 12, when the carriage rolled through Old Brompton to the Hansons' house at Earl's Court, Kensington. The next day Hanson had a long conference with Lord Carlisle and Dr. James Baillie concerning Byron's foot. Baillie later made a full examination and recommended a Mr. Sheldrake, who made some instruments to brace the foot; but these were afterward abandoned for a boot specially constructed for him.

Hanson knew that Mrs. Byron would need assistance for the proper education of her son, and he helped her to draw up a petition to the King, which he asked Lord Carlisle to support. On August 24, 1799, the Duke of Portland replied that Mr. Pitt had been given orders that a provision of £300 a year should be made to her out of the Civil List. Hanson also arranged for Byron to attend a small school in Dulwich run by a Scotsman, Dr. Glennie.

May Gray had been sent back to Newstead, and Hanson begged Mrs. Byron to dismiss the girl. He said that while in Nottingham she "was perpetually beating him [Byron], and that his bones sometimes ached from it; that she brought all sorts of Company of the very lowest Description into his apartments." [n] But Hanson had withheld part of the story. After Byron's death he told Hobhouse: "When [Byron was] nine years old at his mother's house a free Scotch girl used to come to bed to him and play tricks with his person." [n] Byron himself was obviously recalling this period of his boyhood when he wrote in his "Detached Thoughts" in 1821: "My passions were developed very early—so early, that few would believe me, if I were to state the period, and the facts which accompanied it." [n] If Byron was nine years old when this sex play began, it must have started in Scotland and have gone on for some time before he revealed it to Hanson. It seems likely that the worst blows he suffered at the hands of May Gray were psychological rather than physical. The disillusioning experience of seeing her devote her caresses to others after their intimacy may well have roused a maddened jealousy that caused the boy to tell Hanson. This experience with an apparently pious girl who had taught him to read the Bible may have been an additional shock and in part the foundation of his lifelong hatred of cant and hypocrisy in religious people.

The discipline at Dulwich was not too strict. Byron found some agreeable companions, and he slept in Dr. Glennie's own study, where he had access to the books. But he was much behind the other boys in the systematic study of Latin grammar so essential for making any progress in the English schools. He spent the Christmas holidays with the Hanson children at Earl's Court. He had grown fond of the household, where he was admired and catered to by young and old. Hanson and his wife had gone to Newstead and Mrs. Byron accompanied them on their return to London, taking lodgings in Sloane Terrace. She soon made herself obnoxious to Lord Carlisle, who refused to see her again. Her gaucheries and volatile temper made her stay in London an embarrassment for her son and a nuisance to Lord Carlisle, Dr. Glennie, and Hanson.

Byron apparently accompanied his mother to Nottingham and Newstead in the summer of 1800, for that was the date of his "first dash into poetry," inspired by "the ebullition of a passion for my first Cousin Margaret Parker *. . . one of the most beautiful of evanescent beings. . . . My passion had its usual effects upon me: I could not sleep, could not eat; I could not rest; and although I had reason to know that she loved me, it was the torture of my life to think of the time which must elapse before we could meet again. . . ." [n]

It is strange how little account has been taken of Byron's plain statement that his passions were developed very early and that this "caused the anticipated melancholy of my thoughts—having anticipated life." [n] One of the two parallel developments in his relations with women, associated in his mind with Mary Duff and Margaret Parker, stimulated him to a "dash into poetry" and became the constant symbol to him of the ideally beautiful unpossessed love, the sort of image that usually blossoms in adolescence but that in Byron was a dominating vision between the years of eight and twelve. It had numerous embodiments male and female during the rest of his life. The other, the premature sexual awakening, caused disillusionment, the melancholy which springs from physical disgust and the failure of

* Byron was following a family penchant for first-cousin attachments and marriages: his grandfather, the Admiral, had married his cousin Sophia Trevanion; the Admiral's daughter Juliana Elizabeth married William, son of the fifth Baron, her father's brother; Augusta Byron, the poet's half-sister, married her first cousin Colonel George Leigh, son of her father's sister Frances. There were also several marriages of cousins among the Gordons. Byron's first boyish "passion" was for his distant cousin Mary Duff; his second for his cousin Margaret Parker; his third for another distant cousin, Mary Chaworth.

the real experience to measure up to the ideal. The first carried him into love with young girls and boys; the second into the cynical search for "fine animals" like the baker's wife in Venice.

Back at Dulwich, Byron was too distracted to study consistently, and yet his mother, no doubt catering to his whims, kept him at home for extended periods. When she was thwarted in this by Dr. Glennie, she broke out into such an audible fit of temper that she was heard by the boys and the servants. One of his classmates said: "Byron, your mother is a fool." The resigned reply of the embarrassed son was "I know it."[n]

Hanson saw that the only hope was to try to get him into a public school, and with the support of Lord Carlisle he interviewed Dr. Joseph Drury, headmaster of Harrow. Hanson admitted that the boy was ill prepared for a public school, but he said "that he thought there was a *cleverness* about him." Toward the end of April 1801, Hanson took his protégé to Harrow and introduced him to Dr. Drury. He made an unexpected impression. Handsome, with a finely chiseled countenance and sensitive blue-gray eyes, curly auburn hair, and small ears, he was inclined to be haughty and reserved, with a touchy independence of spirit. But Dr. Drury, who had a wide and tolerant knowledge of boys, could perceive behind the shyness a responsiveness to kindness and proper handling. He said later: "I soon found that a wild mountain colt had been submitted to my management. But there was mind in his eye. . . . he might be led by a silken string to a point, rather than by a cable. . . ."[n]

A few months past his thirteenth birthday, Byron was thus launched upon the rough-and-tumble of a public school. He soon discovered that only physical defense would gain him immunity from the animal cruelties inflicted upon any deformity in that environment. In addition, he was just entering upon the emotional and physical eruptions of adolescence. Self-willed and passionate when aroused, he was at bottom soft, almost feminine in his emotional attachments, remarkably generous, and full of boyish ambition and idealism. In the next four years the crucible of Harrow fixed as much as it modified those traits.

CHAPTER IV

1801–1805

Harrow and the Hills of Annesley

At the beginning of the nineteenth century Harrow-on-the-Hill was a pleasant country village eleven miles northwest of the heart of London. At the top of the hill stood the famous school founded in 1571 by John Lyon. It shared with Eton the distinction of a long history and rivaled it in popularity with the aristocracy. A surprising number of young lords and scions of earls and dukes were Byron's contemporaries at Harrow. Dr. Drury, who was fifty-one when Byron entered in 1801, had been with the school for over thirty years, and had been headmaster since 1785. He and his masters had crammed with impartiality into the heads of lords and commoners (the middle class was well represented in the school) a respectable knowledge of Latin and Greek.

When Byron rode up the hill with John Hanson on that April day in 1801, he saw a high, rather ungainly building with small windows and sharp gables on top. A wall separated it from the churchyard of the tall-spired fourteenth-century church of St. Mary's. The shy boy with the brace on his foot could not have been reassured if he saw on the playground the strange boys with tall broad-brimmed black hats, open collars, frock coats with tails, and tight-fitting trousers.

But Drury, foreseeing the embarrassment Byron would suffer if he were placed with boys younger than himself, assigned him his own son Henry as tutor until he should have made sufficient progress to be placed among boys of his own age.

Living in the house of the young master, Byron did not associate much with the other boys, for "a degree of shyness hung about him for some time." [n]

His earliest friends were younger boys and those of a humbler station. Edward Noel Long, who was to be one of Byron's most intimate friends at Harrow and later at Cambridge, arrived at about the same time. Long wrote his father on May 1: "There is another, Ld. Byram [*sic*] a lame fellow just come he seems a good sort of fellow." [n] Byron was also on good terms with Robert Peel, the future statesman. "As a Scholar, he [Peel] was greatly my superior," Byron later recalled; "as a declaimer, and Actor, I was reckoned at least his equal. As a school boy *out* of school, I was always *in* scrapes, and *he never;* and *in School* he *always* knew his lesson, and I rarely; but when I knew it, I knew it nearly as well." [n]

It was inevitable that a lame boy with a great deal of pride should come to blows with his fellows. Taunts at his deformity may have initiated the combats, though he never said so. But Leigh Hunt, probably retailing what he had heard from the poet, said of Byron's lameness that "the usual thoughtlessness of schoolboys made him feel it bitterly at Harrow. He would wake, and find his leg in a tub of water." [n] Yet much of his fighting was in championing smaller boys—George Sinclair, Peel, Lord Delawarr, and William Harness, who was lame from an accident.

Byron's first months of fighting his way left him unhappy, and he hated the school. He described himself as idle but "capable of great sudden exertions . . . but of few continuous drudgeries." [n] By the end of June Dr. Drury had placed him in the fourth form, at the top of the remove, together with Long and Peel.

The summer holidays were a welcome relief. Mrs. Byron had given up her lodgings in Sloane Terrace and had taken a room with a Mrs. Massingberd at 16 Piccadilly. Her son stayed with her occasionally, but spent most of the time with the Hansons. Drs. Baillie and Laurie had devised a shoe for him with a brace round the ankle and they continued to bandage the foot. Hanson had secured from the Court of Chancery a grant of £500 a year for Byron's education, payable in quarterly installments to his mother, whose pension from the Civil List was reduced from

£300 to £200. As her son's expenses increased and his lavish habits grew, his mother's financial difficulties became acute.

At Harrow, Byron was careless and neglected to wear the brace on his foot. The difficulty was that he would never allow it to prevent him from doing what other boys did. He tried every sport and became a fair cricketer. He began to make friends. He was amiable, generous to an extreme with those he liked, and eager for others to like him. All of his older friends were commoners. But earls and dukes were among his younger admirers and protégés. He later counted the Earl of Clare and the Duke of Dorset among "my juniors and favourites, whom I spoilt by indulgence." [n]

He spent the Christmas holidays with his mother but went often to the Hansons. He may have met his half-sister Augusta during that holiday. She was five years his senior and he had never seen her. Mrs. Byron wrote her that Byron "often mentions you to me in the most affectionate manner." [n]

Harrow in the new term was less strange. The adolescent proclivity for versifying was burgeoning in the young Byron. The sentimental emotions and the melancholy moods that stirred him found their proper milieu in the Harrow churchyard, where he used to sit under an elm for hours on a flat blue limestone tomb which covered the remains of one John Peachey, Esq., of the Island of St. Christopher's. There, on the brow of the hill that commanded a view of the valleys and the Middlesex hills, he could daydream or, with the reminders of mortality about him, abandon himself to thoughts of the death of his beautiful cousin Margaret Parker. Why had "The King of Terrors seiz'd her as his prey"?

The daily life of Greek translations became more and more irksome, "The drilled dull lesson, forced down word by word/In my repugnant youth." [n] He sought relief in pranks and got into trouble with Henry Drury. The holidays were welcomed by both master and pupil. Byron went to visit his mother, who had gone back to Bath. Hoping to recapture some of the gaieties that she had known in her girlhood, she took him to a masquerade. Perhaps inspired by some of the travel books he had read in Aberdeen, he dressed as a Turkish boy. Mrs. Byron was forced to write to Hanson on January 19: "Byron *positively* refuses to return to Harrow to be Henry Drury's *Pupil*."[n] But he finally agreed to go back the middle of February as the pupil of Mr. Evans.

His friendship with the Earl of Clare, who was then only eleven, began in this year and lasted in a kind of idealized nimbus for the rest of his life. Byron wrote in his "Detached Thoughts": "My School friendships were with *me passions* (for I was always violent), but I do not know that there is one which has endured . . . till now. That with Lord Clare began one of the earliest and lasted longest. . . ."[n]

Byron wrote his mother on June 23, 1803: "I have been placed in a higher form in this School to day, and Dr. Drury and I go on very well."[n] The headmaster had already begun to recognize some of the qualities of Byron's mind. He told Lord Carlisle: "He has talents, my lord, which will *add lustre to his rank*." The guardian's only reply was "Indeed!!!"[n]

Hanson had finally succeeded in leasing Newstead for the five years of Byron's minority to Lord Grey de Ruthyn, a young man of twenty-three, for £50 a year. Mrs. Byron took a house called Burgage Manor at Southwell, not far from Nottingham. When Byron came down for the summer holiday, he found the manor a pleasant three-story wooden house with a garden and some trees. It faced a small green at the end of the main street of the sleepy little town of three thousand inhabitants. In contrast with Harrow and London it seemed very dull. After a few days he could stand it no longer and rode off to Newstead, where he established himself in the lodge with Owen Mealey, the caretaker.

The young lord soon found a much greater attraction at Annesley Hall, where his cousin Mary Chaworth had grown into a charming young girl in the freshness of early maturity. Byron's satiric wit may have amused her, and his obvious admiration must have flattered the girl, who could have no real romantic interest in him, for she was already engaged to John Musters, a young fox-hunting squire with elegant manners.

But Byron rode over daily from Newstead and in a short time was utterly and miserably in love. Without committing herself, Mary could be amiable and a little flirtatious. Occasional "accidental" physical contacts could be idealized into an unforgettable memory by the adolescent boy, whose erotic impulses had already been stimulated by the sentimental sensuousness of Thomas Moore's verses. "When I was fifteen years of age," Byron later recalled, "it happened that in a Cavern in Darbyshire I had to cross in a boat (in which two people only could lie down) a stream which flows under a rock. . . . The companion of my transit was M. A. C., with whom I had been long in love, and never told it, though *she* had discovered it without." [n]

By the middle of September he was so enamored that he would not go back to Harrow, despite his mother's pleading. When Hanson at the request of Drury asked why, he got a despairing reply from Mrs. Byron: "I cannot get him to return to school, though I have done all in my power for six weeks past. He has no indisposition that I know of, but love, desperate love, the *worst* of all *maladies* in my opinion. In short, the Boy is distractedly in love with Miss Chaworth, and he has not been with me three weeks all the time he has been in this county, but spent all his time at Annesley." [n] But the indulgent mother, remembering her own infatuation for his father, capitulated to her son's wishes and let him stay on until after the next holiday.

Before long, however, the young lover at Annesley was growing restive and moody, for he was forced to realize that "Her sighs were not for him." [n] Mary found the sulky boy a little tiresome as a serious suitor. He sat in idle reverie, toying with his handkerchief; he spent hours firing his pistols at the wooden door under the stairway to the garden terrace. Despite his handsome features, his tendency to corpulence made him appear an awkward schoolboy. The climax came one night when he either heard or someone told him that she said to her maid: "What! me care for that lame boy!" [n] In a spasm of rage he rushed out of the house and returned to Newstead. But he could not put Mary Chaworth out of his mind. He later told Thomas Medwin: "She was the *beau idéal* of all that my youthful fancy could paint of beautiful; and I have taken all my fables about the celestial nature of women from the perfection my imagination created in her—I say created, for I found her, like the rest of the sex, any thing but angelic." [n]

Byron was ready to leave the scene of his chagrin and the home of his ancestors, but Lord Grey had returned by November and made him welcome at the Abbey. Grey was a pleasure-loving spoiled boy eight years older than Byron. His great interest was shooting, and he took his guest on moonlight nights to shoot pheasants on their roosts. Byron stayed on through the holidays, but before his sixteenth birthday something happened that gave him an emotional shock, and he left with the determination never to have anything to do with Lord Grey again. Though he would never reveal the nature of the offense, he hinted at it clearly enough to make it obvious that the sensuous young lord had made some kind of sexual advance which disgusted his younger companion. Hobhouse noted in the margin of his copy of Moore's *Life:* " . . . a circumstance occurred during [this] intimacy which certainly had much effect on his future morals." [n]

At the end of January Byron was back at Harrow. Aside from old and new friendships he had little relish for the school. He was even resigned to returning to Southwell for the Easter holiday. He now found a new confidante in his half-sister Augusta. "I hope you will not attribute my neglect to a want of affection," he wrote, "but rather to a shyness naturally inherent in my Disposition. . . . you are *the nearest relation* I have in *the world both by the ties of Blood* and *affection*." [n] As he grew more critical of his mother, this tie was the more warmly welcomed. His deepest feelings flowed out to Augusta in a revealing correspondence during the next year. "I am not reconciled to Lord Grey, *and I never will be*," he confided. " . . . my reasons for ceasing that Friendship are such as I cannot explain, not even to you, my Dear Sister. . . . They are Good ones, however, for although I am *violent* I am not *capricious* in my *attachments*." [n]

What saved Byron from boredom in Southwell was his meeting with the Pigot family who lived across the green. Elizabeth Pigot, a girl several years older than he, saw him first at a party given by his mother, where he was so shy that he had to be coaxed to play games. She saw him only as "a fat bashful boy, with his hair combed straight over his forehead." [n] But when he called with his mother the next day, Elizabeth broke down his shyness and he felt perfectly at home in the Pigot house.

But he left the following day for Harrow. With a bravura revealing unexpected depths of ambition he wrote his mother: " . . . the way *to riches, to greatness* lies before me. I can, I will cut myself a path through the world or perish in the attempt." [n] The direction of his ambition was already apparent. He dreamed of becoming a Parliamentary orator. During his London holidays he had become enamored of the theater, particularly of the declamation of the most eminent actors, and he had even gone into the gallery to listen to the oratory in the House of Commons. In his mind he did not stop short of emulating a Burke or a Sheridan. His absorbing interest at Harrow now was in the Speech Day performance. He put such energy into the preparation as to win the warm praise of Dr. Drury, who, he recalled in later years, "had a great notion that I should turn out an Orator, from my fluency, my turbulence, my voice, my copiousness of declamation, and my action." [n]

"I always *hated* Harrow till the last year and a half, but then I liked it," he wrote in 1821.[n] He read extensively, and his mind was full of daydreams. His general information was, he said, "so great on modern topics, as to induce the suspicion that I could only collect so much information from *reviews*, because I was never *seen* reading, but always idle and in mischief, or at play. The truth is that I read eating, read in bed, read when no one else reads; and had read all sorts of reading since I was five years old. . . ." [n]

It seems probable that Byron, like Dr. Johnson, "tore the heart out of a book." In a Cambridge notebook he later jotted down a list of the books he had read before the age of fifteen. He mentions Rousseau's *Confessions*, lives of Cromwell, of Charles XII, Catherine II, Newton, and a dozen more; Blackstone and Montesquieu on law; in philosophy, Paley, Locke, Bacon, Hume, Berkeley, Drummond, Beattie, and Bolinbroke ("Hobbes I detest"); in poetry, "All the British Classics . . . with most of the living poets, Scott, Southey, &c.—Some French, in the original, of which the Cid is my favourite.—Little Italian.—Greek and Latin without number"; in divinity, "Blair, Porteus, Tillotson, Hooker,—all very tiresome." As early as 1803 he had discovered the poetry of Alexander Pope, an experience that did more than anything else to fix his poetic taste. He also noted that he had read about four thousand novels, including the works of Cervantes, Fielding, Smollett, Richardson, Henry Mackenzie, Sterne, Rabelais, and Rousseau.[n] Reading this impressive list after Byron's death, his friend Hobhouse wrote: "As Lord Byron says he read these volumes I am inclined to believe the fact, but it is certain he never gave any sign of this knowledge afterward." [n]

In the summer Byron found Southwell more agreeable than he had expected. Through the Pigots he met some of the other Southwell people, including some young ladies who were eager to cultivate the acquaintance of the young lord. But despite his attempts to be agreeable, Byron's efforts to calm the gale of his mother's temper were fruitless. "In former days she spoilt me," Byron wrote Augusta; "now she is altered to the contrary; for the most trifling thing, she upbraids me in a most outrageous manner, and all our disputes have been lately heightened by my one with that object of my cordial, deliberate detestation, Lord Grey de Ruthyn. . . . once she let drop such an odd expression that I was half inclined to believe the dowager was in love with him."[n]

When he could, he escaped to the Pigots. Elizabeth had a disinterested fondness for the boy. With her he did not have to play the suitor and he could be frank and genuine. They exchanged books and wrote verses, lightly flattering, slightly romantic, to each other. Frank tenderness mixed with playfulness in their relationship. But the old pang of his passion for Mary Chaworth was still there. Apparently he returned to Annesley and had some stolen interviews with Mary. He told Medwin later: "I was serious; she was volatile. She liked me as a younger brother, and treated and laughed at me as a boy."[n] They parted on a hill near Annesley which he described in his poem "The Dream" as "crowned with a peculiar diadem" of trees. She was about to be married and her thoughts were elsewhere. The frustration and the emotional crisis left him almost on the verge of hysteria. When his mother, piqued by his comments on Lord Grey, told him one day that his childhood sweetheart Mary Duff was married, he was nearly thrown into convulsions.

The disenchantments of the past year had brought to the surface an adolescent cynicism in the growing boy, a transparent cloak for wounded vanity. After offering Augusta his sympathy for her distress (her uncle General Leigh was putting obstacles in the way of her marriage to his son), he added: "But really, after all (pardon me my dear Sister), I feel a little inclined to laugh at you, for love, in my humble opinion, is utter nonsense, a mere jargon of compliments, romance, and deceit. . . ."[n]

Byron was glad to escape to Harrow in the autumn. Rejected by the girl he loved most desperately, he turned to the reassuring affection of his Harrow friends. To them he did not seem awkward and lacking in the gallantries and graces demanded by fickle young women. Their association was uncomplicated by the vagaries of feminine pretenses. And so Byron developed a penchant for the society of younger boys, especially those like Lord Clare and Lord Delawarr whose handsome faces gave him something of the same aesthetic satisfaction he felt in the presence of beautiful women. If sexual attraction entered into it, he was unaware of it or, thinking of his experience with Lord Grey, put it out of his mind as repugnant and easily sublimated it in terms of affectionate camaraderie.

If Byron had not clearly understood or admitted to himself the sexual implications of these passionate friendships at Harrow, he probably recognized this tendency in himself while at Cambridge, and certainly while he was in Greece on his first pilgrimage. There seems little doubt, if one considers dispassionately the total evidence available, that a strong attraction to boys persisted in Byron from his Harrow days throughout his life. But it seems just as evident that he felt no guilt or shame about any of the friendships formed at Harrow. Hobhouse, however, who was apparently well aware of this tendency in Byron, wrote in the margin of the pages in which Moore was glossing over the Harrow friendships with younger favorites: "M. knows nothing or will tell nothing of the principal cause & motive of all these boyish friend[ships]." Byron's attraction to women, nevertheless, did, on the whole, fulfill his emotional needs much more extensively and through longer periods of his life, though it was not necessarily stronger in individual instances. These facts have long been known. They help to explain much in Byron's character, and throw a great deal of light on his relations with both men and women. Various friends noted the feminine qualities in Byron. Moore recorded in his diary on July 7, 1827: "In the evening some talk with D. Kinnaird about Byron; a great deal of the woman about Byron, in his tenderness, his temper, his caprice, his vanity. Chantrey's remark upon this; the soft voluptuous character of the lower part of his face, and the firmness of the upper part." [n]

In his wide reading Byron had already dipped into some of

the Deistic and skeptical philosophers of the eighteenth century, and in a rebellious frame of mind he had expressed some views not quite orthodox which easily shocked some of the conventional-minded boys. While at Harrow, he told Medwin, "I fought Lord Calthorpe for writing 'D——d Atheist!' under my name." [n]

In his letters to Augusta, Byron constantly recurred to the gulf that had widened between him and his mother. On November 2 he wrote: ". . . she is so hasty, so impatient, that I dread the approach of the holidays, more than most boys do their return from them." [n] And on November 11 he followed up the topic that was weighing on his mind almost to the point of obsession: ". . . she flies into a fit of phrenzy, upbraids me as if I was the most undutiful wretch in existence, rakes up the ashes of my *father*, abuses him, says I shall be a true Byrrone, which is the worst epithet she can invent. Am I to call this woman mother?" [n]

Augusta conspired with Hanson to have Byron spend the holidays in town without arousing the suspicion of Mrs. Byron. He had said his farewells at Harrow, for he had caused so much trouble at the school that Dr. Drury had suggested that he get a private tutor for his final preparation for the University. He enjoyed his freedom in London. He went to Covent Garden to see the "Young Roscius," the boy actor who was making a sensation. Augusta was delighted when she finally arranged for her brother to dine with Lord Carlisle, who, seeing that the boy's views of Mrs. Byron coincided very well with his own, warmed toward him considerably. Augusta wrote with enthusiasm to Hanson: "You will easily believe that he [Byron] is a *very great favourite of mine* . . . the more I see and hear of him the more I *must* love and esteem him." [n]

He returned to Harrow early in February despite Drury's advice, impelled by the fear that his friends would think he had been expelled and by his eagerness to participate in the final Speech Days at the end of the term. But he was soon in trouble again for leading a rebellion against Dr. George Butler, the new headmaster appointed to replace Dr. Drury on his retirement at Easter. Now that he was a leader in the school, the thought of leaving it saddened him. The hold of Harrow on his affections had imperceptibly strengthened as his home ties weakened. "I so much disliked leaving Harrow," he later wrote, "that, though it was time (I being seventeen), it broke my very rest for the last quarter with counting the days that remained."[n]

Byron spent less time in brooding on the Peachey stone now. He was oftener on the cricket field, or at the local inn, "Mother Barnard's," where he lost his self-consciousness in roaring out: "This bottle's the sun of our table."[n] And the coming Speech Days absorbed his interest. For the first one he had chosen the dramatic and passionate speech of Zanga over the body of Alonzo, from Young's tragedy *The Revenge*. He was probably ambitious to emulate Kemble, who was then playing the part to applauding audiences. On the final Speech Day, July 4, he declaimed an impassioned passage from *King Lear*. He put so much nervous energy into the delivery that at the end he was overcome and was obliged to leave the room.

The final day of the term came. Byron exchanged emotional farewells and gifts with his favorites. Henry Long, younger brother of Byron's friend Edward Noel Long, arrived in time to meet Byron descending the steps of the school after carving his name on the wall of the old fourth-form room. Young Long recorded that "during some further conversation, he introduced an oath, and I took an opportunity afterwards to put the question to my brother, do boys at Harrow swear? 'Well,' he said, 'sometimes, you've just heard an instance of it.' "[n]

Byron tried to prolong his school experiences and associations as long as possible. He was most proud of being in the cricket team in the final game of the year against Eton. The match took place in London on August 2, 1805. Byron's foot had so far improved that he could now wear a common boot over a corrective inner shoe, but he still had difficulty in running. Harrow lost, but Byron was still boastful of his performance. After the match the teams dined together and then went to the Haymarket Theatre, where in inebriated high spirits they "kicked up a row."[n]

The next evening Byron set off for Southwell. His schooldays were over, but his thoughts turned back to Harrow and his young admirers there. Still he could not forget Mary Chaworth. When Mrs. Byron, in the presence of Elizabeth Pigot, tauntingly announced that Miss Chaworth was married, "An expression, very peculiar, impossible to describe, passed over his pale face." Then, "with an affected air of coldness and nonchalance" he said, "Is that all?" and changed the subject." But his feelings soon found relief in some stanzas that he showed to Elizabeth Pigot:

Hills of Annesley, Bleak and Barren,
Where my thoughtless Childhood stray'd,
How the northern Tempests, warring,
Howl above thy tufted shade!

Now no more, the Hours beguiling,
Former favourite Haunts I see;
Now no more my Mary smiling,
Makes ye seem a Heaven to me.

On September 23 Byron escaped from Southwell and spent a month in London before going to his new life at Cambridge, where he had already enrolled at Trinity College.

CHAPTER V

1805–1807

Cambridge: *Hours of Idleness*

WHEN I WENT UP TO Trinity, in 1805, at the age of seventeen and a half," Byron wrote many many years later, "I was miserable and untoward to a degree. I was wretched at leaving Harrow, to which I had become attached during the two last years of my stay there; wretched at going to Cambridge instead of Oxford (there were no rooms vacant at Christchurch); wretched from some private domestic circumstances of different kinds, and consequently about as unsocial as a wolf taken from the troop." [n] A sense of being prematurely cast adrift obsessed him. ". . . it was one of the deadliest and heaviest feelings of my life to feel that I was no longer a boy," he wrote in his "Detached Thoughts." "From that moment I began to grow old in my own esteem; and in my esteem age is not estimable." [n]

He had secured rooms in the southeast corner of the Great Court of Trinity, rooms that opened on a wide staircase of the tower round which one might drive a coach and six. Byron always liked spaciousness. That was one reason the great halls of Newstead appealed to him. There was spaciousness in the Court of Trinity too. It was the largest of all the courts in the colleges of England, for Trinity had had royal favor since its foundation by Henry VIII in 1546. In these surroundings Byron began to feel in better spirits immediately. "I am now most pleasantly situated in *Super*excellent Rooms," he wrote his sister on November 6, "flanked on one side by my Tutor, upon the other by an old Fellow, both of whom are rather checks upon my vivacity. I am allowed 500 a year, a Servant and Horse, so Feel as independent as a German Prince. . . ."[n] He was still on the high tide of enjoyment of his situation when he wrote Hanson's son Hargreaves on November 12: "College improves in every thing but Learning. Nobody here seems to look into an Author, ancient or modern, if they can avoid it."[n]

While the conscientiousness of the Reverend Thomas Jones, Byron's tutor, and a few others had raised the morale and scholarly standards of Trinity, there was still a remnant of eighteenth-century contempt for learning which Byron had immediately sensed on his arrival, particularly among the nobility and gentlemen-commoners. Long custom and some lingering rules had given the scions of nobility easy exemption from attendance at lectures and examinations. For the most part they were the ringleaders in breaches of discipline and in all the dissipations then expected of the young aristocracy. There was not, however, the class distinction or snobbery that might have been expected in such an environment. Wordsworth had found Cambridge in 1787–91 more democratic in spirit than the rest of England.

> *And wealth and titles were in less esteem*
> *Than talents, worth, and prosperous industry.*[n]

Byron had felt some snobbish pride in the friendship of his fellow peers at Harrow, but not one of his closest friends at Cambridge was titled. Although he mingled at first with the blasé young idlers, among whom were no doubt many spoiled sons of the nobility, he did not feel comfortable with them. He analyzed his situation with remarkable clarity in a letter to Hanson: ". . . Study is the last pursuit of the Society; the Master [William Lort Mansel] eats, drinks, and sleeps, the Fellows *Drink, dispute and pun;* the Employment of the Under graduates you will probably conjecture without my description. I sit down to write with a Head confused with Dissipation which, tho' I hate, I cannot avoid. . . . after all I am the most *steady* Man in College, nor have I got into many Scrapes, and none of consequence."[n]

Byron's attachment to Edward Noel Long, his Harrow friend who came up to Trinity at the same time, was based on wider interests than were common among his drinking companions. They were both fond of swimming, riding, and reading. They used to dive for shillings in a deep pool of the Cam. They passed the evenings with music, for Long played the flute and violoncello. Riding out to the weir above Grantchester (still called Byron's Pool today) with Long, Byron could escape the depression of spirits that followed the nightly carousings with his too convivial companions. But even among them he stole time to read. It was in the rooms of William Bankes, "father of all mischiefs," that he first read the poetry of Walter Scott.

"I took my gradations in the vices with great promptitude," he later wrote, "but they were not to my taste; for my early passions, though violent in the extreme, were concentrated, and hated division or spreading abroad. I could have left or lost the world with or for that which I loved; but, though my temperament was naturally burning, I could not share in the common place libertinism of the place and time without disgust." [n]

While he had not wasted his substance on light loves, Byron seems to have spent lavishly in other ways, for when he went to London for the Christmas holiday he was badly in need of money. He appealed to Augusta on December 27 to be joint security with him "for a few Hundreds a person (one of the money lending tribe) has offered to advance. . . ." [n] This is the first intimation of Byron's involvement with the usurers, from whom in the next three or four years he borrowed until his debts ran into thousands of pounds. Augusta was frightened and offered to lend him money to pay his debts, but he refused. And on January 7 he hinted at some painful cause of melancholy which he could not disclose. "You know me too well to think it is *Love;* & I have had no quarrel or dissention with Friend or enemy, you may therefore be easy, since no unpleasant consequence will be produced from the present Sombre cast of my Temper." [n]

The specific source of that melancholy is clouded in mystery. But there is a key to it in his later recollections and letters. In his "Detached Thoughts" of 1821, after speaking of his disgust at the libertinism of Cambridge which threw his heart back upon itself, casting him "into excesses perhaps more fatal than those from which I shrunk, as fixing upon [one] (at a time) the passions which, spread amongst many, would have hurt only myself," he says: "If I could explain at length the *real* causes which have contributed to increase this perhaps *natural* temperament of mine, this Melancholy, which hath made me a bye-word, nobody would wonder; but this is impossible without doing much mischief."[n]

But referring to E. N. Long in his diary of 1821, he wrote: "*His* friendship, and a violent, though *pure*, love and passion—which held me at the same period—were the then romance of the most romantic period of my life."[n] And in 1807 he confided to Elizabeth Pigot that while at Cambridge he had become romantically attached to John Edleston, a choirboy at Trinity Chapel. "His *voice* first attracted my attention, his *countenance* fixed it, and his *manners* attached me to him for ever. . . . I certainly love him more than any human being, and neither time nor distance have had the least effect on my (in general) changeable disposition. . . . He certainly is perhaps more attached to *me* than even I am in return. During the whole of my residence at Cambridge we met every day, summer and winter, without passing *one* tiresome moment, and separated each time with increasing reluctance."[n]

Byron wrote to Hobhouse in October 1811: "The event I mentioned in my last [the death of Edleston] has had an effect on me, I am ashamed to think of. But there is no arguing on these points. I could 'have better spared a better being.' Wherever I turn, particularly in this place [he wrote from Cambridge], the idea goes with me. I say all this at the risk of incurring your contempt; but you cannot despise me more than I do myself."[n]

Whatever Byron's feelings may have been later, after the sophistication bred by his Eastern travels, there seems little reason to doubt the truth of his statement that his feeling at the time for Edleston was a "violent, though *pure*, love and passion"—in other words, a romantic attachment. And the best evidence is that the most idealized of Byron's attachments were those that still bore the aura of innocence, such as his love for Mary Duff, Margaret Parker, and Mary Chaworth.

The new term at Cambridge began on February 5, but Byron lingered in London. When the time came, Augusta did not sign as collateral guarantor for his loan, and, apparently piqued, Byron did not communicate with her for some months. In the end Mrs. Massingberd, his landlady at 16 Piccadilly, and her daughter became joint security. Augusta was greatly disturbed, and Mrs. Byron also took alarm, for her son's bills began coming in "to double the amount I expected." [n]

Needing some kind of physical activity, he began to frequent the rooms of Henry Angelo, the famous fencing master, and through him he met "Gentleman" Jackson, the pugilist and ex-champion, who shared rooms with Angelo at 13 Bond Street. Byron was soon taking lessons from them and mingling with their strange assortment of high-class demi-monde associates in theatrical and sporting circles.

He had received a few hundred pounds from the money lenders at ruinous interest. He paid his Harrow debts and also £231 of College bills, but he had no intention of returning. "I happen to have a few hundreds in ready Cash by me," he reported with a kind of malicious glee to his mother; " . . . but I find it inconvenient to remain at College, not for the expence. . . . Improvement at an English University to a Man of Rank is, you know, impossible, and the very Idea *ridiculous.*" And he broke the news that he wanted to spend a couple of years abroad. " 'Tis true I cannot enter France; but Germany and the Courts of Berlin, Vienna & Petersburg are still open. . . ." [n]

His poor mother was hysterical with apprehension. She saw him following in his father's footsteps and ruining himself before he was of age. "That Boy will be the death of me, and drive me mad," she wrote in desperation to Hanson. "I never will consent to his going Abroad. Where can he get Hundreds? Has he got into the hands of Money lenders? He has no feeling, no Heart." [n]

In the meantime, Byron was entering into the pleasures of London which money in his pocket had put within his reach. He frequented the theater. And he later gave an amusing account of an episode of his eighteenth year in London: "There was then . . . a famous French 'entremetteuse,' who assisted young gentlemen in their youthful pastimes. We had been acquainted for some time, when something occurred in her line of business more than ordinary, and the refusal was offered to me. . . . she sent me a letter couched in such English as a short residence of sixteen years in England had enabled her to acquire. . . . But there was a postscript. It contained these words:—'Remember, Milor, that *delicaci ensure everi succés.*' " [n]

Perhaps the Madame had some reason to doubt Byron's "*delicaci*," for he had entered into his dissipations with the reckless cynicism of one who was trying to prove his power over women despite the fact that he was "the little lame boy" or, it may be, to prove to himself that he could find in feminine embraces an escape from his too compelling involvement with Edleston.

By March 10 he had gone through his "hundreds" and was asking Hanson to raise £500 to help him pay his borrowings. By this time he was probably also somewhat bored by his life in town. He was back at Trinity by the middle of April, but his prodigalities began anew. He donated thirty guineas to a collection for a statue of Pitt, who had been a patron of Trinity, and he bought a carriage.

If Byron ever attended a lecture at Cambridge, he found it too dull to mention in his correspondence. Nor did he do any systematic reading, though among his bills for the first term is an item for £20 17s. 6d. for books. But he was busily writing verses. At the end of the term he returned to London, but with no ready cash in his pocket he did not remain long. Against his strongest inclinations he set out for Southwell. Quarrels with his mother were inevitable. He escaped as often as he could across the green to the Pigots, where he had made a fast friend of Elizabeth's brother John, on vacation from his study of medicine at Edinburgh. He was already preparing a volume of his poems and had taken them to the printer John Ridge in the neighboring town of Newark, when a maternal explosion occurred that sent him flying back to London on the 7th of August. The Pigots had assisted his flight in the "Dead of Night" from "Mrs. Byron furiosa."

His mother followed him to London, but he finally persuaded her to return, while he proceeded to Littlehampton on the Sussex coast, to visit his friend Long, then spending the holidays with his family. Long's younger brother Henry has left a convincingly realistic picture of the young lord appearing on the scene with great éclat: "Lord Byron had with him his horses, and his dog Boatswain"—he established himself at the Dolphin Inn. . . . and on the first day of his arrival, he was engaged in firing at oyster shells by the Pier." Sometimes they played cricket, and Byron constantly called Henry, who was recovering the balls, "young shaver." But when he swam he was fond of carrying the boy about on his back.

Young Long recalled that his brother and Byron, having stripped off "every thing excepting their drawers and shirts . . . jumped from the end of the pier . . . into the river, which as it was now nearly low water was running out with fearful rapidity; they shot out to sea and were carried to such a distance as I could barely discern their heads, popping up and down like little ducks upon the sea—by making an immense semicircle, which as the tide runs out very far on that coast, it was absolutely necessary, they at last arrived in safety. . . ." [n]

Byron was back at Southwell in September. There with his carriage and horses, his groom and valet, he no doubt cut a considerable figure, while his mother fumed helplessly at his extravagance. He soon became involved in private theatricals with the Pigots and some of their friends, including Julia Leacroft, the organizer of the performances. Byron of course had the leading role, and mouthed the heroic passages in Cumberland's *Wheel of Fortune.*

At the same time he was paying court and writing verses to several of the Southwell belles. To none of these flirtations did Byron give more than cynical attention. Half of the poems in his privately printed volume, which appeared in November with the title *Fugitive Pieces,* were school exercises, or satires on personalities and practices at Cambridge. The others were essays in gallantry in the manner of Thomas Moore. The frankly erotic poems, like the one "To Mary," were probably inspired by his experiences in London. That unlucky poem, he said, caused him to be "pronounced a most *profligate sinner,* in short, a '*young Moore.*' " [n] But this first volume of Byron had as much realism and satire as sentiment and romance. The mawkishness of the sentimental poems is leavened with such boisterous sophistication as:

> *Why should you weep, like* Lydia Languish,
> *And fret with self-created anguish?*
> *Or doom the lover you have chosen,*
> *On winter nights to sigh half frozen . . .* [n]

Byron had not returned to Cambridge for the autumn term, partly because his finances were not in a state to allow him to live there as he wished, and partly no doubt also because he was pleasantly occupied in Southwell. He had contrived a truce with Mrs. Byron sufficient to make life bearable. The Pigot house had become his adopted home. He had already established the habit of late retiring and late rising that remained with him the rest of his life. His favorite recreations were swimming and firing at a mark with pistols, and these practices too he continued until his death.

It seems incredible that Byron could not have foreseen the repercussions in the respectable clerical society of Southwell to such lines as these in his poem "To Mary":

Now, by my soul, 'tis most delight
To view each other panting, dying,
In love's exstatic posture *lying,*
Grateful to feeling, *as to* sight.

When the Reverend John Thomas Becher, to whom he had presented a copy, objected that the description was "rather too warmly drawn," Byron replied in some verses. His argument was essentially the same one he used later to defend *Don Juan:* his muse, he said, was "the simple Truth." [n] But the same day he called in all the copies he had given to friends and burned the lot. Only four of the volumes escaped the flames. The Reverend John Becher kept his copy.

Byron was soon at work on another volume which he attempted to make "*vastly* correct and miraculously chaste." The artificiality of style did not give him a chance to display his already considerable talents for realism, incisiveness, and humor. *Poems on Various Occasions* was printed in an edition of about one hundred in January 1807.

On January 6 he was at Dorant's Hotel, Albemarle Street, London, trying to raise money and distributing copies of his poems among his friends. Mrs. Massingberd, who was his go-between with the moneylenders, arranged for him to receive £3,000 and to repay £5,000 when he came of age. After paying off his earlier loan, he had little left and he returned to Southwell toward the end of January. He was soon in trouble of another sort. In a reckless mood he had been warmly courting Julia Leacroft. According to Hobhouse, the family "winked at an intercourse between him and [one] of the daughters in hopes of entangling him in an unequal marriage." [n]

Perhaps as a concomitant of his gallantries, Byron had already begun the strict reducing regimen which for the next few months he carried on with almost fanatical zeal. In that time he pared down the stoutness that had persisted since his entrance to Harrow to a slenderness that he maintained with little variation until he relaxed and grew fat again in Venice in 1818. He had been at his heaviest during the autumn of 1806, having reached 202 pounds, a tremendous weight for a boy five feet eight and one-half inches tall. His spartan regime, besides dieting, consisted of "violent exercise, *much* physic, and *hot* bathing." [n]

His financial situation was ever more perilous. His mother, to prevent him from borrowing more from moneylenders, was negotiating a loan of £1,000 among her relations in Nottingham. But between flirting and versifying, Byron kept despondent thoughts at bay, except at intervals. The fact that melancholy generally dominated his verses has given a wrong impression of him as a gloomy youth. But he was full of animal spirits and still boyish a great deal of the time, as Elizabeth Pigot knew.

Byron was proud enough of his versifying to want a larger audience than Southwell afforded. He sent a copy of *Poems on Various Occasions* to be presented to Henry Mackenzie, and was delighted when he received some encomiums from the author of *The Man of Feeling.* Hanson complimented him on his verses but suggested that his true forte was in oratory. Byron replied that he could do nothing in that line until he came of age. "The Fact is I remain here because I can appear no where else, being *completely done* up. *Wine* and *Women* have *dished* your *humble Servant,* not a *Sou* to be *had.* . . ." He continued his rigorous system of thinning. "I wear *seven* Waistcoats and a great Coat, run, and play at cricket in this Dress, till quite exhausted by excessive perspiration, use the Hip Bath daily; eat only a quarter of a pound of Butcher's Meat in 24 hours, no Suppers or Breakfast, only one Meal a Day; drink no malt liquor, but a little Wine, and take Physic occasionally . . . . my Clothes have been taken in nearly *half a yard.*" [n]

He was already deeply engaged in preparing a volume of his poems for publication, rather than for private printing. But when he approached the public, it was with a trepidation that snuffed out most of the sparks of original talent that had occasionally livened the privately printed volumes. What remained was imitative, sentimental, and mawkish. And he added imitations and translations from Anacreon and Virgil; such nostalgic poems as "Lachin Y Gair," recalling the lost romance of his Scottish summers; "Elegy on Newstead Abbey," a too-serious recital of the heroic deeds of his ancestors; and "The Death of Calmar and Orla," an imitation of Ossian. The title, *Hours of Idleness,* was supplied by Ridge, the printer.

He carried the volume in triumph to Cambridge on June 27, when, with an advance on his allowance and prospects of his mother's loan, he went to pay off his College debts. He was delighted that none of his old classmates or friends knew him because he had thinned himself so much. He was now determined to quit Cambridge, he wrote Elizabeth Pigot, "because our *set* are *vanished,* and my *musical protégé* before mentioned has left the choir, and is stationed in a mercantile house of considerable eminence in the metropolis. You may have heard me observe he is exactly to an hour two years younger than myself. . . . He is nearly my height, very *thin,* very fair complexion, dark eyes and light locks. My opinion of his mind you already know;—I hope I shall never have occasion to change it." [n]

His attachment to Edleston had not ceased but had grown stronger. He spoke lightheartedly of it to Elizabeth Pigot, but the emotion shows through. "At this moment I write with a bottle of claret in my *head* and *tears* in my *eyes;* for I have just parted with my *'Cornelian,'* [n] who spent the evening with me. . . . Edleston and I have separated for the present, and my mind is a chaos of hope and sorrow." But the separation was only temporary. ". . . we shall probably not meet till the expiration of my minority, when I shall leave to his decision either entering as a *partner* through my interest, or residing with me altogether." [n]

But a week at Cambridge with new and old friends had made it seem agreeable enough so that he determined to go back for another year. His change of plans frequently seemed casual, but there was always some strong emotional force directing his inclinations. His meeting with John Cam Hobhouse and Charles

Skinner Matthews no doubt fixed his resolve to continue at Cambridge. Both were as full of mischief as Byron himself, but both had uncommon intellectual interests and abilities. Hobhouse, son of Benjamin Hobhouse, M.P. from Bristol, had come up to Trinity in 1806. He had read widely in historical and political fields, had liberal Whig opinions, political ambitions, and literary aspirations.

Matthews, whom he had known slightly, had occupied Byron's spacious rooms during his absence, "and Jones, the tutor, in his odd way, had said, on putting him in, 'Mr. Matthews, I recommend to your attention not to damage any of the moveables, for Lord Byron, Sir, is a young man of *tumultuous passions.*' Matthews was delighted with this; and whenever anybody came to visit him, begged them to handle the very door with caution. . . . Jones's phrase . . . had put him into such a good humour, that I verily believe that I owed to it a portion of his good graces."[n]

There were certain areas in which Matthews, a close friend of Hobhouse, entered into rapport with Byron more readily than did the more sober and less bold John Cam. The freedom of their speculations on all kinds of subjects used to alarm Hobhouse. Byron himself later said that though Matthews was neither dissolute nor intemperate in his conduct, he was "a most decided atheist, indeed noxiously so, for he proclaimed his principles in all societies."[n] But his mischief was generally interfused with wit. He would rouse the Master of Trinity, Lort Mansel, with the taunt: "We beseech thee to hear us, good *Lort!*"—"Good *Lort* deliver us!"[n] In his company Byron was always full of high spirits and facetiousness.

By the middle of July 1807 Byron was back in London. He settled down at Gordon's Hotel in Albemarle Street to enjoy being an author and to enter again into the delights of the town, made more pleasant by his long residence in Southwell. On the 13th he sent a boasting budget of his pastimes and plans to Elizabeth Pigot. Crosby, the London distributor of his poems, published a magazine called *Monthly Literary Recreations,* in the July number of which it "chanced" that there was a laudatory notice of *Hours of Idleness*. In the same number was Byron's review of Wordsworth's *Poems* (2 vols., 1807).

The attention his poems were getting warmed his ego. "In

every Bookseller's I see my *own name*, and *say nothing*, but enjoy my *fame* in *secret*."[n] In intervals of leisure, after two in the morning, he had written 380 lines of blank verse on Bosworth Field. He was full of schemes, one of which was to make a tour of the Scottish Highlands, then hire a boat and visit "the most remarkable of the Hebrides" and perhaps sail as far as Iceland.

When he returned to Cambridge in the autumn, he bought a tame bear and lodged him in the small hexagonal tower above his rooms. He enjoyed the sensation he made when he took bruin for walks on a chain like a dog. He announced with pride to Elizabeth Pigot: "I have got a new friend, the finest in the world, a *tame bear*. When I brought him here, they asked me what I meant to do with him, and my reply was, 'he should *sit for a fellowship*.'"[n] Thomas Jones having died, the Reverend George Frederick Tavell became the mentor of the eccentric young lord. In *Hints from Horace* Byron devoted a couplet to a recognition of the trials of the poor man:

> *Unlucky Tavell! doomed to daily cares*
> *By pugilistic pupils, and by bears . . .*[n]

Although Byron liked to give the impression that he was engaged in constant drinking, gambling, and dissipation, he must have devoted only the fringes of his interest and time to those pursuits, which were the core of Cambridge life. The spur of publication had stimulated a spate of literary activity. "I have written 214 pages of a novel—" he told Elizabeth, "one poem of 380 lines, to be published (without my name) in a few weeks, with notes,—560 lines of Bosworth Field, and 250 lines of another poem in rhyme, besides half a dozen smaller pieces. The poem to be published is a Satire."[n]

Conscious of his comparative neglect of reading since his schooldays, he sat down on November 30 to take stock of the reading he had done before he was fifteen, and compiled an impressive list. "Since I left Harrow," he noted, "I have become idle and conceited, from scribbling rhyme and making love to women."[n] There is evidence, however, that when he did read, it was with care and critical attention. On the flyleaf of his copy of

Owen Ruffhead's *The Life of Alexander Pope*, he scrawled while at Cambridge: "Of Pope's pithy conciseness of style Swift—no diffuse writer himself—has so emphatically said—

> *For Pope can in one couplet fix*
> *More sense than I can do in six.*" [n]

Byron's relish for satire and wit was encouraged by his associates during the new term. Matthews introduced Byron to another Cambridge wit, Scrope Berdmore Davies, then Fellow of King's College. Davies was already well known at the gaming tables as well as in the fashionable drawing rooms in London. A crony of Beau Brummell and other dandies, he preferred the company of men of wit and intellect like Matthews.

With little solid knowledge of political principles, but with liberal leanings and an "opposition" mind, Byron was drawn into the Cambridge Whig Club. It was there perhaps that his friendship and admiration for Hobhouse ripened. But their literary interests drew them even closer together. Each had written a satire. Byron's was the poem which had already reached 380 lines on October 26. This was no doubt the "Dunciad" on all the living authors to which he had given the title "British Bards." Hobhouse had thrown all his ideas concerning the corruptions of political and social life (measured against the stoical virtues of the ancients) into an imitation of the Eleventh Satire of Juvenal.

Another literary friendship that was to be long-lasting was that with Francis Hodgson, just appointed resident tutor at King's College. He shared Byron's enthusiasm for Dryden and Pope, and what particularly interested Byron was that his father had been a friend of William Gifford, onetime editor of the *Anti-Jacobin* and later editor and leading critic of the *Quarterly Review*. Byron had already paid Gifford the compliment of imitating his satires the *Maeviad* and the *Baviad* in his own castigation of modern writers. Hodgson was an excellent classical scholar and had just published a translation of Juvenal. Yet it was a strange friendship. Hodgson's moral earnestness and sometimes humorless conventionality were at complete odds with Byron's scoffing proclivities. But Byron always enjoyed having someone to shock. And Hodgson, knowing that Byron had a good heart, clung to the hope of converting him to orthodoxy, and, like so many of Byron's early friends, came to have a doglike devotion to him.

Byron's new-found intellectual life at the University soon came to an end. With a loan of £20 from Hanson, he spent the Christmas holidays in London. He did not return to Cambridge, except for an occasional visit to his cronies, until he went down for his M.A. the following summer. During his final term at Trinity and in the first months of the following year Byron cemented his friendships with Hobhouse, Matthews, the droll Scrope Davies, and Hodgson. Nothing he carried away from Cambridge was more tangible or more lasting.

CHAPTER VI

1808–1809

English Bards, and Scotch Reviewers

STILL BUSY WITH the revision of his poems and the preparation of a new volume, Byron settled at Dorant's Hotel in London at the beginning of 1808 and was soon enjoying the life of an author and man about town. On January 20 he received an effusively flattering letter from the Reverend Robert Charles Dallas, who claimed kinship with him (Dallas's sister Charlotte had married Byron's uncle, George Anson Byron). Dallas was the sort of person whom Byron in other circumstances might readily have pilloried as a dullard, but politeness and flattery generally neutralized his critical acids. Byron tried to put a damper on any hopes the pious correspondent might have of reforming him: "I have been already held up as a votary of licentiousness, and the disciple of infidelity." [n] Finally Dallas's sanctimonious platitudes elicited a flippant rejoinder intended to shock him: "In morality, I prefer Confucius to the Ten Commandments, and Socrates to St. Paul (though the two latter agree in their opinion of marriage). . . . I believe truth the prime attribute of the Deity, and death an eternal sleep, at least of the body." [n]

This did not stop Dallas, who called upon Byron within a few days, became devoted to him, aided him, sometimes officiously, in putting his poems through the press, and was a frequent caller for several months. But Byron had more congenial friends in several spheres. He began to cultivate his old Harrow associates again. In his insecurity, with no clear goal before him, he clung to the image of Harrow as a symbol of the happiest times of his boyhood. He was soon reconciled with Henry Drury, to whom he had been obstreperous as a schoolboy, and through him with Dr. Butler, the new headmaster, against whom he had rebelled, and all obstacles were removed to his frequent return to the school.

Pinched for money as usual, he felt he could not return to Cambridge. "I am now in my one and twentieth year, and cannot command as many pounds," he complained to Hanson just after his birthday.[n] Lack of cash at this period must have been peculiarly galling to Byron. Generosity was always his greatest extravagance. He had already given £200 to the sycophantic Dallas. Now that he was living as a man about town, entertaining people as careless with money as Scrope Davies and some of his theatrical cronies, he must make a showing even if he had to borrow money for his breakfast. When he had least he was most careless in giving it away. He customarily slipped £5 notes into the embarrassed hands of Henry Long and of Lord Delawarr at Harrow.

Byron's associations at Harrow seem to have been the most innocent of his pastimes, for he soon became involved in excesses in London that undermined his health (already shaken by his excessive dieting) and all but ended his career. He wrote to Becher on February 26: " . . . to give you some idea of my late life, I have this moment received a prescription from Pearson, not for any *complaint,* but from *debility,* and literally *too much Love.*" Then he treated his reverend friend to a little malicious boasting, perhaps with a recollection of Becher's part in the suppression of his early volume where the passions had been "too warmly drawn." "In fact, my blue eyed Caroline, who is only sixteen, has been lately so *charming,* that though we are both in perfect health, we are at present commanded to *repose,* being nearly worn out.—So much for Venus." [n]

To Hobhouse, who had returned to Cambridge, he wrote a similar confession: "I am buried in an abyss of Sensuality. I have renounced *hazard,* however, but I am given to Harlots, and live in a state of Concubinage." Scrope Davies was in town, and also another Cambridge friend, Altamont (later Lord Sligo). "Last night, at the Opera Masquerade, we supped with seven whores, a *Bawd,* and a *Ballet*-master in Madame [Angelica] Catalani's apartment behind the scenes. . . . I have some thoughts of purchasing D'Egville's pupils; they would fill a glorious harem." [n]

The recklessness of his dissipations may have been owing in part to the fact that he felt his fame had been demolished by some ridiculing reviews. He had already been greatly agitated by a caustic critique in *The Satirist,* and the *Monthly Mirror* in January had said that if these *school exercises* had not caused him to be whipped at Harrow, they had "an undue respect for lords' bottoms." [n] Byron was eager to challenge the editor to a duel, but nothing came of it.[n] Now the much more prestigious *Edinburgh Review* had attacked the sensitive vanity of the author. Byron seemed not to be aware that the reviewer would not know his Whig leanings and would attack him as he appeared in his preface, a conceited young lord. He later pretended to have taken the review in his stride, but Hobhouse said emphatically: "this was not the case—he was very near destroying himself." In the end the feeling that predominated was anger, and the desire for revenge. But for the moment his despondency was acute.

Through the spring his excesses continued, until his health was seriously undermined. He spoke of it lightly to Hobhouse, as was the convention of their set: "The *Game* is almost up. For these last five days I have been confined to my room, Laudanum is my sole support. . . . on disclosing the mode of my life for these last two years (of which my residence at Cambridge constituted the most sober part), my Chirurgeon pronounced another quarter would have settled my earthly accounts, and left the worms but a scanty repast." [n]

But at the same time he announced boastingly that he had two "nymphs" in his keeping. One of these, according to Moore, he kept in lodgings at Brompton. This was probably the Miss Cameron whom he "redeemed" for a hundred guineas from a Madame D. She may have been the girl he disguised in boy's clothes and took to Brighton with him in the summer. According to one story current after Byron's death, he passed her off as his brother or cousin, "but the affair had a most ludicrous conclusion, for the young gentleman miscarried in a certain family hotel in Bond Street, to the inexpressible horror of the chambermaids. . . ." [n]

It may be that Byron, in a chivalrous mood when he discovered the girl was pregnant, told his friends he would marry her, for Hobhouse wrote anxiously: "The story of your engagement to Miss (I forget her name) is all over Cambridge."[n] But Hobhouse was relieved to learn that he was dividing his attentions and would probably not be drawn into an unequal marriage. "You will never after all you have said be a Benedict, and as for myself I find my hatred and disgust of that sex . . . every day increasing. You must for certain either have a whore or a termagant. . . ."[n] Byron was in perfect agreement. He would not make the sacrifice even for an heir, he told Augusta.

Byron had a taste for low company which continued throughout his life. He had become a familiar of pugilists through "Gentleman" Jackson and now he arranged a match on Epsom Downs between the popular little boxer Tom Belcher and the Irish champion Don Dogherty, whom he backed. Dogherty was beaten. Although Byron had renounced gambling because he realized that he could not afford it, he liked gamblers and he found the sport exhilarating. In his "Detached Thoughts" he wrote: "I have a notion that Gamblers are as happy as most people, being always *excited*. Women, wine, fame, the table, even Ambition, *sate* now and then; but every turn of the card, and cast of the dice, keeps the Gamester alive. . . ."[n]

Byron's health had improved but his financial situation was hopeless. "*Entre nous*," he wrote to Becher, "I am cursedly dipped; my debts, *every* thing inclusive, will be nine or ten thousand before I am twenty-one."[n] Partly to get away from the extravagance of London, on June 16 he left for Brighton. The chief attraction was sea bathing, in which, as in everything else, he indulged to excess. On July 4 he went to Cambridge to take his degree. " . . . the old beldam [Alma Mater] gave me my M.A. degree because she could not avoid it.—You know what a farce a noble Cantab. must perform."[n]

Hobhouse and Davies were with him when he returned to Brighton. There, with fierce plunges in the sea, the writing of disconsolate verses to one of his London inamoratas, and occasional orgies of drinking, he spent July and August. Surges of melancholia would come over him occasionally, and these moods generally found outlet in verse. The secret dissatisfactions and longings that were covered up in the buffoonery of his letters came out in the poem beginning "I would I were a careless child." The greater his disenchantments, the more pathetically he clung to the dreams of his youth. What never appeared in his letters is apparent in his verses of that summer: that he was emotionally involved beyond what he would admit to his friends with one of his London "nymphs," possibly the blue-eyed Caroline.

Early in September he was back at Newstead. Although his tenant, Lord Grey, had taken little care of the park or the lakes, Byron fell in love with the Abbey all over again and soon strenuously rejected his tentative thoughts of selling Newstead to pay his debts. He was already dreaming of entertaining as lavishly as his ancestors had done. Hobhouse had come and they were planning amusements, but for the time being the house was "filled with workmen, and undergoing a thorough repair," at an expense that was alarming his mother, to whom he wrote grandly, "You can hardly object to my rendering my mansion habitable, notwithstanding my departure for Persia in March (or May at farthest), since *you* will be *tenant* till my return. . . ." [n]

That Eastern voyage he had conceived back in January, when he wrote to his Harrow friend De Bathe: "In January 1809 I shall be twenty one & in the Spring of the same year proceed abroad, not on the usual Tour, but a route of a more extensive Description. . . . are you disposed for a view of the Peloponnesus and a voyage through the Archipelago? I am . . . very serious with regard to my own Intention which is fixed on the Pilgrimage. . . ." [n] In the back of his mind was the desire to take his seat in the House of Lords and then go abroad to enlarge his horizons as preparation for a career in Parliament. That much was most likely to impress his guardian, his attorney, and his mother. But his motives were more complicated. A deep-seated romantic longing for greener fields and fresh experience, and a growing dissatisfaction with the wastrel and dissipated life he was living also stimulated his longing to leave England. He was too weak and easygoing to extricate himself by any but a major break from the routines into which he so easily fell throughout his life.

The direction of his thoughts is traceable in the fact that for a masquerade in Nottingham he had a tailor make him a rich Turkish costume with "Full Trimmed Turban." [n] And of his Eastern tour he wrote his mother: "After all, you must own my project is not a bad one. If I do not travel now, I never shall, and all men should one day or other . . . . If we see no nation but our own, we do not give mankind a fair chance. . . ."[n]

Byron installed as head of his domestic retainers old Joe Murray, who had been the chief servant of "the Wicked Lord." The others included William Fletcher, his valet, and Robert Rushton, a handsome boy, son of one of his tenants, to whom he had taken a great fancy. Byron's favorite dog, Boatswain, and the tame bear he had kept at Cambridge were now at the Abbey. Byron and Hobhouse enjoyed the lordly independence of their life in the decayed baronial mansion. They bathed in the lake and rode through the spacious park. "Hobhouse hunts, etc.," Byron wrote Hodgson, "and I do nothing."[n] But he was not idle, for he was constantly adding to his satire.

When Mary Chaworth, now Mrs. Musters, heard he was at Newstead, she invited him and his guest to dinner at Annesley Hall, which had such poignant memories for him. Byron confessed to Hodgson, "I forgot my valour and my nonchalance, and never opened my lips even to laugh, far less to speak, and the lady was almost as absurd as myself. . . ."[n] Hobhouse saw nothing of this, and Byron, who could not reveal such feelings to his cynical friend, passed off the whole matter with bitter ribaldry. But the emotional disturbance and the chagrin of the experience again found its way into his poetry.

Byron's depression was increased by another disturbing experience. Boatswain, the great Newfoundland dog with which he had romped so often, went mad and died before his eyes. Moore says that "so little aware was Lord Byron of the nature of the malady, that he, more than once, with his bare hand, wiped away the slaver from the dog's lips during the paroxysms."[n] Byron's grief was genuine, and as usual he turned to poetry for an outlet, writing an epitaph in verse to be placed on Boatswain's tomb, which he later erected in the garden at Newstead.

Now he was more eager than ever to leave England. He wrote persuasively to Hanson of the wisdom of his voyage. "I wish to study India and Asiatic policy and manners. I am young, tolerably vigorous, abstemious in my way of living; I have no pleasure in fashionable dissipation, and I am determined to take a wider field than is customary with travellers. . . . A voyage to India will take me six months, and if I had a dozen attendants cannot cost me five hundred pounds; and you will agree with me that a like term of months in England would lead me into four times that expenditure."[n]

Indeed, Hanson had seen enough of Byron's ways to convince him of the truth of the latter statement. But the next proposal must have appalled him. "You honour my debts; they amount to perhaps twelve thousand pounds, and I shall require perhaps three or four thousand at setting out. . . . If my resources are not adequate to the supply I must *sell,* but *not Newstead.*"[n] His hope was set on selling his Rochdale estate in Lancashire, which "the Wicked Lord" had leased illegally. His mood was not brightened by Hanson's reply that the Rochdale estate was in a hopeless legal tangle. He wrote with exasperated humor: "I suppose it will end in my marrying a *Golden Dolly* or blowing my brains out; it does not much matter which, the remedies are nearly alike."[n]

Toward the end of November Hobhouse had left Newstead. Byron had invited several friends for the Christmas holidays, including such disparate characters as Hodgson and Gentleman Jackson, but none of them could come. In the loneliness of the Abbey he returned to his misanthropic meditations. When the gardener brought him a human skull that had been unearthed, it suited his sardonic whim to have it made into a drinking cup. As he touched up the account later, it was "a skull that had probably belonged to some jolly friar or monk of the Abbey about the time it was dismonasteried." He sent it to Nottingham and it returned "with a very high polish, and of a mottled colour like tortoiseshell. . . ."[n] It was set in heavy silver resting on four balls; the jeweller's bill—which did not worry Byron, for he had many larger—was £17 17s. The event was worthy of a poem, "Lines Inscribed upon a Cup Formed from a Skull":

Start not—nor deem my spirit fled:
In me behold the only skull,
From which, unlike a living head,
Whatever flows is never dull.

Byron spent his twenty-first birthday in London, leaving Hanson to represent him at Newstead where the tenants were preparing a manorial fête for the occasion. In a casual sentence he revealed that he had not been without feminine consolation at the Abbey. He was retaining two of the maids to take care of the house, "more especially as the youngest is pregnant (I need not tell you by whom) and I cannot have the girl on the parish." [n] But Byron was never as callous in his human relationships as his letters sometimes suggested. Although he was obviously not in love with the girl [Lucy] and did not pretend to be, he had made a provision for her beyond what, in the code of the time, was considered a young lord's obligation in such a situation: £50 for her and £50 for the child annually. And apparently when the child was born, he wrote a poem "To My Son" in which he hailed his "dearest child of love." [n]

Byron's first concerns when he reached London were to get his satire published and to take his seat with appropriate dignity in the coming session of Parliament. He had written to the Earl of Carlisle of his intention of entering the House of Lords, hoping that his guardian would save him the trouble of presenting credentials by introducing him in the House as a near relation. The Earl merely informed him of the technical procedure, but did not offer to introduce him. Byron was deeply mortified that he was forced by Carlisle's snub to go through the formalities of proving his legitimacy to the Chancellor.

In the meantime he was preparing himself for a career in Parliament by reading political memoirs and history. His bill at the bookseller's went up rapidly. He bought such heavy works as Holinshed's *Chronicles* and Cobbett's *Debates* and *Parliamentary History,* in addition to the *Memoirs of Grammont* and forty-five volumes of *British Essayists.* His extravagance continued to make his mother uneasy. She wrote to Hanson: "I wish to God he would exert himself and retrieve his affairs. He must marry a Woman of *fortune* this spring; love matches is all nonsense. Let him make use of the Talents God has given him. He is an English Peer, and has all the privileges of that situation." [n]

Through February, during the delays before he could take his seat, Byron continued to send Dallas corrections and alterations for *English Bards, and Scotch Reviewers,* the title he had settled on. Dallas had finally arranged for James Cawthorn to bring out an edition of a thousand copies.

When Dallas passed by Reddish's Hotel in St. James's Street on March 13, he found Byron's carriage waiting and went in. Byron was agitated and paler than usual. He was about to take his seat in Parliament, and Dallas accompanied him to the House of Lords. Because of the delays and what he considered the humiliation, he was in a sullen mood. After the ceremony, the Chancellor, Lord Eldon, left the Woolsack and offered his hand in welcome, but Byron merely touched his fingers, and then seated himself for a few minutes on one of the Opposition benches. He later recalled that the Chancellor had apologized for the delay, saying that "these forms were a part of his *duty.*" But he replied, "Your Lordship was exactly like 'Tom Thumb' (which was then being acted). You did your *duty,* and you did *no more.*"[n] But the ungracious behavior was only in part due to pique; he was "born for opposition" and he didn't want the Tory Chancellor to think that he was of his party. And his shyness made him assume a nonchalance he did not feel.

English Bards, and Scotch Reviewers appeared a few days later, though at the author's request, without his name on the title page. With youthful brashness Byron had struck out against almost all contemporary writers, who, compared with Pope or Dryden, or his more immediate model, Gifford, were either "little wits" or "knaves and fools": "The cry is up, and scribblers are my game." He damned "Ballad-monger Southey" for writing too much; Moore, whom Byron had read with avidity as a boy, was upbraided for the immorality of his lays; and Scott accused of writing "stale romance" for money. But despite the imitativeness of the poem, Byron's originality and wit sometimes transcended the limitations of the model. Echoing the current critical views of Wordsworth, he equaled his master Pope in voicing "What oft was thought, but ne'er so well express'd."

The simple Wordsworth . . .
Who, both by precept and example, shows
That prose is verse, and verse is merely prose . . .
And Christmas stories tortured into rhyme
Contain the essence of the true sublime.
Thus, when he tells the tale of Betty Foy,
The idiot mother of "an idiot boy;"
A moon-struck, silly lad, who lost his way,
And, like his bard, confounded night with day, . . .
    all who view the "idiot in his glory"
Conceive the Bard the hero of the story.

To the satire built on his "British Bards" he had added an attack on Francis Jeffrey, editor of the *Edinburgh Review,* imagining him the author of the devastating review of *Hours of Idleness.* But this becomes rather pedestrian except when he calls on the famous hanging judge Jeffries to yield his rope to his namesake, "To wield in judgment, and at last to wear."

Feeling that he had evened the score with the reviewers, and having taken his seat in Parliament, Byron was ready to go abroad. He felt that he would be cutting all his ties, and he clung to his Harrow associates, with whom his bonds were sentimental rather than intellectual. He had commissioned the miniature painter George Sanders to make several portraits to be exchanged with his favorites.

While waiting for Hanson to find money for his voyage, Byron invited several of his more amusing friends, including Hobhouse, Matthews, and Wedderburn Webster, to share the hospitality of his baronial estate. The stories of the unholy orgies carried on there, circulated in Byron's lifetime and later, grew out of what was actually little more than some spirited horseplay spurred on by drafts from Byron's stock of choice wines. Byron recalled: "We went down to Newstead together, where I had got a famous cellar, and *Monks'* dresses from a masquerade warehouse. . . . [We] used to sit up late in our friars' dresses, drinking burgundy, claret, champagne, and what not, out of the *skull-cup* . . . and buffooning all around the house. . . ." [n] Matthews was one of the leaders in this exalted foolery. He always called Byron "the Abbot," and it was he who played the ghost, rising out of a stone coffin to blow out Hobhouse's candle.

As for "Paphian girls" singing and smiling at the Abbey, as Byron proclaimed to the world in *Childe Harold,* they must have been the servant girls reserved for his pleasure when he was alone there. The "Haunted Chamber," the small room adjoining Byron's bedroom on the top floor near the ruined church—in which visitors to the Abbey were said to have seen a headless monk—was occupied by Robert Rushton, the handsome boy whom Byron had taken as a page.

Byron continued to press Hanson to raise the money necessary for his voyage. On April 16 he wrote from Newstead: "If the consequences of my leaving England were ten times as ruinous as you describe, I have no alternative, there are circumstances which render it absolutely indispensable, and quit the country I must immediately."[n] He had booked a passage abroad for the sixth of May from Falmouth, and he urged Hanson to raise money "on any terms." The manner in which he speaks of the urgency suggests some personal impasse more serious than the importunities of his creditors. Later, in Greece, he referred again to some mysterious reasons for his leaving England and not wanting to return there. He assured Hanson that it was not fear of the consequences of his satire that caused his impatience to leave, "but I will never live in England if I can avoid it. *Why*—must remain a secret. . . ."[n] These dark hints in contrast to the open and boastful avowals of his prowess with his "nymphs" in London, or his frank confession to Hanson of his *faux pas* with the maid Lucy, might tempt the speculation that he wished to escape his own proclivities toward attachment to boys, or even that he feared some closer alliance with the Cambridge choirboy Edleston, who had wanted to live with him in London. But we shall probably never know.

Byron arrived at Batt's Hotel, Jermyn Street, on April 25, eager to have news of his satire and to get cash for his journey. There was some prospect of a loan of £6,000 from a Mr. Sawbridge, but negotiations dragged into June and his sailing had to be postponed. In the meantime, he was buoyed up somewhat by the success of his poem, and he was busy preparing a second edition with additional lines, to which he would put his name before he went abroad. But he was in alternate moods of exhilaration and despondency. He made two sentimental Speech Day visits to Harrow. His friend Lord Falkland had been killed in a duel, and Byron, to help his widow, put himself still further into debt by inserting £500 in a breakfast cup at Lady Falkland's so that it would not be discovered until he left.

But with his Cambridge companions he could be scintillating and witty. The cynicism and the nonchalant fatalism of Hobhouse, Matthews, and Davies appealed to Byron more than the socially accepted hypocrisies of others. He had invited both Hobhouse and Matthews to join him on his tour, but only Hobhouse, who had quarreled with his father, accepted the invitation, though he had no money. But Byron, who had less than none—he owed more than £13,000—offered to furnish him with whatever he needed.

Really excited now about his voyage, he was exasperated by the delays in getting the necessary cash. He had written to Hanson: ". . . procure me three thousand pounds . . . if possible sell Rochdale in my absence, pay off these annuities and my debts, and with the little that remains do as you will, but allow me to depart from this cursed country, and I promise to turn Mussulman, rather than return to it."[n] While awaiting Sawbridge's loan, Byron blandly took further money from a usurer, promising an annuity of £400 for seven years.

By June 19 he could wait no longer and announced that he was setting off. He and Hobhouse left for Falmouth with all Byron's servants and equipment. He had brought old Joe Murray, William Fletcher, his faithful valet (who was to serve Byron until his master's death in Missolonghi), and Robert Rushton, "because, like myself, he seems a friendless animal," he told his mother. It was probably while they were in London that Byron and Robert posed in wide-flowing ties for a full-length portrait by Sanders.[n]

He wrote his mother from Falmouth: "I am ruined—at least till Rochdale is sold; and if that does not turn out well, I shall enter into the Austrian or Russian service—perhaps the Turkish, if I like their manners. The world is all before me, and I leave England without regret, and without a wish to visit any thing it contains, except *yourself*, and your present residence."[n] Mrs. Byron, who was taking care of Newstead for him, wrote wistfully to Hanson something she wouldn't have ventured to tell her son: "Lord Grey de Ruthyn has married a Farmer's Daughter, and Smith Wright is to marry a Lady with two hundred thousand pounds!!!"[n]

The disappointing news from Hanson that Sawbridge had remitted only £2,000 was countered by a providential loan of £4,800 from Scrope Davies, who had made a happy winning at the gambling tables. Byron wrote gaily to Henry Drury: "The Malta vessel not sailing for some weeks we have determined to go by way of Lisbon. . . . Hobhouse has made woundy preparations for a book at his return, 100 pens two gallons Japan Ink, and several vols best blank is no bad provision for a discerning Public.—I have laid down my pen, but have promised to contribute a chapter on the state of morals, and a further treatise on the same to be entituled 'Sodomy simplified or Paederasty proved to be praiseworthy from ancient authors and modern practice.' Hobhouse further hopes to indemnify himself in Turkey for a life of exemplary chastity at home by letting out his 'fair bodye' to the whole Divan. . . . P.S. We have been sadly fleabitten at Falmouth."[n]

And to Matthews he wrote, with the buffooning innuendo that was their common language, of the amusing aspects of Falmouth, a sailor's town, and a "delectable region, as I do not think Georgia itself can emulate in capabilities or incitements to the 'Plen. and optabil.—Coit.'[n]. . . We are surrounded by Hyacinths & other flowers of the most fragrant nature, & I have some intention of culling a handsome Bouquet to compare with the exotics we expect to meet in Asia.—One specimen I shall certainly carry off."[n]

On board the Lisbon packet, the *Princess Elizabeth,* on June 30, Byron wrote some rollicking verses for Hodgson, imagining the vessel already at sea and in a storm:

Hobhouse muttering fearful curses,
As the hatchway down he rolls;
Now his breakfast, now his verses,
Vomits forth—and damns our souls.

But the ship did not sail until July 2. Despite the badinage of his letters, Byron's state of mind on leaving his native shores was at once more sober and sentimental and more sensible than appeared on the surface. With due allowance for the distortions and exaggerations of self-dramatization, the essential moods and motives that drove him to travel are recorded in the first canto of *Childe Harold's Pilgrimage*. And shining through the melancholy of that poem is also a fairly faithful record of the *joie de vivre* that the new experiences of travel animated in him.

CHAPTER VII

1809–1810

The Pilgrimage of Childe Harold

THEY HAD A RAPID PASSAGE, arriving at the mouth of the Tagus four and a half days after leaving Falmouth. While Byron's mind turned to romantic contemplation, his rebellious stomach, in spite of the comparatively smooth passage, turned over in a most disconcerting manner. He confessed to Hodgson: "I have been sea-sick, and sick of the sea." [n] The exhilaration and strangeness of being in a foreign land struck the young Englishmen when the Portuguese pilots leaped on board. "I am very happy here," Byron wrote to Hodgson, "because I loves oranges, and talks bad Latin to the monks, who understand it, as it is like their own,—and I goes into society (with my pocket pistols), and I swims in the Tagus all across at once, and I rides on an ass or a mule, and swears Portuguese, and have got a diarrhæa and bites from the mosquitoes." [n]

Hobhouse, who began a diary on the day they landed in Lisbon, recorded mostly the particularities of the dirt, poverty, and ignorance of the country. The Peninsular War was in full swing. Sir Arthur Wellesley was on the frontier and swore he would be in Madrid in a month, and, according to Hobhouse, was "the god of the city." But in spite of the fact that the English were allies and deliverers, there was enough of wartime roguery and violence in the city to make it wise to go armed, especially at night.

On July 11 Byron and Hobhouse set out for Cintra. The village, Byron told his mother, "is, perhaps in every respect, the most delightful in Europe. . . . Palaces and gardens rising in the midst of rocks, cataracts, and precipices; convents on stupendous heights—a distant view of the sea and the Tagus. . . ."[n] But the greatest attraction of all was the Moorish palace, Montserrat, where Beckford, the author of *Vathek*, had lived.

To while away the time in Lisbon, Byron swam the broad estuary of the Tagus, landing below the Belem Castle, a feat which Hobhouse thought more daring than his later swimming of the Hellespont. After two weeks they grew tired of Portugal and decided to travel on horseback to Seville and Cádiz, sending their servants and baggage by ship to Gibraltar. Byron took Robert Rushton with him and they hired a Portuguese servant and guide by the name of Sanguinetti for the trip across the peninsula. The fact that part of the country through which they would travel had recently been a battleground increased the excitement.

In Seville, headquarters of the revolutionary Grand Junta and the allies, and immensely overcrowded, they took lodgings with two unmarried ladies, Josepha Beltram and her sister in the Calle de las Cruzes No. 19. Hobhouse noted ruefully: "went supperless & dinnerless to Bed all 4 in one little room." Byron was more amused than disconcerted. He wrote his mother: "The eldest honoured your *unworthy* son with very particular attention, embracing him with great tenderness at parting (I was there but three days), after cutting off a lock of his hair, and presenting him with one of her own, about three feet in length, which I send, and beg you to retain till my return. Her last words were, *Adios, tu hermoso! me gusto mucho*—'Adieu, you pretty fellow! you please me much.' She offered me a share of her apartment, which my *virtue* induced me to decline. . . ."[n]

Byron was exhilarated by the whole experience in Spain. He wrote to Hodgson of this part of the journey: "The horses are excellent—we rode seventy miles a day. Eggs and wine, and hard beds, are all the accommodation we found, and, in such torrid weather, quite enough. My health is better than in England. Seville is a fine town, and the Sierra Morena, part of which we crossed, a very sufficient mountain; but damn description, it is always disgusting."[n] Later he referred to Seville, the birthplace of Don Juan, as "a pleasant city,/ Famous for oranges and women."[n] At Cádiz, Byron was sufficiently captivated by the

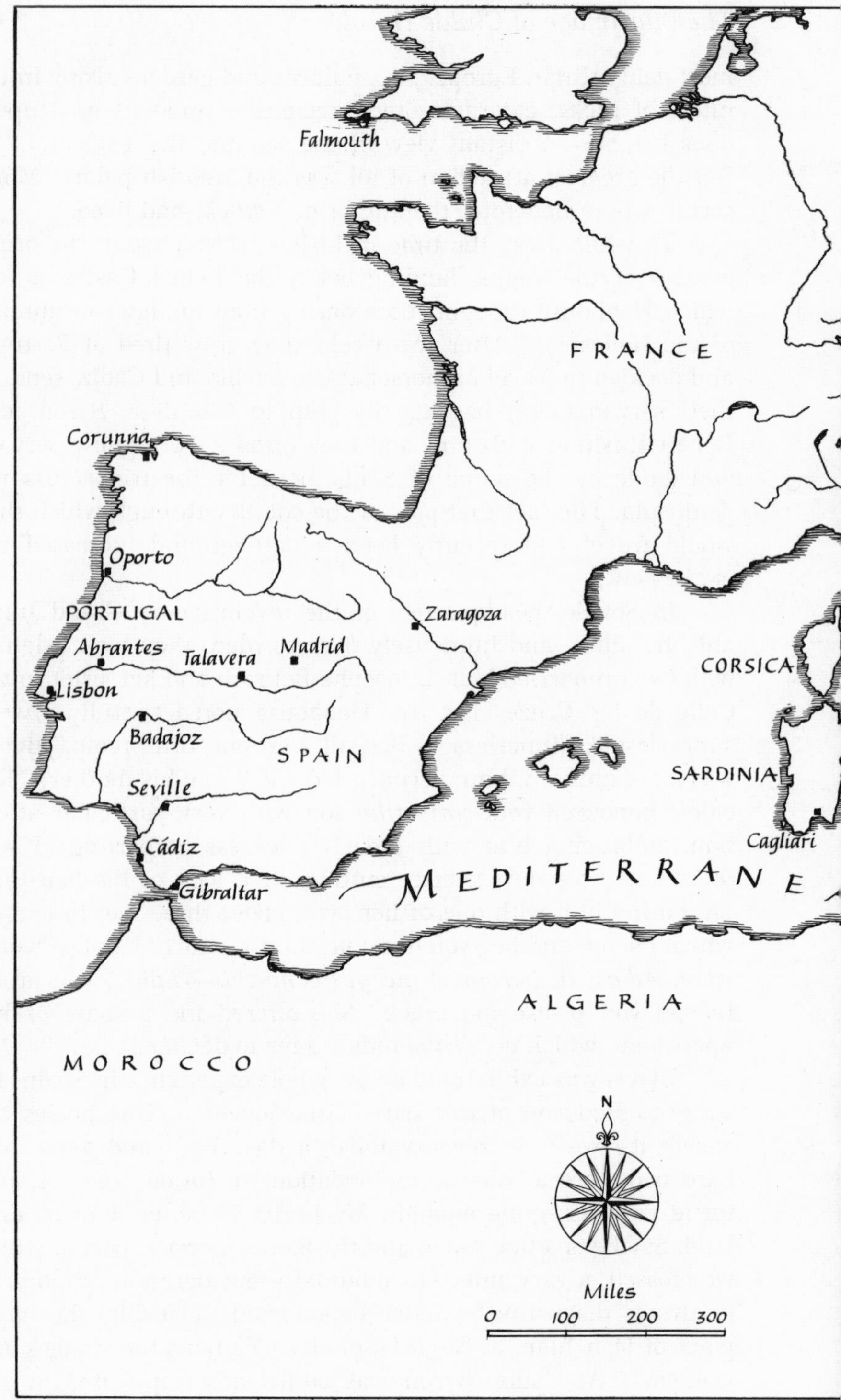
Falmouth
FRANCE
Corunna
Oporto
PORTUGAL
Zaragoza
Abrantes
Madrid
Talavera
Lisbon
CORSICA
Badajoz
SPAIN
SARDINIA
Seville
Cádiz
Cagliari
Gibraltar
MEDITERRANE
ALGERIA
MOROCCO
N
Miles
0
100
200
300

BYRON'S TRAVELS
1809 – 1811
BLACK SEA
TURKEY
Constantinople
SEA OF MARMORA
Abydos
Troy
Tenedos
Lesbos
ALBANIA
ITALY
Tepelene
Jannina
GREECE
Corfu
Prevesa
ÆGEAN SEA
Smyrna
Ephesus
Thebes
Ionian Islands
Kea
Athens
Corinth
Patras
Tripolitza
Girgenti
SICILY
Valetta
Malta
SEA
Crete

picturesque pageantry of a bullfight to devote eleven stanzas of *Childe Harold* to it, but at the same time he was disgusted with the brutality of the performance, being particularly revolted by the "wild plunging of the tortured horse."

His recollection of the city was glowing. "Cadiz, sweet Cadiz!" he wrote to Hodgson from Gibraltar, "it is the first spot in the creation. The beauty of its streets and mansions is only excelled by the loveliness of its inhabitants. . . . Cadiz is a complete Cythera. Many of the grandees who have left Madrid during the troubles reside there, and I do believe it is the prettiest and cleanest town in Europe. London is filthy in the comparison." [n]

Byron wrote his mother that the night before his departure he had sat in the box at the opera with Admiral Cordova's family. Hobhouse recorded in his diary: "B. was in a box with Miss Cordova, a little mad & apt to fall in love. . . ." The Admiral's daughter, Byron wrote, "dispossessed an old woman (an aunt or duenna) of her chair, and commanded me to be seated next herself, at a tolerable distance from her mamma."

The adventurous strangeness of the light flirtation with the dark foreign beauty blossomed soon after in his verses to "The Girl of Cadiz":

Our English maids are long to woo,
  And frigid even in possession;
And if their charms be fair to view,
  Their lips are slow at Love's confession;
But, born beneath a brighter sun,
  For love ordained the Spanish maid is . . .

But in a more realistic mood he confessed: "Certainly they are fascinating; but their minds have only one idea, and the business of their lives is intrigue." [n]

On the *Hyperion* frigate Byron and his party passed Cape Trafalgar on the 3rd of August and the next day found a contrast to the beauties of Seville and Cádiz in Gibraltar, "the dirtiest most detestable spot." [n] Byron and Hobhouse walked up the rock every evening to watch the sun set and to cast eager glances across the strait toward Africa, for Byron hoped to see another continent before he reached Asia. But his hopes were frustrated by a contrary wind.

When the servants and baggage finally arrived from Lisbon, they made hasty arrangements to sail on the *Townshend Packet* for Malta. Byron sent home Joe Murray because he was too old for the rigors of Eastern travel, and Robert Rushton, "because Turkey is in too dangerous a state for boys to enter."[n] Of his servants only the faithful Fletcher accompanied him when he sailed from Gibraltar on August 15. John Galt, who was on board, noted that "Hobhouse, with more of the commoner, made himself one of the passengers at once; but Byron held himself aloof, and sat on the rail, leaning on the mizzen shrouds. . . ."[n] But the third day out his mood had changed and he became playful. He joined the other passengers in shooting at bottles. When night came, however, he withdrew to the railing and sat for hours in silence.

His moodiness may have stemmed from his parting with Robert Rushton, who was much in his thoughts at the time. He had written to his mother, "Pray show the lad kindness, as he is my great favourite. . . ."[n] And he asked the boy's father to deduct £25 a year from his rent for Robert's education. "In case of my death I have provided enough in my will to render him independent."[n] This was the will he had signed on June 14, 1809, bequeathing £25 a year to Rushton for life (to be increased by £25 on the death of Joe Murray). In that will, written in the lugubrious mood of his departure from England, he had requested that his whole library be given to the Earl of Clare, all his lands and property to Hobhouse and Hanson, with a provision of £500 a year for life to his mother. And he expressed the desire "to be buried in the vault at Newstead Abbey with as little Pomp as possible—No Burial service or Clergyman or any Monument or Inscription of any Kind" except the date of his death and his initials. The monument over his dog was not to be disturbed when he was laid beside it.[n]

At Malta, Byron met the romantic Constance Spencer Smith. She was exactly suited to fascinate him. She was three years his senior, with all the attraction of a woman who had lived in foreign courts. Daughter of the Austrian Ambassador at Constantinople, she had married an Englishman, sometime Minister Plenipotentiary to the Porte, who had so incensed Napoleon that his wife twice had to make a dramatic escape from territory held by the French. Byron was captivated, and for the rest of his stay in Valletta was constantly with her. In England all of his amours had been with country girls like Julia Leacroft, or with ballet dancers and chambermaids. Not used to making love to a woman of his own social station, he was probably a little diffident at first, and that reserve, together with the Grecian beauty of his countenance and the charm he could command when he wanted to be agreeable, swept the lady off her feet.

Both Hobhouse and Galt thought that Byron was merely playing the gallant and was not really serious, but it seems that they misjudged the case from his usual flippant remarks at the time, and particularly later, after the passion had cooled. But he wrote Lady Melbourne: ". . . in the autumn of 1809 in the Mediterranean I was seized with an *everlasting* passion, considerably more violent on my part than this [his affair with Caroline Lamb] has ever been—everything was settled—and we . . . were to set off for the Friuli: but, lo! the Peace spoilt everything, by putting this in possession of the French. . . . However we were to meet next year at a certain time; though I told my *amica* there was no time like the present, and that I could not answer for the future. She trusted to her power, and I at the moment had certainly much greater doubts of her than myself." [n]

Byron and Hobhouse took the opportunity to sail on the brig-of-war *Spider*, which was to convoy a fleet of British merchant vessels to Patras and Prevesa. They left on September 19. While the ship plowed through the blue Ionian Sea, Byron felt the excitement of adventure as he neared the islands and then the mainland of Greece. They came to anchor in the harbor of Patras, then a small town backed by a Turkish fortress. Going on shore mainly to feel the soil of Greece under their feet, Byron and Hobhouse practiced pistol shooting in a "currant ground" and then returned to the *Spider*. On the way to Prevesa they saw to the north, across the Gulf of Lepanto, the low-lying town of Missolonghi. Thus on his first day in Greece Byron saw in the distance the marshy town where fifteen years later he was to die.

The first impression of Prevesa was marred by the rain which made the narrow streets muddy and emphasized the bare dinginess of the barrack-like houses. Byron and Hobhouse went ashore on September 29 in their regimental dress, but were soon somewhat bedraggled. Byron adapted himself very well to the inconveniences, but Hobhouse confessed that he would have been willing to return home that first day on Albanian soil. A true John Bull, he wrote: "Properly speaking, the word comfort could not be applied to anything I ever saw out of England." [n]

But the next day the sun came out and the land was transformed as they rode out through olive groves to the ruins of Nicopolis, caught glimpses of the sea, and heard the bleating of sheep and the distant tinkling of bells. On October 1 the travelers started on their journey to Jannina (Greek: Ioannina), Ali Pasha's newly made capital in the heart of the Epirus. Byron never traveled light. Four leather trunks and three smaller ones were weighted down with some of the books he had brought from England. In addition they had a canteen, three beds, and two light wooden bedsteads, a precaution against the bugs and the dampness of the floors. For their horses they had brought four English saddles and bridles. There were now four in their party, for in addition to Byron's servant Fletcher they had taken a dragoman named George.

They arrived at Jannina on the 5th. The setting at the foot of the Pindus mountains was picturesque enough to inspire Hobhouse to unwonted rhetoric: "houses, domes, and Minarets, glittering through gardens of orange and lemon trees, and from groves of cypresses—the lake spreading its smooth expanse at the foot of the city—the mountains rising abruptly from the banks of the lake." [n] But on entering the suburbs they saw an example of Ali's barbarity: a man's arm and part of the side torn from the body hung from a tree.

They called on Captain Leake, official British Resident in Jannina, and found that news of Byron's arrival had gone before him. Living quarters had been prepared at the home of an Italian-speaking Greek, Nicolo Argyri.* Ali Pasha, the ruler of Albania and what is now western Greece, had provided an escort for his guests, whom he begged to follow him to his castle in

* There is now in Jannina, in "Byron Street," a solid two-story house with projecting bars on the upper windows. A plaque in Greek over the door states that Byron lived there in October 1809. It is not, however, the house of Nicolo Argyri, with a courtyard and balconies, pictured in Thomas S. Hughes's *Travels in Sicily, Greece and Albania* (London, 1820). The site is probably the same, not far from the castle of Ali Pasha overlooking the lake.

Tepelene farther north in Albania, where he had gone "to finish a little war."

Ali Pasha's hospitality was not without a motive: he wanted to cultivate the friendship of the English to counter the influence of the French in the Ionian Islands. Before leaving for Tepelene, the young English visitors spent six pleasant days in the town with its mosques and Turkish houses. A tailor called and they tried on Albanian costumes, "as fine as Pheasants." Byron eventually bought "some very 'magnifiques' Albanian dresses. . . . They cost fifty guineas each, and have so much gold, they would cost in England two hundred." [n]

They saw both a Greek wedding procession and the festivities of the Ramadan, or Mohammedan Lent, which began with the firing of pistols and guns at the rising of the moon. They went one evening to a Turkish bath but were frightened away by an old "rubber" (masseur) and did not enter the inner room, where the washing was done, Signor Nicolo said, by *"belli giovani."* They were conducted through the palace of Mouctar Pasha, Ali's eldest son, by Mouctar's son Mahmout, "a little fellow ten years old," Byron wrote, "with large black eyes as big as pigeon's eggs, and all the gravity of sixty," who asked him what he did traveling without a *Lala* (tutor)." [n]

On the 11th they set out for Tepelene. The adventure of that journey was something that Byron never forgot. The gusto of the new experience shines through even the melancholy moods of the second canto of *Childe Harold.* On the first day Byron loitered behind and was overtaken by a sudden thunderstorm with lightning and floods of rain. Two of the horses fell; George, the dragoman, in the excitement "stamped, swore, cried and fired off his pistols, which . . . alarmed the 'valet' into fears for his life from robbers. . . . The whole situation becoming so serious that Ld. B. laughed," Hobhouse recorded. The other members of the party had reached the village of Zitza (Zitsa) high on a slope above the river valley of the Kalamas. Byron, protected by his hooded woolen capote, stopped by the side of some Turkish tombstones to write some stanzas to "Sweet Florence" (Constance Spencer Smith), and did not arrive until three in the morning. They spent the next day resting and visited the monastery above the town. It was "in the most beautiful situation," Byron wrote, "(always excepting Cintra, in Portugal) I ever beheld."[n]

It took another week for them to reach Tepelene, only seventy-five miles from Jannina, for the rains had washed the roads away. It was a strenuous journey, but Byron found it wholly delightful, especially in retrospect. He later recalled that Hobhouse, "when we were wayfaring men, used to complain grievously of hard beds and sharp insects, while I slept like a top, and to awaken me with his swearing at them: he used to damn his dinners daily . . . and reproach me for a sort of 'brutal' indifference. . . ."[n]

Byron was proud to be traveling through a country which no Englishman other than Leake had penetrated beyond the capital. In a note to *Childe Harold* he quoted Gibbon's remark that a country "within sight of Italy is less known than the interior of America."[n] He admired the wild mountain scenery. "The Arnaouts, or Albanese, struck me forcibly by their resemblance to the Highlanders of Scotland. . . . Their very mountains seemed Caledonian, with a kinder climate. The kilt, though white; the spare, active form; their dialect, Celtic in its sound; and their hardy habits, all carried me back to Morven."[n] And, he continued, "the most beautiful women I ever beheld, in stature and in features, we saw *levelling* the *road* broken down by the torrents. . . ."[n]

On October 19 they descended from the passes and saw the towers and minarets of Tepelene just as the sun was setting. Byron, ordinarily chary of description, gave his mother a glowing account of the scene: "The Albanians, in their dresses, (the most magnificent in the world, consisting of a long *white kilt*, gold-worked cloak, crimson velvet gold-laced jacket and waistcoat, silver-mounted pistols and daggers,) the Tartars with their high caps, the Turks in their vast pelisses and turbans, the soldiers and black slaves with the horses, the former in groups in an immense large open gallery in front of the palace, the latter placed in a kind of cloister below it, two hundred steeds ready caparisoned to move in a moment, couriers entering or passing out with the despatches, the kettle-drums beating, boys calling the hour from the minaret of the mosque. . . ."[n]

The Arabian Nights quality in the scene of barbaric splendor made a deep impression on Byron. He was much less moved by the sight of Constantinople, with its more splendid mosques and minarets, or by the Sultan's palace itself, than by the absolute little court that Ali Pasha had established in the inaccessible mountains of Albania. When Byron arrived, Ali held peaceful but despotic sway over the whole of western Greece from the Gulf of Corinth to central Albania.

The Pasha's courtesy to the English visitors was probably increased by his knowledge that the English forces had just taken the neighboring Ionian islands of Ithaca, Cephalonia, and Zante from the French. But Byron was convinced that Ali was most impressed by his rank. Hobhouse recorded dryly, "Ld. B gave me a lecture about not caring enough for the English nobility."

Byron had dressed for the interview "in a full suit of staff uniform, with a very magnificent sabre, etc." He was struck by the personality of Ali, more powerful in his own domain than the Sultan himself, to whom he paid nominal tribute. Ali's very ruthlessness made him the kind of romantic villain Byron was later to picture in his Oriental tales, and the pirate Lambro, the father of Juan's island "bride," owed something to him, for Lambro was "the mildest mannered man/ That ever scuttled ship or cut a throat." [n]

Byron wrote his mother: "The vizier received me in a large room paved with marble; a fountain was playing in the centre; the apartment was surrounded by scarlet ottomans. He received me standing, a wonderful compliment from a Mussulman, and made me sit down on his right hand. . . . He said he was certain I was a man of birth, because I had small ears, curling hair, and little white hands, and expressed himself pleased with my appearance and garb. He told me to consider him as a father whilst I was in Turkey, and said he looked on me as his son. Indeed, he treated me like a child, sending me almonds and sugared sherbet, fruit and sweetmeats, twenty times a day. He begged me to visit him often, and at night, when he was at leisure." [n]

While he was greatly flattered by the Pasha's attention, Byron could not have been wholly unaware that Ali's remarks about his handsome features had a particular meaning more personal and sensual than an interest in his noble birth would have elicited.

Byron left with the blessing of Ali Pasha, an Albanian soldier named Vasilly, whom he later took into his personal service, and an introduction to Ali's son Veli, then Pasha of the Morea (the Peloponnesus). It was largely from Vasilly, who served him with an "almost feudal fidelity," that Byron formed so favorable an opinion of the Albanian character.

The rains had ended when they left Tepelene on October 23, and in four days they were back in Jannina. They spent a busy week in the town and its environs. They visited Ali's palace on the lake, where their host was the twelve-year-old son of Veli Pasha, who had all the poise of his cousin Mahmout. Byron wrote his mother: "They are the prettiest little animals I ever saw. . . . Mahmout . . . hopes to see me again; we are friends without understanding each other, like many other folks, though from a different cause." [n]

Although Byron was inclined to speak jokingly of the writing propensities of Hobhouse, who was busily gathering material for a book of travels, he too had stored impressions of his voyage which he felt a need to express. Those were the thoughts that brought on that "rapt mood" noticed by Galt on the voyage to Malta, or caused him to gaze, as Captain Leake observed in Jannina, "with an air *distrait* and dreamy upon the distant mountains." [n] On the last day of October Byron began a frankly autobiographical poem concerning the adventures and reflections of Childe Burun, a name which he later changed to Childe Harold. The Spenserian stanza he had settled upon no doubt came from his reading parts of the *Faerie Queene* in *Elegant Selections*, an anthology he had carried over the mountains of Albania.[n] Before he had proceeded far, his thinly veiled alter ego, despite the settled gloom of his general mood, was responding with zest to the novelties of his voyage. In the weeks that followed he added to the poem at every pause in the journey.

Byron, now seasoned to the rough life of Eastern travel (Hobhouse and Fletcher never would be), left Jannina with his entourage on November 3. They accepted Ali's offer of an armed vessel from Prevesa to Patras, but neither the captain nor any of the Turkish crew knew how to handle a ship, and when a stiff wind rose, they panicked. Byron described the scene to his mother: "Fletcher yelled after his wife, the Greeks called on all the saints, the Mussulmans on Alla; the captain burst into tears and ran below deck, telling us to call on God; the sails were split, the main-yard shivered, the wind blowing fresh, the night setting in, and all our chance was to make Corfu . . . or (as Fletcher pathetically termed it) 'a watery grave.' I did what I could to console Fletcher, but finding him incorrigible, wrapped myself up in my Albanian capote . . . and lay down on deck to wait the worst." [n] The few Greeks on board got the vessel in hand and made an anchorage on the rocky coast of Suli not far from Parga.

They decided not to trust their lives again to Turkish seamen, but to venture through the robber-infested passes of Acarnania and Aetolia to Missolonghi with a guard of fifty soldiers. After their meal of roasted goat, the Albanians danced around their open fire to the music of their own songs, "bounding hand in hand, man linked to man." One of the songs began: "When we set sail, a band of thieves from Parga . . ." and its refrain was: "Robbers all at Parga." Almost all of Ali's army had been robbers at one time or another, and they might easily return to a profession often allied to patriotism in a country long under Turkish tyranny. The episode found its place in *Childe Harold's Pilgrimage*.

On November 20 the party reached Missolonghi, which stood on a flat, marshy promontory sticking out into the shallow lagoon accessible only to small boats. Fishermen's huts, built on stakes in the water, and fishing nets circled the lagoon. It was not attractive, and Byron nowhere in his letters or poems described the fateful town as it appeared to him on his first visit. At Patras, Byron dismissed his dragoman, George, who had cheated them in a subtle Greek way in his accounts, and hired another Greek, Andreas, who spoke most of the languages then current in the Levant. He had also taken into his service one of his guard, an Albanian Turk named Dervish Tahiri, who was to serve him devotedly during his stay in Greece and to be desolated by his departure.

Following along the blue waters of the Corinthian Gulf, they stopped for several days with Andreas Londos, the Cogia Basha, or Governor of the district, under Veli Pasha. This wealthy young Greek seemed playful as a boy, but at the mention of the name of Rhiga, the Greek patriot who, twenty years before, had attempted to organize a revolution against the Turkish masters, he jumped up suddenly and "clasping his hands, repeated the name of the patriot with a thousand passionate exclamations, the tears streaming down his cheeks." * Byron had begun to see, as he had not in Albania, that there lurked among the Greeks an underlying hatred of their masters which needed only a flame to set it off.

Byron probably had as great an eagerness as Hobhouse to see the home of the muses and to drink from the Castalian Spring. Therefore, instead of following the easier route through Corinth, Megara, and Eleusis, they crossed the Corinthian Gulf and rode up the olive-clad valley to Castri (the site of ancient Delphi) on the slopes of Parnassus. They were disappointed, for the most interesting relics of the temples and the theater had not yet been uncovered. They saw the Castalian Spring and then scratched their names on an ancient column that stood at the entrance to the monastery of the Panagia on the site of the Gymnasium.† Byron, however, was no antiquarian and turned for his inspiration to Mount Parnassus. Seeing a flight of eagles (as one may still see them soaring over Delphi), he "seized the omen" and wrote some stanzas for *Childe Harold,* hoping "Apollo had accepted my homage." [n]

The first view of Athens from a pine-clad hill near Fort Phyle roused Byron to enthusiasm for the living Greece that was a relic of its former self: ". . . the plain of Athens, Pentelicus, Hymettus, the Ægean, and the Acropolis, burst upon the eye at once; in my opinion, a more glorious prospect than even Cintra. . . ." [n] On the evening of Christmas Day they rode down through the olive groves, crossed the Cephisus, passed through an arched gateway, and entered Athens. Since there was no hotel or inn, they took rooms in a double house owned by Mrs. Tarsia Macri, widow of a Greek who had been British Vice-Consul. Their lodg-

* Hobhouse, *Journey,* II, 586. Constantine Rhiga founded the Philike Hetairia, a society to encourage and foster Greek nationalism. He was executed by the Turks in 1798, but his songs, such as "Greeks Arise," an adaptation of the "Marseillaise," did much to arouse the Greeks to thoughts of revolution. When the Greek revolution broke out in 1821, Londos was one of the first to take a lead in the war.

† The names may still be seen on the fallen column, which remains, though the monastery has disappeared. They are very faint, being thinly scratched on the stone, but become visible when water is thrown on the column. See C. W. J. Eliot, "Lord Byron, Early Travelers, and the Monastery at Delphi," *American Journal of Archaeology,* Vol. 71, No. 3 (July 1967), pp. 283–91.

ings, Hobhouse recorded, "consisted of a sitting-room and two bed-rooms, opening into a court-yard where there were five or six lemon-trees, from which . . . was plucked the fruit that seasoned the pilaf. . . ." * The serving was done by the three daughters of the widow Macri: Mariana, Katinka, and Theresa, all under fifteen. Byron referred to them as "the three graces."

Being under the shadow of the Acropolis itself was exciting, though the town, with narrow, squalid streets, was hardly suggestive of its past glories. When Byron arrived, Athens was a town of ten thousand Turks, Greeks, and Albanians crowded into twelve or thirteen hundred houses massed around the north and west sides of the Acropolis and surrounded by a wall. Although there were frequent Western European travelers, the permanent Frank [n] residents consisted of seven or eight families.

Their first wish was to visit the Acropolis, but they were delayed by the necessity of sending a present first to the Disdar, a subordinate of the Waiwode, or Turkish Governor of the town. In the meantime they saw the Theseum and the temple of Olympian Zeus. By the beginning of 1810 the pattern of their life was established. Every day Byron rode out one of the city gates with Hobhouse, either westward to Eleusis with its view of Salamis and Ægina in the distance, or to the monastery of Katerina on Mt. Hymettus. On another day they would go northward to Pentelicus, the mountain from which the ancient Greeks quarried the marble for the great columns and statues on the Acropolis. One of Byron's favorite excursions was to the gemlike harbor of Munichia † where according to legend the tomb of Themistocles stood on a cliff.

Within three weeks they had seen most of the antiquities in and around Athens. Byron's mood on these rides is indicated by what he later told Trelawny (with due allowance for Trelawny's picturesque distortions): "Travelling in Greece, Hobhouse and I

---

* Hobhouse, *Journey*, I, 291. The house where Byron first lived in Athens was partly destroyed in the Greek revolution and disappeared entirely soon after. Today a modern two-story dwelling stands on the spot, in Odos Agias Theklas (near Monasteraki) to the west of the Acropolis. When I first saw it in 1948 a plaque in Greek and English said that Byron's Maid of Athens lived in a house on the site, but the plaque has since disappeared.

† Now called Turcolimani and lined with waterfront tavernas where tourists go to dine in the summer.

wrangled every day. . . . He had a greed for legendary lore, topography, inscriptions. . . . He would potter with map and compass at the foot of Pindus, Parnes, and Parnassus, to ascertain the site of some ancient temple or city. I rode my mule up them. They had haunted my dreams from boyhood; the pines, eagles, vultures, and owls were descended from those Themistocles and Alexander had seen, and were not degenerated like the humans. . . . I gazed at the stars and ruminated; took no notes, asked no questions." [n]

If we may judge from the tone of the sentiments expressed in *Childe Harold,* Byron was at once buoyed in spirit and depressed by the ruins of columns and the relics of a decaying beauty once perfect. But as his impressions began to crystallize, he saw the remnants of Greece's golden age with more sadness than delight. He opened the second canto of *Childe Harold* with an invocation to "august Athena!"

> *Where are thy men of might? thy grand in soul?*
> *Gone—glimmering through the dream of things that*
> *were . . .*" [n]

And he saw the broken columns now as "a Nation's sepulchre!/ Abode of Gods, whose shrines no longer burn." [n]

Yet a new perspective on the relics, and incidentally on the Greeks themselves, came with Byron's first visit to the Acropolis. Delayed by formalities, it was not until January 8 that he climbed the famous hill accompanied by Hobhouse and Giovanni Battista Lusieri, a Neapolitan painter employed by Lord Elgin, who, while British Ambassador at Constantinople, had gained permission to have drawings made and then to remove some of the statues and friezes, which he was shipping to England. The first shipment had gone as early as 1802, but the collection was not opened to public view until 1807 in a museum in Park Lane. The general public response Byron had echoed in *English Bards, and Scotch Reviewers,* where he referred contemptuously to Elgin's "mutilated blocks of art." But seeing them now in their natural setting of the Parthenon and the Erechtheum, he no longer viewed the sculptures that had been removed as worthless stones and "maimed antiques" but as relics of the finest treasures of Greek civilization. He became an ardent defender of the marbles and launched a bitter attack against Lord Elgin for his "vandalism" in some stanzas of *Childe Harold.*

> *Cold is the heart, fair Greece! that looks on Thee,*
> *Nor feels as Lovers o'er the dust they loved . . .*[n]

To dramatize the atrocities of the "plunderers," Byron seized upon the legend of Alaric the Goth, who, terrified by the phantoms of Minerva and Achilles, had spared the city's treasures and monuments.

Hobhouse, who viewed the matter less emotionally, argued that the preservation of these art treasures in London would benefit "an infinitely greater number of rising architects and sculptors."[n] Byron turned his most scathing ridicule upon that argument. He would ever oppose, he said, "the robbery of ruins from Athens, to instruct the English in sculpture (who are as capable of sculpture as the Egyptians are of skating). . . ."[n] His emotional response to the question of the Elgin marbles has been the one adopted by Philhellenes ever since. And this stance no doubt accounted for the hero-worshipping of Byron among both Greeks and foreigners ardent in the cause of Greek independence. It seemed almost that he had foreseen the time when the Greeks would regain their freedom and preserve their own monuments.*

An excursion to Cape Colonni, or Sounion, a high cliff at the tip end of Attica looking over the Ægean, became an indelible memory to Byron. He was accompanied by Hobhouse and his Albanian servant Vasilly on the journey on horseback around Hymettus (there was then no fine road along the Attic coast such as now speeds tourists from Athens in an hour). They arrived on January 23, the day after Byron's twenty-second birthday, and saw the white Doric columns of the ancient temple to

---

* Byron's protest against the spoliation of the Greek treasures moved Harold Nicolson, when he was a young junior clerk in the Foreign Office in 1924, the centenary of Byron's death, to propose to his superiors that it would be a fine gesture of friendship to Greece if the British Museum, which purchased Lord Elgin's marbles in 1816 for £35,000, would send back one of these, the Caryatid, to its original home on the Erechtheum. But they, not being as enthusiastic Byronians as Nicolson, were deaf to the appeal. (See Harold Nicolson, "The Byron Curse Echoes Again," *New York Times Magazine,* March 27, 1949, pp. 12, 13, 33, 35.

Poseidon (then supposed to be that of Minerva) starkly silhouetted against the deep blue sea dotted with steep-sided green islands. These were the "Isles of Greece":

Place me on Sunium's marbled steep,
Where nothing, save the waves and I,
May hear our mutual murmurs sweep . . .[n]

The next goal of the travelers was the plain of Marathon, where the Athenians defeated the Persian invaders in 490 B.C. While Hobhouse was anatomizing the site of the battle, Byron was re-creating a heroic picture which eventually found shape in words that fired Greek national pride and spurred Philhellenic zeal, and which became almost the most quoted of all Byron's lines:

The mountains look on Marathon—
And Marathon looks on the sea;
And musing there an hour alone,
I dreamed that Greece might still be free . . .[n]

Byron had from his arrival formed a more favorable opinion of the modern Greeks than his traveling companion and most of the other Franks with whom he associated in Athens. When the French Consul, M. Fauvel, and the merchant M. Roque (who, according to Hobhouse, supported himself chiefly "by lending money, at an interest from twenty to thirty per cent to the trading Greeks, and in a trifling exportation of oil") came to visit Byron, M. Roque expressed the view common to foreigners in Greece at the time. The Athenians, he said, "are the same *canaille* that existed *in the days of Themistocles!*" This he uttered with "the most amusing gravity," Byron said in a note to *Childe Harold,* adding sarcastically: "The ancients banished Themistocles; the moderns cheat Monsieur Roque; thus great men have ever been treated!"[n]

Byron got along equally well, however, with Greeks and Franks in the close-knit society of Athens, where there was much spontaneous gaiety during the winter. There was frequent dancing and much buffoonery at the Macri House, where his increasing interest in the youngest of the "three graces," Theresa ("12 years old but quite 'nubila,' " Hobhouse noted), made it possible for him to close the account of the emotional strain of his love for Constance Spencer Smith: "The spell is broke, the charm is flown!"

And now a more poignant wrench came when he found it necessary to quit the agreeable life in Athens. He had not given up his intention of going to Constantinople and from there to Persia and India. He had received a traveling firman from Robert Adair, British Ambassador at the Turkish capital. And when the English sloop-of-war *Pylades* offered passage to Smyrna, he seized the opportunity and left with Hobhouse on a day's notice. Parting from Theresa gave him a curious pang. It may have been on the eve of his departure that he wrote, or at least began, his now famous lines:

Maid of Athens, ere we part,
Give, oh give me back my heart!

Perhaps Theresa herself had taught him the refrain, Ζωή μου, σᾶς ἀγαπῶ, which he said was a Romaic expression of tenderness meaning "My life, I love you!" The line, "By that lip I long to taste," suggests that his relations with Theresa had been, if not Platonic, at least in the realm of longing rather than of possession.

Never had he left any place with so much regret. Never had his life fitted into such a tranquil pattern among people who, if not heroic, were at least agreeable; nor had he found before a climate and a setting so conducive to contentment. As he proceeded on his travels, his homesickness for Attica increased. His realistic judgment of the people did not diminish his admiration for them. "I like the Greeks," he wrote Henry Drury, "who are plausible rascals,—with all the Turkish vices, without their courage. However, some are brave, and all are beautiful. . . ." [n]

CHAPTER VIII

1810–1811

The Clime of the East

SHORTLY AFTER ARRIVING IN Smyrna, Byron and Hobhouse set out for the ruins of Ephesus. Byron's only comment on the desolate scene was that "the temple has almost perished, and St. Paul need not trouble himself to epistolize the present brood of Ephesians. . . ." [n] What struck him more was the dramatic barking of jackals heard in that once great but deserted city. Their "mixed and mournful sound" as they "bayed from afar complainingly" seemed to echo fittingly the melancholy of its mouldering marble.

They returned to the hospitality of Mr. Werry, the British Consul-General at Smyrna, to await an opportunity to go on to Constantinople. Byron was disconsolate and uncertain of the future. The lethargy he professed ("the further I go the more my laziness increases," he wrote his mother) stemmed partly from his reflection on the state of his affairs and partly from the climate and tempo of life in the East. He was not as idle as his letter suggested, however, for he was still adding stanzas to *Childe Harold's Pilgrimage*. His thoughts turned back to Attica, where he had felt the presence of ancient Greece.

Where'er we tread 'tis haunted holy ground;
No earth of thine is lost in vulgar mould,
But one vast realm of Wonder spreads around,
And all the Muse's tales seem truly told . . .[n]

On March 28 Byron finished the second canto and laid the manuscript aside. His subsequent experiences in Turkey did not inspire him to continue.

Captain Bathurst invited Byron and his friend to board the *Salsette* frigate for Constantinople. They sailed on April 11, and on the 14th anchored off Cape Janissary or Sigium, a few miles from the entrance to the Hellespont. Detained for a fortnight by contrary winds and by the formality of obtaining a firman to pass the strait, they had ample time to explore the "ringing plains of windy Troy." The authenticity of the tale of Troy seemed important to Byron. He wrote later in his diary: "I have stood upon that plain *daily* . . . in 1810; and if any thing diminished my pleasure, it was that the blackguard Bryant [n] had impugned its veracity. . . . But I still venerated the grand original as the truth of *history* (in the material *facts*) and of *place*. Otherwise, it would have given me no delight." [n]

While the *Salsette* was anchored near the mouth of the Dardanelles, or Hellespont, Byron was eager to try his swimming skill in imitation of Leander. He and Lieutenant Ekenhead made the attempt to cross the channel from the European side, but the coldness of the water and the swiftness of the current obliged them to give up the project. On May 3 they tried again and succeeded. Hobhouse wrote excitedly in his diary: "Byron and Ekenhead . . . now swimming across the Hellespont—Ovid's Hero to Leander open before me." Byron himself added a note to Hobhouse's account: "The total distance E. & myself swam was more than 4 miles the current very strong and cold . . . we were not fatigued but a little chilled; did it with little difficulty." It was a feat in which Byron took unremitting pride. It was not as difficult as his swimming the Tagus at Lisbon, though the associations were more romantic. Perhaps a hundred swimmers since, from college students to Richard Halliburton, have accomplished the crossing of the Hellespont, chiefly because Byron threw glamour over the fabled deed of Leander.

He continued to refer to his exploit in his letters. He told Henry Drury that "the current renders it hazardous, so much so, that I doubt whether Leander's conjugal powers must not have been exhausted in his passage to Paradise." [n] Six days after the event he composed his lighthearted lines "Written after Swimming from Sestos to Abydos." He had not literally acquired the ague, as he asserted humorously in the last line, and the chilling did not dampen his spirits. With an exuberance that flowed into ribaldry he wrote to Drury: "I see not much difference between ourselves & the Turks, save that we have foreskins and they none, that they have long dresses and we short, and that we talk much and they little.—In England the vices in fashion are whoring & drinking, in Turkey, Sodomy & smoking, we prefer a girl and bottle, they a pipe and a pathic. They are sensible people. . . . By the bye, I speak the Romaic or modern Greek tolerably. . . . I can swear in Turkish, but except one horrible oath, and 'pimp' and 'bread' and 'water' I have got no great vocabulary in that language." [n]

Despite the surface gaiety that always burst forth in his correspondence, Byron confessed to the more serious Hodgson: "Hobhouse rhymes and journalizes; I stare and do nothing. . . . We have been very nearly one year abroad. I should wish to gaze away another, at least, in these evergreen climates; but I fear business . . . will recall me. . . . I hope you will find me an altered personage,—I do not mean in body, but in manner, for I begin to find out that nothing but virtue will do in this damned world. I am tolerably sick of vice, which I have tried in its agreeable varieties, and mean, on my return, to cut all my dissolute acquaintance, leave off wine and carnal company, and betake myself to politics and decorum." [n]

At two o'clock on the 13th of May they caught their first sight of Constantinople from the Sea of Marmora, the minarets of the great mosques and the domes and tall cypresses rising gradually out of the mist. Passing the Seven Towers, they anchored at sunset under the gloomy walls near the Seraglio point. At noon the next day they went ashore, passing close under the walls of the Sultan's palace, where they saw two dogs gnawing a dead body. They proceeded to a comfortable hotel in Pera, where all the embassies and the Frankish population were located. At the time no foreigners were allowed to reside within the walls of Stamboul, the old city which lies between the Bosporus and the Golden Horn.

Soon after their arrival they called at the English palace, where Robert Adair, the British Ambassador, cut off from official connection with the French and their satellites, extended general hospitality to most English travelers. Byron declined an apartment but accepted the service of a Janissary for a dragoman, and he and Hobhouse frequently dined at the palace.

Byron's appearance in a shop where he had gone to buy some pipes was observed by an Englishman who happened to be there: "He wore a scarlet coat, richly embroidered with gold . . . with two heavy epaulettes. . . . His features were remarkably delicate, and would have given him a feminine appearance, but for the manly expression of his fine blue eyes. . . . he took off his feathered cocked-hat, and showed a head of curly auburn hair, which improved in no small degree the uncommon beauty of his face."[n]

Byron saw much to justify a growing dislike of the Turks. Their contempt for human life and their arbitrary tyranny seemed revolting to him. And, in strong contrast to his experience in Greece, he had no opportunity to meet the people of the country on a social level. After visiting the wine houses of Galata, the principal mosques, and the bazaars, Byron soon tired of the city and resumed his old habit of riding out each day to some attractive spot in the surrounding country. He was particularly fond of the ride around the land walls, which had stood for a thousand years in a semicircle from the Golden Horn to the Sea of Marmora. He was impressed by the towers and the "Turkish burying-grounds (the loveliest spots on earth), full of enormous cypresses."[n] As spring transformed the gardens and country places along the Golden Horn, Byron frequently rode to the Valley of the Sweet Water, one of the Sultan's pleasure gardens beyond the head of the Golden Horn, or followed the Bosphorus on the European side to the village of Belgrade, where once had lived Mary Wortley Montagu, whose association with Pope increased the romance of her history for him.

All the English had been invited to join the official procession when Adair took leave of the Caimacam, the representative of the Grand Vizier. Byron went to the Ambassador's palace in his gay regimentals, but when he found that his rank was not recognized and that he would have to march behind Mr. Canning, the secretary of the Embassy, he left in a pique. Feeling that he had been insulted, he was unable to gain perspective for three days. In his irritation he threatened to dismiss Fletcher and wrote to Captain Bathurst "to permit me to take a youngster from your ship as a substitute." [n] It took all of Hobhouse's friendly persuasion to prevent him from leaving immediately for Smyrna, but he was brought round by a special invitation from Adair to dine at the palace.

But the remainder of his stay in Constantinople was made gloomy by bad news from England. Hobhouse wrote in his diary on June 6: "a letter from Hodgson to B—tales spread—the *Edleston* is accused of indecency." The second edition of *English Bards, and Scotch Reviewers* had been sold out and Cawthorn was preparing another, but, Byron told Dallas, what happened to his satire would not disturb his "tranquillity beneath the blue skies of Greece," where he proposed to spend the summer and perhaps also the winter. He added "that all climates and nations are equally interesting to me; that mankind are everywhere despicable in different absurdities; that the farther I proceed from your country the less I regret leaving it. . . ." [n] Letters from his mother indicated that his affairs were going badly. The poor woman had been harassed by her son's creditors. Brothers, the Nottingham upholsterer, held a bill for £1,600 for renovating and furnishing rooms at Newstead and was threatening an execution. And Hanson was desperately trying to placate Byron's creditors, who had bills totaling £10,000, and was barely able to pay the £3,000 in annuities due the usurers.

Robert Adair had invited Byron to attend the ceremony of his final audience with the Sultan, but warned him that the Turks did not acknowledge any precedence in the procession. After being assured by the Austrian Internuncia, the authority on diplomatic etiquette, that this was true, Byron wrote Adair accepting the decision without too much grace: "I shall therefore make what atonement I can, by cheerfully following not only your Excellency, 'but your servant or your maid, your ox, or your ass, or anything that is yours'." [n]

Whether disturbed by news from England or by nearer sources of irritation, he evinced a like misanthropy when he wrote to Hodgson the same day (July 4): "Next week the frigate sails with Adair; I am for Greece, Hobhouse for England. A year together on the 2nd July. . . . I have known a hundred instances of men setting out in couples, but not one of a similar return." [n] But it was only a passing mood, for on the same day he could rib Hobhouse good-naturedly about his literary luggage.

The Ambassador's audience took place on July 10. Hobhouse devoted four pages of his diary to a description of the event, but Byron was peculiarly silent about it. The spectacle in the Sultan's palace, a display of pageantry and richness far surpassing anything at Ali Pasha's court, failed to touch him in the same way because he did not feel himself personally involved and because he was only one of a crowd and not a principal actor. When he later praised the Turks, he usually thought of those he had met in Albania. The anonymous stranger who had seen Byron in the shop in Pera, however, reported that the Sultan let his wandering eyes fall on the handsome countenance of the young lord, who "seemed to have excited his curiosity." [n]

The *Salsette* left Constantinople with Adair, Hobhouse, Byron, and his entourage on July 14. During the voyage Adair observed that Byron was laboring under great dejection of spirits. On the 17th the frigate pulled into the harbor of "Zea" (Keos) just off Cape Colonni. Byron and his servants went ashore, and Hobhouse noted sentimentally in his diary: "Took leave, *non sine lacrymis,* of this singular young person, on a little stone terrace at the end of the bay, dividing with him a little nosegay of flowers. . . ."

The intense heat of summer had settled upon Athens on Byron's return, but Greece still pleased him more than Turkey. Constantinople, he said, with all its mosques, "cannot be compared with Athens and its neighbourhood; indeed I know of no Turkish scenery to equal this." [n] He had gone back to his old quarters in the Macri house, but it was not the same. The charm of innocence had flown. "An usual custom here," he wrote his mother, " . . . is to part with wives, daughters, etc., for a trifling present of gold or English arms. . . ." [n] The fact was that the widow Macri was willing enough to part with her daughter to the English lord, but she wanted compensation according to the Greek custom, or a legal marriage. Byron told Hobhouse that " . . . the old woman, Theresa's mother, was mad enough to imagine I was going to marry the girl; but I have better amusement." [n]

Despite the heat Byron set out for Patras on July 21, probably to pick up remittances from Malta from the English Consul Strané. On the 25th he reached Vostitza, where he and Hobhouse had stayed with the Cogia Basha Andreas Londos. There he added to his suite a Greek boy by the name of Eustathios Georgiou, whom he had met on his earlier voyage.[n] The absurd jealous attachment of this youth, who was ready to follow him to England or to "Terra Incognita," he wrote Hobhouse, filled him with amusement. The absurdity was increased when "The next morning I found the dear soul upon horseback clothed very sparsely [sprucely?] in Greek Garments, with those ambrosial curls hanging down his amiable back, and to my utter astonishment, and the great abomination of Fletcher, a *parasol* in his hand to save himself from the heat." They traveled on to Patras and stayed with Strané. Byron added, referring to the boy, "I think I never in my life took so much pains to please any one, or succeeded so ill. . . . At present he goes back to his father, though he is now become more tractable. Our *parting* was vastly pathetic, as many kisses as would have sufficed for a boarding school, and embraces enough to have ruined the character of a county in England, besides tears (not on *my* part) and expressions of 'Tenerezza' to a vast amount. All this and the warmth of the weather has quite overcome me." [n]

Nevertheless Eustathios accompanied him when he set out with Strané for a visit to Veli Pasha in Tripolitza. Veli was even more taken with Byron than his father, Ali Pasha, had been, and he avowed his admiration with less restraint, presenting him with "a very pretty horse." There could be little doubt about Veli's meaning. "He said he wished all the old men . . . to go to his father, but the young ones to come to him . . . 'Vecchio con Vecchio, Giovane con Giovane.' He honoured me with the appellations of his *friend* and *brother*, and hoped that we should be on good terms, not for a few days but for life. All this is very well, but he has an awkward manner of throwing his arm round one's waist, and squeezing one's hand in *public* which is a high compliment, but very much embarrasses *'ingenuous youth.'* " [n]

Byron finally sent Eustathios home from Tripolitza, for "he plagued my soul out with his whims. . . ." [n] When he returned to Athens about August 19, he removed his goods and servants from the Macri house, where his strained relations with the mother of Mariana, Katinka, and Theresa had no doubt dampened the spontaneity of his rompings with the girls,* and took up his residence in the Capuchin monastery at the foot of the Acropolis. The monastery, built around the fourth-century monument of Lysicrates, served as a school for some of the sons of the Frank families and, in the absence of hotels, as a hostelry for travelers.

Byron was immensely entertained by the low comedy of the six "Ragazzi" who lived there, and flattered by the attention they paid him. "The first time I mingled with these sylphs," he told Hobhouse, "after about two minutes' reconnoitring, the amiable Signor Barthelemi, without any previous notice, seated himself by me, and after observing by way of compliment that my 'Signoria' was the 'piu bello' of his English acquaintance, saluted me on the left cheek. . . . But my friend, as you may easily imagine, is Nicolo, who, by-the-by, is my Italian master, and we are already very philosophical. I am his 'Padrone' and his 'amico,' and the Lord knows what besides." After informing Byron that he would follow him across the world, Nicolo added that they should not only live but die together. "The latter I hope to avoid," Byron told Hobhouse, "—as much of the former as he pleases." [n]

Nicolo Giraud, the fifteen-year-old brother of Lusieri's French wife, had become a favorite of Byron before he left for Constantinople and had accompanied him on a number of expeditions. It seems likely that Nicolo had now filled the emotional void caused by Byron's disillusionment with Edleston and with Theresa Macri. Byron, as he said later, always had to have some object of attachment, and in an environment in which from the days of Plato such relationships had been taken for granted and not frowned upon, he turned naturally to the propensity of his schooldays. But he had seen too much in the East to view it any longer with the innocence that accompanied his passionate friendships at Harrow. Yet he could not avoid a lingering English embarrassment, if not the nagging of a Puritan conscience, which accounted for the humorous tone of his letters when he

* Although Byron was still no doubt attracted to Theresa, it was with less romantic ardor, for the bloom of the affair was apparently faded. After his poem was published many legends grew up concerning "The Maid of Athens," frequently distorted by romantic travelers. Theresa eventually married a Mr. Black, but for the rest of her long life she basked in the fame Byron had given her.

referred to these topics, intended in part to throw a smoke screen over the seriousness of his attachment.

There was both a heady exhilaration and a slightly dizzying fear in the experience. He wished Hobhouse there to share the gaiety, "but then," he remembered, "you are so crabbed and disagreeable, that when the laugh is over I rejoice in your absence. After all, I do love thee, Hobby, thou hast so many good qualities, and so many bad ones, it is impossible to live with or without thee."[n] Of his excursions, he said, "Nicolo goes with me at his own most pressing solicitation, 'per mare per terras.' " And he added: "I am about to take my daily ride to the Piraeus, where I swim for an hour despite the heat. . . . it is a curious thing that the Turks when they bathe wear their lower garments, as your humble servant always doth, but the Greeks not. . . ."[n] Moore later wrote that one of Byron's chief delights "was, when bathing in some retired spot, to seat himself on a high rock above the sea, and there remain for hours, gazing upon the sky and the waters. . . ." Moore added that he had become so enamored of these lonely musings "that even the society of his fellow-traveller [Hobhouse] . . . grew at last to be a chain and a burthen on him. . . ."[n] It is not surprising that Hobhouse, with a much closer knowledge of Byron's mind at the time, should have written contemptuously: "On what authority does Tom say this? he has not the remotest grasp of the real reason which induced Lord Byron to prefer having no Englishman immediately and constantly near him."[n] The fact was that Byron felt Hobhouse was too much an embodiment of the British conscience.

Returning one day from his daily bathing at Piraeus Byron encountered a party sent to execute the sentence of the Waiwode of Athens on a girl caught in an act of illicit love. She had been sewed into a sack and was to be cast into the sea. She was a Turkish girl whom Byron undoubtedly knew (though how well, he was careful never to say), and he determined to save her. With threats and bribery (the latter probably more effective) Byron persuaded the Waiwode to give up the girl and sent her off at night to Thebes.* From this event he later derived the central

* This is the story as told by Lord Sligo, who had arrived in Athens after the event, and heard only rumors of it. Byron later, after *The Giaour* was published, asked him to write what he had heard, and

episode of *The Giaour*, the passionate mood of which is some indication of the intensity of the experience. And to his diary he confided: " . . . to describe the *feelings* of *that situation* were impossible—it is *icy* even to recollect them." [n]

It seems evident from Byron's correspondence at the time that he had slipped back into the kind of sexual abandon he had given himself up to in London in the winter of 1808, and for similar reasons—disillusionment with an idealized love and despair of any bright future that would match his boyish dreams. He gave clear hints in his letters to Hobhouse that he was engaged in a number of intrigues in Athens, some of them involving sexual ambiguities. The fact that he refers to them by innuendo and arch facetiousness indicates that they were not the kind of conquests he was wont to speak of with boasting boldness. On August 23 he had written: "I have been employed the greater part of today in conjugating the verb 'ασπαζω' [to embrace]. . . . I assure you my progress is rapid, but like Caesar 'nil actum reputans dum quid superesset agendum,' I must arrive at the pl & opte and then I will write to ———. I hope to escape the fever, at least till I finish this affair, and then it is welcome to try." [n] The "pl & opte" (elsewhere in his letters given more fully as "plen. and optabil. Coit."—see p. 61) was a facetious code, shared by Matthews and others of his circle, meaning an opportunity for sexual gratification. A few weeks later he wrote: "Tell M. [Matthews] that I have obtained above two hundred pl&optCs and am almost tired of them. . . . You know the monastery of Mendele; it was there I made myself master of the first." [n] While these hints, as well as the code phrase, from a passage in Petronius relating the seduction of a boy, might suggest male rather than female conquests, there is sufficient

---

used it to allay rumors that he felt were too near the fact. Although he said that Sligo's account was "not very far from the truth," he added that "one part . . . was more singular than any of the *Giaour*'s adventures." (*LJ*, II, 311. Letter of December 15, 1813, to E. D. Clarke.) Before sending Sligo's letter to Moore, Lord Holland, and others, Byron inked out ten lines of the letter so completely that they could not be read (the MS is at John Murray's). The deleted part, he said, "contained merely some Turkish names, and circumstantial evidence of the girl's detection, not very important or decorous." (*LJ*, II, 258. Letter of September 1, 1813, to Moore.) It may well hold the secret of Bryon's personal interest in the affair.

evidence that Byron did not give up his amours with women of Athens, of all nationalities. With his usual frankness in speaking of his affairs with women, he told Hobhouse before leaving Athens, "I had a number of Greek and Turkish women, and I believe the rest of the English were equally lucky, for we were all *clapped.*"[n]

On September 12, while Byron's mind was still filled with the rescue of the Turkish girl, Lady Hester Stanhope, the strong-minded niece of the younger Pitt, arrived in Athens, and for a few days Byron saw her frequently. He was ill at ease with this odd unwomanly woman. His concluding comment on her to Hobhouse was that he did not admire "that dangerous thing a female wit."[n] The lady reacted as uncharitably to Byron. "I think he was a strange character," she said. ". . . one time he was mopish, and nobody was to speak to him; another, he was for being jocular with everybody. Then he was a sort of Don Quixote, fighting with the police for a woman of the town; and then he wanted to make himself something great. . . . He had a great deal of vice in his looks—his eyes set close together, and a contracted brow. . . ."[n] She used to amuse her friends later by imitating Byron's little affectations, especially his habit of giving solemn orders to his servant in Romaic.[n]

Whether to escape this formidable lady, or for other reasons, Byron left for a second excursion of the Morea in mid-September, taking with him Nicolo Giraud and his two Albanian servants. It was an ill-fated voyage. First he was blown ashore on the Island of Salamis before he reached Corinth. Then he caught a fever at Olympia which seized him violently in Patras, "five days bed-riding with Emetics, glysters, Bark, and all the host of Physic."[n] Later he felt that he owed his life to his faithful Albanians, who threatened death to the physician if he did not recover. Finally on October 2 he could announce that "Nature and Jove" had triumphed over Dr. Romanelli. But Nicolo had caught the fever and Byron cared for him tenderly until he was well enough to travel. Byron was still weakened and emaciated when he returned to Athens. But happy to have lost weight from his illness, he kept up his thinning regimen, taking Turkish baths three times a week, drinking vinegar and water, and eating only a little rice.

During his absence several interesting foreigners had arrived in Athens. Byron became friendly with the whole group, who offered the intellectual conversation he had lacked after Hobhouse went home. His favorites were Dr. Peter Bronsted, a Danish archaeologist, and Jacob Linckh, a Bavarian painter whom he employed to make landscapes for him.[n]

On the whole Byron preferred foreigners to his own countrymen. He could adapt himself to their ways with greater ease than could most Englishmen. He had picked up enough of the languages of the country to talk with the people. He had spoken bad Latin with his servant Andreas Zantachi, but when he left and "that timberhead Fletcher" had been sent home, Byron was thrown back upon the native tongues. By that time, however, he had learned enough Italian, a language in much use in Greece, to get along, and he was studying modern Greek with a master. He was also aided by "tolerably fluent Lingua Franca . . . and some variety of Ottoman oaths of great service with a stumbling horse or a stupid servant."[n]

In addition to Lusieri and Fauvel and their families, who had lived long enough in Athens to be almost natives, Byron was on a footing of easy sociability with official and clerical Turks and Greeks. On November 14 he wrote to Hodgson: "The day before yesterday the Waywode (or Governor of Athens) with the Mufti of Thebes (a sort of Mussulman Bishop) supped here and made themselves beastly with raw rum, and the Padré of the convent being drunk as *we*, my *Attic* feast went off with great *éclat*."[n]

No one could be a more lively companion than Byron when he was in the right mood, but when he stopped to reflect, boredom settled over him. He wrote Hobhouse: " . . . my life has, with the exception of a very few moments, never been anything but a *yawn*. . . . I have now seen the World, that is the most ancient of the ancient part. I have spent my little all, I have tasted all sorts of pleasure (so tell the Citoyen [Matthews]); I have nothing more to hope, and may begin to consider the most eligible way of walking out of it. . . . I wish I could find some of Socrates's Hemlock. . . ."[n]

To relieve boredom, he organized another excursion to Sunium, where he gazed his fill again at the view from the inspiring cliff on which the white columns stand stark against the blue

Ægean and its islands.* Back in Athens Byron was excited to learn from a Greek boatman who had been the prisoner of Mainote pirates that twenty-five of them at the foot of the cliff had meant to attack his party, but had been frightened away by the menacing sight of his Albanians. He was now pleasantly engrossed in the social life of the town. He dined with the English, and "we have had balls and a variety of fooleries with the females of Athens." [n]

In writing to his mother on January 14, 1811, he indulged in some self-justification, first of his motives for sending Fletcher home, and then of his traveling and residence abroad. His English servant had long been a handicap. "Besides, the perpetual lamentations after beef and beer, the stupid, bigoted contempt for every thing foreign, and insurmountable incapacity of acquiring even a few words of any language, rendered him, like all other English servants, an incumbrance." He assured his mother that he had gained immeasurably in becoming a citizen of the world. "Here I see and have conversed with French, Italians, Germans, Danes, Greeks, Turks, Armenians. . . . and without losing sight of my own, I can judge of the countries and manners of others. Where I see the superiority of England (which, by the by, we are a good deal mistaken about in many things), I am pleased, and where I find her inferior, I am at least enlightened. Now, I might have stayed, smoked in your towns, or fogged in your country, a century, without being sure of this, and without acquiring any thing more useful or amusing at home." [n]

On January 20, two days before his twenty-third birthday, he wrote exuberantly to Hodgson: "I am living in the Capuchin Convent, Hymettus before me, the Acropolis behind, the Temple of Jove to my right, the Stadium in front, the town to the left; eh, Sir, there's a situation, there's your picturesque! . . . And I feed upon Woodcocks and Red Mullet every day, and I have three horses (one a present from the Pasha of the Morea). . . ." [n]

---

* If Byron carved his name on the square column at Sunium, which every tourist to Greece now sees, it must have been at this time. But there is strong reason to think that some admirer did the carving at a later time, both from the form of the lettering and from the fact that Byron himself never mentioned it. It is possible, of course, that he scratched it lightly as he had done on the column at Delphi, and that someone else deepened the carving as it is now seen.

Needing literary occupation, Byron turned to writing some notes for *Childe Harold* in which he attempted to formulate his ideas on the Greeks as a people and a nation. When writing the Greek stanzas for the poem, he had expressed the belief that they must trust to their own efforts and their own courage if they would be free. "Hereditary Bondsmen! know ye not/ Who would be free *themselves* must strike the blow?"[n] But after reflection and conversation with both Greeks and Franks, he concluded that they could not rise by their own power from the state of degradation into which they had fallen from centuries of slavery: " . . . the interposition of foreigners alone can emancipate the Greeks. . . ."[n] They had not lost their hope, but they were divided. His views were perhaps influenced by his tutor in the Romaic, Marmarotouri, a scholar and a leader among the Greek patriots, who may have called his attention to "a satire in dialogue between a Russian, English, and French traveller, and the Waywode of Wallachia . . . an archbishop, a merchant, and Cogia Bachi (or primate), in succession; to all of whom under the Turks the writer attributes their present degeneracy."[n] The theme was that the apathy and greed of the privileged classes among the Greeks made them the friends of tyranny. Still, taking a realistic view of the Greeks, Byron tried to eschew the extremes of those who saw them all as "*canaille*" and those who sentimentally overpraised them because of what they had been.

He wrote with feeling and conviction: " . . . it seems to me rather hard to declare so positively and pertinaciously, as almost everybody has declared, that the Greeks, because they are very bad, will never be better. . . . At present, like the Catholics of Ireland and the Jews throughout the world . . . they suffer all the moral and physical ills that can afflict humanity. Their life is a struggle against truth; they are vicious in their own defence. . . . Now, in the name of Nemesis! for what are they to be grateful? . . . to the Turks for their fetters, and to the Franks for their broken promises and lying counsels. They are to be grateful to the artist who engraves their ruins, and to the antiquary who carries them away; to the traveller whose janissary flogs them, and to the scribbler whose journal abuses them. This is the amount of their obligations to foreigners."[n]

Toward the end of January a firman for travel in Syria and

Egypt, for which he had applied, arrived, and this new interest moved Byron to spur Hanson into sending remittances. But, still firm in his resolve not to sell Newstead, he told his mother, "as my only tie to England is Newstead, and, that once gone, neither interest nor inclination lead me northward. . . . I feel myself so much a citizen of the world, that the spot where I can enjoy a delicious climate, and every luxury, at a less expense than a common college life in England, will always be a country to me: and such are in fact the shores of the Archipelago." [n]

To Hobhouse he wrote: " . . . I am off in spring for Mount Sion, Damascus, Tyre and Sidon, Cairo, and Thebes." [n] But remittances were slow in coming, and he gradually lost interest in the project. In the meantime he was stirred to composition again. In February and March he wrote rapidly two poems in the heroic couplet. One was an attempt to follow up the success of *English Bards, and Scotch Reviewers* with a satire on his contemporaries called *Hints from Horace*. The other was a rancorous and rather humorless satire on Lord Elgin as the despoiler of Greece. His feelings on the subject had grown in intensity as he had come to take the side of the Greeks against the foreigners. In couplets more intemperate than the lines in *Childe Harold,* he made Minerva place a curse "on him [Elgin] and all his seed." England was not responsible for him—he came from Caledonia, "land of meanness, sophistry, and mist." [n]

As spring came on a combination of circumstances turned his steps reluctantly toward England. Many of the interesting Franks were leaving, and he gave them a farewell dinner. Their winter in Athens had been "most social and fantastical," he wrote. His irregular life had brought on several ailments. " . . . my health has been changing in the most tramontane way," he wrote Hobhouse on March 5. "I have been fat, and thin (as I am at present) and had a cough and a catarrh and the piles and be damned to them. . . ." [n]

When the actual day of parting came, Byron felt pangs greater perhaps than he had expected. First of all there was a pathetic leavetaking from his faithful Albanians. Dervish took it hardest. He threw down the money which Byron offered him as a parting gift, "and clasping his hands, which he raised to his forehead, rushed out of the room weeping bitterly. From that moment to the hour of my embarkation, he continued his lamentations, and all our efforts to console him only produced this answer, 'M'αφει̌νει̌, 'He leaves me.'"[n] His parting from the "Maid of Athens" may have been tenderer than he let Hobhouse know when he told him that "I was near bringing away Theresa, but the mother asked 30,000 piastres [£600]!"[n]

The transport ship *Hydra*, which he boarded at Piraeus, ironically carried at the same time Byron, the manuscript of his *Curse of Minerva*, a most violent attack against Elgin as the despoiler of Greece, and the last large shipment of Lord Elgin's marbles on their way to England, accompanied by Lusieri, Elgin's agent and Byron's friend. Byron had his own curious cargo. In addition to Nicolo Giraud, whom he intended to put in school at Malta, he had "four ancient Athenian skulls, dug out of sarcophagi—a phial of Attic hemlock—four live tortoises—a greyhound . . . two live Greek servants, one an Athenian, t'other a *Yaniote*, who can speak nothing but Romaic and Italian."[n] The ship was supposed to sail on April 11, but did not get under way until the 22nd.

Byron had left Athens in the midst of spring. All his thoughts turned eastward. Coming from a land where the sun shines but "two months of every year," as he later wrote in *Beppo*, he was first captivated by the balmy air and clear skies of Greece, even in Prevesa. But it was not until he had spent a winter in Athens that the physical environment took a permanent hold on his feelings. He gave a glowing tribute to the land of the citron and olive in some notes to *Childe Harold*: " . . . setting aside the magic of the name . . . the very situation of Athens would render it the favourite of all who have eyes for art or nature. The climate, to me at least, appeared a perpetual spring; during eight months I never passed a day without being as many hours on horseback: rain is extremely rare, snow never lies in the plains, and a cloudy day is an agreeable rarity."[n]

Of course, when Byron speaks of "the clime of the East" he means something more than simply the weather. It includes people, places, moods, and in fact a whole way of life. It is something that is best understood only by one who has lived for some time in that "clime." For Byron, fresh from the cold fogs of England, the clear skies, the turquoise water glistening in the brilliant sunshine became a symbol for the whole climate of

Eastern life. In the purple passages of his Oriental tales the overwhelming presence of the memory of that climate which "o'erflowing teems/ Along his burning page, distempered though it seems," sometimes lends a new and glowing life to the clichés into which his Greek memories too often fall. Through the spate of rhetoric shines a sincerity of enthusiasm for that "climate" which has captivated Philhellenes ever since. The description of the sun setting over the Morea "in one unclouded blaze of living light" which he prefixed to *The Curse of Minerva* (and transferred later more appropriately to *The Corsair*) symbolized his whole Greek experience, the open brightness as opposed to the clouded murkiness of English weather, the freedom and frankness of life and manners in contrast to the English reserve and hypocrisy. It was chiefly his second winter in Athens and its environs that finally fixed the spell of Greece upon Byron's youthful mind. And the indelible imprint of those memories of "the clime of the East" and "the land of the Sun" contributed largely to his lifelong nostalgia for that "greenest island" of his imagination.

Byron disembarked at Malta still suffering intermittently from his maladies. Mrs. Spencer Smith was still waiting patiently for her unhurried lover. Byron later told Lady Melbourne with amusing detachment of their meeting at the palace. "The Governor . . . was kind enough to leave us to come to the most diabolical of explanations. It was in the dog-days, during a sirocco (I almost perspire now with the thoughts of it), during the intervals of an intermittent fever (my love had also intermitted with my malady), and I certainly feared the ague and my passion would both return in full force."[n] As a sequel to the story, Byron told Lady Melbourne that the lady was then (September 1812) writing her memoirs at Vienna, "in which I shall cut a very indifferent figure; and nothing survives of this most ambrosial amour, which made me on one occasion risk my life, and on another almost drove me mad, but a few Duke of York*ish* letters and certain baubles. . . ."[n]

This affair no doubt contributed to his depressed state of mind despite the hilarity of his correspondence. He wrote of his illness to Hobhouse: " . . . the fit comes on every other day, reducing me first to the chattering penance of Harry Gill, and then mounting me up to a Vesuvian pitch of fever, lastly quitting me with sweats that render it necessary for me to have a man and horse all night to change my linen." [n]

He had already arranged to sail on the *Volage* frigate in early June, but as the days dragged out in the oppressive heat, he grew morbidly introspective. His state of mind is reflected in some notes he jotted down giving some reasons "in favour of a Change" in his way of life: "1st At twenty three the best of life is over and its bitters double. 2ndly I have seen mankind in various Countries and find them equally despicable, if anything the Balance is rather in favour of the Turks. 3dly I am sick at heart [here he quoted some lines from Horace's ode "To Venus": "Nor maid nor youth delights me now"]. 4thly A man who is lame of one leg is in a state of bodily inferiority which increases with years and must render his old age more peevish & intolerable. Besides in another existence I expect to have *two* if not *four* legs by way of compensation. 5thly I grow selfish & misanthropical. . . . 6thly My affairs at home and abroad are gloomy enough. 7thly I have outlived all my appetites and most of my vanities aye even the vanity of authorship." [n]

As he sailed on the *Volage* on June 2, the greatest emotional wrench was his parting from Nicolo Giraud, the only being, he now felt, who loved him without guile and with a puppy-like devotion. After he left, Nicolo continued to write him, in Greek, in Italian, and later in English, expressing gratitude "*fine alla morte*." *

Byron whiled away the tedium of the voyage by writing letters to several friends in England to apprise them of his arrival. He had to console Hobhouse, who had not yet been reconciled with his father and was considering joining the militia, and to assure him that he need not worry about his debt (on their parting he owed Byron £818 3s. 4d.). He informed Dallas, his literary agent, that he had an imitation of Horace's *Art of Poetry* ready for Cawthorn, but he said nothing of *Childe Harold*, about the self-revelation of which he was a little nervous.

On July 7, while the frigate was becalmed near Brest, he

* Marchand, I, 274. Giraud was still writing Byron in 1815. From Athens on January 1 of that year he wrote complaining that he had received no answer to his letters. "I pray your excellency to not forget your humble servant which so dearly and faithfully loves you."

wrote Henry Drury, in his usual facetious manner making light of his ailments: "The enclosed letter is from a friend of yours Surgeon Tucker whom I met with in Greece; & so on to Malta, where he administered to me for three complaints viz. a *Gonorrhea* a *Tertian fever;* & the *Hemorrhoides, all* of which I literally had at once, though he assured me the *morbid* action of only one of these distempers could act at a time, which was a great comfort, though they relieved one another as regularly as Sentinels. . . ."[n]

Byron set foot on his native shores once more at Sheerness on the 14th of July, 1811, two years and twelve days after he had sailed from Falmouth. He was perhaps only half aware of the depth of his foreign impressions. On the surface he was as devil-may-care as ever. "I don't know that I have acquired any thing by my travels but a smattering of two languages and a habit of chewing Tobacco," he wrote Augusta.[n] But the effects on his character and career were far more pervasive.

His observations abroad had led him to be more than ever contemptuous of a narrow orthodoxy: "I will bring you ten Mussulmans shall shame you in all goodwill towards men, prayer to God, and duty to their neighbours,"[n] he wrote Hodgson, who was disturbed by his heterodox opinions. His political views had been broadened also by his ability to compare governmental tyrannies at home and in other countries. But, more important than anything else in his Eastern experiences, he had rubbed elbows with life in picturesque surroundings that he would never forget, and these early contacts with all kinds of men he grew to prize as the foundation of his worldly wisdom. Henceforth he was drawn constantly toward the warm lands "where the cypress and myrtle/ Are emblems of deeds that are done in their clime."[n] Many times in the next few years, when the complications of his personal life made him long for escape, he was on the point of leaving again for the shores of the Mediterranean.

"If I am a poet," he told Trelawny, " . . . the air of Greece has made me one."[n] Aside from the perpetual source of literary material most congenial to his spirit which the East had furnished him, there was instilled in him a deep-lying cosmopolitanism. It was not an accident that he chose a passage from *Le Cosmopolite* as a motto for *Childe Harold.* He had been predisposed to become a citizen of the world even before he had traveled; he came home a confirmed one and would always view the prejudices and dogmas of the "tight little island"[n] in the light of his knowledge of "the ways and farings of many men."

CHAPTER IX

1811–1812

Thyrza—A Radical in Parliament

WHEN BYRON ARRIVED IN London on July 14, 1811, he was immediately involved in a whirl of business and a renewal of friendships which left him little time for the melancholy reflections that had haunted him on the long voyage home. His first visitor was Scrope Davies, who came in drunk that same evening with "a new set of jokes." [n] Hobhouse, who had finally succumbed to his father's wishes and joined the militia as captain, sent a welcome from his barracks in Dover. Dallas, having been forewarned that Byron had a manuscript, lost no time in calling. Byron told him he "believed Satire to be his *forte*," and showed him *Hints from Horace*. Dallas, who liked to take credit to himself for having discovered the merit of *Childe Harold*, later recorded that he was disappointed, and asked him whether he had written anything else while he "had been roaming under the cloudless skies of Greece. . . ." [n] Byron then took the manuscript of *Childe Harold* from a small trunk and handed it to him.

But it was only after he had consulted Walter Wright, former Consul-General of the Ionian Islands and author of a poem called *Horæ Ionicæ* which Byron had praised in *English Bards, and Scotch Reviewers*, that the timid Dallas was convinced that *Childe Harold* had great possibilities of popular success. He then praised the poem lavishly and urged Byron to let him find a publisher. There the matter rested while Byron went to Sittingbourne to meet Hobhouse. He was as glad to see him as he had been relieved to part with him the year before. On his return, Dallas, convinced that he had a good thing in the poem (Byron had given him the copyright, having conceived the high-minded idea that a gentleman should not take money for his poetry like a Grub Street hack), was chagrined that Byron now seemed reluctant to have it go to a printer. Byron's hesitation had probably been increased by his conversation with Hobhouse. John Cam had read part if not all of the manuscript in the East, and had warned him of what critics might say about the self-revealing egoism of some of the stanzas.

What troubled Dallas too was Byron's flat refusal at first to omit or alter any of the stanzas expressing skepticism in religion and politics. But convinced that he could get Byron to modify the dangerous parts, he continued to flatter the author with his enthusiasm. Byron was soon persuaded, for he was in fact eager enough to see the poem in print, though without his name. Dallas carried the manuscript to John Murray, who then had a publishing house and bookshop at 32 Fleet Street.

Murray's father had started publishing in 1768. Succeeding to the business in 1795, John Murray II had already, in 1811, by his good judgment and initiative established a high reputation as a publisher. He had brought into his sphere some of the chief literary men of the day: Walter Scott, Isaac D'Israeli, Robert Southey, and William Gifford. Instrumental in founding the *Quarterly Review* in 1808, he had become its publisher. It was fortunate both for Murray and for Byron that Gifford, whom Byron regarded as the greatest critic of the age, was both the editor of the *Quarterly* and Murray's chief literary adviser.

While these negotiations were going forward, Byron was trying futilely to bring some order into his financial affairs, but characteristically was also increasing his debts. He had agreed to buy a carriage for two hundred guineas from his old friend "Bold Webster," who had been the butt of practical jokes at Newstead. Webster had married Lady Frances Annesley, daughter of the first Earl of Mountnorris and eighth Viscount Valentia. Byron wrote wryly to congratulate him: "I shall follow your example as soon as I can get a sufficient price for my coronet." [n]

But the next day (August 1) all this was driven out of his head by news that his mother was seriously ill. He had written on the way home that he would call on her as soon as he had finished his business in town, and added: "I have brought you a shawl, and a quantity of attar of roses. . . ."[n] In fact, he had rather dreaded the meeting, for like his father, he could get along with her better at a distance. Now in this emergency he was completely without money and had to draw £40 on Hanson before he could set out for Newstead. He was still in London when a servant arrived to tell him that Mrs. Byron was dead.

The shock did not strike him immediately. But once he was at Newstead, the sense of loss settled heavily upon him. Now the ties of blood and of early recollections opened the floodgates of emotion to remorse and self-pity. Mrs. Byron's maid found him sitting in the dark by his mother's remains and sighing heavily. He burst into tears and exclaimed, "Oh, Mrs. By, I had but one friend in the world, and she is gone!"[n]

Before Mrs. Byron was buried, another blow struck. Charles Skinner Matthews, the most brilliant of Byron's Cambridge friends, died horribly, enmeshed in a bed of weeds in a pool of the Cam. On the morning of his mother's funeral Byron could not bring himself to follow her remains to Hucknall Torkard Church, but stood in the door of the Abbey until the procession passed out of sight. Then, according to Moore, "turning to young Rushton . . . he desired him to fetch the sparring-gloves, and proceeded to his usual exercise with the boy . . . but, at last,—the struggle seeming too much for him,—he flung away the gloves and retired to his room."[n]

Whatever his mother may have said in anger and exasperation, Byron knew that she had been devoted to him in her fashion. In his absence she had governed his little empire with a firm hand. She dismissed servants to reduce expenses, kept an eye on the others, and was a screaming terror to trespassers. She had a great pride in her son's accomplishments and confidence in his future greatness. He must have been touched by finding among her effects a bound volume of literary reviews and notices of his published poems, together with her own marginal comments.[n]

News of a third death moved him acutely, that of his Harrow friend John Wingfield. Hobhouse was the only one to whom he could write seriously about his feelings: "There is to me something so incomprehensible in death, that I can neither speak nor think on the subject. Indeed, when I looked on the mass of corruption which was the being from whence I sprung, I doubted within myself whether I *was*, or whether she *was not*." [n]

With his thoughts so closely upon death, Byron sat down to write the draft of a will. The estate of Newstead was to be entailed on his cousin George Byron. To Nicolo Giraud of Athens he wished to leave £7,000 to be paid at the boy's reaching the age of twenty-one. Hanson was to get £2,000 and the claims of Davies were to be settled. His library and furniture were to go to Hobhouse and Davies, who were named as executors. And, as in his will of 1809, he requested that his remains be placed without ceremony or inscription beside his faithful dog Boatswain at Newstead.[n] If his heirs should object ("from bigotry, or otherwise"), the estate should go to his sister on similar conditions.[n]

Byron had not seen Augusta since some months before his departure for the East; having heard that she was hurt by his attack on Lord Carlisle in *English Bards,* he had not written to her while he was abroad. But her letter of sympathy on the death of his mother elicited a good-natured reply. He twitted her on the rapid growth of her family: "Notwithstanding Malthus tells us that, were it not for Battle, Murder, and Sudden death, we should be overstocked, I think we have latterly had a redundance of these national benefits, and therefore I give you all credit for your matronly behaviour." [n]

Scrope Davies had been at Newstead. "His gaiety (death cannot mar it) has done me service," Byron wrote Hodgson; "but, after all, ours was a hollow laughter. . . . I am solitary, and I never felt solitude irksome before." [n] To fill up the emptiness, he turned to business. Murray had determined to publish *Childe Harold,* possibly on Dallas's assurance that he could get the author to soften some of the stanzas expressing unorthodox views. Byron had already made one concession. He added a "hypothetical" stanza on immortality:

> *Yet if, as holiest men have deemed, there be*
> *A land of Souls beyond that sable shore . . .*[n]

What concerned him more was that Murray wanted his name on the title page. He was still apprehensive that the poem would reveal too much of his inner emotional life, and that the critics who had been generally receptive to his satire would bear down upon him again as they had on his early romantic verse.

He wanted above all the commendation of Gifford, and he was fearful that as editor of the Tory *Quarterly* and Murray's literary adviser, Gifford would find much to displease him in the sentimental tone and liberal political opinions of *Childe Harold.* And when he learned that Murray had without his consent sought and received Gifford's opinion soon after the manuscript was delivered to him, Byron was furious. He had wanted Gifford's praise free from pressure. "It is anticipating, it is begging, kneeling, adulating," he told Dallas.[n] "I *will* be angry with Murray. It was a bookselling, back-shop, Paternoster-row, paltry proceeding. . . ."[n] But it was too late to do any good, and Gifford's favorable opinion had no doubt encouraged Murray to publish *Childe Harold.*

He reluctantly consented to have his name on the title page, and he increasingly realized that it would be impossible not to be identified with his hero. This added anxiety may subconsciously have influenced Byron in his revisions, for he did eventually agree to modify his harsh pronouncement on the Convention of Cintra and to omit the stanza referring to the "unnatural" love practices of Beckford.[n] The fact is that he was coming to have a much greater liking for *Childe Harold* than for his satires. He put a damper on the publication of *Hints from Horace,* then in the hands of Cawthorn, who was eager for another success like *English Bards,* which had gone into four editions.

Although Byron did not show it on the surface, neither business nor pleasure could quite fill the void in his life. In reply to Dallas's pious consolations, he wrote: "Your letter gives me credit for more acute feelings than I possess; for though I feel tolerably miserable, yet I am at the same time subject to a kind of hysterical merriment, or rather laughter without merriment, which I can neither account for nor conquer, and yet I do not feel relieved by it; but an indifferent person would think me in excellent spirits."[n]

Byron wrote to the ridiculous Webster, who had invited him to pay a visit and observe his married bliss: "I shall invade you in the course of the winter, out of envy, as Lucifer looked at Adam and Eve."[n] And he wrote Augusta with brotherly banter: "The embarrassments [financial] you mention in your last letter I never heard of before, but that disease is epidemic in our family. . . . I don't know what Scrope Davies meant by telling you I liked Children, I abominate the sight of them so much that I have always had the greatest respect for the character of Herod."[n]

Augusta was worried because her husband, Colonel Leigh, had quarreled with the Prince of Wales, whom he served as an equerry. The consequences might be disastrous to their future. Byron's response was: "However, at all events, and in all Situations, you have a brother in me, and a home here. . . . Pray can't you contrive to pay me a visit between this and Xmas? . . . the premises are so delightfully extensive, that two people might live together without ever seeing, hearing or meeting. . . . In short it would be the most amiable matrimonial mansion . . . —my wife and I shall be so happy,—one in each Wing."[n]

In the meantime he wandered about the lonely Abbey, solitary and disconsolate. Dallas and Hodgson were both worried over his skepticism, which had been strengthened rather than weakened by his losses. Dallas continued to argue with him over the freethinking passages in *Childe Harold,* resorting, when theological arguments failed, to the plea of expediency and of danger to his literary reputation. Hodgson was even more earnest.

Byron's reply was open and frank: "I will have nothing to do with your immortality; we are miserable enough in this life, without the absurdity of speculating upon another."[n] But Hodgson was intent upon converting his friend. Taking Byron's own motto, he pleaded: "Crede Byron!" Not trusting his own powers of reasoning, he called on Byron to read Butler's *Analogy* and Paley's *Evidences,* the books that ecclesiastics relied upon to refute the unbelief that sprang from the Enlightenment and from the trust in science.

Byron replied with a little more asperity: "God would have made His will known without books, considering how very few could read them when Jesus of Nazareth lived, had it been His pleasure to ratify any peculiar mode of worship. As to your immortality, if people are to live, why die? And our carcases, which are to rise again, are they worth raising? I hope, if mine is, that I shall have a better *pair of legs* than I have moved on these two-and-twenty years, or I shall be sadly behind in the squeeze into Paradise."[n]

The dullness of his life had not been relieved by the visit of his old Harrow schoolfellow John Claridge. He told Hobhouse:

" . . . there is Scrope B. Davies, with perhaps no better intellects, and certainly not half his sterling qualities, is the life and soul of me . . . but my old friend, with the soul of honour and the zeal of friendship, and a vast variety of insipid virtues, can't keep me or himself awake."[n] But he had other amusements for compensation. He had begun to gather his "little sensual comforts together." He had brought Lucy back from Warwickshire, "some very bad faces have been warned off the premises, and more promising substituted in their stead. . . . Lucinda to be commander . . . of all the makers and unmakers of beds in the household."[n]

Byron finally left for his Lancashire estate near the end of September and was back at Newstead on October 9. News had come in his absence of the death of John Edleston the previous May while he was abroad. He wrote to Dallas: "It seems as though I were to experience in my youth the greatest misery of age. My friends fall around me, and I shall be left a lonely tree before I am withered."[n] The only relief was in poetic composition. He poured out his feelings in a poem to "Thyrza." By using a woman's name he could speak freely of "the glance none saw beside":

> *The whispered thought of hearts allied,*
> *The pressure of the thrilling hand;*
> *The kiss, so guiltless and refined,*
> *That Love each warmer wish forbore.*[n]

The next day he sent off to Dallas a stanza to be added to *Childe Harold,* beginning:

> *There, Thou!—whose Love and Life together fled,*
> *Have left me here to love and live in vain—*[n]

As he had already told Dallas of the death of Edleston, he felt the necessity to cover his tracks: "I think it proper to state to you, that this stanza alludes to an event which has taken place since my arrival here, and not to the death of any *male* friend."[n]

With Hobhouse he could be more frank: "At present I am rather low, and don't know how to tell you the reason—you remember *E.* at Cambridge—he is *dead*—last May—his Sister sent me the account lately—now though I never should have seen him again (and it is very proper that I should not) I have been more affected than I should care to own elsewhere."[n]

Byron made his long-promised visit to Davies, then a Fellow at King's College, Cambridge, in mid-October. It was a pleasure but also an ordeal, for all his old friends except Davies were gone, and the familiar courts were filled with ghostly memories. The Cam where he and Long used to swim, and where Matthews had drowned, was now haunted too, and the choir of Trinity brought back memories that were much too painful. Everywhere he turned, Byron was reminded of his daily walks and water excursions with Edleston. As usual he turned to composition. With this final tribute to the dead chorister he would end *Childe Harold.*[n]

While he was still at Cambridge, Byron received a letter from Thomas Moore, the Irish poet, restating a challenge to a duel he had sent but which Hodgson had withheld. Moore's Irish blood had risen at Byron's derisive reference in *English Bards, and Scotch Reviewers* to his part in a farcical duel with Francis Jeffrey, editor of the *Edinburgh Review,* "When Little's leadless pistol met his eye,/ And Bow-street Myrmidons stood laughing by."[n] Now that Byron was back in England, Moore felt that honor demanded his writing a second letter; but having married in the meantime, Moore was evidently not really interested in an encounter. He hinted that if a satisfactory explanation were forthcoming he would be glad of Byron's acquaintance.

The irony of it was that Byron too would have been glad to meet the author of the pseudonymous poems of Thomas Little, which he had read with such avidity as a boy. After considerable cautious verbal sparring on both sides, Byron was easily able to convince Moore that "*you* were certainly *not* the person towards whom I felt personally hostile."[n] The barb was aimed at Jeffrey, whom he considered his arch enemy because of the review of his poems in the *Edinburgh.* Moore was glad to accept the explanation, and Byron agreed to meet him. Moore hastened to tell his bosom friend Samuel Rogers, the banker poet, and Rogers suggested that the meeting take place at his house.

In London again, Byron felt the eyes of the critics upon him, and, on the verge of making the acquaintance of Moore, Rogers, and others of a higher literary society than any in which he had previously moved, he again had qualms about the self-revealing stanzas of *Childe Harold.* He warned Dallas: "I by no means intend to identify myself with *Harold,* but to *deny* all connection with him. . . . I would not be such a fellow as I have made my hero for all the world."[n]

The eagerly awaited dinner at the home of Rogers took place on November 4. In addition to Moore, Thomas Campbell, author of "The Pleasures of Hope" and "Gertrude of Wyoming," was there. Byron must have felt more excitement than he would let himself show when he entered the door, for Rogers, twenty-five years his senior, and Campbell were the only contemporaries besides Gifford whom he had praised in *English Bards.* They in turn were impressed by the appearance and flattered by the deference of the young lord.

There was a little embarrassment, for Byron was then on one of his strict diets, hard biscuits and soda water, and when Rogers could not provide them he dined on potatoes flattened onto his plate and drenched with vinegar. But when the conversation turned to literary matters, he became animated and charmed his new acquaintances. He hit it off particularly with Moore, who later recalled: "From the time of our first meeting there seldom elapsed a day that Lord Byron and I did not see each other, and our acquaintance ripened into intimacy and friendship with a rapidity of which I have seldom seen an example."[n]

Byron delighted in his new associates because they were not mere Grub Street writers; for the first time he was on an equal footing with those he considered the "first" literary men of the land. But when Byron tried to bring some of his friends into the circle, the result was unfortunate. At the dinner he had arranged with Rogers and Moore, Hodgson was "drunk and sensibilitous." As Byron explained to Hobhouse, Hodgson's friend Bland, "(the *Revd.*) has been challenging an officer of Dragoons about a *whore,* & my assistance being required, I interfered in time to prevent him from losing his *life* or his *Living.* The man is mad, Sir, mad, frightful as a mandrake, and lean as a rutting Stag, & all about a bitch not worth a Bank-token. She is a common Strumpet, as his antagonist assured me, yet he means to marry her. Hodgson meant to marry her, the officer meant to marry her, her first Seducer (seventeen years ago) meant to marry her.

. . . I saw this *wonder*, and set her down at seven shillings worth.[n]

It is not surprising that Moore, who was something of a toady to rank, having risen from the humblest origins (his father was a Dublin grocer—a trade most risible among snobs) to a position of ease in the best drawing rooms in London, should have thought Byron's earlier friends were much beneath him.

Byron did find his new friends stimulating. He wrote Hobhouse: "Rogers is a most excellent and unassuming soul, and Moore an epitomé of all that's delightful."[n] But he was still loyal to his old friends, even when he made sport of them, as he did of Webster. "His wife is very pretty, and I am much mistaken if five years hence she don't give him reason to think so. Knowing the man one is apt to fancy these things, but I really thought she treated him, even already, with a due portion of conjugal contempt, but I daresay this was only the megrim of a misogynist. At present he is the happiest of men, and has asked me to go with them to a tragedy to see his *wife cry!*"[n]

But a few days later he was writing despondently to Hodgson: "To-day is the Sabbath,—a day I never pass pleasantly, but at Cambridge; and, even there, the organ is a sad remembrancer." He heard a song which reminded him of Edleston, whereupon he wrote another poem to "Thyrza," "Away, Away, Ye Notes of Woe." But it was something that now he was striving to forget. "I have many plans," he confessed, "sometimes I think of the East again, and dearly beloved Greece."[n]

In the meantime he was delighted to be getting into the most admired literary circles of the capital. He wrote Hodgson: "Coleridge has attacked the *Pleasures of Hope,* and all other pleasures whatsoever. Mr. Rogers was present, and heard himself indirectly *rowed* by the lecturer. We are going to a party to hear the new Art of Poetry by this reformed schismatic. . . ."[n] And on the 15th of December he wrote his friend Harness: "Tomorrow I dine with Rogers & am to hear Coleridge, who is a kind of rage at present."[n] He had acquired a taste for the theater as early as his Harrow holidays, and now returned to it with zest. He saw Mrs. Siddons and heard Kemble in *Coriolanus*—"he was glorious & exerted himself wonderfully."[n]

But on the 19th he left for Newstead. He had invited Moore,

who could not come, but he took Hodgson and Harness with him. Byron was not in the mood for rioting as he had with Hobhouse and Matthews. They spent their days in literary labors, and when they met in the evenings they had warm arguments on poetry and religion. The young Harness listened with admiration while the more learned Hodgson with "judicious zeal and affectionate earnestness (often speaking with tears in his eyes)" tried to convert Byron to orthodoxy.[n]

But Byron found consolation for these dull evenings in other parts of the Abbey. In the servants' quarters were three pretty girls he had brought into his household in September. His favorite now was Susan Vaughan, a native of Wales, of whom, he wrote Hobhouse, "I am tolerably enamoured for the present."[n] Before he left for London on January 11, 1812, Susan had given, he thought, sufficient proof of her devotion.

Her letters show that she had little education or wit, but considerable vivacity and willingness to please. "Yes," she wrote, "working your bosoms [shirt fronts?] I should think will give me a great deal of pleasure. Anything that's yours I *love* and always shall. Can you doubt it, my dearest friend?"[n] But she was soon writing in a way that may have made Byron uneasy, for it showed how little of a secret their affair was likely to be. Susan had apparently been acting as nursemaid to Fletcher's young sons. She wrote: "You, of course, have not forgot the night you come up to our room, when I was in bed—the time you locked the door. . . . He [George Fletcher] is up stairs with me now. . . . He looks very earnestly at me, and says he: Why, Susan, have you forgot Lord Byron coming to *bed to us*? . . . Don't you remember, Susan, me Lord putting his hand so nicely over your *bosom*? . . . The D——I may have George Fletcher, if he did not *kiss* you besides. . . ."[n]

But the stories he got from Rushton and Lucy, who were both jealous of the favorite, soon convinced Byron that Susan, despite all her protestations, was unfaithful to him after he left. It was a new experience for him to be deceived by a wench upon whom he had lavished so much affection. He wrote her a final letter: "You may also enjoy the satisfaction of having deceived me most completely, and rendered me for the present sufficiently wretched. . . . you threw yourself in my way, I received you, loved you, till you became worthless, and now I part from you with some regret, and without resentment. . . . do not forget that your own misconduct has bereaved you of a friend, of whom nothing else could have deprived you."[n] Susan had inspired at least four short poems (which Byron never published) in which he revealed, as was usual, a truer state of his feelings. His anguish was genuine, but he saw already that "had thy Love outlived today/ My own had fled tomorrow."[n]

As in other moments of depression, he blamed his deformity for his misfortune. "I do not blame her," he told Hodgson, "but my own vanity in fancying that such a thing as I am could ever be beloved."[n] To Hobhouse he wrote: "I have dismissed my Seraglio for squabbles and infidelities."[n] The thought of Newstead was now distasteful. In the shock of his disillusionment he turned once more to memories of Edleston. He confessed to Hodgson: "I believe the only human being, that ever loved me in truth and entirely, was of, or belonging to, Cambridge, and, in that, no change can now take place. . . . I almost rejoice when one I love dies young, for I could never bear to see them old or altered."[n] And another escape was always in the back of his mind. "In the spring of 1813," he announced, "I shall leave England for ever. . . . Neither my habits nor constitution are improved by your customs or your climate. I shall find employment in making myself a good Oriental scholar. I shall retain a mansion in one of the fairest islands, and retrace, at intervals, the most interesting portions of the East."[n]

But this dream was soon pushed into the background, and with the opening of Parliament another came to the fore, that of making a name for himself as a political orator and statesman. Byron had taken his seat in the House of Lords again on January 15. To prepare himself for such a career had been his most satisfying self-justification for his journey to the East. And this constantly held goal, though only occasionally acknowledged, accounted in large measure for his considering literature a secondary pursuit. But, while he was confident enough of his own powers of expression and possessed some basic principles of the rights of peoples, he had misgivings concerning practical political procedure and was aware of his ignorance of particular issues.

In fact there were no issues of consequence before the Parliament at the time. The Whigs were proceeding cautiously with the Prince Regent, who had taken over for his mad father George III a few months before.

For his maiden speech Byron chose to speak in favor of measures that would alleviate the distress of the stocking weavers of Nottingham rather than merely repress their rioting. He sought the advice of Lord Holland, leader of the Moderate Whigs, who was willing enough to encourage a potential Opposition member in the upper house, but who wanted to proceed cautiously. The Tory Cabinet had concocted a bill meting out the death penalty for frame-breaking. Nevertheless, Byron went forward with his preparation of a radical speech that might brand him at the outset of his career as Jacobinical. His recklessness stemmed from a kind of fatalistic anticipation of the failure of his Parliamentary career, arising partly from self-distrust and partly from a realistic conception of the inexorable degradation of political life.

Byron, who, on taking his seat in 1809, had declared his intention to stand aloof from both parties, to speak what he thought, and to preserve his independence, realized now that he was playing a lone hand, for he was held back by aristocratic pride from allying himself openly with the Radical leaders in Parliament whose point of view he more nearly shared. He was now more eager to conciliate and work in harmony with Lord Holland, from whom, however, he did not try to hide his own views. Two days before he made his speech he wrote:

"My own motive for opposing the bill is founded on its palpable injustice, and its certain inefficacy. I have seen the state of these miserable men, and it is a disgrace to a civilized country. . . . The effect of the present bill would be to drive them into actual rebellion. . . . I believe in the existence of grievances which call rather for pity than punishment." Then, concerned with the impression his letter might make on Lord Holland, he added a postscript: "I am a little apprehensive that your Lordship will think me too lenient towards these men, and half a *frame-breaker myself*." [n]

Afraid that he might not be able to control his feelings in an extemporaneous talk on this important occasion, Byron wrote out his speech and memorized it like a Harrow oration. Dallas, who heard him practicing, said: "He altered the natural tone of his voice, which was sweet and round, into a formal drawl." [n]

He had chosen to speak on the second reading of the bill (February 27, 1812). When the day came, he was in a state of high excitement. He launched a direct and radical attack on the injustice, inequity, and cruelty of the bill, making dramatic capital of the misery of the workers. With rhetorical questions and balanced sentences, with rolling periods and reasoned arguments as well as ironic contrasts, he appealed to the feelings and the humanity of the audience. Pitt, Burke, and Sheridan were his models, but he himself recognized that his delivery, "loud and fluent enough," was "perhaps a little theatrical." [n]

He piled up dramatic contrasts as he approached the climax of his argument. "I have been in some of the most oppressed provinces of Turkey; but never under the most despotic of infidel governments did I behold such squalid wretchedness as I have seen since my return in the very heart of a Christian country." Then he asked: "How will you carry the Bill into effect? Can you commit a whole country to their own prisons? Will you erect a gibbet in every field, and hang up men like scarecrows?" [n] The solemn Tory lords must have fumed and felt that they were being forced to listen to a new demagogue quoting passages from Cobbett's *Political Register*.

Byron told Hodgson: "I spoke very violent sentences with a sort of modest impudence, abused every thing and every body, and put the Lord Chancellor [Lord Eldon] very much out of humour: and if I may believe what I hear, have not lost any character by the experiment." [n] "I was born for opposition," he later wrote.[n] Lord Holland congratulated him, but his true feelings were recorded in his *Memoirs:* "His speech was full of fancy, wit, and invective, but not exempt from affectation nor well reasoned, nor at all suited to our common notions of Parliamentary eloquence. His fastidious and artificial taste and his over-irritable temper would, I think, have prevented him from ever excelling in Parliament." [n] The only genuine enthusiasm came from Sir Francis Burdett, leader of the Radicals in the Commons, who stepped up to hear him. "*He* says it is the best speech by a *lord* since the 'Lord knows when,' probably from a fellow-feeling in the sentiments." [n]

Byron sat on a committee that amended the bill, substituting fine or imprisonment for the death penalty, but it was thrown out in the Commons. He took his revenge on the "Framers of the Frame Bill" with a satiric ode which he sent off anonymously to the *Morning Chronicle*, saucy and personal beyond anything he had said in his speech. And a few days later he sent to the same paper some verses whose *lèse-majesté* was even greater, for it struck at the Prince Regent's betrayal of his Whig friends: "Weep, daughter of a royal line,/ A Sire's disgrace, a realm's decay. . . ."[n]

Already uncertain of his position in Parliament, Byron was seeking a freer mode of expression, as well as compensation for what he considered his failure. He was growing impatient with the "Parliamentary mummeries" that bogged down all the business of government. Had it not been for the feeling, imposed half by his own pride and half by the conventions of the time, that writing could not be the serious or main occupation of a gentleman, he might have turned at once to poetry or journalism. As it was, a series of circumstances was forcing him to suppress the form of expression that was most natural to him—satire.

At the beginning of his Parliamentary career he was facing a dilemma. Although pushed by his natural sympathies and his convictions toward a Radical position, he longed for the society of the aristocratic circles of the Moderate Whig camp, of which Holland House was the center. It argues nothing of snobbery in Byron's nature—for when he had become the lion of London society, he never for a moment deserted those early friends such as Hobhouse and Davies, whom Moore, the truer snob, slandered as mere "coffee-house" companions—to say that he had a kind of psychological urge, built upon the whole background of his early life, to be accepted as a social equal in the aristocratic world. Both his pride and his intellect prevented him from being a social climber, but he was flattered by Lord Holland's overtures, and from the time of their first meeting continued to pay him the greatest deference.

It was not surprising then that when Rogers hinted that Lord and Lady Holland would not be sorry if he refrained from any further publication of *English Bards, and Scotch Reviewers*, Byron immediately dropped his work on a fifth edition, together with his *Hints from Horace* and *The Curse of Minerva,* which he had intended to print in the same volume. For many reasons he was not sorry to suppress his early satire. After being brought into the London literary world by Rogers and Moore, he had come to see that his judgments had been youthful, rash, and unfair.

His literary fame now must rise or fall with *Childe Harold.* It had been advertised for publication on March 1, but Murray held it from public sale until the 10th, in the meantime predisposing the public to be eager for it by showing the sheets to various people who spread the word about. Three days after the official publication date, Murray had sold the whole edition of five hundred copies of the handsome quarto. By the middle of the month the author "awoke to find himself famous."

CHAPTER X

1812

The Fame of Childe Harold

EVEN BEFORE the first edition of *Childe Harold* had disappeared from Murray's shelves, Byron had become an object of curiosity and interest in the drawing rooms of the Whig aristocracy. The center of the most recherché society in London was then Holland House, the Kensington mansion of the third Lord Holland and his wife, Elizabeth, whom he had married in 1797 two days after her first husband, Sir Godfrey Webster, had divorced her (naming Lord Holland as co-respondent). In a society in which such irregularities of conduct were taken for granted as prerogatives of an uninhibited upper class, there could be little embarrassment in sitting down to dine with the best company in London at Holland House. Not only the *haut ton* of the aristocracy but also the cream of the talents gathered there. Rogers and Moore were frequent visitors, and Byron soon joined them. His genial and kindly host welcomed him without reserve.

But the Hollands did not monopolize Byron for long. He had become the literary lion of the season and soon was swept into other, more exciting circles. At Melbourne House in Whitehall an erratic and vivacious young lady had been enraptured by the romantic pilgrimage and was burning to meet the author. Lady Caroline Lamb had been married for seven years and had borne a son to her husband, William Lamb, second son of Lord and Lady Melbourne. A creature of impulse, great nervous energy, and intense sensibility, she yet retained a childlike freshness and naïveté that had scarcely been disturbed by marriage and motherhood. In her girlhood she had been something of a tomboy. Born Caroline Ponsonby, daughter of the Earl of Bessborough and of Henrietta Ponsonby, sister of the beautiful Duchess of Devonshire, she was allowed to develop her eccentricities in the permissive atmosphere of Devonshire House, Chatsworth, and Hardwick. Having no formal education, she could scarcely read when she reached her teens, but she developed a facility for writing verses and drawing.

One day Rogers, who was a frequent visitor at Melbourne House, said: "You should know the new poet," and gave her a copy of *Childe Harold* to read. Rogers had told her that "he has a club-foot, and bites his nails," but her reply was, after she had read the poem, "If he was as ugly as Æsop I must know him." She wrote him an anonymous letter: "I have read your Book & . . . think it beautiful. You deserve to be and you shall be happy. Do not throw away such Talents as you possess in gloom & regrets for the past & above all live here in your own Country which will be proud of you—& which requires your exertion." [n] She was offered an introduction at Lady Westmoreland's, but turned away, not wanting to compete with other women who were crowding about. In her journal she wrote of him: "mad—bad—and dangerous to know." [n] That meant she was eager to meet him but on her own terms. Byron's interest was already piqued by her turning away. It was Lady Holland who finally introduced her to him, probably at her own request. Byron was not at first attracted to her physically, at least according to the cold survey he later gave Medwin: "The lady had scarcely any personal attractions to recommend her. Her figure, though genteel, was too thin to be good. . . ." [n]

But he soon found that what she lacked in beauty she made up in vivacity and unpredictability. A romantic attachment to a woman of his own rank and intellect was a new experience for him. He had always been most successful with girls below his social and intellectual level, with those who flattered his ego and looked with awe on his title. And he had come to have a kind of Oriental scorn of women as creatures in no way capable of sharing a man's thoughts or feelings. Among the women he had met thus far in fashionable Whig society, his shyness had caused him to play his own hero, the aloof and melancholy Childe Harold. They did not realize how much his studied politeness and his cynical pose were a mask to hide his lack of ease in an aristocratic society to which he had been a stranger most of his life. The clever acerbities of his undergraduate days, which would have pleased Scrope Davies, were not always appreciated in this company.

When Byron first met Caroline, she was twenty-seven, boyish-looking, with blond curly hair and a frank innocence in her dark hazel eyes. She had a passion for pages, and used to dress in their scarlet and sepia liveries. The engaging Devonshire House drawl and a lisp heightened the startling character of her conversation. Her lack of restraint and carelessness of the world's opinion often shocked him. Caroline probably would have been attracted to Byron in any case, but she was doubly gratified that she had captured the literary lion of the London season, the man who fulfilled her fondest romantic dream. Soon after their first acquaintance she wrote dramatically in her diary: "*That beautiful pale face is my fate.*"[n] Byron was fascinated, and he went again and again to Melbourne House. But he did not succumb immediately, for the giddiness of Caroline's parties and the numerous company put him off.

On his second morning visit (March 25) Byron saw for the first time William Lamb's country cousin Anne Isabella (Annabella) Milbanke, the only daughter of Sir Ralph Milbanke, Lady Melbourne's brother. She had been brought up in seclusion in a house overlooking the bleak cliffs of the North Sea at Seaham in Durham. She was a spoiled child but a very precocious one, who had also been tutored at home and early developed an interest in mathematics, classical literature, and philosophy. She had read widely,* but knew little of the world of fashion when she went to

---

* Two of Miss Milbanke's commonplace books, now in my possession, reveal the seriousness, precision, and self-confidence of her studies and her judgments on books ranging as widely as Bacon's *Advancement of Learning,* which she was reading in 1809, at the age of seventeen, Cowley, Cowper (a favorite), Horace, Massinger, and even some of the more daring writers such as Swift, Bolinbroke, Hume, and Rochefoucauld. Her own comments indicate the complacency of her judgments: "I think self knowledge is not so difficult as to know the place we hold in the opinions of others"; "I presume no one will assert that a man enjoying internally an approving conscience and externally the good opinion of others, is less happy than one whose only gratification is that of a foolish vanity." She quoted with approval Cowper's philosophy in misfortune: "We are forbidden to murmur, but we are not forbidden to regret."

London for the first time in 1811 to acquire social polish while placing herself as decently as possible on the marriage market. But that season was a little disappointing. She had exalted ideas of what she wanted in a husband, and her letters and diary show that she was not a little priggish.

But the season of 1812 was more propitious. She was in her twentieth year, and in spite of her "snub face" she had a dark beauty that was heightened by her pensive reserve. This time she had suitors in plenty, some of them rather troublesome, for she was not genuinely interested. One was Augustus Foster, son of the second Duchess of Devonshire, who hesitated to take a post as Minister to the United States because he did not want to leave her. Another was William Bankes, Byron's Cambridge friend, with £8,000 a year. When Byron presented him a copy of *Childe Harold,* he soon after lent it to Annabella, who had just read it when she first saw the author. She wrote in her diary that night: "His mouth continually betrays the acrimony of his spirit. I should judge him sincere and independent. . . . It appeared to me that he tried to control his natural sarcasm and vehemence as much as he could, in order not to offend; but at times his lips thickened with disdain, and his eyes rolled impatiently." [n]

She listened avidly to the gossip circulated about him: "Mrs. Knight told me authentic anecdotes of Lord Byron which gave me much concern, as they indicated feelings dreadfully perverted." [n] It was already apparent that for the first time she had met a man who aroused more than apathetic interest in her. That she could not approve of him did not lessen her excitement. She wrote her mother: "My curiosity was much gratified by seeing Lord Byron, the object at present of universal attention. . . . It is said that he is an infidel, and I think it probable from the general character of his mind. His poem sufficiently proves that he *can* feel nobly, but he has discouraged his own goodness. . . . I made no offering at the shrine of Childe Harold, though I shall not refuse the acquaintance if it comes my way." [n]

Although Byron did not talk with her on this occasion, he did not fail to notice her. He later told Medwin: "There was something piquant, and what we term pretty, in Miss Milbanke. Her features were small and feminine, though not regular. She had the fairest skin imaginable. Her figure was perfect for her height, and there was a simplicity, a retired modesty about her, which was very characteristic, and formed a happy contrast to the cold artificial formality, and studied stiffness, which is called fashion. She interested me exceedingly." [n]

But for the moment Caroline Lamb occupied his thoughts. At first he was afraid that she was merely leading him on to please her vanity. He took her a rose and a carnation, saying with a half-sarcastic smile that covered his insecurity: "Your Ladyship I am told likes all that is new and rare for a moment." [n] Caroline's impulsiveness was at once a delight and an embarrassment to Byron. From that time on, notes and letters and verses flew back and forth between them. He was soon overwhelmed by her generosity and her abandon. Rogers said: "She absolutely besieged him. . . . she assured him that, if he was in any want of money, 'all her jewels were at his service.' . . . such was the insanity of her passion for Byron, that, sometimes, when not invited to a party where he was to be, she would wait for him in the street till it was over!" [n]

There is evidence, however, that this affair did not absorb Byron wholly. He was much in demand everywhere, and basked in the attention of many women to whom he could be agreeable without making commitments. The Duchess of Devonshire wrote to her son Augustus Foster in Washington: "The subject of conversation, of curiosity, of enthusiasm almost, one might say, of the moment is not Spain or Portugal, Warriors or Patriots, but Lord Byron! . . . [*Childe Harold*] is on every table, and himself courted, visited, flattered, and praised whenever he appears." [n] Before his house in St. James's Street the traffic was held up by a press of carriages bringing notes of invitation. "The genius which the poem exhibited," Rogers said, "the youth, the rank of the author, his romantic wanderings in Greece,—these combined to make the world stark mad about *Childe Harold* and Byron. I knew two old maids in Buckinghamshire who used to cry over the passage about Harold's 'laughing dames' that 'long had fed his youthful appetite.' " [n]

Even the demure and fastidious Annabella Milbanke easily succumbed to his charms. At a party at Lady Cowper's (Lady Melbourne's daughter) she first had an opportunity to talk with him. To her mother she wrote: "I have met with much evidence of his goodness. You know how easily the noblest heart may be perverted by unkindness. . . . Lord B. is certainly very interesting, but he wants that calm benevolence which could only touch my heart." [n] She was unaware how deeply her fate was sealed when she wrote in her diary that she was "convinced that he is sincerely repentant for the evil he has done, though he has not resolution (without aid) to adopt a new course of conduct and feelings." [n]

Byron had a feminine sensitivity to the nuances of sympathetic feeling and an uncanny capacity for displaying that part of his personality which would most engage the person with whom he was talking. This accounted for his friendship with such disparate characters as Hobhouse and Tom Moore, Dallas and Davies, prize fighters, chambermaids, and duchesses. Instinctively he came forward to meet this simple girl on her own level. She felt that she had seen much deeper into Childe Harold than had any of the women who were throwing themselves at him when he asked abruptly at a party: "Do you think there is one person here who dares to look into himself?" Remembering this at a later time, she wrote: "I felt that he was the most attractive person [in the crowd]; but I was not *bound* to him by any strong feeling of sympathy till he uttered these words, not to me, but in my hearing—'I have not a friend in the world!' . . . I vowed in secret to be a devoted friend to this lone being." [n] On April 26 she wrote her mother: "I consider it as an act of humanity and a Christian duty not to deny him any temporary satisfaction he can derive from my acquaintance. . . . He is not a dangerous person to me. . . . *I* cannot think him destitute of natural religion—it is in his heart." [n]

Apparently Byron paid enough attention to her to make Caroline jealous. In her naïveté Annabella had sent some of her poems through Caroline for Byron's opinion. Caroline knew how to deal with this impertinence. She passed along the poems, which she felt would do the writer no good. Byron replied to Caroline with frankness: "She certainly is a very extraordinary girl; who would imagine so much strength and variety of thought under that placid Countenance? . . . I have no hesitation in saying that she has talents which, were it proper or requisite to indulge, would have led to distinction. . . . You will say as much of this to Miss M. as you think proper. I say all this very sincerely. I have no desire to be better acquainted with Miss

Milbank [*sic*]; she is too good for a fallen spirit to know, and I should like her more if she were less perfect."[n]

Annabella was morally smug enough to take that last statement, if Caroline revealed it to her, as a kind of grim compliment. But the "fallen spirit" turned his attention elsewhere and before long Annabella was "wearied with want of tranquillity, and found no pleasure" in London society, and she discontinued her diary.

During all this time Byron's tranquillity was frequently destroyed too, but for reasons unflatteringly remote from Miss Milbanke. Through April and May his affair with Caroline Lamb progressed rapidly to successive heights of wildness and folly. Her utter abandonment of all discretion frequently shocked him and led to quarrels and passionate reconciliations. One of these quarrels, Byron told Medwin, "was made up in a very odd way, and without any verbal explanation. She will remember it."[n]

Byron, too, could be a moody and demanding lover. The waltzing parties, which had made Melbourne House the gayest place in London, were soon abandoned because they gave pain to the lame poet, who could not dance. He could not bear to see Caroline in the arms of another. She said: ". . . he liked to read with me & stay with me out of the crowd."[n] Then he grew jealous of her husband. Bitterness would overcome him, and he would boast of the blackness of his own character; thinking of his deformity, he would cry that William Lamb was to him as an Hyperion to a satyr. He would force her to swear that she loved him better than William. When she hesitated, he shouted: "My God, you shall pay for this, I'll wring that little obstinate heart."[n]

Never did two self-centered egos clash so violently. But their love was torturingly real while it lasted. For Caroline it never ceased to be the greatest and most moving passion of her life. She told Medwin: "I grew to love him better than virtue, Religion—all prospects here. He broke my heart, & still I love him. . . ."[n] Byron wrote honestly to Lady Melbourne after his love had been turned to disgust by Caroline's absurdities: "I do not mean to deny my attachment—it *was*—and it is not."[n] There is genuine tenderness in his few letters to her that have survived. While the passion was still fresh he wrote:

"I never knew a woman with greater or more pleasing

talents, *general* as in a woman they should be, something of everything, and too much of nothing. But these are unfortunately coupled with a total want of common conduct. . . .

"Then your heart, my poor Caro (what a little volcano!), that pours *lava* through your veins; and yet I cannot wish it a bit colder. . . . you know I have always thought you the cleverest, most agreeable, absurd, amiable, perplexing, dangerous, fascinating little being that lives now, or ought to have lived 2000 years ago. I won't talk to you of beauty; I am no judge. But our beauties cease to be so when near you, and therefore you have either some, or something better." [n]

But it was Byron's misfortune that he was impelled to despoil his mistress of those very qualities which had in his romantic imagination made her attractive—her freshness and innocence. When he reproached her for being cold, she wrote: "But was I cold when first you made me yours—when first you told me in the Carriage to kiss your mouth & I durst not—& after thinking it such a crime it was more than I could prevent from that moment—you drew me to you like a magnet & I could not indeed I could not have kept away—was I cold then—were you so? . . . never while life beats in this heart shall I forget you or that moment when first you said you lov'd me—when my heart did not meet yours but flew before it—& both intended to remain innocent of greater wrong." [n]

Spoiled child that she was, Caroline had imagined that she could play with fire without being burned. She had thought she could have the adoration of Byron on her own terms, as she had that of the rest of the world. Once in the game, however, Byron could not stop with a light flirtation, but must carry on until he had conquered her wholly, though he knew and frequently repented the consequences of the steps he seemed fated to take. For a few headlong weeks Byron's political career, his new-found social success, which at first had meant a great deal to his self-esteem, even his literary reputation—all seemed jeopardized by this hectic love affair. He soon realized what a wild spirit he had released by rousing the passions of this *enfant terrible*. She told Medwin: "Byron did not affect—but he loved me as never woman was loved." [n] Once awakened, she could never forget him.

Her indiscretion knew no bounds. Had the affair been carried on secretly and discreetly, no one would have been greatly concerned. Lady Melbourne herself had long been the particular friend of Lord Egremont, whom William Lamb, her second son and Caroline's husband, was said to resemble, and her intimacy with the Prince of Wales was commonly thought to account for the interest he took in her son George. She did not pretend to greater virtue than others, but she was annoyed by Caroline's public display of her conquest. Lady Bessborough too had possessed some of her daughter's recklessness in her youth, but she had followed the code of her class in keeping from public view her early liaison with Lord Granville Leveson Gower. Her later curious affair with Sheridan came nearer to being a scandal because of his indiscretion rather than hers (his last message being that he would be looking up through the coffin lid at her).

But it was apparently Byron himself who proposed the ultimate indiscretion—an elopement—perhaps in the knowledge (or hope?) that Caroline would not have the courage to make such a violent break with her comfortable world, perhaps to test whether she would actually leave her husband for him.

While matters were in this stormy but delicate balance, Byron turned his attention briefly again to politics. Absorbed by his love affair and the social whirl precipitated by the popularity of *Childe Harold*, he had neglected his "senatorial duties" after his maiden speech in February. He attended the House only twice in March and three times in April. His whole concept of political life was that of the orator with independent liberal or radical views whose voice would carry, by its rhetoric and good sense, over the heads of the House to sway the nation as a whole. He had no stomach for active cooperation with any of the Whig leaders; nor could he compromise or exercise the caution which even the most radical of those who espoused popular causes had learned.

Byron spoke again on the first major issue that arose after the Frame Bill, a motion for a Committee on the Roman Catholic Claims, on April 21. His irony was aimed at eliciting sympathy for an oppressed people, the Catholics of Ireland. He concluded with the brash suggestion that Napoleon himself would be most grateful for the ministerial defeat of Catholic emancipation: "It is on the basis of your tyranny Napoleon hopes to build his own." [*]

On the whole the speech was more provocative and defiant, though less rhetorically balanced, than his defense of the frame-breakers. If the peers listened more politely to the author of *Childe Harold* at the height of his popularity than they had to the nervous, unknown young lord making his maiden speech a few weeks before, the speech itself left no marked impression. But his vote did finally give the majority of one needed to pass the motion. He later recorded that he was "sent for in great haste to a Ball, which I quitted, I confess, somewhat reluctantly, to emancipate five Millions of people."[n] But by then his interest in Parliament had subsided.

There was balm enough for his self-esteem in the critical reception given to *Childe Harold.* Even Jeffrey praised the poem in the *Edinburgh Review,* and when Byron wrote apologizing for his unfair attack in *English Bards,* Jeffrey hinted that he could convince him that he was not the author of the review of *Hours of Idleness.* Byron was very willing to bury the hatchet.

The fame of *Childe Harold* had brought Byron a flood of letters from women. Some of them wanted to convert him from skepticism; others wanted him to read their verses. By far the most shamelessly infatuated was Christina, Lady Falkland, widow of his friend Lord Falkland who had been killed in a duel. She imagined Byron was in love with her because out of pity for her plight he had in delicacy left £500 in a teacup for her support. When she read *Childe Harold* she thought all the love passages in it referred to her. "Tell me, my Byron, if those mournful tender effusions of your heart to that Thyrza . . . were not intended for myself?"[n] She was even convinced that the "Maid of Athens" was "your own Christina."[n] Byron finally in desperation turned over her letters to his lawyer, and when she was told that he would neither read nor answer them, she still persisted: "Why, my adored boy, don't you return my affection as you did? . . . Pray do tell me, George," etc.[n]

Although never completely at ease in society, Byron gave himself up to the fashionable world that was wooing him. Among the new friends he made during the first weeks of his fame were two women of beauty, influence, and dominant personality. One was Lady Jersey, a reigning beauty and wit and leading patroness of the fashionable balls at Almacks. She even dared to refuse admittance to the Duke of Wellington when he came late. Byron was soon a favorite at her *haut-ton* parties. The other woman with whom he formed a curious and lasting friendship at this time was Elizabeth, Lady Melbourne, mother of Caroline Lamb's easygoing husband. She emerged from the fracas over her daughter-in-law as Byron's most trusted confidante. She had been a dark beauty as a girl and was still attractive at sixty-two. She was a man's woman: even-tempered and reasonable, pleasantly feminine and even voluptuous, but with a positive distaste for the caprices of pretty women. Tactful and sympathetic, she was never shocked and was never likely to make a scene. She was generally more tolerant of the frailties of both men and women than was common even in Whig society. The feminine traits in Byron's own nature made him the more responsive to the balanced gentleness and sophistication that rendered her a delightful companion and confidante. He perhaps appreciated her the more for the contrast she formed with his own mother in understanding and temper. Yet the pleasure of the association was that she aroused something more than a mere filial fondness in him. He told Lady Blessington: "Lady M[elbourne], who might have been my mother, excited an interest in my feelings that few young women have been able to awaken. She was a charming person—a sort of modern Aspasia. . . . I have often thought, that, with a little more youth, Lady M might have turned my head. . . ."[n]

The affair with Caroline had reached such hectic heights by May that Byron realized he must get away, but he had not the strength to go. He later told Medwin: "I am easily governed by women, and she [Caroline] gained an ascendancy over me that I could not easily shake off. I submitted to this thraldom long, for I hate *scenes*, and am of an indolent disposition. . . ."[n] He wrote Caroline sage advice, knowing it would do little good: "I conformed and could conform, if you would lend your aid, but I can't bear to see you look unhappy. . . . We must make an effort. This dream, this delirium of two months must pass away. . . ."[n] He was already planning to go down to Newstead on June 1, taking with him Hobhouse, "who is endeavouring, like you and every body else," he wrote Moore, "to keep me out of scrapes."[n] Hobhouse—whom Sir Harold Nicolson has aptly called "the balance wheel in Byron's life"—was already deeply concerned for Byron's reputation in the affair, for he knew better than others how far things had gone and what danger there was of an elopement. But even at Newstead there was no escape. Hobhouse noted: "a page come from Lady C. L. with letters for Byron—dreadful body."

Byron returned to London on June 13. In his absence he had been elected a member of the London Hampden Club, a Reform club originally composed of liberal aristocrats like Sir Francis Burdett, who had recommended him. But he felt ill at ease in the dissentient ranks of the reformers. Nevertheless, he found some congenial spirits among them. One of the most active recruiters was Lady Oxford. By mid-June he and Hobhouse were attending her balls and parties. The beautiful and learned Jane Elizabeth Scott, Countess of Oxford, was a rector's daughter brought up in the glow of French Revolutionary thought, whose ardor for popular and radical causes was equaled only by her love for handsome men who by inclination or conversion were devoted to the same causes. Married in 1794, when she was twenty-two, to Edward Harley, fifth Earl of Oxford and Mortimer, she soon tired of being a great lady and devoted herself to Reform movements and movers. Her first enthusiasm, when the Earl, who had absorbed radical ideas in his college days, had subsided into a mild politician and milder husband, was the champion of the people, Sir Francis Burdett. She was completely emancipated from conventional ideas, and indulged in the satisfaction of her instincts with the readiness common among the English aristocracy, but with greater nonchalance. The Princess of Wales, of whom in 1812 she was a bosom friend, excused her for having "granted the last favours to Sir Francis Burdett" by blaming Lord Oxford because he had "left his wife so young and beautiful for above a week in a house alone in the country with so handsome and enterprising a man." But when Lady Oxford admitted everything to the Earl, he "immediately said her candour and frank confession were so amiable that he entirely forgave her."[n] It was scarcely necessary for her to get rid of so agreeable and tolerant a husband.

And so Lady Oxford proceeded, acquiring as a by-product of her amours a family of beautiful children of uncertain paternity who were commonly referred to as the Harleian Miscellany (some manuscripts in the Oxfords' library were published under that title in 1744). Lady Oxford was already tiring of her latest lover, Lord Archibald Hamilton, when Byron met her; but it is doubtful that he, absorbed in his intrigue with Caroline Lamb, gave much attention at this time to the "autumnal charms" of a woman who, though still attractive, was sixteen years his senior.

It is possible that Byron had already been presented to the Princess of Wales. Many of his friends were in her good graces, and Lady Oxford was a constant visitor at Kensington Palace. In any event he shared the general Whig sympathy for the Princess, whose cause furnished a focus for the opposition to the Prince Regent. But when the opportunity presented itself for him to meet the Prince, Byron seized it as eagerly as any Tory. At a party the Prince, informed of the presence of the author of *Childe Harold,* expressed a desire to see him. Byron's embarrassment left him when the Prince engaged him in literary conversation. Their mutual enthusiasm for Walter Scott broke down the poet's reserve. Nevertheless, Byron wrote humorously of the interview to Lord Holland, for he could not allow his Whig friends to suppose that he had capitulated to the enemy.

At the end of July the crisis with Caroline finally came. Hobhouse recorded the whole dramatic story in his diary: "Wednesday July 29. Went to Byron's, No. 8 St. James' Street in expectation of going to Harrow, a scheme he had resolved on to avoid the threatened visit of a Lady—at 12 o'clock just as we were going, several thundering raps were heard at the door & we saw a crowd collected about the door & opposite to it—immediately a person in a most strange disguise walked up stairs—it turned out to be the Lady in question from Brocket. . . . I did think that to leave my friend in such a situation, when . . . every soul in the house servants & all knew of the person in disguise, and not to endeavour to prevent the catastrophe of an elopement which seemed inevitable, would be unjustifiable—accordingly I staid in the sitting room whilst the Lady was in the bed room pulling off her disguise—under which she had a page's dress. . . . at last she was prevailed upon to put on a habit, bonnet, & shoes—belonging to a servant of the house and, after much intreaty did come out into the sitting room. . . ." When Hobhouse insisted on her leaving, she tried to stab herself and Byron had to hold her. Finally Hobhouse got her to consent to go to his rooms to change her clothes, and then to let him accompany her in a coach to the home of a friend, on condition that she be allowed to see Byron again before he left town. Hobhouse's greatest wish, he recorded, was that Byron "should give this lady, who by the common consent of all London has made a dead set at him, no power over him by consenting to any serious folly, and when I knew that every thing had past between them, my next desire was to prevent a public disclosure and an elopement."

Indeed everything had passed between them, and Caroline continued her madness, while Byron alternately succumbed to her headlong folly and urged restraint and prudence. On August 9 she sent him a letter enclosing a gift of her pubic hair with the inscription:

CAROLINE BYRON—
NEXT TO THYRSA DEAREST
& MOST FAITHFUL—GOD BLESS YOU
OWN LOVE—RICORDATI DI BIONDETTA
FROM YOUR WILD ANTELOPE

In her letter she said: "I askd you not to send blood but Yet do—because if it means love I like to have it. I cut the hair too close & bled much more than you need—do not you the same & pray put not scissors points near where quei capelli grow—sooner take it from the arm or wrist—pray be careful. . . ."[n]

There was another, more serious public eruption of the "little volcano" on August 12. Lady Bessborough had tried to persuade Caroline to join her husband in the country and then accompany them to Ireland. When Lord Melbourne came in and reproached her, she threatened to run off to Lord Byron. Melbourne told her to go and be damned, but he did not think Byron would take her. Maddened by that remark, Caroline rushed out not to join Byron but to hide in a surgeon's house, where Byron finally traced her by bribing the coachman and returned her to her family. Byron was relieved when she set out for Ireland with her husband and mother in September. His farewell letter, which she treasured to the end of her days, is an artful mixture of gallantry and self-denial admirably suited to satisfy her sense of what the dramatic situation demanded. She was not wrong in believing that this letter was ample evidence that he was in love with her, but what she could not have understood is that at the same time he was glad to be rid of her. The very fact that she was departing made it easier to avow sentiments which, if he no longer felt them completely, he *had* felt.

"My dearest Caroline,—If tears which you saw and know I am not apt to shed,—if the agitation in which I parted from you . . . if all I have said and done, and am still but too ready to say and do, have not sufficiently proved what my real feelings are, and must ever be towards you, my love, I have no other proof to offer. . . . You know I would with pleasure give up all here and all beyond the grave for you, and in refraining from this, must my motives be misunderstood? I care not who knows this, what use is made of it. . . . I was and am yours freely and most entirely, to obey, to honour, love,—and fly with you when, where, and how you yourself *might* and *may* determine." [n]

Once Caroline was gone, the reaction set in, but he continued to write to her for some time, partly because he knew she expected it and partly because he wanted to prevent further hysterics. Lady Bessborough had learned from the Prince Regent how widely the affair had been talked about and how ridiculous they had all appeared. Lord Melbourne told him that Caroline drove him mad and that Byron had bewitched the whole family, "Mothers & daughter & all." "I never heard of such a thing in my life," the Prince exclaimed, "taking the Mothers for confidantes!" [n]

Byron never thought very highly of Caroline's mother; later he called her "Lady Blarney." But the Prince was right in believing that Byron had made a confidante of Lady Melbourne. Byron revealed to her with amazing frankness and cynical wit the interplay of his emotions and his ego in his relations with Caroline and other women. But he could not submit to her scrutiny the softer sentiments that generally found release only in his poetry.

Before Byron left London for Cheltenham, Newstead had at last been sold. It had been offered at auction on August 14, but on Hanson's advice he rejected all the bids, and the next day Thomas Claughton, a Lancashire lawyer, offered £140,000 for the whole property including the timber, the 3,200 acres of the park and farms, and the furniture. The offer was accepted, but soon it was clear that Claughton had repented and, by questioning the deeds and by other ruses, he delayed paying even the

£25,000 deposit. Byron was no nearer solvency than he had been.

After the strenuous spring and summer, he was glad of the quiet company of the Jerseys, Hollands, Melbournes, and other London friends who had gathered at the fashionable watering place in September. Lord Holland engaged him to write an Address to be read at the opening of the new Drury Lane Theatre constructed after the destruction of the old one in 1809. There had been a contest for the Address, but he had declined to enter it. "I never risk *rivalry* in anything," he told Lady Melbourne.[n] When none of the contributions was found suitable, however, Byron consented to write one to please Lord Holland, but he sweated over it, for he could not write anything to order, and though he was irked, he could not disagree with his friend Perry's pronouncement in the *Morning Chronicle* that it was "in parts unmusical, and in general tame."[n]

Relief from the harrowing emotions and humiliations of his liaison with Caroline Lamb is reflected in a letter to Lady Melbourne: ". . . you will not regret to hear, that I wish this to end, and it certainly shall not be renewed on my part. It is not that I love another, but loving at all is quite out of my way; I am tired of being a fool. . . . It is true from early habit, one must make love mechanically, as one swims. I was once very fond of both, but now as I never swim, unless I tumble into the water, I don't make love till almost obliged. . . ."[n]

He did not like to confess to Lady Melbourne how strong a hold Caroline still had on him. But he needed her help, not only to dispose of the troublesome Caroline, but also to explore the ground in another field. He told her that he had deceived himself and her when he said he was not attached to another. He startled his confidante by saying, " . . . there was, and is one whom I wished to marry, had not this affair intervened, or had not some occurrences rather discouraged me. . . . The woman I mean is Miss Milbanke. . . . I know little of her, and have not the most distant reason to suppose that I am at all a favourite in that quarter. But I never saw a woman whom I *esteemed* so much."[n]

Lady Melbourne was willing enough to see Byron settled in a marriage that would put a stop to the Caroline nonsense, but she could not believe that he was serious, or that her niece, that model of the virtues, could cope with the vagaries of Byron's temperament. To her query he replied: "Miss M[ilbanke] I admire because she is a clever woman, an amiable woman, and of high blood, for I have still a few Norman and Scotch inherited prejudices on the last score, were I to marry. As to *love,* that is done in a week (provided the lady has a reasonable share); besides, marriage goes on better with esteem and confidence than romance, and she is quite pretty enough to be loved by her husband, without being so glaringly beautiful as to attract too many rivals."[n]

He could not quite admit to Lady Melbourne the whole of his complicated feeling for Caroline. He was reluctant to accept her advice that he write her a moderate and friendly letter. That "would be a little too indifferent; and *that* now would be an insult. . . ."[n] It seemed now to him that the only irrevocable road would be marriage, and he urged Lady Melbourne playfully to sound out Annabella, "were it only for the pleasure of calling you *aunt!*"[n]

But a few days of the mild enjoyments of Cheltenham, including a flirtation with an Italian songstress, muted his desire to mate with the estimable Miss Milbanke. "As to Annabella, she requires time and all the cardinal virtues, and in the interim I am a little verging towards one who demands neither, and saves me besides the trouble of marrying, by being married already." An added attraction was that she spoke only Italian, "and she has black eyes, and *not* a very white skin, and reminds me of many in the Archipelago I wished to forget. . . . I only wish she did not swallow so much supper . . . a woman should never be seen eating or drinking, unless it be *lobster salad* and *champagne,* the only truly feminine and becoming viands."[n] But she was lively, and "very fond of her husband, which is all the better, as thus, if a woman is attached to her husband, how much more will she naturally like one who is *not* her husband. . . ."[n] Lady Melbourne knew how to take such persiflage. But an "express" letter from Ireland and the prospect of more scenes made him feel again that a speedy marriage was his only salvation. "If your niece is obtainable, I should prefer her; if not, the very first woman who does not look as if she would spit in my face. . . ."[n]

At this point Lady Melbourne wrote to Annabella, and without naming the suitor asked her what qualities she desired in a husband. This was something upon which her niece had thought long and introspectively. She began by analyzing her own character. "I am never irritated except when others are so. . . . This makes good temper in my companions very necessary for my peace. . . . if I had not acquired the habit of reflecting before I act, I should sometimes have sacrificed considerations of prudence to the impulse of my feelings—but I am not conscious of ever having *yielded* to the temptation which assailed me."[n] As for her husband, "He must have consistent principles of Duty governing strong & *generous* feelings, and reducing them under the command of Reason. . . . I require a freedom from suspicion, & from *habitual* ill-humour—also an equal tenor of affection towards me, not that violent attachment which is susceptible of sudden encrease or diminution from trifles."[n]

Lady Melbourne accused her of being on stilts, but tried out her principles by forwarding Byron's proposal. Even though it was by proxy, it startled her, for he was the one man who had interested her even while her analytical mind dissected and disapproved of him. She took several days to reply, in the meantime writing out a Character of Lord Byron which she had started but put aside some months before. She tried to balance the good and bad in him, and concluded: "He is inclined to open his heart unreservedly to those whom he believes *good*, even without the preparation of much acquaintance. He is extremely humble towards persons whose character he respects, and to them he would probably confess his errors—"[n]

She broke off without finishing it, perhaps because she feared that it was drawing near a conclusion she could not quite face. But her reply, though involved, conveyed the idea that she rejected the offer because of a defect of her own feelings, but did not want to withdraw "from an acquaintance that does me honor and is capable of imparting so much rational pleasure."[n] Byron accepted the refusal good-humoredly, admitting that his heart had not been "much interested in the business." Nevertheless he was intrigued by "the amiable *Mathematician,*" he wrote Lady Melbourne, concluding, "I thank you again for your efforts with my Princess of Parallelograms, who has puzzled you more than the Hypothenuse. . . . Her proceedings are quite rectangular, or rather we are two parallel lines prolonged to infinity side by side, but never to meet."[n]

Amid all the suspense and confusion Byron found time to pen two hundred lines of a satire on waltzing, which he now offered to Murray. Conceived in the prudishness of his libertinism and born in the pangs of the lame watcher on the sidelines of London and provincial balls, the poem had more of bitterness than humor. Horace Hornem, the country squire and supposed author, broke out in paeans to the "Imperial Waltz! imported from the Rhine" that "wakes to Wantonness the willing limbs." It was the slighting references to the royal family, however, that made Byron anxious to preserve his anonymity: the mock homage to the graciousness of George III in begetting George IV; ironic turns of phrase on "princely paunches" and "the royal hip." [n]

Lady Oxford, who had already cast an appraising eye on Byron in London, was now at Cheltenham and invited him to Eywood, the country home of the Oxfords near Presteign. Her calm and ripened charms appealed to him in contrast to the nervous hysteria of Caroline, who was always trying to arouse his sympathy or his jealousy by relating "*how* many lovers were all sacrificed to this brilliant fit of constancy." [n] He was soon established at Eywood as a regular cavalier to Lady Oxford, and he found the situation altogether to his taste. He later told Lady Blessington that she "certainly excited as lively a passion in my breast as ever it has known; and even now the autumnal charms of Lady [Oxford] are remembered by me with more than admiration." [n]

He told Lady Melbourne, who was glad of a liaison that would bar a renewal with Caroline but a little fearful that she would lose her place as his confidante, "Do you doubt me, in the 'bowers of Armida?' I certainly am very much enchanted, but *your spells* will always retain their full force." [n] To Byron the situation was indeed enchanting. In addition to his charming mistress he had the companionship of her lovely daughters. They were just at the ages that excited his romantic sentiments most profoundly. Lady Charlotte Harley, then eleven, was his favorite. No one could have had more poignant sentiments of the beauty of youthful innocence than the disillusioned young lord who had known too early the disappointments of love fading into satiety. His tribute to the child exceeded in warmth of idealization anything he ever wrote of her mother. He prefaced the seventh edition of *Childe Harold* with stanzas to that "Young Peri of the West," under the name of Ianthe.

But of course this idyllic life could not last. A letter came from Caroline, "foolish, headstrong, and vainly threatening herself." She had disgusted him beyond expression, he wrote Lady Melbourne, "and even if I did not love another, I would never speak to her again." Then in candor he continued: "I cannot exist without some object of love. I have found one with whom I am perfectly satisfied. . . . I have engaged myself too far to recede, nor do I regret it."[n]

Then a worse storm broke. On November 9, Lady Oxford received a letter from Caroline, "a long *German* tirade," Byron called it, "evidently to discover on what *terms* we were." It contained "a number of *unanswerable* questions," to all of which he persuaded his mistress to give no reply whatever.[n] He was discovering to what lengths the scorned Caroline would go to make him pay for his apostasy. The same day he wrote her with curt but devastating restraint: "Lady Caroline—our affections are not in our own power—mine are engaged. I love another. . . . my opinion of you is entirely alter'd, & if I had wanted anything to confirm me, your Levities your caprices & the mean subterfuges you have lately made use of while madly gay—of writing to me as if otherwise, would entirely have open'd my eyes. I am no longer yr. lover. . . ."[n]

Shortly thereafter, Caroline returned to England and began pressing Byron for an interview "for the purpose of vindication, from I know not what. . . ."[n] But he had already promised Lady Oxford not to consent to any such meeting, and he delayed his return to London to avoid it. In this amiable atmosphere, "reading, laughing, and playing at blind man's-buff with ye *children,*" he felt relieved that marriage with the "Princess of Parallelograms" had not materialized. "I congratulate A[nnabella] and myself on our mutual escape. That would have been but a *cold collation,* and I prefer hot suppers."[n]

Finally on November 21 Byron left Eywood with regret and stopped at Middleton with the Jerseys on his way to town. Fond as he was of Lady Jersey, there was no enchantress there as at Eywood, where "a print of Rinaldo and Armida was one of the most prominent ornaments."[n] He wrote Hobhouse that "the connection with Lady Caroline Lamb is completely broken off. . . . I am still remote from *marriage,* and presume, whenever that takes place, 'even handed justice' will return me cuckoldom in abundance." [n]

But Caroline was not quiet for long. She did not take her dismissal lightly. First she wanted Byron to return her letters, but when it came to the performance she would not return his. Then she demanded the presents she had given him because she thought he had passed them on to Lady Oxford and wanted to embarrass him. She had gone to her country house at Brocket, where she rode madly on the turnpike and sent him absurd menaces: "You have told me how foreign women revenge; I will show you how an Englishwoman can." [n] Fortunately the revenge was a symbolic one. She gathered some children and had them go through a ritual and recite some verses while she burned "effigies" of Byron's picture and *copies* of his letters (she could not bear to part with the originals).

Byron had arrived at Batt's Hotel in Dover Street on November 30 to find his affairs in the worst shape imaginable. Claughton continued to delay the promised down payment on Newstead, but finally paid £5,000, part of which settled Byron's long-standing debt to Scrope Davies. And now he was besieged by Hodgson, who reproached his old friend for neglecting him and asked for an immediate loan of £500. After transacting some business with Murray, who had moved from Fleet Street to 50 Albemarle Street, just off Piccadilly (where his descendants still carry on the publishing business), he escaped again to Eywood the week before Christmas.

Byron was worn out with Caroline's absurdities. "I begin to look upon her as actually mad, or it would be impossible for me to bear what I have from her already," he wrote his confidante Lady Melbourne.[n] At Eywood, Byron reported "all very happy and serene—no scenes—a great deal of music—good cheer—spirits and temper—and every day convinces me of the *contrast.*" And there was prospect of more pleasure ahead. "We have some talk here of a voyage to Sicily, etc., in the spring. . . ." [n] If that scheme failed, he had some thought of "Levanting" again with Hobhouse. The fever of the East was like an intermittent malaria in Byron's mind; it could be activated by any nostalgic associations.

Looking back over the year that had brought him fame, he could think of nothing pleasanter than his present situation. He wrote to Lady Melbourne on the last day of the year the highest tribute to his "Armida": "I shall not entertain you with a long list of *attributes,* but merely state that I have not been guilty of once *yawning* in the eternity of two months under the same roof—a phenomenon in my history." [n]

CHAPTER XI

1813

Amours in Whig Society

LIFE WAS EVEN MORE IDYLLIC at Eywood as the year 1813 began. Lord Oxford had gone up to London early in January, and Byron remained another fortnight with his lady and her beautiful children. On January 2 he sent Hobhouse a draft on Hanson for one hundred guineas for a portrait of his mistress, to be wrapped "out of sight" and sent to Murray's for him. Two days later he wrote Lady Melbourne: "We go on without any interruptions or disagreeables—very few guests and no inmates—books, music, &c." [n] Byron later recorded in his journal that Lady Oxford had said to him at Eywood: "Have we not passed our last month like the gods of Lucretius?" He ended the entry: "And so we had." [n]

But a disturbing spirit frequently penetrated the placid retreat at Eywood. Caroline Lamb was more than ever determined to make Byron pay for his defection. He had ceased to write to her, but that did not stop the flow of her epistles. She told him that she was having engraved on her livery buttons "*Ne* 'Crede Byron.'" And she forged a letter in Byron's name to get from Murray the one portrait of her former lover that Lady Oxford wanted.

When Byron returned to London the third week in January, he took lodgings at 4 Bennet Street, just off St. James's, and continued to follow closely in the orbit of Lady Oxford. He was immediately swept into the circle of the Princess of Wales. At first he was a little bored with the Princess and slightly piqued with Lady Oxford for taking him there. The serpent had already entered the Eden they had known at Eywood. Byron later told Medwin: "I had great difficulty in breaking with her, even when I knew she had been inconstant to me." [n] She may already have been casting glances at other handsome young men in her London circle. It had become a habit. But Byron had enjoyed her exclusive attention too long not to be annoyed by this. And she may have had her own reasons for chagrin and jealousy. If we may believe one of Lady Byron's later "Statements," her husband confessed (though it should be noted that he often exaggerated his wickedness to shock her) that Lady Oxford had "detected him one day in an attempt upon her daughter, then a child of thirteen, & was enraged with him to the greatest degree." [n]

The Princess was not slow in observing a disturbing ripple in the joys of Armida and Rinaldo. She wrote her lady-in-waiting: "Lady Oxford, poor soul, is more in love this time than she has ever been before. She was with me the other evening, and Lord Byron was so cross to her . . . that she was crying in the anteroom." [n]

But as he became better acquainted with the Princess and less restrained in her company, Byron quite won her over with his charm and gaiety. There was perhaps in her very unrefined earthiness and *grossièreté* something that appealed to him. She concluded: " . . . he is quite anoder man when he is *wid* people he like, and who like him. . . ." [n]

If Byron was sometimes moody, it was because he was beset by irritating situations as soon as he reached London. Claughton was still withholding the payments on Newstead, while the creditors swarmed on every side in the knowledge that a sale had been made. Hanson dissuaded him from letting Claughton give up the purchase, for he feared that it would be impossible to get so good a price on a second sale. What galled Byron was that he could not help the friends who were constantly calling on him. He finally signed a bond with Hodgson for £500, but he could not assist his sister, whose gambling husband was getting her further into debt.

Had not Lady Oxford urged him to attend to his "senatorial duties," Byron would gladly have given up any further appearance in Parliament. He attended several sessions of the House in February, but was bored with the speeches. Toward the end of

March he wrote Augusta that he had "no intention to 'strut another hour' on that stage."[n] Still, he continued to look with regret upon the fading of the boyish dream that had buoyed him up during his wasted youth and his aimless travels. To Augusta he could confess the full measure of his defeat: "You have perhaps heard that I have been fooling away my time with different '*regnantes*'; but what better can be expected from me? I have but one *relative,* and her I never see. I have no connections to domesticate with, and for marriage I have neither the talent nor the inclination."[n]

Escape from England was still his greatest desire, but he was in the agonies of three different schemes. He told Lady Melbourne: "The *first* you know [going with or following after the Oxfords], the second is Sligo's Persian plan. . . . Then there is Hobhouse, with a Muscovite and Eastern proposal also. . . ."[n] In the meantime, Byron was glad to retire to the peace of Eywood, to which he accompanied the Oxfords at the end of March. Caroline Lamb had pestered him for an interview while he was in town. He stopped that by proposing that it should be in the presence of Lady Oxford. And now she wanted a lock of his hair. In a Mephistophelian mood he squared his account by sending her a strand from Lady Oxford's head.

On April 19 Byron hinted at an unexpected complication in his relations with Lady Oxford. "*We* are at present in a slight perplexity," he told his confidante, "owing to an event which certainly did not enter into my calculations; what it is, I leave to your own ingenious imagination. . . ."[n] The suggestion that an addition to the Harleian Miscellany was on the way seems obvious, but as no further mention is made of it, it seems that the alarm was false.

Caroline's silence had not lasted. She was demanding pictures, letters, and trinkets again. Byron wrote Lady Melbourne: " . . . the detestation, the utter abhorrence I feel at part of her conduct I will neither shock you with, nor trust myself to express." A ring she had given him he had transferred to Lady Charlotte Harley, Lady Oxford's daughter, "whom I should love for ever if she could always be only eleven years old, and whom I shall probably marry when she is old enough, and bad enough to be made into a modern wife."[n]

He was back in London at the end of April. On the 29th he

wrote Caroline consenting to an interview, Lady Oxford having withdrawn her interdiction. But he gave her no hope that it would lead to a reconciliation: "You say you will '*ruin* me.' I thank you, but I have done that for myself already; you say you will 'destroy me,' perhaps you will only save me the trouble." [n] Byron left no record of that meeting. He was probably glad to forget it, for he had at the last probably weakened into showing kindness and pity. Caroline, who could well have mistaken Byron's pity for love, later wrote Medwin: "Our meeting was not what he insinuates—he asked me to forgive him; he looked sorry for me; he cried." [n]

In the meantime, Lady Oxford being in the country, Byron found time to see some of his old friends again. He was with Rogers and Moore frequently. The latter took him to see Leigh Hunt, whose imprisonment in the Surrey Gaol for libeling the Prince Regent had made him a martyr of the liberal cause. Hunt was overcome by the unpretentious kindness of the famous noble poet: Byron had brought books that he thought might be useful as background for Hunt's *Story of Rimini,* on which he was working in his flower-decorated prison room. Hunt confessed later, "I had more value for lords than I supposed—." [n] He imagined that with the aid of his prim wife, Marianne, "a good domestic female," he might reform Byron.

But Byron did not give as much thought to Hunt at the time as the latter imagined. He was too preoccupied with other friends and affairs. Hobhouse had left on an extensive Continental tour. Byron wrote to Lady Melbourne: " . . . he is ye oldest, indeed ye only friend I have, and . . . in parting with him, I lose 'a guide, philosopher and friend' I neither *can* nor *wish* to replace." [n] Without the guiding hand of Hobhouse he felt helpless to escape his own weaknesses. He felt that his only recourse was literally to run away from the entanglements which seemed to be closing in on him. In spite of himself, his meeting with Caroline had unsettled him. He could see clearly enough through her ruses, but felt unable to deal with them with adequate harshness, and he could not answer for what might happen if he did not get away. To complicate his feelings still more, he had met Miss Milbanke again—the only girl who had ever refused him. She later wrote in her "Auto-Description": "I was extremely agitated on seeing him—and offered my hand for the first time.

He turned pale as he pressed it. Perhaps—unconscious as I was —the engagement was then formed on my part." [n]

Lady Oxford arrived in London on May 27. It may well have been her encouragement that induced Byron to stand up in the House of Lords on June 1 and present the petition of Major John Cartwright for the right to petition for the "Reform" of Parliament. Cartwright, a Radical who was anathema to Tories and Moderate Whigs alike, had been collecting petitions for reform, but had been obstructed, as Byron said in his speech before the House, "by the interposition of an abused civil and unlawful military force." [n] Just how radical Byron's speech then seemed it is difficult now to realize unless we view it in relation to hysterical periods in our own more recent history when it has taken a brave man to stand up against popular fears and prejudices and speak out for the constitutional rights of free speech. Byron's only defender was the pariah Earl Stanhope, disowned by all parties for his "Jacobinism." The very fact that, like Stanhope, Byron felt that he had burned his bridges behind him as far as Parliamentary influence or success was concerned made it possible for him to speak his mind with a freedom unthinkable to a tactful politician. Nevertheless, he recognized the speech as his swan song in Parliament and as a farewell to the career in public life that he had so long contemplated.

Byron now turned his attention to the publication of *The Giaour,* the Oriental tale he had begun the previous year and to which he was continually adding lines. He offered the copyright to Murray, for he had cooled toward Dallas. Although too polite to send the obsequious parson away, he had begun to find him a great bore and, as he told Hobhouse, "a *damned* nincom. assuredly." [n] His other concern was to get money to follow the Oxfords abroad. He accompanied Lady Oxford to Portsmouth on June 13, but was back in London by the 20th. Lord Oxford had been embarrassed by the open and constant attachment, but when that most patient of husbands complained, his lady brought him to heel: "on *her* threatening to fill up my 'carte blanche' in her own way, he [Lord Oxford] quietly ate his own words and intentions," Byron reported to Lady Melbourne.[n]

On the evening of June 20 he was invited to Lady Jersey's to meet Mme de Staël, the great literary lady of the Continent who had just arrived in London. Along with Sheridan and others he was amazed by the talents of this extraordinary woman, who talked the men into silence. "She interrupted Whitbread . . . she misunderstood Sheridan's jokes for assent; she harangued, she lectured, she preached English politics to the first of our English Whig politicians, the day after her arrival in England." [n] At first he was inclined to spar with her. But he recognized her intelligence, and in the end he came to respect and even to like her, though he kept, as he did concerning most of his friends, a reserve of caustic and cynical judgment which in no way detracted from his liking or loyalty. "She *thought* like a man," he said, "but, alas! she *felt* like a woman. . . ." [n]

Byron gave Lady Blessington an amusing account of how he had once baited that eloquent oracle by telling her that he considered her novels *Delphine* and *Corinne* "as very dangerous productions to be put into the hands of young women. . . . that all the moral world thought, that her representing all the virtuous characters in 'Corinne' as being dull, common-place, and tedious, was a most insidious blow aimed at virtue. . . ." [n] She interrupted him with gesticulations and exclamations, but Byron rushed on delighted to think that he, who had the reputation of a rake, could lecture Mme de Staël on morals.

Byron was a little piqued when the Oxfords sailed without his having a chance to see his *amie* again. "To tell you the truth," he wrote Lady Melbourne, "I feel more *Carolinish* about her than I expected." [n] In the meantime, he was glad of his sister's presence in London. He took her to Lady Davy's on June 27 to see Mme de Staël. "I think our being together before 3d people will be a new *sensation* to *both*." [n] They had not met since before Byron went abroad and had seen each other very little since Augusta's marriage to her cousin Colonel Leigh in 1807. He had invited her to Newstead in the melancholy autumn of 1811, but domestic obstacles had prevented their meeting. She was now the mother of three daughters. When he visited Cambridge, she was away from her home at Six Mile Bottom near Newmarket. Then came the publication of *Childe Harold* and the absorbing occupations of love and fame.

Augusta, five years older than her brother, was soft and voluptuous in face and figure, and though she was not exactly beautiful, she had the handsome Byron profile and large eyes, the long lip that could curl and pout like his own, a tendency to frown as he did and to laugh unrestrainedly at his witticisms. The motherly interest in her "Baby Byron," whom she remembered as a handsome and amusing boy, the willingness to indulge his whims and forgive his weaknesses and foibles, the understanding she displayed with regard to his unhappy early life with his mother and his sensitivity to his lameness—all this added to his feeling that he had found a friend and relative in whose presence he could be unrestrained. Instinctively they understood each other because they were Byrons. And the consanguinity was balanced by the charm of strangeness engendered by their separate upbringing; in their formative years they had escaped the rough familiarity of the brother-sister relationship.

They were both shy in company, but Augusta was proud of her brother's fame and impressed with the easy manner he had acquired in the London drawing rooms. He was so droll and comical and so handsome and highly admired. They developed an easy familiarity. He was soon calling her "Guss," a nickname which he distorted into "Goose" on account of her silly, incoherent gabbling. They laughed together with perfect understanding. It was pleasant to have a sympathetic near relative when one had never had such a luxury. He was fortunately free from any serious liaison, and he took her to the theater and balls and assemblies during July.

In the midst of this calm, Caroline Lamb forced her attention on Byron once more. At a small waltzing party at Lady Heathcote's she seized his hand and pressed a sharp instrument against it, saying, "I mean to use this." Byron replied: "Against me, I presume?" and passed on. Then after supper, according to his own account, he met her again and "told her it was better to waltz; 'because she danced well, and it would be imputed to *me*, if she did not.' " [n] But there may have been more bitterness in his tone or his manner than he was aware of or admitted to Lady Melbourne. Caroline at any rate was maddened by it. She later told Medwin: " . . . he had made me swear I was never to Waltz." When Lady Heathcote asked her to lead the dance, "I did so—but whispered to Lord Byron 'I conclude I may walze [*sic*] *now*' and he answered sarcastically, 'with every body in turn—you always did it better than any one. I shall have a pleasure in seeing you.'" [n] After that she saw Byron going in to supper with Lady Rancliffe and clasped a knife. In passing he said, " . . . if you mean to act a Roman's part, mind which way you strike with your knife—be it at your own heart, not mine—you have struck there already." [n] Then she ran away with the knife, and when some ladies tried to take it from her, cut her hand. The episode was taken up by the scandal columns the next day and Caroline realized that she had gone beyond the pale of the shoddy but inexorable moral code of her own class: she had made a public scene.

Through all this Byron was continuing his preparations to go abroad. The trip now seemed possible, for Claughton was willing to pay the balance of the down payment on Newstead. Byron had already run up fantastic bills for equipment and presents to take with him. In addition to swords, guns, and other military items, and mahogany dressing boxes and writing desks, he ordered a vast number of uniforms, nankeen trousers by the dozen, scarlet and blue staff officers' coats, nine very rich gold epaulets, etc., bringing his tailor's bill up to £896 19s. 6d. To his bill from Love and Kelly, Goldsmiths and Jewellers, he added to the balance brought forward from 1812 (£657 10s.) another £315 for seven fine gold boxes for presents to foreign potentates.[n]

On July 13 he applied to John Wilson Croker, Secretary to the Admiralty, to get him a passage in a ship of war bound for the Mediterranean, but so unsettled was his mind that he could at the same time make plans much nearer home. On that same day he wrote to Moore: "I am amazingly inclined—remember I say but *inclined*—to be seriously enamoured with Lady A[delaide] F[orbes]." [n] But that was only a passing fancy.

Cut loose from any serious attachment for the first time since fame had descended on him, Byron was moving in society more than ever. Looking back at this period later he wrote: "I liked the Dandies; they were always very civil to *me*, though in general they disliked literary people. . . ." [n] It was in the salons of *haut ton* rather than in the Dandy gatherings that Byron was bored. And the salons that patronized literary men were often just as bad or worse. "In general, I do not draw well with literary men," he wrote in 1821, "not that I dislike them, but I never know what to say to them after I have praised their last publication. There are several exceptions, to be sure; but then they have either been men of the world, such as Scott, and Moore, etc., or visionaries out of it, such as Shelley, etc.: but your literary every day man and I never went well in company. . . ."[n] Even if they were personal friends like Matthew Gregory ("Monk") Lewis, he found them tiresome. "Lewis was a good man," he recalled, "a clever man, but a bore, a damned bore. . . ."[n]

There were a few, however, whom Byron genuinely admired for superior talents and individuality. Richard Brinsley Sheridan was one. "Poor dear Sherry! I shall never forget the day he and Rogers and Moore and I passed together; when *he* talked, and *we* listened, without one yawn, from six till one in the morning."[n] Byron admired him as an orator, though he heard him only once in Parliament, but more as a wit. "Poor fellow! he got drunk very thoroughly and very soon. It occasionally fell to my lot to convoy him home—no sinecure, for he was so tipsy that I was obliged to put on his cock'd hat for him: to be sure it tumbled off again, and I was not myself so sober as to be able to pick it up again."[n]

Augusta, after staying about three weeks in London and seeing her brother constantly, had returned to Six Mile Bottom, where Byron visited her twice for several days (her husband was off somewhere following the races), and after the second visit took her back to London with him. On August 5 he made the rather surprising announcement to Lady Melbourne: "My sister, who is going abroad with me, is now in town. . . ."[n] How deeply involved he was in that quarter Lady Melbourne did not know, though he wished and yet feared to tell her. Several times he was on the brink of revealing his secret, but he drew back, though he continued to hint at something dark and forbidding. "When I don't write to you, or see you for some time you may be very certain I am about no good. . . . don't be angry with me—which you will, however; first, for some things I have said, and then for others I have not said."[n] Augusta had gone home and the uncertainty of his mind and plans increased. He was burning with his guilty secret and had an irresistible urge to reveal it. He even wrote to Moore on August 22: ". . . I am at this moment in a far more serious, and entirely new, scrape than any of the last twelve months,—and that is saying a good deal. It is unlucky we can neither live with nor without these women."[n]

Within the next few days he revealed the nature of that scrape so clearly to Lady Melbourne that she was shocked and frightened for him. An intimacy with Augusta, though she was only his half-sister, had implications associated with the dreadful word "incest" which alone could have shocked Lady Melbourne more than the blatant and open scandal of his liaison with Caroline Lamb.*

For Byron there would be a fatal fascination in such an intimacy because it was a "new sensation" and because it was forbidden. The sense that he was fated to succumb to a love that had "something of the terrible" in it is reflected very clearly in the Oriental tales in which he poured out the "lava" of his inner conflicts. He was haunted, too, by a feeling that he could not escape the inheritance of the dark deeds of his ancestors. Had he seen the letters of his father to *his* sister Frances Leigh (mother of Augusta's cousin-husband) which hint at an intimacy like his own with his half-sister, Byron would have been even more convinced that this was his destiny.[n]

Augusta, good-hearted and amiable, was intent only upon giving pleasure to the brother of whom she was fond. She was scarcely aware of abstract moral questions, though she was full of pious phrases and gave Bibles to her family and friends. Byron was too reflective not to think of the dangers and the social consequences, and too self-torturing not to feel remorse. Like many of his contemporaries, he had escaped rationally but not emotionally from the Calvinistic sense of sin that haunted his subconscious mind. But that fatalistic conception of human depravity blended with his own weakness to drive him on to further violation of his inhibitions. Eventually, under the alarmed prodding of Lady Melbourne, he abandoned his project of taking Augusta abroad, but only after he had given up the voyage entirely.

While Byron was occupied, and shaken, by these events, he was surprised to receive a long letter from Annabella Milbanke. On August 22 she sat down to tell him guardedly, under the guise of disinterested friendship, how she felt. "It is my nature to feel long, deeply, and secretly," she told him, "and the strongest affections of my heart are without hope." This fiction that she had another suitor was concocted to justify her refusal of By-

* The extant evidence that Byron had sexual relations with Augusta does not amount to *legal* proof. All that can be said is that the circumstantial evidence in Byron's letters to Lady Melbourne cannot be ignored, and that certain aspects of his life and correspondence cannot be explained sensibly in any other terms.

ron's proposal of the year before. She added some moral advice: "No longer suffer yourself to be the slave of the moment, nor trust your noble impulses to the chances of Life." And then she asked him to keep her letter a secret from Lady Melbourne, who would not "understand the plainness of my intentions."[n]

Three days later she wrote in her commonplace book some thoughts on "the character most interesting to me." Such a one must have: "Active but secret piety—Independence of worldly interests. Undeviating rectitude. Dauntless Sincerity. Pride of Honor. Reserve as to the softer feelings—yet all the capacity for affection which accompanies strong and delicate Sensibility. Generosity and every virtue composing perfect disinterestedness. —Sound Sense and Consistency."

And then she opened a second chapter: "Characters determined by Disappointment—or by the want of that happiness which according to Mad[e] de Stael, consists in the concordance of our situation with our faculties.—Hence arise, in most instances, either Misanthropy or Despondency. . . . Natural benevolence changed to suspicious coldness. Every kind impulse is repelled by the consideration of man's unworthiness."[n]

The shrewd Miss Milbanke perhaps supposed that no one could have guessed that she had a certain young lord in mind when she analyzed the second type of character. Nor was she aware of how tragically inadequate was her conception of Byron's nature.

Eager for any diversion from his present quandary and flattered that he was still in her thoughts, Byron ignored her sermonizing and replied with some words that were exciting beyond Annabella's expectations: "L[y] M. was perfectly correct in her statement that I preferred you to all others; it was then the fact; it is so still." And then followed a confession that startled Annabella and made her regret that she had raised the specter of another lover: "I must be candid with you on the score of friendship. It is a feeling towards you with which I cannot trust myself. I doubt whether I could help loving you. . . ."[n]

Byron had kept the secret of their correspondence as much for his own sake as hers. With her present knowledge of his affairs, Lady Melbourne might not approve. But he soon saw that his confidante was eager to throw Annabella in his way again, probably as an antidote to his more dangerous liaison. She sent him Annabella's specifications for a husband. His reply would have shocked the poor girl. "I return you the plan of A[nnabella]'s spouse elect, of which I shall say nothing because I do not understand it. . . . She seems to have been spoiled—not as children usually are—but systematically Clarissa Harlowed into an awkward kind of correctness, with a dependence upon her own infallibility which will or may lead her into some egregious blunder. I don't mean the usual error of young gentlewomen, but she will find exactly what she wants, and then discover that it is much more dignified than entertaining."[n] Byron knew what her "friendship" meant. He later told Medwin: "The tenor of her letter was, that although she could not love me, she desired my friendship. Friendship is a dangerous word for young ladies; it is Love full-fledged, and waiting for a fine day to fly."[n]

He now wrote Annabella with less restraint. She could take him as he was or leave him: "Your sweeping sentence 'on the circles where we have met' amuses me much when I recollect some of those who constituted that society. After all, bad as it is, it has its *agrémens*. The great object of life is sensation—to feel that we exist, even though in pain. It is this 'craving void' which drives us to gaming—to battle—to travel. . . ."[n]

And now the "craving void," the irresistible desire for "sensation" drove him, despite his better judgment, back to Augusta. He told Lady Melbourne that he intended to leave town on the 9th of September, "and as I am sure you would get the better of my resolution, I shall not venture to encounter you."[n] But he postponed his journey. "I am nevertheless very much perplexed. . . . You say, 'Write to me, at all events'; depend upon it, I will, till the moment arrives (if it does arrive) when I feel that you ought not to acknowledge me as a correspondent. . . ."[n]

Through July and August Byron was busily writing and sending to Murray, that "Anak of stationers," additions to *The Giaour*, that "snake of a poem," which had been "lengthening its rattles every month." First published June 5, it was selling rapidly and was now going into a fifth edition, each with new lines added. The purple passages as well as the hints of secret crimes, which rumor was now willing to ascribe to the author, increased the public interest. For him it was an escape from, or at least a catharsis for, the emotional crisis of recent events.

Yes, Love indeed is light from heaven;
A spark of that immortal fire
With angels shared, by Alla given,
To lift from earth our low desire . . .

I grant my *love imperfect, all*
That mortals by the name miscall;
Then deem it evil, what thou wilt;
But say, oh say, hers *was not Guilt!* [n]

Still in a feverish state of anxiety and perplexity, Byron set off for Six Mile Bottom, probably on September 11. What happened there can only be guessed. Did Byron reveal to Augusta the dangers of their going abroad together? Or had she begun to feel remorse and to draw back from the intimacy they had established? Something of the sort may be surmised from his leaving her on the 13th to go to Cambridge, where he and Scrope Davies drank six bottles of wine in an evening. It is evident that he was seeking some kind of escape, for on the day he arrived in London he wrote to John Murray: "Will you pray enquire after any ship with a convoy *taking passengers*. . . . I have a friend and 3 servants—Gibraltar or Minorca—or Zante." [n]

Shortly after that, he accepted the invitation of his friend Wedderburn Webster to visit him at Aston Hall, near Rotherham. From there on the 21st he reported to Lady Melbourne on that absurd household: "Feeling feverish and restless in town I flew off. . . . The place is very well, and quiet, and the children only scream in a low voice. . . . [Webster] preached me a sermon on his wife's good qualities, concluding by an assertion that in all moral and mortal qualities, she was very like 'Christ!!!' " [n] Byron laughed until Webster was angry.

If Lady Melbourne hoped that her protégé would find a diversion from his dangerous attachment in a flirtation with Lady Frances Webster, she was disappointed, for Byron returned to London after a few days, drawn irresistibly to Augusta. He wrote his confidante: "I have tried, and hardly, too, to vanquish my demon; but to very little purpose, for a resource that seldom failed me before did in this instance. I mean *transferring* my regards to another. . . . and *here* I am—*what* I am you know already." [n] And in the mood of the moment he made a new will, leaving half of his property to his cousin and heir, George Anson Byron, and half to Augusta.

In London he found a letter waiting him from Annabella Milbanke. She had been disappointed by his letter stating that the "object of life is sensation." It was far too "Byronic." He was still fascinated by this strange, intelligent girl, but he would not falsify his character merely to gain her approval. "You don't like my 'restless' doctrines—I should be very sorry if you did; but I can't stagnate nevertheless." Then he turned to a subject which she accused him of having avoided—"an awful one—'Religion.' " He would avoid it no longer: "I was bred in Scotland among Calvinists in the first part of my life which gave me a dislike to that persuasion. . . . If I do not at present place implicit faith in tradition and revelation of any human creed, I hope it is not from want of reverence for the Creator but the created. . . ." [n]

He was now showing her letters to Lady Melbourne, who saw little hope of any diversion there, for no romantic feeling appeared in his analysis of Annabella's self-delusions. He wrote: "The epistles of your mathematician (*A.* would now be ambiguous) * continue; and the last concludes with a repetition of a desire that none but papa and mama should know it; why *you* should not, seems to me quite ludicrous, and is now past praying for. . . ." [n]

Byron was planning to go back to Aston, but he did not tell Lady Melbourne that it was only because he hoped his sister would join him there. He pursued the theme of the farcical Webster, who had written that the Countess he was pursuing was "inexorable." "What a lucky fellow—happy in his obstacles." As for Lady Frances, "She evidently expects to be attacked, and seems prepared for a brilliant defence; my character as a *roué* has gone before me, and my careless and quiet behaviour astonished her so much that I believe she began to think herself ugly, or me blind—if not worse." [n]

Lady Melbourne, however, no doubt saw more clearly than Byron suspected that his interest in Lady Frances was piqued beyond what he would at present admit, being uncertain of her response. And indeed within three days after his return to Aston

---

* This indicates that "A" in his thoughts and his letters to Lady Melbourne now referred to Augusta; he later distinguished them by referring to "your A [Annabella]" and "my A [Augusta]."

he found that his passive attitude was paying dividends, and his interest in the game had increased. He announced: "I have made love, and if I am to believe mere *words* (for there we have hitherto stopped), it is returned." They were in the billiard room when Byron "made a speech." They went on with the game "without *counting the hazards*." He then wrote her a letter to which she wrote an answer, "a very unequivocal one too, but a little too much about virtue, and indulgence of attachment in some sort of etherial process, in which the soul is principally concerned, which I don't very well understand, being a bad metaphysician; but one generally *ends* and *begins* with platonism, and, as my proselyte is only twenty, there is time enough to materialize." Then in a burst of confidence Byron concluded: "I remember my last case was the reverse, as Major O'Flaherty recommends, 'we fought first and explained afterwards.'" He added a postscript to his letter at six that evening: "This business is growing serious, and I think *Platonism* in some peril."[n]

Lady Melbourne perceived that, despite the cynicism of his account, one part of Byron was deeply involved emotionally in the affair, for Lady Frances had the combination of innocence and experience which most appealed to him. But without relinquishing the seriousness of his ardor, he perceived with clear detachment the high comedy and knew that he had a perfect audience in his confidante. He came to savor the reporting of it more than the poignancy of the experience itself. Lady Melbourne could enjoy it because she thought he was now safe from worse entanglements. But when it became serious, he felt that he should justify himself: "Anything, you will allow, is better than the *last;* and I cannot exist without some object of attachment."[n]

The next day he reported: "I believe little but 'l'occasion manque,' and to that many things are tending. . . . We have progressively improved into a less spiritual species of tenderness, but the seal is not yet fixed, though the wax is preparing for the impression."[n] The ironic dénouement came sooner than Byron expected in the spacious ruins of Newstead, where the whole party had gone in the middle of October. He reported to Lady Melbourne that he had been "a little too sanguine as to the *conclusion*. . . . One day, left entirely to ourselves, was nearly fatal—another such *victory*, and with Pyrrhus we were lost—it came to this. 'I am entirely at your *mercy*. I own it. I give myself up to you. I am not *cold*—whatever I seem to others; but I know that I cannot bear the reflection hereafter. Do not imagine that these are mere words. I tell you the truth—now act as you will.' Was I wrong? I spared her. . . . It was not the mere 'No,' which one has heard forty times before, and always with the same accent; but the *tone*, and the aspect—yet I sacrificed much—the hour *two* in the morning— . . . the Devil whispering that it was mere verbiage, etc." [n]

Byron's sentiments were now involved and he was completely hooked, ready for anything—duel, divorce, or scandal. He offered to go away with her, but she declined on his account, she said. "Poor thing—she is either the most *artful* or *artless* of her age (20) I ever encountered. . . . The most perplexing—and yet I can't prevail upon myself to give it up—is the caressing system. In her it appears perfectly childish, and I do think innocent; but it really puzzles all the Scipio about me to confine myself to the laudable portion of these endearments." [n] In quiet desperation Byron drank too much after dinner, and then about midnight, goaded by the boasting Webster, emptied his skull cup, which held more than a bottle of claret, at one draft, and was put to bed by Fletcher. When he had time to reflect on his failure to be "decisive" with Lady Frances, he could not regret his restraint. "I do detest anything which is not perfectly mutual," he wrote his confidante. "Perhaps after all, I was her dupe—if so —I am the dupe also of the few good feelings I could ever boast of. . . ." [n]

Back in London, Byron's passion began to wane, but his loyalty continued. Lady Frances continued to write, with a mixture of boldness and prudence, letters using "two words, 'effusions' and 'soul,' rather oftener than befits out of the circulating library." But he assured Lady Melbourne: " . . . you really *wrong* me too, if you do not suppose that I would sacrifice everything for Ph—. I hate sentiment, and in consequence my epistolary levity makes you believe me as hollow and heartless as my letters are light." [n] But he had already begun to be occupied with other persons and other things. His friend Hodgson was attached to a Miss Tayler, whose mother would not consent to marriage because of Hodgson's debts. Byron rode all night in a post chaise to interview the mother and assure her that Hodgson would soon be free of debt, and then, returning to London, took his friend to Hammersley's Bank and there ordered £1,000 transferred to his credit as an outright gift. This was probably the money he had set aside for his trip abroad.

The agitations of his own frustrated love found relief again in poetic composition. On November 4 he wrote to Lady Melbourne: "For the last three days I have been quite shut up; my mind has been from *late* and *later* events in such a state of fermentation, that as usual I have been obliged to empty it in rhyme, and am in the very heart of another Eastern tale. . . ." [n] He had finished it in a week and he told Moore: "All convulsions end with me in rhyme; and to solace my midnights, I have scribbled another Turkish story. . . ." [n] The theme of incest (Selim and Zuleika were brother and sister in the first draft) had a powerful attraction for him, but he shied away from it at the last and made the lovers cousins. Both Augusta and Lady Frances were very much in his mind when he wrote *The Bride of Abydos*, the title he finally gave the tale.

His preoccupation with Lady Frances had caused him to neglect both Augusta and his mathematical correspondent at Seaham. But on November 8 he wrote an apology to his sister, and he sent a facetious epistle to the "Princess of Parallelograms" two days later. As for mathematics, he wrote, "The only part I remember which gave me much delight were those theorems (is that the word), in which, after ringing the changes upon A B and C D, etc., I at last came to 'which is absurd'—'which is impossible,' and at this point I have always arrived and I fear always shall through life. . . ." [n] In his next letter he made a confession of a more serious sort: "I by no means rank poetry or poets high in the scale of intellect. This may look like affectation, but it is my real opinion. It is the lava of the imagination whose eruption prevents an earthquake. . . . I prefer the talents of action—of war, or the senate, or even of science,—to all the speculations of those mere dreamers. . . ." [n]

On November 14, just after he had sent his new Eastern tale to Murray, Byron began a journal. The first entry was a self-examination and recapitulation of his life, which he now saw as mostly a record of disillusionment and failure. "At five-and-twenty, when the better part of life is over, one should be *something;*—and what am I? nothing but five-and-twenty. . . .

What have I seen? the same man all over the world,—ay, and woman too. . . . I wish one was—I don't know what I wish. It is odd I never set myself seriously to wishing without attaining it—and repenting." [n] In his discontent he thought of marriage, the one thing he had not tried. But at the same time, disillusioned by observation, he shied away from it. The failure of his political career still rankled and contributed to his general dissatisfaction. "I have declined presenting the Debtors' Petition, being sick of parliamentary mummeries." [n] He was going out again a great deal, but enjoying it less. He avoided dinners when he could and wished he were in the country where he could get exercise "instead of being obliged to *cool* by abstinence. . . . I should not so much mind a little accession of flesh. . . . But the worst is, the devil always came with it,—till I starved him out,—and I will *not* be the slave of *any* appetite." [n] He generally found the best company with the Hollands. He went to Drury Lane and to Covent Garden, where he had taken Lord Salisbury's box for the season. But he most enjoyed dining in a small company with the kind of people he liked: J. W. Ward, George Canning, and John Hookham Frere, onetime writers for the *Anti-Jacobin,* and "Conversation" Sharp, "a man of elegant mind, and who has lived much with the best—Fox, Horne Tooke, Windham, Fitzpatrick, and all the agitators of other times and tongues." [n]

Neither social life nor writing, however, could suppress Byron's feeling that his powers were being wasted. He concluded that "no one should be a rhymer who could be any thing better. . . . To be the first man—not the Dictator—not the Sylla, but the Washington or the Aristides—the leader in talent and truth —is next to the Divinity!" [n]

His love affair with Frances Webster was fast degenerating into a kind of comedy which he could not help enjoying while at the same time continuing to feel the serious pangs of the attachment. He sent her his portrait by Holmes, "dark and stern,— even black as the mood in which my mind was scorching last July, when I sat for it [in the first headlong sweep of his passion for Augusta]." [n] Thinking of his sister's undemanding fondness, he told Lady Melbourne: "Do you know I am much afraid that that perverse passion was my deepest after all." [n]

To his journal he could confess that he found most pleasure

in writing to Lady Melbourne—". . . and her answers, so sensible, so *tactique*—I never met with half her talent. If she had been a few years younger, what a fool she would have made of me, had she thought it worth her while,—and I should have lost a valuable and most agreeable *friend.* Mem. a mistress never is nor can be a friend. While you agree, you are lovers; and, when it is over, any thing but friends."[n] He may well have been thinking of his affair with Caroline Lamb.

The Bride of Abydos was published by Murray on December 2, and was an immediate success. Six thousand copies were sold within a month, and Byron was again the literary idol of the London season. When Murray offered him a thousand guineas for the copyrights of his last two Oriental tales, he was tempted because he needed the money, but he still could not violate his own pride by accepting it. He was invited everywhere, but he declined more dinners than he accepted. One night at Lord Holland's he was talking with Thomas Campbell when their host brought out a vessel that looked like a Catholic censer and, approaching Campbell, exclaimed: "Here is some *incense* for you." Campbell, a little piqued at his rival poet's popularity, replied: "Carry it to Lord Byron, *he is used to it.*"[n]

Indecision, purposelessness, and ennui crept over Byron as the days passed. He had taken to smoking cigars, as he had formerly chewed tobacco, to prevent the gnawing pangs of hunger when he abstained from food in order to keep down his weight. On December 7 he wrote in his journal: "Went to bed, and slept dreamlessly, but not refreshingly. Awoke, and up an hour before being called; but dawdled three hours in dressing. When one subtracts from life infancy (which is vegetation),—sleep, eating, and swilling—buttoning and unbuttoning—how much remains of downright existence? The summer of a dormouse."[n]

Dr. John Allen, a friend of Lord Holland, had lent Byron "a quantity of Burns's unpublished and never-to-be-published Letters." They made a curious impression on him. "They are full of oaths and obscene songs. What an antithetical mind!—tenderness, roughness—delicacy, coarseness—sentiment, sensuality—soaring and grovelling, dirt and deity—all mixed up in that one compound of inspired clay!

"It seems strange; a true voluptuary will never abandon his

mind to the grossness of reality. It is by exalting the earthly, the material, the *physique* of our pleasures, by veiling these ideas, by forgetting them altogether, or, at least, never naming them hardly to one's self, that we alone can prevent them from disgusting.'"[n]

Byron was no doubt aware of how closely he had touched here upon the paradox of his own nature. In the need to veil the "*physique*" of his pleasures in some ideal essence in order to escape from the grossness of reality, and in the realistic earthiness that prevented him from ever achieving that goal, he came closer to Burns than he wished to admit.

The demon gnawing at his vitals during the first half of December had been aggravated by his feeling for Augusta and the struggle against it, for no matter how much he fought it, he could not escape the feeling that no woman was so comforting and satisfying to his self-esteem as Augusta, so yielding to his every wish, so sensuous and undemanding, and so motherly and protective at the same time. As his resolution weakened, his letters to Lady Melbourne fell off, for he knew her sentiments and fears on the subject. On the 15th his sister arrived in London, and on the 18th his journal ceased. "It is quite enough to set down my thoughts,—my actions will rarely bear retrospection."[n]

On the day he laid his journal aside, he began another Eastern tale, this one more self-revealing than any he had yet written. Prose could no longer carry the burden. "*I suoi pensieri in lui dormir non ponno*"—"His thoughts cannot sleep within him"—was the motto he chose from Tasso's *Gerusalemme Liberata.* At the head of the first canto of this new tale, *The Corsair,* he placed the famous lines from Dante's *Inferno:*

> *nessun maggior dolore,*
> *Che ricordarsi del tempo felice*
> *Nella miseria . . .**

With Conrad, the hero of *The Corsair,* he could range vicariously over "the dark blue sea" of the lovingly remembered Greek Archi-

* *Inferno,* Canto V. Byron later translated this canto as "Francesca da Rimini," rendering the lines of Francesca:

> *The greatest of all woes*
> *Is to remind us of our happy days*
> *In misery . . .*

pelago. There too he could find another kind of freedom—the expansion of spirit which the creative process gave and which permitted him to look through the veil of fiction at his own ego with a frankness not possible even in his letters to Lady Melbourne. Once started, he wrote feverishly far into the night at his Bennet Street lodgings, and he carried the manuscript with him when he accompanied Augusta home. He had completed the first draft by the 27th, when he was back in London, having written nearly two hundred lines a day.

Before the year ended, two ghosts of Byron's past bobbed up to haunt him. Mary Chaworth-Musters, whose husband, Jack Musters, was now riding after other game than foxes, wrote to the lame boy with whom she had flirted as a girl and who was now a famous poet. If he came into Nottingham he would find "a *very old* and *sincere friend* most anxious to *see you.*" Byron wrote a cautious reply. She had been ill, and she hinted at the infidelity of her husband. "You would hardly recognize in me the happy creature you once knew me. I am grown so thin, pale, and gloomy." [n] This was hardly the letter he wanted from his old sweetheart, and it did not make him eager to see her. He preferred to preserve the dream he had been nursing through the years.

A voice out of the more recent past was that of Annabella Milbanke, who wrote the day after Christmas. She too had been ill, and she did not yet have strength enough to "regain truth" by confessing to her white lie about another attachment, but she wanted to remind him that she was still his "faithful friend." After receiving her previous letter at the end of November he had written in his journal:

"Yesterday, a very pretty letter from Annabella, which I answered. What an odd situation and friendship is ours!—without one spark of love on either side. . . . She is a very superior woman, and very little spoiled, which is strange in an heiress—a girl of twenty—a peeress that is to be, in her own right—an only child, and a *savante*, who has always had her own way. She is a poetess—a mathematician—a metaphysician, and yet, withal, very kind, generous, and gentle, with very little pretension. Any other head would be turned with half her acquisitions, and a tenth of her advantages." [n]

CHAPTER XII

1814

Dangerous Liaisons

The Corsair, WHICH BYRON had written "*con amore,* and much from *existence,*"[n] occupied him during the first days of January. He wrote a dedication to Moore, in which he proclaimed rashly ". . . for some years to come, it is my intention to tempt no further the award of 'Gods, men, nor columns.' " In that dedication he further flouted the public by challenging his readers to seek autobiography in his writing if they wished; he would no longer defend or deny.

Drawn by stronger ties than ever to Augusta since her visit to London in December, Byron was perplexed by the attachment of Lady Frances, who seemed "embarrassed with constancy."[n] As the romance of this country idyl cooled, he was inclined to be chagrined at the frustration of the affair. He told Lady Melbourne, "If people will stop at the first tense of the verb 'aimer,' they must not be surprised if one finishes the conjugation with somebody else—."[n] He was further embarrassed by the overtures of Mary Chaworth-Musters. After receiving a second letter from her, Byron confided to Augusta: "M. has written again—*all friendship*—and really very simple and pathetic—*bad usage—paleness—ill health*—old *friendship—once—good motive*—virtue—and so forth."[n]

Things had become altogether too complicated, not, Byron felt, because he had been aggressive in wickedness, but because he was too eager to avoid hurting the feelings of the women who had become attached to him. He wrote to Lady Melbourne: "I cannot conceive why the D—— I should angle with so many baits for one whom, all the world will tell you, belonged to him probably before he was born. But when they give me a character for 'Art,' it is surely most mistaken. . . ."[n]

Lady Melbourne was hoping for some strong attachment or even marriage to settle him, but the Mediterranean world was enticing him again with memories of his irresponsible youth. Ambition had lost its savor. "I never *won* the world," he told Lady Melbourne, "and what it has awarded me has always been owing from its caprice. My life here is frittered away. . . ."[n] And he confessed: ". . . the kind of feeling which has lately absorbed me has a mixture of the terrible, which renders all other, even passion (pour les autres) insipid to a degree. . . ."[n]

He considered rather speculatively and hopelessly his confidante's remedy. "I wish I were married," he told her, "and don't care about beauty, nor *subsequent* virtue—nor much about fortune. I have made up my mind to share the decorations of my betters—but I should like—let me see—liveliness, gentleness, cleanliness, and something of comeliness—and *my own* first born. Was ever man more moderate?"[n] He continued, "I have no heart to spare and expect none in return; but, as Moore says, 'A pretty wife is something for the fastidious vanity of a *roué* to *retire* upon.' . . . The only misery would be if I fell in love afterwards—which is not unlikely, for habit has a strange power over my affections."[n]

Augusta had arrived in London, and on Monday the 17th they set out for Newstead in his huge coach. An extremely heavy snow had made the Great North Road all but impassable. Once having arrived, they were snowbound in the rambling, empty Abbey. The great park was blanketed in white, and snow weighted down the giant oaks and obliterated the roads. The weather was an excuse for not visiting Mary Chaworth, and the presence of Augusta made existence cozy. He wrote Lady Melbourne: ". . . we never yawn or disagree; and laugh much more than is suitable to so solid a mansion; and the family shyness makes us more amusing companions to each other than we could be to any one else."[n]

The roads did not clear until the 1st of February, but even then Byron was reluctant to leave Newstead. He had done no writing, which meant that he had reached a temporary state of contentment. Before leaving on February 6, he had an enthusiastic letter from Murray announcing the amazing success of *The Corsair,* beyond anything he or the publisher had dreamed of. Murray wrote in high excitement: "I sold, on the day of publication,—a thing perfectly unprecedented—10,000 copies. . . ." [n] In a little more than a month thereafter Murray printed seven editions and sold twenty-five thousand copies. This phenomenal popularity was caused partly by the fine descriptive passages, particularly the lush lines beginning

> *Slow sinks, more lovely ere his race be run,*
> *Along Morea's hills the setting Sun . . .*

Then the swift narrative, sustained by an authentic background derived from personal observation in Greece, heightened the interest. But, most of all, readers were entranced by Conrad, the pirate, "That man of loneliness and mystery," in many of whose traits it was easy to see the thinly veiled portrait of the author. "He left a Corsair's name to other times,/ Linked with one virtue, and a thousand crimes."

In one quarter, however, the publication of *The Corsair* aroused a journalistic storm of hostility. His "Lines to a Lady Weeping," attacking the Prince Regent, had appeared at the end of the volume and were thus identified as Byron's. The Tory *Morning Post* attacked him ferociously as "a sort of R[ichar]d III. —deformed in mind and *body,*" Byron told Murray. "The *last* piece of information is not very new to a man who passed five years at a public school." [n] But when Murray, with his Tory associations and his publisher's fears, omitted the lines from the second edition, Byron insisted that they be replaced. He assured Lady Melbourne: "I have that within me, that bounds against opposition." [n]

Hobhouse had returned from his Continental tour on February 8 and soon after met Byron at Covent Garden. He wrote in his diary: ". . . there I saw and joined my dearest Byron, in a private box. It is long since I have been so happy. I came home with him and sat until near four in the morning." [n] Byron, equally delighted, wrote in his own journal: "He is my best friend, the most lively, and a man of the most sterling talents extant." [n] They met frequently thereafter. On the 19th they saw

Kean in Richard III at Drury Lane. Byron was excited by the performance: "By Jove, he [Kean] is a soul! Life—nature—truth without exaggeration or diminution." [n]

Hobhouse had returned with "ten thousand anecdotes of Napoleon, all good and true." And this set Byron to thinking about the man who had fascinated him since his schooldays. "Napoleon!—this week will decide his fate. All seems against him; but I believe and hope he will win—at least, beat back the invaders. What right have we to prescribe sovereigns to France? Oh for a Republic! . . . The greater the equality, the more impartially evil is distributed, and becomes lighter by the division among so many—therefore, a Republic!" [n]

But neither Hobhouse's company nor the distractions of society and the theater could wean him from his obsessive thoughts. Through February his restlessness increased. He could not sleep and he could not read. He failed to find relief even in writing. In November he had begun a comedy and a novel, but burned them because they "ran into *reality*." [n] Now he tore two pages out of his journal. Discretion seemed more important than confession. And yet his journal was his sole confidante. In it he analyzed his own weakness: "There is something to me very softening in the presence of a woman,—some strange influence, even if one is not in love with them—which I cannot at all account for, having no very high opinion of the sex. But yet,—I always feel in better humour with myself and every thing else, if there is a woman within ken. Even Mrs. Mule, my firelighter,—the most ancient and withered of her kind,—and (except to myself) not the best-tempered—always makes me laugh,—no difficult task when I am 'i' the vein.' " [n]

To add to his self-dissatisfaction, reflection and reading had convinced him that his literary work was of little value. Too much of it was the mere "lava of the imagination" that had been produced to prevent an earthquake in his personal life. He was unhappy at having been diverted from what he thought his true bent in Popean satire, begun so propitiously in *English Bards, and Scotch Reviewers,* by the sudden popularity of his poems of self-revelation like *Childe Harold* and the Oriental tales. He confessed to Moore: ". . . I have lately begun to think my things have been strangely over-rated; and, at any rate, whether or not, I have done with them for ever. I may say to you what I would not say to every body, that the last two were written, *The Bride* in four, and *The Corsair* in ten days,—which I take to be a most humiliating confession, as it proves my own want of judgment in publishing, and the public's in reading things, which cannot have stamina for permanent attention." [n]

Byron was now posing for Thomas Phillips, the popular portrait painter, but when he went into society it was from politeness and inertia rather than inclination. He preferred the wit and intellect he encountered at the home of Rogers, where Sheridan, Mackintosh, and "Conversation" Sharp turned to anecdotes of a former time. With increasing interest in the literature and society of the eighteenth century, Byron delighted more in these vicarious journeys into the past than in the insipid gatherings of the Regency *haut ton*. "*What plays!* what wit!—*hélas!* Congreve and Vanbrugh are your only comedy," [n] he exclaimed after seeing Sheridan's adaptation of Vanbrugh's *Relapse* (*The Trip to Scarborough*).

Through all his disquiet Byron continued his correspondence with Annabella Milbanke, sometimes writing her facetiously and sometimes seriously. Something different from the ordinary feminine allure attracted him to this pretty girl who preached him sermons. Perhaps he delighted a little in seeing how far she was shockable. As for the consolations of religion, he told her, "it is a source from which I never did, & I believe never can derive comfort. If I ever feel what is called devout, it is when I have met with some good of which I did not conceive myself deserving—and then I am apt to thank any thing but mankind. . . . Why I came here, I know not—where I shall go it is useless to enquire. In the midst of myriads of the living & the dead worlds—stars, systems, infinity—why should I be anxious about an atom?" [n]

But still she wrote him her humorless letters. Byron frightened her a little but also piqued her interest by saying that he would like to see her, hinting darkly that he wanted to consult her on some personal problems. She began consulting her parents as to the most suitable time to invite him to Seaham. Commenting on a rumor that she had refused him a second time, she wrote: "In avoiding the possibility of being in a situation to refuse, I cannot consider myself as having refused." [n] That was her practical application of metaphysics to the problem of letting him know that she would be willing to have him propose again. Byron did not miss her meaning. He recorded in his journal on March 15: "A letter from *Bella,* which I answered. I shall be in love with her again if I don't take care."[n]

The bitterest winter on record added to Byron's restlessness and gloom, for he was never quite happy when he could not be out of doors, on horseback and in the sun as he had been in Greece. To keep in exercise, he went back to sparring with his old friend and boxing master, Jackson. "My chest, and arms, and wind are in very good plight," he recorded, "and I am not in flesh. I used to be a hard hitter, and my arms are very long for my height (5 feet 8½ inches). At any rate, exercise is good, and this the severest of all. . . ."[n] On March 28 he moved into new quarters on the ground floor of Albany House in Piccadilly. It was a large apartment, about thirty by forty feet, which he had subleased for a term of seven years from Lord Althorp.

No longer able to resist the appeals of Augusta, who was alone, anxious, and approaching her confinement, Byron set off for Six Mile Bottom on April 2. He remained with his sister until the 7th. Hobhouse and Scrope Davies had expected him at Cambridge on the 5th, but he did not go there. Back in London he wrote Lady Melbourne with ironic seriousness: "[Colonel] L[eigh] was in Yorkshire; and I regret not having seen him of course very much."[n]

Byron, who had maintained an irrational admiration for Napoleon since fighting for his statue at Harrow, was stunned by news of his defeat and abdication. "I mark this day!" he wrote in his journal. "Napoleon Buonaparte has abdicated the throne of the world. . . . Alas! this imperial diamond hath a flaw in it. . . ."[n] Despite his idle boast that he would not publish again, he wrote an *Ode to Napoleon Buonaparte,* ninety lines in one day, and sent it off to Murray. Though it was published anonymously, the inscription to Hobhouse marked it as his, and it was soon the talk of the town.

In the meantime, Hobhouse was determined to make his way to Paris "whilst yet any part of the Napoleon vestiges yet remain." Byron too was enthusiastic and agreed to accompany him, but his loyalty to his sister at the critical time made him give up the project. After anxious days he learned that Augusta had given birth to a daughter on April 15. She named the child

Elizabeth Medora.* Lady Melbourne apparently asked Byron whether the danger he ran in this affair was really worth while, for he replied: "Oh! but it is 'worth while,' I can't tell you why, and it is not an 'Ape,' and if it is, that must be my fault; however, I will positively reform. You must however allow that it is utterly impossible I can ever be half so well liked elsewhere, and I have been all my life trying to make someone love me, and never got the sort that I preferred before. But positively she and I will grow good and all that, and so we are *now* and shall be these three weeks and more too." [n]

Byron's most casual correspondence at this period reflects the depression of his spirits. He remained in a state of indecision whether to go back to Augusta or to accept the invitation to Seaham. In the meantime, he wrote Moore, "I have bought a macaw and a parrot, and have got up my books; and I box and fence daily, and go out very little." [n] This was a foretoken of the strange menagerie of birds and animals that he was to build up around him in the years to come, which served as a kind of escape from the exigencies of human relationships and an outlet for his recurrent misanthropy.

By the time the formal invitation came from Seaham, Byron began to be a little fearful of what it might lead to. "Seriously," he told Lady Melbourne, "if she imagines that I particularly delight in canvassing the creed of St. Athanasius, or prattling of rhyme, I think she will be mistaken. . . . I am not now in love with her; but I can't at all foresee that I should not be so, if it came 'a warm June' (as Falstaff observes), and, seriously, I do admire her as a very superior woman, a little encumbered with Virtue. . . ." [n]

His confidante was aware that one of the chief reasons for his indecision was that he was receiving almost daily letters

---

* When Medora Leigh grew up, she believed that she was Byron's daughter. (See *Medora Leigh: A History and an Autobiography,* edited by Charles Mackay; and Roger de Vivie de Régie, *Le Secret de Byron.*) It is curious, however, that Byron never made any direct reference to his paternity; nor did he show more interest in Medora than in Augusta's other children; and it was unlike him not to acknowledge his illegitimate offspring. But of course this was a special case, and with all his recklessness he must have been aware of the dangers to his sister's if not to his own reputation. It may well be that some of the evidence was destroyed. No positive proof survives on either side of the question.

from Augusta, and she urged him to go. "If you don't like her you may talk only on the Prayer Book & if you should like her that subject will cease to make way for another without any effort." [n] As for the "other A," Lady Melbourne still thought Augusta to blame for the beginning and the continuance of the affair, but Byron came to her defense: ". . . by that God who made me for my own misery, and not much for the good of others, *she* was not to blame, one thousandth part in comparison. She was not aware of her own peril till it was too late, and I can only account for her subsequent '*abandon*' by an observation which I think is not unjust, that women are much more *attached* than men if they are treated with anything like fairness or tenderness." [n]

Byron concluded his letter with a bit of self-knowledge won from experience. "Your niece has committed herself perhaps, but it can be of no consequence; if I pursued and succeeded in that quarter, of course I must give up all other pursuits, and the fact is that my wife, if she had common sense, would have more power over me than any other whatsoever, for my heart always alights on the nearest *perch*. . . ." [n]

To Byron's delight Moore returned to town at the beginning of May, and they went about together a great deal, particularly to the theater, which Byron had come to love more and more since he had discovered the acting of Kean. On the 4th, in response to Moore's request that he write the words for a song, Byron sent him his impassioned stanzas:

I speak not, I trace not, I breathe not thy name,
There is grief in the sound, there is guilt in the fame:

* * *

We repent, we abjure, we will break from our chain,—
We will part, we will fly to—unite it again!

Moore encouraged him in his determination to drown the heaviness of his spirits in social dissipation. On the 7th they saw Kean's first performance of Iago in *Othello*. "Was not Iago perfection? particularly the last look," he wrote Moore the next day. "I am acquainted with no *im*material sensuality so delightful as good acting. . . ." [n]

Byron tried to find distraction in some mild flirtations.

Moore wanted to promote a match with Lady Adelaide Forbes, but Byron was making tentative overtures to another. He sent the Albanian dress in which Phillips had painted him to Miss Mercer Elphinstone (a red-haired girl of a calm disposition whom he had met at Melbourne House) for a masquerade costume.* But his heart was not in these mild courtships. He told Lady Melbourne: ". . . I am trying to fall in love, which I suppose will end in falling *out* with somebody. . . ."[n] Early in May he sent Augusta £3,000 to clear the debts of her wastrel husband.

On May 14 he began a sequel to *The Corsair*. Conrad, the pirate, now called Lara, was the same brooding lonely man. Byron's demons were dispersed by the rapid composition of the poem, which, he later told Murray, "I wrote while undressing after coming home from balls and masquerades, in the year of revelry 1814."[n] He had flung himself into the social stream with abandon, and in the absorption of the moment, for he really liked people, with real and not affected pleasure. He took Hobhouse to "a small party of 100" at Lady Jersey's. He accompanied Moore to see Kean again, and joined in a supper party for the actor after the performance. He was later so affected by Kean's acting of Sir Giles Overreach that he was seized with a sort of convulsive fit.[n]

Out of boredom and curiosity Byron succumbed to one of the many entreaties for an interview that he received from strange young ladies, sometimes brazen, sometimes expressing concern for his soul and his poetry. This girl, Henrietta d'Ussières, was a foreigner and wrote rather amusing letters. She was a Swiss, whose father, she said, had been an active liberal and believer in the doctrines of Rousseau. She wanted to call on the famous poet but was frightened and cautious. He wrote her a remarkable letter of assignation. He could write humorously because he did not care whether she came or not. "Excepting

---

* This Albanian dress, the one in which Byron had sat for his portrait to Thomas Phillips in 1814, is now attractively displayed in the Bath Museum of Costume. Mrs. Doris Langley Moore, the Byron scholar and founder of the museum, discovered it among the possessions of Lord Lansdowne, great-great-grandson of Miss Mercer Elphinstone. The original life-size portrait is in the residence of the British Ambassador in Athens. A smaller copy of it made by Phillips is at John Murray's in London.

your compliments (which are only excusable because you don't know me) you write like a clever woman, for which reason I hope you *look* as *un*like one as possible. I never knew but one of your country—Me de Stael—and she is frightful as a precipice. . . . If you will become acquainted with me, I will promise not to make love to you unless you like it. . . ."[n]

Finally she came and was admitted to the poet's private apartment. For half an hour they talked and she was charmed. She could not have been too hideous, for he ended by making her proposals which shocked her. She retreated and wrote tremblingly, "The first half hour I was so happy! . . . but for the remainder of the evening it was no longer Lord Byron. . . . is it thus you would repay so much admiration—so much esteem?"[n] It is probable that he apologized and was forgiven, for she continued to write and to try to see him, but he was bored, and for him the rest was silence.

And now he entered more fervently than ever into the social whirl. Years later he recalled that summer with nostalgic pleasure. He wrote to Moore from Italy in 1822: "Do you recollect, in the year of revelry 1814, the pleasantest parties and balls all over London?"[n] It was "the summer of the sovereigns." The close of the war on the Continent had brought during June a flock of royalty, statesmen, and generals of the victorious allies to London, among them Alexander, Czar of Russia, the King of Prussia, Metternich, the great hero Blücher, and all their train. The end of a long winter and a long war had loosed the spirit of festivity. Never had London society been gayer. Byron, though he kept a cynical reserve regarding the sovereigns, enjoyed it in his self-forgetful moods more than he pretended. One evening Webster dragged him against his will to a party at Lady Sitwell's, where they saw Byron's cousin, the beautiful Mrs. Wilmot, in mourning with spangles on her dress. The next day he wrote a gemlike lyric about her (later prefixed to the *Hebrew Melodies*):

> *She walks in Beauty, like the night*
> *Of cloudless climes and starry skies* . . .

Moore had left town, and Byron had some thoughts of going to Newstead, partly with the notion of calling on Mary Chaworth, who had written him more than fifty letters and had stirred up recollections that were hard to repress despite his worldly wisdom. But by June Mary was only in the fringe of his desire. What he really cherished was a memory, and he was half attracted, half repelled at the thought of meeting the object of that vision in the too-solid flesh. A sentimental correspondence based on the past was safest. Besides there was a perch near at hand that seemed soft and accessible. At Earl Grey's he had met again Lady Charlotte Leveson Gower, a friend of Augusta. He told himself he was interested in her because of Augusta, but she was very young, very pretty, and shy as an antelope, the qualities which most appealed to him in a woman. But there was the obstacle that she was "one of the tribe of the Carlisle's," and he had never made up his quarrel with his guardian.

Caroline Lamb had grown troublesome once more. A few friendly gestures at public gatherings easily convinced her that she could break down Byron's defenses again. She was aware that he could not be cruel to her when he met her face to face. Lady Melbourne knew it too, and she was alarmed. Caroline had no knowledge of Byron's current amours, but, crazed by neglect and jealousies, she bedeviled her former lover. During June she began to invade his chambers at all hours, indiscreetly unannounced. His detestation was increased by the fact that she did have a curious fascination despite her emaciation. She had grown so thin that he once said in anger he was "haunted by a skeleton." [n] He assured Lady Melbourne that "all bolts, bars, and silence can do to keep her away are done daily and hourly." [n] But these precautions were ineffective. One day she entered his apartment at the Albany, and finding him out, picked up Beckford's *Vathek* from the table and wrote on the first page: "Remember me!" When Byron saw what she had done, in the irritation of the moment he wrote under those words:

Remember thee! remember thee!
Till Lethe quench life's burning stream
Remorse and Shame shall cling to thee,
And haunt thee like a feverish dream!

Remember thee! Aye, doubt it not.
Thy husband too shall think of thee:
By neither shalt thou be forgot,
Thou false *to him, thou* fiend *to me!*

But Byron was not through with her yet. On July 1, though he had little admiration for the Duke of Wellington, he accompanied Hobhouse to a grand masked ball in the Duke's honor at Burlington House. All the *haut ton* was there, and also some of the demi-monde, safe behind dominoes. Byron, dressed as a monk, was annoyed by Caroline's pranks, for she threatened to reveal herself and him, and he "scolded her like her grandfather" for "displaying her green *pantaloons* every now and then." [n]

Caroline's last private interview with Byron may have taken place some time before this. She is a very unreliable witness, though there is generally some grain of truth in her statements. She wrote to Medwin in 1824: ". . . the last time we parted for ever, as he pressed his lips on mine (it was in the Albany) he said 'poor Caro, if every one hates me, you, I see, will never change—No, not with ill usage!' & I said, 'yes, I *am* changed, & shall come near you no more.'—For then he showed me letters, & told me things I cannot repeat, & all my attachment went." [n] The last statement is obviously untrue, for she continued to bedevil him, and her attachment lasted the rest of his life, and hers. It may be, however, that Byron in exasperation did show her some of Augusta's letters, and that in a fit of rage he told her something of his attachment to boys such as Rushton, for during the Byron separation fracas, she told Lady Byron of both these aberrations.[n]

The second day after the masquerade, July 3, Byron left for Six Mile Bottom. He had not seen Augusta since early April, before the birth of her daughter Medora. He did not care for babies in their "mewling and puking" stage, squalling and making messes. After three days he left for Cambridge and opened many bottles with Hobhouse and Scrope Davies. Back in London he was vexed, but helpless to do anything about Claughton's, and Hanson's, procrastination. "I have brought my pigs to a Mussulman market," he wrote Moore. "If I had but a wife now, and children, of whose paternity I entertained doubts, I should be happy, or rather fortunate, as Candide or Scarmentado." [n]

Part of his exasperation was caused by the fact that he wished to finish the business and leave for the seashore with Augusta, who had come to town and was staying in the London Hotel in Albermarle Street. Hodgson, then spending his holiday at Hastings, found him a house, retired and near the sea, but it was July 20 before he could get away. There was another reason for his anxiety to leave London. Mary Chaworth, his once idealized "Morning Star of Annesley," was threatening a visit to the city, and he had no desire to meet her in a London drawing room. He and Augusta escaped to Hastings just before she arrived.

In this house by the sea Byron was nearly happy for three weeks. The ocean itself always revived his spirits. He was reading *Waverley,* which he did not yet know to be Scott's, and which he thought "the best and most interesting novel I have redde since—I don't know when."[n] Hobhouse had written urging him to come to town to vote against a government bill calling for severer enforcement of the laws in Ireland, but conviviality and country pleasures now meant more to him than Parliamentary oratory. To Moore he wrote: "I have been swimming and eating turbot, and smuggling neat brandies and silk handkerchiefs,—and listening to my friend Hodgson's raptures about a pretty wife-elect . . . and walking on cliffs, and tumbling down hills and making the most of the *dolce far-niente* for the last fortnight. I met a son of Lord Erskine's, who says he has been married a year, and is the 'happiest of men' . . . so, it is worth while being here, if only to witness the superlative felicity of these foxes, who have cut off their tails. . . ."[n]

But Byron was already secretly preparing his own fall from bachelorhood. He had continued to receive Annabella's "prim and pretty" letters but had not quite known how to reply. She was perplexed as to how to explain her feelings, and so wrote him a confused letter full of cryptic sentences (it was as difficult for her not to run into abstractions as it was for Byron not to be concrete and direct). She acknowledged an attachment for him, but an "imperfect" one.[n] He sat down immediately to answer her, but, reading her ambiguities again, he was not sure that he understood her at all. "Pray then write to me openly and *harshly,*" he wrote, ". . . you are the last person I would wish to misunderstand." He added: ". . . my memory is still retentive enough not to require the repetition that you are attached to another."[n]

Poor Annabella was back where she had started. How could she ever "regain truth" without confessing that she had told a lie about her attachment to George Eden? Her answer, in spite of its verbiage and analytical nuances, committed her even further while she tried to indicate that she was heart-free without admitting that she was in love with Byron.

In the meantime other plots were developing. While they were at Hastings, Byron and Augusta both came to the conclusion that the only solution for their impasse was for Byron to take a wife. He later told Lady Melbourne: "She wished me much to marry, because it was the only chance of redemption for *two* persons. . . ." [n] Augusta thought her young friend Lady Charlotte Leveson Gower, whom her brother had admired, was much better suited to him than the more austere Miss Milbanke, whose letters he showed her. She began negotiations at once, but the skittish epistles of the young girl left the matter indeterminate, while Byron was growing restive and irritable, not sure that he wanted anything to happen. "I am, in some respects, happy," he wrote Moore, "but not in a manner that can or ought to last. . . ." [n]

Byron and Augusta were back in London by August 10. Two matters had lifted him out of his inertia. Hanson had written that Claughton had finally agreed to sacrifice £25,000 of the down payment and give up the contract for Newstead, and had sent some news that made Byron even more eager to quit Hastings. Mrs. Chaworth, he said, "looks ill and talks of taking the Sea Air at Hastings—She tells me she is separated from Mr. C. —her Children are with her." [n]

On the 10th Byron had written to Annabella. She had asked for an honest avowal of his feelings, and he replied with a frankness that startled her: "I will answer your question as openly as I can. I did—do—and always shall love you; and as this feeling is not exactly an act of will, I know no remedy, and at all events should never find one in the sacrifice of your comfort." [n] He had fairly tossed the matter into Annabella's lap, and she did not quite know what to do with it.

In London, Byron was already thinking of other things. Murray had published *Lara* anonymously in a volume with Rogers's sentimental tale *Jacqueline*. But Byron's authorship was soon known, and Murray had already sold six thousand copies, and when he decided to divorce the two poems, he paid £700 for the copyright of *Lara*. This was the first time Byron had ever accepted money for his own use from the publisher.

The anxiety about his financial affairs, the uncertainty of

the future (Augusta was still in pursuit of the shy "antelope," Lady Charlotte, for him), the apparent hopelessness of his advances to Annabella, who continued to pique his interest more than the pretty but insipid girl of his sister's choice, and the feeling that, after all, no one satisfied him quite so well as Augusta herself—all contributed to put him on edge. Then came Annabella's disappointing reply to his open confession. In her "prim and pretty" style she told him at great length why she ought not to select him as her example on earth and her guide to heaven, but tempered this with the assurance that George Eden had never had a place in her heart and that she had great esteem and affection for her present correspondent. Byron answered with a curtness that would have stopped any girl less self-complaisant than Annabella: "Very well—now we can talk of something else." [n]

On the 20th he signed the papers which terminated Claughton's contract and put Newstead back in his hands, and the following day he departed with Augusta and her children for the Abbey. There he lapsed once more into good-humored ennui. He took time to write at length to Annabella, recommending some historical reading, including the skeptical Gibbon. In the meantime, Byron was enjoying his native woods and lakes. He caught perch and carp in the lake, swam, rowed a boat, and broke soda-water bottles with his pistols.

Miss Milbanke wrote again to say that she would attempt to read the whole of Gibbon, but expressed regret that he was not coming to Seaham. "If we could have met, all my apparent inconsistencies would have been dispelled." [n] Byron replied: "You accuse yourself of 'apparent inconsistencies.' To me they have not appeared—on the contrary, your consistency has been the most formidable apparition I have encountered." [n]

All this time Augusta, the dear "goose," had been corresponding furiously with the "antelope" in a language of innuendoes and backing and starting which Byron confessed he could not understand. Lady Charlotte was even more incomprehensible in her simple way than the "Princess of Parallelograms," some of whose angles might be narrow, but whose lines were straight. Then Augusta's fine scheme blew up and the antelope escaped in a flutter of fear. She was "seized with a panic, on some family scheme . . . of a *compact elsewhere*." [n] The family scheme worked, for Lady Charlotte was married before the end of the year to young Howard, Earl of Surrey, only son of the Duke of Norfolk.

Byron told Lady Melbourne: "I then said to X [Augusta], after consoling her on the subject, that I would try the next myself, as she did not seem to be in luck." [n] The letter he wrote was not a very ardent proposal. "A few weeks ago you asked me a question which I answered. I have now one to propose—to which, if improper, I need not add that your declining to reply to it will be sufficient reproof. It is this. Are the 'objections' to which you alluded insuperable? or is there any line or change of conduct which could possibly remove them? . . . there are few things I would not attempt to obtain your good opinion. . . . Still I neither wish you to promise or pledge yourself to anything; but merely to learn a *possibility* which would not leave you the less a free agent. . . . With the rest of my sentiments you are already acquainted. If I do not repeat them it is to avoid—or at least not increase—your displeasure." [n]

It seems evident that Byron had not intended this as a proposal, but merely as a feeler to determine whether the door was shut to him, as Annabella's ambiguous letters had suggested. He was giving her plenty of opportunity to withdraw, and, not to make his own position too ridiculous, he would not waste love language on anything so tentative. The fateful letter was posted on September 9. In the interim between that day and the 18th, when her reply came, he became increasingly ill at ease and uncomfortable. By the 13th he was no longer sure whether he wanted a favorable reply; in any case, he would steel himself against failure by preparing an escape—the old one, departure for the Mediterranean. There was the possibility of joining Lady Oxford, who was still traveling on the Continent. He turned to Hobhouse: ". . . if a circumstance (which may happen but is as unlikely to happen as Johanna Southcote [*sic*] establishing herself as the real Mrs. Trinity) * does not occur—I have thoughts of going direct and directly to Italy—if so, will you come with me?" [n]

* Joanna Southcott (1750–1814), a fanatical religionist, imagined that she was pregnant by the Holy Ghost and was going to give birth to a new savior, Shiloh. After her death the "pregnancy" was diagnosed as dropsy.

There is little doubt that Byron's letter caused a sensation at Seaham. Their late correspondence had not led Annabella to expect it. She was a clever girl, but she was too innocent to know that even a designing woman of great experience could hardly have pursued tactics better calculated to arouse Byron's interest and curiosity than those she had naturally followed, keeping him at bay until she was sure of his intentions. But his letter melted all her reserve. She refused to see it as a tentative proposal, and considered it a real one. She easily got her parents' consent, for she had always had whatever she wanted. Now she had no doubt that she wanted Byron. She wrote the same day: ". . . I am and have long been pledged to myself to make your happiness my first object in life. . . . I will *trust* to you for all I should look up to—all I can love."[n]

She had sent this letter to the Albany, and it was forwarded to Byron along with a letter from her father. Not knowing whether he was yet in town, she sent another note to Newstead. Annabella later recorded what Augusta told her: "He received it at dinner. . . . His remark to her as he handed the letter across the table, looking so pale that she thought he was going to faint away, was 'It never rains but it pours.' "[n] Augusta said Annabella's letter "was the best and prettiest she ever read."[n]

Byron sat down to write her in a warmer style than that of his restrained proposal—but his letter was still far from being the passionate outpouring of an ecstatic lover. "Your letter has given me a new existence. It was unexpected, I need not say welcome. . . . I know your worth & revere your virtues as I love yourself and if every proof in my power of my full sense of what is due to you will contribute to *your* happiness, I shall have secured my own. It *is* in your power to render me happy—you have made me so already. . . . from the moment I became acquainted my attachment has been increasing, & the very follies—give them a harsher name—with which I was beset & bewildered, the conduct to which I had recourse for forgetfulness only made recollection more lively & bitter by the comparisons it forced upon me in spite of Pride—and of Passions, which might have destroyed but never deceived me."[n]

Long afterward Annabella said of this letter: "I thought that I might now show him all I felt. . . . I wrote just what was in my heart."[n] Certainly while Byron was writing it, he meant what he said, but with what uncanny precision did he unconsciously give his correspondents what they wanted to hear! That letter fed her false hope that she could reform him, that he wanted to be "corrected" by her. By what a narrow margin he had missed one fate and found another! A stroke of the pen could have turned the balance and taken him abroad.

CHAPTER XIII

1814

The Princess of Parallelograms

BYRON'S GREATEST CONCERN was to get Lady Melbourne's blessing on his engagement. Although she probably congratulated herself on having had nothing to do with the second proposal, he credited her with having brought them together. "After all it is a match of *your* making, and better had it been had *your* proposal been accepted at the time. I am quite horrified in casting up my moral accounts of the two intervening years. . . ." But he could not resist a little of the flippancy his confidante was accustomed to. "I wish one or two of one's idols had said No instead; however, all that is over. I suppose a married man never gets anybody else, does he? I only ask for information." [n]

When Lady Melbourne taxed him with lack of seriousness, however, he replied: "You very much mistake me if you think I am lukewarm upon it . . . if I think she likes me, I shall be exactly what she pleases; it is her fault if she don't govern me properly, for never was anybody more easily managed." [n]

Lady Melbourne would have been surprised indeed had she known with what earnestness and what frequency and at what length he wrote to his fiancée. He was determined to convince Annabella (and himself) that her confidence had not been misplaced, that he would try to be everything that she wished. Their dispositions were not so different as she supposed, he said, and even if they were, that need be no obstacle to their happiness. And the next day he continued his clarification and apologia, taking up the matter of religion. "I am rather bewildered by the variety of tenets than inclined to dispute their foundation. In a word, I will read what books you please, hear what arguments you please. . . . You shall be 'my Guide, Philosopher, and Friend'; my whole heart is yours. . . ."[n]

All Annabella's reserves were broken. The reply to her acceptance, she recorded later, "was gratifying beyond words to describe—it made me feel inspired with the purest happiness."[n] But her self-assurance soon melted, and she was a little frightened at the prospect of their meeting. Could she live up to the ideal he had built on the basis of her letters? His confidence in her consistency and his insistence that she should be his guide gave her some uneasiness too. Now that she had surrendered, she wanted him to do the leading. ". . . my ideas wait to be fixed by yours," she told him. "My pursuits easily adapt themselves, and to share them, of whatever kind, must be my greatest pleasure."[n]

But, despite his genuine desire to please and to adapt himself to the wishes of his fiancée, Byron soon began to feel uncomfortable in his new role as a man legitimately engaged to an innocent and inexperienced girl. All his serious love affairs since his boyish attachment to Mary Chaworth had had something of the forbidden and the clandestine in them. He understood better how to make love to a married woman than to a single girl, especially one who knew more of books than of life. This inner disquietude appeared in letters to his sophisticated friends. In writing to Moore he covered his embarrassment with flippancy: "My mother of the Gracchi (that *are* to be), *you* think too strait-laced for me. . . . I must, of course, reform thoroughly. . . . She is so good a person, that—that—in short, I wish I was a better."[n]

Byron lingered a few days at Newstead. Augusta had urged him to go to Seaham at once, but he was in no hurry. He must journey to London first, not only to outfit himself properly for the trip, but also to get Hanson to arrange the sale of Newstead so that he could make a proper settlement on his bride-to-be. Besides, he hated to leave, perhaps for the last time, the ancestral estate he had always loved better than anything else in England. The freshness of early autumn was already enlivening the beauty of the great oaks in the park. As he wandered with

Augusta by the lake or in the cool woods, the melancholy of parting, of upheaval and change, seized him. The new step he was taking would part him not only from the ruined hall and its memories, but also from the only woman who had ever really understood him, who had ever given him unselfish and undemanding love and appreciation. They walked into the "Devil's Wood" back of the Abbey, where the "Wicked Lord" in his misanthropic solitude had set up his leering satyrs. There they carved their names deeply into the bark of an old elm.[n]

The next day (the 21st of September) they left, he for London, Augusta for Six Mile Bottom. Back in town, Byron felt concern for the trouble Caroline Lamb might make when she heard the news. Fortunately she took it calmly and decided to be romantic instead of troublesome. Her letter to him was sentimental and self-sacrificing. Byron was relieved and wrote her with a guarded kindness which she found icy and condescending. She sought relief in writing to Murray: "How has he disposed of the other unfortunates? I speak of them by dozens, you see."[n] She gave a grudging compliment to Annabella: "She is very learned and very good, and the top of her face is handsome. . . ."[n] But in another mood she said that Byron would "never be able to pull with a woman who went to church punctually, understood statistics and had a bad figure."[n]

Lady Melbourne was now more concerned with Augusta, however, than with Caroline. Could she be trusted to withdraw gracefully from Byron's life? Byron defended her, saying that it was she who had urged him to go immediately to Seaham. And when Lady Melbourne's anxiety continued, he assured her: "X is the least selfish person in the world. . . . her only error has been my fault entirely, and for this I can plead no excuse, except passion, which is none."[n] His confidante was justified in her suspicion that his passion would not die so lightly, but she did not know Augusta as well as did the brother. Indeed, Augusta loved Byron quite non-possessively, and wanted genuinely to see him happy. Now she was perfectly willing to go on loving him as a sister with motherly concern for his welfare. What had happened scarcely embarrassed her and made no difference in her feeling for him.

Byron wanted to put his finances in order before he paid his respects at Seaham. He proposed to make a settlement of £60,000, or £3,000 a year, on Annabella, to be secured on Newstead, which he still intended to sell. The money forfeited by Claughton could be used to pay the most pressing debts, and Hanson thought the Abbey would still sell for £120,000. He had heard that Sir Ralph Milbanke was "dipped," having foolishly overspent in electioneering in 1812. Annabella's prospects were chiefly from her uncle, Lord Wentworth. But Hanson could not arrange a time to meet with Sir Ralph's agents, and Byron remained in London and began to fret.

In the meantime the correspondence with Seaham continued. He told Annabella that he still relied on her to help him form a more rational pattern of life. He tried to see embodied in her all the things he had striven for in his pictures of the ideal. He recalled to her how she had appeared to him when he first saw her at Melbourne House: "There was a simplicity—an innocence—a beauty in your deportment & appearance. . . ." And then—oh, what gross rationalizations love can make—he continued: "In very truth—from my heart of hearts, dearest Annabella—I can now tell you that then—at the very time when I became unworthy of being yours—it was to you my attachment had turned. . . ." He concluded with an appeal that must have been disconcerting to a girl who had waited so long for a man whom she could esteem and look up to as superior to herself: ". . . I am whatever you please to make me. I am at least above the paltry reluctance of not submitting to an understanding which I am sure is superior to mine." [n]

The delay week after week (Hanson had skipped off to Devon on business without warning Byron) caused an awkwardness at Seaham, where Annabella had to pacify her parents and quiet her own misgivings. Byron's irritation with Hanson was extreme. He had asked Hobhouse to be his "groomsman," but felt that he could set no date for his departure until business matters were settled.

While he was thus distracted, he had received a letter from a young lady who signed herself "Eliza." There was nothing novel in this. But when she called on him on October 24, all flustered and romantic, he was touched by her innocence and gave her a £50 check as a subscription for her poems. That was better than having to read them. When he told her that he was going to be married, she was so overcome that he sent her home in his own carriage.

Two days later (on Saturday, October 29), Byron left for his first visit to his fiancée. He could not wait longer for Hanson. He stopped at Six Mile Bottom and remained until late Sunday. A germ of uneasiness about the marriage which might separate him from Augusta began to grow in his mind. His correspondence with Annabella had too much self-consciousness in it, too much tortured reflection. Why couldn't the girl be easy and natural? He needed that to overcome his own shyness. Only Augusta could do that, and they could laugh together quite unrestrainedly. Recalling episodes of her married life later, Annabella remembered that he had once told her "he only wanted a woman to laugh, and *did not care what she was besides.*" And at another time he said: "I can make Augusta laugh *at any thing.*" [n]

Byron proceeded northward by slow degrees, stopping at Newstead on the way. At Seaham, Annabella was doing her best to keep her anxious parents from perceiving how agitated she was. He had not said when he would arrive. She tried to hide from them too her chagrin that he had not overwhelmed her with poetry and presents. She would have been even more distressed if she had known how lavish he had been in gifts of jewelry and pictures to other women.

He did not arrive until Wednesday, November 2. Annabella was in her room reading when she heard the carriage. The suspense had put her on edge. She decided that she could not face him while others were watching, and contrived to come down to the drawing room when he was alone there. She found him standing by the chimney-piece. "He did not move forwards as I approached him, but took my extended hand and kissed it." [n] She did not think at all then, or perhaps she would have been hurt that he had not advanced to meet her, though she would have realized later that he was embarrassed by any movement that showed his lameness.

Two days later Byron wrote to Lady Melbourne of Annabella: "She seems to have more feeling than we imagined; but is the most *silent* woman I ever encountered; which perplexes me extremely." [n] Fortunately the ice was broken by the others, who were quite voluble. Whatever qualms the parents had were soon dissipated, for when Byron made an effort to be charming, he always charmed. He even listened patiently to Sir Ralph's tedious stories. The next day Annabella took Byron on her favorite walk along the cliff that faced the cold northern sea. She "tremblingly prest" his arm as he gazed on the rolling waters.[n] But, though he did not say it, the seas he loved washed warmer shores.

When she did not talk, he felt uncomfortably that she was watching him with a critical eye. He reported to Lady Melbourne: "I can't yet tell whether we are to be happy or not. I have every disposition to do her all possible justice, but I fear she won't govern me; and if she don't it will not do at all. . . . I never could love but that which *loves;* and this I must say for myself, that my attachment always increases in due proportion to the return it meets with, and never changes in the presence of its object. . . ."[n] By the fourth day he had thawed Annabella to a certain degree, but was not sure yet that he understood her. His report to his "Tante" was encouraging but not ecstatic: "Annabella and I go on extremely well. . . . She is, as you know, a perfectly good person; but I think, not only her feelings and affections, but her *passions* stronger than we supposed."[n]

Everything seemed to be going smoothly. The lawyers had arrived and had agreed without quibbling. Annabella was to have £20,000 settled on her, and she had certain expectations from her uncle, Lord Wentworth. But after a week the engaged couple were no further ahead in understanding. She could not comprehend his moods, though they were often caused by her own emotional ups and downs. He talked much of Augusta, "with sorrowful tenderness," and when he told her, "You remind me of her when you are playful," she tried to take that as a cue to her behavior, but found it impossible to drop her self-consciousness. He said: "If you had married me two years ago, you would have spared me what I can never get over."[n] Into this statement, made in a moment of pique, she worked all kinds of sinister meanings.

She came to the conclusion that he did not love her, and her overwrought imaginings led her to make a scene and offer to break the engagement. When Byron "fainted entirely away," she later recalled, "I was *sure* he must love me."[n] But Byron was now unnerved. He wrote Lady Melbourne on the 13th: "Do you know

I have grave doubts if this will be a marriage now? Her disposition is the very reverse of our imaginings. She is overrun with fine feelings, scruples about herself and her disposition (I suppose, in fact, she means mine). . . . The least word, or alteration of tone, has some inference drawn from it. Sometimes we are too much alike, and then again too unlike. This comes of system, and squaring her notions to the devil knows what."

Byron had found one way of quieting her upsurges of "feelings"—a silent way which he had tried very successfully with other women, though he had never attempted it before with a girl so innocent as Annabella. He told Lady Melbourne: "For my part, I have lately had recourse to the eloquence of *action* (which Demosthenes calls the first part of oratory), and find it succeeds very well, and makes her very quiet; which gives me some hopes of the efficacy of the 'calming process,' so renowned in 'our philosophy.' In fact, and *entre nous*, it is really amusing; she is like a child in that respect, and quite caressable into kindness. . . ."[n]

Annabella, frightened probably at what these caresses might lead to, apprehensive that her parents might sense what was going on, and dreading further scenes before the wedding, urged Byron to leave after he had been there just two weeks. She was not sure that she could control Byron or herself in his presence, though she told herself that it would be different after they were married. Byron was slightly piqued at being pushed away, and wrote the night after leaving: "If it will give you any satisfaction, I am as comfortless as a pilgrim with peas in his shoes, and as cold as Charity, Chastity, or any other virtue."[n]

Now that he was gone, Annabella could write him with less restraint; she was more at ease and could love the man of her imagination at a distance. "My own dearest, there is not a moment when I would not give my foolish head to see you. I knew it would be so, and think it a salutary chastisement for all my misdemeanours."[n]

Byron met Hodgson and Hobhouse at Cambridge, and was easily persuaded to remain in the vicinity until the 23rd to vote for Dr. Clarke, the Eastern traveler, who was a candidate for the professorship of anatomy. He spent the intervening days at Six Mile Bottom. Stricken by indolence and conflicting emotions, he wrote only once to Annabella, putting off on Augusta the task of keeping her pacified.

When Byron returned to Cambridge and walked into the Senate House to cast his vote, he was applauded by the students in the gallery. Hobhouse recorded: "This is, they tell me, unique. He looked as red as fire. Mansel [then Master of Trinity and Bishop of Bristol] and Dr. Clarke contended for the honour of escorting him."[n] The following day he and Hobhouse left for London, where Byron settled again into his bachelor life at the Albany. On the eve of leaving it forever, he found it good. On the 26th he went with Hobhouse to Drury Lane to see Kean in *Macbeth.* And a few days later they dined *intime* at Douglas Kinnaird's with the great actor, who was in fine form and full of anecdotes. This was the kind of evening Byron enjoyed, and he may well have compared it with his evenings at Seaham listening to Sir Ralph's twice-told tales.

Annabella was writing of the preparation of a wedding cake, and no doubt her parents would have liked a church wedding with all the squirearchy present. But Byron put a damper on that by insisting on a special license so they could be married at home "and mama will lend us a cushion each to kneel upon."[n] Continued delays gave Annabella a vague disquietude which she could ill conceal, and Byron's reassurance had a barb in it: "I am sure I wish we had been married these two years; but never mind—I have great hopes that we shall love each other all our lives as much as if we had never married at all."[n]

In the meantime he had distractions at the Albany. Eliza Francis, the young girl who had called on him before he went north, came again and got a warmer reception. She wrote in her narrative of the episode, the most important event in her life: "*all was sunshine.*" Byron "started from his chair and held out both his hands to me—and impulsively I put both mine into his—then he expressed his wish to be of service to me if he only knew how."

On her next visit she ventured to express a wish that he would introduce her to Lady Byron after his marriage. To that he gave an explicit negative, "lest *though* amiable and unsuspecting herself, those about her might put some jealous nonsense into her head. . . ." While they were talking she heard a noise and asked what it was. " 'Oh, only rats—we have a great many.' It seemed to me wonderful that rats should invade the Albany, but I remarked, 'Well, at any rate you have no children here.' 'Children!' cried Lord Byron, 'don't talk of them [;] you put me in a fever.' "

But he put out his hands once more "and again I placed mine in them. . . . As we stood together I ventured to ascertain the colour of his eyes, and I saw that though the finest eyes in the world they were not *dark* as I had fancied, but the large grey eye—the 'Mary Queen of Scots eye,' which is so beautiful—and his long dark eye-lash made them appear black—I never did behold such eyes before or since, and how long we should have stood—I looking up, and he looking down, I know not, but the door-bell rung, and he let go my hands."

The next two times she called, "his voice and manner were chilling," and then he confessed that he could do nothing for her because of the way in which he was situated. She left him, "standing by the fireplace looking after myself with such an expression of passionate love in his countenance as at once astonished and pained me." She did not return for ten days, but she could not get him out of her thoughts, and she came again to tell him it was her farewell visit. His reply shocked her: " 'Be it so—perhaps it is as well!' . . . he then took my hand and added —'perhaps had we met much oftener, our adventure might have ended as most such adventures do—. . . .' "

Eliza started up to go, but she reeled and almost fainted, and he put his arm around her waist and held her hand. ". . . as I stood with my head bent down, he lightly put aside some little curls which had escaped from under my cap behind and kissed my neck—this completely roused me and I struggled to free my hand, but he then clasped me to his bosom with an ardour which terrified me. . . ."

He reassured her. " 'Don't tremble, don't be frightened, you are safe—with *me* you are safe,' said he impetuously, and throwing himself into an armchair he drew me towards him—for a moment I clung to him—I loved for the first time and this must be my final parting with this transcendent Being. . . . he had drawn me down upon his knee, his arms were round my waist, and I could not escape. . . ." He kissed her cheek and was about to kiss her lips, but she started up, saying "I will go now," but he "clasped me to his bosom with frenzied violence while his passionate looks showed what his feelings were. But he was recalled to his senses by a few gentle words. . . . He opened wide his arms—'Go then,' he said, 'not for the world would I distress you.' " He asked if she would come again, but when she said she must not, he replied: "You are right—but do come, *yet you are very right.*"

As she advanced toward the door, he folded her in his arms again, and once more released her, but, Eliza recalled, "I turned to gaze once more at that Being I was resigning for ever and he stood near with a countenance so expressive of grief that I again flung myself into his open arms," and after another "wild embrace," "with a desperate effort I tore myself for ever from the truly noble Lord Byron." [n]

Byron had applied to the Archbishop of Canterbury for a special license, "because we can be married at any hour in any place without fuss or publicity," he told Annabella, who was guarding her misgivings from her parents and herself. The wedding cake was growing stale, the noble effort of Sir Ralph at an epithalamium was wasting in his desk. On December 24 Hobhouse set out with the reluctant bridegroom. They parted at Chesterford, Hobhouse going on to Cambridge and Byron to Six Mile Bottom. His Christmas was as unhappy as the one at Seaham, for Colonel Leigh was at home and Byron felt restrained. While he was there, he wrote a letter withdrawing from the engagement, but Augusta persuaded him not to send it. He did not pick up Hobhouse until late the next day. Hobhouse recorded in his diary that night: "Never was lover less in haste." [n]

They set out at noon the next day, the weather bitterly cold, snow on the ground. Byron, who had learned to love the warm south, perhaps felt that it was an omen. He "frankly confessed to his companion that he was not in love with his intended bride; but at the same time he said that he felt for her that regard which he believed was the surest guarantee of continued affection and matrimonial felicity. He owned that he had felt considerable repugnance in marrying before his pecuniary affairs were arranged. . . ." [n] That night Hobhouse wrote in his diary: "The bridegroom more and more *less* impatient." [n]

At eight o'clock in the evening, Friday, December 30, a week after leaving London, they finally arrived unannounced.

The strain of waiting had been very great upon everyone at Seaham. Hobhouse's first impression of Miss Milbanke was not favorable. "Miss is rather dowdy looking & wears a long & high dress (as B had observed) though she has excellent feet & ancles —the lower part of her face is bad, the upper expressive but not handsome." [n] Later he found her more attractive. "With me she was frank & open without little airs and affectations—of my friend she seemed doatingly fond, gazing with delight on his bold & animated bust—regulated however with the most entire decorum. B. loves her when present and personally as it is easy for those used to such indications to observe." [n]

The 1st of January was a Sunday, and the wedding was set for the next day. That night Byron said to his friend, "Well, H. this is our last night—tomorrow I shall be Annabella's." According to Moore, Byron "described himself as waking, on the morning of his marriage, with the most melancholy reflections, on seeing his wedding-suit spread out before him. In the same mood, he wandered about the grounds alone, till he was summoned for the ceremony. . . ." [n]

The marriage took place in the drawing room, with only two clergymen and Annabella's former governess Mrs. Clermont in attendance in addition to the family. "Miss M. was as firm as a rock and during the whole ceremony looked steadily at Byron—she repeated the words audibly & well. B. hitched at first when he said 'I George Gordon' and when he came to 'with all my worldly goods I thee endow' looked at me with a half smile." [n]

The ring which he placed on her finger was one found in the garden at Newstead when he was there with Augusta—his mother's wedding ring. The heavy gold band, made for the chubby Mrs. Byron, was too big for the delicate finger of Miss Milbanke. Her mother was on the verge of hysterics, for she had inner misgivings about this son-in-law who would have no proper wedding. She later wrote: "Neither before or *since* Marriage has he made any present to Lady B., not even the *common one* of a diamond Hoop ring. . . ." [n]

There was no reception. Lady Byron left the room and soon returned in her traveling dress. Hobhouse recorded: "Byron was calm and as usual—I felt as if I had buried a friend." [n] The carriage was waiting. The bridal couple had forty wintry miles to travel before nightfall to reach Halnaby Hall in Yorkshire, lent by Sir Ralph for their honeymoon. Hobhouse put a set of Byron's poems bound in yellow morocco in the carriage as a wedding gift to Lady Byron. His diary continues: "when I wished her many years of happiness—she said [']if I am not happy it will be my own fault[']—Of my dearest friend I took a melancholy leave."[n]

CHAPTER XIV

1815

The Fatal Marriage

THE RIDE TO HALNABY was as grim as the winter day. Both Byron and his bride were high-strung, and the excitement had left them emotionally tense. Byron, longing for the warmth of Mediterranean lands, disliked the cold and did not relish the tiresome journey to the bleak Yorkshire hall. He had time to reflect on the freedom he had lost, the innocent girl he had married, the settled routine that was expected of him. Annabella, still upset at leaving the home where she had been the adored and spoiled child for so long, was on the verge of tears, watchful of every nuance of his mood and ready to take offense at the seeming coldness of his self-absorption. With nothing to thaw the ice of their mutual guardedness, the chilling ride increased the irritability of the one and the sensitivity of the other.*

Annabella later said that they rode in silence until Byron, to relieve his feelings, broke out into "a wild sort of singing," perhaps one of the Albanian songs with which he later startled the Shelleys on Lake Geneva. As the carriage clattered into Durham,

* Of what really happened in the carriage, and later at Halnaby, we have only ex parte statements made after the separation, many of them second- and third-hand. Annabella's later statements, as they became more and more entwined with fantasy in her effort to make a case in self-justification, are hardly to be trusted. Byron had already noted, on his first visit to Seaham, that his "least word, or alteration of tone, has some inference drawn from it." (*LBC*, I, 290.) His own account, except for a few remarks to Medwin, was lost when his Memoirs were burned by his over-prudent friends after his death.

bells rang out for the wedding day of Miss Milbanke. Byron, who had been annoyed before by the premature ringing of the bells, said ironically, "Ringing for our happiness, I suppose?" As they proceeded on their way he turned on her ferociously: "It *must* come to a separation! You should have married me when I first proposed."[n]

That was Lady Byron's later remembrance of the events and conversations, as recorded by herself and others in whom she confided. Byron, who had heard some of these accusations, told Medwin: "I have been accused of saying, on getting into the carriage, that I had married Lady Byron out of spite, and because she had refused me twice. . . . if I had made so uncavalier, not to say brutal a speech, I am convinced Lady Byron would instantly have left the carriage. . . . She had spirit enough to have done so, and would properly have resented the affront. Our honeymoon was not all sunshine; it had its clouds . . . but it was never down at zero."[n]

It was after dark when they arrived at Halnaby Hall. The servants were gathered to greet them. But Byron, sensitive about his lame foot, walked away, leaving Annabella to face them. This was another slight that she later magnified. Byron must have soothed his bride's feelings by the silent method he had learned was most effective during his first visit to Seaham, for Moore later told Hobhouse that Byron had recorded in his Memoirs how he "*had* Lady B. on the sofa before dinner on the day of their marriage."[n]

Dinner and wine helped the evening to pass, and Byron was pleased by a glimpse of the library, which was snug and faced south. But he again became bitter and resentful. It had begun to snow during the long journey, and he was not made more amiable by the fact that he had caught a cold. Out of embarrassment about his foot, Byron had always slept apart from his mistresses, and now his shyness made him cruel, or so it seemed to Annabella, who recalled: "He asked me with an appearance of aversion, if I meant to sleep in the same bed with him—said that he hated sleeping with any woman, but I might do as I chose."[n] Again he must have placated her or convinced her that his irritation was only a passing mood, for they retired at last within the crimson curtain of the four-poster bed. Roused from his first sleep and seeing the firelight shining through the red cloth, he thought while looking at his wife "that he was fairly in hell with Proserpine lying beside him!" [n] Byron confessed to Hobhouse after the separation that on that first night he had been seized with a sudden fit of melancholy and had left his bed. When he finally went back behind the red curtains, he stayed there until near noon.

He awoke to look out on the open park with snow and the pond frozen over. When he hobbled down to the library, he found that Annabella had taken fresh umbrage at his neglect. She was on the point of tears, but he said with irony, perhaps thinking that she regretted her marriage, "It is too late now—I hate scenes." Annabella later recalled, "I tried with all the power of affection to 'smile the clouds away' to call out his higher & more generous feelings." [n]

The fact was that Annabella was in love with Byron and forgave him readily when he was kind to her. What frightened her was that his moods changed so unpredictably and so rapidly, and she seemed unaware that her own primness often maddened him. When she relaxed and was no longer the impeccable Miss Milbanke, they had moments of pleasure as poignant as those which had pained her. He became playful and called her "Pippin" because of her round, rosy face. And in return she called him "Dear Duck," an endearment perhaps suggested by "Goose," his pet name for Augusta. Byron was probably not aware how much his melancholy and savage moods frightened his bride. A good deal of the time he found her a pleasant and intelligent companion and felt that they were getting on admirably. On the 7th Byron wrote to Lady Melbourne: "Bell and I go on extremely well so far, without any other company than our own selves. . . . I have great hopes this match will turn out well." [n]

Byron and Annabella spent much of their time in the library, reading and discussing books. Byron set to work again on the *Hebrew Melodies*, which, through the intervention of his friend Douglas Kinnaird, he had promised to Isaac Nathan, who was adapting the music from traditional airs of the synagogues. He had written nine or ten in October "partly from Job &c. & partly my own imagination." [n] The sad wailing complaints of the Old Testament struck a responsive chord in Byron's being. Several of the pieces, including "Herod's Lament for Mariamne" and "By the Rivers of Babylon We Sat Down and Wept," were written at Halnaby, and Lady Byron, pleased no doubt that he should turn his talents to Biblical subjects, copied them out for him in her precise hand.

There is no indication of strain in Byron's genial letters of the early part of January. Still, an undercurrent of touchiness on both sides subtly vitiated the relationship. The ease with which Annabella could be hurt only accentuated Byron's sense of guilt in having married her. His moments of tenderness could not dispel the anxiety she felt when he had disturbing nightmares and rose from his bed to roam the gallery armed with dagger and pistol as if awaiting some attack. One night, she recalled, he came back to her exhausted and haggard. "Seeking to allay his misery," she moved her head so that it rested on his breast. He said gently but with bitterness, "You should have a softer pillow than my heart." [n]

What made her most uneasy was his persistent hinting at crimes from which she would have saved him had she married him sooner. He would say: "I was a villain to marry you. I could convince you of it in three words." [n] When she asked innocently if Augusta knew it, he appeared terrified and agitated, and said, "O for God's sake don't ask her." [n] Like a man irresistibly drawn to the brink of a precipice, he constantly hinted at the thing that obsessed him.

Byron spoke so fondly of his sister that Annabella wrote asking her to come for a visit. Augusta could not leave her children, but she wrote warmly: "I never can express how much I wish you & my dearest B—— all possible happiness." [n] And she tried to warn Annabella of the proper attitude to take toward her brother's moods. But Annabella only exasperated him the more by her meek devotion and "sacrifice." When he accused himself of terrible crimes, instead of laughing him out of it as Augusta would have done, "I answered that I would then consider the burden as mine, whatever it might be—that I only asked to bear it for him here & hereafter. . . ." [n]

Occasionally Annabella assumed some cheerfulness and softened him so that he talked familiarly of his "little foot," saying pathetically that some allowance must be made to him on the Judgment Day, for he had often wished to revenge himself on Heaven for it.[n] She now saw that Voltairean skepticism, which before marriage she had believed was the source of his Satanic pose, influenced only the surface of his intelligence; whereas, deeply ingrained in his unconscious mind, a gloomy Calvinism made him feel that the majority of men and he in particular had the mark of Cain on them and were slated for damnation. After exhausting his powers of reason, wit, and ridicule in trying to refute the arguments of religion, he would often say with violence: "The worst of it is, I *do believe*."[n]

As Byron recognized later with bitterness, Annabella could analyze his weaknesses very well, but that did not help to make their relationship smoother. For with all her sharpness, she lacked the intuitive perceptions of a more easygoing woman like Augusta. She was eager to please and studied his every word and mood with a searching intensity. And sometimes he would say, half in exasperation and half in pity: "If you wouldn't mind my words, we shall get on very well together."[n] When he saw that she took everything literally, he played up to her credulity. He would declare that she had married an exile from heaven, or that he was driven by an invincible force of evil and would, like Zeluco, end by strangling their child.

Instead of laughing at his superstitions, she let him see that she was shocked, and he dramatized them the more. Annabella was rather relieved when the decision was made to return to Seaham after less than three weeks at Halnaby. Her ostensible reason for their leaving so soon was that her parents wished him to spend his birthday (January 22) with them. They had intended to leave on the 20th, but when Byron discovered that the day fell on a Friday he flatly refused to start until the next day. Seeing Annabella's faint smile, he stated in what seemed to her complete seriousness that Friday was the Mohammedan sabbath, which he observed. But when they finally left on Saturday, he was in a good enough humor, believing that he was getting on as well as could be expected with a wife. Looking across at her, he said, "I think you now know pretty well what subjects to avoid."[n]

At Seaham they both relaxed somewhat from the tensions of the first days of their new relationship. She was no longer forced to be alone with him on what she later referred to as his "black days," and he could sometimes forget that she was his wife and consider her an ally against the greater boredom of her parents and the routine of the manor. Not that he was openly lacking in respect to the old people. In fact, he had a kind of Spanish punctilio when he was in a reasonably pleasant humor which had quite won them and their guests.

On his birthday he wrote to Lady Melbourne: "Yesterday I came here somewhat anent my imperial will. But never mind, you know I am a very good-natured fellow, and the more easily governed because I am not ashamed of being so; and so Bell has her own way and no doubt means to keep it. . . ." [n]

After a few days he wrote to Moore: ". . . the treacle-moon is over, and I am awake, and find myself married. My spouse and I agree to—and in—admiration. Swift says 'no *wise* man ever married;' but, for a fool, I think it the most ambrosial of all possible future states. I still think one ought to marry upon *lease;* but am very sure I should renew mine at the expiration, though next term were for ninety and nine years." But then nostalgia for the world he had lost surged up. "Pray tell me what is going on in the way of intriguery, and how the w——s and rogues of the upper Beggar's Opera go on—or rather go off. . . ." [n] To Hobhouse, who had ventured to mention the "expectations" of property from his marriage, he wrote: ". . . don't talk to me of 'expects' . . . the Baronet is eternal, the Viscount immortal, and my lady (senior) without end. They grow more healthy every day, and I verily believe Sir Ralph and Lady Milbanke, and Lord Wentworth are at this moment cutting a fresh set of teeth. . . ." [n]

By Annabella's own record, in her less jaundiced recollections, they shared moments of tenderness and pleasure in each other's company. Once he challenged her to climb up a rock as quickly as he could, and scrambled ahead of her with boyish dexterity, for when he could run, he was never self-conscious about his lameness. Sometimes he showed gratitude to her for small favors—for handing him a book, or getting up in the night to bring him lemonade. She treasured his words on such an occasion: "You are a good kind Pip—a good-natured Pip—the best wife in the world." And she felt sorry for him in his harsher moods. "He inflicted misery, but I felt that he suffered more than he inflicted." Of all his humors during this second, and for her in many ways happier, honeymoon, she remembered with most pleasure his "child-side," when he would speak of himself in the third person as "B." But "after a few minutes it often happened that some careless word of his own would strike some painful chord, and then the man's mind returned with all its wretchedness. He would say 'B's a fool'—'Yes, he *is* a fool,' bitterly—or 'poor B—*poor* B.' "[n]

One reason for Byron's irascibility during his marriage, as he later told Lady Blessington, was that he was constantly bothered by money difficulties. Now he felt that his affairs were being neglected in London. He wrote to Hobhouse, who was trying to find someone to audit Hanson's accounts, "My debts can hardly be less than thirty thousand. . . ." His generosity to Augusta, Hodgson, and others had taken many thousands of Claughton's forfeited £25,000; much more had gone to pay the most pressing debts and interest on the annuities; "the rest was swallowed up by duns, necessities, luxuries, fooleries, jewelleries, 'whores, and fidlers.' "[n] He had urged Hanson to sell Newstead and Rochdale, but the lawyer was still foolishly hoping that Claughton would complete his purchase.

Byron's boredom at Seaham grew measurably as the weeks passed. By March he realized that to straighten out his business affairs going up to London was imperative. When Annabella would not consent to his going alone, he flew into a rage. Apparently he calmed down, however, and acquiesced in her desire to accompany him. While Hobhouse was negotiating for the lease of the London house of the Duchess of Devonshire for his friend, Byron and his bride decided to visit Augusta on their way to town.

In spite of his ups and downs, he had grown fonder of Annabella than he would generally admit; one night before they left he told her: "I think I love you."[n] In the carriage Byron was in an ill-humor—he was generally made irritable by moving—but Annabella had learned something of his moods, and instead of cowering in the seat as she had done on the ride to Halnaby, she managed, before the journey was over, "to get him 'less disagreeable,' as Augusta would say."[n] She could even laugh at the explanation he gave for his irritability as he began to calm down: "I feel as if I were just going to be married."[n] At Wansford, the night before their arrival at Six Mile Bottom, he said, "You married me to make me happy, didn't you?" When she agreed, he continued, speaking with "passionate affection": "Well then, you do make me happy." But, she recalled, "Then again he seemed to pity me for some impending, inevitable misery."[n]

That misery came in full measure during the visit at Six Mile Bottom, which Annabella was to remember with acute anguish through the rest of her life. When the carriage arrived, Byron was in a state of "great perturbation," and Annabella was supersensitive and watchful. As Augusta descended the stairs, the two women met for the first time, each observing the other with the intensest curiosity. Augusta, with her high Byronic forehead, silky dark-brown hair, large brown eyes set in a Grecian countenance, and soft, ample figure, displayed a self-conscious shyness but did not conceal her easygoing kindly disposition. She greeted Annabella with cordiality but did not kiss her. Annabella and Byron both noticed that. When Augusta turned to greet her brother, she observed that he was in one of his blackest humors. Annabella recorded that "He accounted for it by a letter about Newstead which he had just opened."[n]

That night and every night of their stay was a nightmare for Annabella. Byron insisted on staying up with Augusta after his wife had gone to bed. If she lingered, he would take savage delight in insulting her into retiring. "We don't want *you*, my charmer."[n] His cruelty turned upon Augusta as well, probably because he saw that she had firmly determined not to renew their former physical intimacy. Byron's frustration drove him to crude innuendoes about the past that shocked his wife and "sometimes made Augusta ready to sink."[n] He would greet "Guss" in the morning with pointed allusions to her "inflammable temperament" or their stay alone at Newstead.

Annabella was frightened when he came to bed at last and swore at his valet Fletcher while undressing, and once when some movement in her sleep had brought her nearer to him, he woke her with the cry, "Don't touch me!"[n] Annabella did not make allowance for the fact that Byron was drunk on these occasions. And she never learned, as Augusta had learned long since, to mind his saner admonition—not to pay too much attention to his words. Nevertheless, her anguish was real, and Augusta felt genuinely sorry for her and showed her every kindness —"she seemed to have no other view but that of mitigating his cruelty to me,"[n] Annabella confessed. Mainly, Augusta tried to give her advice on how to handle him. His resentment toward them both established a kind of tacit understanding between the sister and the wife.

But in his blacker moods Byron's impulse to torment both women increased to a mania. The evasions of the one and the martyred innocence of the other poisoned all his normal impulses to kindness. He drank to forget, and that made him more uninhibited in his speech. In Annabella's later recollections of this time, part of which she wrote in shorthand, she recorded that he said: " 'A *I know* [you wear drawers]'—or to me, '*I know* A [wears them],' with an *emphasis* perfectly unequivocal. . . . His [personal intercourse with me was less at] S. M. B. than [ever before, but] towards [the end of our visit there it was renewed], yet without any appearance of affection for me, and he signified some reason which did not make the alteration very flattering to me during those three or four days. [I heard from] A——— herself, [that she was in a particular way during those days.] He said once, I *think* oftener, to her in the morning alluding, apparently, to the night before—'So you wouldn't Guss'—mischievously." [n]

His frustration is clearly apparent in the very savagery of his insinuations, and even Annabella was perceptive enough to see that Augusta had not succumbed to his "criminal" wishes, though "Byron's speech and behaviour 'would have brought conviction to any other person.' " [n] It is not surprising that at the end of two weeks both women longed for release from the strain. He was reluctant to move, but finally on the 28th of March the Byrons set out for London. Byron looked back as they drove away and waved passionately to Augusta as long as he could see her.

Before leaving, he had written casually to Moore that Lady Byron showed "some symptoms which look a little gestatory. It is a subject upon which I am not particularly anxious, except that I think it would please her uncle, Lord Wentworth, and her father and mother." [n] Annabella was no doubt relieved to escape, and felt some hope that in their own house things would be better. Now, too, there was the possibility that he would soften to the child that was coming.

Byron's mood did change as soon as they reached London and settled in the Duchess of Devonshire's house, despite the fact that the address in Piccadilly Terrace was No. 13 and he was superstitious. Annabella recorded that "For ten days he was kinder than I had ever seen him."[n] Hobhouse, who had postponed his journey abroad in order to see him (Napoleon had just escaped from Elba, and he was eager to see the excitement in Paris), called the next day. That night he wrote in his diary that Byron "advises me not to marry though he has the best of wives."[n]

Business and publishing affairs soon absorbed Byron's attention. Besides conferring with Hanson on the fate of Newstead, he had to attend meetings with Kinnaird, who was fostering the publication of the *Hebrew Melodies*, and with Murray, who was eager for more from Byron's pen (he had written little since his engagement). His literary reputation was still high. During Easter Week, Samuel Taylor Coleridge had written him a long and flattering letter asking for his assistance with booksellers. He was not offended by Byron's satire in *English Bards,* and he hinted that he would appreciate a recommendation to Murray. Byron replied that he would be glad to comply with Coleridge's request, encouraged the author of *Remorse* to write more dramas, and added an apology for his satire: "The part applied to you is pert, and petulant, and shallow enough. . . ."[n]

Byron was soon back in the swing of his old London life, going to Murray's in the morning for a conference or a chat with the literary group gathered there, attending the theater, and calling on Douglas Kinnaird and even on Lady Melbourne. Annabella did not share much in this life, and she was uneasy. And impelled by a fate as strong as that which Byron felt governed his own destiny, she had invited Augusta to visit them in their new home. Why could she not have accepted the present fact of Byron's kindness to her as an omen? It is impossible not to see in this act a desire for martyrdom that was to make her life with her husband untenable. Byron's attempt to dissuade her was no doubt motivated by a kindness which she could not accept: "You are a fool for letting her come to the house, and you'll find it will make a great difference to *you* in all ways."[n] Augusta arrived at Piccadilly Terrace early in April. But at first the tension was lessened by Byron's other interests in London.

Walter Scott was in town en route to France. Byron and Scott had corresponded after the publication of *Childe Harold* and had grown to have a warm admiration for each other's works. On April 7 Murray recorded proudly in his diary: "This day Lord Byron and Walter Scott met for the first time and were introduced by me to each other. They conversed together for nearly two hours."[n] Among those present were Byron's great idol, William Gifford, James Boswell (son of the biographer of Johnson), and William Sotheby. Murray's son later recalled seeing "the two greatest poets of the age—both lame—stumping downstairs side by side. They continued to meet in Albemarle Street nearly every day. . . ."[n]

They differed on religion and politics, but politely stopped short of open clashes. Scott said he thought that if Byron lived a few more years he would alter his sentiments. "He answered, rather sharply, 'I suppose you are one of those who prophesy I will turn Methodist.' I replied; 'No—I don't expect your conversion to be of such an ordinary kind. I would rather look to see you retreat upon the Catholic faith, and distinguish yourself by the austerity of your penances. . . .' He smiled gravely, and seemed to allow I might be right."[n] Scott's high-principled Toryism was apparently a little irked by Byron's libertarian pronouncements, but he smoothed this over in his recollections, saying that it was Byron's pleasure in exercising his wit and satire against men in office rather than any real conviction that guided him, adding "at heart, I would have termed Byron a patrician on principle."[n] Scott observed Byron's melancholy but did not inquire into its deeper causes. And Byron, as was usual when he entered wholeheartedly into a friendship, sensed the points at which their interests and philosophies collided, and suppressed, without any intention of deception, much in his character and opinions that would have been incompatible with those of the kindly but more conventional Scotsman.

Lord Wentworth died on April 17, but that did not immediately relieve the precarious financial straits of the Byrons. The yearly payment of £700 from the Milbankes by the terms of the marriage settlement was just enough to pay the rent of the Piccadilly house. The considerable number of servants needed to keep up the mansion and the obligation to keep a carriage and coachman increased the expense, and debts mounted. At the first show of opulence in Piccadilly, all Byron's creditors descended upon him.

Some time in April the *Hebrew Melodies* was published by

Braham and Nathan in a large folio selling for one guinea. Despite the price and some critical carping, the work was highly successful. Ten thousand copies of this and a subsequent edition were sold, resulting in a profit of £5,000 for the publishers, and Murray brought out another edition of the poems without the music; but although he was in dire need, Byron would accept no money for the copyright.

One twentieth-century critic, Joseph Slater, has aptly remarked: "Pious persons who bought the *Hebrew Melodies* in the expectation of finding sacred poetry by Lord Byron found instead a book almost as secular as *The Bride of Abydos*. Nine of the poems are Biblical in subject but Byronic in treatment; two are love songs; five are reflective lyrics, neither Jewish nor Christian; and five are expressions of what might be called proto-Zionism." [n] But Byron knew his Bible as well as many of his most pious readers and had a skill in turning its phrases to good account in verses of haunting melancholy.

Those who saw the Byrons during the summer thought them a happily married couple. William Harness observed that at parties, "he would be seen hanging over the back of her chair, scarcely talking to anybody else, eagerly introducing his friends to her. . . ." [n] Murray was much impressed with her: "She is a most delightful creature, and possesses excellent temper and a most inordinate share of good sense." [n] At home, however, Annabella's good sense often deserted her. By her own confessions later, her suspicions of Augusta agonized her. Some possessiveness or familiarity on the part of the sister, or Byron's own insinuations, may have unbalanced her. She wrote after the separation: "There were moments when I could have plunged a dagger in her heart, but she never saw them. . . ." [n] It was a household resting on explosives, and Byron for the most part chose to ignore the danger, and at times even played with fire as if driven by an involuntary compulsion.

Away from Piccadilly Terrace, he continued to have lively interests. He was drawn closer to the life of the theater, which he loved, by his appointment sometime in May as a member of the Sub-Committee of Management of Drury Lane Theatre. Douglas Kinnaird, who was a member, believed his good judgment would be a valuable asset to the Committee in selecting scripts. When Scott returned from France in June and lunched with Byron and the comedian Matthews, he found the poet "full of fun, frolic, wit, and whim: he was as playful as a kitten."[n]

Augusta had left before the end of June, and Annabella relaxed into greater ease and cheerfulness. She wrote afterward of the pleasure Byron could give her in his happier moods: "When he would converse familiarly, there was a sort of conventional language of nonsense between us—which relieved his fears of 'Sermons and Sentiment,' and rather gave play to his Imagination than confined it."[n]

Leigh Hunt had been released from prison, and Byron called on him several times during the summer at his house in the Edgware Road (Maida Vale). Hunt was flattered by the visits and pleased by the simplicity of Byron's manners. He recorded that "with a childish glee becoming a poet," he would ride the rocking horse of Hunt's little boy.[n] "His appearance at that time was the finest I ever saw it. . . . He was fatter than before his marriage. . . ." Hunt caught only a glimpse of Lady Byron, who was waiting in her carriage; "she had a pretty earnest look, with her 'pippin' face."[n] Byron even took the trouble to read Hunt's *The Story of Rimini*, making tactful suggestions in the margin for the deletion of some precious expressions.

Byron's camaraderie with Lady Melbourne was no longer easy, as he was aware that his wife did not approve of the friendship. When Annabella called on her aunt she was chagrined to find Mrs. Chaworth-Musters there. She wrote Augusta: "She asked after B.? Such a wicked-looking cat I never saw. Somebody else [Caroline Lamb?] looked quite virtuous by the side of her."[n] The rival who disturbed her the most was the one who had stirred Byron's romantic imagination. She knew she had nothing to fear now from Caroline, who was playing a role of tragic resignation. In July Caroline went to Brussels and moved on to Paris, where she embarrassed her husband by her flirtations with the Duke of Wellington, and with a number of Army officers.

Hobhouse's exciting accounts of what he had seen in Paris almost persuaded Byron to join him abroad. He was probably prevented from going only by his inertia and lack of funds and by Hobhouse's early return, though a greater obstacle may have been Annabella's disapproval. When Hobhouse arrived late in July, Byron learned to what extent the forces of reaction had

1

1. Byron at about the time he left Harrow for Cambridge.

2*a*

2*b*

2*c*

2a. Admiral Byron, grandfather. 2b. The Byron family coat of arms. 2c. Captain John Byron, father.

3

3. *Mrs. Catherine Gordon Byron, mother.*

4

5

4. *Newstead Priory, Nottinghamshire.*

5. *Harrow School.*

6

6. *Mary Chaworth.*

7

8

7. *Byron, 1807–9.*

8. *John Cam Hobhouse.*

9

10

9. Mrs. Spencer Smith.

10. Ali Pasha.

11

12

11. House of Nicolò Argyri, Ioannina, Byron's residence in 1809.
12. Monastery at Zitsa.

13

13. Byron's Albanian dress.

14

15

14. Athens in Byron's time.
15. Temple to Poseidon, Sunium.

16

17

16. *Franciscan Convent (monastery), Athens, Byron's residence, 1810-11.*
17. *Theresa Macri, the Maid of Athens.*

18

19

18. *Thomas Moore.*
19. *John Murray II, Byron's publisher.*

20

21

20. Lady Caroline Lamb, in page's costume.
21. Elizabeth, Viscountess Melbourne.

22

23

22. *Jane Elizabeth, Countess of Oxford, 1797.*
23. *Annabella Milbanke, 1812.*

24

25

24. Byron, about 1812.

25. Lady Frances Wedderburn Webster.

26

26. *Byron, 1814.*

27

28

27. *Augusta Leigh.*
28. *Ada Byron.*

29

30

29. *Claire Clairmont.*

30. *Percy Bysshe Shelley.*

31

32

31. *The Villa Diodati.*
32. *Byron, 1817.*

33

34

33. 66, Piazza di Spagna, Byron's residence in Rome, May 1817.
34. Byron, 1818.

35

36

35. *The Palazzo Mocenigo, Venice, Byron's residence, 1818–19.*
36. *Margarita Cogni.*

37

38

37. *Byron's summer palace at La Mira.*

38. *Contessa Teresa Guiccioli, aged about eighteen.*

39

40

39. The Palazzo Guiccioli, Ravenna, Byron's residence, 1820–1.
40. The Casa Lanfranchi, Pisa, Byron's residence, 1821–2.

41

42

41. Edward John Trelawny.

42. Leigh Hunt.

writing to him in person? — — — —
Believe me ever & very truly
yours most affectionately
and (since it must be so)
Noel Byron.

43

44

43. *Byron's first signature as "Noel Byron."*
44. *Douglas Kinnaird.*

45

46

45. *Villa Dupuy, Montenero, Byron's residence, May–June 1822.*
46. *Casa Saluzzo, Albaro (Genoa), Byron's last residence in Italy, 1822–3.*

47

48

47. *Byron, Genoa, 1823.*

48. *The Countess of Blessington, about 1820.*

49

50

49. Byron's house, Metaxata, Cephalonia.
50. Prince Alexander Mavrocordatos.

51

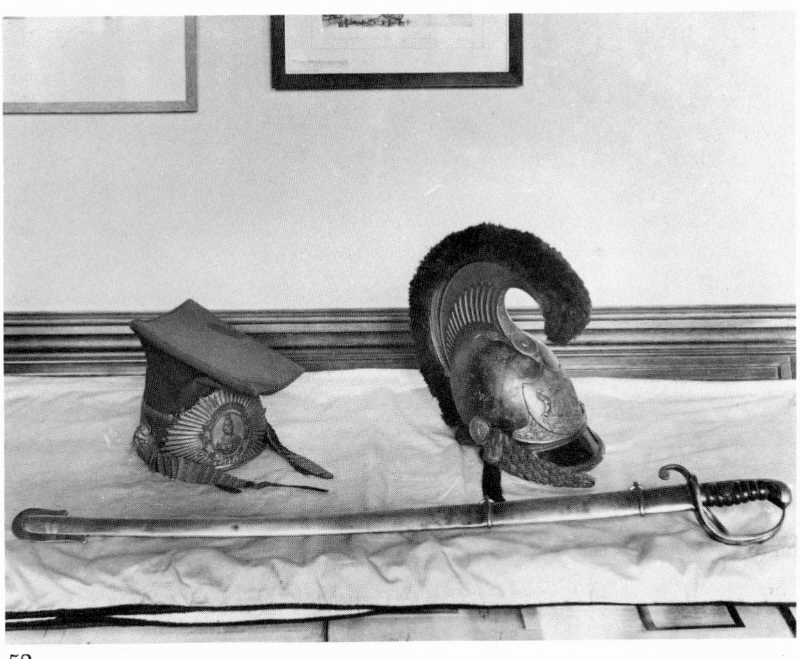

52

51. *Byron's house, Missolonghi.*
52. *Helmets designed by Byron and sword worn by him in Greece.*

53

53. *Statue of Byron at Missolonghi.*

Ra April 26th 1821.

Dear Moray.—

I sent you by
last postis a large packet—which
will not do for publication (I suspect)
being as the Apprentices say—"damned
low!"— I put off also for a week
or two sending the Italian scrawl
which will form a Note to it.
The reason is that letters being opened
I wish to "bide a wee."— — —
Well have you published the trag.?
and does the letter take?— —
Is it true—what Shelley writes me
that poor John Keats died at
Rome of the Quarterly Review?
I am very sorry for it—though I think
he took the wrong line as a poet—
and was spoilt by Cockneyfying and
Suburbing—and versifying Tooke's Pantheon
and Lempriere's Dictionary.— — —

54. *Letter of Byron to John Murray, referring to Shelley and Keats.*

55

56

55. *"Lord Byron shaking the dust of England from his shoes."*
56. *Memorial to Byron in Westminster Abbey.*

(with English Tory blessing) already entrenched themselves in France. He relieved his feelings by writing some excoriating paragraphs on Louis XVIII and Talleyrand, describing the latter as the "living record of all that public treason, private Treachery, and moral Infamy can accumulate in the person of one degraded being."[n]

Annabella's parents, unable to offer the Byrons immediate financial relief (Lord Wentworth's estate, with a supposed income of £7,000 a year, "ate itself up"), had put Seaham at their disposal as a means of helping them to escape duns and the expenses of London living while at the same time providing Annabella with a more comfortable environment for her lying-in. The Noels (the Milbankes had changed their name in compliance with Lord Wentworth's will) were to occupy the estate at Kirkby Mallory in Leicestershire. These arrangements, made in early July, exactly suited Annabella. She knew they were spending beyond their means, and she was uneasy at the temptations which beset Byron in London. She was especially unhappy about his absorption in Drury Lane affairs, his close association with Douglas Kinnaird and other convivial friends, and his familiarity with actors and actresses in the greenroom. But these social distractions from his business worries were the very reasons that made him reluctant to leave London.

Byron had finally persuaded Hanson to put both Newstead and Rochdale up for auction again at the end of July. Farebrother the auctioneer attempted the sale at Garraway's on July 28. Hobhouse accompanied Byron to the auction, "where N[ewstead] was bought in at 95,000 gs the first lot. the bona fide bidding was 79,000 gs. he is much annoyed."[n] Rochdale was bought in too when only £16,000 was offered.

Hobhouse had much opportunity to observe Byron's growing despondency in the months that followed. And yet he noted: "It was impossible . . . for any couple to live in more apparent harmony; indeed, it was the fear of some friends that his Lordship confined himself too much with Lady Byron, and that occasional separation—for they were never seen apart—might be more conducive to their comfort."[n] The specter of Augusta certainly did not seem to be haunting Annabella at this time, for when Byron drew up a new will, which he signed on July 29, 1815, providing that the income from the residue of his estate, after the £60,000 of Lady Byron's marriage settlement was paid, should go to his sister and her children, she wrote to Augusta that the provision was "quite what he ought to make." [n]

But by the end of August Byron's nerves and temper were frayed. It was exasperating for a man with a penchant for generous prodigality to be constantly hounded by the threat of executions and to have no money in sight. He decided to escape by paying Augusta a visit, and the consciousness that he ought not to leave his pregnant wife with the financial worries made him "perfectly ferocious" to her for four days before his departure. She later recorded, however; "As he was starting, he asked my forgiveness, half-earnestly, half-jestingly—but a kind word from him was then too precious to be rigorously examined." [n] Their notes exchanged in his absence indicate an affectionate intimacy on both sides, and this seems to have been normal when the pressure was lifted from Byron's temper.

He returned from Six Mile Bottom, Annabella recalled, "most kind to me, but offended with Augusta," [n] who had defended the Noels against his petulant abuse of them. In the weeks that followed, Byron's spirits were up and down, his alternating kindness, pity, and exasperated harshness to his wife making his conduct unpredictable. His unwillingness to leave for Seaham was no doubt compounded of his increasing annoyance at his parents-in-law for their failure to provide substantial assistance when it was most desperately needed, his consequent reluctance to accept their hospitality, and his growing interest in the affairs of Drury Lane. Aside from buffooning and sometimes flirting with some of the people in the greenroom, he concentrated on the more important business of getting suitable scripts and first-rate actors for the productions.

Byron later recalled the scenes he had to go through: "The authours, and the authoresses, the Milliners, the wild Irishman . . . who came in upon me! . . . Miss Emma Somebody, with a play entitled the 'Bandit of Bohemia,' or some such title. . . . Mr. O'Higgins, then resident at Richmond, with an Irish tragedy, in which the unities could not fail to be observed, for the protagonist was chained by the leg to a pillar during the chief part of the performance." [n]

He tried to get Mrs. Siddons to come to London for the

season, but she would not leave Edinburgh. Drury Lane, during Byron's membership on the Committee, had some of the best dramatic talent of the day. In addition to Kean and Miss Kelly (later much admired by Thomas Hood and Charles Lamb), the Committee had secured the handsome Mrs. Mardyn, who had made her reputation on the Dublin stage. That the season was not better was because of the dearth of good dramatic writing, and Byron tried to find a remedy. His reading of hopeless manuscripts on the Drury Lane shelves convinced him that he must look to poets rather than professional playwrights. He appealed to Scott without success but did secure Maturin's *Bertram.* He attempted to encourage Coleridge to write a drama for Drury Lane, and of course got promises but no performance. Coleridge sent him a copy of *Christabel,* and Byron urged Moore to review it favorably for the *Edinburgh Review.*

But not even the activities of the Committee could free him from the tightening vise of circumstances. Tensed by anxieties, he became the victim again of sleepless nights and nervous fears such as had caused him to walk the floor in the dead of night with his pistols during the honeymoon. It seems probable that Byron was so absorbed in his own miseries that he was unaware of the extent to which Annabella, herself subject to the moods induced by her pregnancy, exaggerated all the words he spoke in irritation at fate rather than at her. When she expressed happiness for the few hours he spared her from his daily and nightly sessions at the theater, he said: "Well, poor thing, you are easily pleased, to be sure"; and he added: "I believe you feel towards me as a mother to her child, happy when it is out of mischief." Again: "If any woman could have rendered marriage endurable to me, you would"; and "I believe you will go on loving me till I beat you." And he often returned to his old reproach: "It is too late now. If you had taken me two years ago. . . . But it is my destiny to ruin all I come near." [n]

He found some relaxation and forgetfulness in sitting late over brandy with Kinnaird and other friends. But even that palled. He wrote to Moore on October 31: "Yesterday, I dined out with a large-ish party, where were Sheridan and Colman . . . Douglas Kinnaird, and others, of note and notoriety. . . . all was hiccup and happiness for the last hour or so. . . ." [n] Afterward he and Kinnaird had to conduct Sheridan down "a damned corkscrew staircase" and deposit him at home. Byron awoke the next day with a headache.

Annabella, who could not take so light a view of these carousings, confessed her anxieties to Augusta: "His [Byron's] misfortune is an habitual *passion for Excitement,* which is always found in ardent temperaments, where the pursuits are not in some degree organized. It is the Ennui of a monotonous existence that drives the best-hearted people of this description to the most dangerous paths, and makes them often seem to act from bad motives, when in fact they are only flying from internal suffering by any external stimulus. The love of tormenting arises chiefly from this Source." [n]

Early in November the inevitable happened: a bailiff entered the house and camped there. Byron was driven to paroxysms of anger and unreason. He had already sold the furniture at Newstead, and now his precious books would have to go. Yet he had property worth over one hundred thousand pounds! Byron later told Medwin that "an execution was levied, and the bailiffs put in possession of the very beds we had to sleep on." [n] But though Lady Byron found this bailiff a "sad brute," Byron apparently made friends with him and perhaps got off the easier for it.

Poor Annabella, who thought she could read Byron's character so well, tried to square his actions and his speech with certain fixed principles, and consequently failed to grasp some of the simplest keys to his behavior. She was determined to read method into his madness, when he was merely giving way under stress to the impulses of a spoiled child and, like the child, was willing to forgive and be forgiven when the "rage" left him. Lady Blessington, after knowing Byron only a short time, observed shrewdly: "He gives me the idea of being the man the most easily to be managed I ever saw: I wish Lady Byron had discovered the means. . . ." [n] And Byron's valet, Fletcher, who had seen his master in all his moods and had by then been witness to his relations with dozens of women of all kinds, remarked with naïve wisdom: "It is very odd, but I never knew a lady that could not manage my Lord, *except* my Lady." [n] Annabella, Byron told Lady Blessington, had "a degree of self-control that I never saw equalled. . . . This . . . self-command in Lady Byron produced an opposite effect on me. When I have broken out, on slight provocations, into one of my ungovernable fits of rage, her calmness piqued and seemed to reproach me. . . ."[n]

Yet the surprising thing is that in the midst of all these maddening provocations Byron could continue to carry on a correspondence of sense and humor. Murray, unaware of the tortures Byron was suffering and making others suffer, wrote Walter Scott: "Lord Byron is perfectly well, and is in better dancing spirits than I ever knew him, expecting every day a son and heir."[n] Actually, Byron felt himself at the end of his rope. Annabella was full of apprehensions. When Hobhouse called, she was sure it was to arrange some scheme for taking Byron to the Continent, for he had said in a mood of depression that as soon as an heir was born, he meant to go abroad, "because a woman always loves her child better than her husband." Taking him literally as usual, she replied with sharp distress: "You will make me hate my child if you say so!"[n]

In bitterness and resignation, while the bailiff was in the house, Byron resolved to sell his library. Annabella was concerned because it hurt her "to see him *in agony*."[n] He had already discussed the sale with a bookseller when the matter came to the ears of John Murray, who immediately sent him a check for £1,500 with the assurance that an equal sum would be at his service in a few weeks. But Byron's pride would not allow him to accept the money. He replied: "I return your bills not accepted, but certainly not *unhonoured*."[n]

Lady Byron had not been unaware of the dangers to one of Byron's nature of the daily contact with actresses at the theater. Byron's first, and perhaps his only, liaison of the greenroom apparently began in November, about the time that he was most harrowed by family and business affairs. He probably would have shied away from any involvement with an actress of repute. He had found adequate occupation for his romantic imagination in poetic composition. All that he wanted from a woman now was physical pleasure, but it was inevitable that he should be harassed by the emotional complications of the simple girl who easily succumbed to his advances. A more heartless rake would have been rid of her sooner; Byron at least preserved her letters. Susan Boyce was a very minor actress at Drury Lane. Her insistence on being treated as a lady was a measure of her vulgarity. She wrote that she wanted his "*confidence* and *esteem*" and she was disconcerted that there was no tender message with the handsome present he sent her.

But, like other women who had been attached to him, she could not forget him, and she appealed for his aid several times after he went abroad. In 1821 she wrote him a pathetic letter signed "the wretched but *unchanged* Susan Boyce." He could then view the affair with detachment: "She was a transient piece of mine," he wrote Kinnaird, "but I owe her little on that score, having been myself, at the short period I knew her, in such a state of mind and body, that all carnal connection was quite mechanical, and almost as senseless to my senses, as to my feelings of imagination. Advance the poor creature some money on my account. . . ."[n]

Byron's feelings were indeed numbed at the time he entered that unsatisfying liaison. Almost frantic with his oppressive financial situation, he became vindictive and cruel toward those for whom he usually had the kindest feelings. Augusta, who had arrived at Piccadilly Terrace on November 15 in response to Annabella's alarming letters, felt the brunt of it. At first he was chilly toward her, and then he began again his pointed remarks and insults to both wife and sister. Sometimes he boasted of his conquests of actresses at the theater, "as much to vex Augusta as you," he said to Annabella.[n]

Byron's heavy drinking contributed to his irrational behavior. His rages became so terrifying that both women were frightened. Annabella took refuge in the belief that he was suffering from temporary insanity, and Augusta readily acquiesced in this view. Augusta, who usually could laugh him out of his tempers, felt she could no longer control him and appealed to Mrs. Clermont, Annabella's former governess, and George Byron, both of whom came to live in the house sometime in December before the child was born. Hobhouse, after calling on Byron on November 25, recorded that "in that quarter things do not go well—strong advices against marriage—talking of going abroad."[n]

But Byron did not confide even to Hobhouse the extent to which, driven by his own insecurity, he made his wife the scapegoat for all his troubles. It is probable that his threats were idle outbursts of frustration and anger, but they were cruel enough to a wife approaching her confinement. Annabella later claimed that only three hours before her labor began, "amid expressions of abhorrence," he told her he hoped she would die and that the child too would perish, and that if it lived he would curse it."[n] And while she was in labor she thought he was throwing soda-water bottles at the ceiling of the room below the one in which she was lying in order to deprive her of sleep. The fact was, that like any nervous husband at such a time, he was trying to allay his anxiety. Hobhouse scotched that story, which circulated during the separation proceedings, finding that "the ceiling of the room retained no mark of blows; and Lord Byron's habit of drinking soda-water, in consequence of taking magnesia in quantities, and of knocking off the heads of the bottles with a poker, sufficiently accounted for the noise. . . ."[n] As for the story of his "having asked his wife when in labour whether the child was dead," Hobhouse put the question direct to Byron. "He answered that he was content to rest the whole merits of his case upon Lady Byron's simple assertion in that respect. 'She will not say so,' he frequently repeated, 'though, God knows, poor thing! it seems now she would say anything; but she would not say that—no, she would not say that.' "[n]

At one o'clock in the afternoon of December 10, Lady Byron's labor ended and a baby girl lay beside her. According to one of the later stories (at third hand), when Byron "was informed he might see his daughter, after gazing at it with an exulting smile, this was the ejaculation that broke from him: 'Oh, what an implement of torture have I acquired in you!' "[n] But in reporting the birth to Francis Hodgson the next day, Augusta said: "B. is in great good looks, and much pleased with his *Daughter*, though I believe he would have preferred a *Son*."[n] And Mrs. Clermont told Hobhouse "a few days after Lady Byron was brought to bed, that she had never seen a man so proud and fond of his child as Lord Byron. . . . Lady Byron herself more than once said to Lord Byron that he was fonder of the infant than she was, adding also what, to be sure, might have been as well omitted, and 'fonder of it than you are of me.' "[n]

The child was baptized Augusta Ada. The second name was a Byron family name in the reign of King John, and Byron was also impressed by the fact that it was the name of Charlemagne's sister and that it was in Genesis (Adah, wife of Lamech). After a while the first name was dropped. However proud Byron was of his daughter, she did not reconcile him to his marriage, as Annabella had for a while vainly hoped. His erratic behavior increased rather than diminished after the child was born. He later wrote of Ada as

The child of Love! though born in bitterness,
And nurtured in Convulsion! Of thy sire
These were the elements . . ."[n]

Byron owned to Hobhouse "that his pecuniary embarrassments were such as to *drive him half-mad.* He said 'he should think lightly of them *were he not married.*' . . . 'My wife,' he always added, 'is perfection itself—the best creature breathing; but, mind what I say—*don't marry.*' "[n]

It is quite possible, however, that Byron was not fully aware of the cumulative impression his conduct under continued irritations, drinking, and loss of temper must have made on his sensitive wife. In one fit of vexation and rage he dashed to pieces on the hearth a watch he had carried since boyhood and had taken to Greece with him. He confessed later to only one really brutal outburst against his wife, though there may have been more. One day when he was beside himself with money worries, he came into a room where she was standing before the fire, and when he came up she said "Am I in your way?" He told Hobhouse: "I answered, 'Yes, you *are,*' with emphasis. She burst into tears, and left the room. I hopped up stairs as quickly as I could ["Poor fellow," Hobhouse interjected, "you know how lame he was"]—and begged her pardon *most* humbly; and that was the only time I spoke really harshly to her."[n]

It is difficult to get a clear picture of Annabella's feelings and impressions of events at this period from her later statements, but some kind of climax seems to have come on January 3, 1816, when Byron went to her room and talked with "considerable violence" on the subject of his affairs with women of the theater.[n] He had apparently talked with her before about the necessity of giving up the expensive establishment in Piccadilly and retiring to the country. She was to precede him while he settled matters in London. On January 6 he wrote her a note, having abstained from seeing her, perhaps to avoid a scene. He asked her to set a date for her departure for Kirkby, where she had been invited by her parents. "As the dismissal of the present establishment is of importance to me—the sooner you can fix on the day the better—though of course your convenience & inclination shall be first consulted—The Child will of course accompany you. . . ."

Byron's story, as told to Hobhouse, was that his wife "had been much offended with this note—that an altercation had ensued of very short duration—that she had declared herself satisfied—and that the affair terminated by a reconciliation that buried the whole matter in silence from that time forwards: that she herself fixed the day of her departure." [n]

But Byron was not aware of all that was going on behind that calm "pippin" countenance. Annabella had conceived the idea that her husband was mentally deranged. She had procured a copy of the *Medical Journal* in which she found a description of hydrocephalus, which she thought fitted his peculiar malady. And she felt it her duty to search his private trunks and letter cases and to study him for "those singularities and obliquities, which she conceived were the proofs and features of that particular insanity under which he laboured." [n] Among other things she found a small bottle of laudanum and a copy of the Marquis de Sade's suppressed novel *Justine*. Then she drew up, Hobhouse later discovered, "a statement of Lord Byron's conduct, including *his sayings* and singularities of manner and look," [n] which she submitted to Dr. Baillie, who at her request came to the house and examined her evidence but would give no decided opinion.

Annabella was so certain of her diagnosis that she asked for an interview with Hanson and sent him the marked pamphlet and her comments. Hanson feared that she had some design of putting her husband under restraint, and he asked her whether she had any personal fear for herself. She answered: *"Oh no, not in the least; my eye can always put down his!!!"* Hanson, who had known Byron a long time and was used to his temper and his temperament, assured her that he "was liable to irritation, and, perhaps, sudden bursts of violence and passion; that he had long been in the habit of indulging in a conversation which was not to be taken 'to the letter.' . . ." [n]

Annabella postponed her journey as long as possible, hoping that something definite could be determined about Byron's mental health. It was a positive relief to her, as she later confessed, to be able to believe that her husband's wicked ravings could be ascribed to a deranged mind. How Annabella's last days in Piccadilly Terrace were spent and what the parting was like must be surmised from little evidence. Byron apparently thought that everything had been smoothed over by his apologies, although, he told Hobhouse, he "recollected being occasionally much annoyed, on lifting up his head, to observe his wife gazing at him with a mixture of pity and anxiety."[n] But he and Annabella, according to Hobhouse, "lived on *conjugal* terms up to the last moment. . . ."[n]

She finally set January 15 for her journey. She would have remained longer, but Captain Byron, who, even more than Annabella herself, took Byron's menaces to the letter, "declared he would not suffer me to remain any longer in the house without himself informing my parents."[n] Byron did not like farewells, and particularly eschewed the sentimental kind. Annabella was more emotional. "The night before I left London," she recorded, "in Mrs. Leigh's presence, he said, very significantly—'*When shall we three meet again*?'—to which I replied '*in Heaven I hope*.' I parted from him that night in a violent agony of Tears and went into the Room where Mrs. Leigh and Mrs. Clermont were—in that State having quite lost the self-command I could in general assume."[n]

Annabella's recollection of her departure was sentimental: "I went down stairs—the carriage was at the door. I passed his room. There was a large mat on which his Newfoundland dog used to lie. For a moment I was tempted to throw myself on it, and wait at all hazards, but it was only a moment—and I passed on. That was our parting."[n] Byron never saw her again.

CHAPTER XV

1816

"Fare Thee Well"

WHEN LADY BYRON LEFT Piccadilly Terrace on January 15, her mind was a whirl of conflicting thoughts, but her heart was filled with pity and tenderness for the man she never quite understood, the most fascinating and exasperating of husbands. Yet it would seem that more than pity, more than concern for the doctor's prescription that she write only on "soothing" topics, prompted her to send this note to Byron when they stopped at Woburn.

> Dearest B.
>
> The child is quite well and the best of travellers. I hope you are *good* and remember my medical prayers and injunctions. Don't give yourself up to the abominable trade of versifying—nor to brandy—nor to anything or anybody that is not *lawful* and *right*.
>
> Though *I* disobey in writing to you, let me hear of *your* obedience at Kirkby.
>
> Ada's love to you with mine.
>
> Pip [n]

And it would be reasonable to assume, as Byron did, that it was her heart rather than her head that directed her pen when she wrote from Kirkby the day after her arrival:

> Dearest Duck,
>
> We got here quite well last night and were ushered into the kitchen instead of drawing-room, by a mistake that might have

been agreeable to hungry people. Of this and other incidents Dad wants to write you a jocose account & both he & Mam long to have the family party completed. Such a W.C.! and such a *sitting*-room or *sulking*-room all to yourself. If I were not always looking about for B, I should be a great deal better already for country air. *Miss* finds her provisions increased, & fattens thereon. It is a good thing she can't understand all the flattery bestowed upon her, 'Little Angel'. Love to the good goose, & every body's love to you both from hence.

Ever thy most loving
Pippin . . . Pip——ip."[n]

Byron and his friends always considered these letters as the clearest evidence that Annabella had no thought of leaving him permanently when she quitted London. But it now seems clear that she was fully determined before she left not to return to her husband if her conviction that he was insane was not confirmed by medical opinion. Mrs. Clermont stated that "She then said if he is insane I will do every thing possible to alleviate his dissease but if he is not in a state to be put under care I will never return to his roof again. The evening before she left London she said 'if ever I should be fool enough to be persuaded to return I shall never leave his house alive.' "[n]

But more conclusive is a letter she wrote to her childhood friend Selina Doyle (who had already become her confidante) on the very evening that she penned the first of those "Pippin" letters, January 15: "Though there is still a doubt as to what must be the *future* ground of conduct, the *present* seems simple enough after the confirmation of a further opinion from Dr. Baillie. To avenge disease on its victim would be as inhuman as disgraceful. . . . On this ground (the future sufficiency of which remains to be tried) I act—and a moral decision must be suspended from such physical causes. . . . But were I now to take the final step, whilst the relations are possessed with this idea, they would desert me—and were the unhappy consequences which they apprehend to Ensue [Augusta feared Byron would commit suicide], what should I feel? . . .

"I was desired to write from hence—and pursuing the plan thus laid down I have done so—a few lines in the usual form without any notice of serious subjects—nor shall I ever commit myself on them. As for my own opinion of Causes, it does coincide with the opinions of others, but under such restrictions as make me fear that I must still undertake the responsibility of that Measure, which Duty, not Timidity now determines me to postpone for a short time." [n]

Augusta was still her stanch ally. She had intended to leave immediately after Annabella had gone to the country, but both Hanson and Le Mann—Lady Byron's personal physician—whom she had asked to examine her husband, urged Augusta to stay a little longer. She sent daily bulletins describing her brother's contradictory behavior and statements, seeing in them further evidence of derangement. So eager was she to believe in it for Annabella's sake and to strengthen her own belief that her brother could not have been so cruel had he been in his right mind, that she lost her own perspective and saw deep significance in his flippant and inebriated remarks. She reported that he kept a pistol on the mantel and had paranoiac feelings about being attacked. He did not write to Annabella because, he said, he was lazy, but asked Augusta to "Tell her as I told Murray that she is the only woman I could have lived 6 months with." [n]

Annabella had told her parents about Byron's "malady" (that was the word she and Augusta commonly used to indicate his supposed insanity), and they had been eager for him to come to Kirkby, where he would have the best of care. Then something happened that changed the whole complexion of events. Exactly how it came about we do not know. Malcolm Elwin suggests that Annabella's mother had seen a letter from Selina Doyle and had asked to read it, and that Annabella then broke down and explained what was meant by Selina's references to "outrages" and "ill treatment." Was it then that she came to realize how deeply she had deceived herself by believing in her husband's derangement? At any rate, it is apparent that she told her parents all that she had withheld from them before concerning his conduct and wild and menacing speech—all, that is, with the exception of her suspicions of Augusta, which she now had come to think unjust. In her first letter to Augusta from Kirkby, she had written ". . . I have much to repair in my conduct towards you. . . . My chief feeling, therefore, in relation to you and myself must be that I *have* wronged you, and that you have never wronged me." [n]

At first it was a relief to throw the burden on her parents, but she soon repented. What she might forgive, they could not, and they became more and more angry, determining that their daughter should never return to the beast who had mistreated her. They induced her to promise that if he proved to be sane, nothing would make her go back to him. They decided that she should have legal as well as medical advice, and on January 18, 1816, she drew up a statement of her husband's offenses for her mother to take to London. But it is evident from the tone of her letter to Augusta, written the same day, that she still clung to the "hope" of Byron's mental illness.

In the next few days there ensued a heart-consuming battle in Annabella between her "reason" and her unreasoned attachment to Byron. He had an irresistible attraction that, if she had let herself go, would have drawn her to him despite all the pain he had caused her. She later wrote: "There were moments when resignation yielded to frenzy—and I would have forgotten myself, my child, my principles, to devote myself to that being who had cast me off." [n] The foolish Augusta sent her an account of all Byron's actions, words, and silences which she thought significant of his mental disturbance. On the 19th Annabella wrote her:

"I think he was so much pleased with my 2nd letter from one expression which acknowledged the power he still has over my affections; and the *love of power* is one principal feature of his Disease or Character. My own conviction of the existence of the former, in any greater degree than many years ago, decreases. . . ." [n]

After she had written out her indictment of her husband, she was emotionally overwrought to the point of being physically ill. She wrote to Augusta: "I have been endeavouring to write off some of my agonies, and have addressed them to B. in the enclosed, which I wish you to read attentively. . . . God bless you and *him!*" [n] But she did not send the enclosure. The next day she wrote: "I mean to break my neck upon my old horse, which is here." [n] And on the 20th: ". . . my presence has been uniformly oppressive to him from the hour we married . . . and in his best moods he has always wished to be away from me. . . . had we continued together he *would* have gone mad." She added plaintively: "Indeed, I have done nothing except on the strictest principle of Duty, yet I feel as if I were going to receive sentence from the Judge with his black cap on. . . . O that I were in

London, if in the coal-hole."[n] That was the day her mother left for London, carrying the document that Annabella felt would seal her doom.

But it was precisely because she always acted on the "strictest principle of Duty" that Byron settled down with a measure of relief to a pleasant bachelor life before taking leisurely steps to break up his expensive establishment (he was already in arrears for half a year's rent). He was quite unaware of what was impending. The two affectionate letters from Annabella left him with the flattering sense that she missed him, but in his relaxed state he left correspondence with her to Augusta.

Two days after his wife left, he dined out and then drank brandy until two in the morning, despite the warnings of Le Mann that his liver was in a bad state. He told Hobhouse: "They want me to go into the country. I shall go soon, but I won't go yet. I should not care if Lady Byron was alone, but I can't stand Lady Noel."[n]

He was easily irritated, however. When Sir James Mackintosh suggested that if he would not take money for his poems, he should have Murray turn it over to some needy authors, Godwin, Coleridge, and Maturin, he readily agreed. But when Murray demurred, Byron countered heatedly: "Had I taken you at your word, that is, taken your money, I might have used it as I pleased; and it could be in no respect different to you whether I paid it to a w[hore], or a hospital, or assisted a man of talent in distress."[n] And he withdrew his manuscripts, but then repented. A week later he had regained enough balance to tell Leigh Hunt, who was bargaining with Murray for the publication of *The Story of Rimini*: ". . . I doubt not he will deal fairly by you on the whole; he is really a very good fellow, and his faults are merely the leaven of his 'trade.' . . ."[n]

Lady Noel in the meantime had gone to Sir Samuel Romilly with the catalogue of her daughter's grievances. He recommended that Byron should not be allowed to remain a moment at Kirkby, and that she put the matter in the hands of a civilian legal adviser. She was referred to Dr. Stephen Lushington, a distinguished barrister of the Inner Temple, who took a personal interest in Lady Byron's cause and became her adviser for the rest of her life. Lady Noel's indignation grew as she consulted her advisers. She was convinced even before she saw Le Mann that Byron was not mad but bad. When Augusta hinted that the announcement of a separation might cause her brother to take his own life, Lady Noel replied: "So much the better; it is not fit such men should live." [n]

On January 22, Augusta, who preferred to think it "malady" rather than "*depravity of heart,*" had so far lost her usual good sense as to see madness in all Byron's actions. "One of the things he did and said last night was desiring George [Byron] to go and live at Seaham, exactly as if it were his own; and even before our dinner he said he considered himself 'the greatest man existing.' G. said, laughing, 'except Bonaparte.' The answer was, 'God, I don't know that I do except even him.' I was struck previously with a wildness in his eyes." [n]

It seems evident that Byron was trying to rib his cousin, who was almost as humorless as Annabella. Shortly afterward, George accused him of cruelty to his wife, and hinted that her parents would take up her defense. Byron "interrupted him with the most animated expressions of exultation and said 'Let them come forward, I'll Glory in it!' " [n] But it was one thing to talk in his usual rattling way of such matters and another to be faced with the cold fact. He, like his wife, was of a divided mind.

Le Mann's report on January 20th that he had "discovered nothing like settled lunacy" left Annabella quite resigned and hopeless, for she knew that a separation must take place. Lady Noel, accompanied by Miss Doyle and Mrs. Clermont, arrived at Kirkby on the 28th, carrying a letter proposing a quiet separation, carefully "corrected" by Sir Samuel Romilly. Sir Ralph copied it and sent it to Byron. On the day the delivery of the letter was expected Annabella's maid, Mrs. Fletcher, noticed that she was "extremely distressed, and almost insensible." [n] Augusta, fearing the effect on her brother, intercepted the letter and sent it back to Annabella with a plea for further deliberation. Sir Ralph, accompanied by Mrs. Clermont, then went to London and had the letter delivered by messenger, on February 2. It was Friday, a day Byron ever considered unpropitious. In a sudden change of mood, uneasy because he had not heard from Annabella, he had just ordered horses to go to Kirkby the following Sunday.

His surprise and agitation on opening the letter were quite unaffected. "*Very recently,*" he read, "circumstances have come to my knowledge, which convince me, that with your opinions it cannot tend to your happiness to continue to live with Lady Byron, and I am yet more forcibly convinced that after her dismissal from your house, and the treatment she experienced whilst in it, those on whose protection she has the strongest natural claims could not feel themselves justified in permitting her return thither." [n] Sir Ralph indicated that he was willing to bring the matter before the public but hoped a separation could be arranged privately.

Remembering the terms on which they had lived during her last days in London and the affectionate and playful tone of her last letters, Byron did not believe that Annabella was herself responsible, and he asked Augusta to confront her with the question. To Sir Ralph he replied candidly and with restraint: "Lady Byron received no dismissal from my house in the sense you have attached to the word. She left London by medical advice. . . . It is true that previous to this period I had suggested to her the expediency of a temporary residence with her parents. My reason for this was very simple and shortly stated, viz. the embarrassment of my circumstances, and my inability to maintain our present establishment. The truth of what is thus stated may be easily ascertained by reference to Lady B.—who is truth itself."

During the past year, he said, he had had "to contend with distress without and disease within," which "may have rendered me little less disagreeable to others than I am to myself. I am, however, ignorant of any particular ill-treatment which your daughter has encountered. . . . for the present at least, your daughter is my wife; she is the mother of my child; and till I have her express sanction of your proceedings, I shall take leave to doubt the propriety of your interference." [n]

Sir Ralph, who was, as Byron had called him, a "good old man," might have taken pause at the moderation of this letter had he not been under the strict surveillance of his legal advisers, and particularly of Mrs. Clermont, who remained at Mivart's Hotel as a kind of confidential secretary reporting everything to Kirkby.

Annabella replied to Augusta's letter, saying that she had given concurrence to her father's proposal for a separation, and adding: "I will only recall to Lord Byron's mind his avowed and insurmountable aversion to the married state, and the desire and determination he has expressed ever since its commencement to free himself from that bondage, as finding it quite insupportable. . . ." [n] Augusta, seeing her brother's agitated state, withheld this letter, and in the meantime he addressed Annabella guardedly: "Will you explain? . . . I shall eventually abide by your decision; but I request you most earnestly to weigh well the probable consequences. . . . I cannot sign myself otherwise than yours ever most affectionately. . . ." [n]

Annabella was forbidden to reply directly. When Hobhouse called on February 5, he found Byron deeply depressed. He showed Hobhouse the "Dearest Duck" letter and "He solemnly protested that Lady Byron and himself had parted friends." [n] Hobhouse offered to write to Lady Byron, and Byron addressed another letter to her: ". . . recollect that all is at stake, the present, the future, and even the colouring of the past. My errors, or by whatever harsher name you choose to call them, you know; but I loved you, and will not part from you without your express and expressed refusal to return to, or receive me." [n]

At Kirkby, Annabella was thrown into an emotional state worse than her husband's by his second letter. Horribly torn between her feelings and what she considered her duty, but irrevocably committed to the latter not only by her promise to her parents but also by her own painfully strong sense of consistency, she suffered nevertheless because she could not tear from her inner consciousness the attachment which had grown as strong as her sense of having been wronged. It must have been at about this time that Mrs. Fletcher reported that her mistress's "distress and agony" were at their height; "that she was rolling on the floor in a paroxysm of grief at having promised to separate from Lord Byron. . . ." [n]

The reply which Annabella wrote was dictated, however, not by her parents but by her reason, which left her even less a free agent. She said she had acted on her own conviction in authorizing her father's proposal for a separation, and she added: "It is unhappily your disposition to consider what you *have* as worthless—what you have *lost* as invaluable. But remember that you believed yourself most miserable when I was yours." [n] This must have cut to the quick because there was a measure of truth in it. But he replied with a resigned desperation:

"Were you then *never* happy with me? did you never at any time or times express yourself so? have no marks of affection, of the warmest and most reciprocal attachment, passed between us? or did in fact hardly a day go down without some such on one side and generally on both? . . . You are much changed within these twenty days, or you would never have thus poisoned your own better feelings—and trampled upon mine." [n]

This was a terrible letter for Annabella to receive and a great trial for her now irrevocable resolution, for she recognized in it the sincerity which she knew to be basic in the character of her husband. It recalled to her some of the happiest moments of her life with him, now cut off forever by that "consistency" and "undeviating rectitude" to which she had committed herself before she became acquainted with the inconsistencies of Byron and of life.

Byron had told Hobhouse on February 9 that his wife had "sat on his knee she kissed him five thousand times before Mrs. L. rather he kissed her—he never lifted up a finger against her. . . . The matter continued inexplicable." [n] But on the 12th Hobhouse "saw Mrs. L. and George B and from them learnt what I fear is the real truth that B has been guilty of very great tyranny—menaces—furies—neglects & even real injuries such as telling his wife he was *living* with another woman—& actually in *fact* turning her out of the house—G.B. suspected she would leave him & told him so a month before she went—but she had no intention of doing it when she went from London—locking doors—showing pistols—frowning at her in bed—reproaches—every thing she seems to believe him to have been guilty of—but they acquit him—how? by saying that he is mad. . . . Whilst I heard these things Mrs. L. went out & brought word that her brother was crying bitterly in his bed room—poor poor fellow." [n]

Later in the day Hobhouse "got him to own much of what I had been told in the morning—he was dreadfully agitated—said he was ruined & would blow out his brains—he is indignant but yet terrified—sometimes says 'and yet she loved me once,' and at other times that he is glad to be quit of such a woman—he said if I would go abroad he would separate at once." [n] Hobhouse found him in the days that followed "a prey to the alternate passions of pity, regret, love, and indignation. . . ." [n]

All sorts of rumors were beginning to fly around London. Hobhouse, who had loyally decided "to work openly to disprove every thing," told Byron the worst that he had heard, "which he received to my astonishment with very little discomposure—poor fellow." [n] He had perhaps grown too numb to care. But his composure was only for the moment and on the surface. He had just written a last appeal to Annabella: "And now, Bell, dearest Bell . . . I can only say in the truth of affliction, and without hope, motive, or end . . . that I love you, bad or good, mad or rational, miserable or content, I love you, and shall do, to the dregs of my memory and existence." [n]

A harmless reference to their child and an inquiry about its welfare alarmed Annabella, for she took it as a hint that he might try to force it from her by legal means. On February 17, after receiving this letter, she wrote to Dr. Lushington, proposing a personal interview: "There are things which I, and I only, could explain to you in conversation that may be of great importance to the thorough understanding of the case." [n] On the 22nd she arrived in London and had a long private conference with the lawyer. It seems fairly clear from Lady Byron's own statements and letters that she then for the first time fully confessed her suspicion of the incest, together with details of Byron's own words and actions which tended to confirm it. Her first statement, written out for her mother to take to London, had contained allegations of acts of adultery and cruelty but had made no reference to incest.*

Lushington was certain that, with Lady Byron's evidence legally excluded, it would be impossible to prove the charge of

* In Lady Byron's pamphlet replying to Moore's account of the separation in 1830, a letter from Dr. Lushington was included, in which the lawyer said that whereas he had previously considered reconciliation possible, he thenceforth thought a separation inevitable and necessary. But the correspondence of the time does not seem to bear this out. Dr. Lushington had not from the first considered a reconciliation possible. Her revelations at that time did not cause him to change his mind. As for the "facts utterly unknown . . . to Sir Ralph and Lady Noel" which Annabella revealed at that time, there is a strong suggestion in the correspondence of February 1816 that she had told her parents the substance of her revelations before she left for London. (See Elwin, p. 417. Letter of February 23, 1816.)

incest in court. His advice, therefore, was to seek a separation, if necessary in court, where an adequate case could rest on Byron's "brutally indecent conduct and language."[n] Part of the evidence would be his crude references to intercourse with Mrs. Leigh as a means of torturing his wife, though no effort would be made to establish the fact of incest.

But Annabella was eager, above all else, to avoid a public hearing of the case. For this reason she and her counsel used every means possible to get Byron's friends to persuade him to agree to a private settlement and a quiet separation. Their efforts were doubled when, in the last week of February, the rumors about Mrs. Leigh and her brother began to be widespread and persistent. It was then that Dr. Lushington and her other advisers urged Annabella to cease all communication with Augusta. But that Annabella would not do. Her chief purpose in revealing the suspicions which had been festering in her mind, but which she had suppressed because of Augusta's undoubted kindness, was to have the instrument of a horrible revelation that would force Byron to accede to a quiet separation and prevent any effort of his to take the child from her (she suspected that he wanted to have Ada put in Augusta's care). But now she found herself in an embarrassing and difficult situation. Augusta seemed to have an ease in coping with the vagaries of her brother in a way that the wife could not, and she had remained to care for him in his supposed "malady" when Annabella had abdicated the duties of a wife. But though Annabella had some deep-seated and unacknowledged jealousy, she could not but remember what she owed to her sister-in-law. Augusta had protected her from his wild and frightening conduct during her pregnancy and she felt, probably mistakenly, that she owed even her life to that protection.

When Annabella finally persuaded her lawyers to let her have an interview with Augusta, however, it was not an indication that she was weakening, but only that she was determined to convince Byron through his sister that she was acting under her own initiative and was not being coerced. She assured both Augusta and George Byron that she would not return—*"no, not if her father and mother would go upon their knees to her so to do."*[n] To Mrs. Leigh's repeated statement that she could not answer for her brother's life if Annabella did not return, the immovable wife replied *"she could not help it, she must do her duty."* [n]

But her implacability only aggravated Byron. He told Lord Holland, whom Lushington had induced to offer mediation: "They think to drive me by menacing with legal measures. Let them go into court, they shall be met there." [n] Nor could he accept Annabella's word through intermediaries. He asked for an interview with her and was refused, but he continued to send her tender and imploring letters, trying to rouse memories of the happier moments of their past: ". . . if I were not convinced that some rash determination—&, it may be, promise—is the root of the bitter fruits we are now at the same time devouring & detesting—I would & could address you no more. Did I not love you—were I not sure that you still love me—I should not have endured What I have already." [n]

But Annabella, who had, as Elwin says, "always prevented herself from perceiving his true character by her habit of drawing inferences to suit her own preconceptions," [n] sought only to find hidden meanings and an intent to deceive in his most sincere appeal. She promptly turned his letters over to Lushington with her analysis of his sinister motives.

During these days of indecision, life went on for Byron, though even his remarkable resilience could not quite stir him to take a very active part in the scenes that generally moved him the most—the gossip at Murray's and the dinners at Kinnaird's, together with the activities of the theater. He had, apparently at the suggestion of Sotheby, sent £100 to the needy Coleridge, though the latter had failed to complete his promised tragedy for Drury Lane.

An event recalling one of the tenderest, and at the same time most cynical, of his romantic intrigues roused him momentarily to the fever of composition. When he learned that Lady Frances Webster's name had been connected scandalously with that of the Duke of Wellington, he wrote sarcastically of it to Murray, but he revived the emotions of the past with the verses:

When we two parted
In silence and tears . . .

Although Byron appeared to be indifferent to the ugly rumors circulating about him, Hobhouse was determined that before the separation papers were signed he would get a disavowal from the quarter most likely to carry weight, from Lady Byron herself. He consequently drew up a memorandum, "a paper of declarations as preamble to the separation in which Lady B disavowed cruelty, systematic unremitted neglect, gross & repeated infidelities—incest & ———," [n] all of which had been subjects of current talk that had come to their ears.*

The paper that was drawn up by Lady Byron's lawyers and signed by her denied that any reports injurious to Byron had been circulated by her family and added that "the two reports specifically mentioned by Mr. Wilmot [Byron's cousin and her intermediary] do not form any part of the charges which, in the event of a Separation by agreement not taking place, she should have been compelled to make against Lord Byron." [n] This statement seemed satisfactory to Byron and Hobhouse, but they failed to see that it was deliberately worded so that Annabella did not commit herself to a denial of the truth of the charges, but only said she would not bring them forward in court, and

---

* Byron himself gave the clearest clue to the unnamed act with which he was charged by rumor. In a letter to Hobhouse of May 17, 1819, he wrote that "they tried to expose me upon earth to the same stigma, which . . . Jacopo is saddled with in hell." (*LBC,* II, 110.) Jacopo Rusticucci, who ascribed his errors to a shrewish wife (*Inferno,* Canto XVI, line 45) was consigned to the third ring of the seventh circle, reserved for sodomites. Hobhouse always professed ignorance of Annabella's reasons for the separation. On Moore's suggestion that it "may have been nothing more, after all, than . . . some dimly hinted confession of undefined horrors, which, though intended by the relater but to mystify and surprise, the hearer so little understood him as to take in sober seriousness" (Moore, II, 791), Hobhouse commented: "Something of this sort certainly, unless, as Lord Holland told me, he tried to ——— her [no doubt referring to an unconventional sexual approach]." (Hobhouse's marginal note in his copy of Moore.) But it is unreasonable to take this as substantial evidence of anything more than that both Lord Holland and Hobhouse were mystified as to the cause. Malcolm Elwin sensibly remarks: "Lord Holland may have confessed that he shared his mystification and dismissed the matter with a crude joke." (Elwin, p. 446 n.) That remark of Hobhouse and the *Don Leon* poems (clever anonymous "curiosa" written by someone with considerable knowledge of Byron's life) are evidence only of the nature of the gossip that was current at the time. The mystery remains. Wilmot, who knew part of the secret, was horrified, but he told Hobhouse it was no "enormity," and Hobhouse's reply was: "indeed I told him it never could be or she would have quitted the house at once." (Marchand, II, 588.) Byron always maintained that he did not know the real reasons for Lady Byron's leaving him, but at Missolonghi he told George Finlay, "The causes were too simple to be soon found out." (Kennedy, p. 308.)

that only because Lushington believed they could not be proved.

Annabella had held to her "undeviating rectitude," but she was near to breaking under the strain. Her mother had written her: "I neither do, or can expect that you should not *feel* and *deeply feel*—but I have sometimes thought (and that not *only lately*) that Your mind is too *high wrought*—too much so for *this* World—only the *grander* objects engage your thoughts, Your Character is like *Proof Spirits*—not fit for common use—I could almost wish the *Tone* of it *lowered* nearer to the level of *us every day people*. . . ."[n] This is one point on which Byron might have found himself in agreement with his mother-in-law!

Augusta too was near a nervous collapse. She wanted without offending Byron and without giving a lever to the gossip mongers to leave Piccadilly Terrace, where she had stayed only to care for her brother and to report his condition and state of mind to Annabella, hoping until the last for a reconciliation. On March 16 she removed to her rooms in St. James's Palace (she had been appointed a lady-in-waiting through the influence of friends close to the Queen).

For several days Byron's moods were alternately up and down, but on the 17th the basis for the legal separation was agreed upon, and on the 22nd Hobhouse found him "in great spirits at prospect of going abroad directly."[n] A devil-may-care mood seized him. Sometime during the hectic days of March he had received a letter in an unknown feminine hand that was striking enough to excite his curiosity. The approach was not that of a sentimental Eliza, nor of the dozens of other women who clothed their proposals in conventional language. This girl said her mind had been formed by his poetry, and she asked this blunt question:

"If a woman, whose reputation has yet remained unstained, if without either guardian or husband to control she should throw herself upon your mercy, if with a beating heart she should confess the love she has borne you many years . . . could you betray her, or would you be silent as the grave?"[n]

After a second appeal, she succeeded in her wish to be "admitted alone and with the utmost privacy."[n] The girl who called on him was not yet eighteen. She had a dark, almost Italian, appearance, and while her face was not quite pretty, her youth and the flashing intelligence of her brown eyes offset her plain features. Her name was Mary Jane Clairmont. Her friends and family called her Jane to distinguish her from her stepsister Mary Godwin, but she called herself Clara or Clare (later Claire).

She had advanced ideas with regard to love, marriage, and the rights of women. These ideas she had imbibed by growing up in the household of the philosopher William Godwin, who had married her mother after the death of his first wife, Mary Wollstonecraft, author of the *Vindication of the Rights of Women*. Claire had accompanied Percy Shelley and Mary Godwin in 1814 on their honeymoon elopement, which took them through France to Switzerland. On their return to England she had lived with them, for the most part, being largely dependent on Shelley's bounty. In fact, her too great fondness for him had already made Mary jealous despite her free ideas, and caused her to long for a cessation of this *ménage à trois*. It may have been Claire's desire to show Mary that she too could capture a poet, and one far more famous than Shelley, that first prompted her to beard the literary lion of all London in his den—that and the fact that she had long idolized this apostle of freedom and sympathetic painter of the lawless passions.

Byron listened to her story, but she was not a ravishing beauty and he was distracted by a thousand irritations. She thought to interest him by pretending to talent in the theater, but he only referred her to Kinnaird. She had written "half a novel" on which she wanted his opinion. And she tried to get his approbation by deriding the institution of marriage, the source of his present distress: "I can never resist the temptation of throwing a pebble at it as I pass by."[n] She succeeded somewhat better when she boasted of her connection with Godwin and the wonder-boy Shelley, who had sent him a copy of *Queen Mab* when it was published in 1813.

Certainly the girl displayed more originality than most of the authoresses who bedeviled him. Besides, there was an innate gentleness and kindness in his nature which Claire had sensed. He had once told Lady Melbourne: "I could love anything on earth that appeared to wish it."[n] He knew she would be troublesome, but he was leaving England soon. Claire pursued her advantage. Before long she was calling on him as often as he would let her. And when he could not see her, he offered his box at Drury Lane to her and Shelley, but she wrote that Shelley could not endure the theater.

Other matters were now claiming Byron's attention. Soon after they had signed the preliminary agreement for the separation, he wrote some verses addressed to his wife, summing up all the sentimental pathos into which his frustrations and regrets now flowed:

Fare thee well! and if for ever,
Still for ever, fare thee well:
Even though unforgiving, never
'Gainst thee shall my heart rebel.
Would that breast were bared before thee
Where thy head so oft hath lain,
While that placid sleep came o'er thee
Which thou ne'er canst know again . . .
When our child's first accents flow—
Wilt thou teach her to say "father!"
Though his care she must forego?

He sent a copy to Annabella, but she was maddeningly silent. Then when she sent back without any answer some letters testifying that Byron had never said anything but good about her, he was furious. The vitriol of his anger found vent in "A Sketch from Private Life," directed against Mrs. Clermont, who, he believed, had been the dominating influence on his wife and the cause of her implacability. It was the bitterest poem Byron ever wrote:

Born in the garret, in the kitchen bred,
Promoted thence to deck her mistress' head; . . .
Quick with the tale, and ready with the lie,
The genial confidante, and general spy . . .

Murray, whom Byron had foolishly asked to print fifty copies to show to friends, had shown both poems secretly to Caroline Lamb, who, it seems, was playing a double game. As soon as she heard of the separation, she wrote to Byron, offering to lie for him to prevent his wife from learning what presumably only she (Caroline) knew of his worst sins: ". . . there is nothing however base it may appear that I would not do to save you or yours from this—do not oh do not believe those who would lead you for one moment to think she knows any thing for certain—be firm be guarded. . . . whatever happens insist upon seeing her . . . see your Wife—& she cannot have the heart to betray you—if she has she is a devil. . . ."[n]

When Byron, suspecting already that Caroline was the source of the rumors that were abroad, failed to answer her, she determined to seek revenge by allying herself with the other side. She sent a series of letters to Lady Byron, hinting at dark secrets which she could reveal to her, and asking for an interview: "*I will tell you that which if you merely menace him with the knowledge shall make him tremble—*."[n] She played on the rumor that Byron would try to take the child. "Above all intimate to *him* that you have the knowledge & proof of Some secret which nothing but dispair shall force you to utter."[n]

Lady Byron, though she distrusted and detested Caroline, took the bait, for that was the very kind of thumbscrew she wished to have on her husband, who was immune to ordinary menaces. The interview took place on March 27 at the home of Mrs. George Lamb, and Annabella took careful minutes of the conversation. Caroline appeared greatly agitated. She made Annabella the judge of what she ought to do. She had made "a solemn promise not to reveal these secrets. . . . his protestations that he would never renew such crimes had prevailed upon her to be silent." This was a mere playing up to Lady Byron's impeccable "rectitude," for Caroline was eager to reveal her secret as she apparently had already to Murray and perhaps others. And Annabella easily rationalized her judgment. "I then said that I conceived *her* promise was released by the infringement of *his*, and that she might now redeem all by giving me this knowledge if as important as she signified to the preservation of my Child—that, neither on earth, nor in Heaven would she, in my opinion, have cause to repent so disinterested an action."[n] Of course, neither Caroline nor Annabella knew whether he had broken his supposed promise, nor did the latter by her own account yet know what the alleged "crimes" were.

Caroline then confessed "That from the time Mrs L—— came to Bennet St. in the year 1813—Lord B—— had given her various intimations of a criminal intercourse between them," first by innuendo and later by an outright avowal, even boasting of the ease of his conquest.[n] Then she said that Byron had told her of "worse crimes": ". . . he had . . . confessed that from his boyhood he had been in the practice of unnatural crime—that Rushton was one of those whom he had corrupted—by whom he had been attended as a page. . . . He mentioned 3 schoolfellows whom he had thus perverted."

Annabella added to her minutes of the conversation to send to Dr. Lushington: "Ly C. L—did not believe that he had committed this crime since his return to England, though he practised it unrestrictedly in Turkey—His own horror of it still appeared to be so great that he several times turned quite faint & sick in alluding to the subject—."[n]

Annabella now had what she needed to justify the adamant course she had irrevocably taken. She wrote to Dr. Lushington: "The result of my interview this morning was . . . to change my strong impression relative to the 1st and 2nd reports, into *absolute* certainty." And she was gratified to hear from her lawyer that he most cordially congratulated her "upon your final escape from all proximity to or intercourse with such contamination."[n] She knew as her lawyer did that if anything of this sort could be convincingly brought forward, even if not proved, Byron would have no chance in court.

During the first days of April Byron was in a fever of activity, seeing his friends, trying to make some settlement of his business affairs, and plunging into festivities which would save him from too much thought. On the 8th his books were sold at public auction. Hobhouse was present and bought £34 worth. Murray bid in some for Mrs. Leigh and for Rogers, and also the screen with the portraits of actors and pugilists, which still remains in the Byron room at 50 Albemarle Street. The total received from the sale came to £723 12s. 6d.

That evening Hobhouse accompanied Byron to Lady Jersey's, where they were introduced to Benjamin Constant. Augusta accompanied her brother on that occasion and was cut by some people, including Mrs. George Lamb, and Byron felt the snubs of the ladies who formerly had crowded around him. Some of the men also avoided him. Only Lady Jersey and Miss Mercer Elphinstone went out of their way to be kind, and he never forgot it. The latter, who had cast coquettish eyes at him in 1812, was a great heiress and independent enough to shake her red hair in the face of public disapproval. According to one story, she "gave him a familiar nod, and said, 'You should have married *me*, and then this would not have happened to you!' "[n]

Byron's volatile temper flared up again when he learned that Annabella had ceased to communicate with Augusta, but had sent a reply through her lawyer. On April 14 Augusta came from St. James's Palace, where she had been living for the past month, to say farewell to her brother. She had stood loyally by him, though she was pregnant again and she felt that her family needed her. Her pregnancy was far advanced, the rumors about her were growing more open and more vicious, and now Annabella apparently had deserted her. She was returning the next day to Six Mile Bottom. It was a touching farewell that aroused all Byron's sincerest feelings. He had written a poetical tribute to her for standing by him, his "Stanzas to Augusta." Others may have thought her weak, but Byron knew her firmness. He later told Lady Blessington: "Augusta knew all my weaknesses, but she had love enough to bear with them. . . . She has given me such good advice, and yet, finding me incapable of following it, loved and pitied me but the more, because I was erring."[n] Remorse for the grief he had brought her overwhelmed him. She presented him with a Bible that he always carried with him. As Byron's premonition told him, on that Easter Sunday they parted never to meet again.

To Byron's surprise and annoyance, Murray had shown his stanzas to Augusta to Caroline Lamb, who wrote him hysterically and hypocritically: ". . . you will draw ruin on your own head and hers if at this moment you shew these. I know not from what quarter the report originates. You accused *me*, and falsely; but if you could hear all that is said at this moment, you would believe one, who . . . would perhaps die to save you."[n] After seeing his "Fare Thee Well," she had written to Murray that Byron was "a poor paltry Hypocrite a mean coward—and a man without a heart."[n] But in another letter (whether before or after it is difficult to determine) she wrote: ". . . be not over angry with *him* whatever his offenses . . . let us still pay worship to the Giaour what though he be fallen—it is yet an Angel

—promise—swear to me—that you will stand firm to him. . . ." [n] But poor Caroline was on the verge of madness, and it was not long before she succumbed completely.

Byron wrote a final letter to Annabella: "I have just parted from Augusta—almost the last being you had left me to part with—& the only unshattered tie of my existence—wherever I may go—& I am going far—you & I can never meet again in this world—nor in the next—Let this content or atone.—If any accident occurs to me—be kind to *her*. . . ." [n] Annabella did not reply. She might have been touched or disturbed by this letter earlier; now she was only concerned with justification for her conduct. She wrote complacently to her mother: "The public feeling has been still more turned against Lord B. by the publication of his verses in the Champion of yesterday—and some comments were added to expose the duplicity of their author—by which a wonderful effect has been produced." [n]

Byron's preparations for going abroad had begun in March. He had engaged a young Dr. John William Polidori as his personal physician.* For the voyage he ordered a huge coach copied from the one Napoleon captured at Genappe. It was built by Baxter for £500. According to Pryse Gordon, "Besides a *lit de repos*, it contained a library, a plate-chest, and every apparatus for dining." [n]

His persistent new acquaintance Claire Clairmont had difficulty in seeing him during these last busy days. To entice his interest, she brought Godwin's talented daughter Mary to see him. Claire had already proposed a plan to meet him alone in Geneva, which appalled him, but now she had a scheme for getting the Shelleys to accompany her there. Mary, who then knew nothing of the liaison, came and was charmed with Byron. Claire could report: "Mary is delighted with you as I knew she would be; she entreats me in private to obtain your address abroad that we may if possible have again the pleasure of seeing

---

* Polidori's sister later married Gabriele Rossetti and became the mother of three famous literary children, William Michael, Christina, and Dante Gabriel Rossetti. Dr. Polidori had literary ambitions and was full of vanity. He spoke English, French, and Italian, and was proud to be the traveling companion of the great Lord Byron. Murray, seeing many guineas in the prospect, offered him £500 for an account of the tour, and Polidori began a diary when they reached Dover.

you. She perpetually exclaims, 'How mild he is! How gentle! So different from what I expected.' "[n]

Byron had sought relaxation and forgetfulness and, to his embarrassment, found love, unwanted and tedious. But although he knew that his kindness encouraged the thing he did not want, he could not be rude to her. She was now ready to play her last card. It was his final week in England. She must act now, she felt, if she was to hold him. She wrote boldly: "I do not expect you to love me; I am not worthy of your love. I feel you are superior, yet much to my surprize, more to my happiness, you betrayed passions I had believed no longer alive in your bosom. . . . Have you then any objection to the following plan? On Thursday Evening we may go out of town together by some stage or mail about the distance of ten or twelve miles. There we shall be free and unknown; we can return early the following morning. . . . I shall ever remember the gentleness of your manners and the wild originality of your countenance."[n]

Whether they went to the country or not, Byron did see her and found momentary solace in her embraces, to his later great regret. His better judgment fought against it, but he had already shown himself weak enough to love "anything on earth that appeared to wish it."

Byron signed the final deed of separation on April 21, saying "I deliver this as Mrs. Clermont's act and deed."[n] The next day his last-minute packing was interrupted by many visitors, all his stanch friends who came to say goodbye. But he took time to write a note to Augusta: "My own Sweet Sis—The deeds are signed. . . . All I have now to beg or desire on the subject is—that you will never mention nor allude to Lady Byron's name again in any shape—or on any occasion—except indispensable business."[n]

Despite Byron's dislike of early rising, there was tremendous activity at an early hour on the 23rd in the great house in Piccadilly Terrace. It was important to get started before the bailiffs came. Besides Dr. Polidori, Byron took with him three servants: a Swiss named Berger; William Fletcher; and Robert Rushton, who had accompanied him as far as Gibraltar on his first journey abroad. Hobhouse and Scrope Davies were going to see him off at Dover. They arrived at eight in the evening and put the Napoleonic carriage aboard for fear the bailiffs would follow and seize it. The wind was contrary the next day, so the sailing had to be postponed, and they passed the time by visiting the grave of Charles Churchill, the eighteenth-century satirist and friend of the republican Wilkes. Hobhouse noted: "Byron lay down on his grave and gave the man a crown to fresh turf it." [n]

News had gone abroad that the celebrated Lord Byron was in Dover, and, Dr. Lushington later reported to Lady Byron, "the curiosity to see him was so great that many ladies accoutred themselves as chambermaids for the purpose of obtaining under that disguise a nearer inspection whilst he continued at the inn. . . ." [n]

The next morning the wind had changed and the captain was eager to get off, but Byron could not rise early. Hobhouse recorded: "however after some bustle out came Byron—and taking my arm—walked down to the Quay." They walked through a line of spectators. "The bustle kept B in spirits—but he looked affected when the packet glided off. I ran to the end of the wooden pier . . . the dear fellow pulled off his cap & wav'd it to me—I gazed until I could not distinguish him any longer—God bless him for a gallant spirit and a kind one. . . ." [n]

CHAPTER XVI

1816

Childe Harold Roams Again

BYRON WAS BOTH EXALTED and cast down by the agitation of the parting. But, as he had told Moore, agitation of any kind always gave "a rebound" to his spirits, and his impressions and reflections were vivified and stored for poetic expression. The sea and the wind and the bouncing ship evoked something of the melancholy he had felt the last time he left England's shores, in 1809. He was Childe Harold again, but a matured and altered Harold,

> . . . *grown agèd in this world of woe,*
> *In deeds, not years, piercing the depths of life,*
> *So that no wonder waits him* . . .[n]

It was, as Byron half realized already, the end of an epoch in his life, but he was not yet aware to what extent it was the beginning of his maturer literary existence. As he left England, never to return, he entered into a freedom of life and expression that transcended the constraints imposed on him by the years of fame. That freedom awoke in him as he headed for the warm lands of the south. Although he planned to stop in Geneva to wait for Hobhouse, his destination was Venice, the "greenest island" of his imagination. And he had intended ultimately to go on to the eastern Mediterranean. Writing from Ravenna in 1820, he said: "I meant to have gone to Turkey and am not sure that I shall not finish with it. . . ."[n]

British restraints departed as soon as he reached Ostend. At their inn, the Cour Impériale, Polidori indiscreetly recorded, "As soon as he reached his room, Lord Byron fell like a thunderbolt upon the chambermaid." [n] They set out the next afternoon in the lumbering Napoleonic carriage, with four horses and a postilion. At Antwerp, Byron admired the famous basins built for Bonaparte's Navy more than he did the paintings. He was particularly severe on the Flemish School's most admired artist. "As for Rubens," he told Hobhouse, ". . . he seems to me . . . the most glaring—flaring—staring—harlotry imposter that ever passed a trick upon the senses of mankind." [n]

At Brussels, Byron met Pryse Lockhart Gordon, who had been a friend of his mother in Scotland. One thing Byron wanted to see more than cathedrals or museums was the field of Waterloo, and Gordon acted as his "cicerone." As he viewed the battlefield, Gordon noted, the poet remained "silent, pensive, and in a musing mood." [n] But before leaving, he and Polidori mounted two saddle horses and galloped over the field, perhaps imagining themselves in a cavalry charge. Byron, according to Polidori, sang "Turkish or Arnaout riding-tunes." [n]

At the Gordons that evening he was in high spirits and charmed the company with anecdotes of his Eastern travels. He consented to compose some verses for Mrs. Gordon's album, in which Walter Scott had written some lines on Waterloo. The next day he returned with the two stanzas: "Stop!—for thy tread is on an Empire's dust," [n] later to be incorporated into the third canto of *Childe Harold.* Already he had begun to put down on paper some of the thoughts that had pursued him since he left England, for only in that way could he find an escape from the imperfection of existence.

'Tis to create, and in creating live
A being more intense that we endow
With form our fancy, gaining as we give
The life we image, even as I do now— [n]

The excitement of travel stirred up in him again the impalpable longings of his youth, which he now associated with the wild freedom of nature and the landscapes and skies beyond the horizon.

Where rose the mountains, there to him were friends;
Where rolled the ocean, thereon was his home . . ."[n]

Having felt while standing on that "place of skulls," "the deadly Waterloo," the vanity of power and the fleetingness of fame, he committed those feelings to paper in the small hours at the Hôtel d'Angleterre. To Byron, Waterloo was not a victory but a melancholy defeat, for Europe was still in fetters and tyranny wielded more power than ever. Yet the individual valor of brave men was memorable and worth recording. The dramatic contrast between the gaiety at the Duchess of Richmond's ball in Brussels on the eve of the battle and the death and destruction that followed made a fine opening for the Waterloo sections of *Childe Harold*.

As for Napoleon, Byron had long been "dazzled and overwhelmed by his character and career." Now more than ever he felt a strong kinship with what he conceived to be the basic springs of the Emperor's character. He was surely thinking of himself when he wrote:

But Quiet to quick bosoms is a Hell,
And there *hath been thy bane; there is a fire*
And motion of the Soul which will not dwell
In its own narrow being, but aspire
Beyond the fitting medium of desire . . ."[n]

On May 6 Byron and his entourage set out in his Napoleonic coach for Louvain on the road to the Rhine.

While he was trying to forget England, neither his friends nor his enemies in England had forgotten him. Hobhouse, Davies, and Kinnaird were trying to quash the ugly rumors that persisted in London, spread apparently by some of those who had either seen or heard of the depositions of Lady Byron to Dr. Lushington. And at least four women lived with the unforgettable image of that handsome face and the memory of his irresistible personality.

On May 9 Henry Colburn published Caroline Lamb's novel *Glenarvon*, a thinly masked satire on the Holland House and Devonshire House circles linked in an impossible combination with a romantic Gothic narrative involving herself and Byron.

The next day Hobhouse wrote: "Glenarvon—the hero is a monster & meant for B. . . . I called on the bitch & was asked whether any harm had been done by her book. . . . she showed me half bawdy pictures of hers of B." [n] She had published one of Byron's letters, slightly altered, in the book, and when Hobhouse intimated that he might publish some of hers, she countered with the threat of publishing all of Byron's letters and her journal of their relations. But Caroline had not painted Byron as dark as she might have in the novel. Although she ascribed murder and kidnapping and a few seductions to the character she had created, once she let herself go, he became a romantic hero, interestingly melancholy, whose genius and charm thrilled her in writing as they had in life.

While Caroline Lamb was thus making a fool of herself, another woman whose thoughts were constantly occupied with Byron retired sedately to Kirkby Mallory in Leicestershire. But Annabella had not gone into the country, as Rogers mistakenly said, "to break her heart." She was already laying plans for correspondence with Augusta on a new footing (she had ceased all communication with her after the first week in April). As she brooded over the past words and actions of Byron and his sister, her opinion that there had been incestuous relations between them became certain and unalterable. Now she had two objects in view: one, to establish the fact absolutely, preferably by getting Augusta to confess, and thus to know for certain whether Byron ever persuaded her to repeat the crime after his marriage; and second, to condition or frighten Augusta against ever again renewing an intimacy with her brother, actually to root out the love she bore him from even her correspondence and her thoughts.

The jealousy which Annabella's principles would not permit her to acknowledge found sublimation in a truly sadistic zeal to extract the sin from Augusta's life. The religious-moral tone of her correspondence, interspersed with expressions of love for Augusta and concern for her spiritual well-being, does not conceal the brutality of her attack upon the foolish, lovable, and impulsive woman. There are few records of the cruelty that wears a benevolent face, of the studied undermining of the peace of mind of a fellow woman, equal to the deliberate assault upon the conscience of Augusta in the correspondence of Lady

Byron and Mrs. Villiers, Augusta's intimate friend, in the months that followed the separation.

While this nemesis of righteousness was being prepared for her, Augusta, having given birth to her son, cut off from all intercourse with Annabella, and feeling desolate in the loss of her brother's society, turned for news of him to Hobhouse, who might go abroad soon and could carry messages for her. She wrote to thank him for the verses of Byron he had sent her, probably the "Stanzas to Augusta." "I think them beautiful," she said simply, "and I need not add, they are most gratifying to me, who doat upon dear B." [n]

Another dark-eyed girl was deeply interested in Byron's journey, and hoped to reach Geneva before him. Claire Clairmont left Dover with Percy Shelley and Mary Godwin on May 3 and wrote to Byron from Paris: "I have taken the name of [Madame] Clairville because you said you liked the name of Clare but could not bear *mont* because of that very ugly woman. And I chuse to be married because I am so [a hint that she already knew or suspected that she was carrying Byron's child] & Madame's have their full liberty abroad. . . . I know not how to address you; I cannot call you friend for though I love you you do not feel even interest for me. . . ." [n]

Byron was proceeding with his leisurely journey up the Rhine. At Cologne he visited the cathedral and St. Ursula's Church, where, according to legend, 11,000 virgins' bones were buried. That legend had always fascinated him and he was to refer to it later in *Don Juan:*

> *Eleven thousand maiden heads of bone.*
> *The greatest number flesh hath ever known.*[n]

Proceeding up the west bank of the Rhine, he was enchanted by the scenery. "The castled Crag of Drachenfels" would have given him "double joy" if Augusta had been there.[n] The travelers crossed into Switzerland at Basel. The field of Morat, where the Swiss defeated the Burgundians in the fifteenth century, gave Byron material for more stanzas for *Childe Harold.* Like other travelers, he picked up a few bones, "as much as may have made a quarter of a hero," he grimly boasted.[n]

They reached the Lake of Geneva (Lac Leman) at Lausanne. Byron was captivated immediately: "Lake Leman woos me with its crystal face."[n] Night had fallen before they arrived at Dejean's Hôtel d'Angleterre on the main road to Geneva, a mile outside the city. Weary from the journey and probably annoyed by the required formality of writing statistical details, Byron put down his age as 100. Claire, who had been keeping anxious watch, for she now knew that she was pregnant by the most talked-of poet of England, saw the register and wrote a note in playful and exuberant relief: "I am sorry you are grown so old, indeed I suspected you were 200, from the slowness of your journey. . . . Well, heaven send you sweet sleep—I am so happy."[n]

But Byron was in no hurry to renew the affair with this importunate girl. The next day he went to Geneva in search of a house or villa that he could rent for the summer. He was directed to the Villa Diodati in the village of Cologny, two miles from Geneva on the south shore opposite their hotel. The villa stood back some two hundred yards from the lake on a hill and commanded a magnificent view of the blue water, with the city to the left and the Jura Mountains furnishing a distant backdrop across the lake in front. The property belonged to Edouard Diodati, a descendant of the Charles Diodati who had been a friend of John Milton. But it seemed too expensive and a little smaller than he had hoped for. He decided to look farther.

Claire had written two more plaintive and sentimental letters, to which Byron apparently sent no reply. Then the following day, when he and Polidori stepped out of their boat on return from their house hunting, he met Claire and Mary with Shelley. When the two poets met on the shore of the Lake of Geneva, one of the most famous friendships in literary history began.

Byron had heard from Claire of the wonderful boy, then only twenty-three, and he had read *Queen Mab.* Shelley was shy with strangers, but so was Byron. Yet the shyness of both vanished once the conversation turned to other than commonplace topics. From this time forward, Byron spent more and more time with the Shelley ménage. The friendship was cemented, and that made it easier for Byron to accept the companionship of the ladies. Neither Mary nor Shelley yet knew of the intimacy Claire had shared with him, and Byron was not eager to have it known. They dined together and went out in the boat. Byron regaled them with stories of the literary men he had known in London.

Mary, who had been enchanted with Byron from the first meeting in London, later recalled with melancholy nostalgia some of the idyllic moments of their moonlight rides on the water: "The waves were high and inspiriting. . . . 'I will sing you an Albanian song,' cried Lord Byron; 'now, be sentimental and give me all your attention.' It was a strange, wild howl that he gave forth; but such as, he declared, was an exact imitation of the savage Albanian mode,—laughing, the while, at our disappointment. . . ."[n]

Out of these evenings, with the stimulus of the sky and the water and the discussions with Shelley, who, himself an ethereal presence, opened up wide vistas in Byron's mind, came new stanzas for *Childe Harold.* Under the spell of Shelley's eloquence, Byron absorbed something of the Wordsworthian pantheistic feeling. No one made Wordsworth's philosophy more appealing to Byron than did Shelley; he too longed to spurn "the clay-cold bonds which round our being cling."[n] But Byron usually ended in a basis of tangible reality, however much he might let his fancy play. He later told Medwin: "Shelley, when I was in Switzerland, used to dose me with Wordsworth physic even to nausea; and I do remember then reading some things of his with pleasure."[n]

During the first week in June, the Shelley ménage settled in a small two-story house at Montalègre, at the foot of the hill of Cologny, only a stone's throw from the lake. And soon after, Byron moved into the Villa Diodati, a couple of hundred yards away. With the expectation of taking more extensive excursions on the lake, Byron and Shelley bought a boat for 25 louis, a small sailing vessel with a keel. It was kept in the little harbor below Shelley's house.

Byron was well pleased with his new home. The little villa was a square structure of gray stone and masonry rising two stories above the basement, with a wrought-iron railing enclosing a balcony that ran around three sides of the *rez-de-chaussée.* There was a grand salon, a room of ample porportions whose windows opened to the front and side balconies. It was decorated in elegant but simple eighteenth-century style, and was cheered by a great fireplace on rainy nights. Byron, who, from the days of his boyhood when he had roamed the ruined halls of Newstead, loved expansiveness, never had a house with a nobler view than that from the balcony of the Villa Diodati.

It was a novelty for Byron to find agreeable persons untrammeled by the conventions of society, well read and intelligent, with sensitive appreciation, ready to discuss any subject under the sun with speculative intensity. When the weather permitted, he and the Shelleys went on the lake in the quiet evening; when it was stormy, they gathered before the fire at Diodati and talked, the conversation ranging from poetry to the appearance of ghosts.

The only discord in the harmony of their lives was created by the vanity and flightiness of young Dr. Polidori, who once challenged Shelley to a duel. Shelley only laughed, but Byron warned the doctor that, though Shelley might have scruples against duelling, he had none and would be glad to take his place. And Byron found relief for his annoyance at the Doctor's "eternal nonsense" by making sly remarks about him such as that "he was exactly the kind of person to whom, if he fell overboard, one would hold out a straw to know if the adage be true that drowning men catch at straws." [n]

Byron had another embarrassment in the presence of Claire, to whom he was afraid to pay any particular attention for fear she would take advantage of it. Nevertheless she induced him to renew his intimate relations with her, though she had difficulty finding opportunities to visit the Villa Diodati as often as she wished, partly because the egotistic Polidori was always in the way. Byron had confessed that his heart always alighted on the nearest perch. He excused himself to Augusta later by saying: "I was not in love nor have any love left for any, but I could not exactly play the Stoic with a woman who had scrambled eight hundred miles to unphilosophize me, besides I had been regaled of late with so many 'two courses and a *desert*' (Alas!) of aversion, that I was fain to take a little love (if pressed particularly) by way of novelty." [n]

Careful as the pair were, gossips were not slow to circulate stories. Byron later told Medwin: "I never led so moral a life as during my residence in that country; but I gained no credit by it. . . . there is no story so absurd that they did not invent at my cost. I was watched by glasses on the opposite side of the Lake, and by glasses too that must have had very distorted optics." [n] He ascribed part of the feeling toward him to the fact that he went so little among the Genevese. The English, who flocked to Geneva in droves during the summer, heard many fantastic stories, such as that the notorious Lord Byron was living with "a Mrs. Shelley, wife to the man who keeps the Mount Coffee-house." [n]

Actually Byron had settled into a very Spartan regime, for he had grown heavy again from the unrestrained feasting of his last days in England. Moore, no doubt drawing from Mary Shelley's memory, says: "His system of diet here was regulated by an abstinence almost incredible. A thin slice of bread, with tea, at breakfast—a light, vegetable dinner, with a bottle or two of Seltzer water, tinged with vin de Grave, and in the evening, a cup of green tea, without milk or sugar, formed the whole of his sustenance. The pangs of hunger he appeased by privately chewing tobacco and smoking cigars." [n] Polidori observed that "he retired to rest at three, got up at two, and employed himself a long time over his toilette; . . . he never went to sleep without a pair of pistols and a dagger by his side, and . . . he never eat animal food." [n] He generally ate alone so that his diet would not be noticed and commented upon.

During one of the evening sessions at Diodati, after a discussion of ghosts and the supernatural and the nature of the principle of life, Byron suggested that they all write ghost stories. He himself began one with its setting in the ruins of Ephesus, but after a few pages left off; Polidori later seized the idea and based his anonymous tale called *The Vampyre* on it, happy to hint that it was Byron's, for that would increase the sale. Mary was the only one to take seriously the pact to write a supernatural story. The result was the frightening tale of the monster created by Frankenstein, which she published the following year.

On June 22 Byron and Shelley embarked in their small open sailboat for a tour of the lake. It was intended as a pilgrimage to sites immortalized by Rousseau. At Meillerie they dined on honey from mountain flowers on the enchanted ground where St. Preux, Rousseau's hero in the *Nouvelle Héloïse,* had spent his exile. On leaving, they ran into a storm. The boat filled with water and seemed about to sink. Byron had some concern for Shelley, who could not swim, telling him that he could save him if he held on to an oar and did not struggle. But, he recalled, Shelley answered "with the greatest coolness, that 'he had no notion of being saved, and that I would have enough to do to save myself, and begged not to trouble me.' " [n]

The next day being calm, they sailed first to the castle of Chillon. While visiting its towers and torture chamber and the dungeons where political prisoners and heretics had been chained to the columns, Shelley was sunk in the depths of melancholy at this monument of "cold and inhuman tyranny." [n] Byron was impressed by the story of François Bonivard, a sixteenth-century patriot who had conspired against the Duke of Savoy and had been confined for some years in the lower dungeon. Before he returned to Diodati, he had composed *The Prisoner of Chillon,* a lyrical dramatic monologue that was to become one of his most popular poems.

At Vevey and Clarens the poets felt themselves again on Rousseau's holy ground. Shelley had just been reading the *Nouvelle Héloïse.* Byron had read it often, and knew it almost by heart. He had already written some stirring lines on Rousseau for *Childe Harold.* For him Rousseau was indeed "The apostle of Affliction, he who threw/ Enchantment over Passion, and from Woe/ Wrung overwhelming eloquence." [n] Byron knew that he was describing himself as well as Rousseau when he wrote:

> *His love was Passion's essence . . .*
> *But his was not the love of living dame,*
> *Nor of the dead who rise upon our dreams,*
> *But of ideal Beauty, which became*
> *In him existence, and o'erflowing teems*
> *Along his burning page, distempered though*
> *it seems.* [n]

But Rousseau symbolized to Byron more than the passionate self. He had inspired the Revolution and set the libertarian principle loose in the world, a principle that, though temporarily thwarted, would not die.

But Byron could turn, with that easy mobility of mind and temper observed by all who knew him well, from the solemnity of Bonivard's fate and the sentiment of Rousseau to the irony and wit of Voltaire and Gibbon. On the anniversary of the day (June 27, 1787) on which Gibbon wrote the last lines of his *History* in the summerhouse at Lausanne, Byron and Shelley visited the spot. After adding some stanzas on these eighteenth-century giants, the one all "fire and fickleness," the other "lord of irony," Byron wrote to Murray the same day that he had completed 117 stanzas of a new canto of *Childe Harold.* Back at Diodati, he spent a few days rearranging and correcting the accumulated stanzas, which had been written on scraps of paper as the inspiration struck him.

On the 4th of July the canto was completed to his satisfaction and he turned it over to Claire for copying. She was eager enough, for it was her one opportunity and excuse to be at Diodati alone with him. She finished the fair copy for the printer by July 10, and then started to copy *The Prisoner of Chillon.* But Byron soon grew tired of her constant pleading for attention. He finally took Shelley into council and urged that she not be allowed to come to Diodati. The Shelleys were planning a tour of Chamouni and Mont Blanc. Claire wanted to see Byron before she left, but he avoided her. Shelley understood the necessity of getting Claire away from Byron, for remaining near him would only make her unhappy.

On his side, Byron no doubt felt some relief when the Shelley party set off on the 21st on a tour that lasted almost to the end of the month. He divided his time between visiting Madame de Staël at her château at Coppet across the lake and extracting verses from his distempered brain in the hours after midnight. On his first visit to Coppet, according to Polidori, who accompanied him, "he was surprised to meet a lady carried out fainting. . . ."[n] Of this incident Byron wrote to Murray: "It is true that Mrs. Hervey (she writes novels) fainted at my entrance into Coppet, and then came back again. On her fainting, the Duchesse de Broglie [Mme de Staël's daughter] exclaimed, 'This is *too much*—at *sixty-five* years of age!' "[n]

Byron was nevertheless pleased with society at Coppet, and found Mme de Staël more agreeable at home than she had been in London, though their mutual *franchises* sometimes brought them into verbal combat. The cultivated Continental group he met there made the atmosphere much more congenial than that of the drawing rooms of Geneva, which were filled with English people. It is true that a few of the guests rubbed him the wrong way. Living at the château was Mme de Staël's great literary friend August Wilhelm von Schlegel, who contradicted everyone and was ridiculously vain. "He took a dislike to me," Byron wrote, "because I refused to flatter him . . . though Madame de Broglie begged me to do so, 'because he is so fond of it. *Voilà les hommes!*' "[n] But Byron formed a cordial relationship with the Abbé de Breme (or di Breme) who, like Pellegrino Rossi, kindled his interest in Italian freedom. Polidori described Breme as a "friend of Ugo Foscolo, enthusiastic for Italy, encomiast in all, Grand Almoner of Italy, hater of Austrians."[n]

After the departure of the Shelley party for Chamouni, alone on the quiet lake or undisturbed in the sequestered Diodati, Byron again felt the urge to write. At the request of Kinnaird, he wrote a "Monody on the Death of the Right Hon. R. B. Sheridan," but the thought of its being mouthed before a theater audience made him self-conscious, as he had been in the Drury Lane Address, and he produced only perfunctory couplets, despite his admiration for Sheridan. News from England, however, brought back the whole stream of his past, which now rolled through his mind in a fevered reverie that found voice in "The Dream," a capsule history of his life from youthful idealism through disillusionment to sad resignation and melancholy despair. In the dream he pictured himself and the Lady of his Love, who was his boy's idealization of Mary Chaworth.

In the same dejected spirit he wrote another dream poem, which he called "Darkness," a terrifying vision of man's last days in a dying universe. All civilization crumbled in the primordial struggle for existence. The altruistic instinct was sunk in every creature but one dog. At about the same time he wrote some verses on "Prometheus," who had been his defiant hero since as a schoolboy at Harrow he had written a paraphrase of a chorus of the *Prometheus Vinctus* of Æschylus. The theme was filling his mind more and more, and the contemplation of his own baffled existence gave it fire.

Titan! to thee the strife was given
Between the suffering and the will,
Which torture where they cannot kill . . .
Like thee, Man is in part divine,
A troubled stream from a pure source;

In his solitary musing upon the failure of life to provide the bright dreams of youth with any satisfying reality, Byron turned again to the vision of Augusta, who had never failed him. He poured out his overflowing feelings in some new verses to her:

Though the day of my Destiny's over,
And the star of my Fate hath declined,
Thy soft heart refused to discover
The faults which so many could find;

But Byron was quite unaware of the dreadful ordeal his sister was undergoing as the prongs of the "Iron Maiden" of Lady Byron and Mrs. Villiers closed upon her. Mrs. Villiers wrote to her partner in the inquisition: "Did you tell of his having betrayed her to others or do you think it possible to do this? Could she once be brought to *believe* this fact, I should hope much from it." [n] Annabella replied: "Except at one period I have always found her much more collected & prepared to repel suspicion than he was—and I have always observed the remarkable difference, that his feelings—distinct from practice—were much more sensitive & correct on all moral questions than hers. She did not appear to think these transgressions *of consequence*. Her self-condemnation has seemed so exclusively attached to what preceded my marriage, that, in opposition to every other probability, it *has* led me to doubt a positive renewal subsequently. . . ." [n]

Augusta was in a sad predicament indeed. To Annabella she wrote piteously: "I only wish *every past & present* thought could be open to you—you would *then* think *less* ill of me than you do now. . . . Dearest A——— *I have not wronged you. I have not abused your generosity.*" [n] But Mrs. Villiers, who was in London and was supposedly Augusta's closest friend, reported every symptom of pain, amendment, or danger in the victim. Her dejection and absence of mind were encouraging, but "I accidentally found yesterday by her question about foreign postage of letters that she was going to write to Ld. B. to-day." [n] Lady Byron proceeded cautiously but with determination. She wrote her coadjutor: "I am now leading her on to promise that she will never renew a confidential intercourse by letter—or any personal intercourse—I find it necessary to gain step by step. . . . She is perpetually relapsing into compromises with her conscience. . . ." [n]

But on July 30 she drove her point home vigorously: "Till you feel that he has in reality been your worst friend—indeed, *not* your friend—you cannot altogether think rightly . . . forgive him—desire his welfare—but resign the pernicious view of being his friend more nearly. . . ." She must always keep in view in writing him "to *rectify* instead of *soothing* or *indulging* his feelings—by avoiding therefore all phrases or *marks* [Annabella remembered the cryptic crosses in Augusta's letters to him] which may recall wrong ideas to his mind . . . and let me also warn you against the levity & nonsense which he likes for the worst reason, because it prevents him from reflecting seriously. . . ." "[n]

It is a measure of the abject state of Augusta's mind at the time that she acquiesced in this. The poor child of nature had now begun to doubt the wisdom of her best impulses and to imagine artificial sins that complicated her simple catechism. The streak of spurious piety in her confounded her other, surer instincts.

Byron in the meantime was diverted by other matters. Mme de Staël had lent him a copy of Caroline Lamb's novel *Glenarvon.* His own portrait in the book did not disturb him. He later wrote to Moore: "It seems to me, that if the authoress had written the *truth,* and nothing but the truth—the whole truth—the romance would not only have been more *romantic,* but more entertaining. As for the likeness, the picture can't be good—I did not sit long enough." "[n]

The Shelley party had returned from Chamouni on July 27. For the next two weeks the boating and the evening discussions at Diodati continued as before. But everything was not quite as it had been. If Shelley and Mary had not known it before, they were now aware of Claire's condition. Shelley was eager to do the best for her, and yet by his own code (he had left his wife, whom he no longer loved, and had cast his lot with Mary) he could not condemn Byron for not wanting to live with Claire. Shelley accompanied her to Diodati to talk the matter over frankly. According to Claire's later statement, "he proposed to place the Child when born in Mrs. Leigh's care. To this I objected on the ground that a Child always wanted a parent's care at least till seven years old. . . . He yielded and said it was best it should live with him. . . . I was to be called the Child's Aunt and in that character I could see it and watch over it without injury to anyone's reputation." [n]

Byron studiously avoided seeing Claire alone, and when she came to Diodati she was always accompanied by Shelley. On August 14, Matthew Gregory ("Monk") Lewis arrived for a visit, and on the 16th Byron accompanied him to Ferney to see Voltaire's château. From this time forward the evenings at Diodati were masculine ones. Shelley came alone, but Byron pacified the ladies by calling occasionally at Shelley's cottage.

In her kind and frank but tactless way Mme de Staël had reopened the old sore of the separation by suggesting that a reconciliation might still be possible. Byron conceded so far as to write a letter expressing his continued love for Annabella, but he had no real hope that this attempt would be more successful than others. How quickly his feelings could change concerning his wife is indicated by the fact that he had begun a prose tale, a thinly veiled allegory of his marital difficulties, and when he heard that Lady Byron was ill, he cast it into the fire. As always when he was troubled, he turned to his sister. Toward the end of August he had received her letter, full of alarms and anxieties, though vague enough, for she could not tell her brother how deeply now she was in Annabella's confidence. In his reply he charged her with "starting at shadows," and added, "do not be uneasy—and do not 'hate yourself' if you hate either let it be *me* —but do not—it would kill me; we are the last persons in the world—who ought—or could cease to love one another." [n]

John Cam Hobhouse and Scrope Davies, whom Byron had expected earlier in the summer, finally arrived on August 26. Shelley called, but Mary and Claire did not meet Byron's cynical guests. Claire was bitterly disappointed that Byron would not even give her a kind word at parting. But the pathos of her farewell letter only steeled his resolution not to yield again to the softness he had once had the weakness to show her. She wrote: "Farewell my dearest dear Lord Byron. Now don't laugh or smile in your little proud way for it is very wrong for you to read this merrily which I write in tears. . . . dearest I shall love you to the end of my life & nobody else, think of me as one whose affection you can count on. . . ." [n] But Claire was never to hear from Byron directly again. Whatever messages he sent came grudgingly through Shelley.

Shelley, Mary, and Claire left for England on August 29. Byron had entrusted to Shelley the manuscript (Claire's transcription) of the third canto of *Childe Harold, The Prisoner of Chillon,* and other shorter poems written during the summer. On that same day Byron, Davies, Hobhouse, and Polidori set out for Chamouni. At one of the inns where they stopped during the tour, Byron noticed that Shelley had written the word "atheist" in Greek after his name. Knowing that other English travelers would see it, he said to Hobhouse: "Do you not think I shall do Shelley a service by scratching this out?"[n] And he proceeded to deface the word with great care. But Shelley had written the same in at least three other inn registers, and English tourists, including Southey, saw and made the most of the scandalous impiety.[n] After this tour, Scrope Davies left for England, taking with him Robert Rushton and various manuscripts.

Byron had heard from his visitors some of the stories that were being told in England about him, and he wrote to reassure Augusta: ". . . as to all these 'mistresses'—Lord help me—I have had but one. Now don't scold—but what could I do? A foolish girl, in spite of all I could say or do, would come after me . . . and I have had all the plague possible to persuade her to go back again, but at last she went." But the heaviness of his present feelings had other causes: ". . . she [Lady Byron]—or rather the Separation—has broken my heart. I feel as if an Elephant had trodden on it."[n] If he had known on what terms his sister was then corresponding with his wife, he would have been doubly shocked.

Despite her apparent compliance, Augusta had kept the way open for continued communication with her brother. She was so evasive that Annabella wanted to get an interview and a full confession. On August 31 she went to London and saw Augusta several times. She had now accomplished her purpose. She wrote exultantly to Mrs. Villiers: ". . . I see all I could wish in her towards you—& the humblest sense of her own situation. . . . She has shown me of her own accord *his* letters to her—having only suppressed them because of the bitterness towards me—they are *absolute love letters*—and she wants to know how she can stop them—."[n]

Mrs. Villiers added her moral suasion to keep Augusta in line. "I told her," she wrote Lady Byron, ". . . that not a letter—

a note—a word should pass between her & him without being submitted to you—that you were her Guardian angel. . . ."[n] And Augusta dutifully wrote to Annabella: ". . . I am anxious to make every atonement. . . . When I write to B. it will be as you advise. . . . My Guardian Angel!"[n]

Byron sensed that something or someone had upset Augusta, but he supposed it was some more of the machinations of Caroline Lamb, and did not dream that his letters were shown to the lady of undeviating rectitude. Some hint that the negotiations through Mme de Staël for a reconciliation were not going well must have reached Byron at about this time, for his sorrow for his wife's illness turned to gall and he wrote some bitter "Lines on Hearing that Lady Byron Was Ill," accusing Annabella of "implacability" and designating her "The moral Clytemnestra of thy lord."

Before leaving on a tour of the Bernese Alps with Hobhouse, Byron finally decided to give Dr. Polidori his *congé*. They parted friends. He told Murray: "I know no great harm of him; but he had an alacrity of getting into scrapes, and was too young and heedless. . . ."[n] And he said later: "I was sorry when we parted, for I soon get attached to people. . . ."[n]

Byron and Hobhouse left Diodati on September 17. Byron decided to keep a journal of the trip for his sister. Her assurances that Lady Byron had been very kind to her rankled, and he wrote her: "*Of* her you are to judge for yourself, but do not altogether forget that she has destroyed your brother. . . . What a fool I was to marry—and *you* not very wise—my dear—we might have lived so single and so happy—as old maids and bachelors; I shall never find any one like you—nor you (vain as it may seem) like me. We are just formed to pass our lives together, and therefore—we—at least—I—am by a crowd of circumstances removed from the only being who could ever have loved me, or whom I can unmixedly feel attached to."[n]

Byron found the mountain scenery superb and exactly suited to his somber mood. The shepherds playing mournfully on their long pipes, the music of the cows' bells, the rushing cataracts, all offered a melancholy balm to his spirit. He wrote in his journal: "Arrived at the foot of the Mountain (the Yung frau, *i.e.* the Maiden); Glaciers; torrents; one of these torrents *nine hundred feet* in height of visible descent. . . . curving over the rock, like the *tail* of a white horse streaming in the wind, such as it might be conceived would be that of the '*pale* horse' on which *Death* is mounted in the Apocalypse."[n]

The high mountains raised Byron's feelings to an unearthly but gloomy ecstasy: "Heard the Avalanches falling every five minutes nearly—as if God was pelting the Devil down from Heaven with snow balls." He closed his journal for the day: "Passed *whole woods of withered pines, all withered;* trunks stripped and barkless, branches lifeless; done by a single winter, —their appearance reminded me of me and my family."[n]

They had ascended the Wengen Alp and had views of the Jungfrau, the Dent d'Argent, "shining like truth," the Kleiner and Grosser Eiger, and the Wetterhorn. On the descent, the glow Byron had felt subsided and he concluded his journal: ". . . neither the music of the Shepherd, the crashing of the Avalanche, nor the torrent, the mountain, the Glacier, the Forest, nor the Cloud, have for one moment lightened the weight upon my heart, nor enabled me to lose my own wretched identity. . . ."[n]

His mood was only temporarily lightened by news from England. Shelley had delivered the manuscript of *Childe Harold* to Murray, who, "trembling with auspicious hope," had carried it immediately to his literary adviser. Gifford, though ill, had sat up until he had read every line. "It had actually agitated him into a fever. . . ."[n] Douglas Kinnaird, who thenceforth acted as Byron's business agent, extracted £2,000 from Murray for the copyrights of *Childe Harold* and *The Prisoner of Chillon*. And Murray had no cause to regret his bargain.

Shelley did not hesitate to convey his confidence in his friend's poetic future. ". . . you are chosen out from all other men to some greater enterprise of thought. . . . *What* it should be, I am not qualified to say." He had once recommended the French Revolution as a theme. "But it is inconsistent with the spirit in which you ought to devote yourself to so great a destiny, that you should make use of any understanding but your own. . . ."[n]

It was good advice, for Byron could follow only his own bent. But first he must free his mind with a poetic catharsis different from anything he had attempted before. All the unhappiness, the sense of guilt, the frustrations, and the dismal brood-ings which had grown out of his reflection during the summer on his relations with Augusta, his marriage, and the separation found relief in a poetic drama that had been conceived in the high Alps and now burned for expression. The conception of Manfred, stimulated first by the passages of Goethe's *Faust* which "Monk" Lewis had translated to him, had something more of the Promethean character than of the Faustian.

But the real drama was within his mind. And the conflict was both personal and cosmic. When Manfred conjures up the spirits, including that of the star which rules his own destiny, he asks from them, not power or pleasure like Faust, but "Forgetfulness." The crux of Manfred's romantic agony is that man is

Half dust, half deity, alike unfit
To sink or soar . . .

Saved by a chamois hunter from self-destruction, Manfred puzzles his benefactor with his strange talk. He envies the simple peasant's acceptance of life, but he is of another order and must long for something "Beyond the fitting medium of desire." Manfred next calls up the Witch of the Alps. Asked what boon he wishes, he replies:

My pang shall find a voice. From my youth upwards
My Spirit walked not with the souls of men,
Nor looked upon the earth with human eyes . . .

But Manfred confesses that there was one who shared his sympathies:

She was like me in lineaments—her eyes—
Her hair—her features—all, to the very tone
Even of her voice, they said were like to mine;
But softened all, and tempered into beauty:
She had the same lone thoughts and wanderings . . .
Her faults were mine—her virtues were her own—
I loved her, and destroyed her!

On the summit of the Jungfrau, Manfred encounters the Destinies and finally Nemesis. But his indomitable mind, which has conjured up the spirits, guides him in refusing to bow down to even the most powerful of them, Arimanes, and they recognize their equal. It is inevitable, for the only spirits with which Manfred could make contact are those of his own mind's creation. He forces them to call up the phantom of Astarte, the one he has loved. The phantom cannot forgive him, for she too is his own creation and he cannot forgive himself. One of the spirits says:

He is convulsed—This is to be mortal,
And seek the things beyond mortality.

The composition had served its chief purpose: Byron had found the most effective relief for his guilt and despair. And he had discovered that his real quarrel with life was that he could not transcend the bounds of mortality; the "half deity" did not compensate for the "half dust."

At half past eleven on the morning of October 5, Byron and Hobhouse left Diodati for Milan, after taking a last look at the lake that for four months had been Byron's chief inspiration. He had little enthusiasm for the voyage, for he had no aim and no destination. He still thought of going to Greece again, but he would first spend some time in Venice.

CHAPTER XVII

1816–1817

Expatriate in Venice

TRAVELING IN Byron's heavy Napoleonic coach, Byron and Hobhouse, with their Italian guide Angelo Springhetti, followed the Simplon Napoleon road over the Alps. Their first impression of Milan was colored by the dirty rooms in L'Ancien Hôtel de San Marco. But that was soon changed by the pleasant society into which they were immediately thrown. They took a box at the Teatro alla Scala, the social center of Milan, and that evening were joined by Polidori, who had traveled over the Alps, and by Monsignore Ludivico di Breme, whom Byron had met at Coppet. Breme told them the gossip of the boxes and deplored the state of Italian literature, limiting the serious poets to Foscolo, Monti, and Pindemonte.

Byron was delighted the next day with the collection of manuscripts in the Ambrosian Library. He was most taken with some letters, "all original and amatory, between *Lucretia Borgia* and *Cardinal Bembo*. . . . I have pored over them and a lock of her hair, the prettiest and fairest imaginable. . . ."[n] He tried without success to get a copy of the letters, but he did filch a hair from the lock and wrapped it in a paper with the motto (from Pope):

> *And beauty draws us by a single hair.*[n]

On October 17, Byron and Hobhouse dined with Breme and his brother the Marquis at the latter's palace. Hobhouse was impressed with the deference paid to Byron. Breme compared him to Petrarch. Among the guests were Silvio Pellico, author of "Francesca da Rimini," the poet Monti, and M. de Beyle (later known by his pen name, Stendhal). Byron did not converse with them that evening, but according to Stendhal, he was in raptures when Monti recited his poem the "Mascheroniana," in praise of Napoleon.

Among other amusing companions in Milan was an Irish soldier of fortune, Colonel Fitzgerald. As Byron told the story to Moore, Fitzgerald had as a young ensign fallen in love with the Marchesa Castiglione, twenty years his senior. After the treaty of peace, he turned up again and flung himself at the feet of the Marchesa, murmuring "in half-forgotten Irish Italian, eternal vows of indelible constancy. The lady screamed, and exclaimed, 'Who are you?' the Colonel cried, 'What! don't you know me? I am so and so,' etc., etc., etc.; till, at length, the Marchesa, mounting from reminiscence to reminiscence, through the lovers of the intermediate twenty-five years, arrived at last at the recollection of her *povero* sub-lieutenant. She then said, 'Was there ever such virtue?' (that was her very word) and, being now a widow, gave him apartments in her palace, reinstated him in all the rights of wrong, and held him up to the admiring world as a miracle of incontinent fidelity, and the unshaken Abdiel of absence." [n]

As a close associate of Napoleon during his Russian campaign, Henri Beyle excited Byron's particular interest. Beyle on his side was fascinated by Byron's personality and impressed with his literary reputation. He observed him closely, but owing to language difficulties had very little conversation with him. Nevertheless, in his later reminiscences he gave some fantastic accounts of the brief encounter which astounded Hobhouse when he read them.[n]

Byron had not heard from Augusta for a month when her letter arrived on October 28. She tried to break the news gently that if he returned to England she could not see him intimately. He replied: "I really do not & cannot understand all the mysteries & alarms in your letters & more particularly in the last. All I know is—that no human power short of destruction—shall prevent me from seeing you when—where—& how—I may please—according to time & circumstance; that you are the only comfort (except the remote possibility of my daughter's being so) left me in prospect in existence, and that I can bear the rest —so that you remain . . . Miss Milbanke appears in all respects to have been formed for my destruction. . . .

"My health is good, but I have now & then fits of giddiness, & deafness, which make me think like Swift—that I shall be like him & the *withered* tree he saw—which occasioned the reflection and 'die at top' first. My hair is growing grey, & *not* thicker; & my teeth are sometimes *looseish* though still white & sound. Would not one think I was sixty instead of not quite nine & twenty?" [n]

His mind was not made easier by a letter from Claire Clairmont. He had hoped that that account was closed, but she was as infatuated as ever. "My darling Albé," [n] she wrote, "I know what you will say, 'There now I told you it would be so. I advised you not. I did every thing I could to hinder you & now you complain of me.' I don't complain of you dearest nor would not if you were twice as unkind. Sometimes I do feel a little angry that you should make me so very wretched for want of sacrificing a little time to tell me how you are & that you care a little for me. . . ." [n]

After receiving these embarrassing protestations, Byron was more firmly resolved never to write to the foolish girl, by whom one act of kindness would inevitably be interpreted as a partiality for her which he could never feel. Although it always made him unhappy and uncomfortable to give anyone pain, and though he liked to have others think well of him, he knew silence was the only course, the one that must cause the least unhappiness in the end.

On the evening of the 28th, while he was in Breme's box at La Scala, word came that Dr. Polidori had got into an argument with an Austrian officer and had been put in the guardhouse. Breme and Byron went down to see what could be done, but the Austrians were adamant, and though they accepted Byron's card for Polidori's bail, the Doctor was forced to leave Milan within twenty-four hours. Byron here had his first view of the Austrian tyranny, and the ideas he had already acquired from Pellegrino Rossi and other Italians in Switzerland were confirmed. His contempt for Austrian rule in Italy was now fixed, and was to govern his attitudes and actions thenceforth. On the other side, the Austrian authorities noted his associations, and from that time his movements were watched by the secret police; though they paid polite respect to his English title and his literary fame, they were constantly suspicious.

Byron took leave of his friends in Milan on November 2. The next morning he and Hobhouse set out in the latter's carriage. Springhetti was engaged to take Byron's two carriages with the luggage to Venice. Following a route that took them through Gorgonzola, Caravaggio, Brescia, and Desenzano, they arrived at Verona on the 6th, where they stopped long enough to see the ampitheater and the supposed tomb of the Capulets. At Vicenza they visited some of the edifices erected by or under the influence of the great Palladio.

But Byron was now so eager to reach Venice that they paused only for dinner in Padua, to the regret of that indefatigable sight-seer, Hobhouse. Following along the Brenta to Mestre the next day (the 10th), they left their carriages and horses at the inn and embarked in a pouring rain in a gondola for the island city. They could see little from their hearselike black box until they were among the lights of Venice. Hobhouse wrote: "The echo of the oars told us [we] were under a bridge and a boatman cried out to us—'the Rialto'—shortly afterwards we landed under the *Hotel of Great Britain* on the great canal and were shown up a magnificent flight of stairs into rooms whose gilding & painted silks showed they belonged to better people in better times. . . ." [n]

Byron took to Venice immediately. It was a magic world, a theatrical setting for life, with a melancholy background of decayed history that touched a chord of sympathy in him. The brilliant social life of Venice was no more. Two or three *conversazioni* were all that remained. Only two coffeehouses were open all night. The colorful costumes had almost disappeared. And yet Venice was still a fascinating place. He felt it as they crossed the lagoon to the Lido, passing the Palladian church of San Giorgio Maggiore and looking back at the fabulous towers. Byron then got his first glimpse of the Adriatic, and against the distant view of the Alps saw Venice all golden under the setting sun.

Deciding to leave the hotel for a private abode, Byron found one to his taste in the Frezzeria, a small alley-like street just off the Piazza San Marco. The lodgings were over the shop of a draper named Segati. Three days later he wrote to Moore: "It is my intention to remain at Venice during the winter, probably, as it has always been (next to the East) the greenest island of my imagination. It has not disappointed me; though its evident decay would, perhaps, have that effect upon others. But I have been familiar with ruins too long to dislike desolation. Besides, I have fallen in love, which . . . is the best or the worst thing I could do. I have got some extremely good apartments in the house of a 'Merchant of Venice,' who is a good deal occupied with business, and has a wife in her twenty-second year. Marianna (that is her name) is in her appearance altogether like an antelope. She has the large, black, oriental eyes, with that peculiar expression in them which is seen rarely among *Europeans*—even the Italians. . . . I cannot describe the effect of this kind of eye,—at least upon me." [n]

So the "*besoin d'aimer*" had returned to him under the mild Italian skies, and it gave a new enchantment to the fabled city which he had been predisposed to like. Within a few days Byron was introduced to the Countess Albrizzi, whose *conversazione* was the center of the literary-social life of Venice. Hobhouse said that she was called the Mme de Staël of Italy, though he added that she was a poor copy but a good-natured woman. Among her friends she numbered Ugo Foscolo and the famous sculptor Antonio Canova.

Byron now wrote to Murray: "Venice pleases me as much as I expected, and I expected much. It is one of those places which I know before I see them, and has always haunted me the most after the East. I like the gloomy gaiety of their gondolas, and the silence of their canals. . . . I have got my gondola; I read a little, and luckily could speak Italian (more fluently though than accurately) long ago. I am studying, out of curiosity, the *Venetian* dialect, which is very naïve, and soft, and peculiar, though not at all classical; I go out frequently, and am in very good contentment." He confessed to Murray also that he was in "fathomless love" with the black-eyed wife of his landlord. ". . . her great merit is finding out mine—there is nothing so amiable as discernment." [n]

He had now fallen into a routine, which he always did easily, and this was one which particularly pleased him. He announced his good fortune to Douglas Kinnaird on November 27: "I have books—a decent establishment—a fine country—a language which I prefer—most of the amusements and conveniences of life—as much of society as I choose to take—and a handsome woman, who is not a bore—and does not annoy me with looking like a fool, setting up for a sage." If he could only arrange his financial affairs in England, he concluded, "you might consider me as *posthumous,* for I would never willingly dwell in the 'tight little Island.'" [n]

Hobhouse had left for an extended tour of Italy, but Byron was too comfortably situated to move. "By way of divertisement [*sic*]," he told Moore, "I am studying daily, at an Armenian monastery [on the island of San Lazzaro, near the Lido], the Armenian language. I found that my mind wanted something craggy to break upon; and this—as the most difficult thing I could discover here for an amusement—I have chosen, to torture me into attention. . . . I try, and shall go on;—but I answer for nothing, least of all for my intentions or my success." [n] And he wrote Murray that his love and his study should last the winter. "The lady has, luckily for me, been less obdurate than the language, or, between the two, I should have lost my remains of sanity." [n]

Byron felt that he had written himself out for the present. England and the passions he had felt there were quickly fading, and he had not adjusted himself enough to his new experiences to write about them. Moreover, in the past his impulse to write had always been roused by unhappiness and frustration, and now that he had achieved a kind of calm contentment, the compulsion was not strong.

He wrote enthusiastically of his new love to Augusta on December 18: "She does not plague me (which is a wonder) and I verily believe we are one of the happiest—unlawful couples on this side of the Alps. . . . This adventure came very opportunely to console me . . . I have been very tranquil, very loving, & have not so much embarrassed myself with the tortures of the last two years and that virtuous monster Miss Milbanke, who had nearly driven me out of my senses. . . . At present I am better—thank Heaven above—& woman beneath. . . ." [n]

The next day Byron received a letter from Augusta, and, amused and a little piqued by her piety, wrote again: "Your letter of the 1st is arrived, and you have 'a *hope*' for me, it seems: what 'hope,' child? my dearest Sis. I remember a methodist preacher who, on perceiving a profane grin on the faces of part of his congregation, exclaimed 'no *hopes* for *them* as *laughs.*' And thus it is with us: we laugh too much for hopes, and so even let them go."[n]

Through all this Byron was continuing his Armenian lessons, and, to requite Father Pasqual Aucher, his preceptor, he offered to bear the expense of printing his Armenian and English Grammar. Although his name appeared on the title page with that of Father Aucher, Byron's part in it must have been little more than that of correcting and clarifying the English explanations, for he knew little Armenian, by his own confession, when it was published. But the intellectual occupation, the unperturbed isolation of the lovely island, where he could read undisturbed in the library, walk unobserved by curious eyes through the quiet cloisters, or sit on the terrace in the sight of Venice or alone under the olive trees, gave him a deep pleasure. The friars, on their side, became attached to him. Father Aucher remembered him as "a young man quick, sociable, with burning eyes." And his memory is kept green among the few monks who remain on San Lazzaro; they continue to print booklets commemorating his sojourn.

Murray had published the third canto of *Childe Harold* on November 18, and *The Prisoner of Chillon and Other Poems* came out in a thin volume on December 5. With the third canto of *Childe Harold,* Byron had captured and captivated his British audience once more. Caroline Lamb begged Murray to let her see it before publication. She observed shrewdly: ". . . whenever he may speak of *himself* Lord Byron will succeed. . . . what he feels he can describe extravagantly well. . . ."[n] Lady Byron read it with the greatest interest. She wrote her friend Lady Anne Barnard: "He is the absolute monarch of words, and uses them, as Bonaparte did lives, for conquest, without more regard to their intrinsic value. . . . His allusions to me in 'Childe Harold' are cruel and cold, but with such a semblance as to make *me* appear so, and to attract all sympathy to himself. It is said in this poem that hatred of him will be taught as a lesson to his child. . . . It is not my duty to give way to hopeless and wholly unrequited affection; but, so long as I live, my chief struggle will probably be not to remember him too kindly."[n]

As for John Murray, he was well pleased with his bargain.

He had sold the booksellers in one evening at a dinner seven thousand copies of *Childe Harold* and a like number of *The Prisoner of Chillon.* Byron himself had a fondness for the third canto which he confessed to Moore: "I am glad you like it; it is a fine indistinct piece of poetical desolation, and my favourite. I was half mad during the time of its composition, between metaphysics, mountains, lakes, love unextinguishable, thoughts unutterable, and the nightmare of my own delinquencies. I should, many a good day, have blown my brains out, but for the recollection that it would have given pleasure to my mother-in-law. . . ."[n]

At Bath on January 12, 1817, Claire Clairmont had given birth to a daughter whom she called Alba, though she left to Byron the choice of a name, thinking foolishly that this would be one way to get him to write her. Byron wrote cavalierly of Claire to Kinnaird: "You know, and I believe saw once, that odd-headed girl, who introduced herself to me shortly before I left England; but you also know that I found her with Shelley and her sister at Geneva. I never loved nor pretended to love her, but a man is a man, and if a girl of eighteen comes prancing to you at all hours, there is but one way—the suite of all this is that she was with *child*—and returned to England to assist in peopling that desolate island. . . . This comes of 'putting it about' (as Jackson calls it) and be damned to it—and thus people come into the world."[n]

Venice continued to please Byron. There was something intriguing to him in a society that put so much energy into its gaieties. "The Carnival is commencing," he wrote Murray on January 2, "and there is a good deal of fun here and there—besides business; for all the world are making up their intrigues for the season. . . . I am very well off with Marianna. . . . I have passed a great deal of my time with her since my arrival at Venice, and never a twenty-four hours without giving and receiving from one to three (and occasionally an extra or so) pretty unequivocal proofs of mutual good contentment."[n]

The frankness of the Italians in love matters amused at the same time that it slightly shocked Byron. The naïve absence of hypocrisy contrasted strongly with the Regency society he had known in England, and at the same time the code of extramarital relations was much stricter. ". . . a woman is virtuous (according to the code) who limits herself to her husband and one lover; those who have two, three, or more, are a little *wild*. . . ."[n]

Byron's life was not as entirely given up to dissipations as he implied to his English correspondents. Sometime during the Carnival he had finished *Manfred*, the poetic drama which he had begun in Switzerland. The festivities ended on February 18, but Byron lingered in the city, despite urgent invitations to join Hobhouse in Rome, for the nightly revels and the literary labor together had left him in a debilitated state. It took just such a mood of wearied pleasure to inspire Byron to write one of his finest lyrics, which he enclosed in a letter to Moore:

So we'll go no more a-roving
So late into the night,
Though the heart is still as loving,
And the moon be still as bright.

For the Sword outwears its sheath,
And the soul wears out the breast,
And the heart must pause to breathe,
And Love itself have rest.[n]

But in his debility there also came upon him a growing dissatisfaction with his aimless life. An attack in the *Edinburgh Review* had brought home to him the precarious state of his literary reputation. Such a blow to his self-esteem undermined his confidence and strengthened his recurring conviction that he and all his contemporaries were on the wrong track when measured against the great model of Pope. He was self-critical enough also to know that his own work failed of the highest polish and imaginative flights even in the genre he had adopted. In such moods his half-formed ambition to try his mettle in political or military action surged up in him.

"If I live ten years longer," he told Moore, "you will see, however, that it is not over with me—I don't mean in literature, for that is nothing; and it may seem odd enough to say, I do not think it my vocation. But you will see that I shall do something or other—the times and fortune permitting. . . . But I doubt whether my constitution will hold out. I have, at intervals, exorcised it most devilishly."[n]

Although Byron still talked of returning to England in the

spring, the thought of his last months in that country were increasingly painful. To Augusta's vague pious hopes (probably for his religious redemption) he replied with quite another subject in mind. "What you 'hope' may be, I do not know, if you mean a reunion between Lady B. and me, it is too late. It is now a year, and I have repeatedly offered to make it up, with what success you know. At present if she would rejoin me to-morrow, *I* would not accept the proposition. I have no spirit of hatred against her, however, I am too sensitive not to feel injuries, but far too proud to be vindictive. She's a fool, and when you have said that, it is the most that can be said for her." [n] It was the thought that his daughter might be taken from him that froze up all sympathy for his wife and her relations.

Byron's life was still without motive and without direction. He had already tired of the formal social life of Venice. He had gone to two or three of the Governor's *conversazioni,* but as he saw there only very plain women and a formal circle, he did not go again. But after he had recovered from the fever that was the aftermath of the Carnival, he found his intellectual energies burgeoning again. He bought a complete set of Voltaire in ninety-two volumes and amused himself by reading the old scoffer. And he was beginning to consider writing a historical drama or dramatic poem. The story of Marino Faliero appealed strongly to him. "There is still," he wrote to Murray, "in the Doge's Palace, the black veil painted over Falièro's picture, and the staircase whereon he was first crowned Doge, and subsequently decapitated. This was the thing that most struck my imagination in Venice—more than the Rialto, which I visited for the sake of Shylock. . . . But I hate things *all fiction;* and therefore the *Merchant* and *Othello* have no great associations to me. . . . There should always be some foundation of fact for the most airy fabric, and pure invention is but the talent of a liar." [n]

On April 9 he was still in Venice and still talking about going to Rome. His indecision made him reckless, and he told Murray that he had contemplated suicide the year before. But now he had some reasons for living. "Besides, when I turn thirty, I will turn devout; I feel a great vocation that way in Catholic churches, and when I hear the organ." [n] And he could be equally facetious in writing to Moore: "My late physician, Dr. Polidori, is here on his way to England, with the present Lord Guilford and the widow of the late earl. Dr. Polidori has, just now, no more patients, because his patients are no more. He had lately three, who are now all dead—one embalmed. . . . Lord Guilford died of an inflammation of the bowels: so they took them out, and sent them (on account of their discrepancies), separately from the carcass, to England. Conceive a man going one way, and his intestines another, and his immortal soul a third!—was there ever such a distribution? One certainly has a soul; but how it came to allow itself to be enclosed in a body is more than I can imagine." [n]

Byron finally got Marianna's consent for his Roman journey and was on his way on April 17. Travel and new sights drew him out of his lethargy. He stopped briefly at Arqua to see the house and tomb of Petrarch, but was more moved by Tasso's cell and Ariosto's tomb in Ferrara. By the time he reached Florence, he had written the burning lines of *The Lament of Tasso.* Inevitably, as he wrote he identified himself with this "eagle-spirit of a Child of Song," who had suffered anguish, but had found resource in "the innate force" of his own spirit.

He spent a day in the two galleries in Florence and came away with grudging praise of a few paintings and sculptures. "The Venus [de Medici] is more for admiration than love; but there are sculpture and painting, which for the first time at all gave me an idea of what people mean by their *cant,* and what Mr. Braham calls 'entusimusy' (*i.e.* enthusiasm) about those two most artificial of the arts." In the Medici chapel he saw only "fine frippery in great slabs of various expensive stones, to commemorate fifty rotten and forgotten carcases." And the church of Santa Croce "contains much illustrious nothing." [n]

He arrived in Rome on April 29 and was greeted by Hobhouse, who had been studying the antiquities diligently for weeks and was glad to act as his cicerone. Byron took rooms in what was possibly a boarding house at 66 Piazza di Spagna, almost opposite the house in which Keats was to live his last days four years later.* Seeing the historic ruins and the environs in

* Vera Cacciatore, Curator of the Keats-Shelley Memorial House in Rome, recently found reports of a meeting of the Memorial Association at which Mr. H. Nelson Gay said he had seen a letter addressed to Byron at 66 Piazza di Spagna. It had been sent to Venice by his publisher John Murray and forwarded to his banker Torlonia in

the Roman spring brought back to him the pleasant equestrian excursions he and Hobhouse had made in the vicinity of Athens. It was a happy thought to bring his saddle horses along, for he would have been very uncomfortable had he been forced to walk over the hills of Rome. Writing to Murray on the 9th of May, he spoke with mounting enthusiasm: "As a *whole, ancient* and *modern,* it beats Greece, Constantinople, every thing—at least that I have ever seen. But I can't describe, because my first impressions are always strong and confused, and my Memory *selects* and reduces them to order, like distance in the landscape, and blends them better, although they may be less distinct." [n] Overwhelmed as he was by the relics of ancient majesty, his mind was busy storing impressions from which in a few weeks the fourth canto of *Childe Harold* was distilled.

Rome was full of English people, and Byron avoided them as well as he could. Unknown to him, however, he was observed by an English party at St. Peter's. Among them was Lady Liddell, a friend of Lady Byron's family. She was horror-struck, and she told her daughter to keep her eyes down; "Don't look at him, he is dangerous to look at." [n]

At Hobhouse's request Byron sat while he was in Rome to the Danish sculptor, Bertel Thorwaldsen, for a bust. When he saw the finished product, he said: "It is not at all like me; my expression is more unhappy." [n] Hobhouse later wrote to Murray: "I would have had a wreath round the brows, but the poet was afraid of being mistaken for a king or conqueror. . . ." [n] Byron's comment was: "I won't have my head garnished like a Christmas pie with holly—or a cod's head and fennel, or whatever the damned weed is they strew round it. I wonder you should want me to be such a mountebank." [n] He felt that the whole thing was embarrassing and that there was something of a "posthumous" character in a bust, but at the same time he took a sheepish pride in being thus immortalized in marble while still alive.*

Rome, who then readdressed it. This letter, dated April 8, 1817, is now in the Murray archives, London. The number on the house has not been changed since Byron's day. The Sculptor John Gibson (1790–1866) later recalled having seen Byron on the balcony which faces the Piazza and the Spanish Steps.

* This is the bust that stands now at the head of the stairs at John Murray's at 50 Albemarle Street. All of Byron's friends thought it the best likeness at the time, and it was from this that Thorwaldsen

In 1812 Byron had witnessed a public hanging of the assassin of Spencer Perceval, the Prime Minister, and now, the day before he left Rome, he was drawn to the macabre and horrible scene of a public execution of three robbers by the guillotine. "The first turned me quite hot and thirsty, and made me shake so that I could hardly hold the opera-glass (I was close, but determined to see, as one should see every thing, once, with attention); the second and third (which shows how dreadfully soon things grow indifferent), I am ashamed to say, had no effect on me as a horror, though I would have saved them if I could." [n]

Before leaving he had received a letter from Shelley on behalf "of a little being whom we—in the absence of all right to bestow a *Christian* designation—call Alba, or the Dawn. . . . what are your plans with respect to the little girl?" [n] In fact, he had no plans, as he told Augusta: "I am a little puzzled how to dispose of this new production . . . but shall probably send for and place it in a Venetian convent, to become a good Catholic, and (it may be) a *Nun,* being a character somewhat wanted in our family. They tell me it is very pretty, with blue eyes and *dark* hair; and, although I never was attached nor pretended attachment to the mother, still in case of the eternal war and alienation which I foresee about my legitimate daughter, Ada, it may be as well to have something to repose a hope upon. I must love something in my old age, and probably circumstances will render this poor little creature a great and, perhaps, my only comfort than [*sic*] any offspring from that misguided and artificial woman, who bears and disgraces my name." [n]

Byron returned to Venice on May 28 and found Marianna Segati delighted to see him. His jaunt across Italy and his Roman experience, together with the news he had lately received from England, convinced him more than ever that he could not happily return to his native land. He was resigned to being an expatriate.

---

made the full-length statue now in the library of Trinity College, Cambridge.

CHAPTER XVIII

1817

La Mira: Harold's Farewell—*Beppo*

ON BYRON'S RETURN TO Venice his first concern was so to arrange his business affairs in England that he could pay his debts and live comfortably abroad. Only "absolute and imperious necessity," he told Kinnaird, would bring him back to that country. He spoke of "the indispensable obligation I feel of disposing of Newstead without further delay, in the course of the present summer, at *any price* which it will bring. . . ."[n] His anxiety to sell the estate was not prompted by any immediate need of money, however, for he now had a sizable income from his poetry. Murray had paid £2,000 for the third canto of *Childe Harold, The Prisoner of Chillon,* and other poems, and he subsequently gave six hundred guineas for *Manfred* and *The Lament of Tasso.*

Augusta's equivocal letters had lessened his desire to return to England. She had now, it seemed, begun to be frightened at shadows—or was there really some sinister influence undermining her love for him? He wrote: "I have received all your letters I believe, which are full of woes, as usual, megrims & mysteries; but my sympathies remain in suspense, for, for the life of me I can't make out whether your disorder is a broken heart or the earache . . . or what your melancholy & mysterious apprehensions tend to . . . whether to Caroline Lamb's novels—Mrs. Clermont's evidence—Lady Byron's magnanimity—or any other piece of imposture. . . ."[n]

To escape the heat and the effluvia of the canals during the summer, Byron had taken a six months' lease on the Villa Foscarini on the left bank of the Brenta River at La Mira, a village about seven miles inland from the river's mouth at Fusina on the Venetian lagoon. The villa, on the dusty road to Padua, was a large boxlike palace considerably altered from the convent that had become the Palladian mansion of the patrician Foscarini family in the early seventeenth century. Marianna Segati also had an excuse for coming to La Mira, for she had friends living nearby. By June 14 Byron was installed in his great palace. One of the chief attractions of the *villeggiatura* to Byron was that he could keep his horses at La Mira and ride at will.

Freed from the distractions of the city, he turned his mind again to literary matters. Murray had hesitated to publish *Manfred,* fearing the public reaction to the poem's unorthodox and daring speculations and its too obvious identification of Astarte with Byron's sister. Byron was anxious about the poem too, but for other reasons. He had poured his heart's blood into it, and had fought out in it, though he had arrived at no very satisfying philosophical conclusions, the metaphysical problems which had long been troubling him. Murray's worst fears were realized when, after its publication on June 16, *Manfred* was reviewed in a London newspaper, *The Day and New Times,* with a pointed reference to its autobiographical significance. Fortunately, however, the major reviews shied away from the forbidden subject of incest and concentrated on the poem's unorthodox speculations.

In the meantime, in the still hours in the empty palace Byron began to capture the essence of his Roman adventure. By July 1 he had written a rough draft of about thirty stanzas of a fourth canto of *Childe Harold.* He had started Harold on his Italian pilgrimage, not in Rome, but in Venice, whose decayed past fitted well into the melancholy mood of the poem. He began with the now famous line: "I stood in Venice, on the 'Bridge of Sighs.' " He was interrupted by a visit from "Monk" Lewis, and went up to Venice for a week with him. Their conversations brought fond nostalgic memories of Byron's London gaieties, and he wrote to Moore: "Ah, Master Shallow, we have heard the chimes at midnight."[n]

But despite the Venetian interlude, he had finished the first draft of 126 stanzas by the 20th. The poem turned out to be not only a panorama of his Italian experience and his journey to Rome, but also, as usual, a history of his deepest feelings and his inner conflicts. Coming to Rome finally in the seventy-eighth stanza, he gave rein to his highest flights of fancy and of rhetoric:

Oh, Rome! my Country! City of the Soul!
The orphans of the heart must turn to thee,
Lone Mother of dead Empires! and control
In their shut breasts their petty misery.[n]

What had touched him most deeply, however, was the site of the supposed fountain of Egeria, the scene of his favorite Latin poet Juvenal's story of Numa and the fountain nymph. The immortal longings roused by the image of human love for a goddess beyond the limitations of human frailty now carried him out of himself in the most poignantly personal stanzas of *Childe Harold:*

Oh, Love! no habitant of earth thou art—
An unseen Seraph, we believe in thee,—
A faith whose martyrs are the broken heart,—
But never yet hath seen, nor e'er shall see
The naked eye, thy form, as it should be;
The mind hath made thee, as it peopled Heaven . . .[n]

But after this rhetorical flight, his Pegasus came down to earth again:

Yet let us ponder boldly—'tis a base
Abandonment of reason to resign
Our right of thought—our last and only place
Of refuge; this, at least, shall still be mine . . .[n]

It was characteristic that Byron should have ended on that note: he always returned from the most airy speculations to reason and common sense. Not that he was the happier for it; it was only an innate compulsion like other forces beyond his control. These nightly bouts with poetry—for he wrote best in the early morning hours—constituted his secret life and his greatest pleasure and gave a quiet satisfaction to his days in that felicitous July of his *villeggiatura*. He rose late, making occasional jaunts to Venice, crossing in his gondola to the Lido to bathe in the Adriatic, and riding at sunset along the Brenta. Before the end of July "Monk" Lewis came to stay with him at La Mita, and on the 31st Hobhouse arrived and joined him on his evening jaunts on horseback.

On one of these rides they met two handsome peasant girls and engaged them in conversation. Byron soon made an assignation with one of them, who was married, but the other flew off from Hobhouse, "not being married," Byron reported, "for here no woman will do anything under adultery." Byron's girl said frankly "that she had no objection to make love with me, as she was married, and all married women did it: but that her husband (a baker) was somewhat ferocious, and would do her a mischief. In short, in a few evenings we arranged our affairs. . . ."[n]

A certain animal fierceness and passionate assurance about this girl, Margarita Cogni, added to the charm of her beauty in Byron's eyes and soon gave her an unprecedented hold on him. He was pleased and amused at her self-confidence and leonine aggressiveness. She was not too much perturbed by his liaison with Marianna or his later affairs with other women, and she openly boasted that he would always return to her. Byron told Murray that the reasons for her ascendancy "were, firstly, her person—very dark, tall, the Venetian face, very fine black eyes—and certain other qualities which need not be mentioned. She was two and twenty years old, and, never having had children, had not spoilt her figure, nor anything else—which is, I assure you, a great desideration in a hot climate where they grow relaxed and doughy, and flumpity a short time after breeding. She was, besides, a thorough Venetian in her dialect, in her thoughts, in her countenance, in every thing, with all their naïveté and Pantaloon humour. Besides, she could neither read nor write, and could not plague me with letters. . . ." When Marianna one evening confronted her, Margarita "threw back her veil (*fazziolo*), and replied in very explicit Venetian, '*You* are *not* his *wife: I* am *not* his *wife: you* are his *Donna,* and *I* am his *Donna: your* husband is a cuckold, and *mine* is another. For the rest, what *right* have you to reproach me? if he prefers what is mine to what is yours, is it my fault?' " [n]

After Lewis left in August, Byron returned to the revision of *Childe Harold*. Finding that Hobhouse approved of this canto more than he did of the metaphysical one completed in Switzerland under the influence of his talks with Shelley, he shared it with his friend and even added stanzas at his suggestion. Soon Hobhouse was engaged in writing historical notes for the poem.

Murray's request that Byron write for him a "civil and delicate declension" of a tragedy which Dr. Polidori had submitted to him elicited some rollicking verses that exercised Byron's sly wit at the expense of his publisher as well as of the egregious Doctor:

Dear Doctor,—I have read your play,
Which is a good one in its way,
Purges the eyes, and moves the bowels,
And drenches handkerchiefs like towels . . .
But—and I grieve to speak it—plays
Are drugs—mere drugs, Sir, nowadays . . .
There's Byron too, who once did better . . .
So altered since last year his pen is,
I think he's lost his wits at Venice,
Or drained his brains away as stallion
To some dark-eyed and warm Italian . . . [n]

Murray's lack of enthusiasm for *Manfred* no doubt still rankled in Byron's mind.

The August days passed pleasantly at La Mira. On weekends Signor Segati appeared regularly, not to disturb his wife's *servente*, but to court another lady nearby, and incidentally to bring Byron and his guests the latest gossip from Venice. On the 29th he told a story which appealed to Byron for its revelation of the quality of Venetian life and morals. It was of a woman who had lost her husband at sea, or so she supposed, and had taken an *amoroso*, a "vice-husband," as Byron facetiously called the *cavalier servente*. After some years a Turk appeared to her and identified himself as her husband, and, Hobhouse recorded, made her three offers: "either to quit your amoroso and come with me—or to stay with your amoroso or to accept a pension and live alone." Hobhouse added: "The lady has not yet given an answer, but M[e] Zagati [*sic*] said I'm sure I would not leave my amoroso for any husband—looking at B. This is too gross even for me." [n]

Byron seized this as the framework of a tale that he could fit into the setting of his whole Venetian experience. In a few days he was at work on a mock-heroic poem that was to open up a new vein of literary activity in him. The form was happily supplied by John Hookham Frere's *Whistlecraft,* a clever satirical poem in the manner and meter of Luigi Pulci, the fifteenth-century precursor of Casti in the use of the adaptable ottava rima. Frere's poem, whose immediate model was Pulci's *Morgante Maggiore,* a mock-heroic romance of monks and giants, rambled with abandoned colloquial ease over diverse subjects, incidents, and characters. Its lack of unity, its digressions, its epigrammatic wit, its ironic deflation of sentiment emphasized in the punch-lines of the couplets at the ends of the eight-line stanzas, the conversational tone, the unheroic portraits of the characters, and the disarming realism of its interpretation of life, all made it an ideal medium for Byron's purpose. It had a special appeal to him, for he was always contemptuous of the canting generalizations and pomposities of English poetry.

With one stroke he freed himself from the fetters of British propriety and the *Childe Harold* manner, and something of the careless and relaxed realism of his letters invaded his verse. Let the critics cavil; he would be himself:

> *I've half a mind to tumble down to prose,*
> *But verse is more in fashion—so here goes!* (*st.* 52)

The beauty of this style of writing was that it was as casual as the country; whatever struck the fancy—description, cynical comment, sentiment, digressions of all kinds—was savored to the full as in a letter, and the story could wait. Having described the Carnival setting, Byron turned to the women:

> *Shakespeare described the sex in Desdemona*
>   *As very fair, but yet suspect in fame,*
> *And to this day from Venice to Verona*
>   *Such matters may be probably the same,*

Except that since those times was never known a
Husband whom mere suspicion could inflame
To suffocate a wife no more than twenty,
Because she had a "Cavalier Servente." (*st.* 17)

The gondola, so convenient for assignations, he described as "Just like a coffin clapt in a canoe," and "sometimes they contain a deal of fun,/ Like mourning coaches when the funeral's done." It was not until the twenty-first stanza that he introduced his heroine, Laura. The name was probably chosen deliberately to mock Petrarch's Platonic and sentimentally veiled love, for Byron's heroine was one who might inspire ogles rather than sonnets. There follows a digression on the charms of married ladies, who, "being natural, naturally please," whereas the single Miss is shy and awkward. "The Nursery still lisps out in all they utter—/ Besides, they always smell of bread and butter."

Freed from the inhibitions of England and the conventions of English modes of writing by this new genre, Byron felt that he owed some tributes to the Italian life and sunshine.

With all its sinful doings, I must say,
That Italy's a pleasant place to me,
Who love to see the Sun shine every day . . .
Not through a misty morning twinkling weak as
A drunken man's dead eye in maudlin sorrow . . .

I love the language, that soft bastard Latin,
Which melts like kisses from a female mouth . . .
(st. 41, 43–4)

His comparisons with England revealed in playful malice some of his deep-seated grudges against that island, "Our cloudy climate, and our chilly women."

Once he took hold of the story, he brought it to its ironic conclusion: Laura and the Count invited her husband in to talk the matter over; she put her husband in the wrong, but took him back quite calmly, while he and the Count, her amoroso, remained good friends.

By October 10 he had finished the poem, which he called *Beppo*, and he returned to adding stanzas to *Childe Harold*. Even as he labored, the recurrent conviction came over him that he and all the modern poets had taken the wrong road. He wrote Murray: "I am the more confirmed in this by having lately gone over some of our classics, particularly *Pope* . . . and I was really astonished . . . at the ineffable distance in point of sense, harmony, effect, and even *Imagination,* passion, and *Invention,* between the little Queen Anne's man, and us of the Lower Empire. . . . if I had to begin again, I would model myself accordingly." [n]

As usual, Byron's literary activities did not interfere with an active social life. William Stewart Rose and the Kinnaird brothers, who had visited him in September and had happily brought Frere's *Whistlecraft,* had gone on their travels, but he saw other Englishmen during the autumn. And he had made the acquaintance of Richard Belgrave Hoppner, British Consul in Venice, and had been immediately taken by his graciousness and his eagerness to be of service. The Consul was the second son of the famous portrait painter John Hoppner, R.A. He himself had studied painting, was an amateur of the arts, and dabbled in literature. He had married a Swiss woman. The Hoppners were proud of the friendship of the poet and paid him the greatest deference. Soon Byron was lending books to Hoppner, and the latter handled much of his business, particularly when he was absent from Venice. Looking forward to a quiet *villeggiatura,* Byron leased Hoppner's villa at Este in the Euganean Hills, but he made only one visit there.

With Hobhouse he lived a quiet country life at La Mira until November, when the chilly nights in the drafty rooms of the old palace drove them back to Venice. The high point of their day was the gondola ride to the Lido to feel the Adriatic breezes and watch the sunset on the lagoon on their return. On November 21, Byron's horses, and hay for them, arrived from La Mira and were ferried to the Lido. From then on, the pleasure of their excursion was increased by a gallop along the sands.

On December 10 Byron received the welcome news that the Newstead estate had at last been sold to his Harrow schoolmate Major (afterward Colonel) Thomas Wildman for £94,500.* The

* After spending upward of £100,000 in repairing and improving the Abbey and the grounds, Wildman sold it in 1860 to William Frederick Webb, a friend of David Livingstone, the African explorer;

prospect of clearing his obligations, which now amounted to more than £30,000, and of having a fixed income was a considerable relief and made him feel easier about incurring other responsibilities. He had finally written to Shelley that he was willing to undertake the care of his daughter by Claire, and had asked that she be sent under proper charge to Italy. Shelley had expected to spend the winter in Pisa and to bring the little girl himself, but he was delayed. He reported that Claire had contemplated christening the child after herself, but "she delays this *important ceremony* until I hear whether you have a predilection for any other name." [n] Byron did indeed. He wrote Kinnaird: "Shelley (from *Marlow*) has written to me about my daughter, (the last bastard one), who, it seems, is a great beauty. . . . will you think of some plan for remitting her here, or placing her in England? I shall acknowledge and breed her myself, giving her the name of Biron (to distinguish her from little Legitimacy), and mean to christen her Allegra, which is a Venetian name." [n]

During the last weeks of Hobhouse's stay in Venice, Byron led a more social life than he ordinarily cared for. He went with his friend to the *conversazioni* of the Countess Albrizzi. They frequently dined at the Pellegrino Inn or at Hoppner's and went to the theater or the opera, mostly to see comedies or farces at the San Benedetto, where Goldoni was a favorite. On the 20th they were at the San Lucca and heard Sgricci, the *improvvisatore*. In the Hoppners' box at the San Moïsè on the 29th they heard "gazza ladra made an opera by Rossini." [n]

On January 7 of the new year Hobhouse took his last ride with Byron on the Lido. In closing his diary for the day he wrote: "passed the evening with Byron, who put the last hand to his Childe Harold, and took leave of my dear friend, for so I think him, at twelve o'clock—a little before my going he told me he was originally a man of a great deal of feeling, but it had been absorbed—I believe the first part of what he said literally—god bless him." The next morning Hobby left for England, carrying Byron's manuscript with him.

---

on Webb's death it was occupied by his descendants until it was purchased in 1930 by Sir Julien Cahn and presented by him to the Corporation of Nottingham to be used as a city park and museum. The Abbey now houses the valuable Roe-Byron Library and many portraits and miscellaneous relics of the poet.

CHAPTER XIX

1818–1819

Don Juan on the Grand Canal

THE CARNIVAL BEGAN IN January, just after Hobhouse left Venice. The previous season, Byron had been too absorbed in Marianna Segati to do much philandering at the ridottos or masquerades. But now, though he still had his rooms at the draper's house in the Frezzeria, some of the *tracasseries* of this black-eyed girl—her jealousies and tantrums, as well as her inclination to make him jealous—were beginning to wear out the freshness of the liaison. According to Moore, what chiefly disillusioned him was the fact that she sold some jewels he had given her.

Byron deliberately sought solace in the Carnival's adventures. Although he missed Hobhouse, a certain restraint fell from him with the departure of his balanced and sensible friend. He was already in a gay Carnival mood when he wrote to Murray, on January 8, a verse epistle full of wit and ribaldry:

My dear Mr. Murray,
You're in a damned hurry
To set up this ultimate Canto;
But (if they don't rob us)
You'll see Mr. Hobhouse
Will bring it safe in his portmanteau.

And he concluded wickedly:

Now, I'll put out my taper . . .
Theres a whore on my right
For I rhyme best at Night
When a C——t is tied close to my Inkstand.

It was Mahomet's notion
That *comical motion*
Increased his "devotion in prayer"—
If that tenet holds good
In a prophet it should
In a poet be equally fair.[n]

In the midst of the masking and fooling, however, Byron had found time to finish copying *Beppo,* and he sent it off to Murray on January 19. But the following week he wrote that the Carnival was still at its height, "and I am in the *estrum* and agonies of a new intrigue with I don't exactly know whom or what, except that she is insatiate of love, and won't take money, and has light hair and blue eyes, which are not common here, and that I met her at the Masque, and that when her mask is off, I am as wise as ever. I shall make what I can of the remainder of my youth, and confess that, like Augustus, I would rather die *standing.*" [n]

It is not surprising that by the middle of February, just after the Carnival had ended, Byron had acquired, to his chagrin, the ancient disease of the votaries of Venus, which had not troubled him since his voyage home from Greece in 1811, when it had alternated with hemorrhoids and a tertian fever in tormenting his passage through "the gut of Gibraltar." He reported to Hobhouse that "Elena da Mosta, a Gentil Donna, was clapt, and she has clapt me; to be sure it was gratis, the first gonorrhea I have not paid for." [n]

His illness temporarily stopped his riding, but not his social activities. There were oratorios by Haydn and Handel at the San Benedetto, and sometime during the early months of the year he had become a regular attendant at the *conversazioni* of the Countess Marina Benzoni (or Benzon), an aging beauty who refused to relinquish the gaieties of her youth and the illusion that at sixty she had the same charm that had captivated Venice and made her the toast of the canals. She had once danced about a liberty tree with Ugo Foscolo in a spontaneous fête inspired by the French Revolution. She was dressed in an Athenian petticoat open along the flanks, with a vest which left her breast free. And Lamberti had made her the heroine of a popular ballad "*La Biondina in Gondoletta.*"[n] The Cavalier Giuseppe Rangone had given up a diplomatic career to serve her, and had remained her *cavalier servente* for thirty years, finally marrying her when he was nearing seventy. When Byron one morning asked the cavalier how his mistress was, he replied with the one glowing word "*Rugiadosa*" ("Dewy").

Her *conversazioni* were more informal than those of the Countess Albrizzi, who was most assiduous in collecting men of letters. That was perhaps one reason for Byron's gradual withdrawal from the Albrizzi circle. He had been disappointed in Pindemonte and many others he encountered there.

Byron soon plunged with more recklessness than ever into new affairs with Venetian women. The middle- and lower-class Italian woman delighted him most—her flashing eyes, her frank abandonment to passion, her peasant humor. To indulge in promiscuous sensual pleasures with these women was for him a kind of revenge upon the cold and mathematical Annabella. For it is apparent that he had a manifest delight in physical pleasures of a nature that to some of his friends, even to Hobhouse, seemed coarse or gross. His slightly sadistic love of boxing and his friendships with "Gentleman" Jackson, the pugilist, and the fencing master Henry Angelo and their pothouse cronies were perhaps remotely related to his penchant for the "fine animals" among the Italian women. But whatever he may have said afterward in detailing these affairs to his friends in England, most of his liaisons and even his most casual encounters were lightened in his own mind at the time by a certain romantic aura. The woman who had the strongest hold upon him at this time, for her liveliness as well as her voluptuousness and beauty, was Margarita Cogni, the baker's wife. He described her as about five feet ten inches tall, with a fine figure, "fit to breed gladiators from."[n]

It was probably his break with Marianna that hastened his search for another habitation. He liked expansive houses, and only his attachment to the Segati could have held him so long in the narrow quarters in the Frezzeria. Measured in English pounds, palaces were cheap in Venice. He had bargained first for Count Gritti's palace.* But he failed to reach an agreement with the Count, and finally settled for a palazzo of the Mocenigo family, into which he moved sometime before the first of June.

The Palazzo Mocenigo, which he took on a three-year lease for 4,800 francs (200 louis, or about £190) a year, was a massive gray building, relic of the days of the merchant princes, just beyond the first sharp turn of the S-shaped Grand Canal as one comes from the Accademia, within sight of the Rialto Bridge and only a few hundred yards from the Piazza San Marco. The third palace (the three buildings presented a solid face to the Grand Canal) was built after 1600. It had three floors above the damp and chilly ground floor, which opened out to the gondola landing. On the second of these upper floors was a great high-ceilinged drawing room. Balconies overlooked the canal from each of the intermediate floors. Dozens of rooms large and small made it possible for Byron to entertain guests and house a considerable number of servants.

An additional reason for his taking more commodious quarters was that his illegitimate daughter was being brought out from England by the Shelleys. Although he tried to hide his paternal feelings under a cynical bravado, Byron was already beginning to display some impatience to see the child. He wrote flippantly to Hobhouse, before he knew the Shelleys were coming: "A clerk can bring the papers [legal papers to be signed in connection with the sale of Newstead] (and, by-the-bye, my *shild* by Clare, at the same time. Pray desire Shelley to pack it carefully), with *tooth-powder, red only;* magnesia, soda-powders, tooth-brushes, diachylon plaster, and any new novels good for anything."[n]

On March 11 the Shelleys left for Italy, taking with them Claire and Byron's daughter, together with an English maid, and Elise, a Swiss nurse. Two days before they left, Claire took her baby to the parish church of St. Giles-in-the-Fields and had her baptized "Clara Allegra Byron, born of Rt. Hon. George Gordon Lord Byron ye reputed Father by Clara Mary Jane Clairmont."[n] She thus joined her own name to the one Byron had chosen and made record of their relationship.

---

* The Gritti Palace is now a favorite hotel of the élite who stop in Venice.

The Shelley party arrived in Milan on April 4 and remained there in the hope that Byron might come to meet them, but he would not stir from Venice. Shelley, perhaps at Claire's prompting, wrote to invite Byron to visit them on Lake Como, where they were seeking a summer residence. But Byron had no desire to renew on the shores of Lake Como the liaison which had discolored his memories of the Lake of Geneva. He merely asked that they send the child to Venice with a nurse. Shelley wrote back urging his visit so that "Clare's pain would then have been mitigated by the prospect of seeing her child with you. . . . you are not so infirm of purpose that soothing words, and gentle conduct need betray you in essential matters further than you mean to go." [n]

In this appeal he showed insufficient knowledge of either Byron or Claire. It was always Shelley's weakness to assume that human nature was more amenable to reason than experience justified, and that the emotions can be put under rational control. But another letter from Byron promising that she should see her child again softened Claire so that she sent Allegra with Elise and Byron's messenger on April 28. And she took the occasion to send him another letter: "I have one favour to beg of you. Send me the smallest quantity of your own dearest hair that I may put with some of Allegra's in a locket. . . . My dearest Lord Byron best of human beings you are the father of my little girl and I cannot forget you." [n]

Poor Claire made it only too clear that she was still in love with Byron, and she was too blinded by her own feelings to realize what impression this desperate pleading for a crumb of kindness would make. If she had convinced him that she was solely interested in the welfare of the little girl and was indifferent to him, he could much more easily have treated her with common courtesy and fairness. The knowledge that she was attempting to use Allegra as a wedge to force herself into his affections made it impossible for him ever to treat her with real kindness.

When Allegra and her nurse arrived on May 2,[n] Byron had not yet moved into his palace, and it is probable that the Hoppners kept her. As soon as he was established in the Palazzo Mocenigo, he brought the child there. Byron developed a growing fondness for his daughter. After she had been with him for three months, he wrote to Augusta: ". . . she is very pretty, remarkably intelligent, and a great favourite with every body; but, what is remarkable, much more like Lady Byron than her [Allegra's] mother—so much so as to stupefy the learned Fletcher and astonish me. . . . she has very blue eyes, and that singular forehead, fair curly hair, and a devil of a Spirit—but that is Papa's."[n]

Murray published *Beppo* anonymously on February 28, and the poem was soon the topic of conversation everywhere. The good humor of the satire won over most of the critics. Byron was pleased and gave Murray authority to put his name to the poem. "It will, at any rate, show them that I can write cheerfully, and repel the charge of monotony and mannerism."[n] As for the fourth canto of *Childe Harold,* Murray "was in raptures," Hobhouse reported, but the publisher was not so enthusiastic about the notes which Hobhouse had concocted. Nevertheless, Byron stuck loyally by his friend and insisted on their inclusion when the poem was published.

He continued to find pleasure in the society of Hoppner and the select English and foreign guests who frequented his hospitable home. It was through Hoppner that Byron met Alexander Scott, a young English bachelor of independent means, who later joined them on their Lido rides. At Hoppner's he also met an interesting soldier of the Napoleonic wars, the Cavalier Angelo Mengaldo. The Cavalier's devotion to the memory of the fallen Napoleon, his republican sympathies, his interest in poetry, and his own literary ambitions all drew him to the English poet. But his self-consuming ego, too much like that of Byron, was a recurrent cause of friction between them. In June Mengaldo entered into a swimming contest with the poet. They had both boasted of their prowess, Byron of swimming the Tagus and the Hellespont, and Mengaldo of crossing the Danube and the Beresina under fire. Byron had kept in practice, frequently dashing into the Adriatic and into the Grand Canal itself. The Countess Albrizzi recorded that he was once seen, "on leaving a palace situated on the Grand Canal, instead of entering his own gondola, to throw himself into the water dressed as he was and swim to his lodging."[n] In order to avoid the oars of the gondoliers, she said, he carried a torch in his left hand when he swam in the canal at night.

The contest took place on June 25. Byron won easily, leaving Mengaldo five hundred yards behind before he got from the Lido to the Grand Canal and then swimming the length of the Canal. "I was in the sea from half-past four till a quarter-past eight without touching or resting," he told Hobhouse, adding, "I could not be much fatigued, having had a *piece* in the fore-noon, and taking another in the evening at ten of the clock." [n]

Through the spring and summer Byron continued his escapades with Venetian women. One who pleased him particularly was an opera singer. He wrote Hobhouse with waggish glee: "She is the prettiest Bacchante in the world—and a piece to perish *in*. The Segati and I have been off these two months, or rather three. I have a world of other harlotry. . . . With regard to Arpalice Taruscelli (the madcap above mentioned) recollect there is no *liaison* only *fuff-fuff* and passades." [n] However lightly Byron may have spoken of the affair, however, he cannot have treated the girl badly, for she continued to have a warm feeling of gratitude toward him for many years after.

His mind stimulated by conversation or lovemaking, Byron generally finished off the night by writing. He concluded a long letter to Moore on June 1: "Good night or rather, morning. It is four, and the dawn gleams over the Grand Canal, and unshadows the Rialto. I must to bed; up all night—but, as George Philpot says, 'it's life, though, damme it's life!' " [n]

Except late at night, however, the Palazzo Mocenigo was not very quiet. Now that he had plenty of room, Byron indulged his fondness for animals, and servants, of which he now had fourteen, all Italian except for Fletcher. He wrote Douglas Kinnaird: "I have got two monkeys, a fox, and two mastiffs. . . . The monkeys are charming." [n] These animals were kept on the ground floor, where he could stop to watch them or play with them on his way to his gondola. Despite minor thievery and petty quarrels, Byron's servants were exceptionally devoted to him. Among his most faithful was Giovanni Battista Falcieri, commonly known as Tita, whom he had taken into his service as gondolier. He was kindly and gentle, and he followed his master as faithfully as a dog, but his prodigious black beard gave him an unmerited reputation for ferocity.

Through the spring and summer Byron's irritation grew at what he considered neglect by his friends in England. Murray did not reply to his letters, though he had written voluminously and amusingly and knew that his publisher took delight in showing or reading his descriptions of Venetian life to visitors at 50 Albemarle Street. And Byron complained that Murray had given no satisfactory account of the reception and sale of his poems. Newstead was sold, but Hanson was procrastinating as usual about sending the papers for signing. And when Byron wrote to Hobhouse and Kinnaird, both of whom were becoming increasingly engrossed in English politics, he got no answer.

Byron's indignation overflowed in his letters. He indulged in some savage plain speaking about his English contemporaries when he wrote to Moore on June 1. Something Moore had told him about Hunt touched the springs of an irritation that he had hitherto suppressed: "He is a good man, with some poetical elements in his chaos; but spoilt by the Christ-Church Hospital and a Sunday newspaper,—to say nothing of the Surrey gaol, which conceited him into a martyr. But he is a good man. When I saw *Rimini* in MS., I told him that I deemed it good poetry at bottom, disfigured only by a strange style. His answer was, that his style was a system, or *upon system*, or some such cant; and, when a man talks of system, his case is hopeless. . . ."[n]

Byron had finally threatened to give his future work to Longman, but a mollifying letter from Murray melted his malice, and a thousand guineas deposited to his account eased his mind. He announced the completion of an Ode on Venice and he added that he had two stories, "one serious and one ludicrous (*à la Beppo*), not yet finished, and in no hurry to be so."[n] This seems to be the first hint that he was already at work on *Don Juan*, the first canto of which he finished in September.[n] And he also announced his intention to write some prose memoirs of his life, "without any intention of making disclosures or remarks upon living people, which would be unpleasant to them. . . ."[n]

Murray had sent an advance copy of the last canto of *Childe Harold* to Lady Byron, and despite her resolutions to be indifferent, she was touched by it. She read the lines:

But there is that within me which shall tire
Torture and Time, and breathe when I expire.[n]

And she wrote: "The passage was probably intended to make a great impression on *me*." In fact, it did. A few days later she was "well, but very *weak*. . . . The new canto is beautiful indeed." Her distress was increased by letters from the Montgomerys, who had seen Byron in Venice and reported him, with malicious delight, "Extremely fat . . . bloated and heavy." [n] Restless and unhappy, she paid a visit to the Abbey, from which Byron had proposed to her in the days when he had filled all her life with romantic dreams.

Cut off from England and his English friends, Byron took his pleasures as they came, and they came in droves of dark-eyed beauties eager for his attentions, some of them for gain, for he had a reputation for generosity, but more of them for the singular attraction of his person, which despite his growing obesity still appealed strongly to women of all sorts. Moreover, he showed a peculiar deference to the sex; there was in his manner a subtle, almost womanly gentleness, of which his cynical letters to his English friends gave no inkling. J. Cordy Jeaffreson observed with a keen perception of Byron's character: "Less harm would have come to him from the creatures, who composed the vagrant harem of the Palazzo Mocenigo, had he possessed the cynical hardness and spiritual grossness to think of them as animals, differing from the brutes only in shape and speech. . . . However dissolute she might be, the woman he regarded with passion became for a moment the object of an affection that was no less tender than transient." [n]

But he was callous to the quarrels of his mistresses, and the éclat of these scandals reverberated through the canals, causing the "*stravagante*" English lord to be talked of by even the gondoliers. English visitors were consumed with morbid eagerness to see him, and even bribed his servants to let them into his house. It is no wonder then that he avoided the English when he met them at an occasional *conversazione*. Aside from these irritations, however, Byron was well contented with his life in Venice. The sale of Newstead would make him independent, far more so than if he had remained in England. "In the two years I have been at Venice," he wrote Wedderburn Webster, "I have spent about *five* thousand pounds, and I need not have spent a *third* of this, had it not been that I have a passion for women which is expensive in its variety every where, but less so in Venice than in other cities. . . . more than half was laid out in the Sex;—to be sure I have had plenty for the money, that's certain—I think at least two hundred of one sort or another—perhaps more, for I have not lately kept the recount." [n] Not all Byron's "Charity" was bestowed on women, however. Hoppner recalled that Byron "sent fifty louis-d'or to a poor printer whose house had been burnt to the ground, and all his property destroyed." [n]

Comfortable as Byron was in his palace, he realized that it was hardly the place to bring up a daughter. Elise, the Swiss nurse of little Allegra, had sent several disquieting reports to the child's mother concerning the quarreling servants and mistresses at the Palazzo Mocenigo. In early August Allegra and her nurse were taken in by the Hoppners. On hearing that her daughter had been sent among strangers, Claire was so upset that she persuaded Shelley to leave with her suddenly for Venice on the 17th. They arrived on the 22nd and went directly to the Hoppners, who agreed to keep Claire's presence a secret.

The next afternoon Shelley called at the Palazzo Mocenigo and was cordially received by Byron, who seemed amenable to Shelley's request that Claire be allowed to see her daughter. Having been led to believe that Claire was in Padua, Byron insisted that Shelley accompany him on his ride on the Lido. He was in an excellent mood. Shelley always stimulated him to the height of his powers. Although Byron loved to twit him on his atheistic views and his transcendental notions, Shelley too was delighted with the conversation and the ride, and later made a poetic record of it in *Julian and Maddalo*. In the preface he spoke of Count Maddalo (Byron) as "a person of the most consummate genius, and capable, if he would direct his energies to such an end, of becoming the redeemer of his degraded country. But it is his weakness to be proud. . . . in social life no human being can be more gentle, patient, and unassuming than Maddalo. He is cheerful, frank, and witty. His more serious conversation is a sort of intoxication; men are held by it as by a spell." [n]

When they returned to Byron's palace, the conversation continued until the small hours of the morning. Byron generously offered Shelley and his family the use of the villa he had leased from Hoppner at Este, where Allegra could visit her mother. The topic of free will and destiny came up again as it had on their ride on the Lido sands, and Julian (Shelley) maintained stoutly:

> *"it is our will*
> *That thus enchains us to permitted ill—*
> *We might be otherwise; we might be all*
> *We dream of happy, high, majestical . . ."*
> *"Ay, if we were not weak—and we aspire*
> *How vainly to be strong!" said Maddalo;*
> *"You talk Utopia."* [n]

During the first three weeks of September, Byron was absorbed in the writing of the first canto of the poem he had started in July. On the 19th he wrote to Moore: "I have finished the first canto (a long one, of about 180 octaves) of a poem in the style and manner of *Beppo,* encouraged by the good success of the same. It is called *Don Juan,* and is meant to be a little quietly facetious upon every thing. But I doubt whether it is not . . . too free for these very modest days." [n] Byron had great plans for his new poem and he wrote *con amore* and with more seriousness of intention than he was willing to acknowledge until he saw how it would go with the public. There was a certain defiance in his choosing the legendary devil's disciple and heartless rake Don Juan for the hero of his mock-heroic epic, and he found additional sport and ironic force in reversing his protagonist's traditional character and making him an innocent creature of circumstance with a well-meaning naïveté akin to that of Candide.

Byron's accumulated observations of the farcical freedoms of Italian manners and his own contacts with the frailties of Venetian women gave him ample background for the rollicking bedroom comedy that is the climactic episode of the first canto, but what he wrote with the most exquisite relish was the description of Don Juan's mother, Donna Inez, a transparent portrait of Lady Byron. Although it is painted in a spirit of amusing caricature, the barb of bitterness is detectable in it:

> *Her favourite science was the mathematical,*
> *Her noblest virtue was her magnanimity . . .* [n]

Her learning and her prim perfection were themes of several stanzas. But since "perfection is/ Insipid in this naughty world of ours," her husband, Don Jose, "like a lineal son of Eve,/ Went plucking various fruit without her leave." [n] This part of the satire reached a climax in the couplet:

But—Oh! ye lords of ladies intellectual,
Inform us truly, have they not hen-pecked you all? [n]

The description of the early training of Juan prepared for the amusing and realistic scene of the innocent seduction of the sixteen-year-old boy by Donna Julia, married and twenty-three. But there was a half-serious Puritan remorse—a curious and not infrequent alloy of his libertine cynicism—in his exclamation about Plato paving the way to immoral conduct and being little better than a go-between. As for Julia,

A little still she strove, and much repented,
And whispering "I will ne'er consent"—consented.[n]

The Dedication sprang from his hearing from some English visitor that Robert Southey, the Laureate, had been spreading stories about him. Always sensitive and suspicious about what was said of him in England, he wrote Hobhouse in hot indignation:

"The son of a bitch on his return from Switzerland, two years ago, said that Shelley and I 'had formed a League of Incest, and practised our precepts with, &c.' He lied like a rascal, for they *were not sisters*. . . . He lied in another sense, for there was no promiscuous intercourse, my commerce being limited to the carnal knowledge of the Miss C." [n]

The Dedication was no less bitter because it was phrased in clever and humorous rhyme. He referred familiarly to "Bob Southey" as an "Epic Renegade," and he lumped all the "Lakers" together, as turncoats who had gone back to Toryism. He made sports of Coleridge's *Biographia Literaria*, "explaining Metaphysics to the nation—/I wish he would explain his Explanation." [n] And as for Wordsworth's "new system to perplex the sages," "he who understands it would be able/ To add a story to the Tower of Babel." [n]

But Southey was the apostate apologist for kings and tyrants, worthy to be classed with "the intellectual eunuch Castlereagh." He was happy to make Southey rhyme with "mouthey." As a Laureate, he was "A scribbling, self-sold, soul-hired, scorned Iscariot." And he added in a note: "I doubt if 'Laureate' and 'Iscariot' be good rhymes, but must say, as Ben Jonson did to Sylvester, who challenged him to rhyme with—

> *'I, John Sylvester,*
> *Lay with your sister.'*

Jonson answered—'I, Ben Jonson, lay with your wife.' Sylvester answered,—'That is not rhyme'—'No,' said Ben Jonson; 'but it is *true.*' " [n]

Meanwhile, Margarita Cogni, "La Fornarina" or baker's wife, had installed herself as Byron's housekeeper at the Palazzo Mocenigo, where she ruled the servants with an iron hand and cut the expenses in half. Boasting to Moore of his leonine Venetian mistress, with "a face like Faustina's, and the figure of a Juno—tall and energetic as a Pythoness, with eyes flashing, and her dark hair streaming in the moonlight—one of those women who may be made any thing," Byron wrote, "I am sure if I put a poniard into the hand of this one, she would plunge it where I told her,—and into *me,* if I offended her. I like this kind of animal, and am sure that I should have preferred Medea to any woman that ever breathed." [n]

But after a time she grew ungovernable. He told Murray, ". . . if I began in a rage, she always finished by making me laugh with some Venetian pantaloonery or another; and the Gipsy knew this well enough, as well as her other powers of persuasion, and exerted them with the usual tact and success of all She-things. . . ." She looked beautiful, Byron said, "in her *fazziolo,* the dress of the lower orders . . . but, alas! she longed for a hat and feathers. . . . I put the first into the fire; but I got tired of burning them, before she did of buying them, so that she made herself a figure." [n] Once when he had gone to the Lido and was overtaken by a squall, on his return he found her "on the open steps of the Mocenigo palace, on the Grand Canal, with her great black eyes flashing through her tears, and the long dark hair, which was streaming drenched with rain over her brows and breast. . . . Her joy at seeing me again was moderately mixed with ferocity, and gave me the idea of a tigress over her recovered Cubs." [n]

When he finally told her that she must go home, she threatened knives and revenge, and returning the next day seized a knife and slightly cut his hand. He then ordered his boatmen to take her home, but she threw herself into the Canal and had to be fished out and carried up the stairs. Finally she was convinced that Byron meant to be rid of her and went quietly.

Byron long relished his memories of her, certainly more than of any other of his Venetian mistresses. "I forgot to mention," he told Murray the following year, "that she was very devout, and would cross herself if she heard the prayer-time strike—sometimes when that ceremony did not appear to be much in unison with what she was then about. . . . One day when she had made me very angry with beating somebody or other, I called her a *Cow* (*Cow,* in Italian, is a sad affront and tantamount to the feminine of dog in English). I called her '*Vacca.*' She turned round, curtesied, and answered, '*Vacca tua, Celenza*' (*i.e. Eccelenza*). '*Your* Cow, please your Excellency.' In short, she was, as I said before, a very fine Animal, of considerable beauty and energy, with many good and several amusing qualities, but wild as a witch and fierce as a demon. She used to boast publicly of her ascendancy over me, contrasting it with that of other women, and assigning for it sundry reasons, physical and moral, which did more credit to her person than her modesty." [n]

In October Mary and Shelley returned to Venice and with some uneasiness left Allegra with the Hoppners, who regaled them with choice bits of gossip concerning Byron and his scandalous affairs with women. Shelley wrote his friend Peacock that Byron was familiar with the lowest sort of women, "the people his gondolieri pick up in the streets. He allows fathers & mothers to bargain with him for their daughters. . . . He says he disapproves, but he endures." [n]

Byron's annoyance at Hanson's delays was reaching a fever pitch when the attorney, his son Newton, and an agent of Major Wildman arrived in Venice with the Newstead papers on November 11. Byron greeted Hanson cordially, and his eyes were filled with tears, for, in spite of his pique because they had brought only one of three boxes sent by Murray and not a single book that he had requested, he was overcome with a flood of memories of his association with the Hansons from his boyhood. The Hansons, on their side, were a little disappointed in him. Newton observed: "Lord Byron could not have been more than 30, but he looked 40. His face had become pale, bloated, and sallow. He had grown very fat, his shoulders broad and round, and the knuckles of his hands were lost in fat." [n]

On November 17, Byron signed a codicil to his will, leaving £5,000 to his natural daughter, Allegra. Hanson carried back to England with him a sealed letter to Hobhouse and Kinnaird instructing them to pay his debts and invest the amount of the marriage settlement in a mortgage or other security. Douglas Kinnaird took over immediately and wrote a letter clarifying Byron's financial situation: "You are to receive £94,500 of which £66,200 is to be paid over to Mr. Bland & myself in order to be laid out in Government Security or real security, & the interest arising therefrom, together with about £200 per an. from S[r] R. Noel to be paid to your annual use—The remaining £28,300 I shall conceive it to be the duty of Hobhouse & myself to apply to the payment of your debts—which by the account transmitted to me appear to amount to about £34,162 leaving a deficiency of funds amounting to about £5860." [n] Hanson proposed that a pro-rata payment be made of Byron's simple contract debts, but that his own bill, amounting to nearly £12,000, should not be docked. Hobhouse and Kinnaird, as Byron's agents, vetoed the proposal, and decided that Hanson should wait for his payment, at least until he itemized his bill. Byron would get the interest (£3,300) from the trust fund during his lifetime, besides £3,000 in interest from April, when the agreement was made, on the purchase money of Newstead.

Byron had sent the manuscript of the first canto of *Don Juan* and was eagerly awaiting the verdict of his friends. He was not without apprehensions, he told Hobhouse, because the poem "is as free as La Fontaine; and bitter in politics, too; the damned cant and Toryism of the day may make Murray pause. . . . When I say *free,* I mean that freedom which Ariosto, Boiardo, and Voltaire—Pulci, Berni, all the best Italian and French—as well as Pope and Prior amongst the English—permitted themselves; but no improper words, nor *phrases;* merely some situations which are taken from life." [n]

Hobhouse breakfasted with Scrope Davies to read and discuss Byron's poem. And in writing to Byron he reported with all the tact he could muster that they both from time to time in the reading exclaimed, *"It will be impossible to publish this,"* but he added, "I need not say that these exclamations were accompanied with notes of admiration at the genius, wit, poetry, satire, and so forth. . . ." He feared that all the stories about Byron's Venetian life would be confirmed, and exaggerated. As for the satire, "Both Scrope and myself agreed that the attack on Castlereagh was much better than that on Southey (which, by the way, has the phrase 'dry-Bob!!'),* but we both agreed that you could not publish it unless you were over here ready to fight him." Hobhouse admitted that he did not see how amputation would save the poem, "more particularly as the objectionable parts are in point of wit, humour, and poetry, the very best beyond all doubt of the whole poem." [n] Even Douglas Kinnaird, who was as free as Byron in his speech, agreed that it could not be published.

It was the feeling of Byron's friends that he had been out of England so long that he was unaware of the growing moral temper of the bulk of the reading public, a development which was in part a general reaction to the profligacy of the court under the Regent and to the moral laxness of the upper classes that Byron had chiefly known during his years of fame in London. But Byron would not acquiesce in this view, and he was averse to cutting, though he conceded it would be better to omit the stanzas on Castlereagh and the two "bobs." "I appeal to Murray at his ledger, to the people, in short, Don Juan shall be an entire horse, or none. If the objection be to the indecency, the Age which applauds the 'Bath Guide,' and Little's poems, and reads Fielding and Smollett still, may bear with that. If to the poetry, I will take my chance. I will not give way to all the cant of Christendom." [n] To Hobhouse's objection that it was too close to the facts of his own life, he replied that "the *Julian* adventure [the bedroom farce with Donna Julia] detailed was none of mine;

* The reference is to the *double-entendre* in the lines in the Dedication: "Gasping on deck, because you soar too high, Bob,/ And fall, for lack of moisture, quite a-dry, Bob!" The term "a dry bob" was well known in the Regency slang of the day. Partridge's *Dictionary of Slang and Unconventional Language* gives the definition: "Coition without (male) emission."

but one of an acquaintance of mine (*Parolini* by name), which happened some years ago at Bassano, with the Prefect's wife when he was a boy. . . ." [n]

Finally Byron appealed to Murray, whose self-interest might be aroused in a *succès de scandale* and who could be persuaded to override his "puritanical committee." ". . . I *protest.* If the poem has poetry, it would stand; if not, fall: the rest is 'leather and prunella,' and has never yet affected any human production. . . ." [n] He asked Murray to print fifty copies for private circulation. But shortly after that, he was insisting on actual publication. "If they had told me the poetry was bad, I would have acquiesced; but they say the contrary, and then talk to me about morality—the first time I ever heard the word from any body who was not a rascal that used it for a purpose. I maintain that it is the most moral of poems; but if people won't discover the moral, that is their fault, not mine." [n]

Byron was further annoyed by the fact that Lord Lauderdale, who had taken his manuscript to London, had carried gossip of his Venetian amours. He wrote with boasting bravado to Hobhouse and Kinnaird:

"Which 'piece' does he mean? Since last year I have run the gauntlet [*sic*]; is it the Tarruscelli, the Da Mosti, the Spineda, the Lotti, the Rizzato, the Eleanora, the Carlotta, the Giulietta, the Alvisi, the Zambieri, the Eleanora de Bezzi (who was the King of Naples' Gioaschino's mistress, at least, one of them), the Theresina of Mazzurati, the Glettenheim and her sister, the Luigia & her mother, the Fornaretta, the Santa, the Caligara, the Portiera Vedova, the Bolognese figurante, the Tentora and her sister, cum multis aliis? Some of them are countesses, and some of them are cobblers' wives; some noble, some middling, some low, & all whores; which does the damned old 'Ladro and porco fottuto' mean? I have had them all and thrice as many to boot since 1817." And Byron's postscript indicated that he was not inclined to change his way of life: "Whatever brain-money you get on my account from Murray, pray remit me. I will never consent to pay away what I *earn,* that is *mine,* & what I get by my brains I will spend on *my* b———cks as long as I have a tester or a t*** remaining. I shall not live long, and for that reason I must live while I can. . . . 'For the night cometh.' " [n]

Despite his protests, Byron had acquiesced temporarily in

withholding *Don Juan* from publication, but he wrote Kinnaird: "This acquiescence is some thousands of pounds out of my pocket, the very thought of which brings tears into my eyes. I have imbibed such a love for money, that I keep some sequins in a drawer, to count and cry over them once a week. . . ." [n]

But before the Carnival was ended, he had decided that he would not be bullied by timid friends; he would trust his own judgment. He discovered that Murray was willing, and even eager to publish the poem, though he hoped to persuade Byron to cut out some of the "indelicacies," and so urged him in a flattering letter. Byron's response was eloquent and trenchant. He had found his own true genius in the rambling satire of *Don Juan,* and he was not to be diverted from it by the flattery of a bookseller or the moral squeamishness of friends. "You sha'n't make *Canticles* of my Cantos," he protested. "The poem will please, if it is lively; if it is stupid, it will fail; but I will have none of your damned cutting and slashing." [n]

Murray had written that Foscolo was "deploring that a man of your genius will not occupy some six or eight years in the composition of a work and subject worthy of you." [n] "I'll try no such thing," Byron retorted; "I hate tasks. And then 'seven or eight years!' God send us all well this day three months, let alone years. . . . And works, too!—is *Childe Harold* nothing? You have so many '*divine*' poems, is it nothing to have written a *Human* one? without any of your worn-out machinery. Why, man, I could have spun the thoughts of the four cantos of that poem into twenty, had I wanted to book-make, and its passion into as many modern tragedies. Since you want *length,* you shall have enough of *Juan,* for I'll make 50 cantos." [n]

Despite the bravado of his letters to his cronies in England, Byron had reached a kind of impasse in his personal life. The pleasures of Venice, though he could not quite admit it to himself yet, had begun to pall on him. Burning the candle to the end of the wick had affected adversely his health and spirits. He had lost most of his zest for adding to the count of his women. Yet during the festivities, when the masking facilitated new intrigues, he had formed for novelty's sake a clandestine liaison with an unmarried girl of eighteen. The great fondness for innocence which clung to him from his youth, when he had idealized Margaret Parker, and later Lady Oxford's eleven-year-old daughter, perhaps prompted him to seek the company of someone less blasé than the sophisticated married women who had been his main diversion during the past year. But his libertine habits, combined with a wide experience of the weaknesses of women, militated against his maintaining the romantic bloom of the affair for long, even though it was stimulated by the need for secrecy and the necessity of climbing a balcony to keep his rendezvous. It was more as Don Juan than as Romeo that he reported the event. The girl, Angelina, wanted to marry him, and when she discovered that he was already married was willing to dispose of his wife by the shortest means. Her "flinty-hearted father," warned by a neighbor, sent a priest and a Commissary of Police to Byron and locked the girl up. Byron later told Medwin that he was indifferent and did not care whether the police officer had come to shoot or to marry him again.[n]

His mind had never been more acute or his creative powers more active, but he was physically and emotionally weary. The sword had, he felt, indeed worn out its sheath. In this indifferent humor he accompanied his friend Alexander Scott to the Countess Benzoni's on an evening in the first days of April. After-theater guests were arriving, and there appeared in the door to the grand salon a petite girl with rich auburn curls falling down to beautifully moulded shoulders. Her bust and arms were plump and full but well shaped, and her complexion was fair and radiantly fresh. She had a voluptuous and yet naïve face, a handsome nose, mouth, and chin, and melting softness in her large eyes. If Byron had looked closely, he might have remembered that he had seen her before, for it was the young Countess Teresa Guiccioli, whom he had escorted to view Canova's "Helen" at the Countess Albrizzi's the year before. She was nineteen and had been married only a little over a year. Her husband, Count Alessandro Guiccioli, fifty-eight, who had exercised his strong will over two other wives before her, had insisted that she come to this *conversazione,* though she was weary.

Her weariness disappeared, however, when she saw the Grecian beauty of Byron's face. But when the Countess Benzoni approached Byron and asked him to meet her, he at first refused. "You know very well," he said, "that I do not want to make any new acquaintances with women; if they are ugly because they are ugly—and if they are beautiful because they are beautiful."

But he allowed himself to be persuaded. The Countess Benzoni presented him as "Peer of England and its greatest poet." His charming smile and "the extraordinary melody of his voice" captivated her. Her bright eyes shone at this "celestial apparition." "

When she told him that she came from Ravenna, he replied that it was a city he wished to visit on account of the tomb of Dante and of Francesca da Rimini. Dante then became the subject of their conversation, for, thanks to the intelligent guidance of the Abbess of the Convent of Santa Chiara at Faenza, where she had gone to school, Teresa had a true love for the great Italian poets of the past which won Byron immediately. It was a theme he was not accustomed to hear from such pretty Italian lips at a *conversazione*. She spoke of Dante and Petrarch with enthusiasm and assurance. When her husband came for her, Teresa later recorded ecstatically. "She rose as if she were coming out of a dream—and in crossing again the threshold of this Palace she was no longer as tranquil as she had been on entering. These mysterious sympathies shake the soul too much and frighten one."

Byron, with greater experience of these emotions, was not at the moment to the same extent shaken in his soul. But he was a believer in fate, and might not have disagreed later with Teresa's statement that "the effect of this meeting was the seal of the destiny of their hearts."

CHAPTER XX

1819

The Countess Guiccioli

WHEN BYRON LEFT the Benzoni's that April evening after his meeting with the Countess Guiccioli, he too was less tranquil than he had been when he entered the salon. Teresa's attractiveness coupled with good breeding and a naïve intellectual enthusiasm free from all the affectations of the "bluestocking" had pleased him first of all. Then her deference toward him as a poet and as a man was a subtle flattery more stirring than the passionate attachment of the "fine animals" he had consorted with in the past months. All his resolutions not to make new feminine acquaintances evaporated, and before they parted he had asked to see her privately. It was not difficult to arrange. Speaking of her first meeting with Byron in her "confession" to her husband, that strange document apparently extracted from her after Byron's death, Teresa said: "I then felt attracted to him by an irresistible force. He became aware of it, and asked to see me alone the next day. I was so imprudent as to agree, on condition that he would respect my honour: he promised and we settled on the hour after dinner, in which you [Count Guiccioli] took your rest. At that time an old boatman appeared with a note, in an unknown gondola, and took me to Mylord's gondola, where he was waiting, and together we went to a *casino* of his. I was strong enough to resist at that first encounter, but was so imprudent as to repeat it the next day, when my strength gave way—for B. was not a man to confine himself to sentiment." [n]

Teresa's roseate reconstruction of the events of these first days is delicately balanced between her desire to let the world know that Byron really loved her and her wish to portray the whole beautiful friendship as Platonic and proper. Byron was more realistic in describing his situation to Hobhouse: ". . . I have fallen in love with a Romagnola Countess from Ravenna, who is nineteen years old, and has a Count of fifty—whom she seems disposed to qualify, the first year of marriage being just over. . . . and I have hopes, sir,—hopes. . . . She is pretty, but has no tact; answers aloud, when she should whisper—talks of age to old ladies who want to pass for young; and this blessed night horrified a correct company at the Benzona's, by calling out to me '*mio Byron*' in an audible key, during a dead silence. . . . What shall I do? I am in love, and tired of promiscuous concubinage, and have now an opportunity of settling for life." [n]

What troubled Byron, however, was that Teresa, despite her indiscretions, very evidently wanted him to become her devoted *cavalier servente*. And although he was inclined to defend the Italian manners against the more hypocritical English, Byron could not help feeling as an Englishman that the office was little better than that of a high-class *gigolo*. He had ridiculed the custom good-humoredly in *Beppo*, and though he realized that the Italians took it seriously as a useful and necessary adjunct of marriages of convenience, he could not but smirk at the fan- and shawl-carrying traditions of the cult. Its most distasteful features in his eyes were the moral pretense that the relationship was Platonic and honorable and the demand that the *servente* display a certain chivalric formality. The gentleman was accepted in society as the *amico* or "friend" of the husband as well as the wife, and the husband was not supposed to be jealous.

The code of *serventismo* was even stricter than that of marriage. The improper conduct of a *dama* and her *amico* was more likely to shock polite society than the mere cuckolding of a husband. Fans were soon fluttering and tongues wagging, but Teresa was too happy to care. Byron, on his side, was persuasive, and he was "not a man to confine himself to sentiment," or to live long on mere "hopes." His private meetings with Teresa, soon known to everyone but her husband, were facilitated by a most faithful and understanding confidante, a governess in Count Guiccioli's household by the name of Fanny Silvestrini, with whom Teresa took long rides in a gondola on the pretext of studying French. And the gondola happened to meet Byron's. Then the lovers often went as far as the Lido or to other islands to view the flamboyant sunsets. Soon, Teresa recalled, that existence seemed natural to her and became necessary.

The ten days of their bliss came to an end when the Count's pressing affairs called him back to Ravenna. But the enamored pair had accomplished much in that time. Byron, who was slightly embarrassed by her flouting of customs for his sake, was even more proud of his conquest, and could not help boasting to Kinnaird: ". . . she is fair as sunrise, and warm as noon, we had but ten days to manage all our little matters in beginning, middle and end; and we managed them; and I have done my duty with the proper consummation."[n]

Count Guiccioli's announcement came suddenly, and Teresa rushed to the theater with a friend and went directly into Byron's box, flouting the etiquette of the *amicizia,* and there in full view of the Venetian gossips, she told him of her chagrin. The opera, Rossini's *Otello,* had begun. "It was in the midst of that atmosphere of passionate melody and harmony," Teresa recalled, that she announced to him that she must leave Venice."[n] The following day they had only a chance for some whispered exchanges as Byron handed her into the gondola, with Count Guiccioli standing by.

The Count was something of an enigma. Said to be the richest man in the Romagna, he was also one of the most cultivated. He had been a friend of Alfieri and was a principal supporter of the theater in Ravenna. But he was also reputed to be somewhat wily and opportunistic. Both in politics and in matrimony he had been shrewd and calculating. During the French occupation of the Romagna, he had realistically preferred putting himself at the head of the *canaille* to losing his head to them, as he cynically expressed it.[n] With the fall of Napoleon and the coming of the Papal regime, he proceeded to make himself agreeable to the Cardinal Legate and the Papal court. But suspicion about his allegiance lingered because by his third marriage he had allied himself with one of the most ardent of the aristocratic "patriots." Teresa's father, Count Ruggero Gamba Ghiselli, and her brother Pietro were among the stanchest supporters of libertarian principles in Ravenna, and soon became leaders in the revolutionary society of the Carbonari.

The foundation of Guiccioli's fortune had been laid in a calculated marriage with the Contessa Placidia Zinanni, a lady much older than the Count but with a very large dowry. One of his housemaids, Angelica Galliani, bore him six children, and when his wife protested, he sent her, not the mistress, away to a lonely country house from which she returned in time to make her will in his favor before dying under circumstances that caused Guiccioli's enemies to whisper "poison" and "murder." Then he married Angelica, and after he had presented a ring to Cardinal Malvasia, some of his children were legitimized. But on the night of his second wife's death he went to the theater as usual, and within a year he was searching for another wife. Because Teresa was young and pretty, he accepted her with the comparatively modest dowry of 4,500 scudi. Though there was nearly forty years' difference in their ages, she seemed to be in love with her husband for a time, but before the year ended, she was disillusioned. She was ready for an *amico* by the time she met Byron, and might have succumbed to something less than the "celestial apparition" which he presented to her.

If not so sentimental at their parting as Teresa, Byron was as disconsolate. She had given him the name of an obliging priest, Don Gaspare Perelli, to whom he could in confidence address letters for her. But she was forced to stop at two of her husband's country estates before arriving in Ravenna. She had left the faithful Fanny Silvestrini behind in Venice to deliver letters and give her news of Byron. On April 18 a letter arrived addressed from Cà Zen on the Po. In sweet sadness she wrote in the best style of Santa Chiara, and it is a measure of Byron's infatuation that he was not critical but only grateful. He replied in a fluent but somewhat rhetorical Italian, quite unlike his usual English letters: "My dearest Love. . . . Perhaps if I loved you less it would not cost me so much to express my thoughts, but now I have to overcome the double difficulty of expressing an unbearable suffering in a language foreign to me. . . . You sometimes tell me that I have been your *first* real love—and I assure you that you shall be my last Passion. . . . Before I knew you—I felt an interest in many women, but never in one only. Now I love *you* there is no other woman in the world for me." [n]

Still lovesick as an adolescent in the first throes of the passion, or at least self-intoxicated to the same degree with the sweet melancholy of separation and longing, Byron wrote again on the 25th: "My Teresa, where are you? Everything here reminds me of you. . . . When I go to the Conversazione, I give myself up to Tedium, too happy to suffer ennui rather than grief. . . . I hear, without the slightest emotion, the opening of that door which I used to watch with so much anxiety when I was there before you, hoping to see you come in. I will not speak of *much dearer* places still, for *there* I shall not go—*until* you return. . . . I did not mean to love any more, nor did I hope to receive Love. You have put to flight all my resolutions—now I am all yours. . . . You have been mine—and, whatever the outcome—I am, and eternally shall be, entirely yours. I kiss you a thousand and a thousand times. . . ." [n]

The Guicciolis had moved on in the meantime to another property of the Count, where Teresa developed a fever, and before she arrived in Ravenna she suffered a miscarriage and had to take to her bed. When she was able to write, she sent word through Fanny that she was ill but was vague about the causes and did not mention Byron's two letters sent to the priest Perelli. Byron began to be uneasy and had disturbing thoughts about the liaison. He began some "Stanzas to the Po," a franker outpouring of his feelings than could have pleased the lady to whom they were addressed:

But that which keepeth us apart is not
Distance, nor depth of wave, nor space of earth,
But the distraction of a various lot,
As various as the climates of our birth.

During the first half of May his disquieting reflections increased with further delays, which in his sensitiveness he ascribed to her unwillingness to give him clear instructions. In the meantime, Hobhouse had warned him against the perils of his new liaison. Byron replied with his usual frankness and some bravado: "The adventure is so far past preventing—that we had consummated our unlawful union with the proper rites four days and daily, previously to *her* leaving Venice. She was with child too, previous to this ingrafting, and to our connection, but miscarried at Pomposa on the road to R[avenn]a, on her return, and is now on her recovery. For anything I know, the affair may terminate in some such way as you hint at, for they are liberal with the knife in R[avenn]a and the Cavalier Conte G., her respected Lord, is shrewdly suspected of two assassinations already. . . . be that as it may, everything is to be risked for a woman one likes."[n]

And in the midst of these uncertainties, Byron turned involuntarily back to the one satisfactory love of his life. With uninhibited fervor he poured out to Augusta his deepest longings for a renewal of what he knew in his inmost mind could not be restored.

"My dearest Love—. . . . I have never ceased nor can cease to feel for a moment that perfect & boundless attachment which bound & binds me to you—which renders me utterly incapable of *real* love for any other human being—for what could they be to me after *you*? . . . we may have been very wrong—but I repent of nothing except that cursed marriage—& your refusing to continue to love me as you had loved me—I can neither forget nor *quite forgive* you for that precious piece of information.—but I can never be other than I have been—and whenever I love anything it is because it reminds me in some way or other of yourself. . . . It is heart-breaking to think of our long Separation—and I am sure more than punishment enough for all our sins—Dante is more humane in his 'Hell' for he places his unfortunate lovers (Francesca of Rimini & Paolo whose case fell a good deal short of *ours*—though sufficiently naughty) in company—and though they suffer—it is at least together. . . . They say absence destroys weak passions—& confirms strong ones—Alas! *mine* for you is the union of all passions & of all affections—."[n]

It is no doubt true that, as the Marchesa Origo emphasizes, Teresa reminded Byron in many ways of Augusta. "To both . . . he showed the same half-humorous, half-mocking tenderness; with both of them he found the release from self-consciousness that brought him gaiety and peace. For Byron did not want women to understand him: Annabella had understood him, and what had that led to?"[n]

Yet it was easy for Byron in his frustrated mood to slip back into his libertine habits of the past months. With relaxed parental vigilance, he was able to renew his adventure with Angelina, though he slipped and fell into the Grand Canal, and then as a drenched Romeo continued his amorous business while perched for an hour on her balcony. But that he could do this in the face of his sincere passion for Teresa added to his self-dissatisfaction and made him wonder the more whether he could commit himself to one woman forever.

In that situation, he was quick to take umbrage at a remark of Hobhouse concerning *Don Juan*. "Mr. Hobhouse is at it again about indelicacy," he wrote to Murray. "There is *no indelicacy;* if he wants *that,* let him read Swift, his great Idol. . . ."[n] But in writing again in reply to Murray's own plea that he avoid "approximations to indelicacy," Byron finally abandoned any pretense that there was none in the poem, saying: ". . . this reminds me of George Lamb's quarrel at Cambridge with Scrope Davies. 'Sir,' said George, 'he *hinted* at my *illegitimacy.*' 'Yes,' said Scrope, 'I called him a damned adulterous bastard'; the approximation and the hint are not unlike."[n]

Uneasy about the vagueness of Teresa's instructions, Byron delayed until the 1st of June before leaving for Ravenna. It was in a very mixed mood that he quitted the island city for this adventure, to which he was drawn by the mingled weakness and fidelity of his nature. Before leaving, he wrote out another draft of his "Stanzas to the Po." The last lines expressed the conflict in his emotions:

'Tis vain to struggle, I have struggled long
To love again no more as once I loved,
Oh, Time! why leave this ~~worst of~~ earliest Passion~~s~~ strong?
To tear a heart which pants to be unmoved?[n]

Byron in his own way was the most constant of men. An inner compulsion kept him from backing down once he had committed himself. And he found it disturbing to observe how strong that "earliest Passion" ("worst of Passions"?) still was.

He paused in Ferrara, where he saw two epitaphs in the Certosa cemetery that threw him back into the *Childe Harold* mood:

MARTINI LUIGI
IMPLORA PACE;

and

LUCREZIA PICINI
IMPLORA ETERNA QUIETE

"That was all," he wrote Hoppner; "but it appears to me that these two and three words comprise and compress all that can be said on the subject,—and then, in Italian, they are absolute music."[n]

At Bologna his morbidity again found outlet in visiting the beautiful cemetery beyond the walls. Although he saw no epitaphs that pleased him so much as those at Ferrara, he did find "an original of a *Custode,* who reminded me of the grave-digger in Hamlet."[n] Then a single hair in the balance of impulses and emotions drew him on to Ravenna. He arrived in his heavy Napoleonic carriage on June 10 during the festival of Corpus Domini (Corpus Christi), and caused quite a stir as he alighted at the mean little hotel with the grand name of Albergo Imperiale in the Via di Porta Sisi, only a few steps from the tomb of Dante.

He had a letter to Count Alborghetti, Secretary to the Papal Legate, which he sent off at once, and he was invited to the Count's box at the theater that evening. When Alborghetti told him that the Countess Guiccioli was at death's door, he was unable to control his emotion and revealed his feelings to the Count by exclaiming that he hoped he would not survive her. But then Count Guiccioli came into the box and gave him better news. That night, repentant for having doubted her love and loyalty, Byron wrote Teresa without reserve: "My sweetest soul—believe that I live for you alone—and do not doubt me. I shall stay here until I know what your wishes really are. . . . I would sacrifice all my hopes for this world and all that we believe we may find in the other—to see you happy. I cannot think of the state of your health without sorrow and tears."[n] At her husband's invitation, he went to see her the next day. They were both extremely agitated, but the circumstances of their meeting were such that they could say little. On returning to the hotel, Byron wrote again: "You are so surrounded. . . . It is impossible for me to live long in this state of torment—I am writing to you in tears—and I am not a man who cries easily. When I cry my tears come from the heart, and are of blood."[n] As long as Teresa was in bed, he had no opportunity for private interviews with her. But she showed a marked improvement as soon as he arrived, and her spirits began to revive.

Having run through the things that might have interested him in the sleepy little town—he cared little for sight-seeing, even with agreeable companions—Byron spent hours brooding in his stuffy room and wrote long impassioned letters to Teresa. The frustration of the situation was almost too much for him. He would have preferred an elopement, "a romance in the Anglo fashion." In fact he actually proposed this remedy, but he knew Teresa would not have the courage. He wrote: "I can already anticipate your answer. It will be long and divinely written—but it will end in a negative. I kiss you from my heart ten million times." [n] Teresa treasured this letter as "a masterpiece of passion, devotion, and generosity." [n] But Byron was right; her answer was negative.

The tension lessened considerably when Teresa was better and was able to ride in her carriage. And of course she took Byron with her. They drove to the forest of umbrella pines that reached from a short distance outside the city to the sea and as far south as Rimini. The sun was setting in an aureole of gold and opal. Teresa recalled that ". . . when they heard from afar the bells of the city it was impossible not to recall the verses of Dante which begin the 8th Canto of the *Purgatory*." [n] It was then that she asked Byron to write something on Dante; he began the next day his *Prophecy of Dante* and dedicated it to her.

The air of the forest, and especially the chance to have some privacy with Byron, improved Teresa's health. One day he saw on her table a copy of Dante's *Inferno*, and they read together what was already a favorite passage of Byron's, and what seemed to parallel their own situation so closely, the episode of Paolo and Francesca. Byron later wrote his own translation of it.

Soon their misunderstandings had been dissolved in a resumption of the relations that had started in Venice—under conditions of danger that made the adventure all the more piquant. Teresa had silenced the doubts of her lover by finding a way to cuckold her husband in his own house. Byron wrote Hoppner: "*She* manages very well—though the local[e] is inconvenient—(no *bolts* and be d——d to them) . . . and *no* place but the great Saloon of his own palace—so that if I come away with a Stiletto in my gizzard some fine afternoon—I shall not be astonished—I can't make *him* out at all—he visits me frequently —and takes me out (like Whittington, the Lord Mayor) in a coach and *six* horses. The fact appears to be, that he is completely *governed* by her—for that matter so am I. . . . By the aid of a Priest—a Chambermaid—a young Negro-boy, and a female friend—we are enabled to carry on our unlawful loves. . . ." [n]

Byron had been too preoccupied with the Guiccioli to pay much attention to Count Giuseppe Alborghetti, Secretary General of the Government of the Lower Romagna. As a lay official second in command under the Cardinal Legate, Alborghetti was in a position of great power and influence, and he was destined to play an important role in Byron's life in Ravenna. His taste for poetry and his knowledge of English probably drew him to the famous English poet, who did finally accept the Count's invitation to meet the Cardinal, Alessandro Malvasia, whom he found agreeable. "He is a fine old fellow," he wrote Lord Kinnaird, "and has been rather loose in his youth, without being much tighter in his age." [n] The Cardinal was well enough pleased with Byron's conversation to arrange a special party for him, and was amazed and angered when the guest of honor sent a lame excuse and did not arrive.

The real reason was that Byron was now seriously worried about his *amica*'s health. He had obtained Count Guiccioli's permission to call Dr. Aglietti of Venice, professor and head of the medical school, to Ravenna to see her. "I greatly fear that the Guiccioli is going into a consumption," he wrote Hoppner. "Thus it is with every thing and every body for whom I feel any thing like a real attachment. . . . I never even could keep alive a dog that I liked or that liked me." Her cough and fever continued, and yet she would not relinquish any of their love trysts for the sake of her health. Byron observed with his usual frankness: "She bears up *gallantly* in every sense of the word, but I sometimes fear that our *daily* interviews may not [*sic*] tend to weaken her (I am sure they *don't strengthen me*) but it is not for me to hint this. . . ." He added feelingly: "If any thing happens to my present *Amica*, I have done with the passion for ever—it is my *last* love." [n]

He felt that like his alter ego, Childe Harold, he had, both physically and emotionally, grown old beyond his years, that he had lived through all the experiences of life, and yet was driven by habit to seek constantly new sensations to quicken his jaded emotions. He confessed to Wedderburn Webster: "At thirty I feel there is no more to look forward to. . . . my hair is half grey, and the Crow's-foot has been rather lavish of its indelible steps. My hair, though not gone, seems going, and my teeth remain by way of courtesy. . . ."[n]

The Guiccioli affair had roused Byron in large part because it had rather surprisingly demonstrated to him that he could still mingle sentiment with passion and that he was not too blasé to respond to genuine attachment. But he was still disturbed by his equivocal situation and could not quite rid himself of a cynical disbelief in the constancy of Teresa. It may have been in self-defense, then, that he flirted tentatively with her friend Geltrude (or Gertrude) Vicari. He confided to Lord Kinnaird: "La Geltruda is gone to Bologna, after pinching her left thigh. . . . I was never permitted to set eyes on her *not no more*."[n]

Teresa's health improved remarkably as she basked in the assurance of Byron's love. And in her joyous confidence she sometimes caused her *amico* the exquisite pain of jealousy. She had only to talk with someone else at the theater and he was in agony. His imagination heated, he wrote from his hotel room: "I have noticed that every time I turned my head toward the stage you turned your eyes to look at that man—and this, after all that had happened today! . . . Let me go—it is better to die from the pain of separation, than from that of betrayal. . . ."[n]

Teresa's comment on this letter years later when she was sorting the notes of the lover she never forgot was this: "Billet de jalousie magnifique—passionné—sublime mais très injuste. Il ne me connaissait encore que depuis trop peu!!!"[n]

But greater tranquillity came to Byron as his *amica* grew stronger and he was able to see her alone more often, particularly during their rides in the Pineta. Teresa recalled these times as wholly idyllic. But such quiet pleasure was boring to the wayward heart of Byron after a time. His thoughts again fastened on his sister or his wife, and it was Teresa's turn to be a little sadly jealous.

She would have been even more chagrined had she seen his letter to Augusta concerning her: "She is pretty—a great Coquette—extremely vain—excessively affected—clever enough

—without the smallest principle—with a good deal of imagination and some passion. . . . She is an Equestrian too—but a bore in her rides—for she can't guide her horse—and he runs after mine—and tries to bite him—and then she begins screaming in a high hat and Sky-blue riding habit—making a most absurd figure. . . ."[n]

It is a mistake, however, to judge Byron's feelings for Teresa solely by his detached and sometimes caustic letters, which were always for him a kind of release for the uninhibited ego and no adequate measure of his capacity for affection and devotion. By the end of July he had finally decided to cut his ties with Venice entirely. But he was perplexed by the problem of what to do with Allegra. He had a fondness for her and would have been glad to have her with him, but he knew that with the uncertainty of his plans and the irregularity of his life he could not give her a proper environment.

A Mrs. Vavassour, a wealthy widow from the north of England, had seen Allegra at the Hoppners and had offered to adopt her, but Byron was not willing to give up his daughter, though he entertained the idea of Mrs. Vavassour taking charge of her education. Nothing came of this, however, and when the Hoppners left for Switzerland in the summer, she was put in charge of Mrs. Martens, wife of the Danish Consul, at La Mira. Elise, the Swiss nurse, had been dismissed after the Shelleys left Venice.

In the meantime Byron had been disturbed by letters from England. Murray had been stalling on the publication of *Don Juan*. On July 15, with some trepidation he sent out the two cantos to the booksellers in a quarto edition with only the printer's name on the title page. Murray's fears concerning the reception were not groundless. Gifford, who was well disposed toward Byron, wrote to the publisher: "I read the second canto this morning, and lost all patience at seeing so much beauty so wantonly and perversely disfigured."[n] Even Douglas Kinnaird reported that *Don Juan* had failed with the public.

Murray had asked Byron for the plan of *Don Juan* in future cantos. He replied: "I *have* no plan—I *had* no plan; but I had or have materials; though if, like Tony Lumpkin, I am 'to be snubbed so when I am in spirits,' the poem will be naught, and the poet turn serious again. If it don't take, I will leave it off where it is, with all due respect to the Public; but if continued, it must be in my own way. . . . Why, Man, the Soul of such writing is its licence; at least the *liberty* of that licence. . . . You are too earnest and eager about a work never intended to be serious. Do you suppose that I could have any intention but to giggle and make giggle?"[n]

Now came another blow. Teresa showed Byron some satirical verses that were being sung in the street about his cuckolding of the Count. She assured him that Guiccioli had only disdain for the anonymous ballad maker, but Byron was uneasy, though the Count remained polite and apparently friendly. Was he so innocent, or so forgiving, or was he merely biding his time? Then the Count announced suddenly that he was going on a projected journey to his property in Bologna, and Teresa must accompany him. She insisted that Byron follow them. He could only obey, but his letter indicated his disquiet: "Farewell, my dearest *Evil*—farewell, my torment—farewell, my *all* (but *not all mine!*) I kiss you more often than I have ever kissed you—and this (if Memory does not deceive me) should be a fine number of times, counting from the beginning. Meanwhile,—you can be sure of me—of my love—and of your power."[n]

He followed dutifully and arrived at the Pellegrino Inn at Bologna on August 10. The next evening he accompanied the Guicciolis to the Arena del Sole to see Alfieri's *Mirra*. The play, upon a theme of incest, affected Byron profoundly. He wrote about it to Murray the next day: ". . . the two last acts . . . threw me into convulsions. I do not mean by that word a lady's hysterics, but the agony of reluctant tears, and the choaking shudder, which I do not often undergo for fiction." Teresa too from fright and sympathy went into hysterics, and, he concluded, "we are all languid and pathetic this morning, with great expenditure of Sal Volatile."[n]

After this unhappy experience they went out very little. Byron visited his *amica* at the Palazzo Savioli in the Via Galleria, a massive palace with a high-ceilinged and elaborately decorated gallery and a many-windowed loggia. They spent the evenings, when the Count went to the theater or to *conversazioni*, under the cool trees or by the fountain in the garden. The calculating Count seemed willing enough to tolerate his wife's *cavalier servente*. Perhaps the fires of passion had burned out in him and he was not really jealous. Perhaps he even liked Byron, though some method and motive appeared when he asked the English lord to try to get him through his friends a post as British Consul or Vice-Consul in Ravenna. Count Guiccioli was aware that his equivocal politics as well as his wealth were watched by the Austrians, and that it would be valuable to have powerful foreign support in the event that political uprisings upset the *status quo*.

The police spies were watching Byron too. They observed that he had moved to the Palazzo Merendoni in the Via Galleria, only a few doors from the Guicciolis' palace, and the report added: "*Byron* is a man of letters, and his literary merit will attract to him the most distinguished men of learning in Bologna. This class of men has no love for the Government."[n] They noted also his request for a passport for a servant to carry a pressing letter to Venice. The letter was not subversive, however, but was addressed to Alexander Scott, urging him to send Allegra to Bologna with a governess accompanied by the clerk Edgecombe.

In the intervals of lovemaking—which never in itself completely satisfied Byron's active spirit—he began to think of carving out a fresh career. He wrote to Hobhouse: "My time has been passed viciously and agreeably; at thirty-one so few years, months, days remain, that 'Carpe diem' is not enough. I have been obliged to crop even the seconds, for who can trust to *to-morrow* . . . I can not repent me (I try very often) so much of anything I have done, as of anything I have left undone." He was thinking of going to England in the spring, but he preferred South America. "Europe is grown decrepit . . . those fellows are fresh as their world, and fierce as their earthquakes."[n]

When Teresa was away for several days with her husband, he had more time for his melancholy self-questioning, and he became physically ill with the conflict of emotions. "I am so bilious," he wrote Hobhouse, "that I nearly lose my head, and so nervous that I cry for nothing. . . . I have had no particular cause of griefs, except the usual accompaniments of all unlawful passions. . . . I feel—and I feel it bitterly—that a man should not consume his life at the side and on the bosom of a woman, and a stranger; that even the recompense, and it is much, is not enough, and that this Cicisbean existence is to be condemned. But I have neither the strength of mind to break my chain, nor the insensibility which would deaden its weight." [n]

Byron's love for Teresa exerted an oppressive compulsion, as much pain as pleasure, which bound him to a fidelity that weathered all the revolts of the free male ego and all reasoned analysis. Wandering through the Palazzo Savioli (she had given him a key), he came upon one of her favorite books, a fat little volume of Mme de Staël's *Corinne,* in small print and bound in purple plush. He used to twit her about her fondness for this sentimental novel, but now he grew sentimental himself and wrote in the margin of it:

"My dear Teresa,—I have read this book in your garden;—my love, you were absent, or else I could not have read it. It is a favourite book of yours, and the writer was a friend of mine. You will not understand these English words. . . . but you will recognize the hand-writing of him who passionately loved you, and you will divine that, over a book which was yours, he could only think of love. In that word, beautiful in all languages, but most so in yours—*Amor mio*—is comprised my existence here and hereafter. . . . my destiny rests with you, and you are a woman, seventeen years of age [*sic*], and two out of a convent. I wish that you had stayed there, with all my heart,—or at least, that I had never met you in your married state. But all this is too late. I love you, and you love me,—at least, you *say so*, and *act* as if you *did* so, which last is a great consolation in all events. But *I* more than love you, and cannot cease to love you. Think of me, sometimes, when the Alps and the ocean divide us,—but they never will, unless you *wish* it." [n]

Allegra arrived before the end of August. "She is English," Byron wrote to Augusta, "but speaks nothing but Venetian. 'Bon di, papa' &c &c she is very droll, and has a good deal of the Byron —can't articulate the letter *r* at all—frowns and pouts quite in our way—blue eyes—light hair growing *darker* daily—and a dimple in her chin—a scowl on the brow—white skin—sweet voice—and a particular liking of Music—and of her own way in every thing—is not that B. all over?" [n]

After the return of the Guicciolis, Byron regained some of his tranquillity. Count Guiccioli seemed amazingly agreeable to his wife's *amico,* invited him to move into a vacant apartment on the ground floor of his palace, and appeared utterly complacent.

But then he asked to borrow a considerable sum of money from his guest. When Byron declined with an excuse, he was angry with Teresa, but she had her recourse. She had a relapse and found that she needed Dr. Aglietti's care and must return to Venice. She even got the Count's permission to let Byron accompany her. The alert director of police reported to Rome that Byron and the Countess had left Bologna on the 12th of September.

The activities of the conspiring pair, however, were not political but amatory. Byron was traveling in his Napoleonic carriage, from which the green paint was beginning to chip. It was laden with his traveling bed and his books as well as his servants and his blue-eyed daughter, and it followed in the dust of Count Guiccioli's coach-and-six, which carried Teresa and her maid and an old manservant. Teresa remembered this trip as one of the happiest of her life. At last she was really alone with her lover. "They made their halts together—they stopped at the same hotels," she recalled with pleasure.[n] One of their halts was to visit the home and grave of Petrarch at Arqua.

Although Byron preferred Dante to Petrarch, and would, Teresa said, have subscribed to the opinion of Sismondi, who said: "I am tired of this veil always lowered," yet he did not want to destroy her illusions and listened with pleasure while she recited Petrarch's verses. They wrote their names together in the visitor's book, and she was pleased when Byron said that their names would never be separated.

Both Byron and his *amica* foresaw what their situation would be in a Venice already seething with gossip. Teresa was even more completely aware than Byron to what extent they had violated Italian conventions, but she could not think of giving up her lover, and on the impulse of the moment proposed that they escape together to the ends of the world. It was Byron who counseled prudence, for reasons which were as mixed as most human motives.

Once in Venice, she found the Palazzo Malipiero on one of the small canals, "disagreeable on account of their exhalations," and within two days she was in the Palazzo Mocenigo. She wrote blandly to her husband, saying that Aglietti had recommended a change of air and asked his permission for Byron to take her to the lakes of Garda and Como. But before she received a reply, she had gone to Byron's villa at La Mira. In her delicate later account she said that she took Fanny Silvestrini with her and that Byron came to La Mira only occasionally and then lived in an entirely separate wing of the building. But the arrangements were not so innocent. Fanny was in Venice, watching the post and instructing the Count's servant Lega Zambelli how to reply to his inquiries about his wife. It was not difficult to arrange, for Fanny was Lega's mistress and eventually he came into Byron's employ.

Byron was puzzled by the Count's easy compliance. But Teresa was happy at La Mira and was in no hurry to go to the lakes. Moreover, she was suffering from two ailments which made her unwilling to move and might have embarrassed the lovemaking of a less ingenuous child of nature. She wrote to her husband that she had piles and that she feared a *prolapsus uteri*, but was reassured by Aglietti.

If Count Guiccioli was sanguine and complacent about Teresa's situation, her father was not. Count Gamba protested to his son-in-law for allowing his wife to be accompanied by a man like Lord Byron, "too gifted, too seductive not to trouble the heart of a young woman and not to excite the observation of the public." [n] So Teresa promised her father, not to leave Byron's house, but to wait at La Mira until her husband came for her.

Byron was still thinking of an escape, but not with Teresa. To Hobhouse he raised the question again of the South American project. He would go there with Allegra. "I am not tired of Italy," he wrote, "but a man must be a Cicisbeo and a Singer in duets, and a connoisseur of Operas—or nothing—here. I have made some progress in all these accomplishments, but I can't say that I don't feel the degradation. Better be an unskilful Planter, an awkward settler,—better be a hunter, or anything, than a flatterer of fiddlers, and fan carrier of a woman. I like women—God he knows—but the more their system here developes upon me, the worse it seems, after Turkey too; here the *polygamy* is all on the female side. I have been an intriguer, a husband, a whoremonger, and now I am a Cavalier Servente—by the holy! it is a strange sensation." [n]

In recent months he had considered the idea of returning to England, but he conceived it possible only if by some heroic gesture he could justify his return and recapture his own self-esteem and the admiration of his countrymen. He had spoken a number of times of coming over to take part in a revolution, for in the year 1819 the discontents and suffering of the people had been increased by the Tory brutality in the Peterloo massacre. To take part with Kinnaird and Hobhouse in a reform movement was not enough. But he realized that "revolutions are not to be made with rosewater. My taste for revolution is abated, with my other passions." [n]

For the present, La Mira was a pleasant place. After riding with Teresa at sunset along the Brenta and conversing or making love in the evening, Byron settled into a routine of writing new verses for *Don Juan* in the early hours of the morning. He was perhaps thinking of his own marriage, and possibly also of Teresa's, but more likely of what would happen to their relationship should they elope and settle into something as fixed as marriage, when he wrote:

> *Think you, if Laura had been Petrarch's wife,*
> *He would have written sonnets all his life?* [n]

On October 7, Thomas Moore arrived on his long-promised visit to Venice. Byron was delighted and in high spirits, for to see Moore was to revive memories of some of his happiest bachelor years in London. Moore noted: "He had grown fatter both in person and face, and the latter had most suffered by the change, —having lost, by the enlargement of the features, some of that refined and spiritualized look that had, in other times, distinguished it." The addition of whiskers and the long hair growing down his neck, together with a foreign-looking coat and cap, made him seem strange and different. "He was still, however, eminently handsome; and, in exchange for whatever his features might have lost of their high, romantic character, they had become more fitted for the expression of that arch, waggish wisdom, that Epicurean play of humour. . . ." [n]

Byron got permission of his *amica* to accompany Moore to Venice, and there established him in the Palazzo Mocenigo, but he himself returned at night to La Mira. On Moore's last day in Venice, however, Byron was permitted by the Contessa to "make a night of it," and did not return until dawn. When Moore stopped at La Mira the next day, Byron presented him with the manuscript of the Memoirs he had begun in Venice the year before. They were not for immediate publication, but Moore might sell them for posthumous appearance. As he described them to Murray, they were intended to be "*Memoranda,* and not *Confessions.* I have left out all my *loves* (except in a general way), and many other of the most important things (because I must not compromise other people), so that it is like the play of Hamlet—'the part of Hamlet omitted by particular desire.' But you will find many opinions, and some fun, with a detailed account of my marriage and its consequences, as true as a party concerned can make such accounts, for I suppose we are all prejudiced." [n]

Although he had no encouragement from Murray, Byron proceeded with the third canto of *Don Juan.* In answer to Murray's account of the English reaction to the first two cantos, he wrote with an exasperated eloquence born of confidence in the creation of his brain. One critic's objection was to the quick succession of fun and gravity in the poem: "we are never scorched and drenched at the same time." Byron replied: "Blessings on his experience! . . . Did he never spill a dish of tea over his testicles in handing a cup to his charmer, to the great shame of his nankeen breeches? Did he never swim in the sea at Noonday with the Sun in his eyes and on his head, which all the foam of Ocean could not cool? . . . Did he never inject for a Gonorrhea? or make water through an ulcerated Urethra? Was he ever in a Turkish bath, that marble paradise of sherbet and Sodomy?" [n]

To Hoppner he wrote: "There has been an eleventh commandment to the women not to read it—and what is still more extraordinary they seem not to have broken it. But that can be of little import to them poor things—for the reading or non-reading a book—will never keep down a single petticoat;— . . ." [n] But underneath the jocular boasting and ribaldry of his tone in a letter to Kinnaird about this time, there is evidence of his unshaken confidence in the merits of the poem as an expression of the rigors of real life. He wrote: "As to 'Don Juan,' confess, confess—you dog and be candid—that it is the sublime of *that there* sort of writing—it may be bawdy but is it not good English? It may be profligate but is it not *life,* is it not *the thing*? Could any man have written it who has not lived in the world?

—and tooled in a post-chaise?—in a hackney coach?—in a gondola?—against a wall?—in a court carriage?—in a vis-à-vis?—on a table?—and under it? I have written about a hundred stanzas of a third canto, but it is damned modest; the outcry has frightened me. I had such projects for the Don, but Cant is [so] much stronger than C*** now-a-days, that the benefit of experience in a man who had well weighed the worth of both monosyllables, must be lost to despairing posterity." [n]

As for his present situation, he could be just as cavalier. "I have been faithful to my honest liaison with Countess Guiccioli, and I can assure you that *She* has never cost me, directly or indirectly, a sixpence. . . . I never offered her but one present—a broach of brilliants—and she sent it back to me with her *own hair* in it (I shall *not* say of *what part*, but *that* is an Italian custom). . . . I have not had a whore this half year, confining myself to the strictest adultery." [n] Replying to a letter of Hoppner telling him of a fantastically distorted story of his abduction of the Countess, he wrote: "I should like to know *who* has been carried off—except poor dear *me*. I have been more ravished myself than any body since the Trojan war. . . ." [n]

Byron went to Venice toward the end of October and was seized with a violent fever, and Teresa hastened in to attend him. While he was still ill and feverish, Count Guiccioli arrived, descending at the gondola landing with his son and several servants. He hoped that staying at Byron's palace would allay gossip in Venice. But within, matters were not so tranquil. A battle of wills ensued between the old Count and his young wife, and they quarreled violently. Finally, Byron told Kinnaird, "he gave her the alternative, *him*, or *me*. She decided instantly for *me*, not being allowed to have both, and the lover generally having the preference. . . . At twenty I should have taken her away, at thirty, with the experience of *ten such years!* I sacrificed myself only; and counselled, and persuaded her with the greatest difficulty, to return with her husband to Ravenna, not absolutely denying that I might come there again; else she refused to go." [n]

There were some terrible scenes, and Guiccioli even came crying to Byron; it was the lover's persuasion rather than the husband's that finally sent her back. Byron felt low and wretched, and lonely, and he thought again of returning to

England. "I will leave the country, reluctantly indeed," he wrote Hobhouse, "but I will do it; for, otherwise, if I formed a new *liaison* she would cut the figure of a woman planted [deserted], and I never will willingly hurt her self-love." [n]

But his enthusiasm for England now was not great. He felt that he could not go back without first fighting a duel with Henry Brougham, the man who had calumniated him on his leaving and who had interfered with Mme de Staël's attempt to reconcile him with his wife. And the equivocal letters of Augusta left him uncertain of his reception even in that quarter. Then Allegra and her nurse fell ill and his journey was delayed. It was the end of November before Dr. Aglietti pronounced Allegra well enough to travel, but Byron still found excuses to postpone the journey. Having made the decision to cut the tie with Teresa, however, he could not deny to himself that there was a certain relief in being free once more from the strongest passions, and, he told himself, perhaps it was better that it should have ended before love could be killed by habit. As usual, he turned to verse to express his feelings:

When lovers parted
Feel broken-hearted,
And, all hopes thwarted,
  Expect to die;
A few years older,
Ah! how much colder
They might behold her
  For whom they sigh . . .
You'll find it torture
Though sharper, shorter,
To wean, and not wear out your joys.

In the delicate balance of motive and will it is not unlikely that inertia played as great a part as inclination in his final decision to remain in Italy. As Fanny Silvestrini reported it to Teresa: "He was already dressed for the journey, his gloves and cap on, and even his little cane in his hand. . . . At this moment mylord, by way of pretext, declares that if it should strike one o'clock before every thing was in order . . . he would not go that day. The hour strikes and he remains!" [n]

The next day a letter from Ravenna decided his fate. It was not from Teresa but from her father. Count Gamba, who had opposed the liaison until now, begged him to come and see his daughter. Psychosomatic illnesses were always useful to Teresa in a crisis. This one broke down the resistance of both her husband and her father. With a mingling of relief and resignation, Byron wrote to Teresa: "F***[anny] will already have told you, *with her accustomed sublimity,* that Love has gained the victory. I could not summon up resolution enough to leave the country where you are, without, at least, once more seeing you. On *yourself*, perhaps, it will depend, whether I ever again shall leave you."[n]

Teresa recuperated rapidly when the cause of the illness was removed. But now Byron took his time about leaving for Ravenna. On December 23 he wrote to Augusta from Bologna, enclosing all his long hair: "You will see that it was not so very long. I curtailed it yesterday, my head and hair being weakly after my tertian."[n] He arrived in Ravenna on Christmas Eve, and was joyously welcomed by a smiling Teresa and her father and friends in the gala atmosphere of the holiday season. All was well, for her *amico* had come home.

CHAPTER XXI

1820

Cavalier Servente in Ravenna

BYRON, WHO HARDLY KNEW what to expect on his return to Ravenna, was at first delighted, a little flattered, and somewhat embarrassed by his reception. He was overwhelmed with attentions by everyone, but he knew on what terms he had come back, for it was evident that Teresa now considered him her acknowledged *cavalier servente*. And she was proud of her triumph, not so much over her husband and her father as over Byron himself. She had rightly sensed that his resistance to this regularizing of their relationship had been more responsible than the attitude of Count Guiccioli for the unhappy struggle in Venice and for the interlude when he had tried to break his chains.

The Count's welcome was suave and polite as ever, though he was aloof, inscrutable, and shrewd, if not sinister. But there was no reserve in the welcome of the other Ravennese, including Teresa's father. The night after his arrival there was a grand reception and ball at the home of her uncle, the Marchese Cavalli, to which Teresa's *amico* received a special invitation. "The G.'s object," Byron wrote to Hoppner, "appeared to be to parade her foreign lover as much as possible, and, faith, if she seemed to glory in the Scandal, it was not for me to be ashamed of it." [n]

After the New Year the Carnival was to begin, and he found himself the center of attention in the provincial town. But within a week or two, old wounds and old pangs began to trouble him again. He recalled that five years before, he had been on his way to be married. On New Year's Eve he wrote Annabella a nostalgic letter to ask her for a portrait of Ada, "something to remind me of what is yours and mine." [n] And soon frictions and misunderstandings began to arise with Teresa. Not being able to see her privately every day, he began to imagine slights, lack of candor, and even familiarities with her husband and friends in his presence designed to torment him. Unable to stand uncertainties and impatient of any dissimulation, he wrote Teresa long letters baring his feelings. She was always able to bring him out of these moods, however, for he was easily managed by any woman who loved him and used her feminine persuasions. In the end what he did was what Teresa wished, though he sulked frequently under the rules of *serventismo*. The weather continued bad and he was deprived of his daily ride and was shut up in the Albergo Imperiale except when he went to see his *amica*.

But she soon contrived to have the Count offer to rent the upper floor of the Palazzo Guiccioli to Byron. His furniture was on the way from Bologna. Byron's hesitancy to accept was motivated by several considerations beyond the thought of the equivocal situation and the gossip it would cause. One was the suspicion that at times Teresa was siding with her husband, or at least that she was making too great an effort to persuade her lover to placate the Count's whims. The sticking point was his resolve not to enter Count Guiccioli's house while he retained a maid whom Byron suspected of being a spy. But on that point she defended her husband, who would not yield. Byron's vexation at the bonds of *serventismo* found vent in a letter to Hoppner: "I am drilling very hard to learn how to double a shawl, and should succeed to admiration if I did not always double it the wrong side out. . . ." [n]

Yet, in a few days, despite his pride, he had accepted the offer on the Count's own terms as the price of regaining an opportunity for intimacy with Teresa. As soon as he was settled in the Palazzo Guiccioli, with its spacious rooms, and had his horses in the stables, Byron's temper improved and he relaxed. The fact that his *amica* was now more accessible also decreased his emotional tension, even though their meetings had to be arranged to coincide with Guiccioli's absence or his naps. Byron soon acquired as his confidential agent one of the Negro pages employed by Guiccioli. This one, from East Africa, was faithful to Teresa; another, who came from the coast of Guinea, played Guiccioli's game and was not to be trusted. The East African carried Teresa's messages and Byron's replies and watched the stairs in a kind of operatic setting.

The Carnival having ended, Byron settled into the routine he liked best, late rising, rides in the forest, the evening with Teresa at the theater or at home, the early morning hours devoted to the exhilarating release of writing. On February 19 he sent off the third and fourth cantos of *Don Juan.* Meanwhile reverberations from the first two cantos were still being heard. Harriette Wilson, the famous courtesan of the Regency, who had seen Byron at a ball in 1814 and had never forgotten him, saw a copy of the poem and sat down to reprimand the author: "Dear *Adorable* Lord Byron, *don't* make a mere *coarse* old libertine of yourself. . . . When you don't feel quite up to the spirit of benevolence . . . throw away your pen, my love, and take a little *calomel.*" [n]

There was keen interest in *Don Juan* in other quarters too. In Florence, Claire Clairmont conceived the idea of writing a satire on it to expose Byron's character, and she continued to write hints for it in her diary. Byron's poem appeared to her "a soliloquy upon his own ill-luck—ungraceful & selfish—like a beggar hawking his own sores about and which create disgust instead of pity." [n] In London, Caroline Lamb went to a masquerade at Almack's dressed as Don Juan, and the *Morning Chronicle* gave a paragraph to her performance the next day.

Byron had little taste for returning to England, what with Hobhouse in jail for writing a pamphlet voted a breach of privilege by the House of Commons, and the Reform movement, which he once had dreams of leading, dragged in the mud of an unwashed *canaille* whose heroes were the demagogues "Orator" Hunt and Cobbett. The arrest of Hobhouse had somehow brought to a focus the strange contradictions of Byron's sympathies balanced against his aristocratic pride. He had early assimilated the eighteenth-century conception of liberalism as a revolt against tyranny which might go even so far as republicanism, but which envisioned an aristocratic or gentlemanly leadership. This concept involved distrust of the mob and lack of sympathy for democratic or proletarian, or even middle-class, control or participation in government. But beyond any philosophical considerations was his pride of birth, heightened by the social insecurity that often troubled him, and even more by the prejudices of his public-school and college training which stressed the importance of breeding and class and which had been stamped upon his subconscious mind too indelibly ever to be erased, even by the detached view of the English character he had acquired abroad.

Byron found an additional reason for not returning to England in the news Hobhouse had sent him of the final debacle of their friend Scrope Davies, who had escaped to Bruges, as Brummell before him had gone to Calais, hopelessly in debt. Byron wrote: "So Scrope is gone—down-*diddled*. . . . Gone to Bruges where he will get tipsy with Dutch beer and shoot himself the first foggy morning. Brummell at Calais; Scrope at Bruges, Buonaparte at St. Helena, you in your new apartments, and I at Ravenna, only think! so many great men! There has been nothing like it since Themistocles at Magnesia, and Marius at Carthage."

He ended his letter to Hobhouse on March 3 with a slightly sheepish boasting: "I have settled into regular *serventismo*, and find it the happiest state of all. . . ."[n] To Teresa Byron was faithful and devoted. He found her quite as delightful a creature as ever, but, disillusioned by certain aspects of her character, he had lost the hope that had filled his imagination during the first months of their liaison of finding in her the perfect companion of mind and spirit. Although from habit he used the language of his earlier passion, his letters and notes suggest that he now accepted her as a fascinating but sometimes wayward and fickle child.

Byron continued to take pride in his daughter, who was thriving and being spoiled by Teresa and the servants. But to Hoppner he wrote: "Allegra is prettier I think, but obstinate as a Mule, and as ravenous as a Vulture. Health good to judge by the complexion, temper tolerable, but for vanity and pertinacity. She thinks herself handsome, and will do as she pleases. . . ."[n]

In spite of moving and quarrels, he had managed to continue his literary labors. Besides two new cantos of *Don Juan*, he had sent Murray his translations of the first canto of Pulci's *Morgante Maggiore* and *Francesca da Rimini* from the *Inferno*, as well as his poem *The Prophecy of Dante*, and a long reply to a criticism of his work in *Blackwood's Magazine,* in which he took occasion to ridicule the Lake Poets and show the superiority of Pope and Dryden to all the lesser poets of his day. He apologized for his own failure to follow Pope on the ground that his literary efforts were not serious attempts in poetry. " . . . almost all I have written has been mere passion . . . my *indifference* was a kind of passion, the result of experience, and not the philosophy of nature. Writing grows a habit, like a woman's gallantry. . . ."[n] And he aimed a parting shot at John Keats, "a tadpole of the Lakes," who in a poem "entitled *Sleep and Poetry* (an ominous title)" had dared to say it was easy to imitate Pope by following "wretched rule and compass vile."[n]

He took time out to compose a ballad accusing Hobhouse of deserting the Whigs and consorting with the mob. Hobhouse was hurt most by Byron's perverse determination to ignore the real issues involved in his arrest and the sacrifices he had made for the principles of liberty and constitutional government. But the ballad was written with a gusto which Hobhouse in another situation might have enjoyed:

> *How came you in Hob's pound to cool,*
> *My boy Hobbie* O?
> *Because I bade the people pull*
> *The House into the Lobby* O . . .

Before Hobhouse received the ballad, he had been released from prison and elected to a seat in Parliament, but it struck him very hard, especially as Murray had circulated it freely and a mutilated copy had already been published in the Tory *Morning Chronicle.* He wrote sadly in his diary: " . . . for a man to give way to such a mere pruriency & itch of writing against one who has stood by him in all his battles & never refused a single friendly office—is a melancholy proof of want of feeling & I fear of principle."[n] But Byron's bantering yet kindly letter of March 29 arrived a few days later, and Hobhouse's resolution to cut his friendship melted.

As the spring wore on, Byron became increasingly absorbed in Italian affairs, even while he viewed them with detachment. He enclosed for Murray's amusement the circular for the Cardinal Legate's *conversazione* of April 9: "The Cardinal himself is a very good-natured little fellow, Bishop of Imola and Legate here, —a devout believer in all the doctrines of the Church. He has kept his housekeeper these forty years, for his carnal recreation; but is reckoned a pious man, and a moral liver." [n]

Byron had told Moore in 1817 that he did not consider literature his vocation. "But you will see that I shall do something or other—the times and fortune permitting. . . ." [n] And now in Ravenna, by the middle of April, time and fortune were thrusting that something in his way, and he was beginning to realize it. His conversations with Count Ruggero Gamba, Teresa's father, an ardent Italian patriot and liberal, had drawn his attention to the growing strength of organizations like the Carbonari. He wrote Murray on the 16th: "I shall think it by far the most interesting spectacle and moment in existence, to see the Italians send the Barbarians of all nations back to their own dens. I have lived long enough among them to feel more for them as a nation than for any other people in existence; but they want Union, and they want principle; and I doubt their success. However, they will try, probably; and if they do, it will be a good cause." [n]

This new feeling must have caused a gradual souring of Byron's relations with the Cardinal, that devout believer in the doctrines of the Church whose temporal power was fortified and supported by the Austrians. On the 23rd he informed Murray: "Last night they have overwritten all the city walls with 'Up with the Republic!' and 'death to the Pope!' etc., etc. This would be nothing in London, where the walls are privileged. . . . But here it is a different thing . . . the police is all on the alert, and the Cardinal glares pale through all his purple." [n]

Byron's political and literary interests were beginning to absorb him more than his lovemaking. He had begun a tragedy based on the career of the Doge Marino Faliero, a patrician who had sided with the people against the tyranny of the Forty, who ruled Venice. "I never wrote nor copied *an entire Scene of that play*," he wrote Murray later, "without being obliged to *break* off —to *break* a commandment, to obey a woman's, and to forget God's. . . . The Lady always apologized for the interruption; but you know the answer a man must make when and while he can. . . . Such are the defined duties of a *Cavalier Servente* or *Cavalier Schiavo*." [n]

In his uncertain situation, Byron was distracted also by consideration for the care and education of his daughter. She was past three years old, and he was aware that she had not had the proper attention and training. But he steeled himself against the importunities of Claire, who had bombarded him with requests to see her child again. She had asked to have her sent to the Shelleys at Pisa, and then had threatened to come to Ravenna. When the Hoppners forwarded him belatedly her first request, he replied with asperity: " . . . I so totally disapprove of the mode of Children's treatment in their family, that I should look upon the Child as going into a hospital. Is it not so? Have they *reared* one? Her health here has hitherto been *excellent,* and her temper not bad; she is sometimes vain and obstinate, but always clean and cheerful, and as, in a year or two, I shall either send her to England, or put her in a Convent for education, these defects will be remedied as far as they can in human nature. But the Child shall not quit me again to perish of Starvation, and green fruit, or be taught to believe that there is no Deity. Whenever there is convenience of vicinity and access, her Mother can always have her with her; otherwise no." [n]

By the middle of May, Byron's relations with Teresa and her husband had reached a crisis. Guiccioli no longer took pains to conceal his resentment. That he was searching for evidence against his wife became clear when Teresa wrote in agitation to say that the Count had broken open her writing desk and gone through it. She believed that Guiccioli was urged and perhaps taunted by some of his friends among the ecclesiastical party, who, suspicious of Byron's politics, wanted to get him out of Ravenna. The climax came when the Count returned one evening to find Byron with the Countess and in extreme irritation asked him to stop his visits. Teresa tried to gloss it over in her account by saying that they were "as usual chatting quietly," but Byron was more frank. He wrote Murray that the trouble arose "on account of our having been taken together *quasi* in the fact, and, what is worse, that she did not *deny* it." [n]

Byron's first impulse was to withdraw and "sacrifice" himself rather than compromise Teresa or embarrass her relations. She only wept and accused him of not loving her. But he could assure her honestly that she misinterpreted his willingness to depart. The underlying reason may have been, as the Marchesa

Origo suggests, his conventionality. He had played the rebel for many years. "But he never questioned—as Shelley did—the essential validity of the social laws." [n] He had referred to himself and Teresa with genuine candor as "those who are in the wrong." [n] He had a sharp and sensitive revulsion, peculiar to fastidious libertines, against the outward show of unconventionality in women.

Teresa was all for leaving the Count immediately and seeking a separation, but Byron counseled her to "Speak to Papa." And in the end it was her father who applied to the Pope for a separation for his daughter. Byron's resolve to stand by her then was no doubt fortified by the attitudes of Count Gamba and his Ravenna friends. On May 20 he wrote to Murray: " . . . the Italian public are on our side, particularly the women,—and the men also, because they say that *he* had no business to take the business up now after a year of toleration. The law is against him, because he slept with his wife after her admission. All her relations (who are numerous, high in rank, and powerful) are furious *against him* for his conduct, and his not wishing to be cuckolded at *three*score, when every one else is at *one*." [n]

Count Gamba was no less influenced in his actions by a genuine liking and respect for Byron, not altogether influenced by Teresa. It seems that he had already come under the spell of the young English lord and would have much preferred him as a son-in-law to the scheming old man who had been unkind to his daughter. Moreover, Byron had consulted him in everything and had offered to act as he thought best for Teresa's reputation, happiness, and station in life. His fondness for Byron was no doubt increased by their essential agreement in politics.

Byron had suspected from the beginning that the clerical party would like to seize the occasion to get him out of the Romagna, though they did not dare to attack an English lord directly. One way of annoying him was to pick quarrels with his Italian servants. Two of his most trusted ones were Lega Zambelli, once in the employ of Guiccioli, who had accompanied him from Venice as his secretary, and his fierce-looking but gentle gondolier, "Tita" Falcieri. In these squabbles Byron was fortunate in having a friend in the inner sanctum of the Cardinal Legate, the Secretary General Count Alborghetti, who—perhaps for pecuniary gain, for he already knew Byron's generosity, but also because of personal admiration and attachment—had become his informant and intermediary. That Alborghetti used what influence he had with the Cardinal in the separation business in behalf of Byron and Teresa seems evident.

Through May and June, Byron continued his daily round of activity on the second floor of the Palazzo Guiccioli, playing with his menagerie, seeing Teresa clandestinely while Morelli and the Negro boy watched the stairs, and writing late into the night. He was deeply disturbed from time to time by what he thought to be Teresa's weakness in acquiescing to the wishes of her husband, with whom her father had counseled her to stay until she had the legal right to leave. Was there something deeper than he could fathom in the Count's hold over her? But he resolved to stick loyally by her to the end. One of his statements impressed Teresa more than anything he had written before. It was the thing she had never been sure about. She later wrote on this letter, preserved among her Byron treasures: *"Promesse!!!! d'être mon Époux!!"* He had written: " . . . my love—my duty—my honour—all these and everything should make me forever what I am *now,* your lover friend and (when circumstances permit) your *husband.*" [n]

On July 6 the Pope wrote his decree granting Teresa her separation from Count Guiccioli because it was "no longer possible for her to live in peace and safety with her husband," [n] but the official news did not come until the 14th. Teresa was to have an allowance from the Count of 100 scudi a month, the equivalent in England, Byron told Kinnaird, of about £1,000 a year. The Cardinal had agreed not to apprise Guiccioli of the Pope's decision until after Teresa had departed, "to avoid violence or scandal." [n] On this last day in the Palazzo Guiccioli, she was "full of fears and anguish," and the Count was suspicious. One cause of her agitation was the thought that she must part from Byron, at least for some time. With the connivance of servants she escaped at four o'clock on the 15th and joined her father, who took her to his country house at Filetto, about fifteen miles southwest of Ravenna. For the lovers it was the end of a chapter. Byron had been transformed from a *cavalier servente,* not into the husband she had dreamed of, but into something much more anomalous: the lover of a "respectable and noble Lady separated from her husband." [n]

CHAPTER XXII

1820

Preparing for Revolution

COUNT GUICCIOLI IN his apartments on the ground floor of the palace was as enigmatic as ever, and common report hinted at the possibility of some sly violence on his part toward either Byron or Teresa. After his evening ride on the day of her departure (July 15), Byron sent his cook Valeriano to act as her bodyguard along with Luigi Morelli, who had accompanied her. He also sent a fond note: "Of my love you cannot doubt—let yours continue.—Remember me to Count G. your father. . . . P.S. It is said that A [Alessandro Guiccioli] cuts a poor figure. Write to me in the finest style of Santa Chiara. Very naughty O. +++++++Be very careful!!" [n]

This tone of affectionate solicitude mingled with teasing, and sometimes scolding, which henceforth characterized his letters, reveals how much Byron had come to consider his relationship with Teresa a calm domestic one. There is no longer any of the emotional anguish of the days when they were living under the same roof in the Palazzo Guiccioli, and when he had felt that she catered too much to her husband's wishes. In all but a few respects he considered himself and wrote as if he were in fact, if not in name, a fond husband. Passion had not died, for she always attracted him strongly as a woman, but his indulgent tenderness did not stand in the way of an open-eyed appraisal of her faults and affectations. Very soon after she left, he began searching for a summer house near Filetto where he could place

Allegra and her nurse, and from which he could make an unobtrusive journey to the Casa Gamba.

In the meantime he returned with some relief to his literary work and his correspondence. He had completed his poetic drama *Marino Faliero*. The theme was one in which he could embody an imaginative concept of the historic past of the decaying city. "Every thing about Venice is," he wrote in the preface, "or was, extraordinary—her aspect is like a dream, and her history is like a romance."

A matter that had begun to absorb his interest more and more was the trial of Queen Caroline, instigated by George IV and his Tory ministers to deprive her of her rights and privileges as Queen and secure a divorce on the grounds of her misconduct with her courier Bergami while she was in Italy. Liberal sentiment had rallied to her and made her trial a popular cause against the King and his ministers. Partly because he remembered with gratitude the kindnesses she had shown him when he had visited her with Lady Oxford in 1813, Byron too took up her cause, though he did not wholly believe in her innocence. He tried through Hoppner and others to find witnesses for her and to discredit those who had been brought from Italy to testify against her.

Byron was feeling the deprivation of lovemaking as keenly as did Teresa. And he took a kind of roguish pleasure in hinting at the physical aspects of their love which she camouflaged in sentiment. He wrote: "This separation from you inconveniences me greatly—you understand," underscoring the words.[n] Count Gamba had brought his son Pietro, just returned from his studies in Rome, to see Byron. "I like your little brother very much—he shows character and talent—Big eyebrows! and a stature which he has enriched, I think, at your expense—at least in those. . . . do you understand me? His head is a little too hot for revolutions—he must not be too rash."[n]

Pietro's naïveté, his sincerity and loyalty, his idealism, and even his impracticality, at which Byron laughed though it sometimes exasperated him, combined with a sense of humor more lively than his sister's, struck a responsive chord in Byron, and they were soon fast friends. Pietro had brought fresh news of the abortive and somewhat ridiculous revolution against the Bourbon tyranny in Naples. Byron wrote to Murray: "The Neapolitans are not worth a curse, and will be beaten if it comes to fighting: the rest of Italy, I think, might stand. The Cardinal is at his wit's end; it is true that he had not far to go." [n]

Through the Gambas, father and son, Byron was during the summer and autumn initiated into the inner meetings of some of the secret societies in the Romagna. Their romantic names, their night meetings in a guarded room or in the forest, their passwords and cabalistic rituals half attracted Byron and half aroused his contempt for their impracticality. But his sympathy for the cause made him bear with the melodrama. He actually allied himself with the "*Turba*" (Mob), composed mostly of workmen, because it seemed most prepared for action. In it he became an honorary "*Capo*" or chief. It also went under the name of "*Cacciatore Americani*" (American Hunters). It seems strange that he, who had so recently ridiculed Hobhouse for allying himself with the mob among the English reformers, should have joined this particular group and been proud of it. But the mob seemed more picturesque in a foreign land, and the Continental deference paid to him as a leader (and later as a provider of arms) made him feel that even revolutionaries here recognized the leadership of gentlemen. But what drew him most confidently into the movement was the fact that all his best friends, the enlightened aristocracy of Ravenna, were moving spirits in the Carboneria.

Byron had finally found a villa for Allegra about six miles from Ravenna. With the pretext of visiting his daughter, he could now make occasional trips to Filetto. His first visit there on August 16 was closely observed by Guiccioli's spies. The Villa Gamba was a spacious family mansion dating from the late seventeenth century. It lay in a flat fertile plain drained by canals on the opposite side of Ravenna from the Pineta and the Adriatic. His pleasant visits to Filetto during the summer and autumn gave Byron the feeling that he had truly found a family life such as he had never known before. He came increasingly to like the whole Gamba clan, their well-bred manners, their warm-hearted affection toward one another, which was easily extended to him. Teresa says that he formed a great fondness for her little sisters. He "caressed them affectionately, and said that he liked *le beau sang* of the family; he felt as if he had become part of it."[n] But he liked the men of the family as much, if not more.

Writing to Moore at the end of August, he said: "What should I have known or written, had I been a quiet, mercantile politician, or a lord in waiting? A man must travel, and turmoil, or there is no existence. Besides, I only meant to be a Cavalier Servente, and had no idea it would turn out a romance, in the Anglo fashion. . . . Now, I have lived in the heart of their houses, in parts of Italy freshest and least influenced by strangers,—have seen and become . . . a portion of their hopes, and fears, and passions, and am almost inoculated into a family. This is to see men and things as they are."[n]

To amuse Teresa in the country when they could not be together, Byron sent her a number of books, mostly in French. One of these touched her to the quick, for it came too close to describing her own situation for comfort. It was Benjamin Constant's novel *Adolphe,* which pictured the tortures of the unequal love affair of Constant and Mme de Staël. Byron later told Lady Blessington that it was "the truest picture of the misery unhallowed *liaisons* produce."[n] Teresa was distressed. "Byron—why did you send me this book? . . . To be able to endure and enjoy that story one must be more remote from the condition of Eleonore *than I am*—and to give it to one's mistress to read, one must be *either very near to* the state of Adolphe, or very far away from it!"[n] Byron refused to take her concern seriously. Discovering her sensitivity, he thought it best to pretend to ignorance of any close parallel with her situation. And another visit to Filetto quieted her anxiety.

Byron himself had his moments of agitation when news arrived that he had appeared in London on the Queen's business, driving a curricle into Palace Yard. " . . . do you think me a coxcomb or a madman," he wrote Murray, "to be capable of such an exhibition? . . . you might as well have thought me entering on 'a pale horse,' like Death in the Revelations."[n]

Isolated in the Palazzo Guiccioli, he eagerly awaited the English post. His opinion of contemporary poetry in England had not been enhanced by the perusal of Wordworth's *Peter Bell.* On the margin of the first page he wrote a burlesquing parody of it. And after reprimanding Murray for not sending Scott's *Mon-*

astery in a packet of books, he wrote: "Instead of this, here are Johnny Keats's *p-ss a bed* poetry, and three novels by God knows whom. . . ."[n] His prejudice against Keats was not lessened by the new volume (*Lamia, Isabella, The Eve of St. Agnes, and other Poems*); indeed, it seems that he cast it aside without reading it.

In his renewed disgust with English literary productions, Byron thought of reviving and publishing his *Hints from Horace,* a sequel to *English Bards* which he had written in Athens in 1811. He considered it his *Dunciad,* exposing the little wits of his time. "I wrote better then than now," he told Murray; "but that comes from my having fallen into the atrocious bad state of the times—partly. It has been kept too, *nine years;* nobody keeps their piece nine years now-a-days, except Douglas K.; he kept his nine years and then restored her to the public."[n]

Through the summer Byron had been annoyed by cajoling and threatening letters from Claire concerning Allegra. Finally he appealed to Shelley: "I should prefer hearing from you—as I must decline all correspondence with Claire who merely tries to be as irrational and provoking as she can be. . . ."[n] Shelley replied that she was unhappy and in bad health and should be treated with as much indulgence as possible. "The weak and the foolish are in this respect like kings; they can do no wrong."[n]

Hoppner, who like his wife had a penchant for gossip, had hinted at some unspeakable misdeeds of Shelley, but Byron came to his defense: "I regret that you have such a bad opinion of Shiloh [a nickname they had adopted for Shelley]; you used to have a good one. Surely he has talent and honour, but is crazy against religion and morality. . . . If Clare thinks that she shall ever interfere with the child's morals or education, she mistakes; she never shall. The girl shall be a Christian and a married woman, if possible. . . . To express it delicately, I think Madame Clare is a damned bitch. What think you?"[n]

Hoppner immediately seized the opportunity offered by Byron's disgust with Claire to relay to him some gossip he had obtained from Elise, Allegra's former Swiss maid, who had married a servant whom the Shelleys had dismissed for misconduct. The story was that Claire was with child by Shelley, that they proceeded to Naples and when the child was born put it in a foundling home. From his general cynical view of human nature and his knowledge of the defiance of conventions in that family, Byron was willing to believe the tale at least tentatively, though he was aware of the questionable character of the evidence. "The Shiloh story is true no doubt," he wrote, "though Elise is but a sort of *Queen's evidence.* You remember how eager she was to return to them, and then she goes away and abuses them. Of the facts, however, there can be little doubt; it is just like them." [n]

The secret societies of the Romagna had been in a ferment, expecting great things since the uprising at Naples in the summer. On August 31 Byron had written to Murray: "We are here going to fight a little, next month, if the Huns don't cross the Po, and probably if they do: I can't say more now. . . . Depend upon it, there will be savage work, if once they begin here. The French courage proceeds from vanity, the German from phlegm, the Turkish from fanaticism and opium, the Spanish from pride, the English from coolness, the Dutch from obstinacy, the Russians from insensibility, but the *Italian* from *anger;* so you'll see that they will spare nothing." [n]

Byron was suspected of furnishing supplies and money to the insurgents. Cardinal Rusconi, who had replaced the easygoing Malvasia, had ample information from his spies to justify the arrest of dozens of the conspirators, but he feared that in the present state of unrest he could not assemble the witnesses to convict them. Rusconi wrote to Cardinal Spina at Bologna: "And also suspected of complicity in this bold plot is the well known Lord Byron . . . on this subject I have given information to his Eminence the Cardinal Secretary of State [Consalvi], but up to now the superior government has taken no measure against him." [n]

Many of the young aristocrats in the Carboneria, like Pietro Gamba, were "hot for revolution," but though Byron spoke with vigor and violence in his letters to England, he generally sided with the elder Gamba and counseled prudence. The news that was seeping through from Naples was not reassuring. The Congress at Troppau, composed of the great European powers, had agreed on a secret protocol affirming the right of collective "Europe" to suppress dangerous internal revolutions. England and France did not go along with the general principle, but remained neutral and acquiesced in the special right of Austria to protect her interest in Italy by crushing the Neapolitan revolution. In consequence, King Ferdinand was invited to attend the adjourned meeting of the Congress at Laibach the following spring. In ignorance of these happenings behind the scenes, however, the Romagnola patriots continued to hope much from the revolution in Naples.

Not being able to read English, Teresa had seen little of Byron's poetry until he sent her a French translation of *Don Juan*. She was rather shocked by it. He wrote Murray: "What do you think a very pretty Italian lady said to me the other day? . . . 'I would rather have the fame of Childe Harold for THREE YEARS than an IMMORTALITY of Don Juan!' The truth is that it is TOO TRUE, and the women hate every thing which strips off the tinsel of Sentiment; and they are right, as it would rob them of their weapons."[n]

Nevertheless he felt that this poem was the medium for his most sincere expression, and that in the end it would find its readers. Writing for his own pleasure and with enormous gusto, he had completed 149 stanzas of a fifth canto and was copying them out by December 9. As usual, he lavished his best efforts and his most lively wit on the digressions which reflected the mood of the moment. In defiance of the moral critics of his earlier cantos, and of Teresa's strictures on the poem for its ridicule of sentiment, he began:

When amatory poets sing their loves
In liquid lines mellifluously bland,
And pair their rhymes as Venus yokes her doves,
They little think what mischief is in hand; . . .
Even Petrarch's self, if judged with due severity,
Is the Platonic pimp of all posterity.

I therefore do denounce all amorous writing,
Except in such as way as not to attract . . .[n]

And to bait his moral readers further, and make his English friends wince, he inserted a stanza which was a pointed reference to the Queen and her courier Bergami. Referring to "the calumniated queen Semiramis," he wrote that she had been accused of "an improper friendship for her horse," but that the tale probably had its source "In writing 'Courser' by mistake for

'Courier.' "[n] He suppressed this stanza at Hobhouse's request, but he was furious when Murray omitted in the first edition another "wicked" stanza:

> *Thus in the East they are extremely strict,*
> *And wedlock and a padlock mean the same . . .*
> *Why don't they knead two virtuous souls for life*
> *Into that moral centaur, man and wife?* [n]

And thrown back among his memories in the loneliness of Ravenna, he began a continuation of his prose recollections. In December he sent off eighteen more sheets to Moore, who was then in Paris, suggesting that he sell the Memoirs for publication after his (Byron's) death. Moore, living abroad to keep out of the way of his creditors, was much pleased with this gift. He subsequently sold them to Murray for two thousand guineas, and in the meantime he apparently showed them to almost everyone he met in Paris.*

Murray had sent Byron the *Quarterly Review* and the *Edinburgh Review* which contained articles that aroused the poet's ire. An article in the *Quarterly* referred to the attack of Bowles on Pope. "Mr. Bowles shall be answered," Byron wrote Murray. "Those miserable mountebanks of the day, the poets, disgrace themselves and deny God, in running down Pope, the most *faultless* of Poets, and almost of men." [n] An article in the *Edinburgh* incensed him even more. That it should praise the milk-and-water poetry of Keats, who had the insolence to attack Pope, was too much for him. He wrote: "The *Edinburgh* praises Jack Keats or Ketch, or whatever his names are: why his is the Onanism of Poetry. . . ." [n] And he recurred to the subject in his next letter: "such writing is a sort of mental masturbation—he is always f--gg--g his *Imagination*. I don't mean he is *indecent*, but viciously soliciting his own ideas into a state, which is nei-

---

* It cannot be said with certainty how many people read the Memoirs. Doris Langley Moore, who has made the closest study of their nature and the circumstances of their burning, lists twenty-two known or probable readers, including Moore himself. (*The Late Lord Byron*, p. 46.) Moore employed two men, and possibly a third, to make copies while he was in Paris. It is known that one copy was burned with the original in 1824. Whether the other copies were completed and what became of them no one knows.

ther poetry nor any thing else but a Bedlam vision produced by raw pork and opium." [n]

Murray had suggested that Byron might want to make some revisions in the new cantos of *Don Juan*. But the poet never had any relish for cold-blooded revisions. Strangely enough for one who so admired the polish of Pope, he made a virtue of the romantic dogma that literary work was best when it came hot from the creative fire. He replied: "I am like the tyger (in poesy), if I miss my first Spring, I go growling back to my Jungle. There is no second. I can't correct; I can't, and I won't." [n]

Because Byron constantly postponed his visits to Filetto, Teresa grew restive in the country, and by the middle of November had persuaded her father to take her back to his town house in Ravenna. Byron was well aware of the dangers to Teresa in the situation, for one of the stipulations of the separation decree was that she should live respectably under her father's roof. He knew that his visits must be cautious and circumscribed. And he knew what was on the government's mind, for he had secret information from Count Alborghetti, who was—for money, favors, or friendship (perhaps a combination of all three)—running close to treason in furnishing Byron with information from the Cardinal's mail, not only on the movement of the Austrians, but also on what concerned more closely himself and his *amica*. "They try to fix squabbles upon my servants," he wrote Kinnaird, "to involve me in scrapes (no difficult matter), and lastly they (the governing party) menace to shut Madame Guiccioli up in a *Convent*." At this threat his indignation rose to the fever pitch: "If they should succeed in putting this poor girl into a convent for doing that with me which all the other countesses of Italy have done with everybody for these thousand years, of course I would accede to a retreat on my part, rather than a prison on hers, for the former only is what they *really* want." [n]

As the menace was abandoned for the time being, it may be assumed that Alborghetti was this time successful in some rather delicate diplomatic maneuvers with the Cardinal. The tension in the town was dramatized on the evening of December 9. Byron was preparing to leave on his nightly visit to Teresa when he heard shots outside his window. Running down with Tita, he found the commandant of the troops, Luigi Dal Pinto, expiring on the ground with five wounds. Byron opened his letter to Moore that night to give an account of the affair:

"As nobody could, or would, do any thing but howl and pray, and as no one would stir a finger to move him, for fear of consequences, I lost my patience—made my servant and a couple of the mob take up the body—sent off two soldiers to the guard—despatched Diego to the Cardinal with the news, and had the commandant carried upstairs into my own quarter. But it was too late, he was gone. . . . Poor fellow! he was a brave officer, but had made himself much disliked by the people. I knew him personally, and had met him often at conversazioni and elsewhere."[n]

Byron was a strange revolutionary. Individual humanity was always stepping in to blur the vision which partisan zealots must see before them. If he could use his influence with both sides to avoid unnecessary violence and savagery, he would do so. In fact, his humanity to the commandant almost jeopardized his standing with the leaders of the Carbonari, and might indeed have done so had it not been for the equal humanity and understanding of the Gambas. Byron might also have been suspected of consorting with the enemy in his odd friendship with Count Alborghetti, who, as Secretary General of the Lower Romagna, must have been allied in the popular mind with the oppressive government, whatever his liberal professions. But in his correspondence with Alborghetti Byron was careful never to compromise his friends of the Carbonari.

As the year ended Byron had settled down to his nightly visits to Teresa, but he seems to have spent as much time in conversation with Pietro and her father as with her, and to have enjoyed it as much. From time to time he dreamed of escape: of returning to England or of engaging in some heroic action. But he knew he could not go back; he himself had changed too much. On December 28, he finally sent Kinnaird the fifth canto of *Don Juan*. It was after all, as his best critical sense told him, the one thing that he could most effectively "put out his powers upon."

CHAPTER XXIII

1821

The Poetry of Politics

THE NEW YEAR BEGAN WITH bad weather, and revolutionary excitement had risen to the fever pitch once more with the Austrians poised for the invasion of Naples. In the midst of alarms and rumors, which served to drive away boredom and stimulate his imaginative faculties, Byron found the usual outlet in writing. But he confessed to Moore that though he was driven to it by his demon, the actual composition was always painful. "I feel exactly as you do about our 'art,' * but it comes over me in a kind of rage every now and then, like ****, and then, if I don't write to empty my mind, I go mad. As to that regular, uninterrupted love of writing, which you describe in your friend, I do not understand it. I feel it as a torture, which I must get rid of, but never as a pleasure." [n]

Practically the only social life Byron indulged in now was his evening visit to Teresa and her family. Because of her precarious position, they did not venture to the theater or to the balls or the Carnival festivities as they had the previous winter when he was her accepted *cavalier servente*. When the weather permitted, Byron took his daily ride about four o'clock, sometimes alone, but often with Pietro Gamba.

His urge to write found outlet for the moment in a journal, which he started on January 4. It was the first he had kept since his tour of the Bernese Alps in 1816 and, like it, was a kaleido-

* Moore had said that he felt about writing "as the French husband did when he found a man making love to his (the Frenchman's) wife: 'Comment, Monsieur,—sans y être *obligé!*'" (*LJ*, V, 215 n.)

scopic chronicle of thoughts and events set down in a prose that was sometimes staccato and sometimes consciously dramatic. On January 6 he wrote:

"What is the reason that I have been, all my lifetime, more or less *ennuyé*? and that, if any thing, I am rather less so now than I was at twenty, as far as my recollection serves? I . . . presume that it is constitutional, as well as the waking in low spirits, which I have invariably done for many years. Temperance and exercise, which I have practiced at times, and for a long time together vigorously and violently, made little or no difference. Violent passions did;—when under their immediate influence—it is odd, but—I was in agitated, but *not* in depressed, spirits. A dose of salts has the effect of a temporary inebriation, like light champagne, upon me. But wine and spirits make me sullen and savage to ferocity—silent, however, and retiring, and not quarrelsome, if not spoken to. Swimming also raises my spirits,—but in general they are low, and get daily lower."

The next day some excitement temporarily dispelled his ennui. Word came that the government was about to strike and that Cardinal Rusconi had ordered a number of arrests. Byron's advice was "Fight for it, rather than be taken in detail," and he offered his house as a refuge for the Liberals in case of need. Exhilarated, he wrote in his journal: "It wants half an hour of midnight, and rains. . . . If the row don't happen *now*, it must soon. . . . Expect to hear the drum and the musketry momently (for they swear to resist, and are right,)—but I hear nothing, as yet, save the plash of the rain and the gusts of the wind at intervals."

The humid weather continued and the roads were impassable, and Byron was thrown back again on reading and his literary pursuits. He sketched the outline for a tragedy on the career of Sardanapalus, an Assyrian king, effeminate, slothful, immersed in luxury and debauchery, but spurred to action by a plot to overthrow him. When he discussed the drama with Teresa, he maintained that love should not be the central theme of tragedy. She pleaded for "a noble passion," which he took lightly. But he wrote in his diary on returning home: "I must put more love into *Sardanapalus* than I intended." Teresa recalled with pride: "The sublime love of Myrrha was conceived that evening."

He was not encouraged to go on with his poetic drama by the reports that, despite his protests, *Marino Faliero,* which he had never intended for the stage, was being put on the boards in London. Much as he had once longed for fame in the theater, he had seen too much of the "insolence" of audiences at Drury Lane to trust his self-esteem to their mercies. At this distance he felt helpless and feared that his friends were not doing enough to stop the production.

He was disappointed too in the hope for some revolutionary action, which seemed now likely to have as its result only defeat or banishment for the rebels. Returning from the Gambas on the 23rd, he wrote in his journal: "The Carbonari seem to have no plan—nothing fixed among themselves, how, when, or what to do."[n] In the meantime the Carnival was in full swing. " . . . the Germans are on the Po," Byron wrote, "the Barbarians at the gate . . . and lo! they dance and sing and make merry. . . ."[n] And Pietro and his father and other Carbonari leaders had gone on a hunting expedition.

He began to think of escape again, to the Ionian Islands (Lord Sidney Osborne, stepson of Augusta's mother, had invited him to Corfu), or to a rendezvous with Hoppner somewhere in the spring. But he knew that if Teresa wished him to stay he could not leave. Queer speculations ran through his mind and were confided to his diary: ". . . 'which is best, life or death, the gods only know,' as Socrates said to his judges. . . . It has been said that the immortality of the soul is a *grand peut-être*—but still it is a *grand* one. Every body clings to it—the stupidest, and dullest, and wickedest of human bipeds is still persuaded that he is immortal."[n]

He could not get on with the drama he had started, but he was planning more ambitious literary projects: ". . . Cain, a metaphysical subject, something in the style of Manfred, but in five *acts*, perhaps, with the chorus; Francesca of Rimini, in five acts"; and a tragedy based on the life of Tiberius.[n] And he jotted down some random thoughts growing out of his current contemplations: "Why, at the very height of desire and human pleasure, —worldly, social, amorous, ambitious, or even avaricious,—does there mingle a certain sense of doubt and sorrow . . . ? I allow sixteen minutes, though I never counted them, to any given or supposed possession."[n]

Despite his feeling that he could make a solid reputation in literature only in dramas following pure classical models, and despite the recent interest in Pope that had caused him to exhume and polish his *Hints from Horace* and write a reply to Bowles's strictures on Pope, Byron was still drawn by a sure instinct back to *Don Juan*. He wrote Murray:

"The 5th is so far from being the last of *D.J.*, that it is hardly the beginning. I meant to take him the tour of Europe, with a proper mixture of siege, battle, and adventure, and to make him finish as *Anacharsis Cloots* * in the French revolution. To how many cantos this may extend, I know not, nor whether (even if I live) I shall complete it; but this was my notion: I meant to have made him a *Cavalier Servente* in Italy, and a cause for a divorce in England, and a Sentimental 'Werther-faced man' in Germany, so as to show the different ridicules of the society in each of those countries, and to have displayed him gradually *gaté* and *blasé* as he grew older, as is natural. But I had not quite fixed whether to make him end in Hell, or in an unhappy marriage, not knowing which would be the severest. The Spanish tradition says Hell: but it is probably only an Allegory of the other state." [n]

Byron was still hopeful of some heroic action on the part of the Italians, and ready to participate in it. His ardor and his hope were not even dampened when his friends, the patriots, returned to his house suddenly and without warning the guns and ammunition he had furnished them, an order having gone out that the government would arrest anyone with concealed arms. On the 18th he wrote in his diary: "I suppose that they consider me as a depôt, to be sacrificed, in case of accidents. It is no great matter, supposing that Italy could be liberated, who or what is sacrificed. It is a grand object—the very *poetry* of politics. Only think—a free Italy!!! Why, there has been nothing like it since the days of Augustus." [n]

But his optimism faded when the Neapolitan revolution collapsed and the plan for the Romagna was bungled, the chiefs betrayed, and all efforts of the Carbonari made a fiasco. His sole comment was: "Thus the world goes; and thus the Italians are

---

* A Prussian Baron, who described himself as *l'orateur du genre humain*. He was active in the Revolution until he fell under the suspicion of Robespierre and was executed in the Terror.

always lost for lack of union among themselves."[n] In his disillusionment Byron did not blame his friends among the Carbonari. Part of his capacity for friendship rested on his wide tolerance of human frailties and his ability to look with a half-cynical, half-humorous eye upon the slightly less than noble characters of those to whom he was attached. He wrote later to Moore, "As a very pretty woman said to me a few nights ago, with the tears in her eyes, as she sat at the harpsichord, 'Alas! the Italians must now return to making operas.' I fear *that* and maccaroni are their forte, and 'motley their only wear.' However, there are some high spirits among them still."[n]

Uncertain about the future and anticipating political turbulence, on March 1 Byron put his daughter Allegra in the convent of San Giovanni Battista in Bagnacavallo, some dozen miles from Ravenna. The nuns had established a school for girls that was drawing children from the best families in the region. He allowed his banker, Pellegrino Ghigi, whose daughter was there, to take her to the convent, because he had found her a little hard to manage—"her disposition is perverse to a degree."[n] He told Hoppner that he did not intend "to give a *natural* child an *English* education, because with the disadvantages of her birth, her after settlement would be doubly difficult. Abroad, with a fair foreign education and a portion of five or six thousand pounds, she might and may marry very respectably. . . . It is, besides, my wish that she should be a Roman Catholic, which I look upon as the best religion, as it is assuredly the oldest of the various branches of Christianity."[n]

The likelihood of any military action having passed, Byron turned again to the drama that expressed most fully his dissatisfaction with the life of slothful self-indulgence. But as the play unfolded under his rapid hand, Sardanapalus became not an indolent wallower in voluptuousness, but a contemplative character whose inaction was owing partly to his humanitarian hatred of war and violence and partly to his contempt for the ends of worldly ambition and the lust for power. Byron's absorbing interest in this drama of the dead past, the thing that kept him at it for hours at a stretch, was generated by the fact that it was like almost everything he wrote *con amore*, an apologia for his own life, an escape from his own self-criticism.

Beneath the calm surface of life in Ravenna hatreds and

resentments were seething. Byron was fortunate that his charities and sympathies for the common people had made him popular in Ravenna, and he had at least the outward respect of the Cardinal and the devoted friendship of the Secretary General. In a few days Alborghetti had an opportunity to show proof of his gratitude for the favors he had received from the famous English poet. Byron's Italian servant Tita got into a heated argument with an officer named Pistocchi. Although they drew knives and pistols, they did not come to actual blows. The servant was arrested, and Byron took the matter to Alborghetti, who informed him that the Cardinal intended to have Tita banished. Byron was indignant: "If the man is to be conducted to the *frontier*—and *lose his bread also*, with a stain upon his character—I beg leave to submit respectfully to the *Cardinal* that I cannot dismiss him from my service. . . . If one is to be punished *both* should be punished."[n]

The matter dragged on, the Cardinal remaining adamant. Byron, who was always indulgent and loyal to his servants, wrote an appeal direct to the Cardinal in terms so forthright as to cause some uneasiness to the more timid Alborghetti. His patience was growing thin when he wrote to the Secretary: "It appears to me that there must be some *clerical* intrigue of the low priests about the Cardinal to render all this nonsense necessary about a squabble in the Street of *words only* between a Soldier and a Servant. . . . If they think to get *rid* of *me*—they shant—for as I am conscious of no fault—I will yield to no oppression; but will go at my own good time when it suits my inclination and affairs."[n]

The affair was pending for three weeks. In the meantime Byron was distracted by other matters. He was heartened by an anonymous pamphlet signed "John Bull" which Murray had sent him. The writer, now known to have been John Gibson Lockhart, later son-in-law of Sir Walter Scott and editor of the *Quarterly Review*, took the author of *Don Juan* to task for a passage in his letter to Bowles in which he belittled his own merit as a poet in comparison with that of Pope. But then he turned to advice that so closely matched Byron's own conception of his forte as to be eminently agreeable: "Stick to Don Juan: it is the only sincere thing you have ever written. . . . it is by far the most spirited, the most straight-forward, the most interesting, and the most poetical; and every body thinks as I do of it, although they have not the heart to say so. . . . I think the great charm of its style is, that it is not much like the style of any other poem in the world. . . . Your Don Juan again, is written strongly, lasciviously, fiercely, laughingly— . . . nobody could have written it but a man of the first order both in genius and in dissipation;—a real master of all his tools—a profligate, pernicious, irresistible, charming Devil. . . ." [n]

Byron had indeed extensive plans for the continuation of the poem, but at the very moment when the encouraging words of "John Bull" might have spurred him to resume writing, he bowed to Teresa's earnest desire that he should give it up. She had seen some quotations in the Milan *Gazzetta* of attacks on Byron's morals in certain English papers and reviews, and she had read the first two cantos in the French translation. He succumbed and promised not to write any more until she authorized it. In telling Murray of the promise wrested from him, he said: "The reason . . . arises from the wish of all women to exalt the *sentiment* of the passions, and to keep up the illusion which is their empire. Now *Don Juan* strips off this illusion, and laughs at that and most other things." [n]

Byron's self-esteem was given a considerable lift in July by the visit of a young American, a friend of Washington Irving, who gave him a notion of the admiration for his poetry across the Atlantic. The young man, he told Moore, was "a very pretty lad—a Mr. Coolidge, of Boston—only somewhat too full of poesy and 'entusymusy.' I was very civil to him . . . and talked with him much of Irving, whose writings are my delight. But I suspect that he did not take quite so much to me, from his having expected to meet a misanthropical gentleman, in wolf-skin breeches, and answering in fierce monosyllables, instead of a man of this world. I can never get people to understand that poetry is the expression of *excited passion,* and that there is no such thing as a life of passion any more than a continuous earthquake, or an eternal fever. Besides, who would ever *shave* themselves in such a state?" [n]

On July 10 a crisis arose in the fortunes of the Gambas. As Pietro was returning from the theater that night he was arrested and conducted to the frontier to be cast into perpetual exile. That he was not put into a dungeon, like so many others, may have been indirectly owing to the influence of Byron and Count Alborghetti. But Byron gradually came to realize that Pietro's banishment, and that of his father shortly after, were part of a deeper design to get rid of himself. The authorities felt certain that Teresa would accompany or follow her father, and that then Byron would also leave the Romagna.

But Teresa was so upset at the thought of leaving Byron in Ravenna, where she imagined that his life was in danger, that she flatly refused to go. It was only with the greatest difficulty that Byron persuaded her to follow her father and brother, who were given asylum in Florence. He succeeded only when he convinced her (Alborghetti had warned him) that she would be shut up in a convent if she stayed. Byron himself was reluctant to leave Ravenna, where hc had put down roots, and at the urging of Teresa he made every effort (though he must have known it was useless) to have the exiles recalled. In the midst of this crisis, Alborghetti announced that he had succeeded in getting the release of Byron's servant. Perhaps the Cardinal felt that, having accomplished his main purpose, he could afford to be generous in a small matter. For he was certain that Byron would eventually follow his *amica.*

After these stormy scenes, Byron settled down with a feeling of relief to think of other matters and to enjoy the brief respite from the strains of an emotional relationship which had governed his life for more than two years, and which, despite the conjugal aspects it had assumed since the Guiccioli separation, had never quite contributed to his peace of mind. The summer wore on and he remained in Ravenna, partly in the forlorn hope of getting the exiles pardoned and recalled, but more because it took a major effort for him to break an established routine. He thought again of returning to England. But he had promises to keep, and, though he might guard in the inner recesses of his mind certain weary longings for freedom from that harrowing "earliest Passion" which he could never take as lightly as his own words sometimes seemed to indicate, he had a stronger impulse to please those who loved and trusted him. In spite of the "heart that pants to be unmoved," he would go to Teresa—but in his own good time.

In the quiet of the Palazzo Guiccioli he began another drama. He called it *Cain.* Although he borrowed from Biblical phraseology, his purpose was not to dramatize the Bible story but to indulge in the farthest realms of speculation on questions of predestination, fate, free will, and the problem of evil. He had first conceived of the drama as on "a metaphysical subject, something in the style of *Manfred.*" But the mood was different. *Manfred* was mainly inspired by remorse and dissatisfaction with events in his past which made him wretched. When, in the words of his hero, he complained that we are "half dust, half deity," he expressed the ultimate romantic revolt against the conditions of life itself. Nothing real in the human and tangible world could ever satisfy one who aspired to the freedom of spirit and the omniscience of deity. In *Cain* Byron went one step farther toward the bleakness of despair. For when Lucifer had taken Cain on a voyage through the spirit world and had shown him things

> *Beyond all power of my born faculties,*
> *Although inferior still to my desires*
> *And my conceptions,*"

he came to the bitter conclusion that even deities may not be happy. All knowledge does not bring all happiness. Nothing remained but a kind of desperate Stoicism—reliance on his own unconquerable will and fortitude born of recognition of the hopelessness of aspiration.

Despite his protestation in the preface that Lucifer's words were those of the character and not of the author, and that it was difficult "to make him talk like a clergyman upon the same subjects," Byron did make Lucifer voice his own speculations as an intellectual rebel of the Age of Reason. Through him he spoke his admiration of

> *Souls who dare look the Omnipotent tyrant in*
> *His everlasting face, and tell him that*
> *His evil is not good!* "

He knew he was inviting the wrath, if not of the Omnipotent, at least of the pious British public.

Murray's reluctance to publish *Don Juan* made it doubtful that he would welcome this new iconoclastic piece. Byron was out of humor with Murray for his delays and evasion of direct commitments. But when Douglas Kinnaird referred to him as a "Tradesman," Byron defended the publisher. "I believe M. to be a good man, with a personal regard for me. But a bargain is in its very essence a *hostile* transaction. . . . even between brethren, [it] is a declaration of war. . . . I have no doubt that he would lend or give—freely—what he would refuse for value received in M.S.S. So do not think [too] hardly of him." [n] And, though Byron continued to twit and to scold Murray, his letters to his publisher were in the main the frankest and friendliest as well as the most interesting of all his letters from Italy.

Shelley had sent a copy of *Adonaïs*, his elegy on the death of Keats, and Byron promptly requested Murray to "omit *all* that is said *about him* [Keats] in any *MSS*. of mine, or publication." [n] And he wrote a note next to the passage attacking the unfortunate poet in the manuscript of his reply to *Blackwood's Magazine:* "My indignation at Mr. Keats's depreciation of Pope has hardly permitted me to do justice to his own genius, which, malgré all the fantastic fopperies of his style, was undoubtedly of great promise. His fragment of *Hyperion* seems actually inspired by the Titans, and is as sublime as Æschylus." [n] But after Shelley's death Byron inserted in *Don Juan* a barbed reference to Keats, tempered, however, with good-humored praise and pity, which concluded with a reference to Shelley's notion that the *Quarterly* review of *Endymion* had killed Keats:

> *'Tis strange the mind, that very fiery particle,*
> *Should let itself be snuffed out by an article.* [n]

Knowing of Byron's imminent departure from Ravenna, Shelley, anxious about Allegra for Claire's sake, hastened to pay him a visit. He arrived at ten o'clock the night of the 6th of August, and he and Byron sat up until five in the morning talking. They had not seen each other since Shelley's visit to the Palazzo Mocenigo in 1818. Byron was doubly glad to see him, for he had been almost completely cut off from English acquaintances since leaving Venice. Shelley reported to Mary: "He has in fact completely recovered his health, & lives a life totally the reverse of that which he led at Venice." [n] He ended the letter with an agitated recital of the lurid gossip which the Hoppners had gleaned from Elise Foggi concerning Shelley and Claire. Why did Byron pass this scandalous tale on to Shelley on the first night of his arrival? Was it because he could not resist the temptation to see what Shelley would say to it? Or was it that, as always when he was with Shelley, he was compelled to respect his integrity, and thought he owed it to him to reveal the gossip that had been spread about him? Perhaps a little of both. Shelley asked Mary to write a refutation to the Hoppners and send it to him in Ravenna so that he could show it to Byron.

Pending a reply and an opportunity to visit Allegra in the convent, Shelley, with Tita as an escort, went to see some of the monuments and churches of Ravenna. He wrote Mary again on the 10th: "Our way of life is this. . . . L.B. gets up at two—breakfasts—we talk read &c. until six then we ride, & dine at eight, & after dinner sit talking until four or five in the morning." [n] Wandering about Byron's quarters in the Palazzo Guiccioli, Shelley encountered an astonishing menagerie. "Lord B.'s establishment consists," he wrote Peacock, "besides servants, of ten horses, eight enormous dogs, three monkeys, five cats, an eagle, a crow, and a falcon; and all these, except the horses, walk about the house, which every now and then resounds with their unarbitrated quarrels, as if they were the masters of it." And later in Byron's "Circean Palace," he reported, "I have just met on the grand staircase five peacocks, two guinea hens, and an Egyptian crane." [n]

Shelley was awed by Byron's power in the new cantos of *Don Juan*. He told his friend Peacock, to whom in 1818 he had written his disapproval of *Childe Harold* and his horror at the dissipations of Byron in Venice: "He lives with one woman . . . and is in every respect an altered man. He has written three more cantos of 'Don Juan.' . . . I think that every word of it is pregnant with immortality." [n]

Shelley during his visit persuaded Byron to give up his plan of taking the Gambas and Teresa to Switzerland and to come instead to Pisa, and he asked Mary to look out for a "large and magnificent" house for him. Shelley himself undertook to write Teresa, who was in Florence with her father and brother, to urge her to accept the Pisan scheme. Teresa was willing enough to accede if Byron would only come to her, and she begged Shelley not to leave Ravenna without him. But that was not an easy thing to accomplish, for Byron was slow in moving and dreaded the dislocation of his life and habits which any shifting of his bulky household entailed.

In the meantime Shelley paid a visit to Allegra at the convent on the 14th. Byron, who complained that her temper was violent, was glad to have the gentle Shelley visit her for him, and he did not go. Shelley spent three hours with her. He wrote Mary: " . . . she has a contemplative seriousness which mixed with her excessive vivacity which has not yet deserted her has a very peculiar effect in a child. She is under very strict discipline as may be observed from the immediate obedience she accords to the will of her attendants—this seems contrary to her nature; but I do not think it has been obtained at the expense of much severity. . . . Her predominant foible seems the love of distinction & vanity. . . ."[n] She was shy at first, but when Shelley gave her a gold chain, she grew more familiar. When he asked her what he should say to Papa, she replied: "Che venga farmi un visitino, e che porta seco la *mammina*."[n] ["That he come to pay me a little visit and that he bring Mama with him."] Shelley was too discreet to deliver that message, though she probably meant Teresa, as she had not seen her own mother since August 1818, when she was under two years old.

On the 16th Shelley received an agonized letter from Mary to Mrs. Hoppner showing how impossible the accusations of Elise were: "Shelley is as incapable of cruelty as the softest woman. To those who know him his humanity is almost as a proverb."[n] Shelley gave the letter to Byron to forward to Hoppner. This was an embarrassment to Byron, who apparently had promised not to reveal the accusations to Shelley. Whether he sent Mary's letter to Hoppner or simply explained to him why he did not believe the story is a question that cannot be answered. But he never again referred to the scandal against Shelley and Claire.[n]

When Shelley returned to Pisa, he found a house for the Gambas, and for Byron a commodious sixteenth-century palace on the Lungarno, the Casa Lanfranchi. Shelley was looking forward to Byron's arrival. He told Mary that he hoped "to form for ourselves a society of our own class, as much as possible, in intellect or in feelings: & to connect ourselves with the interests of that society. Our roots never struck so deeply as at Pisa, & the transplanted tree flourishes not." [n] He had long hoped to get Leigh Hunt to come to Italy and join that society. Byron had earlier mentioned the possibility of bringing Hunt from England to join them in the editorship of a periodical, and Shelley pressed the point now, hoping that Byron would be as generous with Hunt as he had been with Moore, to whom he had presented his Memoirs. But Shelley was reluctant to ask Byron directly for money for Hunt's voyage. Hunt had no such delicacy, for he was, as Shelley already knew, notoriously cavalier concerning the honor he conferred on his friends by accepting their money without expecting to be able to repay it.

Once the house was secured in Pisa, Byron found that a thousand things had to be done before he left Ravenna, and it was two months before he actually got under way. He left most of the burden of packing to Lega Zambelli, his steward, and when Teresa complained, he could blame the delays on him. But he wrote her: "I do not deny that I am leaving very unwillingly —foreseeing very serious evils for you all—and *especially for you*. I will not say more—you will see." [n]

In the meantime, he was not idle in Ravenna. He had finished "The Blues," a satire on the English "bluestockings," or pretentious literary ladies, and now he returned to *Cain* and finished it by September 9. In reading over the newly printed cantos of *Don Juan*, he felt that this was the best thing he had written, and he regretted having promised Teresa to abandon it. But he turned his hand to other matters. He wrote a second letter to Murray replying to Bowles's strictures on Pope, and he sent dedications for his dramas. He dedicated *Cain* to Scott and *Sardanapalus* to Goethe. Then he composed a heated and what he knew would be considered a seditious satire on George IV and on the servility of the oppressed Irish people, who had welcomed and entertained him before the Queen was cold in her grave. This *pièce d'occasion*, which he called "To the Irish Avatar," had been conceived when he read parallel accounts of the funeral of the Queen and the festive reception of the King in Dublin in the *Morning Chronicle*. He knew that it was not his best writing, and he wrote Murray to keep such irritants out of his way, asking him to send "*no periodical works* whatsoever. . . . to keep my mind *free and unbiassed* by all paltry and personal irritabilities of praise or censure. . . . When I was in Switzerland and

Greece, I was out of the way of hearing either, and *how I wrote there!*" [n]

Byron was upset again when the wagons arrived from Pisa for his household goods. He wrote Moore: "I am in all the sweat, dust, and blasphemy of an universal packing of all my things, furniture, etc., for Pisa, whither I go for the winter. . . . It is awful work, this love, and prevents all a man's projects of good or glory. I wanted to go to Greece lately (as every thing seems up here) with her brother, who is a very fine, brave fellow . . . and wild about liberty. But the tears of a woman who has left her husband for a man, and the weakness of one's own heart, are paramount to these projects, and I can hardly indulge them." [n]

The sweating and packing went on until he scarcely had a bed to sleep on, but still he lingered, having the excuse of a light fever to postpone his journey. And "under the crescent of a very young moon" he got off his horse during his ride to walk with a Signora. "But it was not in a romantic mood, as I should have been once; and yet it was a *new* woman . . . and, of course, expected to be made love to. But I merely made a few commonplace speeches." He felt, he told Moore, "a mountain of lead upon my heart." [n]

Yet in the midst of his depression he had been at work upon one of the most high-spirited satires he had ever written—as a single sustained literary expression of irony and wit, the masterpiece of his whole writing career. Since he had seen in the spring Southey's laureate tribute to George III called *A Vision of Judgment,* he had been mulling over a mock-heroic reply. Byron's animosity toward Southey had been growing with the years. Following the suppression of his dedication to Southey in *Don Juan,* he returned to the attack in the third canto with some cutting gibes on the Laureate's turncoat propensities. But it was not yet published when Southey's *Vision* appeared with a preface which made pointed reference to Byron, without naming him, as the leader of the Satanic school of writers whose works "breathe the spirit of Belial in their lascivious parts" and a "Satanic spirit of pride and audacious impiety." [n]

Having purged his ire by means of a skillful counterattack in a long note added to his drama *The Two Foscari,* Byron now caught a brilliant glimpse of the whole episode in its ludicrous proportions and poured out the octaves with inspired zeal. He called the poem *The Vision of Judgment*. Southey's own solemn hexameters dealing serious rewards and punishments, and particularly heaping heaven's praises on the mad old King, furnished material for Byron's satiric hand. He had fun with the realistic picture of the arrival of George at the celestial gate and the hot debate for his soul between the Archangel Michael and Satan:

Yet still between his Darkness and his Brightness
There passed a mutual glance of great politeness.[n]

The comic situation reached its height when Southey was dragged in by the devil Asmodeus, who complained:

"Confound the renegado! I have sprained
My left wing, he's so heavy; one would think
Some of his works about his neck were chained." [n]

Southey loosed a spate of words that frightened angels and devils alike. He said:

He meant no harm in scribbling; 'twas his way
Upon all topics; 'twas, besides, his bread,
Of which he buttered both sides . . .
He had written praises of a Regicide . . .
Then grew a hearty anti-jacobin—
Had turned his coat—and would have turned his skin.[n]

When Southey tried to read his *Vision* to the assembly, he put St. Peter's teeth on edge, and the devils went howling back to hell. St. Peter knocked the poet down, and he fell into his lake. In the confusion, King George slipped into heaven.

And when the tumult dwindled to a calm,
I left him practising the hundredth psalm.[n]

Byron had no sooner finished this satire than he sank again into one of his intermittent fits of melancholy. His thoughts turned with nostalgia to Augusta. He reproached her for "having behaved so *coldly*" and then turned to his liaison with Teresa, which had lasted nearly three years: "I can say that, without being so *furiously* in love as at first, I am more attached to her than I thought it possible to be to any woman after three years —(*except one & who was she can* YOU *guess?*). . . . If Lady B. would but please to die, and the Countess G.'s husband . . . we should probably have to marry—though I would rather *not*—thinking it the way to hate each other—for all people whatsoever."[n]

Byron was so reluctant to leave Ravenna that he eagerly seized every excuse for delay. The bulk of the furniture was gone, but he lingered in the empty palace. When the weather permitted, he went riding daily, and swam in the Adriatic, and he continued writing and waiting for the English post.

When the first load of his possessions arrived at the Casa Lanfranchi in Pisa, alarmed officials of the city and of the Tuscan government as well as the Austrian spies speculated on the purposes of this dangerous Englishman. The President of the "Buon Governo" wrote to the Grand Duke to warn him against this *Signore Inglese*, "who unites birth, a certain pecuniary fortune, literary fame, and a great determination to favor innovations in states."[n]

The spies would have been confirmed in their fear of this dangerous radical if they had read his letter of October 12 to Hobhouse: "Your infamous government will drive all honest men into the necessity of reversing it. . . . I certainly lean towards a republic. All history and experience is in its favour. . . ."[n]

While Byron knew that returning to England was out of the question at the time, his mind went there more and more, for in this blind alley of his life he could not with great pleasure look forward. He sought solace in recollections of the happiest days of his life, certain moments of his childhood in Aberdeen, his schooldays at Harrow, his companionships at Cambridge, and his life in London before his marriage.

To record these memories he began another notebook on October 15, not a diary, but "Detached Thoughts."

"No man would live his life over again, is an old and true saying. . . . At the same time, there are probably *moments* in most men's lives, which they would live over the rest of life to *regain?*"[n] In another note he observed: "I have written my memoirs, but omitted *all* the really *consequential* and *important* parts, from deference to the dead, to the living, and to those who must be both. I sometimes think that I should have written the *whole* as a *lesson,* but it might have proved a *lesson* to be *learnt* rather than *avoided;* for passion is a whirlpool, which is not to be viewed nearly without attraction from its Vortex. I must not go on with these reflections, or I shall be letting out some secret or other to paralyze posterity." [n]

If looking at the past induced melancholy, looking into the future brought troubling speculations: "Of the Immortality of the Soul," he wrote, "it appears to me that there can be little doubt, if we attend for a moment to the action of Mind. It is in perpetual activity. I used to doubt of it, but reflection has taught me better. . . . How far our future life will be individual, or, rather, how far it will at all resemble our *present* existence, is another question; but that the *Mind* is *eternal,* seems as probable as that the body is not so. . . . Man is born *passionate* of body, but with an innate though secret tendency to the love of Good in his Mainspring of Mind. But God help us all! It is at present a sad jar of atoms." [n]

In these "Detached Thoughts" Byron revealed both his indomitable search for an earthly Eden and his realistic view of his limited success. "Padre Pasquale Aucher [his Armenian teacher on the Island of San Lazzaro] assured me 'the terrestrial Paradise had been certainly in *Armenia.*' I went seeking it—God knows where—did I find it? Umph! Now and then, for a minute or two." [n]

Both Shelley and Teresa were eagerly awaiting Byron's arrival. Shelley was disconcerted when he learned that Allegra would for the time being be left at the convent. The Mother Superior heard of Byron's intended departure and invited him to pay his daughter a visit at Bagnacavallo, and she enclosed a letter from Allegra in a large copybook hand in Italian: "My dear Papa—It being fair-time I should so much like a visit from my Papa, as I have many desires to satisfy; will you not please your Allegrina who loves you so?" [n] Byron's only comment was: ". . . sincere enough but not very flattering—for she wants to see me because it 'is the fair' to get some paternal gingerbread—I suppose." [n] If he intended to call on her at the convent before he left, in the confusion of an early morning start he let the opportunity pass. He knew himself a stranger to his daughter, and he did not relish sentimental scenes of parting or the exposure of his embarrassments to the nuns.

At last, on October 29 in the dark of the morning, Byron's Napoleonic carriage rattled through the silent streets of the medieval town that he had entered in the triumph of his *serventismo* nearly two years before. His departure was regretted by Count Alborghetti and many others who had benefited from his generosity. Teresa later told Moore: "His arrival in that town was spoken of as a piece of public good fortune, and his departure as a public calamity. . . ."[n]

In the care of Pellegrino Ghigi, his long-suffering banker, he left "a Goat with a broken leg, an ugly peasant Dog, a Bird of the heron type which would eat only fish, a Badger on a chain, and two ugly old Monkeys,"[n] and his daughter Allegra in the convent at Bagnacavallo.

Between Imola and Bologna, Byron was waked from his drowsiness by a familiar face in an approaching vehicle. It was Lord Clare, his favorite at Harrow, whom he had not seen for seven or eight years. The past rolled up before him. "This meeting annihilated for a moment all the years between. . . . It was a new and inexplicable feeling, like rising from the grave, to me. Clare, too, was much agitated. . . . We were but five minutes together, and in the public road; but I hardly recollect an hour of my existence which could be weighed against them."[n]

At the Pellegrino Inn in Bologna, by prearrangement, Byron met Samuel Rogers, who was on his travels in Italy. It was not so happy a meeting. Byron had written Murray when he heard that Rogers was on the way: ". . . there is a mean minuteness in his mind and tittle-tattle that I dislike, ever since I *found him out* . . . besides he is not a good man: why don't he go to bed? What does he do travelling?"[n] But Byron was more amiable face to face, though Rogers recalled that in their journey across the Apennines, "if there was any scenery particularly well worth seeing, he generally contrived that we should pass through it in the dark."[n] Florence was full of English people. On the morning of November 1, when Byron started on the final leg of his journey to Pisa, Rogers watched him go and then wrote his sister: "I wish you had seen him set off, every window of the inn was open to see him."[n]

Just beyond Empoli, some thirty miles from Florence, Byron's caravan passed the public coach from Pisa. In it was a dark-haired girl who peered out at him without being seen. Claire Clairmont was on her way back to Florence. It was the last time she saw the father of her child.

There is no record of Byron's reception in Pisa, but it was no doubt a warm one. It was the moment for which Teresa had waited despairingly for more than two months. And his arrival was no less welcome to Pietro and his father, and to Shelley, who had been gathering about him a little society congenial in intellect and feelings, which was soon to become a part of Byron's circle in a new routine as pleasant as any he had enjoyed at Ravenna.

CHAPTER XXIV

1821–1822

Shelley and the Pisan Circle

BYRON WAS WELL PLEASED with the palace chosen for him, soon also with the company that Shelley had gathered about him. The Casa Lanfranchi was lighter and less gloomy than the palace of the Guicciolis which he had occupied in Ravenna. The winter climate of Pisa was a relief too, after the snows and slush of the Romagna. Sheltered by hills from the tramontane winds, Pisa enjoyed a truly Mediterranean mildness more like that of the winters he had passed in Greece. The garden was small but pleasant, sunny, and private, and surrounded by high walls. He had only to descend the wide steps to the ground floor and open a back door to be able to pluck his own oranges.

After the first month, he wrote to Murray: "I have got here into a famous old feudal palazzo, on the Arno."[n] But there was nothing Gothic or medieval about the palace, which had been constructed in the sixteenth century of fine Carrara marble in a simple mid-Renaissance design. The marble in aging had taken on a golden hue. There seems to be no truth in the local tradition, which Byron accepted, that the staircase was the work of Michelangelo. The Lanfranchi family had taken the part of the Ghibellines in the civil strife of their day, and Dante mentions one of them in the *Inferno*. These stories increased Byron's interest in the old house, which was said to be haunted as a result of dark deeds in its past.

After his long isolation in the Italian society in Ravenna,

Byron was glad to relax again in an English circle which honored him for his poetry and responded to his wit and literary and worldly conversation. He had no taste for cultivating new Italian acquaintances. Teresa by her situation was effectively cut off from Italian society in this strange city, and saw only the few friends who had been exiled with her father and brother. The Gambas had been given permission for a temporary residence by the Tuscan government. Teresa visited only with Mary Shelley and Mary's friend Jane Williams.

The Shelleys had returned to Pisa from the Baths of San Giuliano a few days before Byron's arrival, and had furnished a flat at the top of the Tre Palazzi di Chiesa, a house facing the Arno on the opposite bank from the Casa Lanfranchi. Shelley's admiration for Byron's poetic genius was increased by his reading *Cain*, which he saw in manuscript shortly after Byron's arrival. Before long, Mary, always exhilarated by the presence of Byron, was writing to her friend Maria Gisborne: "So Pisa, you see, has become a little nest of singing birds." [n]

Just then a good many people were dropping in on the Shelleys, and Shelley had already introduced a number of them to Byron. Edward and Jane Williams, then their closest friends, had arrived in Pisa in January, responding to the urgent invitation of Shelley's cousin Thomas Medwin, who had served with Williams in the Eighth Dragoons in India, and who had come to Italy the previous October to be near his talented cousin. Williams—a half-pay lieutenant with literary leanings and liberal sympathies—having run away with a fellow officer's wife, found it more convenient as well as cheaper to live abroad. Having heard from Shelley something of the "canker of aristocracy" in Byron's character, and nursing the popular legend of the melancholy misanthrope, Williams was agreeably surprised when Shelley took him to the Casa Lanfranchi. "So far from his having a haughtiness of manner," he wrote in his journal, "they are those of the most unaffected and gentlemanly ease—and so far from his being (as is generally imagined) wrapt in a melancholy gloom he is all sunshine, and good humour with which the elegance of his language and the brilliancy of his wit cannot fail to inspire those who are near him." [n]

The next day Byron accompanied Teresa and Pietro to the Shelleys, but thereafter the visiting was always in the other direction, Byron's house becoming the center of a circle which was masculine. Teresa continued her rides with Mary, and with Pietro called on the Shelleys. But Byron saw Teresa only at her own house, though he sometimes met her and Mary when they were riding. Like a magnet, he drew Shelley and his friends into his own orbit of amusements and conversation. Into this circle came another friend of Shelley, John Taaffe, Jr., an Irish expatriate who had spent some years in Italy, having been forced into exile by an unfortunate affair with a woman in Edinburgh. He prided himself on his horsemanship, though he was not a good rider, and he devoted himself to scholarship and writing. He was at work on a magnum opus, a *Commentary on Dante*, which was to be published with his own translation of the *Divine Comedy*. Byron took to him at once and fell in with his scheme so far as to recommend the *Commentary* to Murray.

Thomas Medwin had left Pisa in February but returned on November 14, perhaps with the specific view of meeting through Shelley the renowned Lord Byron. Byron accepted Medwin, as he had Taaffe, with some slightly cynical reservations, as a companion who could furnish him with the worldly conversation that Shelley shunned, and particularly as one who deferred to him and served as a sounding board for his own wit and reminiscence. Soon Medwin, like Taaffe and Williams, was almost a daily caller.

After the Governor of Pisa had refused to allow pistol shooting in the Lanfranchi garden, Byron made his own arrangements with some friends of Dr. Vaccà,* the Castinelli family, who resided outside the city walls. Thenceforth, almost every afternoon, when the weather permitted, Byron and his friends rode out to the Villa la Podera, where they practiced pistol shooting at a target. According to local tradition, part of the attraction of the farmhouse to Byron was the presence of Maria, a beautiful brunette peasant girl. Both Teresa and Mary directed their rides and their walks very frequently toward the pistol-shooting party. It was for Mary, strongly attracted by the intellect and charm of Byron, almost the only opportunity to associate in this man's world for which by temperament and intellectual interests she was eminently fitted. She remembered

---

* Dr. Vaccà, an eminent surgeon, was a friend of the Shelleys.

nostalgically their evenings together at the Villa Diodati and in the boat on Lake Geneva.

In her journal at a later time Mary tried to explain to herself "why Albè, by his mere presence and voice, has the power of exciting such deep and shifting emotions within me."[n] Mary could not admit to herself how deeply she was attracted to Byron, both physically and by subtle responses to his complementary personality. How could she, even with Shelley at her side, be entirely oblivious to the charm that almost every other woman felt in the presence of Byron? Her later novels were filled with heroes who were thinly veiled portraits of him.

Sometime in December Byron began giving weekly dinners at the Casa Lanfranchi for his male friends (the ladies were never invited). Taaffe, Medwin, Williams, and Shelley usually came. Shelley enjoyed the talk until it turned from literature and philosophical subjects to worldly matters, when he generally withdrew. The others talked over their wine until two or three in the morning. With Shelley's other friends Byron never became intimate. Prince Mavrocordatos, the Greek patriot who had given Greek lessons to Mary, had sailed in June to join in the battle for Greek freedom, but his cousin Prince Argiropoli remained in Pisa, and Shelley brought him to meet Byron, thereby kindling anew the latter's enthusiasm for the Greek cause.

If not completely oblivious to the fact that he was obnoxious to the government, Byron was indifferent to how it felt about him, for he had already weathered the displeasure of the government of the Romagna, where fanatics had even posted an *affiche* calling for his assassination. Comfortably adjusted to the pleasant climate and companionship of Pisa, Byron was for a time more contented than he had been for many months. He made himself agreeable to the members of his new circle. Medwin, who had soon begun to take notes on his brilliant conversation, was immediately won over by the friendliness of the great poet. Byron was aware that he was being "Boswellized," but did not refrain from talking freely of his own life and affairs, though he sometimes found pleasure in pulling Medwin's leg.

Medwin noted: "I never met with any man who shines so much in conversation. He shines the more, perhaps, for not seeking to shine. His ideas flow without effort, without his having occasion to think. As in his letters, he is not nice about expressions or words;—there are no concealments in him, no injunctions to secresy [*sic*]. He tells every thing that he has thought or done without the least reserve, and as if he wished the whole world to know it; and does not throw the slightest gloss over his errors. . . . He hates argument, and never argues for victory. He gives every one an opportunity of sharing in the conversation, and has the art of turning it to subjects that may bring out the person with whom he converses. He never shews the author, prides himself most on being a man of the world and of fashion, and his anecdotes of life and living characters are inexhaustible. In spirits, as in every thing else, he is ever in extremes."[n]

Shelley too was drawn by the personality and brilliance of the man whose genius so overawed his own that for the first months of Byron's residence in Pisa the younger poet wrote but little. He had written from Ravenna in August: "I despair of rivalling Lord Byron, as well I may: and there is no other with whom it is worth contending."[n] And later he told Horace Smith: "I do not write—I have lived too long near Lord Byron & the sun has extinguished the glow-worm. . . ."[n] And apropos of *Cain* he wrote: "Space wondered less at the swift and fair creations of God, when he grew weary of vacancy, than I at the late works of this spirit of an angel in the mortal paradise of a decaying body. So I think—let the world envy while it admires, as it may."[n] Byron, on his side, though he did not admire Shelley's poetry greatly, and was inclined to make sport of him occasionally, as he did of his other companions, had a genuine liking for him and respect for his intellect and integrity.

Byron's literary activity had not stopped on his arrival in Pisa, though Medwin wondered how he could find time to write. The poet was annoyed with Murray for treating *Don Juan* as a stepchild, and for his timidity with respect to *Cain*. He would not alter the "impious" passages to make Lucifer "talk like the Bishop of Lincoln. . . . Are these people more impious than Milton's Satan? or the Prometheus of Æschylus?"[n] And, as Byron suspected, Murray was doing well enough with *Don Juan*. Murray's biographer, Samuel Smiles, recorded: "The booksellers' messengers filled the street in front of the house in Albemarle Street, and the parcels of books were given out of the window in answer to their obstreperous demands."[n] Byron was partly mollified when Murray finally offered twenty-five hundred guineas for the last three cantos of *Don Juan* and the three plays, *Sardanapalus, The Two Foscari,* and *Cain,* which were published together on December 19.

Thoughts of his daughter Ada never failed to arouse melancholy reminiscences of the past in Byron. On December 10, her birthday, he wrote Murray: "I wonder when I shall see her again. . . . I have remarked a curious coincidence, which almost looks like a fatality. My *mother,* my *wife,* my *daughter,* my *half-sister,* my *sister's mother,* my natural daughter . . . and *myself,* are all *only children.*" [n] A lock of Ada's hair, sent through Augusta, prompted another letter (finally unsent) to Annabella. He thanked her for the inscription and the date and name, for, he said, he had nothing of her handwriting in his possession except the word "Household" in an old account book. But then he became less sentimental and more realistic: "I burnt your last note, for two reasons:—firstly, it was written in a style not very agreeable; and, secondly, I wished to take your word without documents. . . . We both made a bitter mistake; but now it is over, and irrevocably so. . . . I say all this, because I own to you, that, notwithstanding every thing, I considered our re-union as not impossible for more than a year after the separation;—but then I gave up the hope entirely and for ever. But this very impossibility of re-union seems to me at least a reason why . . . we should preserve the courtesies of life. . . ." [n]

The points at which Byron and Shelley were most likely to disagree touched matters of religion, for Shelley was inclined to be positive in his views, whereas Byron was an uncertain skeptic, who sometimes doubted his own skepticism, as he did once in discussing *Cain.* Shelley exclaimed, according to Trelawny: "I do believe, Mary, that he is little better than a Christian!" [n] Whatever may have been Byron's reluctance to disturb the religious beliefs of others, he was as quick as Shelley to protest against acts of bigotry or inhumanity committed in the name of any religion. When Medwin brought the story of a man who had been taken up for sacrilege and sentenced to be burned alive, Byron exclaimed: "We must endeavour to prevent this *auto da fé.*" [n] Shelley was horror-struck and wanted to mount horses immediately and set off for Lucca to rescue the man. Byron was more cautious and practical. He wrote a letter to Frederick

North, Earl of Guilford, as one who had influence with "these Grand Dukes and Sovereigns—and such people as are able to burn other people still it seems." [n] And he sent Taaffe to Lucca to find the truth of the matter and if possible appeal to the authorities. When he discovered that the man had fled to Florence and had given himself up to the authorities there, who had no intention of burning him, the matter blew over.

At the turn of the year Byron had consented to sit for a bust to the noted sculptor Lorenzo Bartolini. But the likeness only convinced him that, as he approached his thirty-fourth birthday, he had already lived a lifetime and that his youth was gone. One evidence of it was that he no longer desired an all-consuming passion, but was content with the calmer relationship into which he had settled with Teresa. This realization helped to make his life in Pisa pleasant and relaxed. But it was not quite so with Teresa, who, torn from her home and friends, felt that Byron was growing away from her and that she should make an effort to follow his interests more fully. She admired Mary Shelley's wide reading and intellectual ardor, and foolishly thought that Byron would love her more if she emulated that paragon. But Byron had already expressed his views of "ladies intellectual." What appealed to him in Teresa was that she had preserved her youthful beauty and naïve charm.

Early in January, Byron received a letter which revived recollections of a time when his life had been agitated by almost continuous passions. Harriette Wilson, who had met him only once at a masquerade in 1814, the "summer of the sovereigns," had continued to write to him. When in dire need in Paris in 1820, she had asked him for £50. He was easily touched by such appeals. Now she was back in England, deserted by all her lovers, and again in sorry straits. "Do you want an *english maid* who is *not* a *maid*?" she asked, "& whome you need not speak to for a month together, who can amuse herself alone, make your room look comfortable, *pimp* for *you* in *french* but not in ITALIAN, make your tea a *l'anglaise* . . . do anything but mend your shirts for I can't do needle work—if so pray *have me* and I would rather upon my word be your servant & live in your kitchen than wife to anybody else." [n] Byron must have been amused, but there is no surviving evidence of a reply.

On January 14 a new and livening personality entered the

Pisan circle. Edward John Trelawny, a curious combination of salty adventurer and sensitive enthusiast with a longing to associate with literary men, had come to Italy purposely to meet Shelley and Byron, lured by enthusiastic letters from Williams, who had met him in Geneva the previous winter. He was welcomed at the Tre Palazzi, and Mary was particularly struck by his appearance and manner. She referred to him in her diary as "un giovane stravagante—partly natural and partly perhaps put on, but it suits him well, and if his abrupt but not unpolished manners be assumed, they are nevertheless in unison with his Moorish face (for he looks Oriental yet not Asiatic) his dark hair, his Herculean form, and then there is an air of extreme good nature which pervades his whole countenance, especially when he smiles, which assures me that his heart is good. He tells strange stories of himself, horrific ones. . . ."[n]

Trelawny later told some of these stories in his *Adventures of a Younger Son,* which he set before the world as his autobiography. But the facts of his early life, only recently discovered,[n] were quite different. He had gone into the Navy as a boy, but he was never a pirate or privateersman, and he never deserted from the Royal Navy, but returned to England in a British frigate in 1812. Nor, so far as can be ascertained, did he marry an Arab girl or later cremate her on the beach. Most of his vicarious heroisms were no doubt daydreams.

The day after Trelawny's arrival, Williams and Shelley took him to see Byron. They were greeted by Byron's surly bulldog Moretto, Trelawny recalled. Byron's "halting gait was apparent, but he moved with quickness; and although pale, he looked as fresh, vigorous, and animated, as any man I ever saw. . . . he was embarrassed at first meeting with strangers; this he tried to conceal by an affectation of ease."[n]

Trelawny noted that Byron's conversation "was anything but literary, except when Shelley was near him. The character he most commonly appeared in was of the free and easy sort, such as had been in vogue when he was in London, and George IV. was Regent; and his talk was seasoned with anecdotes of the great actors on and off the stage, boxers, gamblers, duellists, drunkards, &c., &c., appropriately garnished with the slang and scandal of that day. Such things had all been in fashion, and were at that time considered accomplishments by gentlemen.

. . . His long absence had not effaced the mark John Bull brands his children with; the instant he loomed above the horizon, on foot or horseback, you saw at a glance he was a Britisher. . . . He seemed to take an especial pleasure in making a clean breast to every new comer, as if to mock their previous conceptions of him, and to give the lie to the portraits published of him."[n] But when Trelawny knew him better he observed: "Lord Byron was nothing in conversation, unless you were alone with him, but then he was rich as a gold mine, in every direction you bored into him you could extract wealth, and he was never exhausted—"[n]

Byron was a little perplexed and embarrassed by Trelawny's emulation at first, as if he had seen a caricature of his own Eastern heroes in this strange character. After the first meeting he told Teresa: "I have met today the personification of my Corsair. He sleeps with the poem under his pillow, and all his past adventures and present manners aim at this personification."[n] But after a few days Byron was quite at ease with Trelawny, who had become an almost daily visitor.

One of the first things Trelawny did was to reanimate the scheme, which Williams and Shelley had been fostering for some weeks, to have a boat built and to spend the summer on the Bay of Spezia. He also interested Byron in the project to the point that he too asked Trelawny to commission his friend Roberts in Genoa to build him a boat with a spacious cabin and to spare no expense in making her "a complete BEAUTY." Byron later regretted that he had told Trelawny to spare no expense, for the boat finally cost ten times his first estimate of a hundred pounds. Shelley modified his demands to a small boat of seventeen or eighteen feet, but "a thorough *Varment* at *pulling* and *sailing!*"[n]

Byron's recent relations with Murray had so irritated him that he had again decided to withdraw from him as a publisher, without quarreling with him personally, if that were possible. According to Medwin, Byron said of the manuscript of *Heaven and Earth,* another "blasphemous" poetic drama dealing with the love of angels for daughters of earth: "Douglas Kinnaird tells me that he can get no bookseller to publish it. It was offered to Murray; but he is the most timid of God's booksellers, and starts at the title."[n]

But news that Murray was likely to be prosecuted for the

publication of *Cain* caused Byron to write his publisher in a half-scolding, half-placating manner: "I can only say . . . that any proceedings directed against you, I beg, may be transferred to me . . . that if you have lost money by the publication, I will refund any or all of the Copyright. . . . If they prosecute, I will come to England. . . ." And he used the situation as a justification for severing publishing connections with Murray. Having confided his spleen to paper in the quiet hours of the morning ("All my malice evaporates in the effusions of my pen . . ." he told Lady Blessington), Byron looked out from his study upon the moonlit night and concluded: "I write to you about all this row of bad passions and absurdities with the *Summer* Moon (for here our Winter is clearer than your Dog days) lighting the winding Arno, with all her buildings and bridges, so quiet and still: what Nothings we are! before the least of these Stars!"[n]

In February news came that Lady Noel had died on January 28. It was an event Byron had long looked forward to, but when it happened, despite his frequent facetious remarks on the longevity and toughness of the old lady, his first reaction carried him into sentimental reflections on the past and sympathy for Annabella. When Medwin called on him, all his servants were in mourning, and Byron told him: "I am distressed for poor Lady Byron! She must be in great affliction, for she adored her mother! The world will think I am pleased at this event, but they are much mistaken."[n]

By the terms of the separation settlement, the income from the Wentworth estates, roughly estimated at £10,000 a year, was to be divided by arbitrators at Lady Noel's death, one to be appointed by each party. Byron immediately wrote to Kinnaird naming Sir Francis Burdett, Hobhouse's close friend in Reform politics, as his referee, and asking that £10,000 insurance be taken on Lady Byron's life, as the Wentworth income would go to other heirs at her death. And as he was by the terms of the will to take the Noel arms, he signed himself for the first time "Noel Byron." The often repeated statement that he thenceforth took a certain pride in the fact that his initials, "N.B.," were the same as those of Napoleon Bonaparte, seems to rest solely on the unreliable evidence of Stendhal, who met him briefly in 1816.[n]

Hanson reported that "the gross Rental of the Wentworth Estates, as handed over to us, is £6336 a year. . . ."[n] With deductions for upkeep and other expenses, Byron's share would be about £2,500. Byron's total income now came to more than £6,000 from the funds and the Wentworth estate. In addition he had been earning more than £2,000 a year by his pen, but that income was beginning to fall off.

Byron could now afford to be generous with Leigh Hunt, whose demands for money, made through Shelley, were increasing. Stranded at Plymouth for the winter with a sick wife and a large family, Hunt, having already drained the ready cash of his brother John, made a desperate appeal to Shelley, who sent him £150. In the meantime, Hunt embarrassed Shelley considerably by appealing directly to Byron for money for his voyage. The defensive familiarity of his tone did not make the request less audacious. There was always a mingling of sycophancy and brazenness in Hunt's letters to Byron which, when their relations became more strained, was deeply annoying. Hunt wrote from Plymouth on January 27:

"My dear Byron, (for I will not abate a jot of my democracy, at least on occasions of letter writing, and especially the present one) Shelley told me some time ago that you were good enough to wish my company in Italy, and that you would have sent me a considerable sum of money to enable me to come over. . . . I might have been somewhat coy in matters of pecuniary obligation to you at that time . . . because from the first hour I knew you, I had got a romantic notion in my head, perhaps a coxcombical one, (and yet not so), of awakening your school-day ideas of friendship again, & shewing you that a man could cultivate your regard, merely from a disinterested love of your intellectual qualities and of that very generosity. . . . I must give you a still better proof perhaps of my boyish notions of friendship, & fairly ask you for your assistance. I would borrow, if possible, (for other purposes besides the mere journey) as much as £250, only you must let me have two years to return it in. . . ." [n]

Shelley, having had experience of Hunt's ways, felt constrained to warn Byron: ". . . I do not think poor Hunt's promise to pay in a given time is worth very much; but mine is less subject to uncertainty, and I should be happy to be responsible for any engagement he may have proposed to you." [n] But Byron felt sufficiently obliged to Hunt and enough interested in the joint literary venture (a new periodical) to supply the money requested despite the gaucheries of Hunt's appeal and his own increasing disinclination to make large disbursements. Byron did not know that Shelley had made the mistake of telling Hunt: "You know Lady Noel is dead & Lord B. is rich, a still richer man." [n]

Byron's newly acquired wealth had, however, made him only more concerned with its conservation. His change in attitude from that of his spendthrift youth was perhaps due in part to the fact that at thirty-four he was experiencing the growing anxieties of age and the need for security. He was increasingly concerned for the time when he would have to provide not only for himself, but also for his child, perhaps for Teresa and her family, and very probably for Augusta and her children.

Trouble was brewing, unknown to Byron, in another quarter. Claire's increasing agitation over Byron's failure to bring Allegra with him or to remove her from the convent when he left Ravenna, moved her to devise wild schemes to rescue her daughter. Shelley and Mary, she felt, were too close to Byron to be trusted with her plans, but she was encouraged by Mrs. Mason (Lady Mountcashell) and other friends in Pisa. Byron ignored two of her letters, one begging him to place Allegra with some respectable family in Pisa, the other asking for a chance to see her daughter before departing for Vienna to join her brother and seek employment there. Byron, as always aroused to brutal resistance and unreasoning contempt by Claire's dramatic appeals for sympathy, was only made more stubborn. In the meantime, Claire came to Pisa.

The Shelleys were sympathetic, but counseled caution, and felt that Claire was exaggerating the evils of the convent. Shelley, urged against his better judgment by her plaintive appeals before she returned to Florence, finally approached Byron on the subject of her anxiety and appealed to him to do something to ease her mind. According to Claire, Byron's only reply "was a shrug of impatience, and the exclamation that women could not live without making scenes." [n] Shelley was genuinely angry, and told the Masons that he could at that moment have knocked Byron down, but afterward he said: "It is foolish of me to be angry with him; he can no more help being what he is than yonder door can help being a door." [n]

From that time on, however, Shelley had an increasing

desire to withdraw from any intimacy with Byron. But for Hunt's sake he must not break with him beofre the new journal was established. And in spite of all, Shelley, like Mary, could not escape feeling attracted to Byron when he was near him, and continued to have an admiration for his poetry which no judgment of his character ever affected. Mary wrote to John Murray after reading Moore's *Letters and Journals* of Byron in 1830: "The great charm of the work to me . . . is that the Lord Byron I find there is our Lord Byron—the fascinating—faulty—childish—philosophical being—daring the world—docile to a private circle—impetuous and indolent—gloomy and yet more gay than any other. I live with him again in these pages—getting reconciled (as I used in his lifetime) to those waywardnesses which annoyed me when he was away, through the delightful & buoyant tone of his conversation and manners—" [n]

Byron, on his side, defended Shelley's character against the attacks of those friends in England who were uneasy at Byron's association with this outcast and atheist. He wrote Moore: "As to poor Shelley, who is another bugbear to you and the world, he is, to my knowledge, the *least* selfish and the mildest of men—a man who has made more sacrifices of his fortune and feelings for others than any I ever heard of. With his speculative opinions I have nothing in common, nor desire to have." [n]

In another letter to Moore, speaking of religion (he had been made touchy on the subject because of attacks on the impiety of *Cain*), Byron said that Catholicism "is by far the most elegant worship, hardly excepting the Greek mythology. What with incense, pictures, statues, altars, shrines, relics, and the real presence, confession, absolution,—there is something sensible to grasp at. Besides, it leaves no possibility of doubt; for those who swallow their Deity, really and truly, in transubstantiation, can hardly find any thing else otherwise than easy of digestion." [n]

On March 8 Byron gave a dinner party as a farewell to Medwin, who left for Rome the next day. It was a convivial affair, but Trelawny was impressed with Byron's abstemiousness in both eating and drinking. "When alone, he drank a glass or two of small claret or hock, and when utterly exhausted at night a single glass of grog. . . . Byron had not damaged his body by strong drinks, but his terror of getting fat was so great that he reduced his diet to the point of absolute starvation. . . . When he added to his weight, even standing was painful, so he resolved to keep down to eleven stone [154 pounds], or shoot himself. . . . He would exist on biscuits and soda-water for days together, then to allay the eternal hunger gnawing at his vitals, he would make up a horrid mess of cold potatoes, rice, fish, or greens, deluged in vinegar, and gobble it up like a famished dog." "

Captain John Hay, Byron's old friend of London and Brighton days, had arrived in Pisa in January, and after returning from a hunting expedition soon replaced Medwin in the circle and joined in the daily ride. On their usual Sunday ride on March 24, an event occurred which disrupted the routine of the whole Pisan circle, and which, trifling in itself, had far-reaching reverberations in the lives of Byron and all those associated with him. The shooting party was returning at a leisurely pace along the road to the city gate. Shelley, Byron, Trelawny, Captain Hay, and Pietro Gamba were riding together; Teresa was some distance ahead in her carriage with Mary Shelley. Those on horseback had stopped to talk with Taaffe, who had just joined them, when a soldier galloped past at a mad speed frightening Taaffe's horse. They all pursued the soldier and overtook him just before he reached the gate. Shelley asked him civilly in Italian what he meant by his conduct, but he was insolent, and Byron, thinking he was an officer, handed him his card as an invitation to fight. Actually he was Stefani Masi, sergeant-major in the Tuscan Royal Light Horse, and he had been hurrying back to Pisa in order not to be late for roll call. The English party crowded around him, the excitement rose, and one of the party, probably the excitable Pietro Gamba, struck him with a riding whip and called him *"Ignorante."*

Masi shouted to the soldiers at the gate to arrest them all, but they rode through, and all escaped except Shelley, who was knocked from his horse and remained insensible for some time, and Hay, who was slashed severely on the nose. Taaffe himself had stayed safely out of the affray. Byron rode ahead to the Casa Lanfranchi and sent Lega off to the police to report the incident, and then returned with a sword stick. He encountered Masi and for the first time learned his name. After some altercation, Masi broke loose and galloped past the palace, where a considerable crowd had gathered. In the confusion, a figure ran down the steps of the Lanfranchi, lunged at the sergeant with a long-handled weapon, and slunk away into the crowd. Masi reeled in his saddle and rode on, but a short time later fell from his horse in front of a café. He staggered up but collapsed and was carried to the hospital.

When Byron arrived back at the Lanfranchi, followed by Trelawny and Shelley with the wounded Hay, he found Teresa in a state of excitement bordering on collapse. After an hour or more of nursing her and Hay, they took her to the Shelleys'. The excitement increased when news came that Masi had been wounded. The next day Byron sent an English physician to offer his services at Byron's expense to the sergeant. He reported that the wound was shallow, but rumors persisted that he was dying, and resentment toward the English circle mounted. Byron distributed alms in front of his palace to conciliate public opinion, and went with his companions on the usual ride.

Two of Byron's servants, Tita and Vincenzo Papi, his coachman, suspected of the attempted assassination, had been arrested. Byron sent Tita, who was devoted to him, and whom he knew to be innocent, a dinner of twelve courses to be shared with his fellow prisoners. Knowing the fantastic stories that would be told in England, Byron sent a letter to Edward Dawkins, British Chargé d'Affaires at Florence, to be forwarded with copies of the depositions of the Englishmen involved in the affair. He was not quite candid when he told Dawkins that he did not know Masi's assailant, for not only Byron but several others knew that his coachman, Papi, had struck down the dragoon. But Byron would protect his servants at any cost. The irony of it was that Papi was questioned and released, while Tita, with his frightening great beard, who had been foolish enough to carry a knife and a brace of pistols into court, was detained.

The affray caused more disruption in the Pisan circle when Taaffe, who did not want to become involved in the affair, said he had not been insulted by the dragoon, and sent to Dawkins a different account from that of the others. Williams was partly successful in bringing about a reconciliation, but most of the group shunned Taaffe and gave him the nickname "False Taaffe" or "Falstaffe." By the end of the week Masi was sufficiently recovered to relieve the anxiety, but the pleasure was gone from the parties at the Lanfranchi. Medwin had already left, and Hay departed for England on April 3. Shelley and the Williamses were contemplating leaving for the summer. Byron himself leased the Villa Dupuy, about seven kilometers from the port of Leghorn on a hill looking toward the bay, for the season, from May to October.

Meanwhile, throughout the excitement he went on with his literary work. He had cajoled Teresa into giving him permission to continue *Don Juan*. When Williams called on him on April 14, he was beginning the sixth canto. On the 20th Samuel Rogers stopped by on his way from Rome. When he arrived at the Lanfranchi, Trelawny was there and rescued him from Byron's bulldog, who stood viciously guarding the stairs. Byron maliciously enjoyed his visitor's terror, and took delight in baiting Rogers, giving him a highly colored account of his (Byron's) delinquencies.

But Byron was sobered by news from Ravenna that his daughter Allegra was suffering from a light fever. Ghigi had sent Dr. Rasi to attend her. At about the same time Claire Clairmont had arrived in Pisa full of new schemes for rescuing Allegra from the convent. Appalled by her boldness, Shelley tried to calm her, while keeping her presence hidden from Byron. Three days after the first news, Ghigi wrote that the fever continued and that Allegra had been bled for what appeared to be consumptive symptoms. From the first news, Byron was "dreadfully agitated," but let no one but Teresa observe his state of mind. He sent a special messenger to Bagnacavallo for more news. On the 18th she was better, but two days later she took a turn for the worse. She died on the 20th. The nuns were in "the greatest affliction," Ghigi wrote to Lega. The report came to Pisa by special messenger on April 22. Lega left it to Teresa to break the news to Byron.

She told him as gently as she could. "'I understand,' said he,—'it is enough, say no more.' A mortal paleness spread itself over his face . . . and the expression such that I began to fear for his reason; he did not shed a tear. . . . He remained immoveable in the same attitude for an hour, and no consolation which I endeavoured to afford him seemed to reach his ears. . . . He desired to be left alone, and I was obliged to leave him." [n]

Whatever regrets Byron may have had for any personal neglect of Allegra, or for having gone counter to Shelley's advice in refusing to remove her from the convent, were overshadowed by an easy identification of her childhood sufferings with his own. A longing came upon him to have her remains placed in the spot so closely associated with his most "pleasing woe," Harrow Church, "where I once hoped to have laid my own," he wrote Murray, asking him to make appropriate arrangements.*

Byron's feelings for Allegra had been mixed indeed during her short lifetime. She was only five years and three months old when she died. At times he could regard her as an extension of his ego, and he admired her beauty and her cleverness and was flattered by the admiration of others for her. But he was repelled when her temperament and her temper reflected his own less agreeable characteristics, and he wanted her out of his sight. The shock to his sensibilities was even greater when she reminded him of her mother. And, as the Marchesa Origo has aptly observed, ". . . there was also a feeling of resentment (unjust, but not wholly unnatural), on behalf of that other child of his, whom he could never see. Allegra, the little bastard, drove in his carriage and sat on his knee, but it was Ada's birthday that he noted in his journal; Ada's miniature that stood on his writing-desk; Ada's education, her disposition and her future, that were always on his lips."

There remained the disagreeable necessity of informing Shelley. The day after the news came, he wrote: "The blow was stunning and unexpected. . . . I do not know that I have any thing to reproach in my conduct, and certainly nothing in my feelings and intentions towards the dead." Byron was still unaware that Claire was in the neighborhood. Shelley's first care was to hurry her off to Lerici, where the Shelleys and the Williamses were looking for a house for the summer. They settled for the Casa Magni across the bay from Lerici before they revealed to Claire the sad fate of Allegra. She seemed to take it better than they had expected, but she released her feelings in an excoriating letter to Byron, upbraiding him for his whole conduct toward her and her child. Byron sent it on to Shelley. His chief need now was to put the whole matter out of his mind as much as possible.

* Murray did his best, but the Rector of Harrow Church objected to placing a tablet in the church proclaiming the paternity of the little bastard: "I feel constrained to say that the inscription he proposed will be felt by every man of refined taste, to say nothing of sound morals, to be an offence against taste and propriety." (Smiles, I, 430–1.) The best Murray could do was to get permission to bury the child just inside the door, but without any tablet to her memory.

He complied with Claire's request for Allegra's portrait and for permission to see the coffin at Leghorn before it left for England (from this last intention Shelley dissuaded her).

Byron found escape for his feelings in taking up the cause of his servant Tita, the order for whose exile had come to his knowledge the night that he learned of Allegra's death. He had used all his influence through Dawkins, but to no avail. In the prison in Florence, Tita was required to shave his offending beard. The spy Torelli recorded in his diary: ". . . when told to shave it off with a razor, he imagined his beard was to be given to his master, Lord Byron; but on being told this was not the case, he wrapped it up most carefully in a sheet of paper."[n] Tita, now no longer a frightening creature, was allowed to change his place of banishment from Bologna to Lucca, and he found his way to the Shelleys at Casa Magni.

Byron was aware that the persecution of Tita, as well as that of the Gambas, was aimed at him. Though he knew that it would be advantageous to the Gambas to get them out of Pisa and keep them quietly at his summer house near Leghorn until the Masi affair blew over, he lingered in the Casa Lanfranchi until past the middle of May. Inertia and low spirits, which had continued to weigh upon him since the death of Allegra, kept him from moving.

The Shelleys and the Williamses were gone, and Trelawny was in Genoa overseeing the construction of the boats. The affair of the dragoon was not ended yet, for the enmity and suspicions aroused in the minds of certain officials of the "Buon Governo" concerning Byron and his dependents and friends had done much to cause the final disintegration of the congenial Pisan circle, which was practically dissolved after Shelley's departure. Shortly after the middle of May, Byron moved the major part of his household and that of Count Gamba to the rambling villa near Leghorn.

CHAPTER XXV

1822

The Drowning of Shelley

THE VILLA DUPUY WAS a low, sprawling country house situated on a slope a little more than four miles south of Leghorn. In the summer its salmon-colored walls, which were not thick, absorbed the hot sun. Its chief virtue was that it had country privacy, was not far from the sea, and commanded a sweeping vista from the terrace through the olive trees to the white houses of Leghorn and the broad expanse of the sparkling Mediterranean. And from his balcony Byron could see the islands of Elba and Corsica.

When he arrived at the suburb of Montenero, where the villa was situated, the Mediterranean squadron of the United States was at anchor in the harbor below. Having for some years been flattered by the attention Americans had paid him, and having several times contemplated a voyage to that new world where he felt that he had a kind of "posthumous" popularity, he sent word that he would like to see an American frigate, and received a cordial invitation from the Commodore, Jacob Jones, to inspect the *Constitution*. A young Harvard graduate, George Bancroft, then twenty-two and returning from his studies in Germany, later to become a distinguished American historian, happened to be in Leghorn and was a witness of the visit, which stirred the whole squadron. He observed that Byron was a little agitated as he came up the gangway, perhaps because of his lameness, but when he was greeted by the eager young Americans, "his manner became easy, frank and cheerful." [n] From the

Constitution he passed on to the *Ontario*, where he was pleased to see a New York edition of his poems. It was a fillip to his ego and a mark of his fame. He told Moore that he would rather have "a nod from an American, than a snuff-box from an emperor." [n]

The following day young Bancroft called on him at Montenero, and Byron plied him with questions about Washington Irving, whose *Knickerbocker's History of New York* had delighted him. Bancroft had also talked with Goethe, and could report that sage's great admiration for *Manfred* and *Don Juan*, which the German poet found "most full of life and genius." [n] Byron even introduced Bancroft to Teresa, and told him that he had just imported a pianoforte from Vienna for her. "The conversation was in Italian, which as far as I could judge, Lord Byron spoke perfectly well." [n]

But Byron was not free from anxiety. Except for the pleasure of looking at the Mediterranean, and the relaxation of the evenings in the garden with Teresa amid the roses and jasmine, heliotrope, and tuberoses when they watched the fishing boats in the bay and the flickering lights on the water, the move to the country house had not solved any of the problems precipitated by the Masi affray. The Gambas were in imminent danger of being exiled from Tuscany, and the likelihood that they would have difficulty finding asylum in any of the Italian states under Austrian domination caused Byron to think of South America again. He had been so impressed by the success of the patriot Simón Bolívar in liberating Colombia and Venezuela from Spanish rule, that, after he had realized the indiscretion of naming his schooner for Teresa, he had decided, in defiance of the tyrannies of Italy, to call it the *Bolivar*.

Shelley's boat had arrived at Lerici on May 12. "The boat sailed like a witch," Shelley wrote Roberts. But the Shelleys were chagrined to find the name *Don Juan* painted on the mainsail. That was the name they had decided on at the suggestion of Trelawny, but Shelley had second thoughts and, according to Mary, wanted to call it the *Ariel*. Then Byron had taken umbrage and had begged Roberts to inscribe the name of the poem on the sail. Shelley and Williams finally cut the piece out. "I do not know what Lord Byron will say," Mary wrote, "but Lord and Poet as he is, he could not be allowed to make a coal barge of our boat." [n] Although Shelley had an increasing desire to withdraw from close association with Byron, it appears that he had not objected to the name *Don Juan,* which Mary, Shelley, and all their friends continued to use in referring to the boat, but only to the disfiguring of the sail.

That Byron was having a boat built at Genoa and that it was to have cannon mounted on it was duly reported to the officials at Florence, Pisa, and Leghorn. President Puccini, acting for the "Buon Governo" in Florence, hastened to give positive orders that Byron was not to be permitted to moor his boat along the coast, but should be required to anchor it at Leghorn and abide strictly by the sanitary laws. So the government was ready for this dangerous craft when it arrived. Trelawny brought the *Bolivar* into Leghorn on May 18, and he was eager to show her to the poet. But when Byron went aboard, Trelawny could see that he had already lost interest in it, and he could not induce him to take it out of the port. The government had so circumscribed its use (he was not allowed to cruise in sight of Leghorn) that it seemed rather futile. So the schooner remained in the charge of Trelawny and the sailors, tied up at the dock, and Byron, sulking at Montenero, was too disconsolate and bored to make what use was possible of his expensive new plaything.

On June 20, Shelley received word of Hunt's arrival in Genoa, and would have set out for Leghorn immediately had it not been for Mary's illness, which delayed him until the 1st of July. His anxiety concerning Hunt's relations with Byron and the new journal continued. "Between ourselves," he wrote Horace Smith, "I greatly fear that this alliance will not succeed, for I, who could never have been regarded as more than the link of the two thunderbolts, cannot now consent to be even that,—& how long the alliance between the wren & the eagle may continue I will not prophesy." [n]

But Shelley was not destined to be present at the meeting of the wren and the eagle, for Leigh Hunt arrived in Leghorn at the end of June or the 1st of July, and was directed by Trelawny to Byron's summer house. "The day was very hot," Hunt recalled; ". . . and when I got there, I found the hottest looking house I ever saw." [n] At the end of his dusty road he found a scene of Italian tragi-comedy at the Villa Dupuy. A quarrel of the servants of Byron and the Gambas had resulted in a knife wound in Pietro's arm and a state of siege, with the malefactor, Byron's servant Papi, "glaring upwards like a tiger." Byron, who was used to Italian excitability, took it in stride. When they went for their ride, the servant came weeping to his master and asked his pardon, but Byron was adamant about dismissing him. The police, whom Byron had indiscreetly sent for, would have forced him to leave anyhow.

"Upon seeing Lord Byron," Hunt wrote, "I hardly knew him, he was grown so fat; and he was longer in recognizing me, I had grown so thin." [n] Hunt fancied himself set down in the midst of a scene from *The Mysteries of Udolpho*. "Every thing was new, foreign, and violent . . . and last, not least, in the novelty, my English friend, metamorphosed, round-looking, and jacketed, trying to damp all this fire with his cool tones, and an air of voluptuous indolence." [n]

For all his coolness, Byron was more agitated than he seemed. It was apparent that the Tuscan government had decided to expel the Gambas and all their household from the state. Counts Ruggero and Pietro Gamba were ordered to appear before a tribunal in Leghorn on July 2. The purpose was made plain in the spy Torelli's report: "This [altercation], together with the fact that Lord Byron's request that his schooner 'Bolivar' should be allowed to embark and disembark people without hindrance along the coast was supported by the English legation, made our Government determine to try to rid Tuscany of this revolutionary fellow, without openly expelling him." [n]

Byron was too concerned with his personal problems to pay much attention to poor Hunt and his family, whose existence depended so completely upon him. Perhaps for that very reason they irritated him. Fortunately, Shelley was on hand to look out for them: the next day he accompanied them to Pisa and saw them settled in the ground-floor apartments prepared for them in Byron's palace. Byron, Teresa, and the remaining servants arrived soon to make preparations for departure. The Gambas remained temporarily at Montenero. They were finally granted an extension until July 8, but Byron's plans were still confused. Shelley now had the unenviable job of trying to rescue Hunt's fortunes or salvage what he could from the wreckage. Hunt, he knew, had counted on the proposed journal for his living. He had spent the whole of the £400 that Byron and Shelley together had advanced to him and was already in debt. As Shelley was out of funds, the burden would fall on Byron, who was preoccupied with arrangements for leaving Pisa. The most that Shelley could do was to get Byron to offer Hunt the copyright of *The Vision of Judgment,* which seemed likely in itself to create enough interest to give the journal a good start.

Byron was sincere in his offer, though it was not entirely motivated by a generous feeling toward Hunt. He had been unsuccessful so far in finding anyone who would risk the publication of a poem whose political *lèse-majesté* was even more dangerous than the levity of its handling of the heavenly hierarchy. The day of his return to Pisa (July 3) he wrote a note to Murray asking him to deliver to Leigh Hunt's brother John (who was to publish the new journal) the manuscript of the *Vision.*

In the exasperation of his situation, Byron was only annoyed that Hunt and his sick wife and numerous unrestrained children had settled in his palace at the moment when he might have to move. Toward the amiable Hunt himself he was not ill disposed, and when the irritation wore off, he was willing to converse with him pleasantly on literary matters. Hunt, on his side, was eager to please and be pleased by his new life.

Mrs. Hunt, however, was determined not to be pleased with Italian manners, and acquitted herself of any obligation to Byron by taking a British middle-class attitude of moral superiority to him and his mistress. Byron sensed her inverted snobbishness and repaid her in kind. Hunt recalled: "My wife knew nothing of Italian, and did not care to learn it. Madame Guiccioli could not speak English." Marianne Hunt pretended a lofty disdain for rank and titles. Hunt recorded that Byron "said to her one day, 'What do you think, Mrs. Hunt? Trelawney [*sic*] has been speaking against my morals! What do you think of that!—'It is the first time,' said Mrs. Hunt, 'I ever heard of them.' " And once, in a pique, Hunt told Byron what Mrs. Hunt had said of an engraving of Harlow's portrait of him, that it "resembled a great school-boy, who had had a plain bun given him, instead of a plum one." It is not surprising that Byron after this spoke of Mrs. Hunt as being "no great things." [n]

On the 7th, after getting a promise from Byron to help Hunt as much as possible with the new periodical, Shelley left for Leghorn, to accompany Williams back to Lerici in their boat. The extent of Byron's intentions is indicated in his letter to Murray instructing him to turn over to John Hunt not only the *Vision* but also the translation of Pulci and any prose tracts. It is significant, however, that in announcing the resumption of *Don Juan* he did not say that he intended to give the new cantos to Hunt for the journal. And he was frank in voicing his misgivings to Moore at the same time that he asked him for a contribution. "He [Hunt] seems sanguine about the matter, but (*entre nous*) I am not. I do not, however, like to put him out of spirits by saying so. . . ."[n]

On the 8th the Gambas found temporary asylum in Lucca. Pending the outcome of their petition for more permanent residence, Teresa returned and with her servants settled into Byron's palace. Byron had previously been rather meticulous in seeing to it that Teresa observed the nominal rules of the Pope's decree by living under her father's roof, but now he had ceased to care. Count Guiccioli had already made the most of the reports that she was living in Byron's house at Montenero (though her father was there), and through his attorney he had succeeded in getting the Pope to rescind his earlier rescript and suspend her allowance, "in order to dissuade the imprudent young woman from a life which, she boasted, made her happy."[n]

Life at the Casa Lanfranchi settled into a pattern agreeable to Byron. Though uneasy about the situation in which he found himself with Hunt, he could not long resist the good nature of his guest on the ground floor, and his desire for literary conversation made him willing to ignore or overlook the snubs and superiorities of Mrs. Hunt and the vagaries of her numerous brood.

Hunt recalled: "Lord Byron, who used to sit up at night, writing Don Juan (which he did under the influence of gin and water), rose late in the morning. He breakfasted; read; lounged about, singing an air, generally out of Rossini, and in a swaggering style, though in a voice at once small and veiled; then took a bath, and was dressed; and coming down-stairs, was heard, still singing, in the court-yard, out of which the garden ascended at the back of the house. . . . My study, a little room in a corner, with an orange-tree peeping in at the window, looked upon this court-yard. I was generally at my writing when he came down, and either acknowledged his presence by getting up and saying something from the window, or he called out 'Leontius!' and came halting up to the window with some joke, or other challenge to conversation. . . . We then lounged about, or sat and talked, Madame Guiccioli with her sleek tresses descending after her toilet to join us." Hunt was too downright to respond easily to Byron's quizzing or his badinage. But he joined Byron when he rode out with Trelawny on their afternoon canter. He conceded that Byron "was a good rider, graceful, and kept a firm seat. . . . We had blue frock-coats, white waistcoats and trowsers, and velvet caps *à la Raphael;* and cut a gallant figure." [n]

Having returned to the writing of *Don Juan,* Byron found it easy to escape from the annoyances of the present into the pleasant creations of his pen. He could look back now at the world's follies and his own with an amused detachment, or with a soft melancholy regret. He was in the midst of the scene in the seraglio in the sixth canto. Part of his pleasure was to share the amusing stanzas with Teresa, for he could translate only what he wished her to hear. According to Teresa, Byron used to write on playbills or odd pieces of paper, "with repeated glasses of gin-punch by his side. He then used to rush out of his room to read to her what he had written, making many alterations, and laughing immoderately." [n]

This pleasant existence was interrupted on the 11th when Trelawny arrived from Leghorn with disquieting news about Shelley and Williams. They had started for Lerici in their small sailing boat with an English boy, Charles Vivien, as sailor, just after noon on the 8th. At about three, a sudden wind or *temporale* came from the Gulf, bringing a violent storm. Roberts, who was watching from the mole, saw them about ten miles out off Viareggio taking in their topsails. Then they disappeared in the haze. When the storm cleared, he and Trelawny looked again but there was no boat on the sea. They questioned fishermen, but nothing could be learned. It was then that Trelawny rode to Pisa hoping to find a letter from the Villa Magni. "I told my fears to Hunt," Trelawny wrote," "and then went upstairs to Byron. When I told him, his lip quivered, and his voice faltered as he questioned me." [n]

Hunt wrote a desperate note to Shelley at the Casa Magni. Mary and Jane Williams read it the next day and started at once for Leghorn with despair in their hearts. They stopped a moment at the Casa Lanfranchi to question Byron, but he knew nothing.

At two in the morning they wakened Roberts in Leghorn and got his story. Trelawny accompanied the ladies back to the Casa Magni, inquiring along the coast as they went. A little boat and a water cask from the *Don Juan* had been found, but they might have been cast over in the storm. Byron gave Roberts free use of the *Bolivar* and joined Hunt in the search along the coast.

On the 16th of July, two bodies were washed ashore near Viareggio. On the 18th another was found and Trelawny arrived in time to identify it before the authorities buried it in the sand. "I knew [it] to be Shelley's which the Poem of Lamia and Isabella open in his jackett Pocket confirmed beyond a doubt. . . ."[n] Trelawny carried the news to the Casa Magni and then took the widows back to Pisa.

The death of Shelley made a greater impact on Byron than he expected. The blow was the more stunning perhaps because he felt a certain remorse for not having appreciated Shelley's qualities of friendship sufficiently and because of his own irritability during Shelley's last visit to Pisa. Although he had never had any strong feeling of accord for Mary, he tried now to make amends by extending every kindness to her. Mary told Maria Gisborne: "Lord Byron is very kind to me & comes with the Guiccioli to see me often."[n]

In reporting the tragedy to Murray, Byron said: "You were all brutally mistaken about Shelley, who was, without exception, the *best* and least selfish man I ever knew. I never knew one who was not a beast in comparison."[n] And to Moore he wrote: "There is thus another man gone, about whom the world was ill-naturedly, and ignorantly, and brutally mistaken. It will, perhaps, do him justice *now,* when he can be no better for it."[n]

Hunt was fully aware that the journal's future and his own were very precarious after the death of Shelley, who had been the catalyst in its conception. Byron asked him to look upon him "as standing in Mr. Shelley's place," but Hunt knew the venture was doomed. "My heart died within me," he wrote. In spite of his conscious intention to be kind to Hunt both because of his promise to Shelley and because Hunt had stood by him, during the unpleasantness of the separation, Byron could not help feeling irritated by the dependence of Hunt on him at a time when he wished to be free to leave Tuscany. This feeling was aggravated by Hunt's half-fawning, half-arrogant manner, and by the knowledge that his friends in England did not approve of the alliance with the "Cockney poet." Acutely proud, Hunt sensed this under Byron's most friendly advances. Even so, their relations might have been less strained had it not been for the Hunt family. When Trelawny first called on them, he found the children, ranging in age from thirteen to a crawling infant, "scattered about playing on the large marble staircase and in the hall. Hunt's theory and practice were that children should be unrestrained until they were of an age to be reasoned with." When Trelawny took his leave, Byron followed him into the passage, "and patting the bull-dog on the head he said, 'Don't let any Cockneys pass this way.' " [n]

Byron later referred to the Hunt children as little Yahoos. But when he complained of their marring the walls with their grimy fingers, Mrs. Hunt recorded in her diary: "Mr. Hunt was much annoyed by Lord Byron behaving so meanly about the Children disfiguring his house which his nobleship chose to be very severe upon. . . . Can anything be more absurd than a peer of the realm—and a *poet* making such a fuss about three or four children disfiguring the walls of a few rooms—the very children would blush for him, fye Lord B.—fye." [n]

But, despite the uneasy truce that existed in the Casa Lanfranchi and the uncertainty of the future, Byron continued through July and August the rapid composition of three new cantos of *Don Juan*. He saw his verse tale now as

> *A nondescript and ever-varying rhyme,*
> *A versified Aurora Borealis,*
> *Which flashes o'er a waste and icy clime.*
> *When we know what all are, we must bewail us,*
> *But ne'ertheless I hope it is no crime*
> *To laugh at* all *things—for I wish to know*
> What, *after* all, *are* all *things—but a* show? [n]

Trelawny, in accordance with the wishes of Mary Shelley, had been negotiating with the health authorities to remove Shelley's remains for burial in the Protestant Cemetery in Rome beside his son William. He finally got permission to cremate the bodies of Shelley and Williams on the beach and then remove the ashes. Trelawny took a certain grim pleasure in preparing for this pagan rite. When Byron and Hunt arrived at Viareggio at noon on August 15, the gruesome business of uncovering the corpse of Williams began. The mutilated body was dragged with boat hooks to the surface of the sand. According to Trelawny, Byron identified him by his teeth. "Lord B. looking at it said—'Are we to resemble that?—why it might be the carcase of a sheep for all I can see'—and pointing to the black handkerchief—said 'an old rag retains its form longer than a dead body—what a nauseous and degrading sight!' "[n]

Byron swam out about a mile from the shore and was seized with a violent sickness. When he returned, Trelawny, who had saved a portion of the jaw bone that had not burned, put the ashes in a box which he gave to Byron to carry to Pisa in his carriage.

The next day the same ceremony was performed for Shelley. Trelawny wanted to preserve the volume of Keats's *Lamia* that had been buried with him, but nothing remained save the leather binding. After he started the fire under the corpse, Trelawny cast oil and spices on the flame while uttering incantations. Trelawny wrote: "Byron, who was standing by my side, said: 'I knew you were a Pagan, not that you were a Pagan Priest; you do it very well.' "[n]

Hunt, who could not bear to witness the gruesome scene, remained in the carriage, and Byron soon wandered away and swam out to the *Bolivar*. When he returned, he found the body consumed by the fire except for the heart, which would not burn. Trelawny preserved it among his relics, later giving it to Hunt, who, after some quarreling, passed it on to Mary. Trelawny placed the ashes in a box and sealed it. Then they all went in the carriage to Viareggio, where, apparently overcome by the two days of fascinating horror, they dined and drank heavily before returning to Pisa. Hunt recalled: "The barouche drove rapidly through the forest of Pisa. We sang, we laughed, we shouted. I even felt a gaiety the more shocking, because it was real and a relief."[n] It is not surprising that Byron was ill. But apparently he suffered more from exposure to the sun than from wine. He had a painful sunburn. Teresa saved the blistered skin that came from his shoulder and arms, and it was among her Byron "relics" when she died many years later.

In the meantime, plans for the new journal were going

forward. Despite some touchiness on Hunt's part, the relations of the partners were outwardly agreeable and at times even cordial. Byron had first suggested the title *Hesperides*, but when the first number appeared, it had been changed to *The Liberal*. Except for Byron's contributions—*The Vision of Judgment*, 'A Letter to the Editor of 'My Grandmother's Review,' " and "Epigrams on Lord Castlereagh"—Hunt wrote most of the first number himself. Byron had tried to get contributions from Moore, but he and other English friends felt that Byron was damaging his reputation by entering this "Unholy Alliance" with "Cockneys."

Possibly in irritation at Moore's refusal, Byron suggested that Hunt turn Moore's *Loves of the Angels* into an exemplification of the joke in his article on "Rhyme and Reason," a facetious proposal that modern versifiers omit all but their rhymes. Seeing that Hunt appreciated that type of wit at Moore's expense, he took delight in repeating it. "And then he would retreat a little, doubling himself up in his peculiar manner, and uttering a kind of goblin laugh, breathing and grinning, as if, instead of his handsome mouth, he had one like an ogre, from ear to ear. Then came the inevitable addition,—'But mind, you must not publish. You know I'm his *friend*.' " And referring to Moore's snobbishness, he would exclaim: "Do but give Tom a good dinner, and a lord . . . and he is at the top of his happiness. Oh . . . TOMMY *loves* a Lord!" " But Byron was just as prone to utter such unmasked truths about his other friends. In his letters to England he did not spare Hunt when annoyed or bored by him.

Beneath the tranquil surface of the life at the Casa Lanfranchi there were anxieties that made Byron dissatisfied with his situation. The Gambas had taken a large house in Genoa for him and expected him and Teresa to join them there, where the government allowed them to live in peace. He would of course move in due time, but he had no idea of making that a permanent residence. Only escape from Italy, he felt, could save him from the narrowing existence which circumstances had forced upon him. Although the domesticated life he had been living with Teresa had begun to bore him a little, he was still fond of her. Schemes for escape accounted for his growing concern over his financial affairs in England and for his parsimony. But he assured his banker, Kinnaird, "my avarice—or cupidity—is *not* selfish—for my *table* don't cost four shillings a day—and except horses and helping all kinds of patriots—(I have long given up *costly* harlotry) I have no violent expences—but I want to get a sum together to go amongst the Greeks or Americans—and do some good. . . ." [n]

Yet he could be generous in larger ways. He wanted to provide for Teresa now that she had lost her allowance from her husband on his account. And he wanted to make a codicil to his will leaving her a substantial amount, but she became hysterical and absolutely refused, not wanting to think of his death, and no doubt suspecting that his motive was a desire to leave Italy, and her.

Mary Shelley departed for Genoa on September 11. Byron, Teresa, and the Hunts were to follow shortly. Almost all the Pisan circle was now gone. Trelawny was at Leghorn, ready to pilot the *Bolivar* to Genoa. Medwin returned to Pisa and remained about ten days. He found Byron sitting with Teresa in the shade of the orange trees in the garden of the Casa Lanfranchi. "He calls her *Piccinina,* and bestows on her all the pretty diminutive epithets that are so sweet in Italian. . . . A three years' constancy proves that he is not altogether so unmanageable by a sensible woman as might be supposed. . . . His spirits are good, except when he speaks of Shelley and Williams." [n]

Medwin noted: "He has almost discontinued his rides on horseback, and has starved himself into an unnatural thinness. . . ." [n] To keep up his stamina, Medwin observed, he drank a pint of gin every night and indulged more freely than usual in wine.

While Byron was in the midst of preparations for moving, Hobhouse arrived on September 15. He had not seen his friend since they parted in Venice in January 1818. Teresa, whom Hobhouse described condescendingly as "a tolerably good looking woman," observed the emotion of Byron on the reunion. "A fearful paleness came over his cheeks, and his eyes were filled with tears as he embraced his friend. His emotion was so great that he was forced to sit down." [n] Still it was difficult for them to get back on their old footing. The presence of Hunt in the house increased Hobhouse's stiffness, for he disapproved of Byron's alliance with Hunt, whom he considered a "legacy" left by Shelley. "He is much changed," Hobhouse noted, "his face fatter and the expression of it injured—For the rest I saw little difference —we were both a little formal." [n] It was perhaps during this visit that Byron turned on Hobhouse suddenly and said: "Now, I know, Hobhouse, you are looking at my foot." Hobhouse, knowing his sensitivity, retorted: "My dear Byron, nobody thinks of or looks at anything but your head." [n]

After a day or two, however, they both thawed and their old ease of manner and friendliness returned. Byron confessed that Hobhouse's letter on *Cain* had made him almost insane. Among the Scherzi of Byron's conversation Hobhouse recorded the witticism that "Cain was right to kill Abel that he might not have the bore of passing 200 years with him." Before Hobhouse left, Byron grew serious again. "He told me he found he had less feeling than usually in his younger days." [n] Hobhouse, grown Parliamentary and cautious, warned him against publishing his epigrams on Castlereagh's death. And Byron parted with his oldest friend with emotion.

When the actual time for moving came, Byron was not in a very happy mood. Everything had gone wrong, and he felt old. The bust that Bartolini had finally completed was a great disappointment. He told Murray: ". . . it may be like for aught I know, as it exactly resembles a superannuated Jesuit." [n]

Byron left in the Napoleonic coach that had carried him to Italy in 1816, accompanied by two other carriages. Hunt and his family rode in another as far as Lerici, and Byron's servants and freight in a felucca from Leghorn. Trelawny pulled into Lerici in the *Bolivar* with Byron's books, papers, and plate. Byron's menagerie included three large geese, which he had intended to eat on Michaelmas Day; but growing fond of them, he spared their lives and carried them in a swinging cage behind the coach.

Teresa's father and brother joined the caravan at Lucca, and the whole party met the Hunts and Trelawny at Lerici. Byron and Trelawny swam three miles to the *Bolivar* anchored in the bay. They were to turn about without boarding and head for the shore, but Byron became violently ill and was seized with a cramp. He would not give up, however, and after resting a few minutes on the ladder of the schooner he swam back in the boiling sun. As a result, he was confined to his bed for four days "in 'the worst inn's worst room,' at Lerici, with a violent rheumatic and bilious attack, constipation, and the devil knows what. . . ."[n]

When Trelawny asked him how he felt, he exclaimed: " 'Feel! why just as that damned obstreperous fellow felt chained to a rock, the vultures gnawing my midriff, and vitals too, for I have no liver.' As the spasms returned, he roared out, 'I don't care for dying, but I cannot bear this! It's past joking, call Fletcher; give me something that will end it—or me!'"[n] Fletcher brought ether and laudanum, which relieved the pain. On the fifth day Byron was weak but able to go on.

To avoid the land journey over the rougher Apennines, they went by boat, Byron and Teresa in one, the Hunts in another, and Trelawny cutting along in the *Bolivar*. The carriages were taken on board the feluccas. "The Sea revived me instantly," Byron wrote; "and I ate the Sailor's cold fish, and drank a Gallon of Country Wine, and got to Genoa the same night after landing at Sestri. . . ."[n]

It was late at night when the carriage, with the cackling geese hanging in their cage behind, rolled into the yard of the palatial Casa Saluzzo on a hill in Albaro high above the harbor of Genoa. Weary and still weak from his illness, Byron was beginning a new life in Italy, his fourth and last residence there. The spy Torelli recorded with some relief when Byron left Pisa: "Lord Byron has finally decided to leave for Genoa. It is said that he is already sated or tired of his Favorite, the Guiccioli. He has, however, expressed his intention of not remaining in Genoa, but of going on to Athens in order to make himself adored by the Greeks. . . ."[n]

CHAPTER XXVI

1822–1823

Exile in Genoa

THE BACK ROOMS OF the Casa Saluzzo looked out on a walled garden. The tall square stone building had a four-sided French roof, a high-ceilinged drawing room, and enough space so that the Gambas could have an apartment separate from Byron's. For it he paid only £24 a year, an item of importance in his economizing mood. Fortunately the Hunts were to share with Mary Shelley the Casa Negroto, a mile down the hill, so that Byron and Teresa were spared the strain of being under the disapproving eyes of the moral Marianne and her brood.

Shortly after arriving, Byron wrote Mary that he had purchased a sofa that had belonged to Shelley in Pisa. "I have a particular dislike to anything of Shelley's being within the same walls with Mrs. Hunt's children. They are dirtier and more mischievous than Yahoos. What they can't destroy with their filth they will with their fingers. . . . With regard to any difficulties about money, I can only repeat that I will be your banker till this state of things is cleared up, and you can see what is to be done [Mary had applied to Shelley's father for support for her child]. . . . Poor Hunt, with his six little blackguards, are coming slowly up . . . was there ever such a *kraal* out of the Hottentot country." [n]

Before he had been a week in his new house, Byron could announce to Murray that he had completed the tenth canto of *Don Juan* and had begun the eleventh. He had now carried Juan to England, and that gave him renewed enthusiasm for the poem. Despite his quarrel with Murray, he still hoped that some arrangement could be made for its publication. But Murray was already chagrined by the order Byron had given to turn over his manuscripts to John Hunt. Leigh's older brother, publisher of *The Liberal*, had apparently taken some liberties at Murray's on the authority of his new alliance with Byron.

Byron now saw less of Hunt, and saw him only at the Casa Saluzzo. Hunt could never quite strike the right note with Byron. He was either attempting to show his independence by some forced jocosity, or he was too stiff and deferential. He tried to cover his embarrassment when he asked for money by a tactless mock-arrogance. On October 24 he wrote: "I must trouble you for another 'cool hundred' of your crowns, & shall speedily, I fear, come upon you for one more. . . ."[n] And when Byron addressed him on occasion as "My dear Leigh," Hunt descended to the bathos of familiarity: "You make me affectionate when you call me Leigh, & so I feel lady-like, & insist upon your coming to *my* house."[n]

The first number of *The Liberal* was published on October 15. *The Vision of Judgment*, which stood boldly as the leading contribution, had been published without the preface in which Byron gave his reasons for attacking Southey. Byron, encouraged by the Hunts to believe that Murray had failed to turn over the preface from malice or jealousy, determined to sever his publishing connections with Murray and withdraw all his manuscripts. He wrote to Kinnaird: "I am . . . not at all sorry to be rid of him, for he was a sad shuffler."[n] Leigh Hunt gleefully told his brother: "Poor Murray is indeed in a deplorable state. . . . He writes to Lord B. how delighted he should be, if his Lordship would but be '*so nobly generous*' as to let him publish works of his 'former glorious description' (admire the invincible impudence lurking at bottom of this adulation); and he adds, in another letter, *that he sits of a morning, for hours, looking at his Lordship's picture!* Imagine the languishing bookseller."[n]

Murray was not slow to let Byron know what was said of the periodical and Byron's connection with it in England, and to plead with him to cease his association with "such outcasts from Society." He continued: "Mr. Kinnaird sent me the 3 Cantos of Don Juan. . . . I declare to you they were so outrageously shocking that I would not publish them if you were to give me your

Estate—Title and Genius—For Heaven's sake revise them—they are equal in talent to any thing you have written—it is therefore well worth while to extract what would shock the feeling of every man in the country and do your name everlasting injury—My company used to be courted for the pleasure of talking about you—it is totally the reverse now—and by a re-action even your former works are considerably deteriorated in sale. It is impossible for you to have a more purely attached friend than I am—My name is connected with your Fame and I beseech you take care of it even for your sister's sake—for we are in constant alarm but she should be deprived of her situation about Court—Do let us have your good humour again and put Juan in the tone of Beppo."[n]

Byron replied with considered firmness: "I shall withdraw from you as a publisher, on every account, even on your own, and I wish you good luck elsewhere. . . ."[n] More trouble ensued when Murray passed around what Byron had said of Hunt and the gossip came back garbled to Leigh. Byron then confessed to Hunt the major part of what he had said, and the latter had to make the best he could of the situation, for he was dependent on Byron's support in the periodical. But Byron never learned discretion. He continued to speak his mind about Hunt to Murray, for the habit of frankness had grown with his long residence in Italy, and despite his quarrel with Murray and his general annoyance at the publisher's timidity and neglect of him, he could not but recognize that he had a closer understanding with Murray than with Hunt.

He upbraided Murray for showing his letter about Hunt, but added: " . . . I confess I did not see anything in the letter to hurt him, unless I said he was 'a bore,' . . . As to any community of feeling, thought, or opinion, between L.H. and me, there is little or none . . . but I think him a good principled and able man, and must do as I would be done by. . . . Alas! poor Shelley! how he would have laughed had he lived, and how we used to laugh now and then, at various things, which are grave in the Suburbs!"[n]

It was no doubt the memory of Shelley that governed Byron's kindness to Mary, for he had little in common with her. He gave her financial aid by hiring her to make clean copies of some of the new cantos of *Don Juan,* which she found an agreeable task, and he asked Hanson to try through Sir Timothy Shelley's solicitor to secure some provision for the maintenance of Mary and her son. Byron's voice charmed Mary, reviving memories of another voice that was stilled. She wrote in her journal: "I do not think that any person's voice has the same power of awakening melancholy in me as Albè's. . . . and I listen with an unspeakable melancholy that yet is not all pain." [n]

Byron had no sooner settled into a routine in Genoa than he began thinking of various roads of escape. Trelawny observed: "The under-current of his mind was always drifting towards the East. . . . his thoughts veered round to his early love, the Isles of Greece, and the revolution in that country. . . ." [n] It was with a view to some such project that he saved his money. He hoped to have £9,000 or £10,000 free and available by the 1st of the year. He chafed at the expense of the *Bolivar,* and Trelawny put her up for the winter. Byron talked of buying an island in the Greek Archipelago or a principality in Chile or Peru. According to Trelawny, "He exhausted himself in planning, projecting, beginning, wishing, intending, postponing, regretting, and doing nothing. . . ." [n] And so Trelawny started out on horseback for a hunting expedition in the Maremma.

During the autumn Byron was reminded of England by two visitors. One was the silly and eccentric James Wedderburn Webster, whose wife, Lady Frances, now separated from him, had been the object of Byron's serio-comic flirtation in 1813, when "Platonism" was imperiled but not lost. Webster was now paying persistent and unwanted court to Lady Hardy, wife of Nelson's Admiral Hardy. Lady Hardy, who had met Byron in London in 1814, had called on him in Genoa and told him something of this ludicrous suit. He was delighted to meet again an amiable and intelligent English woman to whom it was not necessary for him to make love. He wrote her jestingly about Webster and then added more seriously: "I have always laid it down as a maxim—and found it justified by experience—that a man and woman can make far better friendships than can exist between two of the same sex, but *then* with this condition that they never have made or are to make love with each other. . . . Indeed I rather look on love as a sort of hostile transaction, very necessary to make or to break in order to keep the world agoing, but by no means a sinecure to the parties concerned." [n]

Some frank comments of Webster on his appearance may have accounted in part for the thinning regime Byron followed rather strictly during the autumn and winter. He was forced to watch his diet too because of the aftereffects of his illness at Lerici. He rode when the weather permitted, but it was a dreary winter in the stone house with its high ceilings and cold floors. He dined out rarely, with Mr. Hill, the British Envoy, or with the congenial banker Charles F. Barry, the Genoa partner of Webb & Co., who had handled his affairs in Leghorn.

His relations with Teresa were not strained, but she must have sensed a certain aloofness in him that gave her occasional pain. She did not intrude upon him except by invitation, and he preferred to eat alone, especially when he was dieting. When the weather permitted, they walked together in the garden. There may have been times when Teresa could have wished for a more active life. She was still only twenty-three, but her Byron was nearing thirty-five, and in experience felt himself seventy. Teresa had made her choice, however, and was not sorry for it. She fitted herself into his routine and saw him when he wished.

Despite his near quarrel with Byron, Hunt had sent off early in December the copy for the second number of *The Liberal.* Byron had ordered Murray to deliver all manuscripts still in his hands to Hunt, but Murray had already printed two thousand copies of *Werner* and *Heaven and Earth* together. Fearing that he would have another *Cain* on his hands with the latter poem, he then sacrificed the dual publication and hastily published *Werner,* turning the more dangerous poem over to Hunt. *Werner,* based on a German melodrama, but with Byronic characters, soon sold six thousand copies. Byron did not care, and Hunt was glad to have *Heaven and Earth* as a head piece in the second number of his periodical.

When news arrived that John Hunt was being prosecuted for publishing *The Vision of Judgment,* Byron came to his assistance by offering legal aid and expressing a willingness to go to England himself to stand trial if it were necessary. But he wrote to Hobhouse: " . . . all you predicted has come to pass. I have gotten myself into a scrape with the very best intentions (*i.e.,* to do good to those Sunday paper patriots)." [n]

And Byron got into more difficulty with the best of intentions. Mrs. Mason (Lady Mountcashell), a friend of the Shelleys in Pisa, who had encouraged Claire's schemes for the rescue of Allegra from the convent, now appealed directly to Byron for some support for Claire, who had lost her place in Vienna because of rumors connected with her past. Although her letter rubbed him the wrong way with its appeal to his "better nature" and emphasis on his obligations and duties, he might have been willing to help Claire if it could have been done without encouraging her correspondence. In the end he intimated to Mary that if she sent money to Claire without involving him in it, he would reimburse her whenever she needed it. Mary was piqued. She wrote to Jane Williams, who had returned to England: " . . . he has made frequent offers—but it will be a peculiar & most temporary necessity indeed that would make me *borrow* from him—For there after all is the string—it is a loan to me, a gift to C—."[n]

But Byron probably thought she understood his desire not to act directly in anything involving Claire. His readiness to reimburse her seemed to him sufficient evidence of his generosity. He was aware that she would be in possession of a considerable fortune on the death of Sir Timothy Shelley. He would not lay a burden upon her independence by offering her money except in the guise of a loan. He had made loans to many friends which he never expected to be repaid.

It may be that the psychological crux of Mary's pique, the unacknowledged basis of her feeling that Byron was "heartless," was that in her deepest being she wished that he might have been something more to her than a friend. This may have accounted for the condescending pity with which she viewed Byron's enslavement to Teresa. Mary wrote to Jane Williams: "He is kept in excellent order, quarreled with & hen pecked to his heart's content."[n] Perhaps if Mary had had less of this feeling she would have been more willing to call on Byron for help and less touchy concerning the manner in which it was offered.

Byron's thirty-fifth birthday brought only sobering reflections and was attended by illness and abstinence. If he thought wistfully from time to time of past pleasures, he was rather glad than sorry that the drive to indulgence had largely left him. On January 18, four days before his birthday, he wrote to Kinnaird: "I always looked to about thirty as the barrier of any real or fierce delight in the passions, and determined to work them out in the younger ore and better veins of the mine, and I flatter myself (perhaps) that I have pretty well done so, and now the *dross* is coming and I *loves lucre*. For we must love something." [n]

Dr. James Alexander, an English physician residing in Genoa, used to visit Byron frequently and noticed his disconsolate temper during the winter. His morbid sensitiveness to his lameness had not subsided with age and maturity, and it added to his touchiness. He flushed when the doctor glanced at his foot, but another time in confidence he discussed it openly, saying, "That foot has been the bane of my life." And he confessed that he had once gone to London, probably while he was at Harrow, to have it amputated, but the doctor would not perform the operation. Dr. Alexander observed his deep-seated dissatisfaction with his life. Byron used to say that "a man ought to do something more for mankind than write verses." [n]

And yet he continued writing. *The Age of Bronze* was an attempt to deal in a Juvenalian manner with the decadence of the post-Napoleonic world, while *The Island*, based on accounts of the mutiny on the *Bounty*, was a vicarious escape to the South Seas and a world of noble savages. He gave both to John Hunt for publication, but not for *The Liberal*, from which he wished to withdraw without doing damage to the Hunts. He tried to convince himself and the publisher and editor that, because of his growing unpopularity, his connection with the periodical would drag it down. But John Hunt knew that anything of Byron's would keep it going; if it was attacked, it was read. Now he saw that it was doomed and he hoped to salvage what he could from the works Byron permitted him to publish. Leigh was more desperate, for he was wholly dependent on the journal. Byron was eager to get out of the partnership, though he felt a responsibility to Hunt and his family. He wrote Moore: "I cannot describe to you the despairing sensation of trying to do something for a man who seems incapable or unwilling to do any thing further for himself,—at least, to the purpose. It is like pulling a man out of a river who directly throws himself in again." [n]

The routine of Byron's life was interrupted only occasionally by conviviality, and when it was, he usually regretted it, for in his skeleton thinness he could not stand much strain on his constitution. He was content to spend his evenings at his desk.

By the end of March he had finished and sent to Kinnaird the fifteenth canto of *Don Juan,* making ten new ones altogether. He had not yet stipulated a publisher, but he finally entered into a profit-sharing arrangement with John Hunt.

Byron's social life was livened at the beginning of April by the arrival in Genoa of some English visitors. One was Henry Fox, Lord Holland's son, whom he had always liked, partly because he was lame. But some other visitors who arrived about the same time and stayed longer succeeded in stirring Byron from his lethargy. These were "the most gorgeous Lady Blessington," née Margaret Power, and her train, consisting of her husband, the wealthy dilettante Earl of Blessington, her sister Mary Ann Power, and their handsome young friend and traveling companion, Count Alfred D'Orsay.

The Countess, a year younger than Byron, was in the prime of her life. Without apparent warping of her personality, she had triumphed over the poverty and the brutalizing environment of her childhood and early youth, and by sheer beauty, grace, and intellectual charm had won a place in London society that made her house at 10 St. James's Square a rival of Holland House in drawing men of ability and wit. The painter Lawrence had heightened his own fame with a portrait of her that was the sensation of the Royal Exhibition in 1821, a likeness that had given currency to the epithet "most gorgeous," first applied to her by the famous Dr. Parr.

It is possible that the horrible experience of her early marriage in Ireland to Captain Farmer, to whom her father literally sold her at the age of fifteen, "permanently diverted her sexual impulses into another channel," [n] as her biographer has said. If we accept this interpretation it can be argued that her feminine sensibilities, her perceptions and sympathies, had been heightened, while the energies that other beautiful women spent in coquetry she devoted to intellectual pursuits and a detached but not cold observation of life and character. It is probable, however, that her success in pleasing men had been based on qualities less ethereal, for she confessed that for a number of years she had been "a kept mistress." [n]

It is not surprising then that Lady Blessington should have made an impression on Byron, greater perhaps than he would admit. She had an aristocratic bearing less self-conscious than

Byron's own. And he, for his part, could look upon her with unpossessive eyes, although he was always attracted by beauty. Lord Blessington too he soon came to value for his own sake as well as his lady's. Byron found him something more than a dilettante, for he had taste and judgment and sensitivity.

As for Count D'Orsay, he had just the qualities of the beautiful boy (Byron later said he had "the air of a *Cupidon déchaîné*")[n] and of the unaffected dandy to please him. Despite the seeming *ménage à trois*, it is probable that the friendship between D'Orsay and Lady Blessington, which continued throughout her life, was as Platonic on his side as on hers. It is perhaps significant that Byron, who had put horns on a number of husbands and was quick to perceive the situation, did not see any on the Earl's brow.

The "Blessington Circus" arrived at the Albergo della Villa at Genoa on the evening of March 31. The day before, Lady Blessington had recorded in her diary: "Desirous as I am to see 'Genoa the Superb' . . . I confess that its being the residence of Lord Byron gives it a still greater attraction for me."[n] But, like so many others, she had expected to see Childe Harold, and was disappointed. "He is witty, sarcastic, and lively enough . . . but he does not look like my preconceived notion of the melancholy poet. . . . His hair has already much of silver among its dark brown curls; its texture is very silky, and although it retreats from his temples, leaving his forehead very bare, its growth at the sides and back of his head is abundant. . . . He is so exceedingly thin, that his figure has an almost boyish air; and yet there is something so striking in his whole appearance, that could not be mistaken for an ordinary person. . . . I do not think that I should have observed his lameness, had my attention not been called to it by his own visible consciousness of this infirmity. . . . His voice and accent are particularly clear and harmonious, but somewhat effeminate. . . . His laugh is musical. . . ."[n]

When Byron called at their hotel the next day, the frankness of his conversation rather shocked and titillated the Countess. She was startled by "the perfect *abandon* with which he converses to recent acquaintances, on subjects which even friends would think too delicate for discussion."[n] She was shrewd enough to observe that Byron's censure of England and the English was an indication of his nostalgic interest in it. She recorded with gusto his strictures on their mutual friend Moore, and with even more delight what he said of Lady Holland. She had seen enough of the hypocritical moral superiority of women in Whig society to relish his comment on English *cant*. " . . . he says, that the best mode left for conquering it, is to expose it to *ridicule*, the only *weapon*, added he, that the English climate cannot rust." [n]

Byron's interest in the Greek revolution was kindled anew by a visit from Captain Edward Blaquiere, representing the London Greek Committee, of which Hobhouse was a member. He was accompanying Andreas Luriottis, a delegate of the Greek government who had gone to London to seek English aid for the cause. Byron immediately offered to go up to the seat of the newly formed Greek government in July if they thought he could be of any use. But he realized that there were obstacles. " . . . you may imagine that the 'absurd womankind,' as Monkbarns [in Scott's *Antiquary*] calls them, are by no means favourable to such an enterprise. Madame Guiccioli is of course, and naturally enough, opposed to my quitting her; though but for a few months; and as she had influence enough to prevent my return to England in 1819, she may be not less successful in detaining me from Greece in 1823." [n] Nevertheless the Greek scheme absorbed Byron's thoughts more and more. He began inquiries through his banker Charles Barry concerning a vessel to take him to Greece, and he asked Kinnaird to gather his resources for the expedition. But still he did not have the courage to tell Teresa of the plans that were going forward, for he wanted to postpone the scene it would provoke.

The Blessingtons and Count D'Orsay at first somewhat overawed Byron, for they possessed a suavity and ease in society which he had never achieved. Lady Blessington still observed him critically and was on her guard against the flippancy of his tongue, which she had already seen in action on absent friends. He spoke "in terms of high commendation of the talents and acquirements of Mr. Hobhouse; but a latent sentiment of pique was visible in his manner, from the idea he appeared to entertain that Mr. Hobhouse had undervalued him." The "frankness and unbending honesty" of his friend he could praise with enthusiasm, but still the friendship did not warm him as did others, for "he always told me my faults, but I must do him the justice to add, that he told them to *me*, and not to others." [n]

The Countess, like Trelawny, discovered that Byron was best in a *tête-à-tête* with someone with whom he could "think aloud." He said: "An animated conversation has much the same effect on me as champaigne—it elevates and makes me giddy. . . ." [n] When the Countess made some deprecating remark about scandal, Byron replied: "All subjects are good in their way, provided they are sufficiently diversified; but scandal has something so piquant,—it is a sort of cayenne to the mind,—that I confess I like it, particularly if the objects are one's particular friends." [n]

Despite her wariness, Lady Blessington was charmed by Byron's kindness and his attentions. She noticed his charity and the gentleness of his manners to the people he met on his rides. They "seem all to know his face, and to like him; and many recount their affairs, as if they were sure of his sympathy." [n] The key to his inconsistencies, she felt, was his extreme "mobility," his sensitivity to present impressions and his acting on the impulse of the moment and saying what came uppermost in his mind. He regaled the Countess with his ideas and prejudices about women with the same frankness that he had displayed on other matters. "Talking of thin women, he said, that if they were young and pretty, they reminded him of dried butterflies; but if neither, of spiders, whose nets would never catch him were he a fly, as they had nothing tempting." [n] It was a view that was not disturbing to the Countess, for she had ample fleshly endowments. On another occasion he said: "Now, my *beau idéal* would be a woman with talent enough to be able to understand and value mine, but not sufficient to be able to shine herself." [n]

Like many others Lady Blessington was baffled by Byron's dual personality. She was perhaps herself too lacking in "mobility" to believe that he was sincere in both his sentimental and his cynical expressions, that his ineffable longings and his ironic recognition of the unideal nature of the world and himself were but two sides of the same coin. "The day after he has awakened the deepest interest his manner of scoffing at himself and others destroys it," she complained, "and one feels as if one had been duped into a sympathy, only to be laughed at." [n]

Byron warned her: "People take for gospel all I say, and go

away continually with false impressions. . . . Now, if I know myself, I should say, that I have no character at all. . . . But, joking apart, what I think of myself is, that I am so changeable, being everything by turns and nothing long,—I am such a strange *mélange* of good and evil, that it would be difficult to describe me. There are but two sentiments to which I am constant,—a strong love of liberty, and a detestation of cant, and neither is calculated to gain me friends." [n]

His frequent rides with Lady Blessington soon caused Teresa to believe that her *amico* had fallen in love with the English aristocrat. Byron wrote Lady Hardy that Teresa "was seized with a furious fit of Italian jealousy and was as unreasonable and perverse as can well be imagined. God He knows she paid me the greatest compliment, for what little communication I had with this new Goddess of Discord was literally literary, and besides that, I have long come to years of discretion and would much rather fall into the sea than in Love any day of the week." [n]

In the meantime, Byron had heard from Blaquiere and Luriottis, who were both eager for him to go to Greece. And Hobhouse wrote that Byron had been elected a member of the London Greek Committee, and added: "Your proposition was received with unanimous gratitude and delight." [n] Pietro Gamba, Mary Shelley observed, was "half mad with joy at the idea," but Byron, though equally attracted, was slower to move.

He liked routine and was annoyed by any infringement on his habitual ways. Yet Mary Shelley was perceptive enough to see that the object before him was now great enough to move him, though she realized that the Guiccioli was an obstacle. "But he does not seem disposed to make a mountain of her resistance; and he is far more able to take a decided than a petty step in contradiction to the wishes of those about him." [n] He put off from day to day telling Teresa of his plans. He felt in turn sad and angry that his weakness would not let him speak to her frankly about his desire to go. He knew from past experience that her tears could melt his resolution. In the end he left it to Pietro to break the news to her, but that did not soften the blow. "To her a death-sentence would have seemed less terrible." [n] Byron did not make matters easier by suggesting that her husband would forgive her, as he told Hobhouse, "provided that I (a very reasonable condition) did not continue his Sub-agent. . . ."[n]

He wrote to Kinnaird in the same vein: "She wants to go up to Greece too! forsooth, a precious place to go to at present! . . . There never was a man who gave up so much to women, and all I have gained by it has been the character of treating them harshly."[n] His depression of spirits at leaving her was genuine, however, as she recognized. He had only half expressed his feelings to Hobhouse and Kinnaird. On the one hand, he was bored with the life he had been leading and wanted to get away. And the only way to do that, he knew, was to break the ties that had bound him by habit and a factitious domesticity to a woman whose exigent emotional demands he now could match only with kindly half-paternal feelings.

On the other hand, he felt a genuine regret, compounded of a nostalgic sense of the loss of the passion he had experienced and a knowledge of the devotion she gave him and the pain he must cause her. He could face it only by being brusque and casual, and neither action was suited to his nature. In "talking aloud" to Lady Blessington, he revealed much of what was on his mind and the extent to which he was conscious of doing Teresa an injury that he could not avoid: " . . . I am sincerely attached to her; but the truth is, my habits are not those requisite to form the happiness of any woman: I am worn out in feelings; for, though only thirty-six [*sic*], I feel sixty in mind, and am less capable than ever of those nameless attentions that all women, but, above all, Italian women, require. I like solitude, which has become absolutely necessary to me. . . . There is something I am convinced . . . in the poetical temperament that precludes happiness, not only to the person who has it, but to those connected with him."[n] And yet he told Lady Blessington: "Were the Contessa Guiccioli and I married, we should, I am sure, be cited as an example of conjugal happiness. . . ."[n]

His sense of guilt at leaving Teresa made Byron again attempt to make some compensation to her by tangible means when all she wanted was the intangible knowledge of his affection. One day, bringing her a great bundle of his manuscripts which Murray had sent back to him, he said, " . . . perhaps some day they may be prized!"[n] Byron was right—when sold in later years they brought tremendous prices.*

Byron's contradictory views of his Greek venture puzzled Lady Blessington. He had first talked in noble terms of it; then he made sport of his own heroic gesture, with a half-serious archness. And frequently he spoke of his presentiment that he would die in Greece. "I hope it may be in action, for that would be a good finish to a very *triste* existence, and I have a horror to death-bed scenes. . . ."[n]

He was chagrined when the Blessingtons announced their intention to leave Genoa at the end of May. His rides with them had become a necessary part of his existence. They had revived for him some of his pleasantest memories of his heyday in England. He even expressed a wish to return there before going to Greece, but was deterred by what he imagined might be the disagreeable circumstances of his return, including a duel or two he had promised himself with some of his enemies such as Brougham and Southey.

Before the Blessingtons left for Naples, there were sentimental expressions on both sides. The Countess gave up her favorite Arabian horse Mameluke for Byron to take to Greece, though she was put out because he haggled at the price; and she persuaded the Earl to buy Byron's yacht, the *Bolivar* (which he delayed a long time in paying for). At the farewell party tears were shed, by the Countess, according to Teresa, but Lady Blessington transferred them to Byron in her account.

After they left, Byron began serious preparations for his voyage. Toward the end of May he received a letter of credit for £4,000 from Kinnaird, which, with £2,000 already in his hands, he thought would be enough for his current purposes. He had already begun to make purchases for the cause. Through Dr. Alexander he bought medical stores "for 1000 men, for two years." From Zante Blaquiere urged him to come. And now Byron felt the need of that old adventurer Trelawny, who had spent his youth in Eastern seas and who knew his way about a

---

* Whether they were sold in Teresa's lifetime is not known, but Teresa, and Byron, too, would have been astounded by the prices some of his manuscripts brought in the Jerome Kern sale in 1929 (Anderson Galleries, Sale No. 2307, January 7, 1929). The manuscript of *Marino Faliero* sold for $27,000, and cantos XIV and XV of *Don Juan* brought $20,000 (these are now in the Berg Collection of the New York Public Library).

ship. After placing a gravestone over the ashes of Shelley in the Protestant Cemetery in Rome, Trelawny had gone on to Florence and was chafing for some new adventure. He was very willing to join Byron, who was putting up the money for the expedition.

Barry had found a ship, the *Hercules,* which could be chartered after she made a trip to Leghorn. And on the recommendation of Dr. Alexander, Byron engaged for the expedition a young physician by the name of Francesco Bruno, just out of the university. Trelawny was excited by the prospect of accompanying Byron to Greece. But when he arrived, he was less than enthusiastic over plans which he had not made. He was dissatisfied with the *Hercules,* "a collier-built tub of 120 tons, round-bottomed, and bluff-bowed. . . ." [n] Nevertheless, he bent to the task of making preparations, aided by the inept but willing and enthusiastic Pietro.

In a moment when Byron had envisioned the journey as a heroic pilgrimage, he had ordered uniforms for himself and his immediate staff appropriate for landing on Hellenic shores, a resplendent scarlet and gold. He also had three helmets made by Giacomo Aspe in Genoa, one for Pietro Gamba of green cloth in the form of a Uhlan's shako with a figure of Athene on the front, on a base of brass and black leather; and for himself and Trelawny two Homeric helmets, gilt with a towering plume, under which, on his own, were his coat of arms and the motto "Crede Byron." Pietro, the romantic "liberty boy," was no doubt delighted, but when Trelawny showed less enthusiasm, Byron reluctantly put them aside. Nevertheless, he took them to Greece with him.

In the midst of his preparations and the harrowing emotional strain of his parting with Teresa, Byron was ruffled by Hunt's gauche reminders of what he had promised in the way of assistance to Mary Shelley and himself. Byron probably had every intention of fulfilling his promises, but Hunt had a genius for irritating him by reciting what he owed to Shelley and his widow, and he carried tales of what Byron said. In the end, Byron had to use subterfuge to make her accept his money despite her pique. It was the 28th of June, and he was leaving early in July. He wrote Hunt: "I have received a Note from Mrs S with a fifth or sixth change of plan, viz., not to make her journey at all—at least through my assistance on account of what she is pleased to call 'Estrangement,' etc. On this I have little to say. . . . I will advance the money to *you* . . . you can say then that you have raised it as a Loan on your own account. . . ." [n] At the same time he told Hunt that he declined the offer of acting as Shelley's executor and the accompanying legacy of £2,000 stipulated in Shelley's will.

Hunt came back with the information that Mary had refused to take his money and had gone to Trelawny for a loan. Byron's rejoinder to what he considered Hunt's cool officiousness has unfortunately not been preserved, but something of its nature may be surmised by Hunt's long and painful reply. He upbraided Byron for the angry things he had said about Shelley and the franknesses he had indulged in concerning Shelley's views of Hunt's poetry. Then he turned to his own situation, asking for £50 to convey his family to Florence. He also asked to be "exonerated" from the debt of £250 advanced for his passage from England. Byron could not be angry long, and, his better feelings coming to the fore, he sent Hunt a mollifying letter with the promise to furnish him whatever was necessary for his journey to Florence, or to England if he preferred.

Teresa, who liked Mary, was distressed by this quarrel, for which she blamed Hunt, "For he told her [Mary] that Ld. Byron had an antipathy for her—and even for the memory of Shelley, that her visits bored him—that he was very willing to furnish her the means to make her voyage—but that he would prefer not to see her again." [n] If Mary had been less emotionally oriented toward Byron, a reconciliation would have been easier. That she would have melted at any overture on his part seems evident from her reply to Teresa's attempt to smooth matters over: " . . . if he will show me the least sign of friendship and will again be *glad* to help me, I will feel a renewed obligation to him and be grateful." [n] But the matter had gone too far, and Byron, preoccupied with trying to avoid hysterical scenes and reproaches at his imminent parting from Teresa, could not be bothered with the sentimental demands of another woman. But he did send Mary an appeasing note before he sailed and instructed Barry to furnish money for her journey.[n]

There was something more than mere expedience in Byron's solemn promises to return to Teresa, for at least half his nature longed for what he promised. She wanted to believe, but she also had premonitions that she would never see him again. It was in fact Byron's intention at this time to make a reconnoitering expedition to the Ionian Islands, and perhaps also to the mainland, and then return in a few months. He did not, however, rule out the possibility of staying longer if he should be welcomed by the Greeks and could be of any real service to them. Hobhouse wanted him only to seek information for the Committee and to give the moral support of his reputation and prestige to the Greek cause.

In his last hectic days of preparation, Byron had much to be thankful for in his bankers, Douglas Kinnaird in England and Barry in Genoa. Kinnaird had made nearly £9,000 in cash or credits available to him. And he announced that John Hunt's trial for the publication of *The Vision of Judgment* had been put over until the next term and that the publication by Hunt of the new cantos of *Don Juan* was going forward. Barry, in addition to overseeing all the practical details of outfitting the *Hercules* and getting supplies aboard, acted as a buffer between Byron and the Greek exiles, who both at Leghorn and at Genoa increasingly looked upon him as a kind of super Santa Claus. He had already learned how careful he would have to be to guard against the predatory instincts of the Greeks, especially the exiles, who were even more factional and greedy than their compatriots at home. They were eager to get their hands on any money he intended for the Greek cause.

In the last hours before Byron and his companions went on board the *Hercules*, Teresa, half delirious with sorrow and despair, waited patiently in her apartment for her lover to come to her. Count Gamba, her father, had received his passport to return to Ravenna and his family, and he wanted his daughter to go with him. She tried desperately to find some means of remaining in Genoa until her lover returned, but in the end she consented to leave with her father.

On July 13 Byron was ready to leave the Casa Saluzzo. "The fatal day arrived," Teresa recorded. "He must sleep on board in order to set sail the following morning. At 5 o'clock he was to leave Albaro. From 3 to 5 he did not leave Mad^{me} G. He did not wish to leave her alone at the moment of his departure and he had asked Mrs. Shelley to be with her at 5 o'clock." [n] Mary tried to console Teresa and keep up her courage, but she knew it was useless. After Mary had gone, Teresa sat alone and tried to relieve her feelings by writing in a little notebook in which Byron had kept his accounts since she had met him in 1819. "I hear a flute," she scribbled. "What sadness fills me! God help me!" [n] At dawn the next day she was helped to her father's carriage by Barry, while she gathered her strength to look at the sky and observe the direction of the wind.

Byron had gone on board with Trelawny, Count Pietro Gamba, the young Dr. Bruno, and Constantine Skilitzy, whom he had promised a passage back to Greece. In addition to other livestock, they took four of Byron's horses and one of Trelawny's; the faithful bulldog Moretto; and a huge Newfoundland called Lion, which had been given Byron by the retired naval lieutenant Edward Le Mesurier. Five or more servants helped to crowd the small vessel.

By ten o'clock of the 14th they were ready to sail, but there was a dead calm. They all went ashore again and headed for Albaro. But when Barry met Byron and told him that Teresa had already left, he had not the heart to return to the empty house, and directed the party instead to Sestri and the Villa Lomellina, where he had ridden so often with Lady Blessington. They dined on cheese and fruit in the Lomellina garden and then returned to sleep on board.

The next day they started out of the harbor but were becalmed most of the day. Then at night the wind freshened and the old tub rolled so that the horses kicked down their thin partitions, and they hove to and came back to their former berth. Byron had stayed on deck all night in the storm. While Trelawny remained to oversee repair of the damaged stalls, the others went ashore again. This time Byron wanted to visit the Casa Saluzzo once more. A deep despondency settled on him as he climbed the hill with Pietro. " . . . he spoke much of his past life, and the uncertainty of the future. 'Where,' said he, 'shall we be in a year?' " [n] Barry later told Hobhouse that when Byron had been driven back by the storm, "he confessed to him that he would not go on the Greek expedition even then but that *'Hobhouse and the others would laugh at him.'* " [n]

But the die was cast. The weather continued fine. Childe Harold was on his pilgrimage again. In five days they were in Leghorn. Barry was inconsolable at losing a friend who had treated him always with the utmost kindness and never with condescension. On the evening when Byron finally sailed, the banker wrote: "You said that I should be glad when you got off but I hope you don't think so, believe me, My Lord, I am too proud of having known you not to regret most unfeignedly your absence. I cannot cry like the Tailor's boy but I feel the loss as acutely as if I did & most sincerely do I hope that your return to Genoa will not be at a very remote period. . . ."[n] As Lady Blessington prized the *Bolivar* because it had been in Byron's possession, so Barry bought some of Byron's furniture and books. And Byron presented him with some valuable literary autographs, and also a few manuscripts of things he had written in anger and did not intend to publish.

As Teresa proceeded on her journey, her distress increased. She continued to write in the little notebook. The final entry was most agonizing: "I hoped to have the strength to bear this misfortune without dying—but the pain grows every moment and I feel as though I were dying. Send after me Byron—If you would still see [me] in life—Oh that I might flee madly and come at whatever risk. . . ."[n] But Byron had made his irrevocable commitments, and he could not return.

CHAPTER XXVII

1823

Return to "The Isles of Greece"

WHEN THE *Hercules* glided slowly into the port at Leghorn in the afternoon of July 21, Byron was greeted by a salute of thirteen guns from an Ionian vessel. Its commander, Captain George Vitali, had already asked and been granted passage to his homeland by Byron. James Hamilton Browne, a Scotsman who had been dismissed from service in the Ionian Islands because of his Hellenic sympathies, had also asked to join Byron's expedition. He spoke Italian and Romaic, and knew much about the English Residents in command of the Islands. It was on his recommendation that Byron decided to change his first destination from Zante, recommended by Blaquiere, to Cephalonia, then under the command of Colonel Charles James Napier, the only English Resident markedly favorable to the Greek cause.

The now much overcrowded vessel pulled out of the harbor of Leghorn on the 24th and headed south for the Strait of Messina. The weather was fine and all were on deck. This was Byron's farewell to Italy, where, he could now feel, despite his aimlessly drifting course, he had spent some of the happiest, and certainly the most productive, years of his life. He was being swept away toward Greece and an uncertain goal, partly by the compulsion of his own dissatisfaction, but perhaps more by the inevitable demand of circumstances and his own fame, which had combined with his weakness to drive him to do what was expected of him. And yet he had not destroyed all his bridges behind him. He wrote to Barry: "I particularly recommend to your care my own travelling Chariot, which I would not part with for any consideration." [n]

They approached Stromboli on a clear night. Byron sat until morning watching it and exchanging ghost stories with Trelawny and Browne. As Byron went down to his cabin, he said to Trelawny: "If I live another year, you will see this scene in a fifth canto of Childe Harold." [n] Browne observed that during the passage Byron chiefly read the writings of Swift, and supposed that he was thus preparing to write another canto of *Don Juan*. But, except for occasional letter writing, Byron's pen was still now. Browne noted that he also read Montaigne, Voltaire, Grimm's *Correspondence*, and La Rochefoucauld.

By the time the *Hercules* reached the Ionian Sea, Byron's spirits had improved considerably. He easily established a camaraderie that was pleasing to his shipmates. Trelawny concluded: "I never was on ship-board with a better companion than Byron, he was generally cheerful, gave no trouble, assumed no authority, uttered no complaints, and did not interfere with the working of the ship; when appealed to, he always answered, 'do as you like.'" [n]

Every day at noon, Byron and Trelawny, in calm weather, jumped overboard for a swim without fear of sharks, which were not unknown in those waters. And occasionally their exuberance found outlet in boyish horseplay. Once, according to Trelawny, they let the geese and ducks loose and followed them and the dogs into the water, each with an arm in Captain Scott's new scarlet waistcoat.

Byron had brought along three servants whom he particularly valued. These were the Venetian gondolier Tita, who frightened Dr. Bruno; the English valet Fletcher, who had been with Byron on his first journey to Greece; and Lega Zambelli, his steward. Browne says that Byron "sometimes spoke in terms of unqualified praise of the extremely careful and penurious character of old Lega, his Maestro di Casa." [n] Byron also took over from Trelawny a black servant, an American, who was a good cook.

Fletcher, who remembered the discomfort of Greece, thought his master a little mad for wanting to return there. Trelawny recalled his outspoken protest, and Byron's comment on overhearing it: "It's very true—with those who take 'a hog's

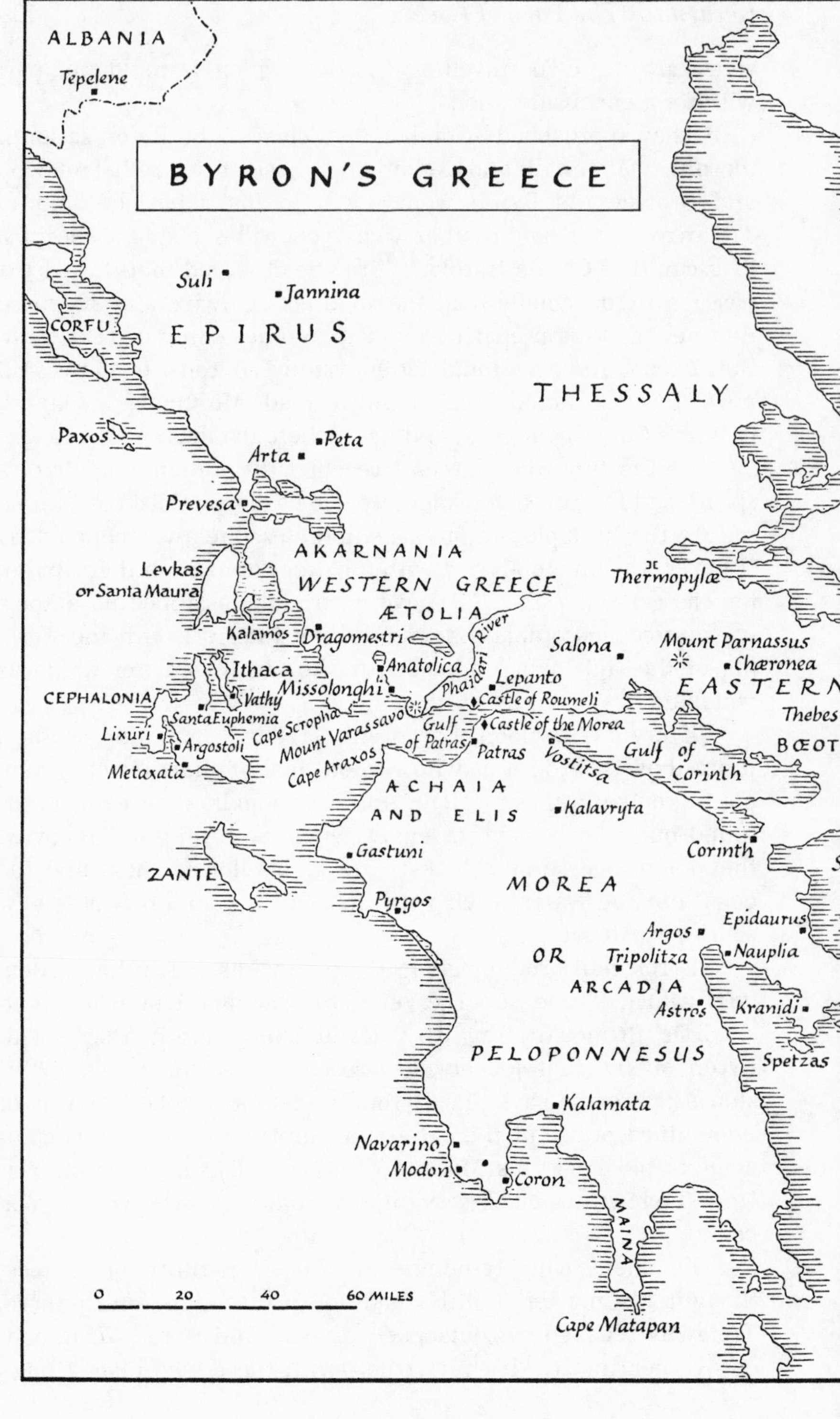

BYRON'S GREECE
ALBANIA
Tepelene
Suli
Jannina
EPIRUS
CORFU
THESSALY
Paxos
Peta
Arta
Prevesa
AKARNANIA
WESTERN GREECE
Levkas
or Santa Maura
ÆTOLIA
Thermopylæ
Kalamos
Dragomestri
Phaidari River
Salona
Mount Parnassus
Ithaca
Anatolica
Chæronea
Missolonghi
Lepanto
EASTERN
CEPHALONIA
Vathy
Castle of Roumeli
Santa Euphemia
Cape Scropha
Castle of the Morea
Thebes
Lixuri
Argostoli
Mount Varassavo
Gulf of Patras
Patras
Vostitsa
Gulf of Corinth
BŒOTI
Metaxata
Cape Araxos
ACHAIA
AND ELIS
Kalavryta
Corinth
Gastuni
ZANTE
MOREA
Pyrgos
Epidaurus
Argos
OR
Tripolitza
Nauplia
ARCADIA
Astros
Kranidi
PELOPONNESUS
Spetzas
Kalamata
Navarino
Modon
Coron
MAINA
0 20 40 60 MILES
Cape Matapan

Samothrace
Mount Athos
Sestos
Abydos
Hellespont
(Dardanelles)
Plains of
Troy
MITYLENE
OR LESBOS
ÆGEAN
SEA
UBŒA
CHIOS
Smyrna
ECE
Marathon
CA
Athens
Colonni
Sunium)
Kea
Paros
Antiparos
NAXOS

eye view of things!' " Trelawny observed: "After a considerable pause—he continued 'I was happier in Greece—than I have ever been before—or since and if I have ever written [well?] (as the world says I have—but which they will pardon my doubting)—it was in Greece—or off [of] Greece. . . .'" [n]

On August 2 they sighted the islands of Cephalonia and Zante. They tacked for Cephalonia. When Byron saw the mountains of the Morea in the distance, he said: "I don't know why it is, but I feel as if the eleven long years of bitterness I have passed through since I was here, were taken off my shoulders, and I was scudding through the Greek Archipelago with old Bathurst, in his frigate." [n] That night they got into the shelter of the roadstead, and the next morning anchored near the town of Argostoli, the island's capital.

Captain John Pitt Kennedy, secretary to the English Resident, Colonel Napier, then absent from the island, came aboard to welcome Byron and his party. The Resident, he said, was ready to serve them in any way that would not compromise his orders of strict neutrality in the war between the Greeks and the Turks.

What determined Byron to remain for the time being at Cephalonia was the news that internal political dissension was rife among the Greeks, that indolence on both sides had almost halted the war, and that the Turks had unobstructed command of the seas surrounding the mainland, whereas the Greek fleet, consisting mostly of armed merchant vessels, was bottled up in the islands off the east coast. The reports were confused and, as he had reason to believe, biased, so that he could see nothing to be gained by moving farther.

Alexander Mavrocordatos had been elected the first President of Greece, under the Constitution of Epidaurus, proclaimed New Year's Day (Eastern calendar; January 13 by the Western calendar), 1822, after the early Greek successes. The government was weak from the first, and the spirit of nationalism was further weakened by later defeats and by the rival claims of chiefs, jealous of their own prerogatives. When the second National Assembly met in February 1823, the members were divided into two parties, one the military party led by Kolokotrones, Ipsilantes, and Odysseus (Ulysses); and the other that of the Primates and the civil leaders such as Petrobey of Maina,

Zaimes, Andreas Londos (whom Byron had met in 1809), and Mavrocordatos. Petrobey became President of the Executive Council, and Mavrocordatos accepted the office of Secretary of State. When the Assembly was dissolved in May, it seemed that the civil party had won. The Executive Council and the Senate had fixed the seat of government at Tripolitza (modern Tripolis), on the central plateau of the Peloponnesus. But when Mavrocordatos was summoned in July to preside over the Legislative Council, he was alarmed by the threats of Kolokotrones and, resigning his office, fled to Hydra.

To get more authentic information, Byron wrote to Marco Botsaris, who had been commended to him by the Metropolitan Ignatius of Arta in Leghorn. Botsaris was in charge of the Greek forces in Acarnania, then battling the Turks north of Missolonghi. In the meantime, Byron and his party remained on board the *Hercules* in Argostoli harbor, to avoid any embarrassment to the English in charge of the Protectorate. The arrival in Cephalonia of the celebrated poet, whose verses had been read by most of the English officers, made a great sensation. He was an object of curiosity to the English and the natives alike. He soon put his horses ashore and went riding regularly every day, presenting, according to one observer, the figure of a Tartar "with his high feather [perhaps his Homeric helmet] and his silver epaulets." [n]

Two days after the arrival of the *Hercules*, Colonel Napier, the British Resident and Governor, returned to the island. He was an able colonial administrator and an ardent Philhellene, who, like Byron, had a "tempered enthusiasm" for the cause and the people with whom Byron was to link his fate. He knew the Greeks and their foibles and was not less devoted to their liberation. Colonel Napier had found a challenge to his administrative abilities in managing the wild Suliote warriors who, with their families, had sought refuge in Cephalonia in 1822 after being exiled from their home on the cliffs of southern Albania. Byron had heard of the heroic defense of their rocky stronghold and had paid tribute to them in *Childe Harold*. They had been scattered over the islands, but some were still serving under Marco Botsaris in the war against the Turks.

Byron was predisposed to like the Suliotes, whom he regarded as the bravest, most faithful, and loyal of the tribesmen, judging them by the two Albanians he had taken into his service on his first visit to the East (for the Suliotes were Albanians). The sight of their weather-beaten countenances and unique dress carried him back to the happy days of his carefree trek through the Epirus in 1809. Here were the brave soldiers he might be proud to lead. He easily succumbed to their blandishments and hired a mob of them as his personal bodyguard and retainers.

Trelawny, however, took a dim view of them: "The morning after our arrival a flock of ravenous Zuliote refugees alighted on our decks, attracted by Byron's dollars. Lega, the steward, a thorough miser, coiled himself on the money-chest like a viper. Our sturdy skipper was for driving them overboard with handspikes. Byron came on deck in exuberant spirits, pleased with their savage aspect and wild attire, and, as was his wont, promised a great deal more than he should have done; day and night they clung to his heels like a pack of jackals, till he stood at bay like a hunted lion. . . ." [n]

Among the English on the island with whom Byron formed a friendship was Dr. Henry Muir, health officer at Argostoli. It was through Muir that he met that earnest evangelical medical officer Dr. James Kennedy, who spent long hours trying to convert to Christianity the admirer of Voltaire and supposed leader of the "Satanic School" of poetry. Kennedy had invited several officers and other Englishmen on the island to his home, where he proposed to demonstrate the truth of the Christian doctrine.

Byron had an almost superstitious awe of the sincerely religious mind. Though he was tough-minded enough to reject the shams of religious pretense and theological inconsistencies, he had not the conviction of his skepticism. He had too great and too obsessive a sense of the mysteries of life and the universe to be quite happy in his negative beliefs. He had wrestled with theological and cosmological problems in *Cain*, in *Heaven and Earth*, and in *Don Juan*, with the curiosity of an explorer of hidden mysteries, and had found the thrill of looking behind the images greater than that of merely breaking them. Moreover, though he would not give up his speculations in forbidden realms, nor his castigation of cant, he was a little sensitive at being thought irreligious by his compatriots. He later told Kennedy that he did not like the appellation of infidel; "he said it was a cold and chilling word." [n]

Byron listened patiently for an hour to Kennedy's arguments, mostly from commentaries, and then began interrupting him with comments and questions. The poet showed a familiarity with the Bible and the commentaries that surprised Kennedy and his guests. "His lordship asked me," Kennedy recalled, "if I thought that there had been fewer wars and persecutions, and less slaughter, misery, and wretchedness in the world since the introduction of Christianity than before."[n] Kennedy's mention of the scriptural simile of the potter and his clay roused Byron to say "that he would certainly say to the potter, if he were broken in pieces, 'Why do you treat me thus?' "[n]

While Byron was waiting for letters from the mainland, he expressed a desire to visit Ithaca, the neighboring island that had long been associated with Homer's Odysseus. He had received no news from England or Italy since arriving. On the eve of departing, he wrote Barry: "Of the Greeks I shall say nothing, till I can say something better, except that I am not discouraged. . . ."[n]

The party, consisting of Byron, Trelawny, Count Gamba, Dr. Bruno, Browne, and several servants, arose at dawn on August 11 and spent nine hours on muleback in a very hot sun. It was a strenuous voyage, but Byron enjoyed it, for its rigors reminded him of his youthful travels in Greece. They crossed the narrow channel between the islands from St. Euphemia in an open four-oared boat, arriving about sunset on the rocky shore of the little island of Ithaca, the two mountainous halves of which are joined by an isthmus. No one was there to meet them, and Byron blithely proposed that they spend the night in one of the caves along the coast, but Gamba found the house of a merchant of Trieste, who offered them hospitality. The next day they were welcomed by Captain Knox, the English Resident, in the capital, Vathy.

Byron was in an excellent mood. After dinner at the Governor's house he engaged in conversation with a stranger, an Englishman by the name of Thomas Smith, and without the least embarrassment discussed his works, Lady Byron, and his daughter Ada. Speaking of the Greeks, he said he had not changed his mind about them. "I know them as well as most people . . . but we must not look always too closely at the men who are to benefit by our exertions in a good cause, or God knows we shall seldom do much good in this world." [n]

The next day the party made an excursion to the so-called Fountain of Arethusa, a grotto and spring a few miles south of Vathy, and on the following day to the "School of Homer" in the northern part of the island. On the fourth day they started the return to Cephalonia. Before leaving, Byron, who had been struck by the plight of the many refugees uprooted from their mainland homes by the war, subscribed to a fund for their relief. And he later brought to Cephalonia a Moreote family, once well-to-do in Patras but now destitute, and provided them with a house and maintenance. This was the family of Chalandritsanos.

While waiting for the boat, Byron spent some time in the water demonstrating swimming feats. The crossing in an open boat under a hot sun, and a considerable banquet at Santa Euphemia after they arrived, played havoc with his frail constitution. When they arrived after dark at the monastery on top of a mountain near Samos where they were to spend the night, he was seized with a paroxysm that almost deprived him of his reason. While the Abbot was delivering an address of welcome, he seized a lamp, crying out, "my head is burning; will no one relieve me from the presence of this pestilential madman?" and rushed into the first room he could find.[n] Dr. Bruno and Trelawny in turn tried to soothe him. He refused any medicine, threatened all who came near him, and tore his bedding and clothes like a maniac. Hamilton Browne finally persuaded him to take some of Dr. Bruno's "benedette pillule." And "with something like childish drivel" he lay down and went to sleep.[n]

Late the next morning he rose quite composed and was exceedingly courteous to the Abbot on leaving. On the journey across the mountains to Argostoli, Smith noted that "lively on horseback, [he] sang, at the pitch of his voice, many of Moore's melodies and stray snatches of popular songs. . . ." [n]

There was still no news from either England or Italy. Byron's future course was no plainer than it had been, and he fell back into his easy habits of riding, swimming, and dining with Colonel Napier and other residents of Argostoli. Pietro wrote again to reassure his sister and to tell her of their pleasant excursion to Ithaca. Byron added his usual postscript in English. He was already divorced from his life in Italy, and his effort to recapture the mood of his attachment was a strain and something of a bore.

Byron was temporarily roused from the convivialities of the island life by the arrival on August 22 of an enthusiastic letter from Marco Botsaris, the Suliote leader, who, with his small band, was then helping to repel the Ottoman forces pressing down the mountain valleys above Missolonghi. "Let nothing prevent you from coming into this part of Greece," he wrote. "The enemy threatens us in great number; but, by the help of God and your Excellency, they shall meet a suitable resistance." [n] But the news a few days later of the death of Botsaris, one of the two Greek leaders who seemed most honest and patriotic, put an effective stop to any plans Byron may have had for leaving immediately for the mainland.

The poet-Philhellene was soon bombarded with petitions from every party on Greek soil with an ax to grind, as well as from individuals who hoped to get a share of the funds he had brought along. Only the healthy cynicism of his view of human nature in general and the Greek character in particular, coupled with a longer view of the ultimate good of liberation of the land, kept him from turning in disgust from the whole project. Among his associates he found a safety valve in commenting satirically on the less amiable Greek traits, but in soberer moments, he, like Colonel Napier, had a large tolerance for the people who had so long been warped by slavery. Count Gamba said that "In his [Byron's] travels during his younger days, he had imbibed a greater personal esteem for the character of the Turks than for that of their slaves." [n] But Byron recognized that the Greek character had been formed by the habits of deceit engendered by the very circumstances of their slavery. Having learned to live by cozening their masters, they carried the habit into all their dealings.

George Finlay, who saw Byron in Cephalonia and was with him later in Missolonghi, noted that "to nobody did the Greeks ever unmask their selfishness and self-deceit so candidly. Almost every distinguished statesman and general sent him letters soliciting his favour, his influence, or his money. . . . Lord Byron made many sagacious and satirical comments on the *chiaroscuro* of these communications. . . . He knew his own character so well, that he remained some time at Cephalonia, not venturing to trust himself among such a cunning and scheming set, fearing lest unworthy persons should exercise too much influence over his conduct."[n]

Byron set down his tempered view of the Greeks without mincing words: "Whoever goes into Greece at present should do it as Mrs. Fry went into Newgate—not in the expectation of meeting with any especial indication of existing probity, but in the hope that time and better treatment will reclaim the present burglarious and larcenous tendencies which have followed this General Gaol delivery. . . . The worst of them is that . . . they are such damned liars; there never was such an incapacity for veracity shown since Eve lived in Paradise."[n]

Byron's disillusionment with the Greeks was no doubt heightened by the growing unruliness and efforts at extortion of the Suliotes he had taken under his protection. To free himself from them, he now offered them another month's pay and passage to Acarnania on the mainland. Afraid of his own softness toward them, Byron let Count Gamba handle the matter for him. He had decided he could not proceed without further information and assurances. He might have been content to remain on the *Hercules,* but Captain Scott wanted to return to England, and other circumstances hastened Byron's removal to a house on shore.

Trelawny and Browne, not sharing Byron's need for caution and prudence as the principal agent for the Greek Committee and as one whose own money and reputation must be thrown into the cause where it would do the most good, had grown impatient of delays and were determined to proceed to the seat of the government in the Morea. Browne thought that Byron was held at Cephalonia principally "through irresolution," or "dislike to locomotion."[n] But to Byron the problem did not seem so simple.*

* In his later accounts, Trelawny was even more critical than Browne of what he considered Byron's procrastination. He wrote in his *Recollections:* "I well knew that once on shore Byron would fall back on his old routine of dawdling habits, plotting—planning—shilly-shallying—and doing nothing. It was a maxim of his, 'If I am stopped for six days at any place, I cannot be made to move for six months.'" (Trelawny, *Recollections*, p. 211.) But at the time Trelawny's critical remarks found vent only in a letter to Mary Shelley, and he was willing enough to have the world know that he was a confidant of the famous poet: " . . . our intimacy has never been ruffled—but smoother than ever and I am as ever most anxious in upholding his great name to the world." (Marchand, III, 1119.)

On the 6th of September Browne and Trelawny embarked for Pyrgos after bidding Byron an affectionate farewell. Byron never saw Trelawny again. There is no doubt that he was fond of the old "pirate," though Trelawny's flamboyance often made him the butt of Byron's jests. He is reported to have said once that if Trelawny would learn to tell the truth and wash his hands, they might make a gentleman of him yet.

Byron, Pietro Gamba, and Dr. Bruno settled down comfortably in a small villa, the smallest one in which Byron had lived since he left his mother's house at Southwell. This villa at Metaxata had a balcony from which Byron could see on clear mornings the outlines of the mainland of the Morea and the clearer green silhouette of the island of Zante to the south. It stood amid vineyards and olive groves in a pretty little village half a mile or more up the island slope from the blue waters of the Ionian Sea, and about four miles from Argostoli. Behind the village loomed the castle of San Giorgio and the bare rocks of the Black Mountain.*

Once settled at Metaxata, Byron had time to consider his situation, and the more he thought about it the less was he inclined to move hastily. A nostalgia for Italy began to surge in him. When at last he received a letter from Teresa, something of his old feeling of playful tenderness returned. To keep up her spirits he wrote: "I shall fulfil the object of my mission from the committee—and then (probably) return into Italy for it does not seem likely that as an individual I can be of use to them. . . . be assured that there is nothing here that can excite anything but a wish to be with you again. . . . I kiss your Eyes (*occhi*) and am most affectly a. a. in e. [your friend and lover forever]" [n]

Knowing his own incapacity to deal with the contradictions of the leaders, Byron turned for advice to Colonel Napier, that hardheaded soldier and administrator. It was because of Napier's abiding faith in the ultimate redemption of the Greeks that Byron trusted him. Napier's feeling was that the only solution was to get together a body of regular disciplined soldiers, English and Germans, from among the Philhellenes, and then gather a

* The house was still standing when I visited Metaxata in 1948, but it was destroyed by the earthquake of 1953. Now a new house stands on the spot on "Byron Street" and across the way is a vine-covered gate with a sign in English saying "Byron's Ivy." Byron, Gamba says, had a bedroom and sitting room, he and Dr. Bruno shared a room, and the servants camped in the kitchen.

few enlightened leaders such as Tricoupi and Mavrocordatos, paying money not to the chiefs but only to the soldiers.

But able and shrewd as he recognized Napier to be, Byron perceived that, in his expectations both of the Greeks and of the author of "The Isles of Greece," Napier was a little too optimistic and naïve. Byron knew his own weaknesses well, and those of the Greeks even better. Finlay acutely observed: "The genius of Lord Byron would in all probability never have unfolded either political or military talent. . . . He regarded politics as the art of cheating the people, by concealing one-half of the truth and misrepresenting the other; and whatever abstract enthusiasm he might feel for military glory was joined to an innate detestation of the trade of war. Both his character and his conduct presented unceasing contradictions. It seemed as if two different souls occupied his body alternately. One was feminine, and full of sympathy; the other masculine, and characterized by clear judgment, and by a rare power of presenting for consideration those facts only which were required for forming a decision." [n]

The journal which Byron had begun in September he discontinued abruptly on the 30th, when he received a letter from Augusta intimating that his daughter Ada was ill. In replying, Byron showed an interest chiefly in his daughter's health and disposition. The reproachful innuendoes of his earlier letters had now disappeared. The fire of passion seemed burned out, and only the brotherly fondness remained.

Pietro had told Teresa that Byron had returned to his hermit's life and was contented with it. But this was not quite true. Most of the English residents and officers of the garrison came out to visit him frequently, and sometimes he rode in to Argostoli. The pious Dr. Kennedy was among those who called. He found Byron eager to resume the conversations on religion, partly from a genuine interest in the subject, and partly, no doubt, for the pleasure of cutting across Kennedy's orthodox arguments with the difficulties that troubled him.

Byron was never rude or sharply sarcastic, but Kennedy was uneasy because he knew that the wits of the garrison were making sport of his efforts to convert Byron, who, it was apparent, did not take the humorless doctor too seriously, though he did not want to hurt his feelings. Only one side of his feeling on the subject, however, is reflected in his facetious remarks to Dr.

Muir: "The fact is, Muir, Kennedy has had a great deal of trouble with us all, and it would be a pity he should lose his time." Then he clasped his hands in a mock-pious gesture, and looking upward, exclaimed: "Oh! I shall begin the 17th Canto of *Don Juan a changed man!*"[n]

Contradictory reports from the mainland continued to come throughout the autumn, and more Philhellenes arrived to confer with Byron. One of these was the young George Finlay, who had come to lend his services to the Greek cause. Byron remarked that his visitor "was far too enthusiastic, and too fresh from Germany," but he liked him none the less for it.

Count Delladecima, Byron's chief adviser among the Greeks on Cephalonia, had turned over to him a report from a friend of Mavrocordatos at Tripolitza, Jean Baptiste Theotoky. This report neutralized the favorable accounts that Browne and Trelawny had given of the Provisional Government in the Morea. What was more likely to deter Byron from any precipitate action, however, was a long memorandum and a letter from Frank Hastings, a British naval officer who had offered his services to the Greeks the previous year, and who had had ample opportunity to observe the strengths and weaknesses of their leaders, particularly of the merchant captains who commanded the ships that served as the Greek Navy. He had hoped that Byron could persuade the London Greek Committee to send out an armored steamboat, which, he believed, alone could help the Greeks to attain mastery of the seas and keep the Turkish fleet from relieving the fortresses they still held in Greece. Captain Hastings reported that the merchant captains and sailors would rather "fail after their own manner than succeed by taking the advice of a Franc."[n] And he warned Byron of the difficulty of forming any regular corps among the Greeks, who were averse to using artillery or anything but their own muskets, and who fought best as irregulars under their own leaders.

Trelawny, in the meantime, had established himself as a confidant and crony of a Greek leader in Attica who called himself Ulysses and who possessed some of the wily characteristics of his namesake. Trelawny wrote disparagingly of Byron to Mary Shelley, picturing himself as a man of action and the poet as one afraid to risk himself and his money among the Greeks. Trelawny then gave some details of his own heroic action. "I have desided on accompanying Ulysses to Negropont [Eubœa] to pass the winter there—their being excellent sport between Turk and woodcock shooting—I am to be a kind of Aidecamp . . . the Gen.[1] gives me as many men as I choose to command —and I am to be always with him—my equipments are all ready —two horses—two Zuliotes as servants—I am habited exactly like Ulysses—in red & gold vest with sheep-skin Capote—gun pistols sabre &c. red cap & a few dollars or dubloons. . . ."[n] So Trelawny had found what he came for—what he had used Byron's expedition to accomplish—adventure in a red and gold vest, with two servants and the companionship of a general—and woodcock-shooting to boot!

That Byron was not idle, however, but was making every useful preparation for helping the Greeks when the time was ripe, is evident from his letters to Kinnaird, to Hobhouse, and to Barry. He wrote to Barry: "I offered to advance a thousand dollars per month for the succour of Messolonghi and the Suliotes under Bozzari (who was since killed) but the Gov.t have answered me . . . that they wish to confer with me previously —which is in fact saying that they wish me to expend my money in some other direction."[n]

Early in November Julius Millingen, a young English doctor, accompanied by three young German Philhellenes, arrived with letters of recommendation from the London Greek Committee. Millingen noted that Byron tried before strangers to give the impression that his own expedition to Greece was governed by prudence, but to those with whom he became familiar he indulged "the natural bent of his mind for adventurous and extraordinary undertakings."[n] Byron took a liking to Millingen and proposed employing him as physician to the Suliote corps he contemplated forming on the mainland.

Dr. Millingen was dubious about Byron's abstemious diet, which the poet said was intended to increase his mental powers, but which the doctor saw was motivated by a fear of corpulence. He not only avoided nourishing food, but "had recourse almost daily to strong drastic pills, of which extract of colocynth, gamboge, scammony, &c. were the chief ingredients; and if he observed the slightest increase in the size of his wrists or waist . . . he immediately sought to reduce it by taking a large dose of Epsom salts. . . ."[n]

Finally, in the first week of November, Byron was on the point of leaving for the seat of the government in the Peloponnesus, though he still had misgivings about what he could accomplish. But at that moment Browne and the two Greek Deputies who were on their way to seek an £800,000 loan in England, arrived at Argostoli, and Byron settled back to view the scene with detachment a little longer. The Deputies, Jean Orlando and the same André Luriottis who had accompanied Blaquiere, were authorized to ask Byron for a loan of 300,000 piastres (£6,000) to activate the Greek fleet. He agreed to give £4,000.

Charles Hancock, an English merchant residing in Cephalonia who had a partnership with Samuel Barff, living at Zante, came forward to cash Byron's bills of exchange. Thenceforward Barff and Hancock, with the latter of whom Byron had already become friendly, handled all his business in Greece. Hancock, like most of the English who met Byron on the island, was immediately captivated by "the affability of his manners, the brilliancy and variety of his conversation, the fascination of his wit."[n] Byron was happy to be doing something for the cause at last. He signed a contract for a loan, "as they apparently decline it as a gift,"[n] he told Kinnaird. And he wrote Bowring: "To say the truth, I do not grudge it now the fellows have begun to fight *again*. . . ."[n]

George Finlay and some of the German officers left for the Peloponnesus, and Browne and the Deputies for England. Shortly after, Colonel Leicester Stanhope arrived in Cephalonia as an agent of the London Greek Committee. Stanhope (later the fifth Earl of Harrington) had served in India, but, unlike the practical soldier and administrator Colonel Napier, he was a doctrinaire Benthamite who believed that everything could be accomplished for the Greeks by establishing republican institutions and setting up printing presses. Stanhope got off on the wrong foot with Byron by introducing the subject of Bentham at their first meeting, for Byron associated the philosophical radicals with all the worst of those who pretended to theoretical knowledge of mankind. When Byron asked whether he had brought any new books, Stanhope mentioned Bentham's *Springs of Action*. Napier recorded that Byron "gave one look into it and said: 'Springs of Action! God Damn his Springs of Action! I know a damn deal more than he does about them'—and then flung the pamphlet in a rage on the floor."[n] According to Hobhouse, Byron also said: "What does the old fool know of springs of action—my—— has more spring in it."[n]

Although Byron was continually irritated by the theoretical vagaries of the "typographical Colonel," as he called him sarcastically, there is evidence that he was relieved to share the responsibilities of the Committee's work with him. And he was glad to have Stanhope precede him into the hornet's nest on the mainland. He gave him a letter to "The General Government of Greece": " . . . I must frankly confess, that unless union and order are established, all hopes of a loan will be vain; and all the assistance which the Greeks could expect from abroad . . . will be suspended or destroyed; and what is worse, the great powers of Europe . . . will be persuaded that the Greeks are unable to govern themselves, and will, perhaps, themselves undertake to settle your disorders in such a way, as to blast the brightest hopes of yourselves and of your friends. And allow me to add once for all—I desire the well-being of Greece, and nothing else; I will do all I can to secure it; but I cannot consent, I never will consent that the English public, or English individuals, should be deceived as to the real state of Greek affairs."[n]

News that the fleet was on the way to Missolonghi and had proceeded as far as Kalamata on the southwestern coast of the Morea was authenticated early in December. And in a few days it was known that Mavrocordatos had joined the expedition. Aware of his responsibility to deliver the money he had promised to pay the fleet, and seeing no possibility of being useful in eastern Greece while the factions were so bitterly embroiled, Byron sent word to the Provisional Government that he had changed his plans and would lend his aid, for the present, to the relief of Missolonghi. Stanhope left by way of Zante, carrying his letters to the government and to Mavrocordatos.

Beset by doubts as to his best course, Byron was now to lose one of his most steadying counselors. Colonel Napier was going on leave to England, hoping to make some arrangements with the Greek Committee for support in case he was able to organize a regular Greek corps. Shortly after he left, the Greek fleet appeared in the gulf and fought an unequal battle with four Turkish ships (the Greeks had fourteen), driving one ashore at Ithaca. Byron did not know at the time that with a shocking disregard for the neutrality of the Ionian Islands, which had harbored many Greek refugees, the rapacious Greek sailors had pursued and murdered the whole crew for the sake of the treasure on board. It was under the cloud of this ignoble victory that Mavrocordatos, the "Washington" of Greece, as Byron had called him, landed at Missolonghi on December 11.

Stanhope arrived there soon after and sent an enthusiastic account, together with a letter from Mavrocordatos, who said: "On reaching Missolonghi I found moreover that everyone was so convinced of the truth of what I now tell you, that you will be received here as a saviour. Be assured, My Lord, that it depends only on yourself to secure the destiny of Greece. . . . I have ordered one of the best ships in our squadron to sail for Cephalonia. . . ."[n] But Byron was too realistic not to make due allowances for Greek rhetoric, and his skepticism was fortified about the same time by another long letter from Frank Hastings, detailing events on the mainland. He knew nevertheless that the time for action had come, but there was much to do before he could uproot himself.

Alone now at Metaxata except for Gamba and Dr. Bruno, whom he pronounced "an excellent little fellow" though somewhat pedantic, Byron fell into a contemplative mood. Having eschewed poetry since coming to Greece, he took up his journal again, confiding to it his speculations on his future course. The Suliotes were eager to enroll under his personal banner and protection. It was an enticing dream, to think that he might become at last a military leader in the cause of freedom. He had not entirely abandoned it when he wrote to Kinnaird on December 23: "For three hundred pounds I can maintain in Greece, at more than the *fullest pay* of the Provisional Government, rations included, one hundred armed men for *three months*." And he urged Kinnaird again to stretch his credit to the limit—"for, after all, it is better playing at nations than gaming at Almack's or Newmarket. . . ."[n] He may have remembered then that the Greek Skilitzi, who had come with him from Genoa on the *Hercules*, "by way of flattery," according to Browne, "used frequently to insinuate that his countrymen might possibly choose Lord Byron for their King."[n]

The Greek vessel sent by Mavrocordatos was forced to return without him, for the English authorities, fearing a violation of neutrality, would not allow it to make any contact with the island. Byron made his own preparations for leaving. The day after Christmas he left Metaxata for the last time and stayed with Charles Hancock in Argostoli waiting for a favorable breeze. He had hired two island boats, one a light, fast-sailing vessel called a "mistico," and the other a larger "bombard" for baggage, horses, and supplies, a number of which had arrived from the English Committee, including a printing press sent at the request of Colonel Stanhope.

On the eve of his embarcation Byron wrote to Bowring: "The supplies of the Committee are, some, useful, and all excellent in their kind; but occasionally hardly *practical* enough, in the present state of Greece; for instance, the mathematical instruments are thrown away—none of the Greeks know a problem from a poker—we must conquer first, and plan afterwards. The use of trumpets, too, may be doubted, unless Constantinople were Jericho. . . ."

But in a postscript he assured the secretary of his earnestness in the cause and his willingness to work with Colonel Stanhope despite the latter's pedantic views: "He came up (as they all do who have not been in the country before) with some high-flown notions of the sixth form at Harrow or Eton, etc.; but Col. Napier and I set him to rights on those points, which is absolutely necessary to prevent disgust, or perhaps return. . . ." [n]

Byron wrote a final appeal for funds to Kinnaird: " . . . I must do my best to the shirt—and to the skin if necessary. . . . Why, man! if we had but 100,000*l.* sterling in hand, we should now be halfway to the city of Constantine." [n] He concluded a note to Hobhouse with the facetious exuberance which the thought of moving into action had kindled in him: "Mavrocordato's letter says, that my presence will '*electrify* the troops,' so I am going over to 'electrify' the Suliotes, as George Primrose went to Holland 'to teach the Dutch English, who were fond of it to distraction.' " [n]

On the 29th they were ready to sail. When Dr. Kennedy came to bid Byron farewell, he found him reading *Quentin Durward.* He promised Kennedy to take along some religious books to distribute in Missolonghi. Hancock and Muir accompanied him in a small boat when he boarded the mistico. He was in high spirits and "mentioned the poetic feeling with which the sea always inspired him. . . ." [n]

Byron took on board with him, in addition to Dr. Bruno, Fletcher, and his Newfoundland dog Lion, the Moreote boy Loukas Chalandritsanos. Byron had been taking care of the boy's mother and sisters since August, when he had brought them over from Ithaca. Loukas, then a handsome boy of fifteen, had been in the fighting band of Kolokotrones, but on hearing of the good fortune of his family, had come over to Cephalonia and had become Byron's favorite. The horses, most of the baggage, all the Committee supplies, and the bulldog Moretto were in the bombard with Gamba, Lega Zambelli, the steward, and the other servants. At Zante Byron put on board an additional eight thousand Levant dollars [£1,600],* which he received from Hancock's partner, Samuel Barff. The ships' papers were made out from Zante to Kalamo, one of the smaller Ionian islands near the Greek mainland.

Toward six o'clock they set sail for Missolonghi, a night's run with a good breeze. Gamba writes: "We sailed together till after ten at night; the wind favourable—a clear sky, the air fresh but not sharp.—Our sailors sang alternately patriotic songs. . . . We were all, but Lord Byron particularly, in excellent spirits. The Mistico sailed the fastest. When the waves divided us, and our voices could no longer reach each other, we made signals by firing pistols and carabines—'To-morrow we meet at Missolonghi—to-morrow.' Thus, full of confidence and spirits, we sailed along. At twelve, we were out of sight." [n]

* The Levant or Maria Teresa dollar was a common medium of exchange in Greece at the time. It was equal in value to 10 piastres, or a fifth of an English pound.

CHAPTER XXVIII

1824

A "Messiah" in Missolonghi

THERE WAS UNIVERSAL REJOICING in Missolonghi when a Zantiote boat brought the news that Byron was sailing for the mainland on December 30. Stanhope wrote to Bowring: "All are looking forward to Lord Byron's arrival as they would to the coming of a Messiah."[n] They knew that this Messiah carried an abundance of dollars. The soldiers—particularly the Suliotes, whose pay was several months in arrears—and the sailors of the fleet were murmuring mutinously. Not even the promise of Byron's dollars could hold them on the afternoon of the 30th, when several Turkish vessels came out of the gulf. The Greek ships at anchor off Missolonghi immediately cut their cables and took flight, leaving the Turks free to patrol the waters in front of the port.

On deck with his dreams, and unaware that the Turks were out, Byron found himself nearer to action than he supposed when at two o'clock in the morning of the 31st a large ship loomed suddenly in front of the mistico. Byron at first thought it a Greek vessel, but the captain of the mistico recognized it as Turkish. Petrified by fear, all on board kept a hushed silence, and even the dogs, Fletcher recalled, "though they had never ceased to bark during the whole of the night, did not utter, while within reach of the Turkish frigate, a sound."[n] The captain turned the rudder sharply and they veered away. The wind had become fresh by three o'clock and the fast-sailing mistico lost the Turk in the dark and kept off the coast until dawn. When daybreak came, they could see two large vessels: one, in the distance, apparently chasing the bombard, and the other between the mistico and the port of Missolonghi. They put into a creek near the Scrofes rocks and Byron landed Loukas and another man to carry a message to Stanhope. He wrote: "I am uneasy at being here: not so much on my own account as on that of a Greek boy with me, for you know what his fate would be; and I would sooner cut him in pieces, and myself too, than have him taken out by those barbarians." [n]

When a Turkish vessel approached, the mistico dashed out and followed the shallow waters along the coast to the north, finding a safe harbor at Dragomestre (now Astakos) before night. The Primates and officers of the town came on board and offered Byron every hospitality, but he preferred to sleep on the boat, where he had considerable money and other things of value.

Mavrocordatos was eager enough to rescue Byron and his precious cargo. He sent three ships to search the coast. The gunboats apparently found Byron at Dragomestre on January 2, but wind and weather kept them from starting on the short journey to Missolonghi until the 3rd. Then he was twice blown onto the rocks in the passage of the Scrofes. Byron had with him Fletcher, Tita, Dr. Bruno, and Loukas, who had returned from Missolonghi in one of the boats. The Turks had gone back to Patras, but the wind continuing contrary, the mistico anchored in the shelter of some islands until morning.

In the meantime, Pietro Gamba had his own adventure. The bombard had been pursued and captured by a Turkish ship and its captain taken on board for questioning. Gamba began thinking of his suspicious cargo: servants, horses, guns, money, a printing press, cannons, and helmets with Byron's arms on them. But what was most dangerous was his own diary and Byron's correspondence with the Greek chiefs. A Turk got into a boat, and before Gamba could see that he was not headed for the bombard, he dropped a bundle of Byron's letters loaded with fifty pounds of shot into the sea. Fortunately when the Turkish captain was about to order the captain of the bombard beheaded and his ship sunk, he recognized him as the man who had saved his life when he was shipwrecked in the Black Sea. He embraced him and took him to his cabin. When they arrived at Patras, the

Turkish captain called Gamba aboard and courteously accepted the telescope and bottles of rum and porter which the Count brought as a present. He recommended him to Yussuf Pasha, commander of the fort. After much Oriental delay and politeness, the bombard was released and proceeded to Missolonghi on the 4th. Gamba was surprised that Byron had not yet arrived.

But that night the mistico also anchored in the port. The next morning Byron put on his red military uniform for the landing and arrived at eleven o'clock to the rejoicing of the whole town. Each ship of the Greek squadron, which had slipped back after the departure of the Turks, fired a salute as he passed. Gamba, filled with emotion, met him as he disembarked: "I could scarcely refrain from tears. . . ." [n]

Mavrocordatos, Colonel Stanhope, and a long line of foreign and Greek officers greeted Byron at the door of the house that had been prepared for him. This was his first meeting with Prince Alexander Mavrocordatos, a squat, unimpressive little man whose dark kindly eyes squinting through the small round frames of his glasses made him look more like a scholar than the military leader he aspired to be. Dr. Millingen described him as "a clever, penetrating, ambitious man. His large Asiatic eyes, full of fire and wit, were tempered by an expression of goodness." [n]

Byron was predisposed to respect and trust the Prince, partly because he had education and breeding, but more perhaps because men such as Colonel Napier and Count Delladecima had assured him that Mavrocordatos was the only man with influence in Greek affairs who could be depended upon for unselfish patriotism. Educated at Constantinople, he came of a long line of Phanariot Greeks who had been Hospodars (Greek rulers under the Turks) in Wallachia and Moldavia, posts which bore the courtesy title of Prince. He had devoted his earlier years to the Oriental languages, and, according to Millingen, he was also "an excellent Greek scholar, spoke and wrote French like a native of France, and was tolerably well acquainted with English and Italian."

For better or worse, Byron had committed himself to aid Mavrocordatos and the forces of western Greece. Though he still maintained his independence from any party, he was soon convinced that the situation here was more propitious for doing something active for the cause than anywhere else in Greece.

Four or five thousand soldiers from various provinces had followed their *capitani* to Missolonghi, where they had assembled for regional conferences on the arrival of Mavrocordatos, and so were available for some strategic action. Mavrocordatos hopefully envisaged the capture of the remaining Turkish forts on the north and south sides of the Gulf of Corinth. The seizure of Lepanto (the commoner Greek name was Naupaktos), the only Turkish stronghold on the north shore, would, he believed, make Patras and the castle of the Morea opposite easy to conquer with the aid of the five Spetziot vessels and the two fireships remaining at Missolonghi.

Byron entered into these schemes at first with fervor, particularly when Mavrocordatos, seeing his eagerness and his willingness to take the Suliotes into his pay, suggested that he lead a force against Lepanto. On the 13th Byron told Hancock that he had undertaken to maintain the Suliotes for a year. After the death of Marco Botsaris in August, the remnant had joined with the Greeks in Missolonghi, assisting in the defense of the town. Byron consented to provide for five hundred, and the government agreed to care for another hundred under Byron's command. Byron was swept along by the patriotic fervor that permeated the town. His dreams of playing soldier had at last come true. Millingen observed: "His house was filled with soldiers; his receiving room resembled an arsenal of war, rather than the habitation of a poet. Its walls were decorated with swords, pistols, Turkish sabres, dirks, rifles, guns, blunderbusses, bayonets, helmets, and trumpets . . . ; and attacks, surprises, charges, ambuscades, battles, sieges, were almost the only topics of his conversation with the different capitani." [n]

Byron was not cast down by the dismal, marshy town or the house that had been provided for him. The presence of the soldiers in their silver trappings and their dirty fustanellas only stimulated remembrances of his happiest days in Greece. He had seen Missolonghi before in about the same season when he and Hobhouse passed through it in 1809. He recognized the dingy houses clustered on the flat, unwholesome promontory which stretched from the marshes of the mainland into the shallow lagoon.

Some three miles offshore, the lagoon is separated from the waters of the luminous gulf by a low line of sand pits and mud dunes reaching from the Scrofes rocks almost to the base of the cloud-capped and precipitous Varassova Mountain (the ancient Chalkis) rising three thousand feet above the water opposite Patras. Near the end of the promontory, at the edge of the oozy lagoon, stood the house in which Byron was quartered, one of the largest private dwellings in the town, the main structure rising two stories above a damp ground floor. The house, which belonged to Apostoli Capsali, one of the Ephores of Missolonghi, had several sheds attached to it around a courtyard, and behind it was an open space where Byron later drilled his Suliote guard, who shared the ground floor and the outhouses with the horses.

At high water or on rain-soaked days the ground about the house was a morass, and it was approachable only by water. The only pleasing prospect was the view to the south toward the open waters of the Gulf across the lagoon. Byron fortunately had that view from his window on the second floor. On a clear day he could see the mountains of the Morea and sometimes the dim outlines of some of the Ionian Islands.

Colonel Stanhope had already established himself on the first floor, where Capsali also retained rooms. Byron had the whole of the second floor, which included a bedroom and a sitting room facing the lagoon, and two or three other rooms for his servants. There was very little furniture. In Turkish fashion, he sat on a cushion on a kind of mattress. Gamba had quarters in another part of the town.

Undisturbed by the cold winter rains, Byron easily fell back into the rigorous way of life he had accepted without complaint when he was a young man seeing Greece for the first time. What comfort he had was supplied by his attentive valet, Fletcher, still grumbling about the lack of English conveniences but always loyal and devoted, and by Tita, who was at hand to offer assistance in every emergency. Lega Zambelli watched the money chests and wrote letters. The black servant acquired from Trelawny was an excellent cook and groom, and the handsome Greek boy Loukas, dressed as a page, was constantly at Byron's side or at his call.

But Byron had little time to think of comforts. The first matter for consideration was the formation of an artillery corps which could aid in the capture or siege of Lepanto. For this, the foreign officers—German, English, American, Swiss, Swedish—

might be most useful. But the greatest hope was placed upon William Parry, the firemaster, who was expected on the *Anne* at any moment with materials and men for manufacturing Congreve rockets and other modern devices of warfare. In addition to his other disbursements, Byron willingly subscribed £100 toward the support of the artillery corps, and—to please Stanhope, though he had grave reservations about it—£50 to help support the printing press which Stanhope had put into the hands of Dr. J. J. Meyer, a Swiss as doctrinaire as Stanhope himself.

The first number of the *Hellenica Chronica* (ΕΛΛΗΝΙΚΑ ΧΡΟΝΙΚΑ) appeared on January 14 (January 2 by the Greek calendar). It bore the motto, from Bentham, "The greatest good of the greatest number." Perhaps Byron overestimated the possible harm the paper could do in embroiling the Greeks, for the subscriptions in the whole country did not exceed forty. Its chief circulation was in the Ionian Islands and in England, and its articles were really directed to readers there.

In the middle of January Byron was more irritated by the ineptness and extravagance of Count Gamba than by the vagaries of Colonel Stanhope. Pietro had foolishly ordered 500 dollars' worth of cloth, exceeding Byron's order for some red cloth and oilcloth. What galled him was that this was at a time when he was trying to husband his resources, despite the many demands on him, for the assault on Lepanto.

Poor Pietro, however, was always the same: enthusiastic, loyal to Byron, and a little homesick. He had written to Teresa after their arrival in Missolonghi that Byron had been received "like a delivering Angel."[11] Despite his concern for the wasting of a few dollars, Byron had his eye on greater objects. He was willing to spend all his income and more for the cause to which he had dedicated himself. He could now count on the whole of the sum to be realized from the sale of his Lancaster estate, Rochdale, which, Kinnaird wrote, had been sold after years of litigation to James Dearden for £11,225.

News from the Morea seemed to favor the formation of a stable government. Both the Legislative and the Executive bodies sent memorials to Byron proclaiming him a benefactor of the nation and apologizing for the internal strife. They expressed the hope that he would give them every assistance with the English loan, and asked him to lend another 20,000 to 30,000 dollars to launch a campaign to secure Candia (Crete). But he had enough to do to keep the government at Missolonghi solvent. In general he was more willing to contribute his money and his services to some exciting action than to give time to routine details, which he turned over to Gamba or Stanhope.

There was potential violence in the atmosphere of Missolonghi. The townspeople were beginning to chafe under the arrogance of the soldiers, who were pressing for the payment of their arrears. The only encouraging news was that Parry had finally arrived at Corfu and was ready to leave for Missolonghi. It was now hoped that the expedition against Lepanto could be organized before serious altercations took place between the troops and the citizens.

On the night of January 18 Byron and his companions heard the noisy discharge of muskets in the streets, a sound that was not uncommon, for the Greeks wasted powder on every occasion of excitement. But this time it was a serious and dangerous disturbance. A citizen had complained because some Suliotes had taken up quarters in his house in his absence. While he was telling his story to Dr. Meyer, a Suliote passed and shot the Greek dead. Mavrocordatos finally got the military chiefs to deliver up the culprit, but the town was in a state of tension.

To add to the confusion, the Turkish fleet had come out of the Gulf again and the five Spetziot ships supposedly guarding Missolonghi pulled anchors and fled before them. Byron was extremely irritated, both by the disturbance in the city and by the flight of the Greek fleet, which might make Parry's arrival with the men and supplies for the artillery corps difficult or dangerous. On the morning of the 21st, ten Turkish men-of-war were cruising in front of Missolonghi. The town was thoroughly blockaded.

A scheme was devised to attack the Turks at night in small boats to damage their rigging and perhaps drive them onto the rocks. All the Europeans volunteered, and Byron insisted on being first in the attack. "He was so determined on this project," wrote Gamba, "that we soon became aware of the folly of exposing such a person on such a desperate enterprise; and we did all in our power to induce him to abandon it: at last we succeeded, but it was with great difficulty, for he was now intent only upon exposing himself to danger, and was extremely jealous that any one should be more forward than himself." [n]

But something more personal was urging Byron to desperate action. The bright dream of personal ambition and heroism that had eluded him since his adolescence at Harrow and his early maturity at Cambridge was intermingled with the frustration of the ideal love, forever sought and forever unattainable, or fading at the touch. Rising to the top of that refulgent image was the recollection of the devoted Cambridge choirboy Edleston, whose hair he still carried in a locket. For in some respects, Edleston, dying early, had more nearly approximated the dream of perfect love than any of the women Byron had known. Perhaps he saw something of Edleston in the dark-eyed, handsome page boy Loukas. But now his emotional involvement was complicated by a frustration that was new to him: apparent indifference to his affection. It was a cruel rebuff that brought home to him that he had indeed "grown agèd in this world of woe," so that the Grecian beauty of the pale face that had been irresistible to men and women alike had now ceased to attract. His greying hair was growing thin, his teeth were loose, his face had returned to a flabby plumpness. It was a sad and disillusioning experience to find that the boy on whom he had lavished expensive gifts did not respond with either affection or gratitude.*

It was something that Byron could not discuss openly with those about him; nor could he confess his chagrin in letters even to his most intimate friends. On the eve of his thirty-sixth birthday he turned to tortured verse for the frankest expression of his inner feelings:

'T is time this heart should be unmoved,
Since others it hath ceased to move:

---

* Doris Langley Moore has summed up the situation well: "In his typical self-destructive way, he [Byron] constantly drew attention to his age, and even to his being older, through the pace at which he had lived, than his actual years. He was aware that, turning thirty-six, oppressed with ill-health, disappointment, and anxiety, he could appear to his attendant of fifteen or sixteen no more than the outworn being he had often pronounced himself to be. He, whom so many had loved, had no other attraction for Lukas than his ability to send him out in the cavalcade with troops to serve under him, gold-embroidered clothes, gilded pistols, and money in his pocket." (*The Late Lord Byron*, p. 177.)

Yet, though I cannot be beloved,
Still let me love!

My days are in the yellow leaf;
The flowers and fruits of Love are gone;
The worm, the canker, and the grief
Are mine alone!

The fire that on my bosom preys
Is lone as some Volcanic isle;
No torch is kindled at its blaze—
A funeral pile.

The hope, the fear, the jealous care,
The exalted portion of the pain
And power of love, I cannot share,
But wear the chain.

But 't is not thus—*and 't is not* here—
Such thoughts should shake my soul, nor now
Where Glory decks the hero's bier,
Or binds his brow.

The Sword, the Banner, and the Field,
Glory and Greece, around me see!
The Spartan, borne upon his shield,
Was not more free.

Awake! (*not Greece—she is awake!*)
Awake, my spirit! Think through whom
Thy life-blood tracks its parent lake,
And then strike home!

Tread those reviving passions down,
Unworthy manhood!—unto thee
Indifferent should the smile or frown
Of Beauty be.

If thou regret'st thy youth, why live?
The land of honourable death
Is here:—up to the Field, and give
Away thy breath!

Seek out—less often sought than found—
A soldier's grave, for thee the best;
Then look around, and choose thy ground,
And take thy Rest.

Byron found an opportunity to convey four Turkish prisoners to the Ottoman fleet on a neutral (British) vessel, at the same time sending a letter to Yussuf Pasha, Turkish commander at Patras, urging him to "treat such Greeks as may henceforth fall into your hands with humanity, more especially, since the horrors of war are sufficiently great in themselves, without being aggravated by wanton cruelties on either side." [n]

On January 26, Captain Yorke of the English gun-brig *Alacrity* came ashore with two officers to demand satisfaction from the Greeks for the seizure of a neutral Ionian caïque. Byron was cordial in his entertainment of the British officers, who found him full of wit and gaiety. The ship's surgeon, James Forrester, observed the strange ménage and primitive surroundings in which he lived. The corridor "swarmed with Mainotes [Suliotes?] and others, armed to the teeth." Tita, with his bushy beard and full livery, ushered them in. They were waited on by Byron's page Loukas, "a young Greek, dressed as an Albanian or Mainote [*sic*], with very handsomely chased arms in his girdle." Byron "rattled away in such a harum-scarum manner, that it required an effort to recollect that he had ever written on a grave or affecting subject." After dinner they amused themselves by firing at bottles. At twelve paces Byron shattered the neck of a bottle no larger than a finger ring. "His precision was the most surprising," Forrester remarked, "because his hand shook as if under the influence of an ague fit. . . ." After each firing, his Newfoundland dog Lion retrieved the bottle. Forrester noted that Byron had a mustache "of a flaxen whiteness." And in this last year of the poet's life he noticed a burr in his speech and "a slight touch of a Scottish accent." [n]

On the 29th the Turkish Squadron returned to the gulf, but the Spetziot vessels had also disappeared and did not return, having gone home despite their promises to stay after the sailors were paid. More troubles ensued. The Suliotes could not easily surrender their independent tribal status to a single command. And Byron soon learned that he had the whole army on his back.

As long as he had money and was willing to use it, neither Mavrocordatos, nor the Governor of the town, nor any of the tribal chieftains, not even such wealthy ones as Stornares with his five hundred thousand cattle, could raise any money for the common cause.

Byron found too that, though he had undertaken to maintain five hundred Suliotes, according to Turkish custom he was expected to furnish rations to twelve hundred, because they counted their families and their livestock. And they evaded their promise to leave the Seraglio, which had been reserved for Parry's use. With Parry and the stores due to arrive any moment, Byron took desperate measures. He used the argument that was most effective. According to Stanhope, "He told them that if they did not quit the Seraglio immediately . . . he would discharge them from his service. The Suliots esteem Lord Byron and his money. They consented." [n]

Amid all his anxieties Byron found his chief consolation in his daily ride. The constant rains had left the streets almost impassable, and the gateway to the mainland through the fortifications was choked with mud. He hired a boy with a boat to ferry him across the lagoon to where his horses were waiting.[n] A mile from the town he had found firm ground for a gallop.

While waiting for Parry's supplies, Byron accepted an invitation from the Primates of Anatolico to visit that town, which had heroically repulsed a Turkish army the previous summer. The party, including Mavrocordatos, Byron, Gamba, and Loukas, set out in a flat-bottomed boat on the morning of Sunday, February 1. As they approached the shore of the town, which was on a fortified island just off the coast, they were saluted by a salvo of musketry and artillery. The women, dressed in their finest clothes, waved from the balconies. They all wanted Byron to remain overnight, but he and Gamba and Loukas returned to Missolonghi, making the three-hour journey in a soaking rain in the open boat. Both Gamba and Loukas were ill from the wetting. Byron was particularly anxious about Loukas and gave up his own bed to him and slept on the floor. His feelings again found vent in agonized verses:

What are to me those honours or renown
Past or to come, a new-born people's cry?

Albeit for such I could despise a crown
  Of aught save laurel, or for such could die.
I am a fool of passion, and a frown
  Of thine to me is as an adder's eye
To the poor bird whose pinion fluttering down
  Wafts unto death the breast it bore so high:
Such is this maddening fascination grown,
  So strong thy magic or so weak am I.[n]

Byron also had other worries. The stores which were arriving daily from Dragomestre had to be carried from the beaches to the Seraglio, but the proud Suliotes would not condescend to act as porters, and he had to hire townspeople to carry them. But even they refused to work on a holiday until he shamed them by himself rescuing the supplies that were being soaked in a heavy rain.

What interested Stanhope most was the safe delivery of the lithographic presses the Committee had sent out. Although skeptical of their utility, Byron bore with this as he did with an "elect blacksmith," sent out with Parry, "entrusted with three hundred and twenty-two Greek Testaments."[n] But an inventory soon disclosed that much which they had expected had not arrived. There were no Congreve rockets, and it would require two months to construct any. This was a blow to the foreign officers, and also to the Greeks, who had expected wonders from these promised weapons.

When Parry, the firemaster, arrived, he was overflowing with energy, but his spirits were dampened by the dismal town and by the news that neither Stanhope nor the government of the town had any funds for the maintenance of the men carrying on his work. He had spent much of his own money to provide for them on his way out. Although it was with some trepidation that he applied to Byron for financial assistance, he was soon put at ease.

Byron was much taken with Parry from the first, and soon was confiding in him the disappointments and harassments he had suffered. The firemaster's sound practicalities were a relief after his experiences with the indecisive Mavrocordatos and the "typographical Colonel." It soon became apparent that the whole financial responsibility as well as the command of the expedition against Lepanto would fall on Byron. The plan for a corps of three thousand was a myth postulated on his ability to provide for them.

The Suliotes were willing to serve while his money was available to them, though their jealousies were not abated. But Byron was still resolved to march as soon as Parry could prepare the artillery corps. He saw some cause for optimism in the reports of two Greeks escaped from Patras who told of dissensions between the European and Asiatic Turks. At Lepanto, conditions seemed favorable for an easy capture of the garrison. Exaggerated accounts of the extent of the preparations at Missolonghi and of Byron's means had shaken the resolution of the troops. An Albanian chieftain had assured a Greek spy that the soldiers would give only token resistance and would capitulate the moment Byron appeared with his forces under their walls. The time seemed ripe to strike.

In these circumstances, Byron saw the necessity of getting the artillery and the Suliote corps in marching order. But when he urged Parry to use all his power to hasten the preparations, the firemaster had to confess that he could not, with the resources at his command, produce what Stanhope through his press had already led the Greeks to expect. Byron reassured him, cheered the workers at the arsenal, and advanced all the money necessary for the project.

He had long conversations with Parry, who quickly concluded that despite his surface optimism Byron was deeply discouraged. "Beyond the walls of his own apartment, where he seemed to derive amusement from his books, and from his dog, Lion; and pleasure from the attachment of his servants, particularly from the attentions of Tita, he had neither security nor repose. He had the ungovernable Suliotes both to appease and control. . . . it was evident to me . . . that he felt himself deceived and abandoned, I had almost said betrayed. He might put a good face on the matter to others, because he would not be thought Quixotic or enthusiastic . . . but in his heart, he felt that he was forlorn and forsaken."[n]

His confidence in Parry having increased daily, Byron found a way of relieving himself of one of his chief worries: he asked Parry to take the responsibility for disbursing all the money he had set aside for the use of the Greeks. Beginning on February 14, Parry added this to his numerous occupations. At this time Byron was disbursing not less than 2,000 dollars a week in rations alone. When Gamba examined the lists of the Suliotes, he found that they had hopelessly padded their rolls. The chieftains had been up to their old tricks of pocketing the pay of nonexistent troops. Moreover, the chiefs, Gamba says, "required that the government should appoint, out of their number, two generals, two colonels, two captains, and inferior officers in the same proportion; in short, that out of three or four hundred actual Suliotes, there should be about one hundred and fifty above the rank of common soldiers. Their object, of course, was to increase their pay. . . . Byron burst into a violent passion, and protested that he would have no more to do with these people."[n]

Byron's burst of temper was not a light thing, and it was, in his present state of tension, a strain on his physical being that brought it near the breaking point. His anger soon passed, but his resolution to withdraw his support from the Suliotes remained. He scribbled a hasty note to Mavrocordatos: "February 15th, 1824. Having tried in vain at great expense, considerable trouble, and some danger, to unite the Suliotes for the good of Greece—and their own—I have come to the following resolution:—

"I will have nothing more to do with the Suliotes. They may go to the Turks, or the Devil,—they may cut me into more pieces than they have dissensions among themselves,—sooner than change my resolution.

"For the rest, I hold my means and person at the disposal of the Greek nation and Government the same as before."[n]

The Suliotes saw that they had gone too far, and finally agreed to form a new corps, three hundred of whom would act under the immediate orders of Byron and his lieutenant, Gamba. But Byron was exceedingly vexed that the plans for the immediate assault on Lepanto had to be postponed. He was calm now but much dispirited. That evening (the 15th), while talking with Parry and others, he was seized with a violent convulsion and fell into Parry's arms: "his countenance was very much distorted, his mouth drawn on one side."[n] Dr. Millingen recorded that while in the fit, "He foamed at the mouth, gnashed his teeth, and rolled his eyes like one in an epilepsy. After remaining about two minutes in this state his senses returned. . . ."[n]

When Gamba and the physicians arrived, he was calm but pale and weak. "As soon as he could speak," Gamba wrote, "he showed himself perfectly free from all alarm; but he very coolly asked, whether his attack was likely to prove fatal? 'Let me know,' he said. 'Do not think I am afraid to die—I am not.'"[n] They carried him up the stairs to his own bed. Gamba believed the attack had been brought on by his vexations and by his abstemious diet.

The next day he was still very weak, but he got up at noon. Parry recommended a more nourishing diet and "stimulant drinks." Dr. Bruno thought he should be bled. Byron would not consent to having a vein opened, but finally allowed Bruno to apply eight leeches to his temples. The blood flowed copiously and when the leeches were removed, it could not be stopped. Byron later wrote to Murray that "they had gone too near the temporal artery for my temporal safety," and that "neither styptic nor caustic would cauterise the orifice till after a hundred attempts."[n] It was not stopped completely until eleven o'clock at night. In the meantime Byron fainted, and later joked about his weakness, saying that he had fainted at the sight of his own blood like a fine lady.

He was up the following day (the 17th), but did not go out. He chafed because his weakness prevented him from joining an expedition to try to capture a Turkish brig-of-war that had gone aground near the city, but he offered to pay the expenses of the venture. Another matter concerned him even more. When urging the Carbonari to action in Ravenna, Byron had quoted with some bravado Marmontel's saying that "Revolutions are not to be made with Rose-water."[n] But now that he was actively engaged in one, he began to see that perhaps his chief usefulness might be found in quenching the flames of cruelty and revenge. Individual humanity always had a stronger power to move him than general principles.

Among the Turkish women and children who had been taken as slaves by some of the wealthier Greeks when their men had been massacred in the first outbreak of the revolution in Missolonghi were the wife and daughter of Hussein Aga. They had appealed to Dr. Millingen to shelter them from the brutality of the Greeks. The little girl, Hatadje, was just nine, the age of Byron's daughter Ada. Her dark eyes and dignified manner pleased him, and he took her under his care as Don Juan had protected the Turkish girl he had rescued in the siege of Ismail. He ordered costly dresses to be made for her and her mother. He thought of sending her to England, perhaps to be a companion to his daughter, or to Teresa in Italy. But in soberer moments he probably realized that Ada's mother would not welcome a little infidel who would talk of Allah and of Ada's father. In the end, Byron sent her with her mother to Cephalonia to the care of Dr. Kennedy and his wife until the mother could join her husband in Patras. At the same time he sent a number of other Turkish women to Prevesa, then in control of the Turks.

The stranded Turkish brig was stripped and burned by the Turks themselves before the Greeks could capture her; Byron had been too weak to join the expedition. The nerves of the foreign officers and men at the arsenal were jittery since the near riot in the town. On the 19th a serious incident ignited the tinder. A Suliote named Yiotes took Botsaris's little boy to look at the machinery and fireworks at the Seraglio. When he was stopped by the guard, a fight was started which ended in the death of Lieutenant Sass, a Swede, and the wounding of Yiotes. The news spread quickly that a foreigner had killed Yiotes. The Suliotes rushed out, and there was fear that the arsenal would be attacked and the town sacked. Byron gave orders that the cannon be drawn up pointing toward the gate. The excited Suliotes gathered around, threatening to attack the house and murder the foreigners. The fury finally subsided, possibly because of the businesslike defensive preparations, and the discovery that Yiotes had not been killed.

In the meantime, Byron sent for the Suliote captains. Stanhope was impressed with Byron's *sang-froid* on this occasion, when, still weak from his illness and bleeding, "with his whole nervous system completely shaken," he confronted "the mutinous Suliots, covered with dirt and splendid attires. . . . Lord Byron, electrified . . . seemed to recover from his sickness; and the more the Suliots raged, the more his calm courage triumphed."[n]

CHAPTER XXIX

1824

A Death for Greece

IN THE LAST DAYS OF February, Byron recovered gradually from his illness, but the spirit of hope that had animated his first weeks in Missolonghi seemed to be slipping away. Dr. Millingen observed a subtle deterioration in his physical condition, and noted the mental depression which frequently seized him. One day when Millingen was trying to prove to him that a total reform of his mode of living might restore his vigor, Byron said with impatience: "Do you suppose that I wish for life? I have grown heartily sick of it, and shall welcome the hour I depart from it. . . . But the apprehension of two things now haunt my mind. I picture myself slowly expiring on a bed of torture, or terminating my days like Swift—a grinning idiot!" [n]

Part of his depression arose from the shock of discovery: despite all he had done for the picturesque mountain soldiers, he could not trust them. The Suliotes now talked openly of leaving Missolonghi on what they thought would be a more lucrative and easier expedition than that against Lepanto. Gamba says: "They talked of marching upon Arta, where they hoped to find considerable booty. They owned that they did not like to fight against stone walls. Lord Byron offered to give them a month's pay if they would go; and they might go where they pleased." [n] A new chagrin awaited Byron when Parry announced that six of the mechanics, frightened by the recent occurrences, had thrown up their jobs and asked to be sent home after only fourteen days of work in the arsenal. Parry was irate, the more so as he had to call on Byron again for aid in paying their passage.

Colonel Stanhope departed for Athens on the 21st, sanguine of his ability to convert the Greeks to unity and constitutional government with his printing press. Byron too, on the collapse of his hopes for the expedition against Lepanto, had contemplated leaving, but he could not uproot himself so easily. When, irritated by the Suliotes, he intimated his intention to depart, the citizens of the town and the soldiers grumbled, and he remained.

The fit that had seized him on the 15th, whatever it was, added to his anxieties, for he was obsessed constantly with the fear of its return, though he wrote nonchalantly about it. He was subject alternately to spells of the deepest depression and almost hysterical high spirits, when he would indulge in some of the practical jokes that Parry has recorded, such as his luring his poor valet Fletcher into attempting to make love to a soldier dressed as a girl.

To cap the week of annoyance and tragic mishaps, at eight o'clock on the evening of the 21st, a severe earthquake shook the flimsy buildings of the town and caused a near panic not only among the Greeks but also among the English and other foreigners, who scrambled to get out of doors. Describing it to Murray the following week, Byron said: ". . . the whole army discharged their arms, upon the same principle that savages beat drums, or howl, during an eclipse. . . ."[n] While Byron laughed at Parry and the others, who were "rather squeezed in the press for precedence" in the scuffle to get out of doors and windows, he had not been quite calm through it all. His first concern had been for his page boy Loukas, whom he sought first around "the tottering hall."

Byron could not quite admit the extent of his defeat, either to his friends in England or to himself. To his pleasure, and embarrassment, he had learned from Hobhouse and Kinnaird that his Greek adventure had made him a hero in England at the moment when everything seemed conspiring to frustrate his being one in Greece. He occasionally revealed the depth of his disillusionment to those nearest him. Stanhope told Hobhouse later: "Byron was sorry now and then that he ever came to Greece. . . . At other times he said he was glad he had come, and talked with enthusiasm of the cause. He would say that it was better being at Missolonghi than going about talking and singing at parties in London, at past forty, like Tom Moore." [n]

After the dismissal of the main body of the Suliotes, Byron kept his own bodyguard, consisting of fifty-six men under Draco and one or two other leaders he trusted most. They were housed in a large outer room, where, their carbines resting against the wall, they lounged about, conversing in their animated way, or sitting on the floor playing cards.

According to Parry, Byron spent a good deal of his time in this room with the soldiers, particularly in wet weather. "On such occasions he was almost always accompanied by his favourite dog Lyon [*sic*], who was perhaps his dearest and most affectionate friend." Byron talked to the animal as if he were a person. "His most usual phrase was, 'Lyon, you are no rogue, Lyon.' . . . The dog's eyes sparkled, and his tail swept the floor, as he sat with his haunches on the ground. 'Thou art more faithful than men, Lyon; I trust thee more.' Lyon sprang up, and barked and bounded round his master. . . . 'Lyon, I love thee, thou art my faithful dog!' and Lyon jumped and kissed his master's hand. . . ." [n]

In the last days of February the weather cleared and Byron was able to ride more often. Partly, no doubt, to keep his Suliote guard exercised and to work off their surplus energies, and partly because he gained some satisfaction from the gesture of marching out in full dress with his own military corps, he frequently took them on a brisk march along the marshy plain behind the city.

To keep up the spirits of the few foreigners, Byron authorized Parry to reorganize the artillery corps, engaging a few Greeks to fill it out. But he realized that he was merely marking time. What made it the more galling was that the Albanians in the Turkish garrison at Lepanto, who had first offered to surrender to him for 40,000 dollars, now agreed to take 25,000. But the Suliotes, excellent mountain warriors, had no stomach for a siege, even one that promised to be so easy.

Toward the end of February, George Finlay arrived from Athens carrying letters from Trelawny and from Odysseus (Ulysses). Byron welcomed him as a man with whom he could talk of things beyond the limited realm of the firemaster. Parry amused him for a time and seemed an excellent antidote to the theoretical Stanhope. But Finlay had lived in a sphere closer to Byron's own, had been to Newstead Abbey, could discuss Goethe and *Manfred,* and yet had a youthful zest for Byron's reminiscences and witty comments on his contemporaries. In these conversations Byron grew animated and gay, full of anecdotes and stories of his former life. As the floodgates of memory opened, he talked freely of his escapades with Hobhouse and Scrope Davies, even of his recollections of Aberdeen and his early love for Mary Duff.

But Finlay had come on a serious mission. He had brought an invitation from Odysseus to Byron and Mavrocordatos, requesting them to meet him at a congress at Salona (Amphissa), where it was hoped the various factions and parties among the Greeks might reach some understanding for the unity and defense of the country. Trelawny added his persuasion. Amid the confusion that surrounded him, Byron had a temporary nostalgia for Trelawny, who had always managed to clear the decks of his chaotic household. Although he shared some of Mavrocordatos's distrust of Odysseus, after a consultation they decided to meet the crafty leader at Salona in two weeks.

During the month of March, Byron's health continued to be precarious, but he carried on his normal riding and exercise as if resolved not to allow physical weakness to govern his life. He was often attacked by vertigoes, and sometimes had disagreeable nervous sensations, which he said resembled the feeling of fear. His volatile spirits were raised by letters from England. But one from Thomas Moore upset him. Moore's letters had generally recalled pleasant memories of his days of fame in London, but Byron was offended when Moore said he had heard that "instead of pursuing heroic and warlike adventures, he was residing in a delightful villa, continuing Don Juan."[n] To have such stories circulating in England, where, Hobhouse told him, he was already a hero of the revolution, annoyed him. He replied rather curtly.

As Byron was living constantly at the edge of his physical and mental strength, the balance of his temper was easily upset. His irritation burst forth at unexpected moments. Even the mild-mannered and suave Mavrocordatos roused him to rudeness. Particularly now that there seemed a chance of uniting the

Greeks, Byron was somewhat annoyed that the Prince continued to show distrust of the other leaders. Desiring to maintain his independence and not be too much influenced by any party, he had deliberately tried to avoid undue intimacy with Mavrocordatos, discouraging his evening social visits and holding chiefly to business.

On the 17th, Byron wrote a cheerful letter to Teresa. He had long ceased to share his confidences with her, and he addressed her with the condescending humor he might have used toward an amiable child: "My dearest T.—The Spring is come —I have seen a Swallow today—and it was time—for we have had but a wet winter hitherto—even in Greece. . . . I do not write to you letters about politics—which would only be tiresome, and yet we have little else to write about—except some private anecdotes which I reserve for 'viva voce' when we meet —to divert you at the expense of Pietro and some others. . . . I write to you in English without apologies—as you say you have become a great proficient in that language of birds.—To the English and Greeks—I generally write in Italian—from a Spirit of contradiction, I suppose—and to show that I am Italianized by my long stay in your Climate." [n]

Aware of the overtures of Odysseus to Byron, the officials of the Greek government at Kranidi in the Morea wrote to invite him to come in person to the seat of government, and proposed as an alternate suggestion that he accept the office of Governor-General of Greece (except the Morea and the Islands). This offer may well have been prompted in part by the advance knowledge that Byron was to be named one of the administrators of the English loan. The purpose was also no doubt to win him away from any alliance with Odysseus, and possibly to undermine the influence and authority of Mavrocordatos in northern Greece. Byron's reply was that he was first going to Salona and that then he would consider their offers.

News of the conclusion of the loan was a spur to Byron's hope, though he still had a realistic vision of the internal obstacles to the success of the Greek cause. Like Finlay, he saw the chief virtues of the Greeks in the common people rather than in their leaders. Parry recalled that Byron had returned from his ride one day unusually pleased. "An interesting countrywoman, with a fine family, had come out of her cottage and presented him with a curd cheese and some honey, and could not be persuaded to accept of payment for it. 'I have felt,' he said, 'more pleasure this day, and at this circumstance, than for a long time past.' "[n]

Byron had his own ideas about the most suitable government for the Greeks. He thought the Swiss or American system would be best adapted to them. "From what I have already said of the different interests and divisions which prevail in Greece," he told Parry, "it is to me plain that no other government will suit it so well as a federation." Yet he would not force the American or any other system on them, but let them work out their own. "There is no abstract form of government which we can call good."[n]

During these intimate talks with Parry, while the rain was making an impassable mire of the streets of Missolonghi, Byron confessed his plans and hopes for the future. But these hopes were short-lived. The Suliotes, having discovered that their expectations of plunder in Arta were not well founded, had returned to Missolonghi. And Mavrocordatos, in order to provide for them, was obliged to ask Byron for another provisional loan. Toward the end of March, applications were made to him for 50,000 dollars in one day.

March 27 had been set for the departure for Salona to meet the other leaders of northern Greece, but the roads were impassable and the rivers unfordable. On the 30th the Primates presented Byron with the citizenship of the town. It was a fine document in the most flourishing Greek, signed by all the notables. But it was only preliminary to a new request for money. Byron was exasperated beyond measure, but he complied, for it was his own decision to remain in Greece and do what he could to the end of his means and his strength. And when they appealed to him personally, he could never withstand them.

It now seems apparent that Byron either suppressed from his letters or molded in the shape of hopefulness all the darker disillusionments of his days in Missolonghi. Those nearest him, however, were aware that he was deeply troubled by the course of events and by his own failures. The rain pelting in the lagoon and in the muddy streets, the crescendo of disagreeable events, the constant drain on his purse and his nerves, the instability of the Greek character, the quarrelsomeness of the foreign Philhellenes, the precariousness of his health, and the constant fear of the recurrence of the frightening fits all depressed his spirits and dampened his usual good humor.

Parry noted that at the beginning of April Byron became irritable. What really oppressed him was the realization that his final and most ambitious hope, that of uniting the Greek leaders, had melted away like that he had earlier entertained of leading the Suliotes against Lepanto. Finlay observed the effect on him of this final blow:

"A mist fell from Lord Byron's eyes. He owned that his sagacity was at fault, and he abandoned all hope of being able to guide the Greeks, or to assist them in improving their administration. . . . Then, too, he began to express doubts whether circumstances had authorized him to recommend the Greek loan to his friends in England. . . . He feared that the proceeds of a loan might be misspent by one party, and the loan itself disowned by another." [n]

On top of the cares and anxieties Byron felt in these last days was the burden of an emotional frustration that drove him once more to seek release in writing. His unrequited love for the boy Loukas Chalandritsanos seems to have inspired the last poem he ever penned:

I watched thee when the foe was at our side,
Ready to strike at him—or thee and me.
Were safety hopeless—rather than divide
Aught with one loved save love and liberty.

I watched thee on the breakers, when the rock
Received our prow and all was storm and fear,
And bade thee cling to me through every shock;
This arm would be thy bark, or breast thy bier.

I watched thee when the fever glazed thine eyes,
Yielding my couch and stretched me on the ground,
When overworn with watching, ne'er to rise
From thence if thou an early grave hadst found.

The earthquake came, and rocked the quivering wall,
And men and nature reeled as if with wine.

Whom did I seek around the tottering hall?
For thee. Whose safety first provide for? Thine.

And when convulsive throes denied my breath
The faintest utterance to my fading thought,
To thee—to thee—e'en in the gasp of death
My spirit turned, oh! oftener than it ought.

Thus much and more; and yet thou lov'st me not,
And never wilt! Love dwells not in our will.
Nor can I blame thee, though it be my lot
To strongly, wrongly, vainly love thee still.[n]

Laboring under the weight of this intolerable feeling, Byron was yet to suffer another shock. There was a rumor that the Turks were landing a force at the village of Krioneri near Missolonghi. And that same day a nephew of George Karaiskakis, a chieftain who had established himself at Anatolico, had been wounded in a quarrel with some Missolonghiot boatmen. The next afternoon, 150 soldiers of Karaiskakis came to seek vengeance, seized two of the Primates as hostages, and took possession of the fortress of Vasiladi at the mouth of the harbor.

It was Byron's coolness and energy, according to Millingen, which brought an end to the siege on April 5. "Gun-boats were sent against Vasiladi in order to dislodge the rebels. Their approach so much intimidated them, that they precipitately abandoned the island." [n] Karaiskakis's soldiers gave up the Primates and were then allowed to embark for Anatolico.

This incident did not have its full impact on Byron until it was over. Exciting events always buoyed him up. But the reaction set in when he contemplated its possible consequences. He feared that if the news of this dissension reached England it would ruin the Greek credit and jeopardize the loan. "But what incensed him most," Millingen observed, "was the weakness and irresolution, exhibited on this occasion by Mavrocordato. . . ." [n]

The sands were running out. Those closely associated with Byron noted the changes that had taken place in him in the course of a few weeks. Pietro Gamba observed how much he chafed under the restraints of the weather, which had prevented him from riding or making the journey to Salona. "In the mean time," Gamba wrote, "My lord, by persevering in the same mode of life, had become very thin; but he was glad of it, being much afraid at all times of the contrary habit of body. His temper was more irritable; he was frequently angry about trifles—more so, indeed, than about matters of importance: but his anger was only momentary." [n]

On Friday, April 9, letters arrived from the Ionian Islands and from England. A letter from his sister giving good news of his daughter filled him with mingled delight and melancholy. He came out of his chamber holding Ada's profile in his hand. Hobhouse had written encouragingly: "Nothing can be more serviceable to the cause than all you have done—Everybody is more than pleased and content—As for myself, I only trust that the great sacrifices which you have made may contribute (which I have no doubt they will) to the final success of the great cause —This will indeed be doing something worth living for—and will make your name and character stand far above those of any contemporary." [n]

According to Gamba, Byron's health had suffered visibly during the preceding day or two. But though the weather was threatening, he insisted on taking his ride, which the rains had prevented for several days. "Three miles from the town," Gamba wrote, "we were overtaken by a heavy rain, and we returned to the town walls wet through, and in a violent perspiration." It had been their practice to dismount at the walls and return by boat, but Gamba urged Byron to continue on his horse the rest of the way, so as not to remain, heated as he was, quietly exposed to the rain and cold in an open boat for another half hour. He would not listen, saying: "I should make a pretty soldier, indeed, if I were to care for such a trifle." [n]

"Two hours after his return home," Gamba wrote, "he was seized with a shuddering: he complained of fever and rheumatic pains. At eight in the evening, I entered his room; he was lying on a sofa, restless and melancholy. He said to me, 'I suffer a great deal of pain; I do not care for death; but these agonies I cannot bear.' " [n]

But Byron did not consider the attack serious enough to deter him from riding out again the next morning an hour earlier than usual for fear it would rain if he waited. He had been feverish during the night, but had slept well; he still had pains in his bones and a headache. He rode a long time through the olive woods with Gamba and his Suliote bodyguard, talking and in good spirits. On his return, however, he scolded his groom for having placed on his horse the wet saddle he had used the day before.

Finlay, then about to leave for Athens, called on Byron that evening with Dr. Millingen. They found him lying on the sofa, complaining of a slight fever and pains. Millingen recalled that "after remaining some few minutes in silence, he said that during the whole day he had reflected a great deal on a prediction, which had been made to him, when a boy, by a famed fortune-teller in Scotland." The prediction was "Beware your thirty-seventh year." He spoke of this circumstance with such emotion that it was apparent it had made a deep impression on his mind. When his guests taxed him with superstition, he replied: "To say the truth, I find it equally difficult to know what to believe in this world, and what not to believe." [n]

Having a healthy dread of the remedies of his medical men, Byron did not call Dr. Bruno until late that night. He then complained of wandering pains over his body and chills alternating with hot spells. During the night he slept little and restlessly, and in the morning Bruno, as usual, recommended bleeding, but when Byron refused firmly, he dosed his patient with castor oil and gave him a hot bath.

Parry came on Sunday the 11th, the second day of Byron's illness, and being alarmed, got his reluctant consent to prepare a vessel to take him to Zante. While the preparations were being made, however, the illness intensified; and by the 13th, when the boat was ready, a sirocco had blown up a veritable hurricane. No vessel was able to leave the port. In the meantime, Dr. Bruno prescribed antimony powder to reduce the fever, as Byron resolutely resisted both bleeding and the application of leeches.

Dr. Millingen was not called in as a consultant until the fourth day of the illness. He agreed with Bruno that bleeding was necessary, but bowed to Byron's strong antipathy to it and thought it could be postponed.

On April 14, Byron arose at noon, as he had done every day since his illness. He was still weak and suffered from pains in his head. He wanted to go riding, but he was persuaded to go back to bed and he remained there. No one was allowed to see him but the two physicians, Count Gamba, the servants Tita and Fletcher, and Parry. At times, Parry suspected, the physicians made excuses to exclude him from the room, saying that the patient was asleep. They knew that he encouraged Byron in his opposition to bleeding, which they now daily urged upon the sick man. Parry noted that the patient's mind frequently wandered in delirium.

That same day Dr. Bruno brought Millingen with him to see whether the two of them could persuade Byron to submit to bleeding, but he became irritated, "saying that he knew well that the lancet had killed more people than the lance." [n] They continued administering pills and cathartics, and at noon the next day returned to demand his blood, but he refused again as peevishly as before. "Drawing blood from a nervous patient," Byron said, "is like loosening the chords of a musical instrument, the tones of which are already defective for want of sufficient tension." [n]

Dr. Bruno pleaded with him again with tears in his eyes "that he would permit me to bleed him, for the sake of all that he held dear in the world," but Byron replied that he did not wish it and "that all my prayers and the chatterings of others were useless." [n] It is difficult to know whether Byron's mind was wandering, whether he was serious, or whether he was merely trying to play a practical joke on the doctors, when he asked Dr. Millingen on this day (the 15th) to search out an old and ugly witch in the town, "in order that she may examine whether this sudden loss of my health does not depend on the evil eye. She may devise some means to dissolve the spell." [n] Millingen was willing to oblige him, but he did not mention the subject again.

Parry, who had been busy during the day, came at seven in the evening, and perceived that Byron was "seriously and dangerously ill." But the sirocco continued to blow, and it would have been impossible to get him to Zante. His situation seemed terribly pathetic to Parry. Despite the number of people about him, there was no one, Parry thought, in whom he could confide. Fletcher, he noted, seemed "to have nearly lost his master's confidence." Both Fletcher and Count Gamba "were so affected, and so unmanned by the situation of Lord Byron, that whenever I saw them they required almost as much attention and assistance as

Lord Byron himself." The same was true of Dr. Bruno, who was so agitated "that he was incapable of bringing whatever knowledge he might possess into use. Tita was kind and attentive, and by far the most teachable and useful of all the persons about Lord Byron. As there was nobody invested with any authority over his household, after he fell sick, there was neither method, order, nor quiet, in his apartments. . . . There was also a want of many comforts which, to the sick, may indeed be called necessaries, and there was a dreadful confusion of tongues." [n]

Parry had a soothing effect on Byron, who asked him to take a chair and sit beside him. He talked to Parry of himself and his family, of his intentions for Greece. "He spoke of death also with great composure, and though he did not believe his end was so very near, there was something about him so serious and so firm, so resigned and composed, so different from any thing I had ever before seen in him, that my mind misgave me, and at times foreboded his speedy dissolution." [n] It is rather curious that it was only to the rough old soldier Parry that Byron talked of religion in his last days. Dr. Millingen recorded: "I did not hear him make any, even the smallest, mention of religion. At one moment I heard him say: 'Shall I sue for mercy?' After a long pause he added: 'Come, come, no weakness! let's be a man to the last.' " [n]

Parry left him about ten o'clock in the evening, and the doctors returned to menace him. He was seized by a violent spasmodic coughing that finally caused him to vomit. Dr. Bruno threatened him with inflammation of the lungs if he did not allow himself to be bled. But it was finally the Doctor's tearful protestations of his devotion and Byron's own weakness that caused him to succumb and promise to yield his veins the following day. But when the doctors came to collect their pound of blood the next morning, Byron said that he had passed a better night than he had expected and therefore would not trouble them. Millingen reminded him of his promise and found an argument that moved him: that the disease might so act on his "cerebral and nervous system as entirely to deprive him of his reason." Then "casting at us both the fiercest glance of vexation, he threw out his arm, and said, in the most angry tone: 'Come; you are, I see, a d——d set of butchers. Take away as much blood as you will; but have done with it.' " The doctors drew out a full pound. "Yet the relief obtained," Millingen noted, "did not correspond to the hopes we had anticipated." [n]

Two hours later they took another pound, "and this was indeed very thin in appearance the same as the first, and with little serum. Immediately after he felt alleviated, more tranquil, and slept a little." [n] But it was the tranquillity of a man whose vital forces had been drained. Parry observed that on this day, the 16th, Byron "was alarmingly ill, and almost constantly delirious. He spoke alternately in English and Italian, and spoke very wildly." [n] Parry implored the doctors not to physic or bleed him, but they reassured him and he left. With Parry gone, there was no one to protect Byron, for even the servants had been won over to the doctors' faith in bleeding. The quality of his pulse remaining the same, Bruno recorded, "we proposed a third bleeding, which we were the more convinced was necessary since his expression became fixed and he complained from time to time of a numbness in his fingers, all of which indicated that the inflammation was mounting to his brain." [n]

In his lucid moments Byron was able still to resist further bleeding, and they plied him with purgatives again. But the next day they took a few ounces of blood, arguing that it would make him sleep. His wild talk during his delirium caused Dr. Bruno to order Tita to remove the stiletto and pistols from beside the bed. It is small wonder that in the confusion of his last days the witnesses should have been at odds in their accounts. Parry discounted most of what was reported of Byron's conversation during the last five days, believing that it was only delirious speech.

The doctors began to have serious apprehensions for the first time on the afternoon of the 17th, and, partly to strengthen their own arguments for bleeding, they called in two other doctors for consultation: Dr. Loukas Vaya, who had been the most trusted physician of Ali Pasha and who was physician and surgeon to the Suliote corps, and Dr. Enrico Treiber, a German attached to the artillery corps. Byron consented to see them only on condition that they would say nothing. After consultation, only Bruno still held out for bleeding. While they were there, the patient apparently went into some kind of shock: ". . . his pulses were weak, contracted but vibrating, and his hands and feet were cold."[n] They gave him some China bark, water and wine to allay his thirst, and applied two blisters on the insides of his thighs (he would not, he said, "allow any one to see my lame foot").[n]

When Parry called on him in the morning, the 18th, Byron was delirious and very ill. It was the Greek Easter Sunday, and, as it was the custom of the people to celebrate that occasion by firing off their muskets, Mavrocordatos, Parry says, arranged "that I should march with the artillery brigade and Suliotes to some little distance from the town, and exercise them, in order to carry the inhabitants along with us."[n] The town guard patrolled the streets, informing the people of the danger to their benefactor and asking them to remain quiet. The scheme worked and Byron was spared the rattle of musketry in his last hours.

Seeing the signs of dissolution rapidly approaching, Dr. Bruno returned to the one remedy he knew, and, getting the consent of the other doctors, applied twelve leeches at the temples and extracted two pounds of blood. For a while the patient was calmer, and when Gamba brought letters insisted on reading them himself. One Gamba withheld. It was from the Archbishop Ignatius and told him that the Sultan had proclaimed him, in full divan, an enemy of the Porte. Another from Luriottis to Mavrocordatos mentioned that the loan was concluded and that Byron was to be at the head of a commission for its disposal. This pleased him, for he knew that his name and fame had largely contributed to the success of the loan.

It was the middle of the afternoon before Byron realized, possibly from the weeping of the servants and the perturbation of the doctors, that he was in mortal danger. He told Millingen: "Your efforts to preserve my life will be vain. Die I must: I feel it. Its loss I do not lament; for to terminate my wearisome existence I came to Greece.—My wealth, my abilities, I devoted to her cause.—Well: there is my life to her. One request let me make to you. Let not my body be hacked, or be sent to England. Here let my bones moulder.—Lay me in the first corner without pomp or nonsense."[n]

Gamba wrote: "Dr. Millingen, Fletcher, and Tita were round his bed. The two first could not contain their tears, and walked out of the room. Tita also wept, but he could not retire, as Byron had hold of his hand; but he turned away his face.

Byron looked at him steadily, and said, half smiling, in Italian —'Oh questa è una bella scena.' " He became delirious soon after and began to talk wildly, Gamba recorded, "as if he were mounting a breach in an assault. He called out, half in English, half in Italian—'Forwards—forwards—courage—follow my example —don't be afraid,' &c." [n]

When Parry returned, everything was in confusion. Parry got Byron to take some bark the doctors had prescribed. He found the patient's hands deadly cold. "With the assistance of Tita," he wrote, "I endeavoured gently to create a little warmth in them; and I also loosened the bandage which was tied round his head. Till this was done he seemed in great pain, clenched his hands at times, gnashed his teeth, and uttered the Italian exclamation of *Ah Christi!* . . . after it was loosened, he shed tears. I encouraged him to weep, and said, 'My Lord, I thank God, I hope you will now be better; shed as many tears as you can, you will sleep and find ease.' He replied faintly, 'Yes, the pain is gone, I shall sleep now,' and he again took my hand, uttered a faint good night, and sank into a slumber; my heart ached, but I thought then his sufferings were over, and that he would wake no more." [n]

But he did wake again, to talk sometimes wildly and sometimes calmly and pathetically to those about him. "I wished to go to him," Gamba wrote, "—but I had not the heart. Mr. Parry went, and Byron knew him again, and squeezed his hand, and tried to express his last wishes. He mentioned names, as before, and also sums of money: he spoke sometimes in English, sometimes in Italian. From those about him, I collected that . . . he could be understood to say—'Poor Greece!—poor town!—my poor servants!' Also, 'Why was I not aware of this sooner?' and 'My hour is come!—I do not care for death—but why did I not go home before I came here?' At another time he said, 'There are things which make the world dear to me [*Io lascio qualche cosa di caro nel mondo*]: for the rest, I am content to die!' " *[n]

* The ending, "*Per il resto son contento di morire,*" the Marchesa Origo says, should be translated: "as to the rest, I am *glad* to die." (Origo, p. 383 n.) A literal translation of the first part would be: "I leave something dear in the world." But it is still a little ambiguous. The Marchesa Origo implies that he meant *someone,* and suggests that it could have been a veiled message to Teresa. It is equally possible to suppose that he meant *something:* his work, his efforts

As Byron came to realize that his medical men could do nothing for him, he did not hesitate to express his anger at them in his lucid moments. But, moved by Fletcher's tears, "he took his hand," according to Hobhouse, "and began to talk kindly to him, saying he was sorry he had done nothing for him by his will, but Mr. Hobhouse would be his friend and see him provided for. He then expressed an anxiety to do something for his favourite *chasseur*, Tita, and his Greek boy, Luca, but Fletcher told him to speak of more important concerns."[n] He did apparently manage to provide for Loukas by giving him the receipt for the 3,000 dollars he had lent to the town of Missolonghi, and, knowing from his own experience that such a claim was only a problematical asset, he also ordered that he be given the bag of Maria Teresa dollars that he habitually kept in his room.[n]

He attempted to tell Fletcher his last wishes: "Oh, my poor dear child!—my dear Ada! my God, could I but have seen her! Give her my blessing—and my dear sister Augusta and her children;—and you will go to Lady Byron, and say——tell her every thing—you are friends with her." His voice trailed off and he kept muttering things which Fletcher could not understand, but then he would raise his voice and say: "Fletcher, now if you do not execute every order which I have given you, I will torment you hereafter if possible."[n]

Thereafter Byron grew delirious, with only intervals of lucidity, though he attempted again to give his last orders to Fletcher, who could not understand a word. It is not surprising that his strength was waning fast. For the doctors on top of all the bleeding had concocted another purgation, this time a clyster of "senna, three ounces of Epsom salts, and three of castor oil."[n] Byron got out of bed a little before six in the evening to relieve himself, and coming back said, "The Damned Doctors have drenched me so that I can scarcely stand."[n]

This was the last time he left his bed. At about six o'clock on Sunday the 18th Fletcher heard him say: "I want to sleep now," and he turned on his back and shut his eyes.[n] These were his last words, and he scarcely moved again. The doctors now had him in their power, and they applied leeches to his temples.

---

for the liberation of Greece? And, of course, we have only Pietro's second-hand report, perhaps from someone who did not understand Italian very well.

The blood flowed from his already impoverished veins all night.

Not long after Byron had entered this comatose state, more letters arrived from England, from Hobhouse and Kinnaird, with the most cheering news. Hobhouse wrote: "Your monied matters, Kinnaird will tell you, are going on swimmingly; you will have—indeed you have—a very handsome fortune; and if you have health, I do not see what earthly advantage you can wish for that you have not got. Your present endeavour is certainly the most glorious ever undertaken by man. Campbell said to me yesterday that he envied what you are now doing (and you may believe him, for he is a very envious man) even more than all your laurels blooming as they are."[n]

But Byron was now beyond envy. He did not move during the next twenty-four hours. Tita and Fletcher watched by his bed. At six o'clock on the evening of the 19th (Easter Monday), Fletcher recorded, "I saw my master open his eyes and then shut them, but without showing any symptoms of pain, or moving hand or foot. 'Oh! my God!' I exclaimed, 'I fear his lordship is gone.' The doctors then felt his pulse, and said, 'You are right—he is gone.' "[n]

CHAPTER XXX

1824

"The Remembered Tone of a Mute Lyre"

ON MONDAY EVENING, Parry recorded, "At the very time Lord Byron died, there was one of the most awful thunder storms I ever witnessed. The lightning was terrific. The Greeks, who are very superstitious, and generally believe that such an event occurs whenever a much superior, or as they say, a supreme man dies, immediately exclaimed, 'The great man is gone!' "[n] Byron himself might have been moved by such a portent. And his detached spirit must have enjoyed the mad medley of bickering doctors and weeping servants about his deathbed, displaying a gamut of emotions worthy of a scene in *Don Juan.*

The grief, however, was not feigned. The servants had never had a better master, and would look in vain for another as kind and generous. Fletcher, who had been with him longer than all the others, regretted his loss more deeply than the attempted rhetoric in his letter to Byron's sister might suggest. The black servant, his secretary Lega Zambelli, and Tita Falcieri knew not where to turn. Tita, who during Byron's last days had been his favorite and had seldom left his room, wrote to his parents: "With tears in my eyes, I announce . . . the death of my good master and my second father."[n]

The doctors, despite their differences, were not free from honest tears, and Pietro Gamba was desolated. Since he had first met Byron in Ravenna in 1820, he had been his constant companion, friend, admirer, and disciple. Parry, who had known Byron so short a time, mourned him none the less deeply. He noted also how sincere was the sorrow of the Greeks. "No persons, perhaps," he wrote, "after his domestics and personal friends, felt his loss more acutely than the poor citizens of Missolonghi. His residence among them gave them food, and ensured them protection."[n]

There is no doubt that Mavrocordatos's personal grief for the loss of Byron was sincere, but with it was mingled a great anxiety for the consequences to himself and the cause he had espoused. Mavrocordatos was only too aware of the forces of greed and rivalry that Byron's death would release. He immediately issued a proclamation on behalf of the Provisional Government of Western Greece, calling for the firing of minute guns and for general mourning. At sunrise on the 20th, those who had been wearied by grief and long vigils were wakened by the cannon of the fortress booming over the still lagoon at mournful intervals.

It had already been decided to embalm the body and send it back to England. At nine o'clock the physicians gathered for their gruesome task. But they paused a while, "in silent contemplation," Millingen says, of this abused clay which still bore witness to the physical beauty which had attracted so many men and women. Millingen continues: ". . . the only blemish of his body, which might otherwise have vied with that of Apollo himself, was the congenital malformation of his left foot and leg.* The foot was deformed, and turned inwards; and the leg was smaller and shorter than the sound one. . . . there can be little or no doubt, that he was born club-footed."[n] A legend persists in Missolonghi that the Greek woman who was employed to lay out the body told her daughter on returning from the house by the lagoon that the corpse of Milord was "white like the wing of a young chicken."[n]

But the doctors soon allowed their wonder to succumb to their clinical curiosity. The crude embalming process required the removal of the viscera, but, moved probably by the desire to settle their disputes concerning the cause of death, they extended their activities to a general autopsy. They started sawing and hacking at the noble head. Dr. Bruno recorded in his clinical

* The witnesses best qualified to know, including his mother, said it was the right foot, but as Millingen wrote his memoirs some years after the personal observation, the error is not surprising.

diary, "the bones of the cranium were found very hard without any traces of the sutures like the bones of a person of 80 years. . . ." [n]

An experienced diagnostician of the present day, Dr. Nolan D. C. Lewis of the New Jersey Neuro-Psychiatric Institute, after examining Dr. Bruno's records and other medical evidence of Byron's last illness and death, said that "the autopsy was as crude as the therapy afforded him in the light of modern techniques and methods. . . . Therefore it is probable that we shall be forever in the dark concerning a number of the pertinent medical facts. . . ." But in the light of the total recorded statements he ventured the opinion that "the immediate cause of death was uremic poisoning, a metabolic disorder with terminal symptoms described for Byron's last days, with his death hastened at the end by the numerous bleedings and purgings with strong cathartics." *

A tin-lined chest of rough wood was prepared to receive the body. The heart, brain, and intestines were placed in separate containers. The citizens and soldiers paid their last respects on the 22nd at rites in the church in which Marco Botsaris was buried. A black mantle served as a pall, and over it was placed Byron's Homeric helmet and sword and a crown of laurel. The funeral oration, pronounced by Spiridon Tricoupi, son of a Primate of Missolonghi, was a fine example of Greek oratory. But if the rhetoric was somewhat excessive, the feelings stirred by it were genuine enough among the Greeks who idolized Byron. Of

---

* In his summary comments Dr. Lewis said: "The chronic condition of the bones of the skull and of the meninges and of the brain secondarily could well be due to a constitutional weakness or predisposition to such changes which were precipitated and perpetuated by the various excesses during his short but very intense life. . . . In the face of this chronic situation there were added at the end the factors of exposure to dampness, high fever and some form of associated secondary infection (La Grippe?) bringing on the acute uremic attack and producing the more acute changes in the intracranial structures. Thus apparently in the brain there was an acute inflammatory process superimposed upon an old chronic one with adhesions to the skull and brain sufficient to account for his symptoms of fits, headaches and vertigo. The chronic inflammatory process in the skull and the brain coverings, and the terminal cerebral congestion could both have been the result of a combination of different causes and could well have been the source of his convulsions, which were not epileptic, in my opinion, but symptomatic of a local irritation." (Marchand, III, 1233–4 n.)

the many klephtic ballads about him sung among the soldiers, one must have been composed soon after his illness and death:

Missolonghi groaned and the Suliots cried
For Lord Byron who came from London.
He gathered the klephts and made them into an army . . .
The klephts gave to Byron the name of father
Because he loved the klephts of Roumele . . .
The woodlands weep, and the trees weep,
The castle of Missolonghi groans,
Because Byron lies dead at Missolonghi.[n]

As the news spread, almost every town in Greece had its own memorial service for Byron. At Anatolico, at Salona, at Argos, at Nauplia, and in the islands, his name had come to stand for disinterested patriotism more completely than that of any native Greek. In each town Greek rhetoric flowed, but the feelings of the people were deeper than the oratory could convey. And his death did more, perhaps, to unite Greece than all his living efforts. With the final winning of Greek independence, his name became even brighter. Almost every Greek town has a "Byron Street," and his statue stands in the most imposing position in the Garden of the Heroes at Missolonghi.

The Legislative Body at Argos proclaimed May 5 a day of mourning throughout the land. The Executive Body at Nauplia called likewise for mourning "because Byron does not walk any more on the Greek land, which he had loved so much years ago, and because Greece is grateful to him for ever, and the Nation must give him the name of a father and benefactor. . . ." And in announcing the event to the Greek Committee in London, it said that "Lord Byron, to the misfortune of Greece, has passed to the everlasting tabernacles." [n]

Trelawny heard the news while he was on the way to Missolonghi. He entered the silent, gloomy town on the 24th or 25th. His account of uncovering the body while Fletcher was out of the room is unreliable in the extreme. But it has been quoted (from his *Recollections* written long after the event) by uncritical biographers so frequently that it has acquired the picturesque standing of a legend hard to refute. Trelawny wrote that "to confirm or remove my doubts as to the cause of his lameness, I uncovered the Pilgrim's feet, and was answered—the great mystery was solved. Both his feet were clubbed, and his legs withered to the knee—the form and features of an Apollo, with the feet and legs of a sylvan satyr."[n] That he saw the foot at all is doubtful, and he himself contradicts this later by speaking of the lameness of Byron's right foot.

The Greeks would have been glad to keep Byron's body in the land of which he had been made an honorary citizen. Several times he had expressed a desire to be buried in foreign soil, on the Lido at Venice or in Greece. He had once said, "my bones would not rest in an English grave."[n] But latterly he had felt a nostalgia for his native land and had told Fletcher, Parry, and others that if he died in Greece he would like his body sent home. Stanhope had wanted to place his remains in the Temple of Theseus or in the Parthenon in Athens, but several boats had already come to transport the casket and Byron's household and effects to Zante. The Missolonghiots, however, pleaded for some part of the "honorable cadaver" and their wish was granted. The jar containing his lungs was deposited in the church of San Spiridione. And so the Greeks did retain part of Byron's mortal remains.

The coffin, which had been placed in a large cask containing 180 gallons of spirits, was put on board the *Florida* in Zante, with Colonel Stanhope in charge, and with Byron's servants and dogs aboard. It sailed on May 24th and arrived in the roadstead of the Downs in the Thames estuary on June 29th.

Pietro Gamba had wished to accompany the remains of the man who had been dearer than a brother to him, but he sailed for England on another ship to avoid embarrassment to Byron's relatives and friends because of the well-known liaison of the poet with Pietro's sister. He had not the heart to break the news to Teresa, then staying with friends in Bologna, but left that task to his father. She bore it "with grief, but dignity."[n]

The first news of Byron's death reached England on May 14, in letters and dispatches to Douglas Kinnaird. He wrote immediately to Hobhouse, who opened the letters and in "an agony of grief" learned the melancholy details. Despite the years when they had lived separate lives, Hobhouse felt the loss keenly, for his memories of Byron were wrapped up with the associations of his youth. Opposite a passage in Moore's life of

Byron, he wrote later: "of all the peculiarities of Byron his laugh is that of which I have the most distinct recollections." [n]

Hobhouse sent for Kinnaird and Sir Francis Burdett. They were both strongly affected. Sir Francis consented to break the news to Mrs. Leigh and to take her Fletcher's letter. But in the depth of their sorrow Byron's closest friends turned their attention to protecting his reputation from his own indiscretions. Hobhouse recorded: "After the first access of grief was over I then determined to lose no time in doing my duty by preserving all that was left to me of my friend—his fame—my thoughts were turned to the Memoirs of his life given to Thomas Moore & deposited by him in Mr. Murray's hands for certain considerations." [n]

The news had already been given to the papers. Among those most shocked by the account was Mary Shelley. She wrote in her journal on the 15th: "Albè—the dear, capricious, fascinating Albè—has left this desert world! God grant I may die young!" [n] Captain George Byron, the poet's cousin, who had succeeded to the title, went down to the country to see Lady Byron. He reported that she was "in a distressing state. . . . She wished to see any accounts that had come of his last moments." [n]

Hobhouse's whole attention now was turned to getting hold of the Memoirs and seeing them destroyed. Strangely enough, he found a stanch ally in John Murray, who had already paid two thousand guineas to Moore for the manuscript. Moore resisted, but he was faced with stubborn opposition. Even his determination to salvage part of it before it was burned was thwarted. His argument that to destroy it without previous perusal or deliberation (Hobhouse had never read it) "would be throwing a stigma upon the work, which it did not deserve," [n] was met only by panic zeal for Byron's reputation on the part of Hobhouse and Murray. Moore's attempt to save the manuscript by putting it into the hands of Mrs. Leigh failed because Hobhouse had already played upon her fears. Lady Byron too, though she did not want her name brought into the affair, was eager to see destroyed the Memoirs which told Byron's side of the separation story. She was represented by Wilmot Horton and Colonel Doyle.

In the great high-ceilinged parlor of Murray's house, which was also the office of the publishing firm, a solemn squabble took place over the Memoirs which Byron had started in Venice to enlighten and shock the public after his death. He would have been amused by the fact that the chief defenders of his honor and fame were Hobhouse, who had been a constant gadfly tormenting him to suppress parts of *Don Juan*, and John Murray, the "most timid of God's booksellers"; while his good friend Moore—for selfish reasons it may be—was the only one to defend the right of posterity to Byron's own account of his life. It is impossible not to recognize the sincerity and admire the unselfish loyalty of Hobhouse and Murray, but it is also impossible, after the passing of years, not to wish that their squeamish apprehensions had not triumphed over the saner counsels of Moore. If the manuscript could only have been hidden away or lost sight of for more than a hundred years like the Boswell papers! With Moore protesting to the last, Wilmot and Doyle solemnly tore up the original manuscript and the copy made for Moore and burned them in the fireplace.[n]

In an interim of the activity that had engaged him since the news of Byron's death arrived, Hobhouse abandoned himself to fond memories of his friend. "Indeed," he wrote, "I see by the papers that the regret is universal. . . . no man ever lived who had such devoted friends. His power of attaching those about him to his person was such as no one I ever knew possessed—no human being could approach him without being sensible of this magical influence—There was something commanding but not overawing in his manner—He was neither grave nor gay out of place and he seemed always made for that company in which he happened to find himself."[n]

The news of Byron's death, Allan Cunningham wrote in the *London Magazine*, "came upon London like an earthquake."[n] The loss was felt most deeply perhaps among those who had not known him personally: the serious-minded younger generation with poetic instincts. The impact of what Swinburne, and later Matthew Arnold, was to call the "sincerity and strength" of Byron is seen in the reactions of those who, as eminent Victorians, were later to repudiate his influence. Alfred Tennyson, a boy of fourteen at Somersby in Lincolnshire, wandered out disconsolately and wrote on a rock: "Byron is dead."[n] Jane Welsh, then being courted by Thomas Carlyle, wrote to him: " . . . Byron is dead! I was told it all at once in a roomful of people. My God, if they had said that the sun or the moon had gone out of the heavens, it could not have struck me with the idea of a more awful and dreary blank in the creation. . . ." [n] Carlyle wrote that Byron's was "the noblest spirit in Europe"; he felt as if he "had lost a Brother." [n]

On July 2 Hobhouse boarded the *Florida* in the Thames estuary and accompanied the remains up the river with the most melancholy reflections: "I was the last person that shook hands with Lord Byron when he left England at Dover in 1816—I recalled him waving his cap as the packet bounded off on a swelling sea. . . ." [n] When the undertaker came aboard and took the coffin out of the barrel of spirits, Hobhouse could not bear to look at that once handsome face. He merely leaned against the coffin, Byron's Newfoundland dog at his feet.[n]

The body lay in state for several days in the house of Sir Edward Knatchbull, 20 Great George's Street, and was seen by only a few of Byron's friends and relations. Hobhouse was less affected by the sight than he had expected to be, for the face "did not bear the slightest resemblance to my dear friend—the mouth was distorted & half open showing those teeth in which poor fellow he once so prided himself quite discoloured by the spirits—his upper lip was shaded with red mustachios which gave a totally new character to his face—his cheeks were long and bagged over the jaw—his nose was quite prominent at the bridge & sank in between the eyes . . . his eye brows shaggy & lowering . . . his skin was like dull yellow parchment. . . . It did not seem to be Byron—I was not moved so much scarcely as at the sight of his hand writing or any thing that I knew to be his. . . ." [n]

Several people, including Stanhope, had urged burial in St. Paul's or Westminster Abbey. But Hobhouse had consulted with Mrs. Leigh and acceded to her wish that her brother be buried in the family vault in Hucknall Torkard Church near Newstead. And he was irritated that Murray (so he thought—actually it was Kinnaird) [n] had on his own initiative, but in Hobhouse's name, applied to Dr. Ireland, Dean of Westminster, and thus given him an opportunity to refuse burial in the Abbey.

Fletcher, despite his genuine grief at the loss of his master, enjoyed his role of chief mourner and the attention paid him as one who had heard the poet's last words and wishes. It seems too that he was willing to remember, or at least hint at, things which would enlist the interest of those who had been most vitally involved with Byron. When he came to Lady Byron in July with his story of Byron's death, she walked about the room, "sobbing so that her whole frame was shaken, while she implored him to remember the words muttered earnestly, unintelligibly, 'for nearly twenty minutes.' "[n]

Hobhouse had made every effort to provide respectable attendance at the funeral procession when the hearse and the mourning coaches left London for Nottingham on July 12. But there was a reluctance on the part of the great families, particularly those actively connected with the government, to be seen in the procession, though a large number of empty carriages were sent out of deference to Hobhouse and his friends. Despite the acclaim in the newspapers, there was an undercurrent of timidity among the great which stemmed partly from the feeling that, though Byron's actions in aiding Greek independence might be applauded privately, the British government was still neutral and should not give official recognition to a supporter of a rebel cause. Moreover, the Greek Committee, whose representative he had been, had for its chief supporters, aside from a few classical-minded Philhellenes, mostly Radicals and Radical Whigs. But a deeper timidity really arose from the half-acknowledged association of social ostracism which had clung to Byron's name since the days of the separation, and which had grown with rumors about his life in Italy. It was not what he had done but what he had frankly proclaimed to the world that made him in many eyes no longer an Englishman, or an English gentleman. And the fact that Mrs. Leigh was his nearest of kin and the chief mourner did not increase the eagerness of the beau monde to be seen among the public mourners.

There was no lack of people in the streets to watch the forty-seven carriages pass. The day was fine, and the crowds increased as the procession proceeded along Oxford Street and up Tottenham Court Road. No ladies were in the carriages, though many watched from windows. Augusta had neither the heart nor the strength, moral or physical, to enter the mourning coach, and sent her husband in her place. Hobhouse wrote: "George Leigh—Capt. Richard Byron [the new Lord Byron was reportedly ill at Bath]—Hanson & myself went in the first coach. Burdett—Kinnaird—Bruce—Ellice—Stanhope— & Trevanion (one of the family) in the second—Moore—Rogers—Campbell—and Orlando the Deputy in the last." The empty carriages followed. Hobhouse concluded pathetically: "On the whole as much honour was done to the deceased as circumstances would admit of—He was buried like a nobleman—since we could not bury him as a poet." [n]

Mary Shelley watched the procession as it passed her house and wrote to Trelawny: " . . . connected with him in a thousand ways, admiring his talents & with all his faults feeling affection for him, it went to my heart when the other day the herse [*sic*] that contained his lifeless form, a form of beauty which in life I often delighted to behold, passed my window going up Highgate Hill on his last journey. . . ." [n]

At the edge of the city the empty carriages turned back, and only the undertaker and his assistants accompanied the cortège of mourners on the slow progress northward. The hearse with its sable escort was four days on the way. In every town the interest was intense, and it grew as they approached the Blackmoor's Head Inn at Nottingham. The black plumes were covered with dust, but silent crowds watched the procession roll into the inn yard. The bell of St. Mary tolled.

Hobhouse was reminded of Byron's high spirits when he visited him at Newstead in 1809. Other memories followed: "Of the five that often dined at Byron's table at Diodati near Geneva—Polidori—Shelley—Lord Byron—Scrope Davies & myself—the first put an end to himself—the second was drowned—the third killed by his physicians—the fourth is in exile—!!!" [n]

Byron's old friend Francis Hodgson and Colonel Wildman, the owner of Newstead Abbey, joined the mourners when the procession started for Hucknall on the 16th. The mournful bell tolled as they left the inn yard. The pomp—the pages, the mutes, the rich black silk velvet pall, the black horses with their plumes—satisfied a sense of fitness in John Cam Hobhouse, M.P., but his thoughts carried him constantly back to other, carefree times when he had ridden about these regions with Byron.

When the coffin was carried to the family vault, Hobhouse wanted it to rest on the casket of the poet's mother, but that was too mouldered to hold it, and Byron's was laid instead on that of the fifth ("Wicked") Lord Byron. One side of the multiform personality of Byron would have been pleased with this ending:

his bones had come back to rest with those of his ancestors. And another facet of his spirit would have seen "a deal of fun,/ Like mourning coaches when the funeral's done,"[n] in the solemn pageantry which ended with the reading of the Church of England service over his sunken visage.

But in *Childe Harold* Byron had written his own epitaph in terms more sincere and more moving than any words spoken over his corpse in Greece or in England:

But I have lived, and have not lived in vain:
My mind may lose its force, my blood its fire,
And my frame perish even in conquering pain;
But there is that within me which shall tire
Torture and Time, and breathe when I expire;
Something unearthly, which they deem not of,
Like the remembered tone of a mute lyre,
Shall on their softened spirits sink, and move
In hearts all rocky now the late remorse of Love.[n]

EPILOGUE

Post Mortems

There was something in Byron's restless spirit that did continue to breathe when he expired, that moved his close associates to devotion to his memory and to contention with others, but scarcely ever to indifference. Few men have had a more far-reaching influence beyond the tomb. Hobhouse soon felt this. He wrote: "poor Byron—he always kept his friends in hot water during his life and it seems his remains will be of no easy management after his death." [n]

No sooner had the news of his demise been published than a dozen women who had been intimate with Byron, and indiscreet enough to bare their hearts in letters, were beseeching Hobhouse to return their correspondence. Among the first of these was Caroline Lamb. But when it came to giving up Byron's letters to her, she could not part with them, and Hobhouse kept hers as insurance that she would not publish the poet's letters in another novel. Caroline wrote to Murray, asking him to tell her every particular and adding, "I am very sorry I ever said one unkind word against him." [n] She wanted to see Fletcher, perhaps to find out whether Byron had mentioned her on his deathbed. "That beautiful pale face" did indeed haunt Caroline Lamb until her dying day.

Lady Frances Webster asked to have her letters to Byron destroyed. But Hobhouse redeemed himself with posterity in a measure for his part in the destruction of the Memoirs by neither returning nor destroying her letters or those of dozens of other women who eagerly sought to recover the evidence of their indiscretions. And while he resolutely opposed all biographies and memoirs of Byron, including Moore's, he as stanchly preserved Byron's own letters and papers; whereas Moore, who alone had pleaded for the saving of the Memoirs, after bowdlerizing Byron's letters to himself when he printed them in his life of Byron, either destroyed them, or left that task to his literary executor, for they have vanished.[n]

Throughout his long life, Hobhouse considered himself Byron's chief friend and the protector of his reputation. He refuted the misstatements of Dallas and Medwin and other memoirists, and withheld letters and other documents from Moore, who was commissioned by Murray to write the official biography of Byron.[n] In later years Hobhouse married Lady Julia Hay, and subsided from the radicalism of his youth into a somewhat stiff respectability. He was active in social and political life, was at various times in the Cabinet, and was raised to the peerage by Queen Victoria in 1851, as Baron Broughton de Gyfford.*

Thomas Moore recouped his losses from the destruction of the Memoirs by publishing his *Letters and Journals of Lord Byron, with Notices of His Life* (1830), which, despite omissions voluntary and involuntary, gave a broad view of Byron's character and personality that has been the mainstay of biographers ever since. The chief merit of the work was that the author let Byron speak for himself in his most amusing letters to Moore and Murray and in his journals.

Pietro Gamba, after following Byron's body to London, wrote and published his *Narrative* of Byron's last days, and then, being still an exile from his native Romagna, returned to Greece. He died of typhoid fever in 1827 on the isthmus of Methana and was buried in the fortress of Diamantopoulos, which was later destroyed. Only his book and a few letters remain of this most faithful of Byron's followers.

John Murray, in addition to publishing Moore's "Life" of Byron, continued to put out edition after edition of Byron's works, buying back copyrights that had gone out of his control, and remained an enthusiastic Byronian throughout his life, as have all his descendants. The present head of the firm, Mr. John Grey Murray, still at 50 Albemarle Street, has an enormous collection of the poet's manuscripts, letters, and memorabilia.

---

* The after-lives of those men and women most closely associated with Byron make a fascinating story. It has been told entertainingly and in detail by Doris Langley Moore in *The Late Lord Byron.*

Of Byron's servants, Fletcher, in later years, having found the small annuity which Hanson and Hobhouse arranged for him inadequate, started a macaroni factory with Lega Zambelli. When it failed in 1835, he applied to Hobhouse for help. He frequently sent similar appeals to Augusta Leigh, and sometimes to Murray. Fletcher's son later married Zambelli's daughter. "Tita" Falcieri was for some time a domestic in the employ of Benjamin Disraeli, himself in his youth an ardent admirer of Byron.

Loukas Chalandritsanos, the favorite who had caused Byron so much emotional distress in his last months, fared badly after the death of his patron despite the benefits Byron tried to shower upon him during his fatal illness. He too died early and probably without being able to collect that promissory note from the Greek government at Missolonghi which Byron had given him, for his sisters in 1832 appealed for assistance to Byron's daughter, hoping that she, "born of a Philhellene father, will pity our misfortune." They spoke of Byron's charity to all suffering Greeks, and added: "Among those who were thus charitably treated was one of our brothers named Lukas, who was very much loved by the unforgettable Lord Byron, but who died in the midst of the war and in the midst of the happiness which Byron had procured for him. . . ."[n]

Trelawny, after trying unsuccessfully to divert to his favorite, Odysseus, material and money of the Greek Committee that had been at Byron's disposal, returned to join that chieftain. He alternately tried to impress upon the world the closeness of his friendship with Byron, and his superiority to the poet. He wrote grandly to Mary Shelley: " . . . I am again, dear Mary, in my *element*, and playing no *second* part in Greece. . . . But I am sick at heart with losing my friend [Byron],—for still I call him so, you know, with all his weakness, you know I loved him." But he ended: "No more a nameless being, I am now a Greek Chieftain, willing and able to shelter and protect you. . . ."[n]

A few months later, however, when Byron's reputation in Greece was even greater than it had been in his lifetime, Trelawny wrote again: "I wish he [Byron] had lived a little longer, that he might have witnessed how I would have soared above him here, how I would have triumphed over his mean spirit."[n]

Joseph Severn, the friend of Keats, who saw Trelawny in Rome in 1823, had referred to him as "Lord Byron's jackal." [n]

Trelawny married Odysseus's sister, and when things got difficult retired to his chief's secret cave on the side of Mount Parnassus. There he was shot by a treacherous companion, but after a long time he recovered and was rescued by an English party, and finally returned to England, where he lived to extreme old age, glorying in his early adventures and associations with poets and heroes of the Greek revolution. In his *Recollections* he glorified Shelley, and himself, at the expense of Byron, and wrote many picturesque things about both which biographers have often been tempted to quote without sufficient skeptical reserve. He lived on until 1881, and died at the age of eighty-nine, the longest-lived of all the Romantic generation.

Augusta Leigh inherited the residue of Byron's property (the bulk of it—the £60,000 of the marriage settlement—went to Lady Byron under the terms of the separation), but she was always in financial difficulties, partly because of her own impecuniosity, partly because of her gambling husband. Despite the relentless efforts of Lady Byron to make her duly repentant, she continued to nourish an affection for the memory of her darling brother. She sometimes cut out his signature for admiring friends, but she could not bear to part with his letters. She eventually quarreled with Annabella, not over Byron but over business affairs. Lady Byron's implacable "kindness" extended to befriending Augusta's daughter Medora, encouraging her to think that she was Byron's daughter. Medora bore two children to her sister's husband, Henry Trevanion, and finally retired to France, married a Frenchman, and brought up a family proud to be descended from the famous poet. Before Augusta died in 1851, Lady Byron "granted" her a final interview at which she expected another confession—namely that she had prejudiced her brother against his wife. But Annabella was disappointed; Augusta did not confess for the simple reason that it was not true.

Lady Byron divided her later years between good works and "confidences" about her marriage, which she shared with a surprising number of people, while giving the impression to the world that she bore her wrongs in silence. Among those to whom she bared her secrets was Harriet Beecher Stowe, who some years after Lady Byron was dead, published her sensational revelations of the incest in a garbled account of her conversations with Annabella. Lady Byron's own account is still extant in the numerous "Narratives" written in her later years, when self-justification was the obsession of her days. She kept copies of all her letters and of any that came to her hands which had a bearing on her case.

Byron's daughter Ada, "though born in bitterness," did, as he had predicted, come to love him. Knowledge of her father, and his picture, had been kept from her in her childhood, but she was weaned from her mother's influence by her husband, Lord King (later Lord Lovelace), and came to revere her father's poetry and his memory. Byron might have been somewhat chagrined, however, had he known that she would come to be an even greater mathematician than her mother, though her confidence that knowledge of numbers would make her a sure winner at the races was doomed to disappointment. When she died at the age of thirty-five, she was buried at her own desire in the family vault at Hucknall Torkard beside her father.

Claire Clairmont retired to Florence in her later years, nourishing her hatred of Byron into an obsession. Ironically, she had been converted to the Roman Catholic faith, but that did not soften her diatribes against Byron in her correspondence with the aging Trelawny, who accused her of having a "bee in her bonnet." She too became something of a legend in her last years because of her connection with Byron and Shelley and the rumor that she possessed valuable letters and papers (she could not have had any of Byron's letters, for he studiously avoided writing to her). But on this assumption Henry James made her the central character of *The Aspern Papers*. She died in 1879 at the age of eighty-one, leaving instructions for this curious epitaph: "In misery she spent her life expiating not only her faults but also her virtues." [n]

Teresa Guiccioli recovered from the immediate grief which Byron's death caused her, but the memory of the years she had shared with him remained the dominant force of her long life. She went back to her husband in 1826, but soon separated from him again. She spent several winters in Rome, where she had a brief affair with Byron's handsome lame friend Henry Fox, Lord

Holland's son. She also flirted with the French poet Lamartine, whose admiration for Byron made a strong appeal to her. She likewise philandered lightly with a number of other Englishmen in Italy, including the Earl of Malmesbury, who left a record of her recollections of Byron in his memoirs.

She had long wished to go to England, and in the spring of 1832 she made her first pilgrimage to Byron's homeland. There she met Lady Blessington (of whom she had been so jealous in Genoa), John Murray, Augusta Leigh, and others who had been close to Byron, and she made a sentimental journey to Newstead Abbey. She later spoke affectionately of Mrs. Leigh, the "*nearest* and *dearest* relative of him—whom I have rather *worshipped* than loved. . . ."[n]

In later years Teresa lived much in Paris. Count Guiccioli died in 1840, and after a long courtship the Marquis de Boissy led her to the altar in the chapel of the Luxembourg, a bride of forty-seven. She was still handsome, but the simplicity of her manners, which had pleased Byron, had passed into affectation. Many visitors of later years have reported the absurdity into which she was carried by her Byron-worship. She kept a portrait of her poet lover in her salon, and she would stand before it and exclaim: "*Qu'il était beau! Mon Dieu, qu'il était beau!*"[n] The Marquis, with French complacency, was proud of his wife's liaison with the famous poet, and when asked if she was related to the Countess Guiccioli who had once been connected with Lord Byron, replied with a beaming smile: "*Comment donc, mais c'est elle-même, c'est elle!*"[n] It is also reported that he used to introduce his wife as "*La Marquise de Boissy ma femme, ancienne maîtresse de Byron.*"[n]

After the Marquis's death in 1866, Teresa devoted herself to spiritualism and talked with the spirits of both Byron and her husband. She happily reported: "They are together now, and are the best of friends."[n]

In the 1830's, after Moore's "Life" had increased Byron's fame, there was some agitation to have a monument placed in Westminster Abbey. This caused a great furor in the press, but the ecclesiastical authorities again rejected the proposal. When a subscription was finally taken to commission a statue of Byron by Thorwaldsen, it was without a home until finally accepted for the Library of Trinity College, Cambridge, in 1843. It too had been offered to Westminster and refused by the Dean. For 145 years the Abbey was unsullied by any reminder that Byron ever lived. In 1954 a plaque was unveiled there to the memory of Shelley and Keats. Then in 1968 the Dean, the Very Reverend Eric Abbott, approved a petition by the Poetry Society for a Byron memorial in the Abbey. And finally on May 8, 1969, a "Ceremony of Dedication of a Memorial to Lord Byron" was solemnly held in the Abbey under the auspices of the Poetry Society. William Plomer, President of the Society, said appropriately at the unveiling: "One can imagine that Byron's shade, if present here today, may be wearing a slightly sardonic smile."

Notes

An explanation of abbreviations is given as part A of the Bibliography (page 514).

Notes to Chapter I

p. 3, l. 23 Pepys, *Diary*, entry of April 26, 1667.

p. 5, l. 21 *LJ*, VI, 231–2.

p. 6, l. 34 Quoted, Moore, I, 614 *n.*

p. 7, l. 15 *Ancient Ballads and Songs of the North of Scotland . . .* With explanatory notes by Peter Buchan, Edinburgh, 1875, I, 251.

p. 7, l. 31 Prothero, "The Childhood and School Days of Byron," p. 67.

Notes to Chapter II

p. 9, l. 3 The number of the house was later changed to 24. Toward the end of the nineteenth century the house, which bore a metal medallion indicating that it had been the poet's birthplace, was torn down. The large drapery establishment of John Lewis & Co. later occupied the site. During the blitz of the Second World War almost the whole street was bombed out. It has been rebuilt but no trace remains of Byron's birthplace.

p. 9, l. 8 Marchand, I, 24.

p. 9, l. 25 For the evidence on Byron's club foot see my article "Byron's Lameness: a Re-examination," *Keats-Shelley Memorial Bulletin,* VII (1956), 32–42. Various physicians and surgeons have written on Byron's lameness, arguing that he was spastic, that he had Little's Disease, or a dysplasia, but most of these have not made a sufficiently careful evaluation of the biographical evidence.

p. 10, l. 2 *LJ*, I, 11 *n.*

p. 10, l. 12 Symon, p. 19.

p. 11, l. 9 Medwin (ed. Lovell), pp. 56–7.

p. 11, l. 26 Maurois, pp. 32–3. Quoted from Captain Byron's letters to his sister in the Lovelace papers.

p. 11, l. 31 Symon, p. 36.

p. 12, l. 3 *LJ*, I, ix.

p. 12, l. 9 Prothero, "The Childhood and School Days of Byron," p. 71.

p. 12, l. 15 *LJ*, VI, 232 *n.*

p. 12, l. 19 Medwin (ed. Lovell), pp. 55, 57.

p. 12, l. 24 Symon, p. 38.

p. 12, *l.* 26 *LJ*, I, 11 *n.*

p. 12, *l.* 32 Moore, I, 10.

p. 13, *l.* 8 *LJ*, V, 99. Letter of October 16, 1820.

p. 13, *l.* 12 Symon, p. 63.

p. 13, *l.* 29 *LJ*, V, 406.

p. 14, *l.* 25 Gamba, p. 149; Moore, I, 255 *n.*

p. 14, *l.* 33 *LJ*, V, 391. Letter of October 9, 1821.

p. 15, *l.* 5 Moore, I, 10.

p. 15, *l.* 13 Ibid., p. 19.

p. 15, *l.* 28 *LJ*, II, 347–8. From Byron's journal of November 26, 1813.

p. 16, *l.* 4 Moore, I, 20.

p. 16, *l.* 9 Marginal note in Hobhouse's copy of Moore.

p. 16, *l.* 28 Moore, I, 68.

p. 16, *l.* 36 *Don Juan*, X, 17.

Notes to Chapter III

p. 17, *l.* 10 Moore, *Prose and Verse*, p. 416.

p. 18, *l.* 37 Hanson narrative, Murray MSS. Marchand, I, 50.

p. 19, *l.* 5 *LJ*, I, 6–7.

p. 19, *l.* 17 *LJ*, I, 7–8. Letter of March 13, 1799.

p. 20, *l.* 18 *LJ*, I, 10 *n.* Letter of September 1, 1799.

p. 20, *l.* 22 Hobhouse notes titled "Lord Byron" with his manuscript diary of the summer of 1824. Marchand, I, 57.

p. 20, *l.* 26 *LJ*, V, 450.

p. 21, *l.* 19 *LJ*, V, 449–50.

p. 21, *l.* 23 *LJ*, V, 450.

p. 22, *l.* 10 Moore, I, 32.

p. 22, *l.* 26 Moore, I, 38–9.

Notes to Chapter IV

p. 24, *l.* 3 Moore, I, 39.

p. 24, *l.* 9 Marchand, I, 66.

p. 24, *l.* 15 *LJ*, V, 454.

p. 24, *l.* 22 Hunt, *Lord Byron*, I, 151.

p. 24, *l.* 28 *LJ*, V, 453.

p. 25, *l.* 12 Moore, I, 43.

p. 25, *l.* 17 Pratt, p. 5.

p. 25, *l.* 32 *Childe Harold*, IV, 75.

p. 26, *l.* 1 Hanson narrative, Murray MSS. Marchand, I, 72.

p. 26, *l.* 10 *LJ*, V, 455.

p. 26, *l.* 13 *LJ*, I, 15.

p. 26, *l.* 16 Moore, I, 39.

p. 27, *l.* 7 *LJ*, V, 441.

p. 27, *l.* 17 *LJ*, I, 16 *n.* Letter of October 30, 1803.

p. 27, *l.* 22 "The Dream," line 63.

p. 27, *l.* 29 Moore, *Prose and Verse*, p. 431; also Moore, 1, 56.

p. 27, *l.* 36 Medwin (ed. Lovell), p. 61.
p. 28, *l.* 12 Marchand, I, 80 *n.*
p. 28, *l.* 20 *LJ*, I, 19–20. Letter of March 22, 1804.
p. 28, *l.* 27 *LJ*, I, 23. Letter of March 26, 1804. Corrected from text in *Sharpe's London Magazine.*
p. 28, *l.* 33 Moore, I, 65.
p. 28, *l.* 39 *B-SP*, I, 10. Letter of May 1804.
p. 29, *l.* 11 *LJ*, V, 453.
p. 29, *l.* 13 *LJ*, V, 445.
p. 29, *l.* 20 *LJ*, V, 452.
p. 29, *l.* 37 Moore, I, 95–8.
p. 29, *l.* 40 Marginal note in Hobhouse's copy of Moore. Marchand, I, 85.
p. 30, *l.* 12 *LJ*, I, 43. Letter of November 2, 1804.
p. 30, *l.* 22 Medwin (ed. Lovell), p. 61.
p. 30, *l.* 38 *LJ*, I, 35. Letter of October 25, 1804.
p. 31, *l.* 38 Moore, *Memoirs*, II, 624.
p. 32, *l.* 5 Medwin (ed. Lovell), pp. 63–4.
p. 32, *l.* 10 *LJ*, I, 43.
p. 32, *l.* 16 *LJ*, I, 46. The date is given as November 4 in *Sharpe's London Magazine.*
p. 32, *l.* 30 Marchand, I, 93. Letter of January 31, 1805.
p. 33, *l.* 2 *LJ*, V, 445.
p. 33, *l.* 6 Moore, I, 67.
p. 33, *l.* 23 Marchand, I, 97–8.
p. 33, *l.* 33 *LJ*, I, 71. Letter of August 4, 1805, to Charles Gordon.
p. 34, *l.* 1 Moore, I, 57.

Notes to Chapter V

p. 35, *l.* 9 *LJ*, I, 151–2. Letter of November 19, 1820, to John Murray.
p. 35, *l.* 13 *LJ*, V, 445.
p. 36, *l.* 2 *LJ*, I, 81.
p. 36, *l.* 6 *LJ*, I, 83.
p. 36, *l.* 22 Wordsworth, *The Prelude*, Book IX, lines 231–2.
p. 36, *l.* 35 *LJ*, I, 84–5. Letter of November 23, 1805.
p. 37, *l.* 16 *LJ*, V, 445–6.
p. 37, *l.* 22 *LJ*, I, 92.
p. 37, *l.* 31 *LJ*, I, 94.
p. 38, *l.* 3 *LJ*, V, 446.
p. 38, *l.* 7 *LJ*, V, 169. Diary of January 12, 1821.
p. 38, *l.* 18 *LJ*, I, 133–5. Letter of July 5, 1807.
p. 38, *l.* 25 *B-SP*, I, 124. Letter of October 22, 1811.
p. 39, *l.* 2 *LJ*, I, 95 *n.* Letter of January 11, 1806.
p. 39, *l.* 20 *LJ*, I, 95–7. Letter of February 26, 1806.
p. 39, *l.* 27 *LJ*, I, 95 *n.* Letter of March 4, 1806.
p. 39, *l.* 39 *LJ*, V, 575. (In the second letter to Murray on the Bowles-Pope controversy.)
p. 40, *l.* 37 Marchand, I, 115. This seems to be the first mention of

Byron's favorite Newfoundland dog, which he probably acquired at Southwell. On Boatswain's tomb at Newstead Byron recorded that he was born in May 1803.

p. 41, l. 12 Marchand, I, 116. From a MS "reminiscence" of Byron by Henry Long in the Berg Collection, New York Public Library.

p. 41, l. 31 LJ, I, 113. Letter of January 13, 1807, to John M. B. Pigot.

p. 41, l. 38 "To a Lady, Who Presented to the Author a Lock of Hair, Braided with his Own, and Appointed a Night in December to Meet Him in the Garden."

p. 42, l. 22 "Answer to some Elegant Verses sent by a Friend to the Author, complaining that one of his descriptions was rather too warmly drawn." *Poetry*, I, 115.

p. 43, l. 4 Marchand, I, 124. Noted in the margin of his copy of Moore.

p. 43, l. 15 LJ, I, 127. Letter of April 1807 to John M. B. Pigot.

p. 43, l. 40 LJ, I, 126–7. Letter of April 2, 1807.

p. 44, l. 25 LJ, I, 132. Letter of June 30, 1807.

p. 44, l. 30 Edleston had given Byron a Cornelian stone about which he wrote a poem. See *Poetry*, I, 66–7.

p. 44, l. 35 LJ, I, 133–4. Letter of July 5, 1807.

p. 45, l. 17 LJ, I, 156. Letter of November 19, 1820, to John Murray.

p. 45, l. 25 LJ, I, 338. Letter of August 21, 1811, to R. C. Dallas.

p. 45, l. 28 LJ, I, 160.

p. 46, l. 2 Marchand, I, 135. Letter of August 2, 1807, to Elizabeth Pigot.

p. 46, l. 15 LJ, I, 147. Letter of October 26, 1807.

p. 46, l. 20 Hints from Horace, lines 229–30.

p. 46, l. 30 LJ, I, 147. Letter of October 26, 1807.

p. 46, l. 36 Moore, I, 98.

p. 47, l. 5 The copy of Ruffhead is now in the Berg Collection, New York Public Library.

Notes to Chapter VI

p. 49, l. 13 LJ, I, 170. Letter of January 20, 1808. Such an accusation was leveled against Byron in *The Eclectic Review* (Vol. III, part 2, pp. 989–93).

p. 49, l. 19 LJ, I, 173. Letter of January 21, 1808.

p. 50, l. 10 LJ, I, 174–5. Letter of January 25, 1808. He had paid off with a new loan £3,000 of the £3,300 due to moneylenders.

p. 50, l. 33 Marchand, I, 147.

p. 51, l. 2 Marchand, I, 147; *B-SP*, I, 40. Letter of February 27, 1808.

p. 51, l. 9 Monthly Mirror, n.s., III (January 1808), 30.

p. 51, l. 10 Marchand, I, 144–5. This is the first record of Byron's sending a challenge to a duel. There is no evidence that he actually fought a duel, but he came near it several times, and he thought about it often and sent several challenges. Each time he was prevented by friends, or by explanations or apologies.

p. 51, *l.* 27 Marchand, I, 150.
p. 51, *l.* 38 *Blackwood's Magazine* (November 1824), p. 532.
p. 52, *l.* 2 Joyce, p. 10.
p. 52, *l.* 8 Joyce, p. 12.
p. 52, *l.* 21 *LJ*, V, 425.
p. 52, *l.* 25 *LJ*, I, 187.
p. 52, *l.* 31 *LJ*, I, 218. Letter of March 18, 1809, to William Harness.
p. 53, *l.* 17 *LJ*, I, 193. Letter of October 7, 1808.
p. 53, *l.* 25 *LJ*, I, 176. Letter of February 2, 1808.
p. 53, *l.* 38 Marchand, I, 158.
p. 54, *l.* 2 *LJ*, I, 195. Letter of November 2, 1808.
p. 54, *l.* 12 *LJ*, I, 197. Letter of November 3, 1808.
p. 54, *l.* 19 Ibid., p. 198.
p. 54, *l.* 29 Moore, I, 154.
p. 55, *l.* 2 *LJ*, I, 199–200. Letter of November 18, 1808.
p. 55, *l.* 9 Ibid., p. 200.
p. 55, *l.* 15 *LJ*, I, 205–6. Letter of December 17, 1808.
p. 55, *l.* 27 Medwin (ed. Lovell), pp. 64–5.
p. 56, *l.* 3 Marchand, I, 165.
p. 56, *l.* 11 Moore, I, 104–5; Marchand, I, 166.
p. 56, *l.* 32 *LJ*, I, 206 *n.* Letter of March 4, 1809.
p. 57, *l.* 11 *LJ*, V, 432.
p. 58, *l.* 25 *LJ*, I, 153–5. Letter of November 19, 1820, to John Murray.
p. 59, *l.* 2 Marchand, I, 175.
p. 59, *l.* 11 *LJ*, VI, 446. Letter of November 12, 1809.
p. 60, *l.* 7 *LJ*, I, 222. Letter of April 26, 1809.
p. 60, *l.* 18 Sanders put them in an artificial stance by the sea with a romantic mountain background. This was the picture used as a frontispiece in Moore's life of Byron.
p. 60; *l.* 24 *LJ*, I, 225. Letter of June 22, 1809.
p. 60, *l.* 29 Marchand, I, 180 *n.* Letter of June 17, 1809.
p. 61, *l.* 5 Marchand, I, 182. Letter of June 25, 1809.
p. 61, *l.* 10 The Latin abbreviation Byron quoted (with some confusion of cases and genders) in this letter and several times later is a phrase in the *Satyricon* of Petronius (para. 86, sec. 4): *"coitum plenum et optabilem"* ("complete intercourse to one's heart's desire"). In Petronius the narrator tells how he overcame the reluctance of a boy. I am indebted to Professor Gilbert Highet for tracing the quotation.
p. 61, *l.* 14 Marchand, I, 181–2. Letter of June 22, 1809.

Notes to Chapter VII

p. 62, *l.* 6 *LJ*, I, 233. Letter of July 16, 1809.
p. 62, *l.* 14 Ibid.
p. 63, *l.* 3 *LJ*, I, 237. Letter of August 11, 1809.
p. 63, *l.* 30 *LJ*, I, 238. Letter of August 11, 1809.
p. 63, *l.* 38 *LJ*, I, 234. Letter of August 6, 1809.

p. 63, *l.* 40 *Don Juan,* I, 8.
p. 66, *l.* 12 *LJ,* I, 234–5. Letter of August 6, 1809.
p. 66, *l.* 31 *LJ,* I, 235. Letter of August 6, 1809.
p. 66, *l.* 35 Marchand, I, 194.
p. 67, *l.* 7 Marchand, I, 195. Letter of August 13, 1809, to Hanson.
p. 67, *l.* 12 Galt, p. 51.
p. 67, *l.* 20 *LJ,* I, 242. Postscript dated August 15 to letter of August 11, 1809.
p. 67, *l.* 23 *LJ,* I, 243. Letter of August 15, 1809, to Mr. Rushton.
p. 67, *l.* 34 William H. Marshall, "The Byron Will of 1809," *The Library Chronicle* (University of Pennsylvania), Vol. XXXIII, No. 2 (Spring 1967), p. 104. The will is in the collection of Byroniana given the library by Mr. and Mrs. Meyer Davis.
p. 68, *l.* 23 *LBC,* I, 77. Letter of September 15, 1812.
p. 69, *l.* 5 Hobhouse, *Journey,* I, 40.
p. 69, *l.* 26 Hobhouse, *Journey,* I, 52.
p. 70, *l.* 11 *LJ,* I, 256. Letter of November 12, 1809, to Mrs. Byron.
p. 70, *l.* 22 *LJ,* I, 287. Letter of July 4, 1810, to Hodgson.
p. 71, *l.* 2 *LJ,* I, 249. Letter of November 12, 1809, to Mrs. Byron.
p. 71, *l.* 11 *LJ,* V, 115. Letter of November 9, 1820, to John Murray.
p. 71, *l.* 16 *Poetry,* II, 174.
p. 71, *l.* 21 Ibid.
p. 71, *l.* 24 *Poetry,* II, 177.
p. 71, *l.* 38 *LJ,* I, 249–50. Letter of November 12, 1809.
p. 72, *l.* 23 *Don Juan,* III, 41.
p. 72, *l.* 35 *LJ,* I, 250–1. Letter of November 12, 1809.
p. 73, *l.* 15 Ibid., p. 257.
p. 73, *l.* 23 J. H. Marsden: *A Brief Memoir of the Life and Writings of the Late Lieutenant William Martin Leake . . .* (London, 1864), p. 32.
p. 73, *l.* 29 Byron later justified his use of the Spenserian stanza by citing the precedent of Beattie and other eighteenth-century followers of Spenser who had found the stanza adaptable to great varieties of narrative and reflective poetry, but there seems little doubt that his recent reading of Spenser was decisive.
p. 74, *l.* 7 *LJ,* I, 253–4. Letter of November 12, 1809.
p. 75, *l.* 21 *LJ,* V, 450.
p. 75, *l.* 27 *Poetry,* II, 189.
p. 76, *l.* 14 The term "Franks" was used generally in the Levant to designate all Western Europeans.
p. 77, *l.* 9 Trelawny, *Records,* p. 27.
p. 77, *l.* 18 *Childe Harold,* II, 2.
p. 77, *l.* 20 Ibid., II, 3.
p. 78, *l.* 4 Ibid., II, 15.
p. 78, *l.* 12 Hobhouse, *Journey,* I, 347 *n.*
p. 78, *l.* 15 *LJ,* V, 547. In the first letter on Bowles.
p. 79, *l.* 6 *Don Juan,* III, "The Isles of Greece," following stanza 86.
p. 79, *l.* 17 Ibid.
p. 79, *l.* 31 *Poetry,* II, 190.
p. 80, *l.* 31 *LJ,* I, 266. Letter of May 3, 1809.

Notes to Chapter VIII

p. 81, l. 5 *LJ*, I, 268.
p. 81, l. 23 *Childe Harold*, II, 88.
p. 82, l. 13 Jacob Bryant's *Dissertations concerning the war of Troy* . . . , 1796, argued that no such city existed.
p. 82, l. 16 *LJ*, V, 165–6. Diary of January 11, 1821. It was not until the 1870's that the researches and discoveries of Heinrich Schliemann established the location of Troy as the modern Hissarlik, a village not far from the Dardanelles.
p. 82, l. 38 From the original letter in the library of Trinity College, Cambridge, dated May 3, 1810.
p. 83, l. 13 Ibid.
p. 83, l. 25 *LJ*, I, 271–2. Letter of May 5, 1810.
p. 84, l. 13 *The New Monthly Magazine*, XVII (1826), 310–11. The author is not identified.
p. 84, l. 26 *LJ*, I, 282. Letter of June 28, 1810, to Mrs. Byron.
p. 85, l. 5 Marchand, I, 244.
p. 85, l. 18 *LJ*, VI, 451–2. Letter of June 23, 1810.
p. 85, l. 31 *LBC*, I, 9.
p. 86, l. 1 *LJ*, I, 286.
p. 86, l. 15 *The New Monthly Magazine*, XIX (1827), 147.
p. 86, l. 29 *LJ*, I, 292. Letter of July (21?), 1810, to Mrs. Byron.
p. 86, l. 33 Ibid., pp. 292–3.
p. 86, l. 39 *B-SP*, I, 81. Letter of August 23, 1810.
p. 87, l. 5 A number of letters in Greek from Eustathios to Byron are among the Byron papers at John Murray's. The first one, dated January 1, 1809 [meant for 1810] indicates that Byron had asked to have the boy sent to him in Athens, but, ill with a fever, he could not then come.
p. 87, l. 22 *B-SP*, I, 75–6. Letter of July 29, 1810.
p. 87, l. 35 *B-SP*, I, 78. Letter of August 16, 1810, to Hobhouse.
p. 87, l. 37 Ibid.
p. 88, l. 21 *B-SP*, I, 80. Letter of August 23, 1810.
p. 89, l. 9 Ibid., p. 82.
p. 89, l. 14 Ibid., pp. 81–2.
p. 89, l. 21 Moore, I, 254.
p. 89, l. 26 Marginal note in Hobhouse's copy of Moore.
p. 90, l. 4 *LJ*, II, 361. Journal, December 5, 1813.
p. 90, l. 21 *B-SP*, I, 82; Marchand, I, 258 *n.*
p. 90, l. 28 *B-SP*, I, 87. Letter of October 4, 1810; Marchand, I, 258 *n.* Hobhouse was discreet enough not to tell Matthews of Byron's sexual deviations (see Moore, *The Late Lord Byron*, p. 90 *n*).
p. 91, l. 6 Marchand, I, 270. Letter of May 15, 1811.
p. 91, l. 13 *B-SP*, I, 85. Letter of October 4, 1810.
p. 91, l. 20 Meryon, III, 218–19.
p. 91, l. 22 A. W. Kinglake, *Eothen*, p. 97.
p. 91, l. 30 *B-SP*, I, 83. Letter of October 2, 1810, to Hobhouse.
p. 92, l. 6 A good brief account of foreigners in Athens during

Byron's sojourn is in William A. Borst, *Lord Byron's First Pilgrimage*, pp. 136–7 *n.*

p. 92, *l.* 18 *LBC*, I, 29. Letter of January 20, 1811, to Hodgson.

p. 92, *l.* 27 *LJ*, I, 307.

p. 92, *l.* 37 *LBC*, I, 20–2. Letter of November 26, 1810.

p. 93, *l.* 8 *LBC*, I, 25. Letter of January 10, 1811.

p. 93, *l.* 27 *LJ*, I, 308–9. Corrected from the MS in the Morgan Library.

p. 93, *l.* 34 *LBC*, I, 29–30.

p. 94, *l.* 7 *Childe Harold*, II, 76.

p. 94, *l.* 12 *Poetry*, II, 192.

p. 94, *l.* 19 Ibid., p. 199.

p. 94, *l.* 39 Ibid., pp. 190–1.

p. 95, *l.* 9 *LJ*, I, 310–11. Letter of January 28, 1811. Date corrected from the MS in the Morgan Library.

p. 95, *l.* 11 Marchand, I, 267. Letter of February 1, 1811.

p. 95, *l.* 24 *Curse of Minerva*, lines 164, 138.

p. 95, *l.* 33 *B-SP*, I, 92.

p. 96, *l.* 2 *Poetry*, II, 176.

p. 96, *l.* 5 Marchand, I, 269–70. Letter of May 15, 1811, to Hobhouse.

p. 96, *l.* 16 *LJ*, I, 318. Letter of July 7, 1811, to Henry Drury. (Date corrected from the MS in the Berg Collection of the New York Public Library.)

p. 96, *l.* 32 *Poetry*, II, 188.

p. 97, *l.* 29 *LBC*, I, 78. Letter of September 15, 1812.

p. 97, *l.* 35 Ibid.

p. 98, *l.* 3 *LBC*, I, 32. Letter of May 15, 1811.

p. 98, *l.* 20 Borst, p. 149.

p. 99, *l.* 9 Marchand, I, 276. From the original letter in the Berg Collection of the New York Public Library.

p. 99, *l.* 16 *LJ*, II, 31. Letter of September 9, 1811.

p. 99, *l.* 21 *LJ*, II, 22. Letter of September 3, 1811.

p. 99, *l.* 31 *The Bride of Abydos*, lines 1–2.

p. 99, *l.* 36 Trelawny, *Records*, p. 27.

p. 100, *l.* 3 A phrase from a song written by Thomas Dibden, which Byron was fond of using when he wished to belittle the provincialism of England.

Notes to Chapter IX

p. 101, *l.* 6 *LBC*, I, 41. Letter of July 15, 1811.

p. 101, *l.* 15 Dallas, *Correspondence*, pp. 117–18.

p. 102, *l.* 36 *LJ*, II, 4 *n.* Letter of July 29, 1811.

p. 103, *l.* 1 *LJ*, I, 312. Letter of June 25, 1811.

p. 103, *l.* 13 Moore, I, 274.

p. 103, *l.* 24 Ibid.

p. 103, *l.* 34 Ibid., p. 275.

p. 104, *l.* 1 *LBC*, I, 44. Letter of August 10, 1811.

p. 104, l. 11 LJ, I, 327–30. Letter and draft of will dated August 12, 1811. The will is now in the library of the University of Texas.

p. 104, l. 12 LJ, I, 331. Letter of August 20, 1811.

p. 104, l. 22 LJ, I, 332. Letter of August 21, 1811.

p. 104, l. 26 LJ, I, 339. Letter of August 22, 1811.

p. 104, l. 33 Childe Harold, II, 8.

p. 105, l. 9 LJ, II, 41. Letter of September 17, 1811.

p. 105, l. 11 LJ, II, 45. Letter of September 23, 1811.

p. 105, l. 20 LJ, II, 47–8. Letter of September 26, 1811. Byron also suppressed the stanza which began: "Frown not upon me, churlish Priest! that I/ Look not for Life, where life may never be . . ." (*Poetry*, II, 103–5 *n.*)

p. 105, l. 33 LJ, I, 333. Letter of August 21, 1811.

p. 105, l. 37 LJ, II, 16. Letter of August 31, 1811.

p. 106, l. 3 LJ, II, 10–12. Letter of August 30, 1811.

p. 106, l. 13 LJ, II, 13–14. Letter of August 30, 1811.

p. 106, l. 23 LJ, II, 18–19. Letter of September 3, 1811.

p. 106, l. 38 LJ, II, 36. Letter of September 13, 1811.

p. 107, l. 5 LBC, I, 47. Letter of September 20, 1811.

p. 107, l. 11 LJ, II, 46. Letter of September 25, 1811, to Hodgson.

p. 107, l. 18 LJ, II, 52. Letter of October 11, 1811.

p. 107, l. 25 Poetry, III, 30–4. For a discussion of the identification of *Thyrza*, see Marchand, I, 296 *n.*

p. 107, l. 29 Childe Harold, II, 9.

p. 107, l. 33 LJ, II, 58. Letter of October 14, 1811.

p. 108, l. 3 Marchand, I, 297.

p. 108, l. 14 Childe Harold, II, 95–8. For a discussion of other poems to Edleston, see Marchand, I, 313 *n.*

p. 108, l. 22 English Bards, lines 466–7. Moore and Jeffrey took a liking to each other and became friends, and Moore was eager to live down the attempted duel.

p. 108, l. 32 LJ, II, 62–3. Letter of October 27, 1811.

p. 109, l. 5 LJ, II, 66. Letter of October 31, 1811.

p. 109, l. 25 Moore, *Prose and Verse*, p. 424.

p. 110, l. 2 Marchand, I, 305–6. Letter of November 16, 1811.

p. 110, l. 10 LBC, I, 60. Letter of November 16, 1811.

p. 110, l. 18 LBC, I, 56. Letter of November 3, 1811.

p. 110, l. 26 LJ, II, 85. Letter of December 8, 1811.

p. 110, l. 32 Ibid., p. 83.

p. 110, l. 35 Pratt, p. 98.

p. 110, l. 38 Ibid.

p. 111, l. 8 L'Estrange, p. 13; Hodgson, I, 219–20.

p. 111, l. 14 Marchand, I, 310. Letter of December 25, 1811.

p. 111, l. 20 "To Lord Byron," p. 26. Letter of January 12, 1812.

p. 111, l. 31 Ibid., pp. 33–4. Letter of January 20, 1812.

p. 112, l. 4 Doris Langley Moore: *The Great Byron Adventure* (pamphlet, 1959), p. 14. The date, here given as January 20, 1812, should be January 28 (see Elwin, p. 138, and *"To Lord Byron,"* pp. 58–9).

p. 112, l. 8 Moore, *The Great Byron Adventure*, p. 13.

p. 112, l. 12 Hodgson, I, 221.

p. 112, l. 13 *B-SP*, I, 132. Letter of February 10, 1812.

p. 112, l. 20 *LJ*, II, 100–1. Letter of February 16, 1812. Byron embodied this same idea in a poem beginning "And thou art dead, as young and fair" (*Poetry*, III, 42).

p. 112, l. 26 *LJ*, II, 100.

p. 113, l. 37 *LJ*, II, 103–4. Letter of February 25, 1812.

p. 114, l. 3 Dallas, *Correspondence*, III, 15.

p. 114, l. 13 *LJ*, II, 105. Letter of March 5, 1812, to Hodgson.

p. 114, l. 21 *LJ*, II, 429.

p. 114, l. 29 *LJ*, II, 105. Letter of March 5, 1812.

p. 114, l. 30 *Don Juan*, XV, 22.

p. 114, l. 36 Holland, p. 123.

p. 114, l. 40 *LJ*, II, 105. Letter of March 5, 1812, to Hodgson.

p. 115, l. 10 *Poetry*, III, 45.

Notes to Chapter X

p. 118, l. 18 Elwin, p. 141.

p. 118, l. 22 Morgan, II, 200.

p. 118, l. 29 Medwin (ed. Lovell), p. 216.

p. 119, l. 17 Mayne, p. 151.

p. 120, l. 21 Mayne, *Lady Byron*, p. 36. Diary of March 25, 1812.

p. 120, l. 25 Ibid.

p. 120, l. 34 Ibid., pp. 36–7. Letter of March 26, 1812.

p. 121, l. 3 Medwin (ed. Lovell), pp. 33–4.

p. 121, l. 8 *LJ*, II, 451.

p. 121, l. 17 Rogers, pp. 234–5.

p. 121, l. 27 Foster, pp. 375–6.

p. 121, l. 34 Rogers, p. 232.

p. 122, l. 2 Mayne, *Lady Byron*, p. 38.

p. 122, l. 6 Ibid., p. 39.

p. 122, l. 22 Ibid., p. 39.

p. 122, l. 27 Ibid., p. 41.

p. 123, l. 2 *LJ*, II, 121. Letter of May 1, 1812.

p. 123, l. 16 Medwin (ed. Lovell), p. 216.

p. 123, l. 22 *LJ*, II, 452. Letter to Medwin (November ?, 1824).

p. 123, l. 28 Cecil, p. 156.

p. 123, l. 34 *LJ*, II, 452. Letter to Medwin (November ?, 1824).

p. 123, l. 36 *LBC*, I, 111. Letter of November 26, 1812.

p. 124, l. 11 *LJ*, II, 116–17. The letter is undated.

p. 124, l. 24 Marchand, I, 341.

p. 124, l. 38 *LJ*, II, 452. Letter to Medwin (November ?, 1824).

p. 125, l. 40 *LJ*, II, 438, 442–3.

p. 126, l. 10 *LJ*, V, 431. "Detached Thoughts."

p. 126, l. 28 *"To Lord Byron,"* p. 17.

p. 126, l. 29 Ibid., pp. 18–19.

p. 126, l. 33 Ibid., p. 19.

p. 127, l. 24 Blessington (ed. Lovell), p. 132.

p. 127, l. 30 Medwin (ed. Lovell), p. 216.

p. 127, l. 35 Marchand, I, 349.

p. 127, l. 38 LJ, II, 123. Letter of May 20, 1812.

p. 128, l. 34 Glenbervie, II, 81. From the diary entry of October 28, 1810.

p. 130, l. 22 Elwin, p. 146.

p. 131, l. 15 LJ, II, 135–9. Undated, but the context indicates it was soon after Caroline ran away (August 12, 1812).

p. 131, l. 24 Airlie, p. 131.

p. 132, l. 10 LBC, I, 72. Letter of September 10, 1812.

p. 132, l. 16 Morning Chronicle, October 12, 1812; *LJ,* II, 172 *n.*

p. 132, l. 25 LBC, I, 72. Letter of September 10, 1812.

p. 132, l. 36 LBC, I, 74–5. Letter of September 13, 1812.

p. 133, l. 9 LBC, I, 79. Letter of September 18, 1812.

p. 133, l. 14 LBC, I, 85. Letter of September 25, 1812.

p. 133, l. 17 LBC, I, 82. Letter of September 21, 1812.

p. 133, l. 29 LBC, I, 84. Letter of September 25, 1812.

p. 133, l. 32 LBC, I, 87. Letter of September 28, 1812.

p. 133, l. 37 Ibid., p. 88.

p. 134, l. 7 Airlie, p. 137.

p. 134, l. 13 Ibid.

p. 134, l. 25 Mayne, *Lady Byron,* p. 49.

p. 134, l. 31 Airlie, p. 142. Letter of October 12, 1812.

p. 134, l. 39 LBC, I, 91, 93–4. Letters of October 17 and 18, 1812.

p. 135, l. 13 The Waltz was printed in a few copies for private circulation but was not published during Byron's lifetime.

p. 135, l. 20 LBC, I, 93–4. Letter of October 18, 1812, to Lady Melbourne.

p. 135, l. 26 Blessington (ed. Lovell), p. 149.

p. 135, l. 31 LBC, I, 99. Letter of October 30, 1812.

p. 136, l. 11 LBC, I, 103–4. Letter of November 9, 1812.

p. 136, l. 16 LBC, I, 104–5. Letter of November 10, 1812.

p. 136, l. 25 Airlie, pp. 151–2. This was the letter which Caroline published, somewhat garbled, in her novel *Glenarvon,* attributing it to the hero of which Byron was the model.

p. 136, l. 28 LBC, I, 108. Letter of November 16, 1812.

p. 136, l. 35 LBC, I, 110, 107–8. Letter of November 14, 1812.

p. 136, l. 40 LBC, I, 111. Letter of November 26, 1812. Armida was the sorceress in Tasso's *Gerusalemme Liberata* in whose palace Rinaldo forgot his vow as a crusader.

p. 137, l. 4 LBC, I, 112. Letter of November 27, 1812.

p. 137, l. 13 LBC, I, 119. Letter of December 21, 1812, to Lady Melbourne.

p. 137, l. 32 LBC, I, 124. Letter of December 31, 1812.

p. 137, l. 36 LBC, I, 118. Letter of December 21, 1812.

p. 138, l. 7 LBC, I, 124.

Notes to Chapter XI

p. 139, l. 9 LBC, I, 128. Letter of January 4, 1813.

p. 139, l. 12 LJ, II, 325. Journal, November 17, 1813.

p. 140, l. 4 Medwin (ed. Lovell), p. 70.

p. 140, l. 13 Elwin, p. 163.
p. 140, l. 19 Bury (1908), II, 287.
p. 140, l. 25 Bury (1908), II, 280.
p. 141, l. 2 *LJ*, II, 198. Letter of March 26, 1813.
p. 141, l. 10 Ibid., p. 197.
p. 141, l. 15 *LBC*, I, 142. Letter of March 18, 1813.
p. 141, l. 27 *LBC*, I, 148. Letter of April 19, 1813.
p. 141, l. 39 *LBC*, I, 145. Letter of April 5, 1813.
p. 142, l. 5 *LBC*, I, 152.
p. 142, l. 11 *LJ*, II, 452. Letter of November ?, 1824.
p. 142, l. 21 Hunt, *Lord Byron*, I, 4.
p. 142, l. 30 *LBC*, I, 156. Letter of May 24, 1813.
p. 143, l. 2 Mayne, *Lady Byron*, p. 55.
p. 143, l. 11 *LJ*, II, 445.
p. 143, l. 30 *B-SP*, I, 159. Letter of January 17, 1813.
p. 143, l. 37 *LBC*, I, 160. Letter of June 21, 1813.
p. 144, l. 5 *Murray's Magazine*, January 1887.
p. 144, l. 11 Blessington (ed. Lovell), p. 24.
p. 144, l. 18 Ibid., pp. 25–6.
p. 144, l. 25 *LBC*, I, 161. Letter of June 29, 1813.
p. 144, l. 28 *LJ*, II, 227. Letter of June 27, 1813.
p. 145, l. 31 *LBC*, I, 163. Letter of July 6, 1813, to Lady Melbourne.
p. 145, l. 39 *LJ*, II, 453. Letter of November ?, 1824.
p. 146, l. 3 Ibid.
p. 146, l. 20 Marchand, I, 398–9. Murray MSS.
p. 146, l. 27 *LJ*, II, 230. Letter of July 13, 1813.
p. 146, l. 32 *LJ*, V, 423. "Detached Thoughts."
p. 147, l. 1 *LJ*, V, 435. "Detached Thoughts."
p. 147, l. 4 *LJ*, V, 418. "Detached Thoughts."
p. 147, l. 10 *LJ*, II, 320. Journal, November 16, 1813.
p. 147, l. 16 *LJ*, V, 413. "Detached Thoughts."
p. 147, l. 23 *LBC*, I, 168.
p. 147, l. 31 *LBC*, I, 172–4. Letter of August 20, 1813.
p. 147, l. 37 *LJ*, II, 251.
p. 148, l. 15 Doris Langley Moore, *The Great Byron Adventure*, p. 38.
p. 149, l. 5 Mayne, *Lady Byron*, pp. 57–9.
p. 149, l. 20 From a commonplace book of Annabella Milbanke now in my possession.
p. 149, l. 35 *LJ*, III, 398–9. Letter of August 25, 1813.
p. 150, l. 10 *LBC*, I, 177–8. Letter of September 5, 1813.
p. 150, l. 15 Medwin (ed. Lovell), p. 34.
p. 150, l. 22 *LJ*, III, 400. Letter of September 6, 1813.
p. 150, l. 27 *LBC*, I, 179. Letter of September 8, 1813.
p. 150, l. 31 *LBC*, I, 179–80. Letter of September 9, 1813.
p. 151, l. 8 *The Giaour*, lines 1131–4, 1141–4. These lines first appeared in the fifth edition, published August 25, 1813.
p. 151, l. 20 *LJ*, II, 265. Letter of September 15, 1813.
p. 151, l. 28 *LBC*, I, 180–1.
p. 151, l. 38 *LBC*, I, 183. Letter of September 28, 1813.
p. 152, l. 15 *LJ*, III, 401–3. Letter of September 16, 1813.
p. 152, l. 23 *LBC*, I, 184. Letter of September 28, 1813.

p. 152, l. 33 *LBC*, I, 186. Letter of October 1, 1813.
p. 153, l. 17 *LBC*, I, 190–3. Letter of October 8, 1813.
p. 153, l. 30 *LBC*, I, 198. Letter of October 13, 1813.
p. 153, l. 35 *LBC*, I, 201–2. Letter of October 14, 1813.
p. 154, l. 9 *LBC*, I, 203–4. Letter of October 17, 1813.
p. 154, l. 18 *LBC*, I, 204–5. Letter of October 17, 1813.
p. 154, l. 27 *LBC*, I, 209. Letter of October 21, 1813.
p. 154, l. 36 *LBC*, I, 213. Letter of October 23, 1813 (postscript dated "Monday" [October 25]).
p. 155, l. 10 *LBC*, I, 214.
p. 155, l. 13 *LJ*, II, 293. Letter of November 30, 1813.
p. 155, l. 28 *LJ*, III, 404.
p. 155, l. 34 *LJ*, III, 405. Letter of November 10, 1813.
p. 156, l. 4 *LJ*, II, 313.
p. 156, l. 9 *LJ*, II, 318. Journal, November 14, 1813.
p. 156, l. 15 *LJ*, II, 328. Journal, November 17, 1813.
p. 156, l. 24 *LJ*, II, 341–2. Journal, November 24, 1813.
p. 156, l. 30 *LJ*, II, 338, 340. Journal, November 23, 1813.
p. 156, l. 37 *LJ*, II, 350. Journal, November 27, 1813.
p. 156, l. 39 *LBC*, I, 218. Letter of November 25, 1813.
p. 157, l. 7 *LJ*, II, 343. Journal, November 24, 1813.
p. 157, l. 21 *LJ*, II, 365. Journal, December 6, 1813.
p. 157, l. 32 *LJ*, II, 369. Journal, December 7, 1813.
p. 158, l. 5 *LJ*, II, 376–7. Journal, December 13, 1813.
p. 158, l. 23 *LJ*, II, 377. Journal, December 14, 15, 16, 1813.
p. 159, l. 19 *LBC*, I, 223 *n.*, 224–5 *n.* Letters of December 24, 1813; January 7, 1814.
p. 159, l. 39 *LJ*, II, 357. Journal, November 30, 1813.

Notes to Chapter XII

p. 160, l. 2 *LJ*, II, 382. Journal, February 18, 1814.
p. 160, l. 11 *LBC*, I, 224. Letter of January 8, 1814, to Lady Melbourne.
p. 160, l. 16 *LBC*, I, 232. Letter of January 13, 1814.
p. 160, l. 21 *LJ*, III, 7. Letter undated, but probably about January 8, 1814.
p. 161, l. 4 *LBC*, I, 226. Letter of January 10, 1814.
p. 161, l. 10 Ibid.
p. 161, l. 13 *LBC*, I, 228. Letter of January 11, 1814.
p. 161, l. 20 *LBC*, I, 234. Letter of January 13, 1814.
p. 161, l. 25 *LBC*, I, 237. Letter of January 16, 1814.
p. 161, l. 37 *LBC*, I, 241. Letter of January 29, 1814.
p. 162, l. 5 Smiles, I, 223. Letter of February 3, 1814.
p. 162, l. 26 *LJ*, III, 27. Letter of February 7, 1814.
p. 162, l. 30 *LBC*, I, 243. Letter of February 11, 1814.
p. 162, l. 35 Broughton, I, 84.
p. 162, l. 38 *LJ*, II, 382. Journal, February 18, 1814.
p. 163, l. 3 *LJ*, II, 385–6. Journal, February 19, 1814.
p. 163, l. 12 *LJ*, II, 383–4. Journal, February 18, 1814.

p. 163, l. 18 *LJ*, II, 323. Journal, November 17, 1813.
p. 163, l. 29 *LJ*, II, 389–90. Journal, February 27, 1814.
p. 164, l. 5 *LJ*, III, 56. Letter of March 3, 1814.
p. 164, l. 15 *LJ*, II, 398. Journal, March 10, 1814.
p. 164, l. 31 Elwin, p. 190.
p. 164, l. 39 Elwin, p. 191. Letter of March 12, 1814.
p. 165, l. 4 *LJ*, II, 401.
p. 165, l. 13 *LJ*, II, 401. Journal, March 17, 1814.
p. 165, l. 24 *LBC*, I, 249. Letter of April 8, 1814.
p. 165, l. 30 *LJ*, II, 409–10. Journal, April 9, 1814.
p. 166, l. 10 *LBC*, I, 251. Letter of April 25, 1814.
p. 166, l. 16 *LJ*, III, 70. Letter of April 20, 1814.
p. 166, l. 29 *LBC*, I, 253–4. Letter of April 29, 1814.
p. 167, l. 3 Marchand, I, 448.
p. 167, l. 12 *LBC*, I, 254–5. Letter of April 30, 1814.
p. 167, l. 19 *LBC*, I, 255. Letter of April 30, 1814.
p. 167, l. 35 *LJ*, III, 81. Letter of [May 8, 1814].
p. 168, l. 8 *LBC*, I, 257. Letter of May 16, 1814.
p. 168, l. 16 *LJ*, VI, 77. Letter of June 6, 1822.
p. 168, l. 23 Moore, I, 553.
p. 169, l. 6 *B-SP*, I, 286. Letter of June [18], 1814.
p. 169, l. 13 *"To Lord Byron,"* pp. 135–6.
p. 169, l. 21 *LJ*, VI, 80. Letter of June 8, 1822.
p. 170, l. 25 Glenbervie, II, 302.
p. 170, l. 26 *LBC*, I, 262. Letter of June 28, 1814.
p. 171, l. 8 *LBC*, I, 263. Letter of July 2, 1814.
p. 171, l. 17 *LJ*, II, 453.
p. 171, l. 24 Moore, *The Late Lord Byron*, pp. 241–3.
p. 171, l. 35 *LJ*, III, 104. Letter undated, but about July 10, 1814.
p. 172, l. 11 *LJ*, III, 110. Letter of July 24, 1814, to Murray.
p. 172, l. 23 *LJ*, III, 117–18. Letter of August 3, 1814.
p. 172, l. 31 Mayne, *Lady Byron*, p. 100.
p. 172, l. 36 Mayne, *Lady Byron*, p. 101. Letter of August 1, 1814.
p. 173, l. 8 *LBC*, I, 273–4. Letter of October 4, 1814.
p. 173, l. 16 *LJ*, III, 120. Letter of August 3, 1814.
p. 173, l. 24 Marchand, I, 466. Letter of July 30, 1814.
p. 173, l. 31 Mayne, *Lady Byron*, p. 103.
p. 174, l. 15 Mayne, *Lady Byron*, p. 104. Letter of August 16, 1814.
p. 174, l. 28 Elwin, p. 205. Letter of September 2, 1814.
p. 174, l. 31 Elwin, p. 205. Letter of September 7, 1814.
p. 174, l. 40 *LBC*, I, 274. Letter of October 4, 1814.
p. 175, l. 6 Ibid., pp. 274–5.
p. 175, l. 18 Mayne, *Lady Byron*, p. 111.
p. 175, l. 36 *LBC*, I, 266.
p. 176, l. 14 Elwin, p. 208. Letter of September 14, 1814.
p. 176, l. 21 Elwin, pp. 208–9.
p. 176, l. 22 *LBC*, I, 269. Letter of September 23, 1814.
p. 176, l. 37 Elwin, p. 209. Letter of September 18, 1814.
p. 176, l. 40 Mayne, *Lady Byron*, p. 112.

Notes to Chapter XIII

p. 178, l. 12 LBC, I, 270. Letter of September 23, 1814.

p. 178, l. 17 LBC, I, 277. Letter of October 7, 1814.

p. 179, l. 5 Mayne, *Lady Byron,* p. 444. Letter of September 20, 1814.

p. 179, l. 8 Mayne, *Lady Byron,* p. 114.

p. 179, l. 17 Ibid., p. 446. Letter of September 22, 1814.

p. 179, l. 31 LJ, III, 139–40. Letter of September 20, 1814.

p. 180, l. 9 Irving, *Abbotsford and Newstead Abbey,* p. 68. That part of the tree containing their names was later cut out and is now preserved at Newstead Abbey.

p. 180, l. 19 "To Lord Byron," p. 68.

p. 180, l. 21 Ibid., p. 67.

p. 180, l. 23 Ibid., p. 68 *n.*

p. 180, l. 31 LBC, I, 276. Letter of October 7, 1814.

p. 181, l. 27 Mayne, *Lady Byron,* pp. 448–9. Letter of September 26, 1814.

p. 182, l. 16 Elwin, p. 166.

p. 182, l. 31 Mayne, *Lady Byron,* p. 122.

p. 182, l. 39 LBC, I, 287. Letter of November 4, 1814.

p. 183, l. 5 Mayne, *Lady Byron,* p. 123.

p. 183, l. 16 LBC, I, 287–8. Letter of November 4, 1814.

p. 183, l. 21 LBC, I, 288. Letter of November 6, 1814.

p. 183, l. 33 Mayne, *Lady Byron,* p. 124.

p. 183, l. 39 Mayne, *Lady Byron,* p. 123.

p. 184, l. 18 LBC, I, 289–90.

p. 184, l. 28 Mayne, *Lady Byron,* p. 126. Letter of November 16, 1814.

p. 184, l. 34 Mayne, *Lady Byron,* p. 128.

p. 185, l. 8 Hobhouse diary, November 23, 1814.

p. 185, l. 21 Mayne, *Lady Byron,* p. 137. Letter of December 3, 1814.

p. 185, l. 26 Ibid., p. 139. Letter of December 5, 1814.

p. 187, l. 14 Marchand, II, 496–500. From the manuscript narrative of Eliza Francis.

p. 187, l. 28 Broughton, I, 191.

p. 187, l. 37 Broughton, II, 195.

p. 187, l. 38 Broughton, I, 191.

p. 188, l. 6 Marchand, II, 504. From the manuscript diary, Berg Collection, New York Public Library.

p. 188, l. 11 Ibid.

p. 188, l. 19 Moore, I, 599.

p. 188, l. 26 Marchand, II, 505.

p. 188, l. 35 Mayne, *Lady Byron,* 152 *n.*

p. 188, l. 38 Marchand, II, 506.

p. 189, l. 5 Ibid.

Notes to Chapter XIV

p. 191, l. 6 Mayne, *Lady Byron,* p. 160.
p. 191, l. 17 Medwin (ed. Lovell), p. 36.
p. 191, l. 26 Hobhouse diary, May 15, 1824.
p. 191, l. 36 Elwin, p. 251.
p. 192, l. 2 Stanley T. Williams, *The Life of Washington Irving,* I, 455, note 75. Irving, who read Byron's Memoirs (later burned), recalled this incident as there recorded.
p. 192, l. 14 Elwin, p. 252 *n.*
p. 192, l. 30 *LBC,* I, 293.
p. 192, l. 37 Mayne, *Lady Byron,* p. 469. Letter of October 20, 1814.
p. 193, l. 15 Mayne, *Lady Byron,* p. 165.
p. 193, l. 19 Ibid.
p. 193, l. 21 Elwin, p. 256.
p. 193, l. 27 Elwin, p. 254. Letter of January 4, 1815.
p. 193, l. 34 Elwin, pp. 252–3. Annabella's statement of March 1817.
p. 193, l. 39 Mayne, *Lady Byron,* p. 167.
p. 194, l. 7 Stowe, *Lady Byron Vindicated,* p. 302.
p. 194, l. 15 Maurois, p. 229.
p. 194, l. 34 Mayne, *Lady Byron,* p. 166.
p. 195, l. 8 *LBC,* I, 295.
p. 195, l. 19 *LJ,* III, 175–6. Letter of February 2, 1815.
p. 195, l. 25 *LBC,* I, 296. Letter of January 26, 1815.
p. 196, l. 4 Mayne, *Lady Byron,* p. 172.
p. 196, l. 15 Marchand, II, 521. Letter of January 26, 1815.
p. 196, l. 29 Maurois, p. 231.
p. 196, l. 34 Mayne, *Lady Byron,* p. 173.
p. 196, l. 36 Ibid., p. 174.
p. 197, l. 2 Ibid.
p. 197, l. 17 Ibid., p. 175.
p. 197, l. 22 Ibid., p. 176.
p. 197, l. 26 Ibid., p. 177.
p. 197, l. 32 Ibid.
p. 197, l. 39 Ibid., p. 176.
p. 198, l. 19 Elwin, p. 295. The words in brackets are Lord Lovelace's transcriptions of Annabella's shorthand.
p. 198, l. 24 Mayne, *Lady Byron,* p. 176.
p. 198, l. 34 *LJ,* III, 188. Letter of March 27, 1815.
p. 199, l. 2 Mayne, *Lady Byron,* pp. 180–1.
p. 199, l. 7 Marchand, II, 527.
p. 199, l. 21 *LJ,* III, 192. Letter of March 31, 1815.
p. 199, l. 35 Mayne, *Lady Byron,* p. 181.
p. 200, l. 4 Smiles, I, 267.
p. 200, l. 9 Smiles, I, 267–8.
p. 200, l. 18 Moore, I, 616.
p. 200, l. 24 Ibid.
p. 201, l. 15 Slater, p. 86.

p. 201, *l.* 22 L'Estrange, p. 24.
p. 201, *l.* 24 Hogg, p. 104. Letter of April 10, 1815.
p. 201, *l.* 30 Mayne, *Lady Byron*, p. 181.
p. 202, *l.* 2 *The Journal of Sir Walter Scott*, I, 52.
p. 202, *l.* 9 *Astarte*, p. 1 *n*. From narrative of Lady Byron, dated March 1817.
p. 202, *l.* 15 Hunt, *Autobiography*, p. 253.
p. 202, *l.* 19 Hunt, *Lord Byron*, I, 6.
p. 202, *l.* 28 *LJ*, III, 210 *n*. Letter of Tuesday [August 1815].
p. 203, *l.* 6 *LJ*, III, 209 *n*. From a manuscript apparently written for some newspaper, but not published in Byron's lifetime.
p. 203, *l.* 30 Hobhouse diary, July 28, 1815.
p. 203, *l.* 37 Broughton, II, 201.
p. 204, *l.* 3 *LJ*, III, 210 *n*.
p. 204, *l.* 13 Mayne, *Lady Byron*, p. 187.
p. 204, *l.* 18 Ibid., p. 188.
p. 204, *l.* 38 *LJ*, V, 442–3. "Detached Thoughts."
p. 205, *l.* 34 Mayne, *Lady Byron*, p. 190.
p. 205, *l.* 39 *LJ*, III, 242–3.
p. 206, *l.* 13 Mayne, *Lady Byron*, p. 194.
p. 206, *l.* 20 Medwin (ed. Lovell), p. 38.
p. 206, *l.* 34 Blessington (ed. Lovell), p. 122.
p. 206, *l.* 38 Moore, II, 223 *n*.
p. 207, *l.* 3 Blessington (ed. Lovell), p. 181.
p. 207, *l.* 10 Smiles, I, 286.
p. 207, *l.* 17 Mayne, *Lady Byron*, p. 191.
p. 207, *l.* 20 Ibid., p. 190.
p. 207, *l.* 26 *LJ*, III, 249. Letter of November 14, 1815.
p. 208, *l.* 14 Marchand, II, 550. Letter of August 23, 1821.
p. 208, *l.* 24 Mayne, *Lady Byron*, p. 196.
p. 208, *l.* 35 Marchand, II, 552.
p. 209, *l.* 3 Mayne, *Lady Byron*, p. 197.
p. 209, *l.* 13 Broughton, II, 279.
p. 209, *l.* 20 Broughton, II, 280.
p. 209, *l.* 26 Stowe, *Lady Byron Vindicated*, p. 306.
p. 209, *l.* 29 *LJ*, III, 291–2. Letter of December 11, 1815.
p. 209, *l.* 35 Broughton, II, 280.
p. 210, *l.* 7 *Childe Harold*, III, 118.
p. 210, *l.* 12 Broughton, II, 201–2.
p. 210, *l.* 27 Marchand, II, 556.
p. 210, *l.* 33 *Astarte*, p. 39.
p. 211, *l.* 5 Ibid.
p. 211, *l.* 11 Broughton, II, 215.
p. 211, *l.* 20 Broughton, II, 250.
p. 211, *l.* 24 Broughton, II, 251.
p. 211, *l.* 37 Broughton, II, 253–4.
p. 212, *l.* 8 Broughton, II, 255.
p. 212, *l.* 10 Broughton, II, 215–16.
p. 212, *l.* 15 Fox, p. 102.
p. 212, *l.* 23 Elwin, p. 409.
p. 212, *l.* 29 Mayne, *Lady Byron*, p. 202.

Notes to Chapter XV

p. 213, l. 18 Fox, p. 98. In the first draft of the letter Annabella had written: "Let me hear of *your* obedience at Kirkby—though *I* disobey you in writing to you instead of to Augusta—My love to her." (Elwin, p. 351.)

p. 214, l. 12 Elwin, p. 351.

p. 214, l. 23 Elwin, p. 350.

p. 215, l. 4 Elwin, pp. 351–2.

p. 215, l. 19 Elwin, p. 354. Letter of January 17, 1816.

p. 215, l. 38 *LJ*, III, 294. Letter of January 18, 1816.

p. 216, l. 17 Fox, p. 104.

p. 216, l. 26 *LJ*, III, 297. Letter of January 19, 1816.

p. 216, l. 32 *LJ*, III, 298.

p. 216, l. 34 *LJ*, III, 298. Letter of January 19, 1816.

p. 217, l. 1 *LJ*, III, 298–9.

p. 217, l. 17 Broughton, II, 202.

p. 217, l. 26 *LJ*, III, 257. Letter of January 22, 1816.

p. 217, l. 31 *LJ*, III, 259. Letter of January 29, 1816.

p. 218, l. 4 Broughton, II, 207.

p. 218, l. 13 Fox, pp. 105–6.

p. 218, l. 19 Fox, p. 108.

p. 218, l. 30 Broughton, II, 264.

p. 219, l. 7 Broughton, II, 209.

p. 219, l. 31 Broughton, II, 211–13.

p. 220, l. 4 *LJ*, III, 302. Letter of February 3, 1816.

p. 220, l. 9 Mayne, *Lady Byron*, p. 210.

p. 220, l. 13 Broughton, II, 217.

p. 220, l. 19 Broughton, II, 219. Letter of February 5, 1816.

p. 220, l. 31 Broughton, II, 220.

p. 220, l. 39 Broughton, II, 236. Letter of February 7, 1816.

p. 221, l. 9 Mayne, *Lady Byron*, p. 212. Letter of February 8, 1816.

p. 221, l. 21 Marchand, II, 576.

p. 221, l. 33 Marchand, II, 576–7.

p. 221, l. 39 Marchand, II, 577. Hobhouse diary, February 12, 1816.

p. 222, l. 2 Broughton, II, 259.

p. 222, l. 7 Marchand, II, 579. Hobhouse diary, February 16, 1816.

p. 222, l. 13 Broughton, II, 258. Letter of February 15, 1816.

p. 222, l. 20 Fox, p. 110.

p. 223, l. 3 Fox, p. 59.

p. 223, l. 39 Broughton, II, 290.

p. 224, l. 2 Broughton, II, 260.

p. 224, l. 6 Ilchester, p. 277. Letter of February 23, 1816.

p. 224, l. 15 Elwin, p. 423. Letter of March 4, 1816.

p. 224, l. 18 Elwin, p. 423.

p. 225, l. 6 Marchand, II, 586. Hobhouse diary, March 7, 1816. Hobhouse never committed the word indicated by the dash to his diary.

p. 225, l. 14 Fox, p. 112. The statement is dated March 9, 1816.

p. 226, *l.* 10 *Astarte,* pp. 55–6. Letter of March 3, 1816.
p. 226, *l.* 23 Marchand, II, 590.
p. 226, *l.* 35 *LJ,* III, 429. The letter is undated and signed E. Trefusis. It was probably written sometime in March.
p. 226, *l.* 37 *LJ,* III, 430.
p. 227, *l.* 29 *LJ,* III, 433.
p. 227, *l.* 37 *LBC,* I, 111. Letter of November 26, 1812.
p. 229, *l.* 6 Elwin, p. 419.
p. 229, *l.* 13 Moore, *The Late Lord Byron,* p. 233.
p. 229, *l.* 16 Ibid., p. 234.
p. 229, *l.* 34 Moore, *The Late Lord Byron,* p. 240.
p. 230, *l.* 2 Ibid., p. 241.
p. 230, *l.* 13 Ibid., pp. 243–4.
p. 230, *l.* 20 Moore, *The Late Lord Byron,* p. 244 *n.*
p. 231, *l.* 5 Hazlitt, *Conversations of James Northcote,* No. 15. Paraphrased from Northcote by Hazlitt.
p. 231, *l.* 22 Blessington (ed. Lovell), p. 198.
p. 231, *l.* 33 *LJ,* II, 450.
p. 231, *l.* 36 Marchand, II, 596.
p. 232, *l.* 2 Marchand, II, 600 *n.*
p. 232, *l.* 9 *Astarte,* pp. 51–2. Letter of April 14, 1816.
p. 232, *l.* 16 Elwin, p. 465. Letter of April 15, 1816, to Lady Noel.
p. 232, *l.* 23 Pryse Gordon, *Personal Memoirs,* II, 328.
p. 233, *l.* 2 Marchand, II, 604–5.
p. 233, *l.* 17 *LJ,* III, 435–6.
p. 233, *l.* 24 Marchand, II, 605. Hobhouse diary, entry of April 21, 1816.
p. 233, *l.* 31 Marchand, II, 606. Letter of April 22, 1816.
p. 234, *l.* 6 Marchand, II, 608. Hobhouse diary, entry of April 24, 1816.
p. 234, *l.* 12 *Astarte,* p. 53.
p. 234, *l.* 21 Marchand, II, 608. Hobhouse diary, entry of April 25, 1816.

Notes to Chapter XVI

p. 235, *l.* 11 *Childe Harold,* III, 5.
p. 235, *l.* 23 *Astarte,* p. 112.
p. 236, *l.* 4 Polidori, p. 33.
p. 236, *l.* 11 *LBC,* II, 5. Letter of May 1, 1816.
p. 236, *l.* 17 Pryse Gordon, *Personal Memoirs,* II, 323.
p. 236, *l.* 20 Polidori, p. 213. Letter of May 11, 1816, Polidori to Hobhouse.
p. 236, *l.* 26 *Childe Harold,* III, 17–18.
p. 236, *l.* 34 *Childe Harold,* III, 6.
p. 237, *l.* 2 *Childe Harold,* III, 13.
p. 237, *l.* 23 *Childe Harold,* III, 42.
p. 238, *l.* 4 Marchand, II, 615.
p. 239, *l.* 11 Broughton, II, 363. Letter of May 21, 1816.
p. 239, *l.* 22 Marchand, II, 618. Letter of May 6, 1816.

p. 239, *l.* 29 *Don Juan*, X, 62.

p. 239, *l.* 32 Byron incorporated the verses on the Drachenfels in the third canto of *Childe Harold*, after stanza 55.

p. 239, *l.* 37 *Poetry*, II, 297.

p. 240, *l.* 2 *Childe Harold*, III, 68.

p. 240, *l.* 12 Marchand, II, 620. Letter of May 25, 1816.

p. 241, *l.* 10 Moore, II, 23–4.

p. 241, *l.* 18 *Childe Harold*, III, 73.

p. 241, *l.* 23 Medwin (ed. Lovell), p. 194.

p. 242, *l.* 20 Moore, II, 29.

p. 242, *l.* 34 *Astarte*, p. 267. Letter of September 8, 1816.

p. 242, *l.* 40 Medwin (ed. Lovell), p. 11.

p. 243, *l.* 5 Glenbervie, II, 160. Entry of July 3, 1816.

p. 243, *l.* 15 Moore, II, 30 *n.*

p. 243, *l.* 19 Polidori, *The Vampyre*, pp. ix–x.

p. 244, *l.* 2 *LJ*, IV, 297. Letter of May 15, 1819, to John Murray.

p. 244, *l.* 7 Shelley, *Essays, Letters from Abroad*, II, 73. Letter of July 12, 1816.

p. 244, *l.* 20 *Childe Harold*, III, 77.

p. 244, *l.* 28 *Childe Harold*, III, 78.

p. 245, *l.* 27 Polidori, *The Vampyre*, p. xiii.

p. 245, *l.* 31 *LJ*, IV, 300–1. Letter of May 15, 1819.

p. 246, *l.* 4 *LJ*, V, 337. Letter of August 4, 1821, to John Murray.

p. 246, *l.* 8 Polidori, p. 147.

p. 247, *l.* 13 *Astarte*, p. 218. Letter of June 19, 1816.

p. 247, *l.* 22 *Astarte*, p. 220. Letter of June 28, 1816.

p. 247, *l.* 27 *Astarte*, pp. 223–4. Letter of July 3, 1816.

p. 247, *l.* 32 *Astarte*, p. 239. Letter of July 18, 1816.

p. 247, *l.* 38 *Astarte*, p. 245. Letter of July 28, 1816.

p. 248, *l.* 12 *Astarte*, pp. 247–8.

p. 248, *l.* 26 *LJ*, IV, 12. Letter of December 5, 1817.

p. 249, *l.* 2 Grylls, *Claire Clairmont*, p. 262.

p. 249, *l.* 26 *Astarte*, p. 265. Letter of August 27, 1816.

p. 249, *l.* 38 Marchand, II, 646.

p. 250, *l.* 10 Broughton, II, 9.

p. 250, *l.* 14 The episode is discussed in detail by Gavin de Beer, "An 'Atheist' in the Alps," *Keats-Shelley Memorial Bulletin*, IX (1958), 1–15.

p. 250, *l.* 25 *Astarte*, pp. 266–7. Letter of September 8, 1816.

p. 250, *l.* 38 *Astarte*, p. 257.

p. 251, *l.* 2 *Astarte*, pp. 259–60. Letter of September 15, 1816.

p. 251, *l.* 5 *Astarte*, pp. 261–2. Letter of September 17, 1816.

p. 251, *l.* 20 *LJ*, III, 379. Letter of November 1, 1816.

p. 251, *l.* 21 Medwin (ed. Lovell), pp. 106–7.

p. 251, *l.* 33 *Astarte*, pp. 271–3. Letter of September 17, 1816.

p. 252, *l.* 3 *LJ*, III, 357–8. Journal, September 22, 1816.

p. 252, *l.* 10 *LJ*, III, 359–60. Journal, September 23, 1816.

p. 252, *l.* 19 *LJ*, III, 364. Journal, September 29, 1816.

p. 252, *l.* 25 Smiles, I, 365. Letter of September 12, 1816, Murray to Byron.

p. 252, *l.* 36 *LBC*, II, 19. Letter of September 29, 1816.

p. 253, *l.* 18 *Childe Harold*, III, 42.

Notes to Chapter XVII

p. 255, *l.* 17 *LJ*, III, 376. Letter of October 15, 1816, to John Murray.

p. 255, *l.* 21 Hobhouse diary, entry of October 15, 1816.

p. 256, *l.* 24 *LJ*, IV, 27. Letter of December 24, 1816.

p. 256, *l.* 32 Doris Langley Moore, in *The Late Lord Byron*, has given a detailed account of Hobhouse's exposure of the falsities of Stendhal's reminiscences of Byron, from an unpublished manuscript in the Hobhouse papers. See Chapter XI, "An Imaginative Frenchman," pp. 372–95.

p. 257, *l.* 10 *Astarte*, pp. 277–8. Letter of October 28, 1816.

p. 257, *l.* 13 Albé (sometimes written Albè) was the nickname the Shelleys had given Byron during their sojourn at Geneva, perhaps because of his outlandish Albanian war songs, or, it has been suggested, as a playful corruption of L.B. (Lord Byron).

p. 257, *l.* 20 Marchand, II, 666. Letter of October 6, 1816.

p. 258, *l.* 25 Marchand, II, 669. Hobhouse diary, November 10, 1816.

p. 259, *l.* 14 *LJ*, IV, 7–8. Letter of November 17, 1816.

p. 259, *l.* 36 *LJ*, IV, 14, 16. Letter of November 25, 1816.

p. 260, *l.* 7 *LBC*, II, 24.

p. 260, *l.* 16 *LJ*, IV, 9–10. Letter of December 5, 1816.

p. 260, *l.* 20 *LJ*, IV, 19. Letter of December 4, 1816.

p. 260, *l.* 36 *Astarte*, pp. 279–80.

p. 261, *l.* 4 *B-SP*, II, 378.

p. 261, *l.* 29 *"To Lord Byron,"* pp. 78–9. Letter of October 13, 1816.

p. 261, *l.* 39 Stowe, *Lady Byron Vindicated*, pp. 307–9.

p. 262, *l.* 10 *LJ*, IV, 49. Letter of January 28, 1817.

p. 262, *l.* 24 Marchand, II, 681. Letter of January 20, 1817.

p. 262, *l.* 34 Marchand, II, 678–9. This letter, with omissions, is in *LJ*, IV, 38–43. An omitted portion is supplied from the Murray MSS.

p .263, *l.* 2 *LJ*, IV, 40. Letter of January 2, 1817, to John Murray.

p. 263, *l.* 19 Enclosed in letter of February 28, 1817, to Moore. *LJ*, IV, 60.

p. 263, *l.* 37 *LJ*, IV, 62–3. Letter of February 28, 1817.

p. 264, *l.* 11 *Astarte*, p. 283. Letter of February 25, 1817.

p. 264, *l.* 33 *LJ*, IV, 92–3. Letter of April 2, 1817.

p. 264, *l.* 39 *LJ*, IV, 99.

p. 265, *l.* 11 *LJ*, IV, 101–2. Letter of April 11, 1817.

p. 265, *l.* 30 *LJ*, IV, 113–14. Letter of April 26, 1817, to John Murray.

p. 266, *l.* 11 *LJ*, IV, 119.

p. 266, *l.* 20 *Astarte*, p. 17.

p. 266, *l.* 24 Elze, p. 221.

p. 266, *l.* 26 Smiles, I, 391. Letter of December 7, 1817.

p. 266, *l.* 30 *LBC*, II, 56. Letter of June 20, 1817, to Hobhouse.

p. 267, *l.* 10 *LJ*, IV, 126. Letter of May 30, 1817, to John Murray.

p. 267, *l.* 14 *LBC*, II, 52–3. Letter of April 23, 1817.

p. 267, *l.* 27 *LJ*, IV, 124. Letter of May 27, 1817. Words after "comfort" supplied from proof sheets at John Murray's.

Notes to Chapter XVIII

p. 268, *l.* 7 Marchand, II, 696. Letter of May 30, 1817.
p. 268, *l.* 24 *Astarte*, p. 285. Letter of June 3, 1817.
p. 269, *l.* 38 *LJ*, IV, 148. Letter of July 10, 1817.
p. 270, *l.* 9 *Childe Harold*, IV, 78.
p. 270, *l.* 20 Ibid., IV, 121.
p. 270, *l.* 28 Ibid., IV, 127.
p. 271, *l.* 18 *B-SP*, II, 473. Letter of August 1, 1819, to Murray.
p. 272, *l.* 2 Ibid., 473–74.
p. 272, *l.* 24 *B-SP*, II, 415–16. Enclosed in letter of August 21, 1817.
p. 273, *l.* 4 Hobhouse diary, entry of August 29, 1817.
p. 275, *l.* 9 *LJ*, IV, 169. Letter of September 15, 1817.
p. 276, *l.* 11 *LBC*, II, 62. Letter of December 17, 1817.
p. 276, *l.* 17 *LBC*, II, 65. Letter of January 13, 1818. According to Teresa Guiccioli, Byron took the name Allegra from a Jewish lady, perhaps one of the daughters of the Jewish family who were his neighbors at La Mira.
p. 276, *l.* 26 Hobhouse diary, entry of December 29, 1817. Byron had a fondness for Rossini. See Leslie A. Marchand: "Byron and Rossini," *Opera News*, Vol. 30, No. 20 (March 19, 1966), pp. 6–7.

Notes to Chapter XIX

p. 278, *l.* 10 Marchand, II, 722.
p. 278, *l.* 21 Marchand, II, 723. Letter of January 27, 1818.
p. 278, *l.* 30 Marchand, II, 724. Letter of February 23, 1818.
p. 279, *l.* 5 Meneghetti, pp. 133–4. See also Iris Origo, "The Lady in the Gondola, a Portrait of Contessa Marina Benzon," in *A Measure of Love*, pp. 91–114.
p. 279, *l.* 36 *LJ*, IV, 215. Letter of March 16, 1818, to Moore.
p. 280, *l.* 30 *LBC*, II, 71. Letter of March 25, 1818.
p. 280, *l.* 36 *LJ*, IV, 123 *n.*
p. 281, *l.* 13 *LBC*, II, 74. Letter of April 22, 1818.
p. 281, *l.* 25 Marchand, II, 734.
p. 281, *l.* 36 Letter of May 5, 1818, to Hobhouse, in the possession of Mr. Robert H. Taylor.
p. 282, *l.* 7 *LJ*, IV, 250. Letter of August 3, 1818.
p. 282, *l.* 13 *LJ*, IV, 218. Letter of March 25, 1818.
p. 282, *l.* 38 Albrizzi, *Ritratti*, No. XXIII, quoted, *LJ*, IV, 440 (my translation).
p. 283, *l.* 7 Marchand, II, 739.
p. 283, *l.* 15 Marchand, II, 740.
p. 283, *l.* 24 *LJ*, IV, 239–40.

p. 283, *l.* 30 *LBC*, II, 106. Letter of March 6, 1819.
p. 284, *l.* 21 *LJ*, IV, 237.
p. 284, *l.* 27 *LJ*, IV, 245. Letter of July 10, 1818.
p. 284, *l.* 29 The manuscript of the first few stanzas (later made a "Dedication" and suppressed before publication) is dated July 3, 1818.
p. 284, *l.* 32 *LJ*, IV, 246. Letter of July 10, 1818.
p. 284, *l.* 37 *Childe Harold*, IV, 137.
p. 285, *l.* 4 Mayne, *Lady Byron*, p. 277.
p. 285, *l.* 24 Jeaffreson, p. 264.
p. 286, *l.* 2 Marchand, II, 747. Letter of September 8, 1818.
p. 286, *l.* 5 Moore, II, 266.
p. 286, *l.* 32 *Julian and Maddalo*, Preface.
p. 287, *l.* 7 *Julian and Maddalo*, lines 170–3, 177–9.
p. 287, *l.* 15 *LJ*, IV, 260.
p. 287, *l.* 34 *Don Juan*, I, 12.
p. 288, *l.* 2 *Don Juan*, I, 18.
p. 288, *l.* 5 *Don Juan*, I, 22.
p. 288, *l.* 14 *Don Juan*, I, 117.
p. 288, *l.* 25 Marchand, II, 752–3. Letter of November 11, 1818.
p. 288, *l.* 31 *Don Juan*, Dedication, 2. Byron wrote in his copy of *Biographia Literaria*, however: "I was very much amused with Coleridge's Memoirs. There is a great deal of Bonhommie in that book, and he does not spare himself. Nothing, to me at least, is so entertaining as a work of this kind—as private biography." Quoted in "Lord Byron's Books—A Catalogue of Books, selected from the Library of the late Lord Byron (which were sold by Auction by Mr. Evans, on Friday, July 6, 1827,) and purchased by J. Brumby, Bookseller, 14, Mary-le-Bone St., Piccadilly, near Glasshouse Street, Golden Square."
p. 288, *l.* 34 *Don Juan*, Dedication, 4.
p. 289, *l.* 11 *Poetry*, VI, 7 *n*.
p. 289, *l.* 23 *LJ*, IV, 262. Letter of September 19, 1818.
p. 289, *l.* 33 *LJ*, IV, 332. Letter of August 1, 1819.
p. 290, *l.* 2 Ibid., 333–4.
p. 290, *l.* 26 Ibid., 335–6.
p. 290, *l.* 34 Shelley, *Letters*, ed. Frederick L. Jones, II, 58. Letter of December 17 or 18, 1818.
p. 291, *l.* 7 *LJ*, IV, 267 *n*.
p. 291, *l.* 22 Marchand, II, 760–1.
p. 291, *l.* 40 *LBC*, II, 90. Letter of November 11, 1818.
p. 292, *l.* 16 Marchand, II, 764–5. Letter of January 5, 1819.
p. 292, *l.* 33 *B-SP*, II, 439. Letter of January 19, 1819, to Hobhouse and Kinnaird.
p. 293, *l.* 3 *LBC*, II, 101. Letter of January 25, 1819.
p. 293, *l.* 9 *LJ*, IV, 277. Letter of January 25, 1819.
p. 293, *l.* 16 *LJ*, IV, 279. Letter of February 1, 1819.
p. 293, *l.* 39 Marchand, II, 767–8. *B-SP*, II, 440. Letter of January 19, 1819.
p. 294, *l.* 5 *LBC*, II, 103. Letter of January 27, 1819.
p. 294, *l.* 17 *LJ*, IV, 283. Letter of April 6, 1819.
p. 294, *l.* 20 *LJ*, IV, 283 *n*. Letter of March 19, 1819.

p. 294, l. 29 *LJ*, IV, 284. Letter of April 6, 1819.

p. 295, l. 15 Medwin (ed. Lovell), p. 75.

p. 296, l. 5 Marchand, II, 774–5. The account of the meeting and the quotations come from Teresa Guiccioli's manuscript "Vie de Lord Byron en Italie," freely translated from her not-too-perfect French.

Notes to Chapter XX

p. 297, l. 24 Origo, p. 40.

p. 298, l. 14 *LBC*, II, 106–7. Letter of April 6, 1819.

p. 299, l. 13 *B-SP*, II, 444. Letter of April 24, 1819.

p. 299, l. 20 Guiccioli, "Vie," pp. 67–8.

p. 299, l. 32 *I Guiccioli*, I, 3.

p. 300, l. 38 Origo, pp. 44–5. Letter of April 22, 1819. This and subsequent letters of Byron to Teresa in Italian I give in the translation of the Marchesa Origo. The Italian text is printed in the Appendix of her *The Last Attachment*.

p. 301, l. 13 Origo, pp. 47–8.

p. 302, l. 5 Marchand, II, 785. Letter of May 17, 1819.

p. 302, l. 28 *Astarte*, pp. 81–3. Letter of May 17, 1819.

p. 302, l. 35 Origo, p. 13.

p. 303, l. 8 *LJ*, IV, 295. Letter of May 15, 1819.

p. 303, l. 15 *LJ*, IV, 304–5. Letter of May 20, 1819.

p. 303, l. 26 Marchand, II, 789.

p. 304, l. 6 *LJ*, IV, 310. Letter of June 6, 1819.

p. 304, l. 11 *LJ*, IV, 313. Letter of June 7, 1819, to Murray.

p. 304, l. 31 Origo, p. 66. Letter of June 10, 1819.

p. 304, l. 38 Origo, p. 67. Letter of June 11, 1819.

p. 305, l. 13 Origo, p. 70. Letter of June 14, 1819.

p. 305, l. 14 Origo, p. 69.

p. 305, l. 23 Guiccioli, "Vie," pp. 137–40.

p. 306, l. 7 Marchand, II, 795. Letter of June 20, 1819.

p. 306, l. 19 *B-SP*, II, 461. Letter of July 5, 1819.

p. 306, l. 38 *LJ*, IV, 325–6. Letter of July 2, 1819. See also Marchand, II, 797.

p. 307, l. 7 *LJ*, IV, 323. Letter of July 2, 1819.

p. 307, l. 17 *B-SP*, II, 461. Letter of July 5, 1819.

p. 307, l. 26 Origo, p. 76. Undated letter.

p. 307, l. 30 Origo, p. 76.

p. 308, l. 6 Marchand, II, 802. Letter of July 26, 1819.

p. 308, l. 34 Smiles, I, 404.

p. 309, l. 6 *LJ*, IV, 342–3. Letter of August 12, 1819.

p. 309, l. 21 Origo, p. 102. Letter of August 7, 1819.

p. 309, l. 32 *LJ*, IV, 340–1. Letter of August 12, 1819.

p. 310, l. 14 *LJ*, IV, 455.

p. 310, l. 30 *LBC*, II, 121–2. Letter of August 20, 1819.

p. 311, l. 2 *LBC*, II, 123. Letter of August 23, 1819.

p. 311, l. 28 *LJ*, IV, 350. Letter of August 25, 1819.

p. 311, l. 36 *Astarte*, pp. 294–5.

p. 312, l. 18 Guiccioli, "Vie," p. 219.

p. 313, l. 21 Guiccioli, "Vie," p. 260.
p. 313, l. 37 LJ, IV, 357. Letter of October 3, 1819.
p. 314, l. 8 Ibid., p. 358.
p. 314, l. 18 Don Juan, III, 8.
p. 314, l. 32 Moore, II, 248.
p. 315, l. 12 LJ, IV, 368–9. Letter of October 29, 1819.
p. 315, l. 27 Marchand, II, 807.
p. 315, l. 32 Marchand, II, 823.
p. 316, l. 8 Marchand, II, 823–4. Letter of October 26, 1819.
p. 316, l. 16 Ibid., p. 824.
p. 316, l. 20 LJ, IV, 370. Letter of October 29, 1819.
p. 316, l. 36 LBC, II, 126–7. Letter of November 16, 1819.
p. 317, l. 4 LBC, II, 129. Letter of November 20, 1819.
p. 317, l. 38 Origo, p. 142.
p. 318, l. 12 Moore, II, 290.
p. 318, l. 18 LJ, IV, 389–90.

Notes to Chapter XXI

p. 319, l. 21 LJ, IV, 393. Letter of December 31, 1819.
p. 320, l. 3 Astarte, p. 298. Letter of December 31, 1819.
p. 320, l. 30 LJ, IV, 400. Letter of January 31, 1820.
p. 321, l. 17 "To Lord Byron," pp. 159–60.
p. 321, l. 24 Marchand, II, 840.
p. 322, l. 21 B-SP, II, 504–5.
p. 322, l. 35 B-SP, II, 510. Letter of March 31, 1820.
p. 323, l. 9 LJ, IV, 488.
p. 323, l. 12 LJ, IV, 493.
p. 323, l. 32 Marchand, II, 847. Diary entry of April 16, 1820.
p. 324, l. 4 LJ, V, 6. Letter of April 9, 1820.
p. 324, l. 7 LJ, IV, 62. Letter of February 28, 1817.
p. 324, l. 20 LJ, V, 10.
p. 324, l. 29 LJ, V, 18–19. Letter of April 23, 1820.
p. 324, l. 40 LJ, V, 90–1. Letter of October 8, 1820.
p. 325, l. 20 Marchand, II, 851.
p. 325, l. 35 LJ, V, 28. Letter of May 20, 1820.
p. 326, l. 3 Origo, p. 174.
p. 326, l. 5 LJ, V, 32. Letter of May 24, 1820, to Moore.
p. 326, l. 20 LJ, V, 28.
p. 327, l. 21 Origo, pp. 185–6. Undated.
p. 327, l. 24 Origo, p. 188.
p. 327, l. 30 Guiccioli, "Vie," p. 414 bis. Marchand, II, 861.
p. 327, l. 40 Marchand, II, 861.

Notes to Chapter XXII

p. 328, l. 11 Origo, p. 193.
p. 329, l. 27 Origo, p. 198. Letter of July 26, 1820.
p. 329, l. 33 Origo, p. 198. Letter of July 29, 1820.

p. 330, *l.* 3 *LJ*, V, 57. Letter of July 22, 1820.
p. 331, *l.* 1 Origo, p. 199.
p. 331, *l.* 12 *LJ*, V, 70–1. Letter of August 31, 1820.
p. 331, *l.* 20 Blessington (ed. Lovell), p. 91.
p. 331, *l.* 25 Origo, p. 214. Letter of August 26, 1820.
p. 331, *l.* 34 *LJ*, V, 77. Letter of September 21, 1820.
p. 332, *l.* 3 *LJ*, V, 93. Letter of October 12, 1820.
p. 332, *l.* 15 *LJ*, V, 77–8. Letter of September 23, 1820. "Keep your piece nine years" was the advice of Pope to a Grub Street scribbler. (*Arbuthnot*, 1, 40.)
p. 332, *l.* 20 Marchand, II, 874. Letter of August 25, 1820.
p. 332, *l.* 23 *LJ*, V, 497. Letter of September 17, 1820.
p. 332, *l.* 33 *LJ*, V, 73–5. Letter of September 10, 1820.
p. 333, *l.* 7 *LJ*, V, 86. Letter of October 1, 1820.
p. 333, *l.* 18 *LJ*, V, 68–9.
p. 333, *l.* 29 Marchand, II, 378–9.
p. 334, *l.* 14 *LJ*, V, 96–7. October 12, 1820.
p. 334, *l.* 31 *Don Juan*, V, 1–2.
p. 335, *l.* 1 *Don Juan*, V, 61.
p. 335, *l.* 7 *Don Juan*, V, 158.
p. 335, *l.* 23 *LJ*, V, 108–9. Letter of November 4, 1820.
p. 335, *l.* 28 Wise, II, 18. Letter of November 4, 1820. Wise has supplied the omission in *LJ*, V, 109.
p. 336, *l.* 2 Marchand, II, 886. Letter of November 9, 1820.
p. 336, *l.* 10 *LJ*, V, 120. Letter of November 18, 1820.
p. 336, *l.* 32 *LBC*, II, 163–4. Letter of November 22, 1820.
p. 337, *l.* 12 *LJ*, V, 134–5. Letter of December 9, 1820.

Notes to Chapter XXIII

p. 338, *l.* 13 *LJ*, V, 214–15. Letter of January 2, 1821.
p. 339, *l.* 18 *LJ*, V, 155–6.
p. 339, *l.* 29 *LJ*, V, 157–8.
p. 339, *l.* 39 *LJ*, V, 173. Journal entry for January 13, 1821.
p. 339, *l.* 40 Guiccioli, "Vie," p. 526.
p. 340, *l.* 14 *LJ*, V, 183.
p. 340, *l.* 16 *LJ*, V, 183–4. Diary of January 24, 1821.
p. 340, *l.* 29 *LJ*, V, 186–7. Diary of January 25, 1821.
p. 340, *l.* 34 *LJ*, V, 189. Diary of January 28, 1821.
p. 340, *l.* 40 *LJ*, V, 190. Diary of January 28, 1821.
p. 341, *l.* 21 *LJ*, V, 242–3. Letter of February 16, 1821.
p. 341, *l.* 33 *LJ*, V, 205.
p. 342, *l.* 1 *LJ*, V, 208. Diary of February 24, 1821.
p. 342, *l.* 11 *LJ*, V, 272. Letter of April 28, 1821.
p. 342, *l.* 19 Green, *Keats-Shelley Journal*, V, 101. Letter to Hoppner, February 10, 1821.
p. 342, *l.* 27 *LJ*, V, 264. Letter of April 3, 1821.
p. 343, *l.* 16 Marchand, "Lord Byron and Count Alborghetti," p. 1001.
p. 343, *l.* 28 Ibid., p. 1002.

p. 344, l. 8 Strout, *John Bull's Letter to Lord Byron,* pp. 82, 90–1.
p. 344, l. 21 LJ, V, 321. Letter of July 6, 1821.
p. 344, l. 36 LJ, V, 318. Letter of July 5, 1821.
p. 346, l. 18 Cain, Act II, scene i, lines 81–3.
p. 346, l. 32 Cain, Act I, scene i, lines 137–40.
p. 347, l. 8 B-SP, II, 658–9. Letter of July 14[?], 1821.
p. 347, l. 14 LJ, V, 331. Letter of July 30, 1821.
p. 347, l. 21 LJ, IV, 491 *n.*
p. 347, l. 27 *Don Juan,* XI, 60.
p. 347, l. 37 Shelley, *Letters,* ed. Jones, II, 316. Letter of August 7, 1821.
p. 348, l. 16 Ibid., II, 322. Letter of [August 10], 1821.
p. 348, l. 25 Ibid., II, 330–1. Letter of August [10?], 1821.
p. 348, l. 32 Ibid., II, 330. Letter of August [10?], 1821.
p. 349, l. 15 Ibid., II, 334–5. Letter of [August 15], 1821.
p. 349, l. 18 Ibid., p. 335.
p. 349, l. 27 Ibid., II, 337. Letter of August 10, 1821.
p. 349, l. 33 For further details see Marchand, II, 925–6 *n.*
p. 350, l. 1 Shelley, *Letters,* ed. Jones, II, 339. Letter of [August 16], 1821.
p. 350, l. 19 Origo, p. 279.
p. 351, l. 2 *LJ,* V, 374–6. Letter of September 24, 1821.
p. 351, l. 12 *LJ,* V, 364–5. Letter of September 19, 1821.
p. 351, l. 21 *LJ,* V, 386. Letter of October 1, 1821.
p. 351, l. 36 Southey, *Poetical Works* (1838), X, 206.
p. 352, l. 9 *Vision of Judgment,* 35:7–8.
p. 352, l. 14 Ibid., 86:1–3.
p. 352, l. 22 Ibid., 96:2–4; 97:1, 7–8.
p. 352, l. 28 Ibid., 106:7–8.
p. 353, l. 8 *Astarte,* pp. 307–8. Letter of October 5, 1821.
p. 353, l. 21 Marchand, II, 936.
p. 353, l. 27 *LBC,* II, 203–4.
p. 353, l. 40 *LJ,* V, 439.
p. 354, l. 8 *LJ,* V, 446–7.
p. 354, l. 20 *LJ,* V, 456–7.
p. 354, l. 27 *LJ,* V, 436.
p. 354, l. 36 Origo, *Allegra,* pp. 84, 118.
p. 354, l. 39 Ibid., p. 119.
p. 355, l. 11 Moore, II, 550.
p. 355, l. 15 Marchand, II, 940–1.
p. 355, l. 25 *LJ,* V, 463.
p. 355, l. 32 *LJ,* V, 372. Letter of September 20, 1821.
p. 355, l. 36 Rogers, *Table Talk,* p. 237.
p. 355, l. 40 Clayden, I, 321.

Notes to Chapter XXIV

p. 357, l. 14 *LJ,* V, 486–7. Letter of December 4, 1821.
p. 358, l. 18 *Letters of Mary W. Shelley,* I, 150. Letter of November 30, 1821.

p. 358, l. 38 Williams, p. 109. Entry of November 5, 1821.

p. 360, l. 5 *Mary Shelley's Journal,* p. 184. Entry of October 19, 1822.

p. 361, l. 12 Medwin (ed. Lovell), pp. 265–6.

p. 361, l. 18 Shelley, *Letters,* ed. Jones, II, 323. Letter of [August 10], 1821.

p. 361, l. 20 Ibid., II, 423. Letter of [May 21?], 1822.

p. 361, l. 24 Ibid., II, 376. Letter of January 12, 1822.

p. 361, l. 35 *LJ,* V, 469–70. Letter of November 3, 1821, to Murray.

p. 361, l. 40 Smiles, I, 413.

p. 362, l. 11 *LJ,* V, 491–2. Letter of December 10, 1821.

p. 362, l. 25 *LJ,* V, 479–80. Letter of November 17, 1821.

p. 362, l. 31 Trelawny, *Records,* p. 45.

p. 362, l. 38 Medwin (ed. Lovell), p. 180.

p. 363, l. 3 Sotheby sale catalogue, October 29, 1968, p. 115. Shelley added an impassioned plea to Byron's letter, now in the Pforzheimer Library, New York.

p. 363, l. 38 Marchand, III, 959–60.

p. 364, l. 15 *Mary Shelley's Journal,* p. 165. Entry of January 19, 1822.

p. 364, l. 18 See Lady Anne Hill: "Trelawny's Family Background and Naval Career," *Keats-Shelley Journal,* Vol. V (Winter 1956), pp. 11–32.

p. 364, l. 31 Trelawny, *Recollections,* pp. 24–5.

p. 365, l. 6 Ibid., pp. 36–7.

p. 365, l. 10 Cline, p. 76.

p. 365, l. 17 Origo, p. 298.

p. 365, l. 30 Trelawny, *Letters,* p. 2.

p. 365, l. 39 Medwin (ed. Lovell), p. 155.

p. 366, l. 15 *LJ,* VI, 16–18. Letter of February 8, 1822.

p. 366, l. 25 Medwin (ed. Lovell), p. 111.

p. 366, l. 38 "Lord Byron en Italie," in Stendhal: *Racine et Shakespeare* (Paris, 1854), p. 266.

p. 366, l. 40 Marchand, III, 971. Letter of April 8, 1822.

p. 367, l. 33 Marchand, III, 972.

p. 367, l. 38 Shelley, *Letters,* ed. Jones, II, 389. Letter of February 15, 1822.

p. 368, l. 5 Ibid., p. 390. Letter of February 17, 1822.

p. 368, l. 35 Dowden, II, 486.

p. 368, l. 39 Dowden, II, 487.

p. 369, l. 15 *Letters of Mary W. Shelley,* ed. Jones, II, 29. Letter of January 19, [1830].

p. 369, l. 23 *LJ,* VI, 32–3. Letter of March 4, 1822.

p. 369, l. 32 *LJ,* VI, 39. Letter of March 8, 1822.

p. 370, l. 6 Trelawny, *Recollections,* pp. 45–8.

p. 372, l. 36 Moore, II, 615.

p. 373, l. 3 *LJ,* VI, 52. Letter of April 22, 1822.

p. 373, l. 20 Origo, pp. 312–13.

p. 373, l. 25 *LJ,* VI, 53–4. Letter of April 23, 1822.

p. 374, l. 12 Ross, p. 760.

Notes to Chapter XXV

p. 375, *l.* 25 Bancroft, pp. 191–3.
p. 376, *l.* 4 *LJ*, VI, 82. Letter of June 8, 1822.
p. 376, *l.* 10 Bancroft, p. 199.
p. 376, *l.* 14 Bancroft, p. 206.
p. 376, *l.* 40 *Letters of Mary W. Shelley*, I, 171. Letter of June 2, 1822, to Maria Gisborne.
p. 377, *l.* 31 Shelley, *Letters*, ed. Jones, II, 442. Letter of June 29, 1822.
p. 377, *l.* 37 Hunt, *Lord Byron*, I, 14.
p. 378, *l.* 9 Ibid., I, 15.
p. 378, *l.* 14 Ibid., I, 17–18.
p. 378, *l.* 25 Ross, p. 761.
p. 379, *l.* 36 Hunt, *Lord Byron*, I, 44–6.
p. 380, *l.* 9 *LJ*, VI, 97. Letter of July 12, 1822.
p. 380, *l.* 21 Origo, p. 309.
p. 381, *l.* 9 Hunt, *Lord Byron*, I, 64–5, 72–3.
p. 381, *l.* 21 Malmesbury, I, 32.
p. 381, *l.* 36 Trelawny, *Recollections*, p. 119.
p. 382, *l.* 12 See Marchand, "Trelawny on the Death of Shelley," p. 17. See also Marchand, III, 1017.
p. 382, *l.* 22 *Letters of Mary W. Shelley*, I, 185. Letter of August 15, 1822.
p. 382, *l.* 26 *LJ*, VI, 99. Letter of August 3, 1822.
p. 382, *l.* 29 *LJ*, VI, 99. Letter of August 8, 1822.
p. 383, *l.* 12 Trelawny, *Records*, pp. 99–100.
p. 383, *l.* 21 *Bulletin and Review of the Keats-Shelley Memorial, Rome*, No. 2 (London, 1913), pp. 72–3.
p. 383, *l.* 32 *Don Juan*, VII, 2.
p. 384, *l.* 9 Trelawny, *Letters*, p. 8.
p. 384, *l.* 22 Trelawny, *Letters*, p. 270. Letter of December 18, [1878], to W. M. Rossetti.
p. 384, *l.* 35 Hunt, *Autobiography*, ed. Morpurgo, p. 328.
p. 385, *l.* 25 *Tatler* (Hunt's periodical), January 15, 1831.
p. 386, *l.* 5 Cline, p. 190. Letter of September 12, 1822.
p. 386, *l.* 23 Medwin (ed. Lovell), p. 253.
p. 386, *l.* 26 Medwin (ed. Lovell), p. 266.
p. 386, *l.* 36 Moore, II, 614.
p. 387, *l.* 3 Marchand, III, 1030.
p. 387, *l.* 7 Gronow, I, 154.
p. 387, *l.* 15 Marchand, III, 1032.
p. 387, *l.* 23 *LJ*, VI, 117. Letter of September 23, 1822. The Bartolini bust is now in the National Portrait Gallery, London.
p. 388, *l.* 3 *LJ*, VI, 121. Letter of October 9, 1822.
p. 388, *l.* 10 Trelawny, *Recollections*, p. 151.
p. 388, *l.* 19 *LJ*, VI, 122. Letter of October 9, 1822.
p. 388, *l.* 30 Marchand, III, 1036.

Notes to Chapter XXVI

p. 389, l. 21 *LJ*, VI, 119–20. Letter of October 6, 1822.

p. 390, l. 14 Marchand, III, 1038.

p. 390, l. 18 Ibid.

p. 390, l. 27 Marchand, III, 1039. Letter of November 2, 1822.

p. 390, l. 34 Brewer, p. 155. Letter of October 26, 1822.

p. 391, l. 13 Marchand, III, 1040. Letter of October 29, 1822. The three cantos of *Don Juan* which so shocked Murray were VI, VII, and VIII, which carried Juan through the adventures of the harem and the horrors of the battle of Ismail.

p. 391, l. 16 *LJ*, VI, 138. Letter of November 18, 1822.

p. 391, l. 36 *LJ*, VI, 157. Letter of December 25, 1822.

p. 392, l. 7 *Mary Shelley's Journal*, p. 184.

p. 392, l. 12 Trelawny, *Recollections*, pp. 148–9.

p. 392, l. 20 Trelawny, *Recollections*, p. 156.

p. 392, l. 40 Gore, pp. 44–5. Letter of November 10, 1822.

p. 393, l. 38 *LBC*, II, 238. Letter of December 14, 1822.

p. 394, l. 15 Marchand, III, 1050. Letter of February 19, 1823.

p. 394, l. 31 Marchand, III, 1051. Letter of December 5, 1822.

p. 395, l. 3 *LJ*, VI, 163.

p. 395, l. 15 Marchand, III, 1052.

p. 395, l. 36 *LJ*, VI, 182. Letter of April 2, 1823.

p. 396, l. 29 Sadleir, p. 140.

p. 396, l. 37 Blessington (ed. Lovell), p. 12.

p. 397, l. 8 *LJ*, VI, 180. Letter of April 2, 1823.

p. 397, l. 19 Blessington, *Idler*, I, 289.

p. 397, l. 34 Blessington, *Idler*, I, 393, 395–6.

p. 397, l. 39 Ibid., II, 5.

p. 398, l. 8 Blessington (ed. Lovell), p. 13.

p. 398, l. 23 *LBC*, II, 255. Letter of April 7, 1823.

p. 399, l. 2 Blessington (ed. Lovell), pp. 54, 62.

p. 399, l. 7 Ibid., p. 106.

p. 399, l. 12 Ibid., p. 76.

p. 399, l. 17 Blessington, *Idler*, II, 19.

p. 399, l. 26 Blessington (ed. Lovell), p. 117.

p. 399, l. 30 Ibid., p. 110.

p. 399, l. 39 Ibid., p. 219.

p. 400, l. 8 Ibid., p. 220.

p. 400, l. 17 Gore, p. 50. Letter of May 17, 1822.

p. 400, l. 22 Marchand, III, 1069. Letter of April 29, 1823.

p. 400, l. 31 *Letters of Mary W. Shelley*, I, 226. Letter of May 10, 1823, to Trelawny.

p. 400, l. 37 Origo, p. 337. Guiccioli, "Vie," pp. 1574–5.

p. 401, l. 2 *LBC*, II, 258. Letter of May 19, 1823. (See Marchand, III, 1071 *n.*)

p. 401, l. 7 *LBC*, II, 260. Letter of May 21, 1823.

p. 401, l. 31 Blessington (ed. Lovell), p. 49.

p. 401, l. 33 Ibid., p. 74.

p. 401, l. 39 Origo, p. 344.

p. 402, l. 8 Blessington (ed. Lovell), p. 221.
p. 403, l. 13 Trelawny, *Recollections*, p. 167.
p. 404, l. 3 Moore, *The Late Lord Byron*, p. 408.
p. 404, l. 26 Guiccioli, "Vie," p. 1366.
p. 404, l. 32 Origo, p. 331.
p. 404, l. 37 See Marchand, III, 1085, and Doris Langley Moore: "Byron, Leigh Hunt, and the Shelleys," *Keats-Shelley Memorial Bulletin*, No. X (1959), pp. 20–29.
p. 405, l. 39 Guiccioli, "Vie," pp. 1590–1.
p. 406, l. 4 Pratt, "An Italian Pocket Notebook of Lord Byron," p. 209.
p. 406, l. 34 Gamba, p. 12.
p. 406, l. 37 Broughton, III, 153.
p. 407, l. 8 Marchand, III, 1089.
p. 407, l. 20 Pratt, "An Italian Pocket Notebook of Lord Byron," p. 211.

Notes to Chapter XXVII

p. 409, l. 2 *LJ*, VI, 236. Letter of July 24, 1823.
p. 409, l. 7 Trelawny, *Recollections*, p. 187.
p. 409, l. 20 Ibid., p. 191.
p. 409, l. 34 Browne, "Voyage from Leghorn," pp. 64–5.
p. 412, l. 5 Marchand, III, 1098.
p. 412, l. 12 Trelawny, *Recollections*, p. 201.
p. 413, l. 23 Moore, *Prose and Verse*, p. 432.
p. 414, l. 17 Trelawny, *Recollections*, p. 202.
p. 414, l. 40 Kennedy, p. 342.
p. 415, l. 8 Kennedy, p. 64.
p. 415, l. 11 Kennedy, p. 66.
p. 415, l. 18 *LJ*, VI, 255. Letter of August 10, 1823.
p. 416, l. 1 *Medora Leigh*, pp. 57–8.
p. 416, l. 23 Browne, "Narrative," p. 396.
p. 416, l. 28 *Medora Leigh*, p. 63; Marchand, III, 1112.
p. 416, l. 33 *Medora Leigh*, p. 63.
p. 417, l. 10 Gamba, p. 32.
p. 417, l. 28 Gamba, p. 4.
p. 418, l. 3 Finlay, VI, 325–6.
p. 418, l. 12 *LJ*, VI, 246–7.
p. 418, l. 31 Browne, "Narrative," p. 399.
p. 419, l. 29 Origo, pp. 361–2. Letter of September 11, 1823.
p. 420, l. 18 Finlay, VI, 324–5.
p. 421, l. 5 *LJ*, VI, 430.
p. 421, l. 30 Marchand, III, 1130.
p. 422, l. 8 Ibid., p. 1131.
p. 422, l. 21 *LJ*, VI, 268. Letter of October 25, 1823.
p. 422, l. 29 Millingen, p. 4.
p. 422, l. 40 Millingen, p. 8.
p. 423, l. 19 *LJ*, VI, 427. Letter of June 1, 1824, Charles Hancock to Henry Muir.

p. 423, l. 21 Marchand, III, 1135. Letter of November 10, 1823.
p. 423, l. 23 LJ, VI, 286. Letter of December 13, 1823.
p. 424, l. 1 Marchand, III, 1136.
p. 424, l. 3 Ibid.
p. 424, l. 21 Gamba, p. 60.
p. 425, l. 14 Nicolson, p. 174.
p. 425, l. 34 LJ, VI, 287, 289.
p. 425, l. 38 Browne, "Voyage from Leghorn," p. 64. Although Byron sometimes alluded to the offer in a facetious style, he was no doubt flattered by it.
p. 426, l. 24 LJ, VI, 293. Letter of December 26, 1823.
p. 426, l. 28 Notes and Queries, 4th series, IV, September 25, 1869, p. 250.
p. 426, l. 34 LBC, II, 286. Letter of December 27, 1823.
p. 427, l. 2 LJ, VI, 429. Letter of June 1, 1824, Charles Hancock to Henry Muir.
p. 427, l. 27 Gamba, pp. 69–70.

Notes to Chapter XXVIII

p. 428, l. 5 Stanhope, p. 60.
p. 428, l. 33 Moore, II, 704.
p. 429, l. 9 LJ, VI, 297. Letter of December 31, 1823.
p. 430, l. 13 Gamba, p. 84.
p. 430, l. 22 Millingen, p. 65.
p. 430, l. 35 Millingen, p. 66.
p. 431, l. 29 Millingen, p. 90.
p. 433, l. 28 Origo, p. 374. Letter of January 8, 1824.
p. 435, l. 2 Gamba, p. 124.
p. 437, l. 11 Gamba, p. 132.
p. 437, l. 33 Medwin, *The Angler in Wales,* II, 198–212.
p. 438, l. 16 Stanhope, p. 103. Letter of February 4, 1824, to Bowring.
p. 438, l. 21 According to a tradition still persisting in Missolonghi, Byron gave a pair of Turkish slippers to the boy, Costa Ghazis. They are now an heirloom of a Missolonghi family. (See Patrick Leigh Fermor, *Roumeli,* pp. 160–9.)
p. 439, l. 8 This was one of the manuscripts found among Byron's papers when he died. The exact date of composition is not known, but the sentiment is similar to that expressed in the poem written on his thirty-sixth birthday. It was first published in *Murray's Magazine,* Vol. I (February 1887), p. 146.
p. 439, l. 20 LJ, VI, 314. Letter of February 5, 1824, to Charles Hancock.
p. 440, l. 36 Parry, pp. 27–8.
p. 441, l. 15 Gamba, p. 169.
p. 441, l. 30 LJ, VI, 326 *n.*
p. 441, l. 39 Parry, p. 43.
p. 442, l. 3 Millingen, p. 118.
p. 442, l. 8 Gamba, p. 176.

p. 442, l. 21 LJ, VI, 334. Letter of February 25, 1824.
p. 442, l. 32 LJ, V, 10. Letter of April 16, 1820.
p. 443, l. 39 Stanhope, 2nd edn., p. 537.

Notes to Chapter XXIX

p. 444, l. 12 Millingen, pp. 119–20.
p. 444, l. 21 Gamba, p. 191.
p. 445, l. 26 LJ, VI, 335. Letter of February 25, 1824.
p. 446, l. 3 Broughton, III, 60. Diary entry of July 2, 1824.
p. 446, l. 21 Parry, pp. 74–5.
p. 447, l. 32 Moore, II, 741–2 *n*.
p. 448, l. 21 Origo, p. 380.
p. 449, l. 4 Parry, p. 166.
p. 449, l. 13 Parry, p. 174.
p. 450, l. 17 Finlay, VI, 327.

p. 451, l. 10 This poem, found among Byron's papers at Missolonghi after his death, was first published in *Murray's Magazine*, Vol. I (February 1887), pp. 145–6. Although the poem written on his thirty-sixth birthday is printed last in E. H. Coleridge's edition, both internal and external evidence (supplied by Coleridge himself) indicates that the poem here quoted (Coleridge gave it the bracketed title ["Love and Death"]) was the last one Byron wrote. Coleridge's footnote quotes a notation by Hobhouse: "The last he ever wrote. From a rough copy found amongst his papers at the back of the 'Song of Suli.' Copied November, 1824.—John C. Hobhouse." (*Poetry*, VII, 85 *n*.) The internal evidence, such as the reference to his illness of February 15 and the earthquake (February 21), clearly dates the poem some weeks after the one written on his birthday.

p. 451, l. 24 Millingen, p. 124.
p. 451, l. 32 Millingen, p. 127.

p. 452, l. 6 LJ, VI, 434. Letter of Gamba to Augusta Leigh, begun August 17, 1824.

p. 452, l. 18 LBC, II, 292. Letter of February 12, 1824. (Date and text corrected from MS.)

p. 452, l. 30 Gamba, pp. 248–9.
p. 452, l. 36 Ibid., p. 249.
p. 453, l. 17 Millingen, p. 129.
p. 454, l. 11 Marchand, III, 1215.
p. 454, l. 17 Millingen, p. 131.
p. 454, l. 22 Marchand, III, 1215–16.
p. 454, l. 28 Millingen, pp. 139–40.
p. 455, l. 9 Parry, pp. 112–13.
p. 455, l. 17 Parry, pp. 120–1.
p. 455, l. 23 Millingen, p. 141.
p. 456, l. 3 Millingen, p. 132.
p. 456, l. 7 Marchand, III, 1219.
p. 456, l. 11 Parry, p. 124.

p. 456, l. 19 Marchand, III, 1220. There is considerable disparity in the accounts of the various witnesses, even the doctors, concerning both the number of bleedings and the quantity of blood taken. I have followed Bruno's diary for the most part, since it is the most nearly contemporary account.

p. 457, l. 1 Marchand, III, 1223. Dr. Bruno's diary.

p. 457, l. 4 Millingen, p. 133.

p. 457, l. 11 Parry, p. 126.

p. 457, l. 36 Millingen, p. 141. Fletcher later told Hobhouse that Byron had said to him, "it is not worth while to take such a body as this home," but that he afterward added, "Perhaps, on the whole, it would be better to do so." (Broughton, III, 60.)

p. 458, l. 6 Gamba, pp. 260–1.

p. 458, l. 21 Parry, p. 127.

p. 458, l. 34 Gamba, pp. 264–5.

p. 459, l. 9 Broughton, III, 58.

p. 459, l. 14 Marchand, III, 1227. See also the letter of Pietro Gamba to Hobhouse, in Moore, *The Late Lord Byron*, pp. 179–81.

p. 459, l. 23 *Westminster Review*, II (July 1824), 256.

p. 459, l. 29 Marchand, III, 1228.

p. 459, l. 32 Ibid.

p. 459, l. 35 Broughton, III, 58–9.

p. 460, l. 12 *LBC*, II, 299. Letter of March 15, 1824.

p. 460, l. 20 *Westminster Review*, II (July 1824), 257.

Notes to Chapter XXX

p. 461, l. 7 Parry, p. 128 *n*.

p. 461, l. 20 Marchand, III, 1230.

p. 462, l. 5 Parry, p. 137.

p. 462, l. 27 Millingen, pp. 142–3.

p. 462, l. 31 Nicolson, p. 190.

p. 463, l. 3 Marchand, III, 1232.

p. 464, l. 10 Notopoulos, pp. 39–40.

p. 464, l. 30 Marchand, III, 1236.

p. 465, l. 4 Trelawny, *Recollections*, p. 224.

p. 465, l. 11 *LJ*, IV, 315. Letter of June 7, 1819.

p. 465, l. 33 Origo, p. 387.

p. 466, l. 2 Marchand, III, 1244.

p. 466, l. 13 Hobhouse diary, entry of May 14, 1824.

p. 466, l. 18 *Mary Shelley's Journal*, p. 194.

p. 466, l. 21 Hobhouse diary, entry of May 15, 1824.

p. 466, l. 30 Moore, *Memoirs*, I, 493.

p. 467, l. 16 The best account of the Memoirs and their burning is given by Doris Langley Moore in her first chapter of *The Late Lord Byron*.

p. 467, l. 27 Hobhouse diary, entry of May 16, 1824.

p. 467, l. 29 *London Magazine*, Vol. X (August 1824), p. 119.

p. 467, l. 37 *Tennyson, A Memoir*, by his son, I, 4.

p. 468, l. 2 D. A. Wilson, *Carlyle Till Marriage*, p. 328.

p. 468, l. 4 Ibid., p. 327.

p. 468, l. 10 Hobhouse diary, entry of July 2, 1824.

p. 468, l. 13 Hobhouse took Byron's dog Lion under his care, and was much upset when the Newfoundland died in 1825. (Moore, *The Late Lord Byron*, p. 196.)

p. 468, l. 28 Hobhouse diary, entry of July 6, 1824.

p. 468, l. 34 Moore, *The Late Lord Byron*, p. 207.

p. 469, l. 6 Mayne, *Lady Byron*, p. 297. Mrs. Moore (*The Late Lord Byron*, p. 150) found no source for this statement in the Lovelace Papers.

p. 470, l. 6 Hobhouse diary, entry of July 12, 1824.

p. 470, l. 13 *Letters of Mary W. Shelley*, I, 298. Letter of July 28, [1824].

p. 470, l. 27 Hobhouse diary, entry of July 15, 1824.

p. 471, l. 3 *Beppo*, stanza 20.

p. 471, l. 16 *Childe Harold*, IV, 137.

Notes to Epilogue

p. 472, l. 8 Hobhouse diary, entry of July 1, 1824.

p. 472, l. 18 Smiles, I, 437. Letter of July 13, 1824.

p. 473, l. 5 Bertrand Russell has written me that his grandfather, Lord John Russell, Moore's literary executor, burned many papers before his death, and that this Victorian practice was repeated by his son, Bertrand Russell's father. It seems incredible that Byron's letters should have been destroyed. But none of them remains in the Russell archives.

p. 473, l. 11 Doris Langley Moore has given convincing evidence that Hobhouse's jealousy of Moore, to whom Byron had given the Memoirs without even suggesting that he let Hobhouse read them, was probably the strongest reason for Hobhouse's irrational eagerness to destroy them. (*The Late Lord Byron*, Chapter I.)

p. 474, l. 23 Moore, *The Late Lord Byron*, pp. 182–3.

p. 474, l. 34 Marshall, *Life and Letters of Mary W. Shelley, II*, 115–16. Letter of April 30, 1824.

p. 474, l. 39 Ibid., p. 117.

p. 475, l. 2 William Sharp: *Life and Letters of Joseph Severn* (London, 1892), p. 135.

p. 476, l. 34 Herbert Huscher: "Claire Clairmont's Lost Russian Journal and Some Further Glimpses of Her Later Life," *Keats-Shelley Memorial Bulletin*, No. VI (1955), p. 47.

p. 477, l. 13 Quoted, Henry Sotheran & Co., Catalogue No. 12, 1899. No correspondent indicated.

p. 477, l. 22 *Athenaeum*, April 5, 1873, p. 439.

p. 477, l. 27 Origo, p. 415.

p. 477, l. 29 *Athenaeum*, October 9, 1869, p. 465.

p. 477, l. 33 Mary R. Darby Smith, *Recollections of Two Distinguished Persons: La Marquise de Boissy and the Count de Waldeck*, p. 16.

Bibliography

Sources Referred to in the Notes

A. Sources Referred to by Symbols and Abbreviations

Astarte—Lovelace, Ralph Milbanke, Earl of: *Astarte: A Fragment of Truth Concerning George Gordon Byron, Sixth Lord Byron,* recorded by his grandson. New edition by Mary Countess of Lovelace. New York, 1921.

B-SP—*Byron, A Self-Portrait. Letters and Diaries, 1798–1824,* ed. Peter Quennell. 2 vols. London, 1950.

LBC—*Lord Byron's Correspondence,* ed. John Murray. 2 vols. New York, 1922.

LJ—*The Works of Lord Byron. A New, Revised and Enlarged Edition, with illustrations. Letters and Journals,* ed. Rowland E. Prothero. 6 vols. London, 1898–1901.

Marchand—Marchand, Leslie A.: *Byron: A Biography.* 3 vols. New York, 1957.

Medora Leigh—*Medora Leigh: A History and an Autobiography,* ed. Charles Mackay. New York, 1870.

Moore—Moore, Thomas: *Letters and Journals of Lord Byron: with Notices of His Life.* 2 vols. London, 1830.

Nicolson—Nicolson, Harold: *Byron, The Last Journey, April 1823–April 1824.* London, 1924.

Origo—Origo, Iris: *The Last Attachment.* New York, 1949.

Poetry—*The Works of Lord Byron. A New, Revised and Enlarged Edition, with illustrations. Poetry,* ed. Ernest Hartley Coleridge. 7 vols. London, 1898–1904.

Pratt—Pratt, Willis W.: *Byron at Southwell.* Austin, Texas, 1948.

"To Lord Byron"—Paston, George, and Peter Quennell: *"To Lord Byron," Feminine Profiles Based upon Unpublished Letters, 1807–1824.* New York, 1939.

Williams—*Maria Gisborne & Edward E. Williams, Shelley's Friends, Their Journals and Letters,* ed. Frederick L. Jones. Norman, Okla., 1951.

B. Other Published Sources

[AIRLIE] MABELL, COUNTESS OF AIRLIE: *In Whig Society, 1775–1818 . . .* London, 1921.

Athenaeum, The, October 9, 1869, p. 465; April 5, 1873, p. 439.

BANCROFT, GEORGE: "A Day with Lord Byron," in *History of the Battle of Lake Erie and Miscellaneous Papers.* New York, 1891.

BEER, GAVIN DE: "An 'Atheist' in the Alps," *Keats-Shelley Memorial Bulletin,* No. IX (1958), pp. 1–15.

Blackwood's Edinburgh Magazine, review of Medwin's *Conversations*, XVI (November 1824), 530–6.

BLESSINGTON, MARGUERITE, COUNTESS OF: *The Idler in Italy*. 2 vols. London, 1839.

[———]: *Lady Blessington's Conversations of Lord Byron*, ed. Ernest J. Lovell, Jr. Princeton, N.J., 1969.

BORST, WILLIAM A.: *Lord Byron's First Pilgrimage*. New Haven, Conn., 1948.

BREWER, LUTHER A.: *My Leigh Hunt Library: The Holograph Letters*. Iowa City, 1938.

BROUGHTON, LORD [JOHN CAM HOBHOUSE]: *Recollections of a Long Life*, ed. by his daughter, Lady Dorchester. 6 vols. London, 1909–11.

BROWNE, JAMES HAMILTON: "Narrative of a Visit to the Seat of War in Greece," *Blackwood's Edinburgh Magazine*, XXXVI (September 1834), 392–407.

———: "Voyage from Leghorn to Cephalonia with Lord Byron . . . ," *Blackwood's Edinburgh Magazine*, XXXV (January 1834), 56–67.

BRYANT, JACOB: *Dissertations Concerning the War of Troy* . . . London, 1796.

BUCHAN, PETER: *Ancient Ballads and Songs of the North of Scotland* . . . 2 vols. Edinburgh, 1875.

[BULL, JOHN]: *John Bull's Letter to Lord Byron*, ed. Alan Lang Strout. Norman, Okla., 1947.

Bulletin and Review of the Keats-Shelley Memorial, Rome, No. 2. London, 1913.

BURY, LADY CHARLOTTE [CAMPBELL]: *The Diary of a Lady-in-Waiting*, ed. A. F. Steuart. 2 vols. London, 1908.

CECIL, DAVID: *The Young Melbourne*. London, 1939.

CLAYDEN, P. W.: *Rogers and His Contemporaries*. 2 vols. London, 1889.

CLINE, C. L.: *Byron, Shelley and their Pisan Circle*. London, 1952.

DALLAS, R. C.: *Correspondence of Lord Byron with a Friend* . . . Philadelphia, 1825.

DOWDEN, EDWARD: *The Life of Percy Bysshe Shelley*. 2 vols. London, 1886.

Eclectic Review, Vol. III, Part 2, pp. 989–93.

ELWIN, MALCOLM: *Lord Byron's Wife*. New York, 1963.

ELZE, KARL: *Lord Byron, A Biography*. London, 1872.

FERMOR, PATRICK LEIGH: *Roumeli*. London, 1966.

FINLAY, GEORGE: *A History of Greece from its Conquest by the Romans to the Present Time, 146* B.C. *to* A.D. *1864*. Vols. 6 and 7: *The Greek Revolution*. Oxford, 1877.

FOSTER, VERE: *The Two Duchesses* . . . London, 1898.

FOX, SIR JOHN C.: *The Byron Mystery*. London, 1924.

GALT, JOHN: *The Life of Lord Byron*. Philadelphia, 1830.

GAMBA, COUNT PETER [PIETRO]: *A Narrative of Lord Byron's Last Journey to Greece*. London, 1825.

[GLENBERVIE]: *The Diaries of Sylvester Douglas (Lord Glenbervie)*, ed. Francis Bickley. 2 vols. London, 1928.

GORDON, PRYSE LOCKHART: *Personal Memoirs*. 2 vols. London, 1830.

GORE, JOHN: " 'When We Two Parted': A Byron Mystery Re-Solved," *Cornhill Magazine*, LXIV (January 1928), 39–53.

GREEN, DAVID BONNELL: "Three New Byron Letters," *Keats-Shelley Journal*, V (Winter 1956), 97–101.

[GRONOW, CAPTAIN R. H.]: *The Reminiscences and Recollections of Captain Gronow, 1810–1860*. 2 vols. London, 1900.

GRYLLS, R. GLYNN: *Claire Clairmont, Mother of Byron's Allegra*. London, 1939.

GUICCIOLI, ALESSANDRO: *I Guiccioli—Memorie di una Famiglia Patrizia*. 2 vols. Bologna, 1934.

HAZLITT, WILLIAM: *Conversations of James Northcote*. No. 15. *The Complete Works of William Hazlitt*, Centenary Edition, XI. London, 1930–4.

HILL, ANNE: "Trelawny's Family Background and Naval Career," *Keats-Shelley Journal*, V (Winter 1956), 11–32.

HOBHOUSE, JOHN CAM: *A Journey through Albania and Other Provinces of Turkey in Europe and Asia, to Constantinople, during the Years 1809 and 1810*. 2nd. edn. 2 vols. London, 1813.

[HODGSON, REV. FRANCIS]: *Memoir of the Rev. Francis Hodgson, B.D.*, by his son, the Rev. James T. Hodgson. 2 vols. London, 1878.

HOGG, JAMES: *Memorials of James Hogg, the Ettrick Shepherd*, ed. by his daughter, Mrs. [M.] Garden. London, [1884].

HOLLAND, HENRY RICHARD VASSALL, third LORD HOLLAND: *Further Memoirs of the Whig Party, 1807–1821*. New York, 1905.

HUNT, LEIGH: *Lord Byron and Some of His Contemporaries . . .* 2nd edn. 2 vols. London, 1828.

[———]: *The Autobiography of Leigh Hunt*, ed. J. E. Morpurgo. London, 1949.

HUSCHER, HERBERT: "Claire Clairmont's Lost Russian Journal and Some Further Glimpses of Her Later Life," *Keats-Shelley Memorial Bulletin*, No. VI (1955), pp. 35–47.

ILCHESTER, EARL OF: *The Home of the Hollands*. London, 1937.

IRVING, WASHINGTON: *Abbotsford and Newstead Abbey. The Works of Washington Irving*, Bohn's Standard Library, III. London, 1885.

JEAFFRESON, JOHN CORDY: *The Real Lord Byron*. London, 1884.

JOYCE, MICHAEL: *My Friend H. John Cam Hobhouse*. London, 1948.

KENNEDY, JAMES: *Conversations on Religion with Lord Byron . . .* London, 1830.

KINGLAKE, A. W.: *Eothen*. Oxford (Clarendon), 1917.

[LAMB, LADY CAROLINE]: *Glenarvon*. 2nd edn. 3 vols. London, 1816.

L'ESTRANGE, REV. A. G.: *The Literary Life of the Rev. William Harness*. London, 1871.

The London Magazine, "Robert Burns and Lord Byron," X (August 1824), 117–22.

MALMESBURY, EARL OF: *Memoirs of an Ex-Minister*. 2nd edn. 2 vols. London, 1884.

MARCHAND, LESLIE A.: "Byron's Lameness: a Re-examination," *Keats-Shelley Memorial Bulletin*, No. VII (1956), pp. 32–42.

———: "Byron and Rossini," *Opera News*, Vol. XXX, No. 20 (March 19, 1966), pp. 6–7.

———: "Trelawny on the Death of Shelley," *Keats-Shelley Memorial Bulletin*, No. IV (1952), pp. 9–34.

MARSDEN, J. H.: *A Brief Memoir of the Life and Writings of the Late Lieutenant William Martin Leake* . . . London, 1864.
MARSHALL, MRS. JULIAN: *The Life and Letters of Mary Wollstonecraft Shelley.* 2 vols. London, 1889.
MARSHALL, WILLIAM H.: "The Byron Will of 1809," *The Library Chronicle* (University of Pennsylvania), Vol. XXXIII, No. 2 (Spring 1967), pp. 97–114.
MAUROIS, ANDRÉ: *Byron.* London, 1930.
MAYNE, ETHEL COLBURN: *Byron.* New York, 1924.
———: *The Life and Letters of Anne Isabella Lady Noel Byron* . . . New York, 1930.
[MEDWIN, THOMAS]: *Medwin's Conversations of Lord Byron* . . . , ed. Ernest J. Lovell, Jr. Princeton, N.J., 1966.
MENEGHETTI, NAZZARENO: *"Lord Byron a Venezia."* Venice, [1910].
MERYON, C. L.: *Memoirs of Lady Hester Stanhope.* 3 vols. London, 1845.
MILLINGEN, JULIUS: *Memoirs of the Affairs of Greece* . . . London, 1831.
Monthly Mirror, new series, Vol. III, No. 30 (January 1808).
MOORE, DORIS LANGLEY: "Byron, Leigh Hunt, and the Shelleys," *Keats-Shelley Memorial Bulletin,* No. X (1959), pp. 20–9.
———: *The Great Byron Adventure* (pamphlet). Philadelphia, 1959.
———: *The Late Lord Byron.* Philadelphia, 1961.
MOORE, THOMAS: *Memoirs, Journal, and Correspondence,* ed. by the Right Hon. Lord John Russell. 2 vols. New York, 1858.
———: *Prose and Verse* . . . London, 1828.
MORGAN, SYDNEY (OWENSON) LADY: *Lady Morgan's Memoirs.* 2 vols. London, 1862.
Murray's Magazine, January, February, March, 1887.
The New Monthly Magazine. "Recollections of Turkey," No. 1, XVII (1826), 305–14; No. 2, XIX (1827), 137–49.
NICOLSON, HAROLD: "The Byron Curse Echoes Again," *The New York Times Magazine,* March 27, 1949, pp. 12–13, 33, 35.
Notes and Queries, 4th series, Vol. IV, Sept. 25, 1869, p. 250.
NOTOPOULOS, JAMES A.: "New Sources on Lord Byron at Missolonghi," *Keats-Shelley Journal,* IV (Winter 1955), 31–45.
ORIGO, IRIS: *Allegra.* London, 1935.
———: *A Measure of Love.* New York, 1957.
PARRY, WILLIAM: *The Last Days of Lord Byron* . . . London, 1825.
[PEPYS, SAMUEL]: *Diary and Correspondence of Samuel Pepys,* ed. Lord Braybrooke and Mynors Bright. 10 vols. New York, 1884.
[POLIDORI, JOHN WILLIAM]: *The Diary of John William Polidori,* ed. William Michael Rossetti. London, 1911.
[———]: *The Vampyre, A Tale.* London, 1819.
PRATT, WILLIS W.: "An Italian Pocket Notebook of Lord Byron," University of Texas *Studies in English,* XXVIII (1949), 195–212.
PROTHERO, R. E.: "Childhood and School Days of Byron," *The Nineteenth Century,* XLIII (January 1898), 61–81.
[ROGERS, SAMUEL]: *Recollections of the Table Talk of Samuel Rogers* . . . ed. by the late Rev. Alexander Dyce. New Southgate, 1887.
ROSS, JANET: "Byron at Pisa," *The Nineteenth Century,* XXX (November 1891), 753–63.

Sadleir, Michael: *The Strange Life of Lady Blessington.* Rev. American edn. New York, 1947.

[Scott, Sir Walter]: *The Journal of Sir Walter Scott.* The text revised from a photostat in the National Library of Scotland. Ed. by J. G. Tait. (Completed by W. M. Parker.) Edinburgh, 1950.

Sharp, William: *Life and Letters of Joseph Severn.* London, 1892.

Sharpe's London Magazine, new series, Vols. XXXIV and XXXV (1869).

[Shelley, Mary W.]: *The Letters of Mary W. Shelley*, ed. Frederick L. Jones. 2 vols. Norman, Okla., 1944.

[———]: *Mary Shelley's Journal*, ed. Frederick L. Jones. Norman, Okla., 1947.

Shelley, Percy Bysshe: *Essays and Letters from Abroad* . . . 2 vols. London, 1840.

[———]: *The Letters of Percy Bysshe Shelley*, ed. Frederick L. Jones. 2 vols. New York, 1964.

Slater, Joseph: "Byron's Hebrew Melodies," *Studies in Philology*, XLIX (January 1952), 75–94.

Smiles, Samuel: *A Publisher and His Friends: Memoir and Correspondence of the Late John Murray* . . . 2 vols. London, 1891.

Smith, Mary R. Darby: *Recollections of Two Distinguished Persons: La Marquise de Boissy and the Count de Waldeck.* Philadelphia, 1878.

Southey, Robert: *Poetical Works* (1838). Vol. X.

Stendhal [Marie Henri Beyle]: "Lord Byron en Italie," in *Racine et Shakespeare.* Paris, 1854.

Stanhope, Colonel Leicester: *Greece in 1823 and 1824; Being a Series of Letters, and Other Documents on the Greek Revolution* . . . London, 1824.

———: *Greece in 1823 and 1824* . . . New edn. London, 1825.

Stowe, Harriet Beecher: *Lady Byron Vindicated, A History of the Byron Controversy* . . . London, 1870.

Symon, J. D.: *Byron in Perspective.* New York, 1925.

Tatler, The (Leigh Hunt's periodical), January 15, 1831.

[Tennyson]: *Alfred Lord Tennyson, A Memoir, by His Son.* 2 vols. New York, 1897.

Trelawny, Edward John: *Recollections of the Last Days of Shelley and Byron.* London, 1858.

———: *Records of Shelley, Byron and the Author.* The New Universal Library. London, [n.d.] (first published 1878).

[———]: *The Letters of Edward John Trelawny*, ed. H. Buxton Forman. London, 1910.

Westminster Review, II (July 1824), 225–62. (Ostensibly a review of *The Deformed Transformed*, but the running head throughout is "Lord Byron in Greece.")

Williams, Stanley T.: *The Life of Washington Irving.* New York, 1935.

Wilson, David Alec: *Carlyle Till Marriage (1795–1826).* London, 1923.

Wise, T. J.: *A Bibliography of the Writings in Verse and Prose of George Gordon Noel, Baron Byron* . . . 2 vols. London, 1932–3.

Index

A NOTE ABOUT THE AUTHOR

LESLIE ALEXIS MARCHAND was born near Bridgeport, Washington, on February 13, 1900. He studied at the University of Washington (A.B., 1922; M.A., 1923), Columbia University (Ph.D., 1940), the Sorbonne, and the University of Munich. He taught first at the University of Washington, then at the Alaska Agricultural College and School of Mines (now the University of Alaska), at Columbia University, and from 1937 to 1966 at Rutgers, where he was Professor of English. He was Fulbright Professor at the University of Athens (Greece) in 1958–9, and has been a visiting professor at the University of California at Los Angeles, the University of Illinois, Hunter College, New York University, Arizona State University, Hofstra University, and Harvard. He has had research grants from the Rutgers Research Council and the ACLS. A Guggenheim Foundation Fellowship enabled him to do research for the present book in Europe in 1968–9. He has contributed numerous articles and reviews to professional journals, as well as to *The New York Times Book Review, Saturday Review,* and *Life International.* His previous books include: *The Athenaeum: A Mirror of Victorian Culture* (1941); *Byron: A Biography,* 3 vols. (1957); and *Byron's Poetry: A Critical Introduction* (1965). He is married and now lives in Englewood, Florida.

A NOTE ON THE TYPE

This book was set in a typeface called Primer, designed by Rudolph Ruzicka for the Mergenthaler Linotype Company and first made available in 1949. Primer, a modified modern face based on Century broadface, has the virtue of great legibility and was designed especially for today's methods of composition and printing.

Primer is Ruzicka's third typeface. In 1940 he designed Fairfield, and in 1947 Fairfield Medium, both for the Mergenthaler Linotype Company.

Composed, printed, and bound by
Kingsport Press, Inc., Kingsport, Tennessee.
Typography and binding design by

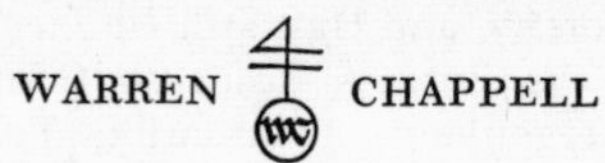